T3-BUM-994

THE RISE OF THE CHRISTIAN RELIGION

A STUDY IN ORIGINS

MACMILLAN AND CO., Limited
LONDON · BOMBAY · CALCUTTA · MADRAS
MELBOURNE

THE MACMILLAN COMPANY
NEW YORK · BOSTON · CHICAGO
DALLAS · SAN FRANCISCO

THE MACMILLAN CO. OF CANADA, Ltd.
TORONTO

THE RISE OF THE CHRISTIAN RELIGION

A STUDY IN ORIGINS

BY

CHARLES FREDERICK NOLLOTH, M.A., D.Litt.

ORIEL COLLEGE, OXFORD

EXAMINING CHAPLAIN TO THE BISHOP OF ROCHESTER

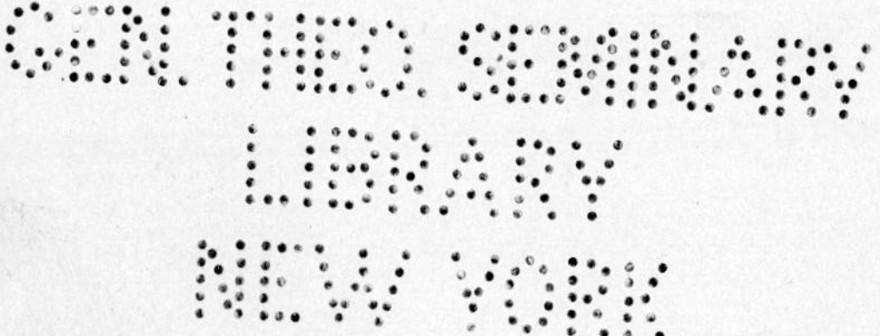

MACMILLAN AND CO., LIMITED

ST. MARTIN'S STREET, LONDON

1917

GLASGOW: PRINTED AT THE UNIVERSITY PRESS
BY ROBERT MACLEHOSE AND CO. LTD.

VXORI

IN OMNI LABORE MEO

PARTICIPI ATQVE ADIVTRICI

PREFACE

The present work is an attempt to trace the rise and early course of the Christian Religion, and is, in some sort, a sequel to *The Person of Our Lord and Recent Thought* (Macmillan), which I wrote a few years ago.

In a subject so vast and many-sided, it stands to reason that, if anything useful and satisfying is to be said, the choice of topics must be strictly limited. Thus, while the Person and the Mission of the Founder of Christianity naturally dominate and control the situation, there is no intention to present another 'Life of Christ.' The aim is rather to deal with certain movements of thought which are central for any clear understanding of early Christianity, and to emphasize events that form epochs in its history.

Hence, after a brief survey of the literary evidence at our command, there is a discussion of some of the chief contributions of Jewish, Greek and Roman religious thought and practice to the preparation for the Gospel, and of the state of things which, in consequence of that preparation, prevailed at the dawn of the Christian era.

In the course of the historical investigation which follows, I have endeavoured to show that while our Lord was in a certain sense the heir of the ages which preceded Him, He constituted a fresh and unexampled element in human history, which the past was powerless to produce and which no theory of development can explain.

Another result of our inquiry emerges in the conviction that the Christian Religion as it reached, with the end of the first century, the close of its formative period, was, on the whole, what its Founder intended it to be—that, in other words, as it left the hands of the Apostolic Witnesses of its origin, it was in theory wholly, and largely in fact, in agreement with the mind of Christ.

The substance of the book was in manuscript before the war. Recent events have tended to deepen the distrust, already prevailing in many quarters, of the methods adopted by certain schools of criticism. I believe that one result of the present upheaval in Europe will be a considerable modification of the respect hitherto paid in this country to those methods.

The present work is intended not only for the professed student of theology but for the educated layman.

As in the case of the earlier book, it has been thought advisable to translate passages of German works cited in the notes, with a view to the requirements of a wider circle of readers.

The Rev. Dr. H. J. White, Professor of New Testament Exegesis at King's College, London, has very kindly read the proofs. I have to thank him for many valuable criticisms and suggestions. To other friends I am indebted for help in verifying quotations and in the preparation of the Index.

C. F. NOLLOTH.

CHISLEHURST, February, 1917.

CONTENTS

CHAPTER XXVIII.

CHAPTER XXIX.

INTRODUCTION

No event in the history of mankind is of so surpassing a magnitude, either in itself or in its effects, as the entrance into the world of the Christian Religion; in itself, because of the historic facts to which it points as its *raison d'être*: in its effects, because it claims to touch and influence every department of human thought and energy, and more than this, has made good that claim among the more progressive and enlightened peoples.

Christianity is thus the dominating factor of human experience. All other interests pale before it. All events take their colour from their relation to it. However strenuously the attempt may be made to separate provinces of thought and action from its sanction or its influence, sooner or later the judgment of Christianity has to be faced. We must consider what it has to say upon our enterprise. We cannot keep them apart.

It is easy to show why this is so. The Christian Religion is the most complete expression of that conscious relation of God and man which is the distinguishing trait of humanity. It brings out the central fact of man's nature and being—his likeness to God. Struggle as he may, he can never rid himself of the consequences of this overmastering element of his life. He belongs to God; he is like God; God is his destiny. As the streams flow into the ocean, human life in all its relations sets towards the boundless and the infinite—towards the love of God. That is why Christianity, as the highest point in which this characteristic of human life is exemplified, touches everywhere the deepest springs and the most varied forms of human activity.

Christianity is therefore the supreme interest of mankind. Nor is this position at all affected by the fact that there are vast sections of people who have either never heard of it, or having heard have declined to accept it. Facts are no less facts for their non-acceptance by the generality of men. They are not established by counting heads. There have been many epochs in human affairs, during which some Athanasius has stood alone against the world, and men have come to realize in after years that the solitary was in the right and the world was wrong. Never is it safe to infer that truth must needs be with the greater number.

Besides, it would not be difficult to show that, even when their differences from Christianity are most profound and far-reaching, the testimony yielded to it by adverse or alien sections of thought is often most real and striking. Often we can see that rudimentary and imperfect tendencies in other religions point towards it, and find their completion and fulfilment only where Christ is known and honoured. The Buddhist's abnegation of all personal aims finds its truest expression in the assertion of St. Paul, 'I live, yet not I, but Christ liveth in me.' His longing for union with the infinite, for immersion in the whole of things, is, if he but knew it, only to be satisfied by conscious communion with God in Jesus Christ. The Kaffir's sense of guilt, as it takes the form of devil-worship under stress of fear, is a mute and unconscious appeal to the Cross of Calvary, to the One offering for the sins of the world.

If, then, the Christian Religion is the dominating factor of human life, it becomes a matter of no slight importance that we should form a true judgment upon its rise and early fortunes. All great movements need to be estimated by the character of their object and purpose, and by the pure and unmixed nature of their early enthusiasms, rather than by the course of their later developments, when alien interests have had time to penetrate them. This is especially the case with Christianity. Its adherents claim that it is from above; that it is something of heaven that has stooped to earth; that it is a Divine force plunged into the midst of human circumstance. If its true nature is to be investigated, the stream should be analysed at its source, not where, in its ever-widening career, it has received tributary accretions from other centres of influence.[1] That

[1] In the opening passages of his famous Chapter xv. Gibbon seems to feel the fairness of such a consideration; but, as it has been pointed out, he confounds 'in one undistinguishable mass the *origin* and *apostolic* propagation of the Christian religion with its later progress.' *Decline and Fall of the Roman Empire*, vol. ii. p. 152, n. *a*.

source is the Person of Jesus Christ. Christianity is Christ in action. If we would know, to any practical purpose, something of the character, the meaning and the object of the Christian Religion, we have to study the mind of Christ as it is unfolded for us in His teaching and His life, and as it is illustrated and reflected in the lives and in the teaching of His first followers.

In the course of our investigation, questions of a highly contentious nature will arise. In dealing with them, there has been an effort to do full justice to the facts which emerge, and to give full weight to rival points of view.

We start with a high sense of the historical value of the sources which lie before us in the writings of the New Testament, giving their authors that credit for substantial accuracy of statement and for entire honesty of purpose which appears to be their due; while refusing to *à priori* judgments of merely hypothetical character the right to set aside evidence of proved authenticity and weight.

In an inquiry of this kind, it can hardly be avoided if certain conclusions cause pain or disappointment to the reader. Cherished convictions and old-established views are not lightly parted with. Anything that seems to conflict with them is certain to incur a certain feeling of resentment. But at least, the writer may urge that he has not willingly said a word to unsettle or disturb an earnest seeker after truth.

And after all, it is the aim of all honest historical investigation to arrive at truth. Recent events in world-history have strongly emphasized its paramount importance. A people that has for years been the victim of illusion knows the bitterness of the awakening, when facts that have been held at arm's length have come to assert themselves.

There is equal need for a fearless dealing with truth and fact, when we study the entrance into the world of the greatest phenomenon in all its long history—the Religion of Christ. As we write, men are being brought face to face with eternal realities as never before. Justice, righteousness, truth loom the larger for the despite that has been done to them.

It is hoped that the following pages will help to clear the vision of some who wish for light upon what passed at the dawn of that new day which broke upon the world nineteen centuries ago.

CHAPTER I

THE SOURCES—I. JEWISH AND PAGAN

There are two main sources of our knowledge of Christian origins—literary and institutional, documents and Christian customs. The one supplements and completes the other. We have besides the confirmatory evidence of the personal experience of the Christian, not so much for the rise, as for the character, of Christianity; not for its history, but for the adequacy with which it makes good its claims.

The documentary sources are to be sharply distinguished. They are found both in profane and in sacred literature, but in very unequal proportion. There is perhaps no great movement in history so little noticed in the literature of the time, apart from the literature which it has itself produced, as Christianity. This is partly to be explained by its lowly beginnings and by the unworldly character of its claims and of its methods. The remote and secluded scene of its origin, far from the centres of world-power and commerce, hedged it round from common observation. Moreover, its kinship with Judaism, rising as it did out of the heart of that religion, was long a cause of confusion in the minds of the surrounding peoples; while the fact that its Founder suffered death by crucifixion made it appear an impossible thing in the eyes of the ordinary citizen of the Empire. But, however it may be accounted for, the fact remains that the Kingdom of God came 'not with observation'; and it would be strange if it were not employed for their own ends by the foes of Christianity. Not only is the poverty of the allusions made much of, but most of the references that have come down to us are assailed by doubt. They are assigned to the interested activity of some Christian interpolator; and thus we are said to owe our knowledge of the rise of our religion solely to the 'prejudiced' evidence of Christians.

That this is not an extreme view of the case can be seen at once by referring to some of the latest exponents of liberal criticism. They make the demand that Christianity must be certified by its enemies, or by those who are indifferent to it. Christians themselves are said to be 'interested' parties, and their interest mars the force of their evidence.[1]

But what is the nature of this interest? It makes all the difference whether it is selfish—for ambition or gain—or whether it rests on moral and spiritual grounds. The first disciples had everything to lose and nothing to win, from a worldly point of view, when they went forth to preach the Gospel, or sat down to commit to writing their impressions of the Person and Life of Christ. They were cutting themselves off from fellowship with the adherents of their own historic faith on the one hand and, on the other, they were setting themselves in opposition to the ruling power. If they gave their witness, it was because they could do nothing else. 'We cannot but speak the things which we have seen and heard.' [2]

And who is more likely to be in a position to certify the facts of a great movement? One who enters heartily into its spirit and meaning, or one who stands aloof, cold and unmoved, irresponsive to its call and untouched by its message? When to these considerations we add the fact that to bear witness was to go in hourly peril of life and liberty, we must admit that such 'interest' as was displayed by the first Christian preachers and writers is no disqualifying factor, when we come to estimate the value of their evidence.[3]

But, to return to non-Christian allusions to the rise of our religion: for it is not so easy to get rid of them as some suppose. They are of two kinds, Jewish and Pagan. Of these, the Jewish literary allusions are of the scantiest description. They could hardly be otherwise, considering the known attitude of Judaism in the first Christian century. A loyal and zealous Jew might

[1] J. Weiss has some excellent remarks upon this subject. *Jesus von Nazareth*, p. 93.

[2] Acts iv. 20. Cf. *The Historic Personality of Christ*, 1911, p. 6, by the present writer.

[3] Cf. Heitmüller, *Jesus*, 1913, pp. 5, 6.

persecute, like Saul. He would not perpetuate in writing the tenets and practices which he abominated. To ignore was the best repudiation which he could give of a 'sect everywhere spoken against.'[1] So it came to pass that of the two most famous Jewish writers and historians of the first century A.D., one, Philo of Alexandria, is wholly silent, while in the case of the other, Josephus, the indications of knowledge or interest are of the slightest.

The silence of Philo is the more disappointing from his advantageous position with regard to Christianity. He was our Lord's contemporary, and as he was in Palestine in the year A.D. 39, at a time when Jerusalem was ringing with the voices of the Apostolic preachers of Christ and the Resurrection, we can hardly suppose that a man of such keen intelligence and such profound interest in religion as Philo is shown to be by his writings, could have failed to have his attention drawn to the new movement.[2] Yet, not only is he silent, but criticism has not got the task of dealing with any suspicious cases of interpolation in his writings such as are freely assigned to the text of Josephus. Can we account for this silence? During his life-time, the cause of Christianity had not advanced sufficiently to attract much attention from a man like Philo, passionately attached as he was to his own faith. Besides, he died about A.D. 40, soon after his return from Palestine. Had he lived, his further writings might have betrayed first-hand acquaintance with the rise of Christianity, although, from inclination or policy, he would be disposed to ignore it.

Josephus was not only a man of very different character, but he lived at a later period. During an interregnum in the Governorship of Judaea, following upon the death of Festus, the High Priest Annas, one of the sons of the Annas of the Gospel story of the Passion, seized the opportunity to kill St. James the Lord's brother. Josephus was living in Jerusalem at the time, and was about twenty-four years old. The event created a deep impression, for St. James was held in reverence for his high character both by Jews and Christians. Josephus thus alludes to it, 'he (Annas) assembled the Sanhedrin of judges and brought before

[1] Acts xxviii. 22.

[2] But *v.* Renan, *Vie de Jésus*, p. ix; S. Reinach, *Orpheus*, p. 227, E.T. Cf. Batiffol, *Orpheus et l'Évangile*, 1910, p. 19, n. 3.

it the brother of Jesus, who was called Christ, whose name was James, and some others.'[1]

There is very little in the early Rabbinic literature of the Christian era which refers directly to Christianity. But a few allusions to our Lord are assigned to the first century and to the early part of the second. There is enough to show that the Rabbis of this period 'were well acquainted with the Person of Christ and for a time were friendly to Him.'[2]

It would be incorrect to speak of a 'conspiracy of silence,' but the general absence of reference to the Christian religion, which is apparent in the strictly Jewish literature of the first hundred years after the Resurrection, marks the existence both of repugnance and contempt on the part of Jews for the very name of Christian.[3] The cross was 'a stumbling block' to many. It was incomprehensible to them that the crucified Nazarene should be regarded as the Christ of God; while their hatred was inflamed by the knowledge that the downfall of their race, the

[1] Joseph. *Antiq.* xx. 9, § 1, τὸν ἀδελφὸν Ἰησοῦ τοῦ λεγομένου Χριστοῦ (Ἰάκωβος ὄνομ' αὐτῷ). *v.* Batiffol, *Orpheus et l'Évangile*, p. 13. This is perhaps the only passage in his works, in which there is clear testimony to the Person of our Lord, and its authenticity is disputed by Schürer. Two great authorities, however, have recently (1910) declared for its genuineness: Jülicher, *Hat Jesus gelebt?* p. 19, and Batiffol, *Orpheus et l'Évangile*, p. 16, n. 2.

The reference of Josephus to John the Baptist, *Antiq.* xviii. 5, § 2, is generally admitted to be genuine. *v.* Schürer, *Geschichte des Jüdischen Volkes*, i. p. 438, n. 24. The interpolation of passages in *Antiq.* xviii. 3, § 3, is possible; but Renan regards the section as 'authentique dans son ensemble. Il est parfaitement dans le goût de Josephe.' *Vie de Jésus*, p. xl. Cf. Scholten in 'Flavius Josephus en Jezus' (*Theologisch Tijdschrift* for 1882, pp. 428-451). Recently, the genuineness of the passage has been upheld by critical scholars of authority: Harnack in *Internat. Monatschrift für Wiss.* 1913, pp. 1037-1068; Burkitt in *Theol. Tijdschrift*, 1913, pp. 135-144. Heitmüller is therefore hardly justified in saying that 'it is certainly a Christian interpolation.' *Jesus*, 1913, p. 3. J. Weiss had already said that he was not aware of any clear and absolute necessity to reject the passage. *Jesus von Nazareth*, p. 88, n. 1.

For political motives for the silence (comparatively speaking) of Josephus *v.* *The Historic Personality of Christ*, p. 8. Cf. Bousset, *Was wissen wir von Jesus?* p. 16; Heitmüller, *Jesus*, p. 4; Whiston, *Josephus*, Dissertation I. As Burkitt says, 'The hypothesis of a Christian interpolation (*Antiq.* xviii. 3, § 3) raises more serious difficulties than it solves.' *Op. cit.* p. 144.

[2] Chwolson, *Über die Frage ob Jesus gelebt hat*, 1910, pp. 12, 13. Cf. Strack, *Jesus, die Häretiker und die Christen*, 1910, pp. 23*, 25*.

[3] *v.* Batiffol, *Orpheus et l'Évangile*, p. 29.

destruction of their Temple and their capital, were directly traced by the Christians to the rejection of our Lord.[1]

Under these circumstances, we can hardly wonder if there was little desire to discuss or record what was happening in the Apostolic Church. The Jew, who was not won over by the preaching of the Gospel, remained impassive and silent, if he was not stirred to open hostility. The book of Acts records many occasions of this hostility, and St. Paul was only shielded from it by openly appealing, as a Roman citizen, to the protection of the Emperor.

When we turn for evidence to Pagan writers, we find an almost equal poverty of allusion; but the causes are different. In the first place, it is to be remembered that 'the entire literary tradition for the period of the early Emperors has perished until we come to Tacitus and Suetonius.'[2] Of course, that lost literature may have contained many references to Christ and Christianity; but judging from the attitude of the ordinary Roman citizen to the new religion, it is not likely that sufficient interest was taken in it by the writers of the day. For the preaching of the Cross was 'foolishness' to the Graeco-Roman world at large; and the idea that an obscure Jew of Galilee could ever become the central Figure of a religious movement claiming the adherence of mankind was not thought worthy of consideration. Besides, what chiefly deterred men from thinking seriously of it was the exclusive claim which the religion made upon all who would receive it. The Roman was used to practise a complaisant attitude in religion. He had his favourite cult, but he

[1] *v.* Wernle, *D. Quellen des Lebens Jesu*, p. 4; Nolloth, *The Person of Our Lord and Recent Thought*, p. 13.

Something has been made of the absence of any reference to Christ in the perished work of Justus of Tiberias, a contemporary of Josephus. Photius read it in the ninth century, and was surprised that it did not mention Christ; but as it was a chronicle of the Jewish rulers from Moses to Agrippa, it is not surprising, as J. Weiss says (*Jesus von Nazareth*, p. 91, n. 2), that Christ is not named.

[2] J. Weiss, *Jesus von Nazareth, Mythus oder Geschichte?* p. 86; *Die Geschichtlichkeit Jesu*, 1910, p. 6. His statement that Tacitus is the oldest witness to Christ in Roman literature is not quite accurate, as the famous letter of the younger Pliny to Trajan is a few years earlier than the *Annals* of Tacitus. The impression conveyed by Wernle (*D. Quellen des Lebens Jesu*, p. 3) should be qualified by mention of Pliny's letter, the evidence of which is all the more valuable, that it is so clearly undesigned and occurs in the midst of a question of a practical character.

was by no means intolerant of other forms of worship. It appeared mere fanaticism to expect a man to adopt a new religion which condemned every other as sacrilegious and profane. To use a modern phrase, the Roman was 'not bigoted.' When the Orontes had begun to flow into the Tiber, an easy reception for foreign cults was guaranteed. But then, they were not, like Christianity, despotic and exclusive. They accommodated themselves to their new conditions on the principle of 'live and let live.' It was the rigid, unbending claim of Christianity to be the sole expression of the relation between man and God that surprised and angered the Roman man of the world.

And there was another reason for this failure to give a large place in their literature to the religion of Christ. For a long period it was popularly confounded with Judaism, and regarded either as a sect of that religion, or as a new development of it. If Jews were tolerated, they were held in little esteem under the early Empire. They were turbulent and fanatical, requiring at times the force of the state to keep them in check, and always a source of anxiety to the authorities.[1] It was, therefore, improbable at the outset that the Christian Faith would make for itself any considerable place in Roman literature.

But when we open the earliest Roman books that have come down to us from the period of about seventy years after the death of Christ, we meet with authentic evidence of Christianity, and that of the most telling and positive kind. The younger Pliny was Governor of Pontus and Bithynia under the Emperor Trajan. In a letter addressed to Trajan, he asks for direction in dealing with Christians, of whom there appear to have been a large number under his administration. The whole letter is full of interest; but there is one passage of surpassing value, when we consider the author, the early date—A.D. 112—and the contents. He tells Trajan that the Christians 'are accustomed to meet together before dawn, and to sing antiphonally a hymn of praise to Christ as God.'[2] Here we have not only direct non-Christian evidence, and that of a cultivated Roman of high rank, for the historical Personality of our Lord; but we also have the assurance that He was being addressed by believers as

[1] Cf. Acts xviii. 2.

[2] *Epist.* 96, 'quod essent soliti stato die ante lucem convenire carmenque Christo, quasi Deo, dicere secum invicem.'

God, and worshipped. The authenticity of the letter is beyond doubt, and is further supported by the attitude of detachment and indifference to the Christian Faith which the writer shows. His only concern was the correct handling of a difficult matter from an official point of view. There is no sign of interest or of sympathy with the adherents of this new and strange religion. It is the characteristic Roman attitude of the time.

The first mention of Christ or Christianity by any Roman historian that has come down to us is contained in the passage of the *Annals*, in which Tacitus writes, 'The Founder of that name, Christus, was put to death in the reign of Tiberius by the Procurator, Pontius Pilate.' Thus, like Pliny, the Roman historian unconsciously lends his voice to swell the recital of the Creed of Christendom.[1] From the one writer we learn the Passion, from the other, the Godhead of Christ. Their entire disinterestedness, standing as they do outside the Religion and untouched by its appeal, increases the force of their witness. No one can say that they speak by book.

When we add to their allusions that of Suetonius,[2] writing three or four years after Tacitus, we have exhausted all the pagan evidence of the first two or three generations of the Christian era that has come down to us. It is little enough, but from the reasons given above, its meagreness is fully explicable. Our knowledge of the conditions of the time would at once render any copious, interested recital from such sources suspicious. We have enough to act as an external check upon the conclusions which we draw from the literature of the Canon and from the writings of the early Fathers. An Apostle once asked, 'Lord, how is it that Thou wilt manifest Thyself unto us and not unto the world?'[3] And when risen, it was to His own who loved Him and were capable of faith, that He appeared. The world, which 'knew Him not,' did not see Him. In analogy to the

[1] Tac. *Annals*, xv. 44, written A.D. 115-117. For the authenticity of the passage, see Nolloth, *The Historic Personality of Christ*, pp. 11 f.; Heitmüller, *Jesus*, p. 3, 'Every unprejudiced person will recognise this narrative as a complete testimony to the historical character of the Figure of Jesus'; von Soden, *Hat Jesus gelebt?* 1910, p. 11; J. Weiss, *Jesus von Nazareth*, p. 86.

[2] *Claudius*, 25. He speaks of Chrestus, meaning Christus. Cf. Bousset, *Was wissen wir von Jesus?* p. 16. So Loman; *v.* Rovers, *Stemmen uit de vrije gemeente*, pp. 51-64; Heitmüller, *Jesus*, p. 179.

[3] Jo. xiv. 22.

principle which governed His personal manifestation, we are prepared to meet with little reflection of His life and work in the mirror of profane literature. It was not held up to Him. The Roman superciliously passed Him by. He did not enter into his thoughts. To the cultivated and materialistic citizen of the Empire, the rise of the Christian Faith was not worth a moment's consideration.

A deeper reason for the comparative silence of the pagan world lay in the principle that spiritual things are 'spiritually discerned.' The risen Christ belonged, though still human, to the world of spirit; 'the Lord is that Spirit.'[1] And it was among His own people that He sought His witnesses. As, in the days of His flesh, He had silenced the confession of demons who knew Him, so would He not require the witness of men who served other gods. It was a standing law of His Kingdom that it was to be spread by those who were of it. 'Ye shall be witnesses unto Me in Jerusalem . . . and unto the uttermost part of the earth,'[2] said the risen Saviour to those who loved and followed Him.

While, then, we welcome every ray of light, from whatever quarter, that falls upon the rise of our religion, we have no need to be disconcerted at the small extent of what may be called independent testimony. Its poverty is explained both by the conditions of the time and by the nature of the case.

[1] 2 Cor. iii. 17. [2] Acts i. 8.

CHAPTER II

THE SOURCES—II. CHRISTIAN

WHEN we turn for our knowledge of Christianity to the New Testament, we are at once confronted with a problem of discrimination. The material is abundant, but how is it to be used? Are the Epistles of St. Paul to come first, or shall we go to the Gospel narratives? A short time ago, the priority of the witness of St. Paul could be regarded as assured. It could be said that his Epistles contain the earliest literary testimony to Christ and Christianity that has come down to us; and that the chronological order of studying our subject is the only right one. That position might be challenged, while admitting the soundness of its data. But in the present state of criticism, we have no security for their soundness.[1] The last few years have witnessed a considerable movement of thought with regard to the chronology of the writings of the New Testament, and this in two directions.

In the first place, there is a strong tendency to place the composition of the Synoptic Gospels themselves farther back; and secondly, the primitive material that underlies them is regarded by some as belonging not only to the generation, but (at least in one portion) to the life-time of our Lord. We shall have to deal separately with these questions.

First, as to the date of the Synoptic Gospels in their present form. There is no critical position more generally recognized than that St. Mark forms the groundwork of St. Matthew and St. Luke. The greater part of the Second Gospel is incorporated in the text of the First and Third Gospels. If, therefore, we can arrive at the approximate date of the latter Gospels, we shall get

[1] *v.* below, p. 23.

a *terminus ad quem* for the composition of St. Mark. It must have been written before them, because they embody it. Can we assign a *terminus ad quem* to either the First or the Third Gospel? It matters little for our present purpose which we choose. If both incorporate St. Mark, it suffices to fix a date for one of them. Lower than that date St. Mark cannot go.

Take St. Luke; for there is the advantage of having another work by him, later than the Gospel and presenting characteristics which point to the date of its composition. It is practically certain that St. Luke wrote the Book of Acts.[1] That 'the former treatise' of which the writer speaks is the Gospel there can be no doubt.

There is little to show the date of the composition of Acts until we come to the last chapter. There we are confronted with a serious literary problem. How is it that a book, which displays consummate art and skill in narration, comes so abruptly to so ineffective a conclusion? The writer has been telling the story of the first stages of the Christian Church. Great events—the Ascension, Pentecost, the

[1] For a different view see J. Weiss, *D. Aufgaben der N.T^en Wissenschaft*, p. 33, 'In spite of Harnack, the fact will remain that the Lucan writings as a whole are works of a man of the post-apostolic generation, however much that is old the author has taken up into his work.' But this view is in direct conflict with the best recent criticism. 'L'auteur du troisième Évangile est le même que celui des Actes.' Loisy, *Jésus et la Tradition Évangélique*, 1910, p. 17. *v.* below, p. 15, n. 1. Loofs regards St. Luke as author of the Acts. *What is the Truth about Jesus Christ?* p. 91. J. Weiss considers it certain that the writer of the Acts was familiar with Josephus, whose *Antiquities of the Jews* belongs, at the earliest, to the year 94. He accordingly places the composition of Acts in the post-apostolic period. 'It cannot have been published by a close companion of Paul.' *Das Urchristentum*, i. pp. 4, 5. Against this view, we have to set not only the great authority of Harnack, but the fact that St. Luke's indebtedness to Josephus is not proved, while many of Weiss' examples of a late tone of thought and expression in the book would not be generally acknowledged; they fail to prove his point. He admits that the sources from which the writer has drawn his materials are of great historical value, and reflect the earliest and pre-Pauline condition of things. The Christology especially he regards as untouched by Paulinism (p. 7). But the present attitude of criticism lends no colour to Weiss' assertion that the Lucan authorship is, in spite of Harnack's championship, untenable. Zahn, alluding to the absence of any reference in Acts to St. Paul's Epistles, remarks that this proves that 'the writer stood near enough to, and in sufficiently long connection with, the Apostle to be able to dispense with the study of his Epistles with a view to the enrichment of his historical knowledge.' *Einleitung in d. N.T.* ii. p. 418.

calling of the Gentiles—unroll themselves before us. Great figures stand out upon the glowing canvas. One would look naturally for some synthesis—a summing up—at the conclusion of the story. Turning to the closing verses, we get the interesting information that St. Paul, though a prisoner, was living for two years at Rome in his own hired house, receiving and teaching all who came to him. Nothing more, and so the great recital ends. Why does it thus end? There is no satisfactory reply but that the writer has got to the end of his knowledge. He wrote no more because he knew no more. He depicts the state of things down to the time of writing. If he ever wrote more, the writing has perished.[1]

The Martyrdom of St. Paul took place in the year 65 or 66.[2] How long after he had been living for two years at Rome 'in his own hired house' we do not know. If we accept the authenticity of the Pastoral Epistles, there was a second term of imprisonment following upon a course of missionary activity in Crete and probably in Spain.[3] In that case the composition and promulgation of the Book of Acts must be placed no later than A.D. 61 or 62, and very possibly a year or two earlier. Thus 'the first treatise'—the Gospel—is thrown back to a still earlier date. The expression 'first treatise' seems to refer to a writing, not of yesterday, but of a date considerably earlier. Besides,

[1] Cf. Salmon, *Introduction to the N.T.* p. 329; Harnack in *Theol. Literaturzeitung* for 1911, p. 110, 'Preponderating grounds speak for the fact that it was written in the year in which it breaks off.' K. Lake thinks that the trial of St. Paul probably came to an end after two years—the point at which Acts breaks off—owing to the non-appearance of Jewish accusers. *Theologisch Tijdschrift* for 1913. Ramsay thinks that, as no prosecutors appeared, no trial took place. 'At the expiry of a certain period the case against him fell, and he was set free.' *The Teaching of Paul*, 1913, p. 367.

[2] We have no precise data to enable us to fix the exact year. For a comparative table of various theories, *v.* Turner in Hastings' *D.B.* i. p. 424. Lightfoot's date, A.D. 67, has recently been adopted by Edmundson, *The Church in Rome in the First Century*, pp. 148 f. 240.

[3] For the certainty that St. Paul was released from his first imprisonment, *v.* Harnack, *Chronologie*, i. p. 240; 2 Tim. iv. 16; Gwatkin, *Early History of the Church to* A.D. 313, i. p. 59, n. 1, 'St. Paul's release from Rome is anticipated by himself (Phil. ii. 24; Philem. 22) and seems proved by the Pastoral Epistles, which are decisive if genuine (which to myself does not seem seriously doubtful) and not far from decisive even if spurious.' Spitta, who regards Romans as a composite work, places chap. xvi. between St. Paul's first and second imprisonment. *v.* A. Schweitzer, *Geschichte der Paulinischen Forschung*, p. 117.

it is hardly likely that two such important compositions would be written consecutively, or within a brief interval of time. Everything points to the lapse of years, rather than months between them. We may therefore assign the Gospel to the closing years of the fifth decade, about A.D. 57 or 58.[1] Before applying this result to the date of the composition of St. Mark, we may inquire whether it is possible to fix a probable date for the First Gospel.

Here we have much less to go upon. Not only is the authorship of the Gospel uncertain, but there is no other book by the same writer with which to compare it, or to aid our inquiry. The general tradition of the Church from Irenaeus onwards ascribes it to St. Matthew. But when the literary study of the Gospels began, and attempts were made to determine their mutual relation and to trace their origin, doubt was at once cast upon the tradition, until at length it has become widely held that, in spite of its title and of the common belief of the Church, our present Gospel is not the work of the Apostle.

Two considerations led to this result. It was thought that an Apostle—an eye-witness—would not have based his own Gospel on the work of one—St. Mark—who was neither an Apostle nor an eye-witness of the life of Christ. It was also felt that the Gospel shows every indication of being a work originally written in Greek, not a translation of the writing which Papias ascribes to St. Matthew.[2]

[1] Harnack assigns A.D. 59 as the date of Acts. Loofs thinks A.D. 61 or 62 more probable, but adds 'earlier than the Acts, hence before 61 or 62 A.D., the Gospel of Luke must have been written.' After referring to the views of Harnack on the date of St. Mark and the Logia, Loofs remarks, 'Even if I were convinced (that he was right), I should be sure that Harnack would not do away with the later dates which are defended by liberal theologians. The very interest in a purely human life of Jesus will prevent the critics from ... admitting so early a date to the Gospels.' *What is the Truth about Jesus Christ?* p. 91. A more extraordinary charge—or is it a personal confession?—of subjectivity it would be difficult to imagine. A writing is found to belong to a certain year; but this must not be admitted lest a pet theory should suffer. Besides, Loofs himself remarks, 'The Gospel of John really throws insurmountable obstacles in the way of describing a purely human life of Jesus.' *Ib.* p. 98.

[2] In Euseb. *H.E.* iii. 39. *v.* B. Weiss, *D. Leben Jesu*, i. p. 52, 'Our Matthew is no doubt an original Greek writing.' So Dean Robinson, *The Study of the Gospels*, p. 17; McNeile, *The Gospel according to St. Matthew*, 1915, p. xxviii, 'Though Hebraic to the core, it is quite clearly a Greek composition.'

These considerations require testing. At first sight they appear formidable. The use of St. Mark by the author of the First Gospel is certain. It forms the groundwork of his narrative, and, according to Papias, embodies as the staple of its material reminiscences of the teaching of St. Peter. Now St. Matthew (supposing him to be the author of the First Gospel) would be well aware of the origin of a writing which he incorporated in his own Gospel and treated with great respect, preserving its order and in many cases its actual expressions. He was not himself a man of much mark among the Apostles. His call came comparatively late.[1] In framing his own Gospel, it was a help to be able to use historical material, which had the authority of an original Apostle of the rank of St. Peter.[2] But there is another side to the question. The fact that here and there the First Gospel modifies, omits and deals somewhat freely with St. Mark, suggests that its author was a man of some position in the community. Otherwise, he would hardly have ventured to alter what proceeded from so high a quarter. It seems reasonable, therefore, that an Apostle should employ a Gospel writing which proceeded mainly from the teaching of St. Peter as the narrative basis of his own Gospel, while, at the same time, his own position as a disciple and eye-witness would qualify him to amend his written authority from his own stores of direct experience.[3]

The other difficulty in the way of the assignment of the First Gospel to St. Matthew is purely literary. If we follow Papias in this matter and accept his assurance that 'Matthew compiled the oracles in the Hebrew (Aramaic) tongue,' we are met by the fact that the First Gospel has every appearance of having been written originally in Greek. There is no indication that it was translated from another language. But does this mean that, if we accept the statement of Papias that Matthew wrote the oracles in Hebrew, other persons

[1] Matt. ix. 9 and 11. *v.* Zahn, *Einleitung in d. N.T.* ii. p. 260.

[2] His narrative of what passed at Caesarea Philippi points in that direction. Matt. xvi. 18, 19. Not without significance is the fact that St. Luke, though, as he says, he had perfect knowledge of all things from the first, made Mark the groundwork of his own Gospel.

[3] The above considerations appear to lessen the force of Dr. McNeile's contention that 'One who could write with the paramount authority of an eyewitness would not have been content to base his work on that of a secondary authority.' *St. Matthew*, p. xxviii.

translating them according to their ability, we are necessarily precluded from holding that St. Matthew also wrote a Gospel, the first copy of which was in the Greek language, and that that work and our own First Gospel are one and the same thing?

Before we endeavour to answer that question, we must see what Papias means by *τὰ λόγια*. The expression is usually understood to refer to 'sayings,' 'discourses': and a comparison of 'Q,' as arrived at by analysis of the non-Marcan element common to St. Matthew and St. Luke,[1] shows that if the *λόγια* of Papias refers to that element 'Q,' the writing certainly consisted mainly of sayings rather than of narrative. But the usual term for 'sayings' was not *λόγια* but *λόγοι*;[2] and if speeches and sayings of our Lord comprised the main part of 'the oracles,' it stands to reason that there would not have been wanting some connecting threads of narrative, showing the occasion and place of the utterances and setting them in an historic framework.[3]

May we not reconcile the literary peculiarities of the First Gospel with the statement of Papias, and follow the tradition from Irenaeus onwards, by regarding it as a Greek writing of St. Matthew,[4] in which he incorporates his own Aramaic, but translated, notes of Christ's sayings with the Petrine narrative of St. Mark, adding other material from special sources unknown to St. Luke? The ordinary employment and life of St. Matthew as a publican ensured his familiarity with the two languages—the Aramaic of the Syrian peasants, and the Greek of the merchants in the Galilean towns.[5] It is now thought that St. Mark's

[1] 'Q' = Quelle (source) is a non-committal designation given to the material common to St. Matthew and St. Luke which is not derived from St. Mark.

[2] Matt. vii. 28; Mk. viii. 38; Lk. vi. 47, ix. 28.

[3] Cf. B. Weiss, *D. Leben Jesu*, i. p. 30; Zahn, *Einleitung in d. N.T.* ii. p. 262.

[4] The manner in which the First Gospel deals with the Apostle Matthew strongly points to his authorship. In its list of the Apostles, it places him *after* St. Thomas: in the other lists, he comes *before* that Apostle. No one but St. Matthew himself would, in giving a detailed list of the Apostles, hand down to all time the name of one of them in connection with the hated trade of publican (Matt. x. 3). In Mk. ii. 14 and Lk. v. 27, the publican whom Christ called to discipleship, and who made Him a feast in his house, is named Levi. In the First Gospel, when the same series of events is described, the publican is identified with Matthew the Apostle (Matt. ix. 9 f.). *v.* Zahn, *Einleitung in d. N.T.* i. pp. 258, 9.

[5] *v.* Zahn, *Einleitung in d. N.T.* ii. p. 259; Carr in *Expositor* for 1910, p. 553.

Gospel was first written in Aramaic, being afterwards translated at Rome into Greek; [1] and this consideration lends colour to the suggestion that the First Gospel is composed of materials which were put together in the first instance in the Aramaic language—St. Matthew's own λόγια and the Second Gospel.

It should be remembered that when Papias wrote it would be known whether St. Matthew was the author. If Papias made no statement, we may conclude, from the belief which prevailed a few years later, that the writer was thought to be St. Matthew. If, on the other hand, he attributed the Gospel to another source, we may be sure that Eusebius would have recorded the fact. So far as we know, the only name ever assigned to it was that of St. Matthew.[2]

[1] This opinion was formed by W. C. Allen and published in 1900 in *Expositor*, p. 442 f. Wellhausen believes in an Aramaic original of St Mark. *Einleitung in d. drei Ersten Evangelien*, pp. 35, 37. He observes that the other Synoptic writers might have seen the Aramaic text, but as a rule they used the Greek. Blass also thinks that St. Mark wrote in Aramaic. *Philology of the Gospels*, 1898, p. 196 f. So too Allen in *Expository Times*, July, 1910, and in *Oxford Studies in the Synoptic Problem*, p. 293. (For the date of St. Mark, *v.* Allen in *Expository Times, ib.*) *v.* Chwolson, *Über die Frage ob Jesus gelebt hat*, 1910, pp. 4, 5.

[2] Dean Armitage Robinson, who says that 'our St. Matthew is demonstrably composed out of two Greek books,' thinks that 'if a sufficiently early date could be established for the book, then we might accept the tradition of its authorship in spite of the puzzling statement about its having been written in Hebrew.' *The Study of the Gospels*, pp. 18, 19. But it remains a question whether the reference of Papias is to the Gospel or to a collection of sayings. The latter explanation now finds most favour; and if we adopt it, we have not got the 'Hebrew' difficulty to deal with. Papias himself notes how freely and generally translations of St. Matthew's 'Hebrew' were being made. According to Zahn, Papias is referring to oral translation during public worship, and it is not the whole Gospel, but the sayings of Jesus contained in it which are the subject of translation. *Einleitung in d. N.T.* ii. p. 263. Our Greek St. Matthew, he considers, is a translation made from the Hebrew (Aramaic) St. Matthew by an unknown writer in the province of Asia rather before A.D. 90 than after A.D. 100. *Ib.* p. 265. He also remarks that we are not indebted to Papias alone for the information that the Gospel first appeared in Hebrew. 'Origen, in whose writings no trace of any acquaintance with the work of Papias is to be found, speaks as confidently as Irenaeus of the original language of the Gospel of Matthew.' About A.D. 180, Pantaenus, the founder of the catechetical school at Alexandria, met with a Hebrew Gospel which passed as St. Matthew's, in India (South Arabia ?) (Euseb. *H.E.* v. 10, 3). Zahn, *ib.* p. 266. Burkitt says, 'What the work was to which Papias alludes is very doubtful; it is certain that our Gospel according to Matthew is a Greek work, based upon Greek sources, one of them being in fact our Gospel according to Mark.' *The Earliest Sources for the Life of Jesus*, 1910, p. 38, n. 1.

But, if that Apostle wrote both the 'oracles' in Aramaic and the Greek Gospel which incorporates them, a considerable time must have elapsed between the composition of the two works. Some think that our present Gospel was written too late for it to be possible for the Logia to be the work of the same man. The use of the term ἐκκλησία [1] and the Trinitarian formula in our Lord's parting words [2] are held to show a tone of thought which requires a late date. But it has been proved that there is no anachronism in placing the word ἐκκλησία (*i.e.* its Aramaic form) in our Lord's mouth; [3] while, as regards the Three-fold Name, its use by St. Paul shows that the idea was already familiar to the primitive community. So striking a co-ordination of Father, Son and Holy Spirit must have required nothing short of the highest authority for its employment.

There is some ground for thinking that St. Luke was acquainted with the First Gospel before writing his own.[4] As we have seen, he probably wrote it about A.D. 57-60. On this theory, St. Matthew would have to be placed about A.D. 54-57, after the Greek version of St. Mark, but before the composition of St. Luke. If we can assign such a date to our Greek First Gospel, there is no reason to be alleged, on the score of time, against St. Matthew's authorship both of the Hebrew 'oracles' and of the Gospel as we now possess it.

So far, we have been working back to the probable date of the Second Gospel from consideration of the dates of the First and Third. We may sum up this part of our inquiry as follows. There is good ground for thinking that the Third Gospel was in existence by the years A.D. 57-60, and some probability that St. Matthew's Gospel in Greek had been written a few years earlier. If this be so, St. Mark, which lay in its Greek form

[1] Matt. xvi.; xviii. *v.* Von Dobschütz, *Probleme des apost. Zeitalters*, p. 10.

[2] Matt. xxviii. 19. Cf. 2 Cor. xiii. 14. *v.* below, p. 469.

[3] For the use of ἐκκλησία, *v.* Hort, *The Christian Ecclesia*, pp. 8, 9. He considers it was employed by Christ. Cf. Wellhausen in Matt. xvi. 18, who says that the word passed from the Jewish to the Christian community, and in its Aramaic original could indicate either. We have no need to suppose that the term is due to a later interpolation. On the unity of the Gospel, *v.* Allen in *Dict. of Christ*, art. 'Matthew,' p. 146.

[4] *v.* Robinson Smith in *Hibbert Journal* for April, 1912. On the other hand, McNeile considers that the First and Third Gospels 'appear to be quite independent and neither shows distinct signs of priority.' *St. Matthew*, p. xxvi.

before the First and Third Evangelists, is put back to about A.D. 50.[1]

If these dates can be upheld—and there is every probability that further investigation will strengthen their claim on our reception of them—we have in our present Gospels historical material which was committed to writing well within the generation immediately following upon the Resurrection; writings which could be investigated and checked by living witnesses of our Lord, and could be compared with the oral teaching that was being given in the churches by the Apostles and Evangelists; teaching which was gradually taking a set form and to which believers generally were expected to give their whole-hearted allegiance. The importance of this critical position can hardly be over-estimated. When we read the Gospels, we have an ever-growing certainty that we are face to face with the work of Apostolic witnesses to Christ; and that their accuracy [2] has the double guarantee of early composition and harmony with the body of Apostolic teaching, which was being orally given in Jerusalem, in Antioch and elsewhere.[3]

[1] Sanday places it ten years before St. Luke. Streeter thinks that 'Q' was written twenty years before St. Mark. *Oxford Studies*, p. 219. If Harnack's suggestion of *c.* A.D. 60 for St. Luke is taken, this would bring 'Q' to much the same date—the life-time of Christ—which has been suggested by Ramsay, Salmon and Chwolson. But, of course, it must be remembered that the writers above mentioned might not give their adherence to all the links in this chain. *v.* Sanday in *Oxford Studies*, p. xviii; Allen, *Expos. Times*, July, 1910, p. 444.

[2] Dr. P. Gardner speaks of 'modern historical criticism' as 'destroying our confidence in the literary records of early Christianity.' *The Ephesian Gospel*, 1915, p. 355. As will be gathered from what has been said above, the actual state of the case appears to be the exact opposite to this view. Whatever view we take of the position of Schweitzer as a critic, we have to admit that his work has done much to expose the failure of 'liberal' theology to discredit the trustworthiness of the Gospels. But that its tendency was and is destructive there can be no doubt. *E.g.* he asks, 'How can anyone cut out the feeding of the multitudes and the Transfiguration, as narratives of secondary origin, without destroying the whole of the historical fabric of the Gospel of Mark?' *Von Reimarus zu Wrede*, p. 305, E.T.; cf. *ib.* p. 331. 'Modern historical theology with its three-quarters scepticism is left at last with only a torn and tattered Gospel of Mark in its hands.' *Ib.* p. 307. But recent writings of the 'religious-historical' school show that Schweitzer's attack has by no means put an end to the methods which he has exposed; still less has it silenced the efforts of negative criticism to eliminate the 'supernatural' conception of the Person of our Lord from the Christian Faith.

[3] Cf. Acts ii. 42, *τῇ διδαχῇ τῶν ἀποστόλων*. *v.* Carr in *Expositor*, 1910, p. 547 f., who strikingly brings out the definite character of this teaching. Cf. Heb. ii. 3.

There is at present a tendency to depreciate the value of the oral element in the transmission of our Gospels, partly from the necessary lack of positive proof as compared with the evidence of existing documents; partly, perhaps, from the undue weight assigned to it by some scholars.[1] Yet we may at least regard it as a very real check and criterion of the written Gospels: for we may be sure that no writings which lacked the consent and adhesion of living Apostles and Teachers, would have won acceptance from the Church as authoritative. We may, therefore, regard the Gospels as coming to us with the authority of careful and conscientious writers, who have at their back the whole weight of the *διδάχη τῶν ἀποστόλων* to confirm, to restrain and to authenticate their message.

Secondly. Behind the Gospels as they have been handed down to us, there was not only oral, but written support. Analysis of their contents discloses the existence of two main sources. The Petrine teaching which forms the chief portion of St. Mark is one. The other is 'Q,' the non-Marcan element—largely composed of sayings—common to St. Matthew and St. Luke. The progress of investigation tends to throw both of these ancient sources far back towards the days of our Lord's public ministry. The peculiar freshness of the portions of St. Mark that are evidently due to St. Peter points to an experience which is recent and vividly remembered.[2] Then, too, the frequent occurrence of

[1] Such as Bp. Westcott and in the present day Dr. A. Wright.

[2] *E.g.* In the feeding of the 5000, the people sitting down in companies are still before the mind of St. Peter, looking like flower beds among the green grass, *ἀνέπεσον πρασιαὶ πρασιαί*, lit. 'they were reclining garden-beds, garden-beds.' In Mk. ii. 1, *ἐν οἴκῳ* (*al. lect. εἰς οἶκον*) 'at home,' 'indoors' (Swete), points to the direct manner of speech of St. Peter as he talked of the familiar house. On the descent from the Mount of the Transfiguration, the scene is described as it would be by one of those who came down with our Lord (*e.g.* by St. Peter). St. Mark speaks of Christ coming to the rest of the disciples and seeing a great crowd (ix. 14). Then there are minute touches which point to recollections of an eye-witness scattered throughout the Gospel; Mk. xii. 41.

Apart from these internal signs of freshness, all that we know of St. Mark's own career points to the probability that he committed his notes of St. Peter's preaching to writing at a very early date. The son of the Mary (sister of Barnabas) at whose house in Jerusalem Christians were gathered together on the night of the Passover, A.D. 44, when St. Peter was delivered from prison, St. Mark must have heard the Apostle preach not long after Pentecost. The house of his widowed mother plays a great part in early tradition. It was probably the scene of the last Passover and of the appearances of Christ to the disciples after His Resurrection. St. Peter was in the habit of frequenting the house. The damsel Rhoda at once recognized his voice, Acts xii. 13. As

Aramaisms not only points to the probability that the first draft of the Gospel was in that language, but to the desire to link the Greek Gospel on to the teaching of the Apostle, and to reproduce his actual words, here and there, in the midst of the general Greek texture of the later version.

When, to the evidence of the early committal to writing of the Petrine reminiscences of St. Mark, we add that of 'Q,' we get a remarkable amount of certainty that the Synoptic Gospels are placed upon a bedrock of authentic tradition. 'Q' is now recognized as our earliest Gospel source. There is considerable probability that it contained words of our Lord taken down at the moment of utterance. No one among the Apostles would be more likely to take notes of what He said than St. Matthew. His business as a tax-gatherer involved a system of accounts accurately put down at the moment of each transaction. His call to Apostleship took away from the man his employment. But it did not do violence to habits long formed and, in their way, of great value. He who once noted the receipt of money, now records the precious sayings that fell from his Master's lips. He has become 'a tried banker';[1] and the coinage, which he

St. Mark soon after this was quite old enough to be chosen by St. Paul and St. Barnabas as their minister (ὑπηρέτης), Acts xii. 25; xiii. 5, is it not probable that many of his notes of the preaching of St. Peter at Jerusalem were already made in Aramaic by that time? *v.* Zahn, *Einleitung in d. N.T.* ii. pp. 204, 217, n. 7. Out of those early notes the first draft of his Gospel would be constructed; and material and place both suggested the continued use of Aramaic. What then was the probable occasion of the composition of the present Greek Version? It was the general belief of antiquity that the Second Gospel was written in Rome. St. Mark was there during St. Paul's first imprisonment. But its use by SS. Matthew and Luke as the basis of their Gospels requires an earlier date for its translation into Greek than the visit to Rome would permit. It is possible that a final revision, occasioned by renewal of intercourse at Rome with St. Peter, may have led to the belief that the Gospel was originally composed there. That belief rests mainly on Clem. Alex. *Hypotyp.* in Euseb. *H.E.* vi. 14, and hardly appears to be of sufficient weight to negative the conclusions to which we have been led. The presence of variations in the use of St. Mark by the First and the Third Evangelist supports the hypothesis of a version of the Gospel other than that which has come down to us. Cf. Stanton, *The Gospels as Historical Documents*, ii. p. 43; *Oxford Studies in the Synoptic Problem*, Essay XIII. Zahn favours the theory of the Roman origin of the Gospel (*Einleitung*, ii. p. 208). It would be interesting to know his present attitude in view of the researches of Harnack and others in Gospel chronology.

[1] *Γίνεσθε τραπεζῖται δόκιμοι*, an apocryphal saying of our Lord preserved by Origen, *in Joann.* xix. and elsewhere. Cf. Ps. cxix. 72.

handles and passes down for the use of all ages, is from the mint of heaven.[1]

To sum up this analysis of the sources at our disposal: there is good ground for believing that, behind the Synoptic Gospels in their present form, two ancient documents were already in existence, the record of Christ's sayings of which Papias speaks, and which is now thought to have been put into writing by St. Matthew during the Public Ministry, and the Aramaic notes of the preaching of St. Peter made by his 'interpreter' St. Mark, forming the original copy of the Second Gospel. Thus, along with the probability that our Gospels assumed their present shape at an earlier date than we had thought, *their underlying substance* may now be regarded as belonging to the life-time of our Lord and the few following years.

One result of this new movement of thought in the chronology of the Gospels is the need for reconsidering their relation to the Pauline Epistles. Hitherto, the writings of St. Paul (1 Thess. 2 Thess. Galat.) have been regarded as the earliest documentary evidence that has come down to us in its original form. 1 Thess. has been placed in A.D. 51;[2] Galatians in A.D. 50-55.[3] As a

[1] The age of 'Q' is a subject of deep interest. The writing stopped short before the Passion. It contains no record of the sayings of the last days of Christ's life. How is this to be explained? Ramsay in *Expositor*, May, 1907, says that 'Q' was written down during the public ministry. Salmon in the same year takes a similar view. *The Human Element in the Gospels*, p. 274. Harnack believes 'Q' to be our oldest Gospel source. *Beiträge zur Einleitung in d. N.T.* ii. 1907, p. 171. The silence of 'Q' as to the Passion has more recently been accounted for by the prevailing belief in the nearness of the Parousia and by the fact that the circumstances were too well known to need a record. Streeter in *Oxford Studies in the Synoptic Problem*, p. 215. The earlier explanation is the simplest; and it is being made the more probable by the present tendency to work back to a very early date for the primitive material of the Gospels. Streeter himself (*Oxford Studies, ib.*) considers twelve years after the Crucifixion a probable date for such a document as 'Q.' The theory advocated by some recent writers that Mark had seen 'Q' and made some use of it points in the same direction. It has been observed that shorthand, which Cicero employed during the trial of Catiline, was much in vogue during the first century A.D. (*Hibbert Journal* for April, 1912, p. 723). It was an accomplishment which the publican Matthew would, of all the Apostles, be the most likely to possess, and the period was one of great literary activity in the Jewish world. These considerations, while they do not prove, go far to commend the opinion that the common, non-Marcan material of the First and Third Gospels was committed to writing within the time of our Lord's public ministry.

[2] By Sanday in *D.B.* ii. p. 648: by Turner in *D.B.* i. p. 423.

[3] By Turner in *D.B.* i. p. 423.

consequence of the general belief that St. Paul is, in this respect, the earliest witness to the origin of Christianity, many writers begin their works on Christian doctrine or practice with his Epistles, the Gospels being relegated to a later stage of evidence. That this method was to be defended at a time when the priority of St. Paul was regarded as certain, may well be admitted, however unnatural[1] it might appear. That it requires reconsideration in view of the facts which have been referred to, must now be conceded. The Gospel of St. Mark in its present form is now held, on good grounds, to proceed from a period *as early as* (*if not earlier than*) the first of the Epistles of St. Paul; while in its first, Aramaic shape, it belongs to a period well before the date of any of the Pauline writings.[2]

When we pass from the Synoptic Gospels to that of St. John, we enter a field of criticism in which there is scarcely any general agreement. Certain main positions in the Synoptic problem are almost universally admitted. But in the case of the Fourth Gospel, authorship, date, historical value, are still regarded as open questions. Private convictions, however strongly grounded, must therefore be restrained from dogmatically asserting themselves. We cannot use the Fourth Gospel as a source of our knowledge of the rise of Christendom as freely as we use the Synoptics. To do so would at once prejudice our conclusions in the minds of those who are unable to follow our critical course. At the same time, there is a growing disposition to regard the Fourth Gospel as containing history; while it is also felt that the deepest characteristics of our Lord's life and ministry, and some of the most certain elements of His Self-consciousness are nowhere more vividly brought out than in St. John.

In many cases its historical worth is assured by comparison with the Synoptic narratives; and, as we shall find as we proceed, *it is the same Christ that all the Gospels present for our acceptance.*

We must first face the fact that we have a double tradition of Jesus, that of St. John and that of the Synoptic writers.[3] Each

[1] 'Unnatural,' because the narrative of an event ordinarily precedes discussion of its meaning.

[2] *v.* above, p. 12.

[3] Wernle, *Einführung in das Theologische Studium*, 1908, p. 144.

strain regards its subject from a different point of view. There is strong temptation, which some critics have failed to resist, to magnify the differences and to lose sight of what is common to the two aspects. However, full recognition must be given to the—at first sight—disconcerting fact that, when the three Synoptic Gospels had become fairly established in the use of the chief Churches, another Gospel was presented, which not only takes a different line in its treatment of the subject, but contains a large number of statements which are difficult to reconcile with the Synoptic outline of events already in the possession of the Church.

Is it not a most perplexing thing that, about the close of the first century, when all but one of the original witnesses of our Lord's life had passed away, a fresh account of Him should suddenly be launched upon the Church, containing so much that, to men familiar with the existing tradition, appeared to give quite a different version of the facts?[1] Besides, we have to bear in mind that, even to this day, no complete reconciliation of these differences has been effected. There are still outstanding problems that defy every attempt at solution. The Johannine question is still in the forefront of those trials to faith and patience, which form a large part of our present discipline.

Before we can come to any decision as to the use of the Gospel as an authority, we must see how we stand as regards authorship, date, internal and external testimony.

Does it bear the marks of being an authentic document? It seems natural to ask, first of all, who wrote it. That is generally the first question that meets one who offers us a book on any subject. We may be certain that, when Churches distant from the birthplace of the Gospel were made aware of its existence, and when its strangeness and its independence were realized, men asked 'To whom do we owe this new account of the life and death of the Lord?' Now, at that late date in the rise of the Christian Faith, when men had for several decades been accustomed to a certain clear and well-defined outline of the way of life, anything that appeared to cross, or run counter to, received truth would be challenged peremptorily as to its authority. And of one thing we may be perfectly sure. None

[1] 'Le quatrième Évangile est une œuvre à part, et pour tout dire, unique.' Batiffol, *Orpheus et l'Évangile*, p. 194.

but a man of Apostolic rank would gain a hearing for so revolutionary a narrative as the Fourth Gospel is still felt by many to be. We may go farther, and say that no less a personality than one of 'the chiefest Apostles' would be listened to with such a message. Men would reasonably ask for the highest credentials before receiving what presented so fresh and novel a view of the course of our Saviour's ministry and of the manner of His teaching. The answer to the question was at once forthcoming. No other name than that of John, son of Zebedee, was ever whispered as the author until we come to recent times;[1] while the fact of the gradual acceptance of the Gospel, wherever it was brought, points to the universal opinion—may we not say knowledge?—of its origin.

Does the Gospel itself throw any light upon the question of its authorship? When we compare St. John with the other three Gospels, we are struck with the fact that whereas the Synoptics have much to say about John the son of Zebedee and his close intimacy with our Lord, the Fourth Gospel does not once mention him by name. But it speaks frequently of a 'disciple whom Jesus loved,' and seems to identify him with the John who occupies so prominent a place in the other Gospels. It is difficult to avoid the conclusion that the John, son of Zebedee, of the Synoptics, the loved disciple and 'he who wrote these things,' of the Fourth Gospel, are one and the same man. The restrained allusions to the loved disciple, coupled with what we know of his position among the Apostles, are exactly what we might expect from an author who was referring to himself with the diffidence of a high-souled man like St. John. The Gospel compared with the Synoptics thus confesses to its authorship. It is by the man who veils his identity and is unwilling to come openly forward, who yet asseverates his capacity to bear witness and leaves to the judgment and common sense of the whole Church the naming of the author of its last Gospel.[2]

[1] The assignment of the authorship to Cerinthus by the sect called the Alogi is a vagary which hardly deserves mention. *v.* p. 44.

[2] Spitta, who regards the Fourth Gospel as a composite work, discusses the various occasions on which the nameless disciple, whom Jesus loved, is mentioned in the Gospel, and draws the conclusion that he is the author of the oldest part—the underlying source of the Gospel. He shows that this disciple is closely connected with St. Peter, who, in the Synoptic Gospels, is constantly mentioned along with the sons of Zebedee as standing closely to our Lord.

The date of the Fourth Gospel is not easy to determine; but everything conspires to place it near the close of the first century. St. John 'lived until the times of Trajan';[1] and tradition concurs with internal indications in pointing to the Fourth Gospel as a work of the writer's extreme old age.[2] We may, perhaps, assign it to the closing decade of the first century and to the year 95 or thereabouts. The solemnity of the asseverations of truth, the reference to the mistaken interpretation of our Lord's words in chap. xxi., which seems to be made under the influence of an impression of the impending close of life, incline one to set the Gospel down as the work of the Evangelist's last

James, one of these sons, is not so connected with Peter. The nameless disciple is therefore in all probability St. John, and he it is who is the writer of the original, underlying source of the Gospel. *Das Johannes-Evangelium*, p. 457.

If we examine the arguments of the most recent opponent of the Johannine authorship, Dr. P. Gardner, *The Ephesian Gospel*, 1915, we find that they are partly hypothetical in character, although most dogmatically expressed, and partly dependent on questions of literary taste and judgment. Thus, 'that he (the author) was John the son of Zebedee is so improbable that we may regard this view as set aside.' 'As a literary composition it is quite beyond the powers of the fisherman of Galilee,' p. 54. 'It is indeed very doubtful whether the fisherman of Galilee would have had sufficient literary training to write any continuous composition,' p. 69. It suffices to reply that, according to our information, if the son of Zebedee was in his youth a Galilean fisherman, in later years and to extreme old age he was a dweller in such cities as Jerusalem and Ephesus. Again: 'It seems quite incredible that if the Apostle John were the actual writer of the Gospel, he should have designated himself in it by the phrase, "the disciple whom Jesus loved,"' p. 71. It has been well replied that 'as soon as Professor Gardner's improbables and impossibles are examined by someone else, they have a way of passing into the possible and the probable.' *Expos. Times*, Aug. 1915, p. 482.

[1] Trajan reigned A.D. 98-117. *v.* Iren. *Haeres.* ii. 22, 5; iii. 3, 4; Euseb. *H.E.* iii. 23. An indirect proof of its composition in the first century is the foolish attribution of the authorship of the Gospel to the heretic Cerinthus by a sect of about A.D. 170. Cerinthus was at Ephesus about the time that St. John was said to be living there. *v.* Zahn, *Einleitung in d. N.T.* ii. p. 454; *D. Evangelium des Johannes*, p. 15; B. Weiss, *Bibl. Theologie des N.T.* p. 583.

[2] Irenaeus speaks of the residence of St. John at Ephesus. *Haeres.* ii. 22, 5; iii. 3, 4, etc., so too Polycrates of Ephesus (A.D. 196), in Euseb. *H.E.* iii. 31, 3; v. 24, 3. It is also referred to by G. Hamartolus in his *Chronicon* (*v.* Lightfoot-Harmer, *The Apostolic Fathers*, p. 519) in a passage in which he quotes Papias as to the death of St. John by martyrdom. It is therefore probable that Papias spoke of the residence of St. John at Ephesus. 'If John had lived at Ephesus for many years in his old age, the tradition that he was the author of the Fourth Gospel could not easily be pushed aside.' F. Loofs, *What is the Truth about Jesus Christ?* p. 104.

years. The fact that hardly any trace of its existence is to be found in the sub-Apostolic writers of the next few years makes it probable that it was of such recent origin, and—as compared with the Gospels already in the use of the Church—of such strange and novel content, that it had not yet gained a place in general acceptance. It was probably retained in certain circles in Asia and hardly known in Rome and the West. But that it must have been written at about the turn of the century is clear from the fact that it is quoted in A.D. 125 by the Gnostic, Basileides.[1] On the whole, a date before A.D. 100 appears most probable.

Much skill and labour have recently been expended on the attempt to distinguish strata (*Schichte*) of various periods in the Gospel.[2] The book is thought to be composite, containing historical elements of great value embedded in editorial note and comment by one or more hands.[3] Criticism has set itself the task of disentangling the original (Johannine) element from these later accretions.[4] But the attempt fails through the impossibility of ever attaining agreement upon the limits of the old and the new, as well as through the difficulty of hitting upon a criterion for discriminating between what belongs to the original draft of the work and what is editorial. There can be no finality in what is so purely subjective.

Then, in direct opposition to any theory of strata or of the editing of an *Ur-Johannes*, we have the strong testimony to the essential unity of the work which is given by Holtzmann, Jülicher and others.[5] 'The work, apart from interpolations[6]

[1] Harnack says, 'that it was not written later than c. A.D. 110, is an assured historical truth.' *Gesch. der altchristl. Literatur. Chronologie*, i. p. 674. Zahn thinks that the Gospel was written and put into circulation before the year 100. *Einleitung in d. N.T.* ii. p. 503. F. Loofs concurs in the view of Harnack, as to date. *What is the Truth about Jesus Christ?* p. 101.

[2] By Wendt, Wellhausen, Spitta, etc.

[3] Thus Wendt considers that St. John is the author of the source which has been edited in the Fourth Gospel. *Die Lehre Jesu*, p. 41.

[4] For a discussion of these theories (as put forward by Wendt and Briggs) see Sanday, *The Criticism of the Fourth Gospel*, p. 22 f. For criticism of Wendt's principles of distinguishing later additions, *v.* Schmiedel in *Encycl. Bibl.* ii. col. 2555. 'The difficulties in the way of partition theories seem to be insuperable.' Inge in *Dict. of Christ*, i. p. 889.

[5] Holtzmann, *Einleitung in d. N.T.* p. 431; Jülicher, *Einleitung in d. N.T.* p. 354.

[6] *E.g.* v. 4; vii. 53–viii. 11.

. . . and the concluding chapter added by way of supplement,[1] is, in form and substance, in arrangement and thought, an organic whole, without additions or omissions, "the seamless coat."'[2]

The elders of Ephesus have, indeed, added a solemn note of confirmation (vv. 24, 25) to the concluding chapter, moved perhaps by the author's insistence upon the truth of what he has written; but the very fact that they are so impressed with its historic value would suffice to deter them from altering or emending, or in any way editing, a work for which they had conceived so deep a reverence.[3]

It is from the characteristic peculiarities of the Gospel itself that the strongest arguments against its authentic and trustworthy nature are brought. Two of these characteristics are especially prominent. In style and contents, the sayings and speeches attributed to our Lord differ widely from those reported by the other Evangelists. Are we placed in the dilemma of rejecting the Johannine recital if we accept the Synoptic report?

Now, the difference between the two accounts—Synoptic and Johannine—is certainly very great; and the question is further complicated by the fact that the Fourth Evangelist is not always careful to mark the transition from our Lord's words to his own reflections based upon the words.[4] The most striking point of dissimilarity is the absence of that teaching by parable, which forms so leading a feature of the discourse of Christ in the Synoptic Gospels. In St. John you find pictorial, descriptive, allegorical representation, but nowhere actual parable. Does the reason of this difference lie in the mental attitude of the Fourth Evangelist himself, as distinct from that of the other writers? Was St. John

[1] But this view is rejected by many (Lightfoot, Harnack, Wernle, etc.). Holtzmann himself acknowledges that there is no proof that the Gospel was ever published without chap. xxi. (*Evangelium des Johannes*, p. 308). Zahn considers chap. xxi. a supplement. 'No historical writing of the N.T. and few histories of antiquity possess what is so clearly a conclusion as the Fourth Gospel contains in chap. xx. 30 f.' *Einleitung in d. N.T.* ii. p. 492.

[2] Holtzmann, *Einleitung*, p. 431. Zahn thinks that the concluding chapter was added before the Gospel left the circle for whom it was composed. *Einleitung in d. N.T.* ii. p. 493.

[3] Schmiedel considers that this guarantee of truthfulness is against the Apostolic origin of the Gospel. *Encycl. Bibl.* ii. col. 2543.

[4] *v.* below, p. 36, n. 2.

disposed to assimilate what our Lord taught by figure and image rather than that which took the form of a story? Having before him the threefold Synoptic narrative of the teaching, he was not inclined to add to its wealth of parable; but he may well have been concerned to bring out and to perpetuate teaching, which it is quite probable that our Lord gave in the form in which St. John has handed it down. It is true that we are told that 'without a parable spake He not unto them.'[1] For 'the multitude' it was the most appropriate and telling vehicle of instruction. But there were many occasions—in discourse with individuals and with disciples—in which the parable was not suitable for His purpose. St. John has preferred to seize upon what passed on those occasions. The dialogue was a form of discourse which seems to have specially appealed to his own tone of mind. As 'the disciple whom Jesus loved,' he appears to have been at hand when the rest of the Apostles were absent. He seems to have overheard the discourse with Nicodemus. Did he alone linger with Jesus at the well of Sychar, when 'the disciples had gone away unto the city to buy meat'? His power to report what was said on these occasions finds its simplest explanation in his presence. He, whether alone of all the disciples he was present, or alone was able to enter into and retain it, reports the great High Priestly Prayer, which Christ prayed aloud to His Father on the eve of His death. In the repeated assurance of his special nearness to the human heart of Jesus, should we not see an explanation of his capacity to narrate what was most intimate and reserved of his Master's utterances, not a mere boast of privilege?[2] The disciple, whom Jesus loved, was one in whom He found a sympathy that was not forthcoming in the other disciples. And love is the key to knowledge. In the tie of mutual affection, which bound St. John and his Lord, we have an explanation of the peculiar characteristics of the Fourth Gospel. It does not indeed remove all our difficulties; but it goes some way towards accounting for the marked con-

[1] Matt. xiii. 34, that is 'to the multitudes,' τοῖς ὄχλοις. Cf. Mk. iv. 11, 'Unto them that are without, all these things are done in parables.'

[2] Schmiedel regards the designation (John xiii. 23, etc.) as fatal to the view that it applies to the author of the Gospel. 'One can hardly understand how it is possible to have sympathy for a writer who claims for himself such a degree of superiority as is implied in this designation.' *Encycl. Bibl.* ii. col. 2544. The mention of such a piece of criticism is sufficient to refute it.

trasts, which meet us as we compare the Synoptic and the Johannine records of our Lord's sayings.

If the temperament of the writer and the fact of his peculiar intimacy with our Lord throw light upon the contrasts, which his Gospel presents to the Synoptic narrative of Christ's sayings, we have also to take into account the distinct purpose of his work.

St. Clement of Alexandria [1] has told us that St. John wrote, not to add to the Synoptic history of our Lord's life, but to convey the inner, spiritual meaning of His appearance among us. Origen [2] carries this idea out in a description of the character of the Gospel with a boldness which few serious critics would be inclined to imitate, although they might agree with his main conclusions.

The Gospel was written, according to its author's own declaration, that men 'might believe that Jesus is the Christ, the Son of God, and believing might have life through His Name'; [3] that is, to prove the Messiahship and the Divine Sonship of Jesus. In view of this double attestation of the author's purpose—that of his own words and that of such well-informed writers as St. Clement—the attempts which have been made to detect other purposes in the writing of the Gospel have little weight. The frequent allusions to ideas which were soon to become characteristic of Gnosticism,[4] have been thought to indicate that opposition to that incipient heresy was a chief motive with St. John. But it has been pointed out [5] that the Gospel bears

[1] In Euseb. *H.E.* vi. 14, *τὸν μέντοι Ἰωάννην ἔσχατον, συνιδόντα ὅτι τὰ σωματικὰ ἐν τοῖς Εὐαγγελίοις δεδήλωται, προτραπέντα ὑπὸ τῶν γνωρίμων, Πνεύματι θεοφορηθέντα, πνευματικὸν ποιῆσαι Εὐαγγέλιον.*

[2] *De Princ.* iv.; *Comment. in Joan.*

[3] xx. 31. Cf. 1 Jo. v. 13. 'It seeks to answer the question *who* it was that appeared upon earth, and suffered on Calvary and rose from the dead and left disciples who revered and adored Him.' Sanday, *The Criticism of the Fourth Gospel*, p. 205.

[4] *E.g.* Jo. v. 37; xiv. 17; xvii. 3, 25.

[5] By Wrede, *Charakter und Tendenz des Johevang.* 1903, p. 59; Jülicher, *Einleitung in d. N.T.* p. 359, and others. *v.* Holtzmann, *Evangelium des Johannes*, p. 29, 'In Gnosis there is to be found no influence capable of determining the aim of the Gospel.' Yet, if it is true that the refutation of Gnosticism was not the main object of the Evangelist, it is no less true that the Docetic tendencies which were early prevalent among Gnostics were repugnant to him. *v.* V. Dobschütz, *Probleme des Apost.-Zeitalters*, p. 94; P. Gardner, *The Ephesian Gospel*, p. 81.

no trace of any hostility to what was, within a few years of its composition, to become a religious philosophy of extraordinary influence. The Gospel is not an anticipatory apologetic. It is an authoritative statement of the historic and ever-living significance of the Son of God. Still less can we go with those who regard it as a polemic directed against followers of John the Baptist, who had not given in their adhesion to Christ. The Gospel is indeed full of hostile references to 'the Jews.' The writer, Jew as he was and intimately acquainted with the Judaism of Palestine, is singularly detached in his allusions to his own people and to their rejection of the claims of Christ. He writes in the manner of one who looks back upon the wilfulness of his countrymen sadly and sternly; almost as if their hardness of heart had estranged him, so that in becoming a Christian, he had lost his tie of blood-relationship with his people and had become one of another race. It was to impart the certainty of what they rejected—the Divine Messiahship of Jesus—that he was writing his Gospel. The continued obstinacy of the Jews, at the time of its composition, would have made the Apostle all the more stern and determined in his record of the nation's action during our Lord's ministry, and of their part in securing His condemnation.[1]

[1] It is worth considering whether the hostile attitude of the Fourth Gospel towards 'the Jews' lends any colour to the statement imputed to the perished work of Papias, *An Exposition of the Oracles of the Lord*, by Philip of Sidè and G. Hamartolus, that John, as well as James, was 'killed by Jews.' See the fragments of Papias in Lightfoot-Harmer, *The Apostolic Fathers*, pp. 518-19. It is to be noticed that Papias is not reported to have said when or where John was martyred, but ὅτι ὑπὸ Ἰουδαίων ἀνηρέθη. It is conceivable that when the unfriendly attitude of the Gospel had become known at Ephesus, there was a sudden outburst of anger in the large Jewish colony of the city, and that the old Apostle then met his death. If we take the natural sense of the assurance or prophecy of Mk. x. 39, we must admit that, if it was fulfilled, as we know it was in the case of St. James, *red* martyrdom was the baptism which awaited the other brother. Now, we have ample proof in Gal. ii. 9, that, eight years after the death of his brother James, John the son of Zebedee was present at the council of Jerusalem (Acts xv. 1 f.). If we attach any weight to the general tradition, we have to admit that there is good reason for thinking that the words of Papias have been misunderstood. When G. Hamartolus quotes Origen in support of his statement, and we turn to his commentary on St. Matthew (p. 719, ed. Bened.), we find no mention of the death of St. John, but only of his bearing witness (μαρτυροῦντα) to the truth by banishment to Patmos. Hamartolus also quotes Eusebius to the effect that 'John received Asia as his lot, where also he made his residence and died at Ephesus.' (Cf. Euseb. *H.E.* iii. 31, quoting a letter of Polycrates.) Harnack thinks that 'what

But there is nothing to show that those disciples of the Baptist, who, as time went on, declined to join forces with the Christians, were ever of such importance in numbers or influence as to form an adequate object for the attack of the Fourth Evangelist. They come before us occasionally in the Acts,[1] but give the idea of being but a small body, and ready to embrace the full revelation of the Gospel, when it is definitely brought to them.

Objection has also been taken to the authentic character of the Fourth Gospel on the ground that its portrait of Christ differs from that in the Synoptics. The Man of Sorrows has become the God. And with this transfiguration of His Person, there is also the 'unhistorical' representation of the faith of His disciples, who, instead of a gradual approach to the conception of His Messiahship and Sonship such as the Synoptic Gospels teach, come at once to a full confession of His Godhead.[2] The Gospel is said to exhibit the belief of the period of its composition.

To this objection it may be replied that the difference between the Johannine and the Synoptic portrait of our Lord has been exaggerated. It is admitted that the Synoptic Gospels present Christ as the Son of God, and that the primitive Church worshipped Him from the first, paying Him divine honour. If these conceptions pervade the Fourth Gospel to a greater extent than the other Three, if the Self-consciousness of our Lord is revealed in a way which is hardly equalled in the less direct statements recorded in the Synoptics, it is what we should expect from the circumstances and the character of the respective writers, and from the objects which they set before themselves in writing. The interest of the Fourth Evangelist was mainly directed upon the Person of our Lord. The previous Evangelists had less care for theological conceptions. They endeavoured to show how

Papias really wrote must be left undecided (*dahingestellt*).' *Geschichte der alt-christ. Liter.* pt. ii. *Chronologie*, i. p. 666. Cf. F. Loofs, *What is the Truth about Jesus Christ?* p. 103. Moffatt remarks that Mk. x. 39, if fulfilled, obliges us to 'admit that He (Christ) foretold a martyrdom for the two men, and also that this had come to pass by the time Mark's Gospel was published.' *Introduction to the Literature of the New Testament*, p. 603. This latter statement does not necessarily follow from the fact of the mention of the incident related by St. Mark; *v.* below, p. 47; and Ramsay in *Expos.*, July 1911, p. 72 f.

[1] Acts xviii. 24; xix. 3. *v.* Zahn, *Einleitung in d. N.T.* i. p 558.

[2] *v.* below, p. 41.

Christ lived during His ministry, what He taught, how He suffered and rose again. In the course of their narratives, we find few theological definitions or statements. They write as men who seem hardly conscious of the significance of what they report. And it is just this absence of theological intention which gives their extreme value to the Synoptic Gospels. There is little trace of reflection in their narratives. They report what Christ said and did, but seldom speak of the logical consequences for faith and life of the occurrences which they report.

If St. Matthew and St. Luke tell us of the unique knowledge of the Father claimed, according to His own words, by Christ, they do not soliloquize, as St. John would have done, upon the bearing of such language upon the mystery of His Person. If St. Matthew goes on to report His divine invitation to every weary and heavy-laden child of man to come to Him and find rest, he lets the words and the extraordinary claim of sufficingness, which they convey, speak for themselves. St. John could hardly have reported them without reference to the majesty and the true nature of the Speaker. It is in keeping with his purpose, not only to select for narration words and events which, like these isolated sayings in the Synoptic Gospels, reveal the secret of Christ's Personality, but to draw attention to them and to hover in thought about their meaning.

But the difference of manner and of object in writing should not blind us to the essential unity of idea that subsists between the Fourth Gospel and the Synoptics. It is the same Christ and Saviour, Who is revealed in each type of narrative. The perspective from which He is regarded is different. The Person is the same. Holtzmann[1] seems to think that the Johannine Christ is simply the exponent of Christian thought at the time the Gospel was written. If that were the case, we should have no alternative but to reject those early confessions of disciples which we find in the very first chapter of the Gospel. They, too, would be but the expression of the Church of the Evangelist's own age and of his own convictions, not the utterances of the men to whom they are attributed. We should have to abandon

[1] *Neutest. Theologie*, ii. p. 399. Cf. P. Gardner, *The Ephesian Gospel*, p. 335. 'Though the Fourth Gospel contains valuable historic material, yet what is its main treasure, the speeches of our Lord contained in it, belongs not to the lifetime of the Founder, but to the early experience of the Church.' If this is the case, the 'treasure' must surely lose the chief part of its value.

the Gospel as an authoritative source of information of what Christ said and what He did. Everything would come to us through the mediating prism of the Evangelist's own devout mind. We should not see the original beams of the true light because of the varied hues into which it was broken. It would be a study of a Personality, not the record of words and deeds. That the writer had in view the instruction and edification of his friends and disciples may be freely admitted. His object was not to add to the existing biographies of Christ. He had a distinct theological purpose. The tradition of the composition of his Gospel which we owe to Clement of Alexandria is borne out by the language of the Gospel itself. 'The bodily things' having already been recorded, he sets to work to compile a 'spiritual Gospel.' He presupposes his readers' knowledge of the Synoptic writings;[1] and where he finds it necessary, he supplements, corrects, goes behind the facts related, in order to emphasize their significance, lifts the life of the Master into a position in which it can be understood. Reflection and meditation, under the guidance of the Spirit, bring to light what passed unnoticed when the material of the earlier Gospels was being collected and set in order. If there is creation in the composition of the Fourth Gospel, it is the creation not of invention but of perception. The main object in writing is to produce certainty.[2] Impressed with the eternal worth and significance of the Person and the work of Christ, the last of the original witnesses places on record his own impressions. He tells what he saw of 'the Word of Life,' and by his choice of the material at his command, brings out the vital elements of His manifestation. And his narrative is eloquent of his purpose. It was not written down within a short space of time from the events which it records. It has passed through the retort of reiterated reflection. It is not a mere epitome of the life of an interesting Personality. It is the testimony of one who knows, to the reality of the life and work among men of the Eternal Son of God. 'The Word was made flesh and dwelt among us and we beheld His glory.' And in the First Epistle which forms a corollary to the Gospel, the same writer continues, 'The Life was manifested and we have seen It and bear witness.'

[1] *v.* Zahn, *Einleitung*, ii. p. 507.
[2] Jo. xix. 35.

The presence of 'theological' purpose[1] in the Fourth Gospel is, as we think, perversely regarded as taking from the historical value of its contents. Rather ought the importance of its subject, as conceived by the writer, to have the effect of ensuring accuracy of statement. Writing at the close of his long life, with the past and its wonderful experiences standing out with indelible distinctness, discerning with the mind of a seer the unimaginable triumphs of the cause whose inception he had witnessed, if ever a man was the organ of the Spirit of God, it was he who gave to the Church the Fourth Gospel.[2]

Again, in the Fourth Gospel, Jerusalem is the scene of visits, which find no place in the Synoptic narrative. While it is silent on so central an event as the institution of the Eucharist, it contains recitals like the raising of Lazarus, which, transcendent as is their interest, are not named by the earlier writers. Can we regard narratives which thus differ, now in omission, now in inclusion, as equally appealing to our confidence and equally necessary for a complete representation of what happened? The simpler way of dealing with the situation is to say 'no,' and to take our attitude accordingly. But we shall soon come to realize that the truth is not to be arrived at so easily; that it is not a mere question of taking one

[1] Yet 'the theologian among the Apostles, according to preparatory training, mode of thought and speech, is not John but Paul.' Zahn, *Das Evangelium des Johannes*, p. 7.

[2] It has been urged that the way in which the Evangelist passes from recital of fact to meditation, is a serious hindrance to our acknowledgment of the historical character of the Gospel. But it will be found on examination of the instances of this habit that the main point of the narrative of fact—the deed, or the account of the speech or saying—is clearly indicated. When the writer glides almost imperceptibly into meditation, though we cannot lay our finger on the dividing clause with unfailing certainty, the presumably meditative element contains no new, or at least no contradictory ideas. Cf. Westcott in Jo. iii. 16-21. 'It adds no new thoughts.' Thus in Jo. iii. the narrative of the discourse with Nicodemus passes with no clear dividing line into the Evangelist's own meditation. But we can say with considerable probability that Christ ceases to speak at verse 15 and that v. 16 begins the comment of the writer. Cf. Holtzmann, *Evangelium des Johannes*, p. 90, 'Here the Evangelist speaks, not Christ.' So in i. 16-19, the words are not the Baptist's, but the Evangelist's. There is similarity of expression (*e.g.* μονογένης) to that used by the Evangelist in iii. 16. These are the only instances in the Gospel of passages which we cannot, with complete certainty, assign to their author. It is hyper-criticism to allege their presence as taking from the historical character of the narrative, as P. Gardner appears to do. *The Ephesian Gospel*, p. 122.

view and leaving the other; that possibly the truth resides in each, and that only by combining the two will a complete and satisfying representation be obtained.

It is admitted that the writer of the Fourth Gospel had the other three before him.[1] He would thus be well aware that his own account of Christ differed, in many important particulars, from the more or less homogeneous and consistent narrative of the Synoptics; and that this difference would naturally lead to the questioning of his authority, when the contents of the two streams of evidence came to be compared.[2] Moreover, it was a case of one authority confronted with three;[3] and these three already established in the confidence of the Church, and soon to be included in the list of authoritative writings which was to form the Canon of the New Testament.[4] The three first Gospels were everywhere being read at the Sunday gatherings for worship, and were thus entering into the mind and affection of Christian people, as giving a true—if incomplete—story of the life and sayings of our Lord. And now appears this fourth account. It might be supposed that the new Evangelist would be careful to confine his recital within the limits of time and place adopted by the Synoptic writers. Writing so much later, it would seem prudent to preserve a structural harmony between his own Gospel and the rest. But he does nothing of the sort. He launches out with a scheme which is entirely original. He is careless of the difficulty which his readers may find in reconciling it with the threefold narrative already in existence. Does not this fact of itself afford a large support to the assignment of the Gospel to an authority of the first rank, an Apostle, and one of the inner circle? Who but a writer conscious of unique standing and no less unique opportunities, as a disciple and witness, would

[1] Clem. Alex. in Euseb. *H.E.* vi. 14.

[2] This fact partly accounts for the small use of the Fourth Gospel which is made by the Apostolic Fathers. *v.* above, p. 28.

[3] Three separate writers, but as regards the strictly narrative portion of the Synoptics, the actual authority pitted against that of St. John is one—that of the Petrine-Mark Gospel.

[4] The silence of the Synoptic Gospels is thought by some to be destructive of the historical character of the raising of Lazarus; but that event is in close connection with Jerusalem, and our Lord's Ministry there. It does not come within the Galilean framework of the Synoptic writers. *v.* Headlam, *The Miracles of the N.T.* p. 228.

have ventured to present the Church with a Gospel so evidently distinct in form and material from the Gospels which it already possessed and valued? Nothing is more certain than that a writer of inferior authority, an 'elder' John of Ephesus[1]—if there were such a person—would at least endeavour to recommend his narrative by some sort of agreement with the plan and scope of the rest. And it is almost equally certain that, had he not done so, his Gospel would have fallen out of the circle of accepted writings, as was the case with so many which failed to gain a place within the Canon. The spiritual excellences of the writing might indeed have won for it a certain reverence, yet the disparities from the received Gospel scheme would have proved too strong for it to acquire a permanent place among the Scriptures. But if the author were known to be John, son of Zebedee, the loved disciple, his knowledge and authority would compel a hearing for its presentment of the facts. And when once a hearing was gained for it and men began to appreciate its worth and, recognizing the soundness of its claim to first-hand knowledge, felt that it was not to be discredited by its real or apparent discrepancies with the other Gospels, it quickly took its place among the sacred writings. Moreover, it seemed to be the Gospel which was wanted to complete the number foreshadowed in prophecy[2] and symbolized by the four quarters of the world[3] and the cardinal winds of heaven.

Discrepancies in contrasted writings may be of such a character as to exclude all prospect of reconciliation. In that case, we have to come to a decision and firmly reject one account or the other. Is that the case, when we compare the Fourth Gospel with the Synoptics? We can say, beforehand, that if a rejection must be made, it is not the Synoptic writings which must go. Their age and their consistency with one another, both in point of view and to a large extent in material, would forbid such a course. Must the Fourth Gospel be sacrificed on the altar of consistency? Are discrepancies so marked that we cannot assign any historical value to the book?

Let us look at them, or at least at the most typical examples. The course of Christ's public life is quite differently conceived in the two kinds of writing. The Synoptic scene is Galilee with

[1] *v.* below, p. 48, n. 1. [2] Ezek. i. 5 f.

[3] Iren. *Adv. Haeres.* iii. 11, § 8.

a final week at Jerusalem;[1] the whole ministry lasting but a little more than a year. The Johannine scene is still Galilee, but there are visits to Jerusalem for feasts, and the ministry is spread over a period of about three years. More startling is the contrast between the gradual advance to full recognition of the Divine claims of Christ, as the Synoptics describe it, and the way in which His Divinity is accepted and confessed from end to end of the Fourth Gospel. It will suffice for our present purpose to concentrate attention on these two main points of difference, asking ourselves whether a writer who placed himself in so marked an attitude of opposition—not to say contradiction—to a record which had already gained for itself the belief of the Christian community, could be regarded as an eye-witness of what he relates.

But first it should be remembered that no one would be more conscious of the apparent lack of agreement in the two versions than the author of the Fourth Gospel himself. This obvious fact is generally ignored. But it is of supreme importance for the forming of a right judgment. It is against reason to think that a writer desirous to be heard and to influence would voluntarily expose himself to the charge of violently distorting received history. He would at once be pulled up by the expostulations of his readers; *unless*, and here is the point of the whole problem, *he was aware that he was in possession of truth that could not be denied*, and that by reason of his own personal authority and opportunities for knowledge as an eye-witness, and on the strength of his known reputation for truthful speech and fairness of mind, his position was impregnable.

Now his method gives us the impression that this was the case. He corrects and modifies Synoptic statements silently, by the presentation of other points of view. But he does not correct in a didactic or superior manner, and he never refers directly to the view which he means to modify. He simply gives his own account. He takes it for granted that his competence and his truthfulness will be admitted. He speaks as one who *must* know, and he expects the assent of reasonable men. This assent he has freely received from those who, in every age of the Church, from

[1] But the passage Lk. ix. 51–xviii. 14 (or 31 ?) is a departure from the rest of the Synoptic tradition, and gives scope for visits to Jerusalem which are named in the Fourth Gospel. *v.* Plummer, *St. Luke*, p. 260; Moffatt, *Introduction to the N.T.* p. 541.

Justin Martyr and Irenaeus to our own day, have most deeply penetrated into the mind of Scripture. In the language of one of the latest who have spoken, the Fourth Gospel is a writing 'which to many has ever appeared the most trustworthy that the New Testament, nay all literature, possesses dealing with the Person and the history of Jesus.' [1]

What do these supposed discrepancies amount to? It is often taken for granted that two accounts contradict, when one merely supplements the other. The Synoptic narrative is a Galilean record, until the last days. The reasons for this limitation are not easy to produce. But whatever they may be, the limitation is there. Does St. John give the lie to this narrative by his mention of several visits to Jerusalem for feasts? Not only is there nothing in the Synoptic recital to forbid such an addition to the sphere of our Lord's activity; but we can find sayings and statements in that recital which positively require the visits to Jerusalem that St. John narrates. The 'how often' of the great lament is meaningless without them.[2] The judgment upon Jerusalem and the Jews is inexplicable if they had had no experience of the work and teaching of our Lord in their streets, until the week of their final rejection of Him. Had we no Fourth Gospel, we should have had to map out for ourselves some such visits, and some such extended duration of the public ministry. It requires but the exercise of common sense, not keenness of critical faculty, to divine that the Fourth Gospel is giving us history, provided that the Synoptic record is to be relied upon. Although in the Synoptics we cannot say that a longer period for their narratives than a little over a year is actually demanded, the 'great interpolation' in the Marcan groundwork, which we find in the Third Gospel, is probably a record of several months. This would extend the period which the general course of the Synoptic narrative allows. There is also a vagueness as to notes of time in the Synoptic recital which does not permit us to bring a charge of contradiction against St. John. The visits to Jerusalem are *implied*, if not *stated* by the Synoptic record. St. John records them.[3]

[1] Spitta, *Das Johannes-Evangelium als Quelle der Geschichte Jesu*, 1910, p. 466.

[2] Matt. xxiii. 37; Lk. xiii. 34; xix. 42.

[3] F. Loofs also takes this view: 'A word of Jesus in the "collection of sayings" (Matt. xxiii. 37; Lk. xiii. 34) speaks volumes in favour of John's

The other charge of discrepancy is perhaps of a more serious character. If we except one or two instances of confession of Christ as Son of God in St. Matthew, there is no generally attested utterance on the subject by any disciple, in the Synoptics, until we come to the great day at Caesarea Philippi. Turn to the Fourth Gospel, and in the first chapter you have confessions of far-reaching character not only from John the Baptist, but from Nathanael at his first meeting with our Lord. Christ is at once Son of God and Messiah.[1] Can we accept this view of the effect of our Lord upon those who come in contact with Him, in face of the slowly evolved expressions of faith which the Synoptic version records? It is sometimes said that the memory of the Fourth Evangelist was at fault. He was so fully impressed with the truth, which was now the common possession of the whole Church, that he unconsciously referred his own mode of thought to men who had not even begun so to think of Jesus of Nazareth. This is to charge the writer with serious inaccuracy. Does the impression of a slowly evolved recognition of Christ's Divine claims, which we undoubtedly get from the Synoptic narrative, exclude the possibility of such early confessions of faith as those of the Fourth Gospel?

Before we attempt to answer that question, a consideration of a more general character requires mention. People take note of sayings and incidents which correspond with their own mental outfit and tally with their own experience, just as the striking of a certain chord brings out music of the same key, that is latent in a room. 'Like is known by like.' There is acceptance and response. To other impressions, to music of another key, there is no answer.

No one can read the Fourth Gospel without perceiving that the writer was peculiarly sensitive to certain characteristics of our Lord's Person, and to the effect which they had upon those with whom He came in contact. Two things St. John had grasped and made his own with a strength of conviction which had no rival. One was the Deity of Christ. The other was the

statement, and what the Synoptic Gospels tell us of Jesus' doings and sayings in Jerusalem hardly fits into the frame of the few days during which Jesus, according to them, dwelt in Jerusalem.' *What is the Truth about Jesus Christ?* p. 110.

[1] 'Jesus is here the same, unchanged from the beginning to the end.' Schmiedel, *Das vierte Evangelium*, p. 27.

complete historical humanity of the Son of God.[1] The two facts come out in full force in the Prologue of the Gospel. Critics, who admit this, think that it accounts for the confessions which the Evangelist places in the mouths of men at the very beginning of the Ministry. Such confessions, they would say, are unhistorical. They are reflections of the Evangelist's own passionate belief. He attributes his own thought to others, and supposes a faith which belonged to a future stage of experience.

But, happily, we are not left without information from other sources which bears directly upon the subject. At the time of Christ's birth, Messianic expectation was keenly felt by many of the faithful in Israel. Simeon and Anna and Zacharias are witnesses who cannot be set aside. And the truth of St. Luke's narrative of the reality and fervour of the expectation is confirmed by his later report of the way in which 'all men mused in their hearts of John whether he were the Christ, or not.' The hope of Messiah was in the air. In that hope and in the fervour with which it was held lay the probability that some at least of the more thoughtful minds would see, when confronted with Jesus of Nazareth, that 'God had indeed visited His people.' Here and there would be men who, like Nathanael, entertained the highest conception of the Messiah's Person,[2] and their utterances might well leave on so impressionable a mind as that of St. John an ineffaceable recollection. If the confession of the Baptist is still more striking, if its terms belong to a still more exalted conception of Jesus Christ, it is what we might anticipate from the insight and the inspiration of one in whom his contemporaries recognized the emergence of a prophet—a phenomenon in the life of their people unknown for the last 400 years.

We therefore take it that the statements of the Fourth Gospel as to early confession of the Person and the Mission of Christ are borne out partly by the idiosyncrasies and the character of the Evangelist himself, partly by the state of expectation which is known to have existed among the Jews at the

[1] 'It is the undying merit of the Fourth Gospel to have brought securely to earth again the form of Christ which threatened to evaporate in Docetic mist.' V. Dobschütz, *Probleme des Apos. Zeitalters*, p. 94.

[2] This conception had been prepared for in O.T. passages as well as in Apocalyptic utterances. *v.* below, p. 69.

time, and partly by the personality of those who make the confession.[1]

Another point of difference between the Synoptics and the Fourth Gospel is concerned with the matter of style. The Christ of St. John speaks in language which is said to be touched with Hellenistic (Alexandrian) modes of speech. There is an abstract tone, which is foreign to the pictorial language of the Synoptics. Certain words play a great part in the discourses of Christ as well as in the language of the Evangelist himself. These phenomena lie on the surface and have to be accounted for. The discourses of Christ in the Fourth Gospel 'plainly bear the stamp, not of the authentic manner of speech of Jesus, but of the speech of the author of the source.'[2] It is easy to say that the writer has composed the discourses and placed them in the mouth of our Lord, much as Thucydides supplied the speeches of Pericles and other historical characters with whom he deals. But the spiritual depth, the lofty and comprehensive character of the discourses forbid such a theory. It is the same Christ who speaks. The root conceptions are in substance those which belong naturally to the Christ of the Synoptics.[3] There is the same insistence on the worth of the human soul and on the righteousness of God. It is neither a new religion nor a new moral code which appears in the Fourth Gospel.

And yet there are differences of style and treatment, and

[1] The confession of the Baptist, 'Behold the Lamb of God,' and 'This is the Son of God,' Jo. i. 29, 36, 34, is supported by the narrative of Matt. iii. 17; Mk. i. 11, in which a voice from heaven says, 'This is My beloved Son.' The voice was heard by the Baptist, and would confirm the intuition which, as a prophet, he already possessed. Jo. i. 33.

[2] Wendt, *Die Lehre Jesu*, p. 42, who believes in a Johannine source edited by the writer of the Gospel. P. Gardner remarks that 'the Fourth Evangelist . . . says that a man must be born of water, as well as of the Spirit, before he can enter into the Kingdom of God.' He apparently assumes that the whole incident of the interview with Nicodemus is an invention of the Evangelist. *The Religious Experience of St. Paul*, p. 109. In his more recent work, *The Ephesian Gospel*, 1915, Gardner again and again refers sayings of our Lord to the Evangelist, especially the longer discourses: 'We feel that it is not the visible and audible Jesus Who is speaking, but the Christ Who is the life of the Church,' p. 115. Cf. pp. 88, 185, 219, 230. But 'the Christ Who is the life of the Church' is after all not the speaker. It is the Evangelist, according to Gardner, who is responsible for the form and apparently for the substance of what is said.

[3] *v.* Abrahams in *Cambridge Biblical Essays*, p. 181; Burkitt, *The Gospel History and its Transmission*, p. 237.

varieties of emphasis on essentials in the two types of Gospel. However conscientiously a writer may seek to record sayings which live in his memory, however earnestly he may try to produce them in their original freshness of outline, yet in spite of himself his transcript will gather modifications in style and manner through the action of his own experience and circumstances. The Evangelist, a Jew of Palestine, long a stranger to his native land, and exposed to the new forms of culture and expression which everywhere met him in a city like Ephesus; feeling, too, the effects and the advantages which his knowledge of the Greek language afforded him, would unconsciously introduce his own modes of thought and expression into his narrative of the sayings of his Master. But, with all allowance for some such modification, the thoughts, the expression, the mind, are those of Jesus Christ. It is He Who is speaking, and we feel that we can trust the report. It is borne out even by the evidence of the Synoptics.[1]

Another difficulty in the way of assigning the authorship of the Fourth Gospel to St. John is the paucity—if not entire absence—of quotations from it to be met with in the writings of the Apostolic Fathers. Apart from the precariousness of the argument from silence, which has been frequently demonstrated, it is to be borne in mind that a Gospel which is conceived on an entirely different plan from the Synoptic Gospels would naturally have to make its way gradually towards full acceptance by the Church. The Synoptic Gospels were already established in its confidence. The mere fact that the sect of the Alogi, obscure and unimportant though they were, rejected the Fourth Gospel and ascribed it to the heretic Cerinthus, is proof that it had to

[1] *E.g.* cf. such instances of common imagery and sayings as those cited by Westcott, *Gospel of St. John*, p. lxxxii. 'The claims of the Lord which are recorded by the Synoptists, if followed to their legitimate consequences, involve the claims recorded by St. John.' *Ib.* p. lxxxiv.

Gardner, after contrasting the Johannine with the Synoptic picture, says of that of the Fourth Gospel, 'We see that such a figure could not historically have existed.' *The Ephesian Gospel*, p. 90. If that be the case—and we think it contrary to the best critical estimates—it is difficult to understand 'of what infinite value the spiritual teaching of the Evangelist has been to the Church in every age of her history,' p. 91. Spiritual teaching founded on an imaginary and false foundation can never be anything but misleading. You cannot have it both ways; a Gospel untrue to history and fact is no Gospel in the ordinary sense of the word. But this Gospel is almost passionate in its claim to hand down the certainty of what it records.

struggle for its reception. Certain phrases of writers, such as the author of the Epistle to Diognetus, Ignatius and the narrator of the martyrdom of Polycarp,[1] seem to show a knowledge of Johannine language which was probably derived from the Gospel itself. But on the whole, the Gospel, if known, is hardly referred to.[2] The first undoubted reference comes from a quarter which we should hardly have anticipated. Basileides, the Gnostic, who lived about 125 A.D.,[3] quoted St. John i. 9 as 'that which is said in the Gospels.'[4] A few years later, in A.D. 146,[5] Justin Martyr in his First Apology shows acquaintance with the Gospel.[6] The first writer to assign it definitely to St. John is Theophilus of Antioch, who died A.D. 180.[7] In the latter half of the second century the evidence of its acceptance throughout the Church is complete.[8]

[1] *v.* Lightfoot-Harmer, *The Apostolic Fathers*, p. 568 (Index, St. John). With regard to Ignatius, *v.* Sanday, *The Criticism of the Fourth Gospel*, p. 242; F. Loofs, *What is the Truth about Jesus Christ?* p. 101, 'The letters of Ignatius show that Ignatius was influenced by the sayings of Jesus reported in the Fourth Gospel.' M. Rackl finds in Ignatius *literary dependence* (not merely that of tradition) on St. John. *D. Christologie des heil^{n} Ignatius*, 1914.

[2] 'That between the composition and publishing of the book there lay an interval, during which the author kept it in his own hand and let it become known only to his friends and guests and to the community of the place in which he was living, was in accordance with ancient custom.' Zahn, *D. Evang. des Joh.* p. 12.

[3] 'In point of antiquity, he holds a rank intermediate between that of Clement of Rome and Polycarp.' Westcott, *History of the Canon of the N.T.* p. 293.

[4] The statement that Basileides quoted Jo. i. 9, is contained in the *Refutation of All Heresies*, by Hippolytus, vii. 22. (Origen, *Philosophumena*), Τοῦτο φησὶν (Βασιλείδης) ἔστι τὸ λεγομένον ἐν τοῖς Εὐαγγελίοις. 'The fact (of this recognition of the teaching of St. John) itself belongs to an earlier date; for this belief cannot have originated with him, and if we go back but one generation, we are within the age of the Apostles.' Westcott, *ib.* p. 295.

[5] According to Hort, *Journal of Class. and Sacred Philology*, iii. 191.

[6] 'The Gospel is known to Justin Martyr.' Loofs, *What is the Truth about Jesus Christ?* p. 101. Westcott gives a list of parallels in *History of the Canon of the N.T.* p. 168, n. 1. Cf. B. Weiss, *Das Leben Jesu*, i. p. 80, who speaks of 'an undoubted allusion to the history of Nicodemus' in *Apol.* i. 61. 'That Justin used the Gospel I think we may take as at the present time generally admitted.' Sanday, *The Criticism of the Fourth Gospel*, p. 246. Justin Martyr 'became a Christian at Ephesus about the year A.D. 130.' Zahn, *D. Evang. des Joh.* p. 15.

[7] He quotes St. John i. 1-3 and ascribes the passage to St. John. *Apologia ad Autolycum*, ii. 22. *v.* B. Weiss, *Das Leben Jesu*, i. p. 81.

[8] 'No Gospel comes to us with stronger external evidence of its acceptance by the Church.' J. A. Robinson, *The Study of the Gospels*, p. 127. 'It was everywhere received and circulated as a work of the Apostle John.' Zahn, *D. Evang. des Joh.* p. 13.

Now, that epoch is connected with the time in which the Gospel was composed by two remarkable lives—Polycarp, Irenaeus. Polycarp was a hearer of St. John; Irenaeus, a disciple of Polycarp. Fixed tradition thus bound the latter half of the second century with the Apostle. This link will have had influence in determining the attitude of the Church to the Fourth Gospel, and in ensuring its practically universal acceptance.[1] We therefore conclude that the absence of clear allusions to the Gospel in the few years (before Basileides gives his testimony) which immediately followed its composition is no proof that it is unauthentic.

A statement has been attributed to Papias according to which both the sons of Zebedee suffered martyrdom at the hands of the Jews. Now we know that St. James was put to death by Herod in the year A.D. 44. Papias does not say that St. John suffered at the same time. At the Council of Jerusalem, in or about A.D. 49, we find him taking part in its deliberations along with St. James, the Lord's brother and St. Peter. If, therefore, St. John was put to death, a number of years must have elapsed since the death of his brother: how many, we do not know. The Book of Acts contains no allusion to his death—an unaccountable omission if it occurred, and by violence, during the period covered by that work. Moreover, the next time that the Apostle is identified with any place, we find him at Ephesus.[2] If Papias was correct in saying that he was killed by the Jews, the martyrdom occurred, in all probability, in that city, and presents no obstacle to the received authorship of the Gospel.

[1] Heracleon, c. A.D. 170, is the first commentator on the Gospel of whom we have knowledge. *v.* Salmon in Murray's *Dict. of Christian Biography, sub v.* 'Heracleon.' He was a Gnostic of the School of Valentinus. *v.* Clem. Alex. *Strom.* iv. 9.

[2] Justin Martyr, who was himself at Ephesus at the time of his conversion, about A.D. 130, in ascribing the Apocalypse to John the Apostle, indirectly connects the writer with Ephesus or its neighbourhood; for the letters to the Seven Churches were written by a resident. Καὶ ἐπειδὴ καὶ παρ' ἡμῖν ἀνήρ τις ᾧ ὄνομα Ἰωάννης, εἷς τῶν ἀποστόλων τοῦ Χριστοῦ ἐν ἀποκαλύψει γενομένῃ αὐτῷ κ.τ.λ. *Dialog. cum Tryph.* 81, c. About A.D. 190, Polycrates, Bishop of Ephesus, writing to Victor, Bishop of Rome, speaks of 'John, who leaned upon the Lord's breast,' as having fallen asleep at Ephesus. In Euseb. *H.E.* v. 24. If, as we have concluded, the son of Zebedee was the loved disciple, this is high authority for St. John's residence there.

But when we come to look more closely into the supposed statement of Papias, we can only come to the conclusion that, as alleged against the Johannine authorship of the Fourth Gospel, it is of no account. His work appears to have perished during the early part of the Middle Ages. Two writers, one in the fifth, the other in the ninth century, saw or heard of it. It is mentioned in what appears to be an epitome of the earlier writer, Philip of Side.[1] The writer of the ninth century,[2] who cites Papias, appeals to Origen for confirmation of his quotation. When we turn to Origen,[3] we find not only that he makes no such statement, but that he draws a clear distinction between the killing of St. James by Herod and the banishing of St. John by 'the King of the Romans' to the island of Patmos; and he speaks of John as 'witnessing (*μαρτυροῦντα*) for the word of truth.' It was this word *μαρτυροῦντα* which probably caused the mistake of the monk George, and led him to think that the two brothers suffered martyrdom together. There is, therefore, no reason to deny the Apostolic authorship of the Gospel on the ground that St. John was martyred, and at so early a date as to render it impossible.[4]

[1] In a fragment first printed in 1888. *v.* Lightfoot, *The Apostolic Fathers*, pp. 518, 519.

[2] The monk Georgius Hamartolus, in a fragment published in the year 1862.

[3] *Comment. in Matt.* p. 719 (ed. Bened.).

[4] It is strange that Moffatt remarks that 'the second fragment of Papias . . . corroborates the first by proving . . . that he died early as a martyr.' Again, Moffatt says, 'The evidence for the early martyrdom of John the son of Zebedee is threefold . . . (*b*) the witness of Papias . . .' *Introduction to the Liter. of the N.T.* pp. 601, 602. But as we have already seen (*v.* above, p. 32), the statement ascribed to Papias does not say *when* St. John was killed by the Jews, and thus does not exclude a residence at Ephesus in his old age. But if John, son of Zebedee, was killed by the Jews, it seems difficult to account for the absence of any reference to the event in the writings of the men who must have known of it, such as Irenaeus. *v.* Harnack, *Alt-christ. Literatur-Geschichte*, ii. *Chronologie*, i. p. 666. Harnack considers that these late reports of a perished narrative carry no weight as against the general early tradition of the prolonged life of the Apostle. It is also to be noticed that G. Hamartolus apparently read in his copy of the work of Papias that St. John lived at Ephesus, for he states the fact in the fragment of his *Chronicon* (Lightfoot, *The Apostolic Fathers*, pp. 519, 531). He also speaks approvingly of the statement of Eusebius that 'John received Asia by lot, where also he made his residence and died at Ephesus.' *Ib.*

For a criticism of Moffatt's argument for the martyrdom of St. John from the Calendar of the Church of Edessa, *c.* A.D. 411, and from other Calendars,

Besides, the general belief that the writer's name was John can only be explained on the ground that he was either the Apostle or the other John of Ephesus, who is mentioned by Papias after his enumeration of eye- and ear-witnesses of Christ.[1] But how could a Gospel, which so clearly appears to be the work of an Apostle and an eye-witness,[2] be set down by the Churches of Asia to a John, who was not an Apostle, and then, within a few short years, be ascribed afresh, as we know it was, to John the son of Zebedee? [3] As Zahn observes, 'The idea must come to nothing on the mere ground of the absurdity of its consequences.' [4]

It stands to reason that the purpose of the Gospel—if we can ascertain it—has a direct bearing upon the question of its value as a record of the Saviour's Life and Teaching. If, as we have seen, it aims at giving an interpretation of our Lord's life on earth rather than an historical summary of what He said and did, we shall look for ideas rather than for facts. Not that we shall not find facts everywhere from beginning to end, facts too that are related in a manner which reveals the eye and ear of one

v. Pullan, *The Gospels*, p. 304 f. Cf. J. H. Bernard in *Irish Church Quarterly*, vol. i. So far is the martyrdom from being proved from these sources that under the date of June 6th is found the entry, 'At Alexandria, Arius the Presbyter.'

[1] In Euseb. *H.E.* iii. 39. *v.* Lightfoot, *The Apostolic Fathers*, pp. 516, 528. This 'elder' John, who was apparently living in the time of Papias, is a very elusive personage. Now he seems to come within the range of history; now again to vanish into a double of the son of Zebedee. Those who, like V. Dobschütz, *Probleme des Apost. Zeitalters*, p. 91 f., attribute to him the authorship of the Gospel, have to account for the fact that, besides the son of Zebedee, there was another John who, although not mentioned in the Gospels, was present on eventful occasions in Christ's life and claimed the credence due to a first-hand authority upon the subject. Dom Chapman, O.S.B., has shown good reason to regard John, son of Zebedee, the Elder John, the loved disciple and the John who wrote the Gospel as one and the same man. *John the Presbyter and the Fourth Gospel*, 1911.

[2] *v.* above p. 26 f.

[3] Zahn, *D. Evang. des Johan.* p. 14. Cf. F. Loofs, *What is the Truth about Jesus Christ?* p. 103, 'Even the most improbable statements of later writers have been believed by some scholars in order to render this tradition (of the Johannine authorship) suspicious.' *v.* Illingworth, *The Gospel Miracles*, p. 176.

[4] *Op. cit.* p. 13. 'That the John of Asia Minor was the Apostle remains still the more probable supposition (*v.* Zahn, *Forschungen*, vi. 1900, pp. 175 f.).' Porter in Hastings' *D.B.* iv. p. 265. Gardner admits that the authority of St. John is behind the Gospel, but he withholds from the Apostle the attribution of authorship. *The Ephesian Gospel*, p. 42.

who was present: but we shall not look for what St. Clement calls 'the bodily things,' although in the silent acquiescence in the Synoptic narrative of those things which the Fourth Evangelist so often manifests, and in the points of contact with that narrative in which he shows firmly that he has an independent and sometimes a varying knowledge, there is many a trace of his sense of the historical foundation on which his Gospel rests.

But it is a meditation rather than a narrative, an old man's revelation of his view of an ever-living and unforgotten past, the record of an experience. It is Jesus, the Lord, not as He seemed to the world, nor even as He appeared to disciples at the moment, but as He became manifested to a devout and intimate and devoted follower through the enlightening power of the Spirit. The Fourth Gospel is the Gospel of '*Christ manifested in remembrance*,'[1] in accordance with His own promise, as the writer recalls it.[2] And it is this character, as conveying the illumination of reality, the spiritualizing of historic fact, deepening and widening, without obscuring or belittling, the actuality of past events, that has made the Fourth Gospel so dear to the people of God through all the Christian ages. The value of the Synoptic narrative lies in the literal, non-theological presentation of Christ as He appeared and spoke to those who walked with Him in the days of His flesh. Its value lies in that absence of interpretation which is one of its chief characteristics. The value of St. John's Gospel lies in the inspired interpretation which it places upon the subject of its narrative. It shows us Christ as revealed by the Holy Ghost; the same Christ, but as on the Mount, transfigured.

And those who, in the pursuit of a reverent criticism, have most deeply investigated the problems which must arise whenever the two great streams of Gospel narrative are brought into comparison with one another, freely admit the surpassing value of the Gospel which completes the fourfold presentation of what Christ was and is, as Son of Man and Son of God. They acknow-

[1] *v.* Newman, *Parochial and Plain Sermons*, vol. iv. serm. 17.

[2] Jo. xiv. 26. The words Τὸ Πνεῦμα τὸ Ἅγιον . . . ὑπομνήσει ὑμᾶς πάντα ἃ εἶπον ὑμῖν are not to be deprived of their actual meaning, as P. Gardner suggests. *The Ephesian Gospel*, p. 264. The interpretation which he proposes would be tautological. It is contained in the preceding words, ὑμᾶς διδάξει πάντα.

ledge that it is St. John who gives us the fullest and truest portrait of our Redeemer.[1] Ὁ ἐπιστήθιος 'the man who lay upon (the Saviour's) breast,'[2] has penetrated most deeply to the truth of His Divine-human Being. He knew Christ as no one else had known Him, and out of the fulness of his store of memories, like a wise householder, he has brought forth things new and old—old in their setting in the long historic past, new in the light shed upon them by the beams of the Spirit who inspired him.

We shall therefore use the Fourth Gospel as an authority of the highest value for the study of the mind of Christ, for light on the mystery of His Person, and as the record of an eye-witness of certain historic scenes and events of His public ministry. In cases in which the evidence appears to conflict with that of the other Gospels, we shall have to consider which account seems to bear upon its face the closest resemblance to truth; but we shall keep in mind the difficulty of forming a competent judgment on the respective merits of narratives which, from different points of view and at various periods of time, relate with characteristic brevity occurrences of the distant past. We do not know enough to be able always to assign their precise value as history to those Gospel recitals which appear to be contradictory. We may be certain that a method, which excludes a narrative as untrustworthy on the plea that it is a doublette, or that it does not appear to agree in all points with another version of the same story, is unsatisfactory. It rests on no scientific basis. It is purely subjective.

A more reverent, as well as a more scientific, dealing with the narratives will lead us to suspend our judgment in the presence of what appears to be contradictory. A fuller knowledge may show that, in some cases, each account is but a separate facet of one precious jewel of truth. Besides, is it not well to bear in mind that no one would be more quick to notice differences or contradictions than the Evangelist himself? He wrote with the other Gospels before him; and the knowledge that his friends and disciples in the Church of Ephesus would be fully alive to

[1] *E.g.* Spitta, *Das Johannes-Evangelium*, p. 401 (speaking of the *Grundschrift*), 'A source of special importance, perhaps the most important of all for the history of Jesus.' *Ib.* p. 459, 'Perhaps the oldest Gospel sketch that we possess.' Cf. B. Weiss, *Leben Jesu*, i. p. 105; Headlam, *The Miracles of the New Testament*, p. 180; E. Abbott, *The Fourfold Gospel*, pt. viii.

[2] *v.* Origen *in Joan.* xiii. 23; Zahn, *Einleitung in d. N.T.* ii. p. 488.

the contrasts presented by his narrative would heighten his sense of responsibility.[1]

In spite of certain differences in treatment of their subject-matter, the First Epistle of St. John presents remarkable similarities of language, thought and style to the Fourth Gospel. We cannot say which was the earlier composition, but it was no long space of time that intervened. Recent criticism has failed to shake the evidence, external and internal, which assigns the Epistle and the Gospel to the same authorship. Nor has any sufficient reason been produced for attributing the Second and Third Epistles to another writer.

The authorship of the Apocalypse is still one of the most perplexing problems of New Testament criticism. It stands alone of its kind. For several centuries it failed to obtain complete recognition as a member of the Canon. Here was a book claiming three times over in its first chapter to be written by 'John.' He is God's 'servant.' He is 'brother and companion in tribulation' to 'the seven churches which are in Asia.' He 'was in the isle that is called Patmos for the word of God and for the testimony of Jesus Christ.' The only personage answering to this self-designation and description of whom we have any real knowledge is John son of Zebedee, to whom with the ancient Church and with many of the more learned critics of the present day, we have seen reason to assign the substance, and probably the authorship, of the Fourth Gospel. The difficulties in the way of assigning to a single writer works of so varied a character, style, language and contents have been pointed out as long ago as the middle of the third century by Dionysius of Alexandria, the successor of Origen in the catechetical school of that city.[2] His criticism is as able as it is reverent. It draws attention to the reiterated mention of the writer's name,[3] so unlike the practice of the author of the Fourth Gospel and the Johannine

[1] It is difficult to enter into the mind of a critic who can write, 'He (the Fourth Evangelist) is not a writer who feels it incumbent upon him to narrate nothing that is untrue; if it suits his purpose, he does so.' Schmiedel, *Das Vierte Evangelium*, p. 43.

[2] In an Epistle preserved by Eusebius, *H.E.* vii. 25.

[3] Yet, as Dionysius says, the author does not speak of himself (as so often in the Gospel) as *τὸν ἠγαπημένον ὑπὸ τοῦ Κυρίου μαθητήν*, or *τὸν ἀναπεσόντα ἐπὶ τὸ στῆθος αὐτοῦ*, or *τὸν ἀδελφὸν Ἰακώβου*.

Epistles. While the Gospel and First Epistle are written in excellent Greek, the Apocalypse abounds in solecisms, in ungrammatical expressions and uncouth turns of language. Dionysius adds that he does not mention these things in ridicule, but only by way of criticizing the dissimilarity of the writings.[1]

The verdict of Dionysius was all the more daring from the fact that, from Justin Martyr [2] onward to Origen, the Apocalypse had been attributed to the Apostle St. John.

The criticism of Dionysius takes no note of the similarities existing between the language of the Fourth Gospel and the Apocalypse. Yet they are frequent and of considerable importance.[3] In his enumeration of points of difference, he hardly gives any weight to the consideration that the subjects, the purpose and the occasion of the two writings differed *toto coelo* from one another. On the whole, recent criticism is inclined to agree with the statement of Irenaeus [4] that the Vision of St. John was beheld towards the close of the reign of Domitian. If that date must be adhered to, the difficulty of single authorship seems insuperable. But is this necessary? There is internal evidence to show that certain passages were written in the reign of Nero and before the fall of Jerusalem.[5] The uncouthness of style, as

[1] *διάλεκτον μέντοι καὶ γλῶσσαν οὐκ ἀκριβῶς ἐλληνίζουσαν αὐτοῦ βλέπω, ἀλλ' ἰδιωμασίν τε βαρβαρικοῖς χρώμενον, καί που καὶ σολοικίζοντα. Ἅπερ οὐκ ἀναγκαῖον νῦν ἐκλέγειν· οὐδὲ γὰρ ἐπισκώπτων, μή τις νομίσῃ, ταῦτα εἶπον, ἀλλὰ μόνον τὴν ἀνομοιότητα διευθύνων τῶν γραφῶν.* Dion. '*Ep.*' in Euseb. *H.E.* vii. 25.

[2] *Dialog. cum Tryph.* 81.

The book was known to Irenaeus as the work of 'John' or 'John the Disciple of the Lord.' *Adv. Haeres.* v. 26, 1; 28, 2. It is quoted as Scripture in the letter of the Churches of Vienne and Lyons, *c.* A.D. 177 (in Euseb. *H.E.* v. 1). There is little doubt that to Irenaeus 'John the Disciple of the Lord' was the Apostle. The 'John the Elder' of Papias is little more than a shadow, 'who has the critical notes and art of Eusebius to thank for his existence.' Zahn, *Einleitung in d. N.T.* ii. p. 490. When Dionysius speaks of two tombs at Ephesus bearing the name of John, he is careful to add that he speaks on hearsay, *φάσιν*.

[3] *v.* Swete, *The Apocalypse*, pp. cxxiii f

[4] *Haeres.* v. 30, § 3. *οὐδὲ γὰρ πρὸ πολλοῦ χρόνου ἑωράθη, ἀλλὰ σχεδὸν ἐπὶ τῆς ἡμετέρας γενεᾶς, πρὸς τῷ τέλει τῆς Δομετιανοῦ ἀρχῆς.* But *v.* Edmundson, *The Church in Rome in the First Century*, p. 164 f.

[5] 'Chapter xi. 1, 2, must have been written before 70 A.D.' Bousset, *Encycl. Bibl.* Art. 'Apocalypse,' col. 205.

v. Westcott, *St. John*, p. lxxxvii. Both Dr. Lightfoot and Dr. Hort concurred in the view of Dr. Westcott, a consensus of opinion which it is difficult to set aside. *v.* Hort, *St. Peter*, p. 2; *Judaistic Christianity*, p. 160; Lightfoot,

compared with the Greek of the Gospel and First Epistle, points to the early effort of an Aramaic-speaking writer to express himself in a language which, after long residence in Ephesus, he may well have made his own. If, bearing in mind signs of early composition, we can bring ourselves to set aside the late period assigned by Irenaeus and place a generation between the two works—and only if that interval can be defended—the Apocalyptist and the Evangelist may come together in a single personality.[1]

It is difficult to rate too highly the historical value of the Book of Acts.[2] For the story of the first days of the infant Church, its spiritual equipment and its early struggles; for the momentous gain to the Apostleship which resulted from the conversion of St. Paul; for the conflict between Judaic exclusiveness and the larger vision which was granted to the Apostle of the Gentiles, we turn to it with the certainty that we are treading on sure ground. Its general trustworthiness has been so fully proved in the course of recent archaeological research[3] that our estimate of its value is not disturbed by the few remaining difficulties that still await solution.[4] We shall, therefore, employ Acts as an historical document of the first order.

The authenticity of the four practically undisputed Epistles of St. Paul[5] will be assumed. Of the rest, 1 Thessalonians is certainly genuine and, if not the earliest, is at any rate among

Biblical Essays, p. 52. Harnack regards the Apocalypse as a composite work—a Jewish writing edited by a Christian. He thinks that the finished work and the Gospel may both be by the same hand. *Geschichte der altchrist. Literatur*, ii. *Chronologie*, i. p. 675. Cf. J. Weiss, *Die Offenbarung Johannis*, 1904, p. 162.

[1] 'To ascribe two writings, one of which is fervently apocalyptic while the other definitely rejects apocalyptic ideas, to the same writer is a patent absurdity.' P. Gardner, *The Ephesian Gospel*, p. 45. The force of this contention is lessened by the above consideration of an interval of time between the two works. The apocalyptic feeling in the earlier Epistles of St. Paul has disappeared in his later writings. A generation elapsing between the Apocalypse and the Fourth Gospel might well account for a similar phenomenon.

[2] *v.* above, p. 13; below, p. 392.

[3] Especially Sir W. M. Ramsay's works, *passim*.

[4] Such as the account of the Council in chap. xv., as compared with Gal. ii.

[5] Galatians, Romans, 1 and 2 Corinthians.

the earliest of New Testament writings.[1] The difficulties incurred by the attempt to prove that 2 Thessalonians is not the work of St. Paul are so great that its reception is the only course that our present state of knowledge warrants. Both Epistles will be freely employed.

The genuine character of the Epistle to the Philippians is evident throughout. Its extreme importance in the development of the Christology of the Apostolic age heightens our appreciation of its authenticity.

The Epistle to the Colossians will be employed as a complete and integral work of St. Paul. It is of the highest importance for the cosmical position of Christ.[2] The authenticity of the Epistle to the Ephesians is less assured; but it will be cited as containing the mind if not, in every phrase, the language of the Apostle.

The beautiful Epistle to Philemon betrays its Pauline authorship in every line, and is closely linked with the Epistle to the Colossians in date and in place of origin.

The Pastoral Epistles are thought by many to reflect a more advanced stage of doctrine and of custom than existed during the life-time of St. Paul. But they are full of his spirit, and will be employed under the limitations which the present critical position appears to demand.

The mystery which still surrounds the authorship of the Epistle to the Hebrews in no way detracts from its value as a genuine document of the critical period which saw the destruction of the Temple. It is strange that we are unable to name the writer of what is perhaps the most scholarly, and is among the most valuable of the Epistles of the New Testament.[3] Like the Apocalyptists of the second and first centuries B.C., he was content

[1] *v.* above, p. 23.

[2] i. 15 f. Our Lord is represented as the goal and object, as well as the agent, in creation. On the relation of this passage to other and earlier cosmical passages in the writings of St. Paul, *v.* Moffatt, *Introduction to the Literature of the N.T.* p. 155.

[3] The definition of faith, Heb. xi. 1, is one of the profoundest passages in the New Testament. Various attempts have been made to paraphrase it. Remembering that it is here concerned with the apprehension of spiritual things, the meaning appears to be as follows: Faith gives you the actual possession of what you are looking forward to in hope; it proves the reality of what

to express the truths which were borne in upon him, without thought of personal fame or even recognition.[1]

There is good reason to regard the Epistle of St. James as the work of the Lord's brother. The absence of specific Christian thought and the thoroughly Jewish character[2] of the writing point to an early date. At the same time, the Epistle is full of quotations of, or allusions to, sayings of our Lord.[3] These two characteristics reveal the work of a man, who, while deeply impressed with the teaching of Christ to which he had actually listened, did not feel himself called upon to formulate Christian doctrine. What we know of St. James of Jerusalem corresponds with the impression conveyed by the Epistle. He was perhaps the last of the primitive Christian leaders to part with his devotion to ideas and practices of the old faith. A certain similarity to writings like 'the Shepherd' of Hermas[4] does not warrant the transference of the authorship to the beginning of the second century. In the absence of any clear indication to the contrary, we shall consider the Epistle as a genuine writing of the first generation of the Church, reflecting the life of a time of transition from Judaic Christianity to the gradually acquired freedom of the Gospel.

you cannot see. Believe and you already have. Cf. xii. 22. 'Ye are come unto mount Sion.' You are already in heaven. With this view St. John is in entire agreement. 'This is life eternal.' 'He that hath the Son hath life. Faith makes the future present and visualizes the invisible.

[1] The names of Barnabas and Apollos almost equally commend themselves, as we think of the authorship. The latter especially as a man 'mighty in the Scriptures' seems to have possessed the gifts demanded by such a work. 'No one suits the impression which we receive of the author of Hebrews so well as Apollos... But every sound treatment of the question of authorship goes back to the point of Origen, *τίς δὲ ὁ γράψας τὴν ἐπιστολὴν, τὸ μὲν ἀληθὲς, Θεὸς οἶδεν.* Zahn, *Einleitung in d. N.T.* ii. p. 155.

[2] Cf. Jam. ii. 2, where *τὴν συναγωγὴν ὑμῶν* may refer to Christian attendance at the Jewish synagogue. *v.* J. Weiss, *Das Urchristentum*, i. p. 40. There is less distinctive Christian teaching in this Epistle than in any other New Testament writing. The atmosphere is prevailingly Jewish. So much is this the case that the theory of a Jewish writing to which a few Christian touches have been added is not without plausibility.

[3] 'The Epistle contains more reminiscences of the sayings of Jesus than any other apostolic letter. It is like a Sermon on the Mount among the Epistles.' Holtzmann, *Einleitung in das N.T.* p. 476. *v.* Resch, *Agrapha: Ausser-canonische Evangelienfragmente*, p. 252 f.; Mayor on Jam. i. 12.

[4] With Jam. i. 6-8 cf. *Pastor*, Mand. ix. Jam. iv. 6 is quoted by Clem. Rom. c. xxx. *v.* Mayor, *The Epistle of St. James*, p. xlviii f.

The First Epistle of St. Peter bears the marks of its Apostolic origin,[1] while the evidence of its early use and recognition is abundant.[2] As might be expected, if the writer is St. Peter, great stress is laid upon the death and resurrection of Christ.[3] For so short an Epistle, the allusions are very numerous. They give the impression that the writer was profoundly impressed with the significance of the redemptive work of the Saviour; and we are hardly surprised that special mention of the teaching of our Lord is absent. The eschatology of the Epistle points to an early date, when the expectation of an immediate return of Christ was widely held.[4] Much has been said about Pauline influence upon the writer of the Epistle: yet it is difficult to discover any idea which a man with the experience of St. Peter need have borrowed from another writer.[5] Contact with Pauline thought is, at any rate, no argument against the traditional authorship of the letter: [6] while there is much which agrees well

[1] 'In the Petrine Epistle we have proof that there was a Christendom whose authenticity is unassailable, because it proceeds from the first witnesses of Christ.' B. Weiss, *Der erste Petrusbrief*, p. 65. For the correspondence between the condition of things mirrored in the Epistle and the time of Nero—rather than a much later period which would be fatal to the Petrine authorship—we have the assurance of Mommsen and need no other. The view of J. Weiss that, as 'we can no longer look upon the Epistles of Peter and James as genuine writings of these original Apostles, we have no *direct* witnesses to the religion of the oldest Jewish-Christian community' is contrary to the facts of the case. *Christus: die Anfänge des Dogmas*, p. 7. Besides, apart from these Epistles, the early letters of St. Paul furnish direct evidence on the subject.

[2] The presence of language and idea of 1. Pet. in Clement of Rome is clear and striking; *e.g.* 1 Pet. ii. 9; Clem. Rom. lix. δι' οὗ ἐκάλεσεν ἡμᾶς ἀπὸ σκότους εἰς φῶς. If we may trust Eusebius, Papias of Hierapolis spoke of the First Epistle of Peter, and alluded to the mention of St. Mark, 1 Pet. v. 13. *v.* Chase in Hastings' *D.B.* iii. p. 780. Later on, the attribution of the Epistle to St. Peter is universal. 'Very few of the apostolical writings are better attested.' Lightfoot, *Galatians*, p. 355.

[3] 1 Pet. i. 2, 11, 19; ii. 21 f.; iii. 18; iv. 1, 13; v. 1, refer to the death. The resurrection is alluded to in i. 3, 11, 21; iii. 21.

[4] *v.* 1 Pet. iv. 7.

[5] In idea, if not in phraseology, there is likeness between Gal. ii. 20 and 1 Pet. ii. 24. For resemblances of language between 1 Pet. and Eph. *v.* Moffatt, *Introduction to the N.T.* pp. 382 f.

[6] *v.* Chase in Hastings' *D.B.* iii. p. 788. B. Weiss reminds us that 'The doctrinal language of all New Testament writers is founded on the colloquial Greek which was common to the East and is formed on the model of the Greek version of the Old Testament which was in general use; hence there was much that was common property.' *Der erste Petrusbrief*, p. 59. He points out

with the impression of the teaching of St. Peter conveyed by the Acts of the Apostles.[1] The burden of proof lies with the opponents of the traditional authorship. Hitherto they have failed to sustain it.[2] We are inclined to place the composition of the Epistle in the year A.D. 63 or 64, during the Apostle's residence in Rome and but a short time before his martyrdom in the garden of the Vatican.[3]

The case of the Second Epistle of St. Peter stands on a very different footing. While it is unmentioned by any writer before Origen, the internal evidence is, on the whole, adverse to Petrine authorship. Allusions to the great redemptive acts of Christ, which abound in the First Epistle, are here absent. Likeness to the 'Apocalypse of Peter'[4] suggests similarity of origin and date. There is considerable agreement in regarding the work as the pseudonymous creation of a writer of about the middle of the second century.[5] Under these circum-

that sayings of our Lord and their bearing upon Christian faith and practice were at an early period brought by writing into a more or less fixed shape. *Ib.* p. 64.

[1] With 1. Pet. i. 10, cf. Acts ii. 16; iii. 18, 21. With 1 Pet. ii. 6 f. cf. Acts iv. 11.

[2] 'It cannot be a matter of indifference whether we possess a written document which shows how the preaching of salvation and its application to life unfolded itself in the case of one of the original Apostles.' B. Weiss, *ib.* p. 64.

[3] *v.* Zahn, *Einleitung in d. N.T.* ii. pp. 18, 19, and Anmerk. 4. B. Weiss, who says that Peter 'must have come to Rome towards the end of his life, since his martyrdom there rests on unassailable tradition,' considers that the Epistle could not have proceeded from Rome at such a time in view of its omissions. He takes 'Babylon' to be the actual city on the Euphrates. *Der erste Petrusbrief*, p. 44 f. Bigg, *Epistles of St. Peter and St. Jude*, p. 87, places the date of the Epistle between A.D. 58 and 64.

[4] This likeness is perhaps exaggerated by some writers. There is, for instance, very little common ground between 2 Pet. i. 16 f. and the description of the scene upon the Mount in the 'Apocalypse of Peter' (Akhmîm Fragment, § 4 f.). In the fragment preserved by Macarius Magn. (No. 5 in Preuschen, *Antilegomena*, p. 88) the passing away of the heavens recalls Isaiah xxxiv. 4, and is more akin to Revel. vi. 13, 14, than to 2 Pet. iii. 10 f.

[5] Among supposed evidences against the Petrine authorship, it is often alleged that the similarity of the Epistle in part to the Epistle of Jude is fatal to the idea of apostolic authorship. But we have no means of determining whether a man like St. Peter would hesitate at making free use of another work, especially if its author were a near kinsman of Christ. The allusion to St. Paul's Epistles as Scripture is regarded as clear evidence of a late date. So Weinel, 'about or after A.D. 150.' *Bibl. Theologie des N.T.* p. 572. But, as Harnack suggests (*Dogmengesch.* i. p. 110), it is not clear that γραφή always denotes what we

stances, the Epistle will not be used as authoritative Scripture with the same freedom with which the other New Testament writings will be employed.[1]

There is nothing to be said against the probability that the short Epistle of 'Jude a servant of Jesus Christ and brother of James'[2] was written by the kinsman of our Lord who is mentioned in St. Mark vi. 3.[3] The fact that this Epistle and 2 Peter contain a certain amount of material which shows that one writer borrowed from the other,[4] and that 2 Peter is apparently a work of the middle of the second century, makes it very probable that the Epistle of St. Jude is the work of a person of consideration living in the first age of the Church. If this be admitted, we have no ground for rejecting the author's claim in v. 1.

understand by Canonical Scripture. *v.* Zahn, *Einleitung in das N.T.* ii. p. 99; Bigg, *The Epistles of St. Peter and St. Jude, ad loc.* p. 302.

The warning against 'scoffers in the last days,' 2 Pet. iii. 3 f., is thought to argue a much later date than the Apostolic age. 'The fathers' of the Church had fallen asleep. Unless we regard the warning as prophetic, the state of things can only be placed at a date when St. Peter and his fellow Apostles had passed away. This is perhaps a sign that the Epistle is a pseudonymous writing of the second century. *v.* Peake, *A Critical Introduction to the N.T.* p. 98. On the other hand, Bigg, *Epistles of St. Peter and St. Jude, ad loc.* considers that οἱ πατέρες, like the phrase in Heb. i. 1, Acts iii. 13, refers to the fathers of the Old Covenant. 'No forger would have fallen into so obvious and fatal a blunder' as to mean the founders of the Christian Church. Then, again, the theory that 2 Pet. i. 16, is an allusion to the Petrine element of the Second Gospel, and is designed to draw attention to the person of St. Peter, is too far-fetched to be alleged against the genuineness of the Epistle. It is therefore an over-statement of the case against it, to say with M. Jones, 'It is no longer possible to regard 2 St. Peter as an authentic Petrine Epistle.' *The New Testament in the Twentieth Century.*

[1] It should be noted that Zahn not only assigns to 2 Pet. priority to the Epistle of Jude, but places it before 1 Pet. and about A.D. 60-63.

'. . . The deficiency of external evidence forbids the use of the Second Epistle in controversy.' Lightfoot, *Galatians*, p. 355.

[2] Jude 1.

[3] But Jude 17, 18 seems to point to a period which was already far gone.

[4] In the opinion of Zahn, *Einleitung in d. N.T.* ii. p. 74 f., Jude was written about A.D. 75 and *after* 2 Pet. Bigg also regards 2 Pet. as the earlier writing of the two. *Op. cit.* p. 216 f.

CHAPTER III

THE PREPARATION: JUDAISM

SPEAKING generally, the coming of Christ was prepared for both consciously and unconsciously. The conscious preparation was under the direct inspiration of the Holy Spirit, and found its chief expression in Hebrew prophecy. The unconscious preparation was under the guiding of God's Providence. But its action was unmarked by those who shared it. It lay rather in the disposal of world-history, in the gradual evolution of thought, in the processes of government and administration. The conscious preparation is associated with a single people and a single land:[1] the unconscious was spread over the wide field of the Roman Empire, and owed much of its efficacy to the pervasive influence of the Greek language.

It may, of course, be argued that in such a subject there is a tendency to read backwards from the event to the antecedent circumstances, and to let it colour the preceding years with tones reflected from itself. We may so magnify its importance as to be unable to read earlier history apart from it, and to allow no independent weight to matters which had intrinsic importance in their day. We may carry the theory of continuity too far, and see links in the chain of circumstance where an unprejudiced mind would only find unrelated and distinct phenomena.

Yet, when all allowance is made for possible exaggeration under the spell of a great conviction, the marks of preparation for Christ, both conscious and unconscious, which history shows, are too evident to be mistaken.

[1] *v.* Schürer, *Geschichte des Jüd. Volkes*, i. p. 1. 'In the fulness of the times the Christian Religion sprang out of the bosom of Judaism.'

It is quite true that, if there is such preparation in His case, He stands alone in this experience. No other child of man has been the object of so many converging lines of thought and activity as are claimed for Him. The great men of history—the heroes of achievement and leaders of thought—if, as is no doubt the case, their lives have been moulded and shaped by circumstances preceding their birth, have been but factors in the current of events which has borne them into prominence. They have been part of the process of development, not the goal of it. Not so with Christ. The lines have so converged upon Him as their aim and object, that we may almost say they had no part to play in history but to go forward and meet in His Person. Touched and affected as He was by the social conditions into which He entered, acquainted as others of His people with the moral and intellectual possessions of His race and time, He was singularly free from dependence upon them. He lived in the world which had helped to form Him and which gave Him His surroundings. He was in it, but not of it. He was never in subjection to the moral and intellectual standards of His time. When we speak of the preparation for Christ we must remember this.

We may again subdivide the preparation for Christ. There was personal preparation—that which contributed to His own life and modes of thought. And there was the external and impersonal preparation which affected His work and its extension in the world.

The personal preparation was almost entirely Jewish. That people gave Him His mother, His home, His education, His religion, His Bible. All religion, like the light, has risen in the East. Christ was a child of the East; and to understand Him, we have to penetrate into modes of thought and expression that seem strange to Western minds.

If Christianity was to take root so far more freely in the West than in the East, the choice of an Eastern family and home for the Saviour appears remarkable. It remains a matter of wonder that He who was to make all things new, the Reformer and Remodeller, found a home among the folding hills of Palestine with a people whose greatness lay in the past, and who clung with invincible tenacity to that which 'decayeth and waxeth old' and 'is ready to vanish away.'

Why, if He was to bring in a new heaven and a new earth, and to inspire with fresh life whatever made for the redemption and amelioration of man, did He pitch His tent by a backwater, and not by the flowing stream of life which was so soon to widen out into the nations of the modern world ?

The answer is partly to be found in the nature of the work that He came to do. The clue to His hidden life, so remote from the great centres of thought and action, to the choice of mother and home, lay in the spiritual character of that life and of its purpose. 'The Kingdom of God cometh not with observation.' To have entered the world of politics or literature or administration would have indicated a desire to compete with it, and would have added a fresh rival to those that were already jostling one another in the market places and the schools of the world-wide Empire. If He was to reveal God, to bring in a kingdom of righteousness and to redeem and quicken the dead souls of sinful men, He must concentrate Himself upon that work and enter life where it was somewhat sheltered from the world; where, with all that sufficed for human experience, He could yet be withdrawn from contact with currents of thought and feeling that would hinder the carrying out of His purpose.

But the needful seclusion and detachment was a small part of what the Jewish people could contribute in preparing for Christ. Along with its shortcomings, its obstinacy and stubbornness, it combined a singular genius for religion. In a way unexampled before or since, the soul of the people was steeped in intense religious fervour. Religion was its life. All else was subordinated. Again and again, from the call of Abraham with which their life as a people and a Church began, they were making decisive acts of choice for God. They lived with Him ; and His Fatherhood was to them a reality as was nothing else. It is often said that Christ came to reveal God as the Father of men.[1] This was certainly not His purpose, so far as His own people were concerned. That truth was already the main factor of their lives.[2] It was rather because they possessed it that He became one of them in race and rearing. There was already a foundation principle on which He could work, a rock on which

[1] *E.g.* by Harnack, *Das Wesen des Christentums*, p. 91. *v.* below, p. 297.

[2] 1 Chron. xxix. 10 ; Is. lxiii. 16 ; Ps. lxviii. 5, ciii. 13 ; Jer. xxxi. 9.

He could build His Church. With the Jews, He could begin at a riper stage of religious development than with any other people. They had already in their keeping the bud from which the full flower of the absolute religion could break out into its perfection.

This position of pre-eminence in religiousness and in adaptability for His purpose had been carefully and patiently won through long ages of anticipation. Great heroes and prophets had each contributed his own share to the work. There were times in the history of the people when Heaven and earth were very near to one another, when the face of God was almost visible, and men walked with Him as a Friend. There were heights and depths of spiritual experience which have never been surpassed even under the ministry of the Holy Spirit. The troubled heart and conscience turns instinctively to the Psalms to express and relieve its burden. To stand with Moses on Sinai, or with Isaiah in the Temple, is to feel to the full the awe of the Divine presence.

If, then, 'our Lord sprang out of Judah,'[1] it was because that people was of all peoples the best adapted to receive Him. Far behind other nations in much that stirs our interest —in art, in secular literature, in commerce—they possessed just those qualities which formed a point of contact for the new influence that was to work in the hearts of men. The Jews afforded the most likely seed-plot for the Gospel. They had been trained to expect a heavenly visitation. No one people could enter into and grasp the message of salvation as they. They had nothing to unlearn. All that they possessed was true, as far as it went. They had but to receive what was the logical outcome and goal of their historic past.

Nothing to unlearn so far as regards the fabric and staple of their religion, as received at the hands of their heaven-taught leaders and prophets. At every stage of their history, some new truth or principle of life was added. But in the process of its development we have to note, as is always the case in a religion which is vital and therefore capable of adaptation to fresh needs and conditions, the gradual accretion of elements which are not essential and which tend to obscure or stifle those parts which are. Hence our Lord's complaint against the Pharisees for

[1] Hebr. vii. 14.

'making the Word of God of none effect through tradition.'[1] In this sense there was much to unlearn, not in the religion but in its practice, not in the kernel but the husk.

This clouding of essential principle and vital fact by the trivial and external thwarted our Lord at every step. It accounts for His otherwise excessive sternness towards Scribes and Pharisees. Conviction of sin, with repentance and amendment, was impossible in the case of men steeped in complacent satisfaction with their own righteousness. The Kingdom of Heaven had readier access to the outcasts of society than to them. His dealing with them is a warning to every age that to be content with one's own standard and way of life, to feel no desire for better things, bars effectually all the ministry of Divine grace.

The Jewish people were trained for their part in world-history by their religion. Of that religion, their public worship was the central feature. Its chief characteristics were their intense realization of the sole majesty and the Fatherhood of God, and their sense of personal sin with its correlative, the need of atonement.

The belief that there is but one God was only gradually arrived at. When fully attained, it was held with passionate fervour. However often the people fell away into idolatry, they always came back, under the guidance of prophets and the teaching of adversity, to the creed which was the unique glory of their race. In the pre-prophetic period, they let their personal belief carry them no farther than the limits of their own race. Their feeling could be expressed in the words of Joshua, 'As for me and my house, we will serve the Lord.'[2] They did not dispute the idea that there might be other gods. Jehovah alone was *their* God. They had not arrived at the full monotheistic standpoint. When the period of the pre-exilic prophets is reached, we get many indications that the conception of God is extended to embrace universal dominion. He is no longer the God of Israel only, with rival deities outside the cult of the chosen people. He stands alone, the God of heaven and earth.[3]

Another characteristic of their worship was the expression which it gave to the sense of personal sin and to the need of atonement. In no other religion is this feature so constant

[1] Mk. vii. 13. [2] Josh. xxiv. 15.
[3] *v.* Kautzsch, in Hastings' *D.B.* v. p. 680.

and so pervading an element. Sacrifice was the central act of their worship. The priesthood was the leading class of the community. The claim of purity was the most pressing of all the requirements which their religion laid upon them. To render themselves pleasing and acceptable to God by taking part in daily acts of cleansing and in propitiatory offerings, culminating in the intensified rites of the weekly Sabbath and of the greater Feast Days of the year, formed the chief part of the religious life of all who had access to the Temple, either by residence in Jerusalem and its neighbourhood, or by special visits from their more distant homes.

But it was on the Day of Atonement that the sense of sin and the need of forgiveness reached their climax among the Jewish people. Every part of the ritual concentrated the mind on the idea of guilt. The longing after God, which was the most persistent factor in the spiritual life of the nation, was represented by the entrance, on that day alone in all the year, of the High Priest into the Most Holy Place. But that entrance was bought by sacrifice. The sacred spot which symbolized the presence of God could not be approached until expiation had been made. Not the people and not the ordinary priests might go in there; and the High Priest himself only on that day and then 'not without blood.'[1] Nothing could have more vividly brought home to the people the reality of sin, the insurmountable barrier which it presents to communion with God, the need for its conquest, and the inadequate and preparatory character of the dispensation under which they lived. It showed that the way into the inner shrine of God's Presence was not yet thrown open,[2] that their religion must necessarily be imperfect, typical, prophetic, until it should please God to inaugurate 'a better covenant.' That at least was, according to the writer to the Hebrews, the teaching of the Holy Spirit. How far it was grasped by the people generally, it is now impossible to say. But we can see how the restrictions which were placed upon their worship, and the importance assigned to sin as a bar to grace, would make the more thoughtful realize the temporary and unsufficing character of their religion, and look forward with eagerness to the dawn of a better day. It was its recognized inadequacy to be a satisfying expression of religious feeling,

[1] Hebr. ix. 7. [2] Hebr. ix. 8.

coupled with its witness to the primal facts of the religious consciousness, that gave Judaism its pre-eminence among the conditions which prepared the world for its Saviour. No other *milieu* more adapted for His purpose could He have chosen than the people whose worship centred in the Temple, and whose every act typified at once their sense of need and their hope of deliverance. In a word, the Jews were of all races the best equipped for receiving, in the fulness of the times, the Person of the world's Redeemer. It is one of the paradoxes of history that a people so fitted by their history and their institutions for God's greatest gift and whose whole past was a preparation for it, should have turned against Him when He came.

Another element of their religious life was the gift of prophecy. Every wise and experienced man is, to a certain extent, a seer. From his knowledge of the past and of the conditions of success or failure, he can often picture the future. But his estimate must always remain provisional. Forces and conditions of which he has had no experience may come into play, modifying the action of what is familiar to him. There can be no certainty in his forecast; and it is this which distinguishes him from the true prophet. He goes solely on his own interpretation of the past and the present, when he projects his thought into the future. The prophet, on the other hand, speaks less from his own acquired experience than from a source of knowledge which is given to him; which, while it uses and does not crush out his own faculties of perception, yet lifts for him the veil that hides the future.

The prophetic gift was of a twofold character, predictive and didactic. At different times one of these gifts has been magnified at the expense of the other. The apologetic value of the predictive element in prophecy led people to lose sight of the moral teaching of the prophets and of their spiritual influence. Nowadays, the pendulum has swung in the opposite direction. The predictive element, which is after all the really constitutive one, is thrust into the background.[1] Yet it is a factor in Jewish life which cannot be ignored. The vision of the future was the distinctive burden of the prophetic message, and the prophets themselves appealed to the fulfilment of their predictions as the guarantee that God had spoken by them.[2] The object of their

[1] *v.* A. B. Davidson in Hastings, *D.B.* iv. p. 118.

[2] 1 Kings xxii. 28. Cf. Ezek. ii. 5, xxxiii. 33.

vision was the coming of the Kingdom of God. Beyond the inevitable times of disaster and captivity, they saw the dawn of a brighter day.

What was the origin of this central conviction of Jewish thought? If we cannot derive it from the Protevangelium[1]—for the tradition of the Fall left few traces of itself in the other Old Testament writings—we may at least regard that promise as pointing to an early conviction of the standing enmity which exists between good and evil, and of the future victory of good to be realized in the heart of humanity. If the heel of the woman's offspring is to be bruised, it is the head of the evil one, the centre of his thought and action, which is to suffer. In the one case, the organ of activity may be crippled; in the other, it is the vital part of being. It is, perhaps, in the person of Abraham, and in the experiences which are attributed to him, that we meet with the earliest form of the conviction. Here we have to do with an historic groundwork, however freely the piety of later times and the well-known desire to account for present circumstances have built upon and around that central kernel of fact. We may at any rate see in his migration from his old home, in his devotion to God, in his heroic faith and unfailing hopefulness, an example to all who, through varying fortunes, have maintained their trust in God and in His promises. Our Lord gave expression to that estimate of the historic faith of the patriarch, when He said 'Your Father Abraham rejoiced to see My day: and he saw it and was glad.'[2] His faith rested on the persuasion that God would one day bring in for mankind through the instrumentality of a descendant of his own a time of glory and prosperity. By faith Abraham saw 'the day of the Messiah,' in the fulfilment of God's promise that he should have a son.[3] Thus he was 'the father of all them that believe,'[4] the person in whom the Messianic hope of the far-off future first took up its abode. It is impossible to mistake the importance

[1] Gen. iii. 15.

[2] Jo. viii. 56. It should be observed that the recital of this colloquy is closely bound up with the record of a definite stage in our Lord's career, which marked the beginning of His Passion. The effect of His teaching about Abraham was that the Jews 'took up stones to cast at Him,' v. 59.

[3] So Zahn, in Jo. viii. 56. According to Westcott *in loc.* 'My day' is probably the historic manifestation of the Christ.

[4] Rom. iv. 11, 16.

which the New Testament writers assign to the position of Abraham in the gradual evolution of the Messianic idea. It is confined to no one school of thought, but pervades the New Testament from end to end. His person looms through the dimness of the past as the great originator, through his own gifts of faith and hope, of the longing and looking for that condition of things, to which later ages gave the name of the Kingdom of God. In a very true sense, all who look for the reign of righteousness, to whatever period of history they belong, are the children of 'faithful Abraham.'[1]

The next great step in the progress of the Messianic idea was taken by Moses. As regards the historical character of the records of his life in their main outlines, we may say with Kittel,[2] 'If the events of that period are, as a whole, beyond dispute, they demand for their explanation such a personality as the sources give us in Moses.' If we did not find him in the history, we should have to invent him. No such movement as that of the Exodus, no such event as the giving of the covenant, no such religious crisis as the choice of Jehovah by the united Israelitish clans, could have taken place except under the leadership of a mighty and commanding figure. All the sources of our knowledge of the time represent such a personality to have existed in Moses. 'The foundation upon which, at all periods, Israel's sense of its national unity rested was religious in its character. It was the faith which may be summed up in the formula, Jehovah is the God of Israel, and Israel is the people of Jehovah. Moses was not the first discoverer of this faith, but it was through him that it came to be the fundamental basis of the national existence and history.'[3] The importance

[1] Gal. iii. 9. Kittel remarks that 'the patriarchal period, especially that of Abraham, must be regarded as the necessary presupposition for the Mosaic period. . . . If . . . Israelite tradition, both in history and prophecy, goes further back than Moses and finds in the patriarchs the first roots not only of the possession of the land, but also of the people's higher worship of God, this can only be accounted for by assuming that memory had retained a hold of the actual course of events. It may therefore be assumed that the person of Abraham rests on a historical background.' *History of the Hebrews*, E.T. i. p. 174. *v.* Ryle in Hastings' *D.B.* i. p. 16.

[2] *History of the Hebrews*, E.T. i. p. 239.

[3] Wellhausen, *Proleg. to Hist. of Israel*, p. 433. Cf. Kittel, *op. cit.* i. p. 240, 'Israel became a nation at the Exodus. Moses created it. Without him, Israel would have remained what it was before.'

of Moses in the preparation for Christ is thus due, not so much to the definite grasp and expression of the hope of a Divine deliverer, as to the foundation which he laid, in the worship of the One God, for all that was to be involved in that hope. St. Peter, indeed, does not hesitate to give a full Messianic meaning to the words which the Deuteronomist puts into the mouth of Moses; [1] but we cannot say that they were so understood at the time they were spoken. Rather must we see the significance of Moses for the gradual evolution of Messianic thought in his work of purifying and elevating the religious life and conceptions of the Messianic people. The Christian Church to-day owes to that great personality the religion out of which it rose and which made its own existence possible. 'The importance of the personality of Moses can hardly be exaggerated.' [2] He marked one of the chief stages in the long way of preparation that led to Christ.

Between the time of Moses and the erection of the monarchy, the prophetic gift was exercised on matters of a more or less temporary character. Samuel is the most conspicuous instance. He was the last of the Judges, and laid down his office on the establishment of the monarchy, for which, like John the Baptist, he had prepared the way, by designating the first holder of the office. Loyal and faithful to God, he was yet destitute of vision. He was a man of his time and did not look beyond the period which he inaugurated. What is true of him is true of others who, possessing the prophetic gift, employed it on the circumstances of their day. It is not until we come to the great literary prophets of the eighth century that we catch a glimpse of the extended vision, the wider interest, the broader outlook upon life. Only then does the Messianic idea begin to find expression. Its burden is the coming in of a better time. The prophets are the preachers of hope. In the course of time the vision takes fresh forms and shapes. It becomes difficult to western minds to trace the connection between its different stages. The future glory of Israel, with the discomfiture of their foes, is the main feature of the prospect. One figure stands out pre-eminent, the King, of David's line. And here the vision seems to vary. Now it is a line of Davidic

[1] Acts iii. 22; Deut. xviii. 15.

[2] Kautzsch, 'Religion of Israel,' *D.B.* extra vol. p. 625.

kings, whose dynasty is not to fail ;[1] then again, it is one ideal prince of David's house, who is to reign for ever.[2] So entirely does this Personage embody features which afterwards came to be connected with the Messiah that, though the Name itself is not applied, we cannot help recognizing in Him the Hope of Israel, the Lord's Anointed.

Then emerges the conception that Jehovah Himself will be present with His people. He comes in Person to be their Saviour and to reign over them.[3] When the house of David and the monarchy had lost their significance in the crushing disasters of the Captivity, the way was open for more spiritual thoughts of deliverance.[4] How God's presence was to be brought about we are not told ; but the conception of the Messianic future was widely extended in two very important directions. The world at large was included in the sphere of the Messianic reign.[5] The individual began to claim his share in the glories of the future kingdom.[6] Moreover, the older view of the kingdom itself, which took its colour and form mainly from mundane conceptions, became spiritualized. Heaven is its true home. *There* is the New Jerusalem awaiting the faithful. There, too, dwells from all eternity in communion with God, the Messiah.[7]

On the return from the Exile, the figure of a personal Messiah of David's line passes into the background. Zechariah, it is true, told of the Just One, who would ride into Jerusalem as a King, bringing salvation. But after Zerubbabel, the line of David was no longer in the mind of the people. It had ceased to produce any conspicuous representative. The figure of a son of David fades from the Messianic picture. Besides, the Greek ascendancy, under the successors of Alexander the Great, had brought the nation into contact with the thought and interests of a far wider world.[8]

[1] *v.* Schürer, *op. cit.* ii. p. 528, and n. 16. Cf. Jer. xvii. 25 ; xxii. 4 ; xxxiii. 17.

[2] Schürer, *ib.* p. 500. Cf. Is. vii. 14-16 ; ix. 6, 7 ; xi. ; Mic. iv. v.

[3] Is. vii., ix., xi., xxiv. 23.

[4] Ezek. xxxvii. 27. *v.* Bousset, *D. Religion des Judentums*, p. 277.

[5] *v.* Schürer, ii. p. 500 ; *Encycl. Bibl.* iii. p. 3058.

[6] *v.* Schürer, ii. p. 501 ; Bousset, *D. Religion des Judentums*, p. 239.

[7] Schürer, ii. p. 503.

[8] Zech. ix. 9. But 'there are indications which seem to show that the prophecy is *pre-exilic.*' Driver, *Liter. of O.T.* p. 348. Cf. *Test. of Levi*, 8. *v.* Bousset, *Die Religion des Judentums*, p. 256 ; Holtzmann, *Neutestamentliche Theologie*, i. pp. 89, 103.

Then, again, after the victory of the Maccabaean princes, and when the chief power had passed into the hands of the High Priest of the house of Levi, the line of David as the family of Messiah entirely lost its significance. In spite of prophecy, Messianic hopes became concentrated upon the priestly tribe. Many thought that the Messianic age had already dawned.[1]

But it was only for a time that the national hopes were thus turned aside from their true object. In restoring the ancient form of the Messianic idea, a great part was played by the apocalyptic writers of the second and first centuries B.C. The figure of a Son of David comes forth once more.[2] The Gospels attest its continuance as the prevailing type of belief in our Lord's day.[3]

In the book of Daniel, we find what is probably the first distinct mention of the Messiah by name—'the Anointed One, the Prince.'[4] If the 'One like unto a Son of Man'[5] refers in the first instance to the 'Saints of the Most High' (vv. 22, 27), yet that representative Figure cannot be dissociated from Messianic ideas, and we find from allusions in 1 Enoch 46 and 4 Ezra 13[6] that a definite Messianic interpretation was placed upon the phrase.[7]

The Person of the Messiah is almost entirely absent from the apocryphal books of the Old Testament, although the Messianic hope is still in evidence.[8] Under Hasmonaean influence, the

[1] *v.* Bousset, *ib.*; Charles, *Apocrypha and Pseudepigrapha of the O.T.* ii. pp. 282, 9.

[2] *v.* especially *Ps. of Sol.* xvii. 5, 7, 8, 23, 'Behold, O Lord, and raise up unto them their king, the Son of David.' *Test. of Judah*, xxiv. 5, 6; *Book of Jubilees*, xxxi. 18 f. *v.* Charles, *op. cit.* ii. pp. 9, 294, 630.

[3] In the *Assumption of Moses*, which is probably the work of a Pharisee contemporary with Christ, a Messianic Kingdom is referred to (x. 8, 9), but there is no personal Messiah. That conception had been degraded by worldly and political views. The writer is much like one of the old Hasidim. *v.* below, p. 230, n. 1; Charles, *op. cit.* ii. pp. 407, 11, 12.

[4] Dan. ix. 25. *v.* Stanton in Hastings' *D.B.* iii. p. 353.

[5] Dan. vii. 13.

[6] *v.* Box in Charles, *The Apocrypha and Pseudepigrapha of the O.T.* ii. p. 616.

[7] *v.* Schürer, ii. p. 506; Bousset, *Die Religion des Judentums*, p. 255, n. 2, 'The Figure of a personal Messiah appears, but the writer himself interprets it allegorically.' 'Thus in Enoch, this title is the distinct designation of the personal Messiah, and the Greek equivalent must have been ὁ Υἱὸς τοῦ ἀνθρώπου and not Υἱὸς ἀνθρώπου.' Charles, *op. cit.* ii. p. 214.

[8] *E.g.* in Ecclus. l. 24; Judith xvi. 17; Tobit xiv. 5. Cf. the description of the New Jerusalem in xiii. 15 f. On the Messianic future in the Book of Wisdom, see Charles, *Apocrypha and Pseudepigrapha of the O.T.* i. pp. 529, 531.

author of 1 Maccabees is content to dispense with the hope of a Davidic dynasty.[1] The actual title of Messiah appears in the earlier apocalyptic literature.[2] In the Sibylline Oracles of about the year B.C. 140, we find mention of a heaven-sent King;[3] and in the Ethiopian Book of Enoch, the Messiah is symbolized by the image of a white bullock.[4] In the Psalms of Solomon, generally assigned to a period closely following the capture of Jerusalem by Pompey (B.C. 63), a Messiah of David's line is clearly named.[5] Thus, as Schürer remarks, the Messianic hope remained down to the time of Christ.[6] At times it became dim and seemed almost to fail as a living hope, but it revived again, and when we come to the hour of the Saviour's birth, we find it strongly held in quiet places among the faithful.

How great a part in the preservation of the Messianic hope was played by the apocalyptic writings of the second and first centuries B.C. is only gradually being realized. We have been accustomed to speak of the silence of the voice of prophecy from Malachi to Christ. Certainly there was no open, recognized successor of the old prophetic line. The reign of law was paramount. God had spoken His last word. So men thought; and as the Canon of the books of the Law—the Pentateuch—was finally closed in the time of Ezra, and the Canon of the prophetic books by about 200 B.C., no official recognition was to be expected by writers who laid claim to the gift of vision, or who were conscious that they had a message from God.[7] Even the book of Daniel only found a place in the third division of the Canon among the Hagiographa, some time during the second century, and not among the prophets; for the second division—that of prophecy—was complete, and no addition to it could be entertained. It was this hard and rigid attitude of official

[1] *v.* Schürer ii. p. 507.

[2] 1 *Enoch* xlviii. 10; lii. 4. 'Now for the first time . . . applied to the ideal Messianic king that is to come.' Charles, *op. cit.* ii. p. 185. But *v.* above, p. 70.

[3] *Orac. Sib.* iii. 49, 50. 'A holy prince shall come to wield the sceptre over all the world unto all ages of hurrying time.' *Ib.* 652. 'And then from the sunrise God shall send a king.' For the date of these sayings, *v.* Charles, *op. cit.* ii. p. 372.

[4] 1 *Enoch* xc. 37. [5] *Ps. of Sol.* xvii. 23, 5. [6] *Ib.* p. 505.

[7] Cf. Ryle, *The Canon of the O.T.* p. 192, 'Revelation, it was thought, had ceased with prophecy. . . . There was no room for recent writings, there was no confidence in their authority.'

Judaism which was accountable for the peculiar, pseudonymous character of the apocalyptic literature of the time. To gain a hearing, the writer sank his personality in that of some saint or hero of a past age. Daniel, Enoch, Moses, the twelve Patriarchs, Solomon, Isaiah are all at different times made to stand sponsor for the visionary and prophetic outpourings of men of the second and first centuries B.C. who felt the burdens of the age and seemed to hear the voice of God speaking by them to their fellow-men. The literary artifice was adopted in all innocence. The great name seemed to give a sanction to the utterances attributed to it, and which might be supposed to be in accordance with the mind of the ancient worthy.[1] The actual writer only cared that men should take heed to his message. He was content to be unknown. And in this carelessness of personal fame or reputation we cannot help seeing the mark of men who feel that God is speaking through them. The true, prophetic fire burns in sayings which stand out by themselves in the midst of much that, to our thinking, is confused and grotesque. And what gives to this curious class of literature its singular interest for the student of Christian origins is the deep impression which it made upon the minds both of our Lord Himself and of the New Testament writers. It is hardly too much to say that while the apocalyptic writings reach back to the Old Testament prophets, they form the true perspective through which we may approach the Gospel. Both in idea and in actual phrase, they live again in the language of Christ. From St. Mark to Revelation and the Fourth Gospel, they supply thought or figure of speech. This use of them by our Lord and the Apostolic writers is a witness to the extent of the familiarity with which their contents were regarded in the first age of the Church. When He employed an apocalyptic term or illustration, He could reckon upon awakening a memory in the minds of His hearers. It gave Him a common ground of access to them. He would be understood. Thus, in the characteristically apocalyptic passage in which He replies to St. Peter's brusque question, 'What shall we have?' the promise of the twelve thrones, which will await the Apostles, is to be realized 'when the Son of Man

[1] Cf. Burkitt, *Jewish and Christian Apocalypses*, p. 6. 'Both authors and readers believed that if any Revelation from God was true, it could not be new. It must have been given to the great saints of antiquity.'

shall sit on the throne of His glory'—almost the very words of Enoch, 'When they see that Son of Man sitting on the throne of His glory.'[1] The promise itself seems suggested by Enoch, 'I will seat each on the throne of his honour.'[2] In Christ's reference to Judas, 'It had been good for that man if he had not been born,' we can hardly help finding an echo of the saying in Enoch, 'It had been good for them—those who have denied the Lord of Spirits—if they had not been born.'[3] A remarkable instance appears in our Lord's saying, 'He hath committed all judgment unto the Son.' In Enoch we read, 'The sum of judgment was given unto the Son of Man.'[4] Thus from each of the great streams of Gospel tradition come words of Christ framed, both as to substance and detailed expression, on the writing of this unknown Apocalyptist of the second century.[5] If our Lord Himself shows His indebtedness—so to speak—to the Book of Enoch, we can hardly wonder that its influence is traceable throughout the New Testament. Not only is the Book itself expressly named and quoted by St. Jude[6] in his Epistle, but, as we might well imagine, the borrowings of idea or phrase in the great Christian Apocalypse—the Book of Revelation—are frequent.[7] When St. Peter declares before the rulers that 'there is none other name . . . (than that of Christ) whereby we must be saved,' he is repeating what Enoch had said of 'the Son of Man,' 'In His Name they are saved.'[8]

Very remarkable, too, are the parallels between the *Book of the Secrets of Enoch* and sayings of Christ in the Sermon on the Mount and elsewhere. That book was being written about the dawn of the Christian era,[9] and it is therefore impossible to say on which side lay the borrowing. If we may judge by the analogy of the relation between 1 Enoch and the Gospels, we

[1] 1 En. lxii. 5; Matt. xix. 28.
[2] 1 En. cviii. 12.
[3] 1 En. xxxviii. 2; Matt. xxvi. 24.
[4] 1 En. lxix, 27; Jo. v. 22.
[5] 'It is when you study Matthew, Mark and Luke against the background of the Books of Enoch that you see them in their true perspective.' Burkitt, *Jewish and Christian Apocalypses*, 1913, p. 21.
[6] Jude 6; 1 En. xii. 4. Jude 14; 1 En. lx. 8, i. 9.
[7] With 1 En. lxii. 14, compare Rev. iii. 20. With 1 En. xlvii. 2, compare Rev. vi. 10. With 1 En. li. 1, compare Rev. xx. 13.
[8] Acts iv. 12; 1 En. xlviii. 2, 7.
[9] *v.* Charles, *Apocrypha and Pseudepigrapha of the O.T.* ii. p. 429. It is now generally referred to as 2 Enoch.

may incline to the view that 2 Enoch also was known to our Lord and to the Apostolic writers.[1]

The work called *The Testaments of the Twelve Patriarchs* is assigned to the closing years of the second century B.C.[2] It was well known to our Lord. St. Paul, too, adopts much of its phraseology. The beautiful passage in the *Testament of Gad*, 'Love ye one another from the heart; and if a man sin against thee speak peaceably to him, and in thy soul hold not guile; and if he repent and confess, forgive him,' has clearly moulded the thought of our Lord's saying about forgiveness of an offending brother.[3] The great saying, which describes the principle on which the verdicts of the Last Judgment will be given, closely follows the experience of the patriarch Joseph as described in his *Testament*: 'I was beset with hunger and the Lord Himself nourished me. I was alone and God comforted me: I was sick and the Lord visited me: I was in prison and my God showed favour unto me.'[4]

The Apocalypse of Baruch was written by orthodox Jews not long before the fall of Jerusalem, in 50-70 A.D. and within a few years subsequently.[5] Its interest is largely due to the fact that its composition was partly contemporaneous with that of the New Testament. Unlike most of the earlier Apocalypses, it

[1] Cf. Matt. v. 9, 'Blessed are the peacemakers,' and 2 En. lii. 11, 'Blessed is he who implants peace and love.' With Matt. xxv. 34, 'Inherit the kingdom prepared for you from the foundation of the world,' compare 2 En. ix. 1, 'This place (Paradise) O Enoch is prepared for the righteous . . . for eternal inheritance.' With John xiv. 2, 'In My Father's house are many mansions,' compare 2 En. lxi. 2, 'In the great time (to come) . . . are many mansions prepared for men.' For a Pauline parallel compare Eph. iv. 25, 'Speak ye truth each one with his neighbour,' with 2 En. xlii. 12, 'Blessed is he in whom is truth, that he may speak truth to his neighbour.' *v.* Charles, *op. cit.* ii. p. 428.

The expression 'Joanit stations of light' in the description of Enoch's ascent into the Seventh Heaven (xx. 1), if it is an allusion to the Book of Revelation, as Dr. Charles thinks (*ib.* p. 441), implies the author's borrowing from the N.T. book.

[2] By Charles (*op. cit.* ii. pp. 289, 290), to the reign of the Priest-king John Hyrcanus. So too, F. C. Burkitt, who remarks that 'for the first time since Solomon, an Israelite Monarch was ruling over the whole of the Promised Land.' *Jewish and Christian Apocalypses*, p. 35.

[3] *Test. of Gad* vi. 3; Matt. xviii. 15; Lk. xvii. 3. *v.* Charles, *op. cit.* ii. p. 293.

[4] *Test. of Joseph* i. 5, 6; Matt. xxv. 35, 36.

[5] According to Burkitt, after the fall of the city. 'I really do not see why it should be regarded as composite.' *Jewish and Christian Apocalypses*, pp. 40, 41.

conceives of the Messianic kingdom as temporary: but it gives no consistent representation. In one part there is a Messiah; in another, there is a kingdom but no Messiah. These different conceptions may be due to the composite character of the book,[1] and to the effect of the fall of Jerusalem upon the writers.

The Apocalypse of Ezra is generally regarded as a composite work,[2] which took its final form after the fall of Jerusalem. Here we meet with the curious idea that Messiah, after a reign on earth of 400 years, 'and all in whom there is human breath,' will die.[3] As in 2 Baruch, the outlook is largely eschatological. There will be a General Resurrection 'and the Most High shall be revealed upon the throne of judgment.'[4] Indeed, it is the deep-rooted expectation of the coming judgment that is the most strongly marked feature of these later Jewish Apocalypses.

We shall hardly be wrong, if we assign to the early apocalyptic writers a chief part in preserving and continuing the spiritual teaching of Hebrew prophecy, until it found its fulfilment in the Person of Christ. Although one only—Daniel—found a place in the sacred Canon, and as we look for guidance and instruction, we are often met by what appears confused and uncouth to Western minds, we cannot help seeing that a strain of true piety and stedfast faith runs through them. They came from hearts that longed for the manifestation of God. They touched hearts that yearned for the Coming One. And when He came, and coming, used their language and responded to their hopes, He was owned and recognized by the men whose religion they had done so much to sustain.[5]

Simeon was 'waiting for the consolation of Israel.' Anna 'spake of Him to all them that looked for the redemption of Jerusalem.'[6] At the appearance of the Baptist, 'all men mused

[1] *v.* Charles, *op. cit.* ii. p. 474 f.

[2] But not by F. C. Burkitt, *Jewish and Christian Apocalypses*, p. 42.

[3] *v.* 4 Ezra vii. 29, 30.

[4] *Ib.* 33. So, too, in the contemporary or rather later *Books of Adam and Eve* xlix. 3; xxvi.; xxviii.; *Apoc. of Moses* xxxvii. 5; xliii. 2; xli. 3. *v.* Charles, *op. cit.* ii. p. 132.

[5] 'We read Enoch to get the mental background of the apostles and of the crowds that listened to our Lord.' Burkitt, *Jewish and Christian Apocalypses*, p. 31.

[6] Cf. Is. xl. 2; Lk. ii. 25, 38.

in their hearts of John, whether he were the Christ or not.' Even the Samaritan at the well was possessed of the same widespread expectation, 'I know that Messias cometh Which is called Christ.'[1] We may see in this attitude of expectancy the failure of the legalism of the last four or five centuries to crush the prophetic spirit in Judaism. Scribe had pitted himself against prophet: but the man of vision, unable to gain a hearing among people who, convinced of the perfection and completeness of the law, rejected all movements of the Spirit Who in time past had spoken unto their fathers by the prophets, found an outlet for the fire which consumed him in apocalyptic, hiding himself under a great name of a former age.[2] The apocalyptic literature of the two pre-Christian centuries—Daniel, Enoch, Psalms of Solomon—played, we may be sure, a great part in keeping alive in Israel the expectancy of such men as Simeon. It prepares us too for those startling confessions of our Lord's Messianic rank which, according to the Fourth Gospel, meet us so early in His career.[3]

The known prevalence of the apocalyptic standpoint, among the quietists and more spiritual of our Lord's contemporaries, makes the attitude to which St. John bears witness entirely reasonable. The prophetic mantle had fallen upon the shoulders of those unknown writers, and the use which our Lord and His Apostles made of their works is a proof that they were regarded as men 'borne along by the Holy Spirit.'[4] They formed the last stage of the literary preparation by which the Jewish world made ready for its Messiah—the last link in the long chain of written prophecy, of which the Baptist proclaimed the fulfilment when he looked 'upon Jesus as He walked,' and said 'Behold the Lamb of God.'

[1] Lk. iii. 15. Cf. Matt. xi. 3; Jo. iv. 25.

[2] *v.* Charles, *Apocrypha and Pseudepigrapha of the O.T.* vol. ii. p. viii; *ib.* p. 9, 'Since the law was the ultimate and complete expression of absolute truth, there was no room for any further revelation.'

[3] Jo. i. 41, 45, 49; cf. ii. 11; iv. 29, 42. With Jo. i. 41, 'We have found the Messiah, which is, being interpreted, the Christ' (margin, 'the Anointed'), compare *Ps. of Solomon* xvii. 36, 'All shall be holy and their king the Anointed of the Lord,' *i.e.* 'The Lord's Christ.' Cf. Lk. ii. 11.

[4] ὑπὸ Πνεύματος Ἁγίου φερόμενοι, 2 Pet. i. 21.

CHAPTER IV

THE PREPARATION: THE DISPERSION: PHILO

THE Jews of the Dispersion, living in cities and towns of the Empire, largely outnumbered those who remained in Palestine. Various causes had led to this Dispersion. The Assyrian and Babylonian conquerors had violently carried away multitudes into captivity in the far eastern provinces.[1] From that captivity the Ten Tribes had not returned, but had become so merged in the people surrounding their place of exile[2] as to be lost to history. Later, about B.C. 350, the Persian King Artaxerxes Ochus brought many prisoners from Jerusalem and settled them on the shores of the Caspian Sea. Under the successors of Alexander the Great, the 'Diadochi,' efforts were made to get the Jews who were living in their dominions to mix freely with the inhabitants of the country. Large numbers of Jews left Palestine of their own accord and joined the communities of their people in the cities of the Graeco-Roman world. About 140 B.C. the Sibyl declares that they abound in every land and on the shores

[1] Nehardea in Babylonia was the place to which the captives of the conquered kingdom of Judah (and Benjamin) were taken. *v.* Schürer, *op. cit.* iii. p. 7, and in Hastings' *D.B.* extra vol. art. 'Diaspora,' p. 92.

[2] Nisibis on a tributary of the Euphrates was, according to Josephus, a stronghold to which the captives from Israel were taken. It was in the district named in 2 Kings xvii. 6; xviii. 11, as the destination of the Ten Tribes. Scripture contains no account of any return; and although it was the general belief that, at the beginning of the Messianic kingdom, the dispersed of Israel would return to their own land (*v. Ps. of Sol.* xi. 3; 1 Baruch iv. 36, 37; v. 5-9; Is. xlix. 22; lx. 4, 9; *Ps. of Sol.* xvii. 34, 28; 2 Baruch lxxvii. 1-7; lxxviii. 7), doubts were felt by individual writers. Thus Deut. xxix. 28 was interpreted as meaning that the Ten Tribes would not come back. *v.* Schürer, *ib.* ii. p. 538; O. Holtzmann, *Neutestamentliche Zeitgeschichte*, p. 178.

of every sea.[1] Josephus[2] quotes Strabo the Geographer as saying that they had come to every city, and that the spot was not easy to find which had not admitted the race and of which they had not taken possession. Philo[3] quotes the letter of Agrippa to the Emperor Caligula, as saying that Jerusalem had become the capital of many lands besides Judaea, because of the colonies which it had sent out to them. In Alexandria, under the Diadochi, a district of the city was apportioned to the Jews. They were in Rome, as we learn from Cicero,[4] before B.C. 62, for at that time Jewish money was being sent to Jerusalem from Italy. As early as the time of Judas Maccabaeus, an embassy had arrived at Rome to form an alliance.[5] After the conquest of Jerusalem by Pompey in B.C. 63, large numbers of captive Jews were sold into slavery in Rome. Many of these, on obtaining their freedom, joined the already existing Jewish colony in the district across the Tiber, whose inhabitants still show traces of their origin. Mourning Jews surrounded the funeral pyre of their protector, Julius Caesar.[6] Not until the reign of Tiberius did the large Jewish colony begin to suffer from oppressive restrictions and, in consequence of a charge afterwards recognized as false, banishment from the city.[7] They were to be found in Rome again under Caligula, and except for the Edict of Claudius,[8] which forbade their assemblies and caused many of them to leave the

[1] Πᾶσα δὲ γαῖα σέθεν πλήρης καὶ πᾶσα θάλασσα. *Orac. Sib.* iii. 271. 'In the time of the Diadochi, the Jewish people, which had led a retired life for 200 years, was plunged anew into the ferment of world-history.' Holtzmann, *N.T. Theologie*, i. p. 119.

[2] *Antiq.* xiv. 7, 2; cf. *Bell. Jud.* ii. 16, 4.

[3] *Legat. ad Caium*, § 36 (Mangey, ii. p. 587).

[4] *Pro Flacco*, 28.

[5] 1 Macc. viii. 17-32.

[6] Sueton. *Julius*, 84. *v.* Schürer, *op. cit.* iii. p. 30.

[7] Tac. *Ann.* ii. 85; Sueton. *Tiber.* 36; Joseph. *Antiq.* xviii. 3, 5.

[8] The Edict, referred to in Acts xviii. 2, which threatened banishment, and by its forbidding assemblies for worship, drove many (*e.g.* Aquila and Priscilla) to forsake their homes, does not appear to have been executed to its full extent. Dio Cassius (lx. 6), referring to it, speaks of the difficulty of banishing such large numbers of people without creating tumults, and implies that abstinence from public meeting for worship was all that was required. This restriction placed upon their worship would suffice of itself to expel many pious Jews from the city. *v.* Schürer in Hastings' *D.B.* art. 'Diaspora,' p. 98. *Id. Geschichte des Jüd. Volkes*, iii. p. 31.

city, they do not appear to have been again deprived of their right of dwelling.

We must now inquire into the effect produced upon the religious and moral condition of the Jews by their sojourn in a strange land. This will lead to the question whether the Jews themselves came to exercise any appreciable influence upon the people of the countries in which they had made their home. We shall then be in a position to estimate the contribution of the Dispersion to the readiness of the world for the Gospel.

It may at once be said that the Jew of the Dispersion remained, on the whole, true to his religion and its obligations. The intense longing for Jerusalem and the Temple found pathetic expression. But the separation caused by banishment from the centre of worship led to changes in religious custom and experience which were epoch-making. Only at the great festivals, and then if his home were not far distant, could the Jew of the Dispersion 'stand within the gates of the daughter of Zion.' How did he supply the place of the Temple worship, and maintain his connection with the religion of his race? It should be borne in mind that Judaism, after the return from the Captivity, was dominated by the Law, rather than by the observances which clustered round the Temple and its Priesthood. The influence of the Scribe was paramount. The Law, with its interpretation and application to conduct, was supreme in public estimation. And this change in the expression of religious thought and feeling tended to reconcile the Jew of the Dispersion to the consequences of his separation from the old worship. He still maintained his connection with the Temple and its ceremonial by the payment of tithes, which were annually conveyed to Jerusalem by persons of authority appointed for the purpose:[1] but it was only at rare intervals, if ever, that he was able to take part in the actual worship. How did he set about supplying its place?

The peculiar and distinct character of his race naturally inclined the Jew of the Dispersion to live in close community with his fellow-countrymen. Thus he was led to devise some means of meeting together for the reading of the Law and for prayer, by which he might at least keep in touch with the general religious life and hopes of his people. The result was the Synagogue, which quickly arose in every town and village in which

[1] *v.* Philo, *De Monarchiâ*, ii. 3.

any number of Jews were congregated.[1] It was distinctly a layman's form and method of worship. Every Jew of a certain age could take part in the reading of Scripture, in the prayers and in the words of exhortation, if called upon to do so by the 'ruler' of the Synagogue. We have instances of this both in the Gospels and in the Acts.[2] But for our present purpose the importance of the Synagogue lies in the great opportunity which it afforded to the Gentile to become acquainted with the religion and ethics of Judaism, and so to be ready for the message of the Gospel; [3] while at the same time it gave Jewish Christians, who in the early days of the new Faith were still frequenters of the Synagogue, a vantage ground from which they could make known that message to their fellow-countrymen. Thus in two different ways the Dispersion, owing to its remoteness from the old centre of religious worship, became a great factor in the preparation for Christ; and this largely through the opportunities afforded by the worship of the Synagogue.

[1] The actual circumstances that led to the rise of the Synagogue are unknown. We find it in existence, not only in centres of the Dispersion, but in Palestine. The place of its origin, as well as the date, are alike matter of conjecture. But there is little doubt that distance from the central place of worship was the determining factor, and that an institution, which was found to be beneficial in other lands, was brought home to Palestine by the influence of those who had had experience of it elsewhere.

[2] Lk. iv. 16 f.; Jo. vi. 59; Acts xiii. 14 f.; xvii. 2.

[3] The Jew of the Dispersion became an effective missionary. We have evidence of this in the allusions to proselytism which occur in the New Testament. Cf. Matt. xxiii. 15; Acts ii. 10; xiii. 43. Gentiles, who had been drawn towards the stern monotheism of their Jewish fellow-citizens and by the higher standard of morals which accompanied it, were allowed to attend the worship of the Synagogue. Cf. *Apoc. of Baruch* i. 4, 'I will scatter this people among the Gentiles that they may do good to the Gentiles.' The class of Gentile hearers which came to be called οἱ σεβόμενοι or οἱ φοβούμενοι τὸν Θεόν formed a favourable seed-plot for the reception of the Gospel. Nicolas, a proselyte of Antioch, was one of the Seven Deacons, Acts vi. 5.

'For the sake of these "devout," Paul in all probability retained the practice of going to the Synagogue on the Sabbath Day whenever he came to a new city. He sought to form a connection with these Gentile elements that were most predisposed to receive his Gospel.' H. Wendt in *Hibb. Journal*, Oct. 1913, p. 158.

'Everywhere in the Greco-Roman Empire were men who in the God of Israel found the resting place for all thought that sought after God, and in the accompanying moral law and the belief in recompense, the truly reasonable religion which healed the troubles of the world.' Holtzmann, *Neutest. Theologie*, i. p. 119.

So fully was the Synagogue found to meet the requirements of the people, not only in far distant lands but in Palestine, that the system spread everywhere. Even in Jerusalem itself a number of Synagogues sprang into being, answering to the wants of different sections and communities.[1] There would be few at the dawn of the Christian era to whom the ancient language of the Scriptures was familiar. The reading of the Law and the Prophets was therefore interpreted.[2] The Septuagint version was regarded as of equal authority with the original Hebrew, and was employed to explain it in large areas of the Dispersion.[3]

Another great service was performed by the Synagogue. It prepared the way for that loosening of the ties of the old worship, which was to follow upon the destruction of the Temple. It recalled men's minds to the ethical elements of their religion, in the Law and the Prophets, which had been too much obscured through the sacrificial observances of the Temple. When we remember the character of the Priesthood in the hands of the Sadducees, with their indifference to the spiritual side of their religion and their worldly outlook, we can understand how, in the century before the birth of Christ, the process of detachment from the Temple worship went on apace. The Synagogue was gradually superseding, in influence and in its ministration to the needs of the devout Jew, those formal acts of religious observance, which were so soon to be rendered impracticable and obsolete. We need to think of this gradual detachment when we try to estimate the effect of the destruction of the Temple and the complete closing of the age-long worship which it enshrined. The warning voices of prophets, who had pleaded for obedience rather than sacrifice, and who had proclaimed in clearest terms the demands of God

[1] 'The Jewish Dispersion had Synagogues in Jerusalem (Acts ii. 5, etc.) propagating its doctrines; the country people congregated there. . . . In these circles, quite removed from Pharisaic and Sadducean party life, Christianity grew up.' Friedländer, *D. relig. Bewegungen*, 1905, p. 16.

[2] *v.* Zahn, *Einleitung in das N.T.* i. p. 7.

Greek was the language used in the Synagogues over a large part of the Jewish Dispersion. In Palestine and perhaps to some extent in the region of Babylon, the Hebrew Scriptures were interpreted not in Greek but in Aramaic. *v.* Bacher in Hastings' *D.B.* iv. p. 641; cf. below. p. 90.

[3] On its use in the Synagogues as contributing to the formation of the prophetic Canon, *v.* Ryle, *The Canon of the O.T.* p. 127.

upon His people, were now recalled.[1] It was realized that God could be worshipped without recourse to the 'sacrifices, which they had offered year by year continually.'[2]

And if the Synagogue helped to smooth the way for the passing of the old Temple worship, it formed a model for the meeting together of the early Christian communities. If we except the chief object of such meeting—the Breaking of the Eucharistic Bread—almost every other element of early Christian worship was taken over bodily from the ordinary Sabbath rite of the Synagogue. The same version of the same Scripture, the prayers, the 'word of exhortation,' appear in the new worship with the new elements produced by the fulfilment of the ancient promise. The Name of the Messiah, with all that It meant to His followers, permeates the whole. The felt presence of His Spirit quickens the pulse of every worshipper. Here and there the Synagogue became for a time a Christian Church. Apostles are bidden to speak in the course of the ordinary worship, and the walls echo to the Gospel of Jesus and the Resurrection.[3] What happened at Antioch was repeated, we may be sure, elsewhere. But the connection was soon broken. The growing prejudice of reactionary Judaism soon banished the Name of Christ from the Synagogue. The experience at the Pisidian Antioch is renewed in Iconium, in Thessalonica, in Berea, in Corinth.[4] Everywhere there is at first a welcome and the Gospel is preached. But everywhere the preaching of the Cross is 'to the Jews a stumbling block,' and the welcome turns to contempt and rejection. It was in the Synagogue at Antioch, after the Jews had rejected the

[1] 1 Sam. xv. 22; Ps. xl. 6; Hos. vi. 6. Cf. Hollman, *Welche Religion hatten die Juden als Jesus auftrat?* p. 42. *v.* Judith xvi. 16.

[2] 'The Jewish Church contained within it, in the prophetical teaching, a set of principles which at least involved the conclusion that sacrifice was unnecessary, from which it was no long step to the position that it should be discontinued.' Paterson in Hastings' *D.B.* iv. p. 343. Cf. Matt. xii. 7. Hollman remarks, 'With all the external devotion that existed, detachment from the Temple worship had quietly come about. Jesus had no occasion to oppose it; in Essene circles the separation had resulted. Therefore the destruction of the Temple brought about no serious crisis.' *Op. cit.* p. 42. 'Even Jeremiah, the most pessimistic of the prophets, holds out the hope of pardon. But the forgiveness will be an act of free grace and not conditioned by sacrifice.' H. P. Smith in *American Journal of Theol.* Oct. 1911, p. 538. 'The narrative books (of the O.T.) lay no stress on sacrifices as a condition of forgiveness.' *Ib.* p. 539.

[3] Acts xiii. 15, 44.

[4] Acts xiv. 1 f.; xvii. 1 f.; 10 f.; xviii. 4 f.

Gospel, that St. Paul spoke the momentous words, 'Lo, we turn to the Gentiles.'[1] Thus the Synagogue formed the bridge by which the Gospel passed from the Jewish to the Gentile world. If it prepared the way for a wider offer of the message of salvation, it became the earliest scene of its proclamation.

A chief element in the Greek preparation for the Gospel was the influence of the Jewish Dispersion. Scattered as they were in all the chief centres of population, the Jews began to enter upon a different mode of life. From being peasants and artisans they took to merchandise ; and this change of occupation brought them into contact with the various races who gathered in the market-places of the great cities. The Greek language was the common medium of intercourse, and with it came to the Jew new forms of culture, of philosophy, of religious belief which, if they did not alienate him from his own faith, at least tended to widen his outlook. Then, when the language, with its accompaniments of thought and habit, had taken hold upon the stedfast Jew, he in turn began to exercise upon the Greek world an influence, at first subtle and hardly recognized, yet of ever increasing power, which ripened and prepared it for the Gospel. The effect of this reciprocal influence made itself chiefly felt in Alexandria. If we want to study its clearest manifestations, we have to look for them in Philo. No other writer of the Dispersion has left us so complete a view of his philosophy or of his religion. We see in him the result of that gradual blending of Judaism with Hellenism which had been going on for centuries, wherever the people of God had come into close contact with the heathen populations of the great cities in which they made their home. Philo is a singularly attractive, and withal, a pathetic figure. Appearing on the stage of history at a critical time—his career extends from about B.C. 20 to A.D. 50—he exemplifies the utmost degree of sympathy with world-culture consistent with a firm hold upon the faith of his fathers. He is at once philosopher and theologian, Greek and Jew.[2] Wide as was his learning, he never lost his faith in the Divine guidance of his own people.

[1] 1 Cor. i. 23 ; Acts xiii. 46.

[2] Cf. Weinel, *Bibl. Theologie des N.T.* 1911, p. 36. 'Judaism and the Porch are intertwined in him in remarkable conjunction, besides his mysticism.'

There is no spirit of compromise to be traced in his writings. His mind, always open to the vivid impressions which met him in his daily life in Alexandria, was never disturbed by what he heard or read. His view of God and man was too surely grounded for that. He was a Jew first; and if he could not reconcile much of the Greek thought, which he had mastered, with the teaching of his own religion, and if in the early stories of his Scriptures, he found details which wounded his moral sense, he had at hand a ready instrument to apply—his system of allegorical interpretation. As the Greek philosophers dealt with the popular mythology, so Philo dealt with everything in his own sacred Scriptures that seemed to refuse a literal interpretation. Yet such was his veneration for them, that he regarded them as literally inspired, transferring even to the Septuagint version the same verbal accuracy that he attributed to the original Hebrew writings. More than this—and it was one of his most distinctive beliefs—he traced the wisdom of the Greek, as he found it in Plato and the Stoics, to undeveloped seeds of thought in the books of Moses; thus bringing philosophy in all its ramifications under the same inspiring influence which created the Hebrew Scriptures, and referring all the wisdom of man to the inbreathing of the Spirit of God. It is needless to point out how far-fetched and strained would be the results of such a system of interpretation. It was repellent to the mind of his fellow-countrymen; and Philo seems never to have found sympathy or following among them. He stands, a lonely figure, reaching back to the past and to his own people a hand which was not taken; while for the future, it was not until his works began to be studied by the writers of the Church that his ideas and methods received recognition. He lives again in Clement of his own Alexandria and in Origen, and his allegorical system was eagerly studied and imitated by writers both of the East and the West.[1] The very fact that he was held in high esteem by Christians undoubtedly led to neglect of his works by his own countrymen, in the early centuries of our era; while his fusion of Greek learning with the old faith tended to make him still more unpopular with his own nation,

[1] Many of Philo's writings have perished. It is due to his popularity with the Fathers of the Church that a large number of them have been preserved. Schürer, *op. cit.* iii. p. 490.

when their strife with Rome had reached its height.[1] The influence of the Rabbis of Palestine became predominant in Judaism, and the writings of Philo, together with the use of the Septuagint, fell into abeyance.

A chief element of the philosophy of Philo was his dualistic conception of the universe. Like Plato, he saw a complete antagonism between the spiritual and the material, between the soul and the body, between God and the world. The eternal and infinite could never come into contact with the perishable and the finite. It is possible that Persian ideas of the evil of matter combined with Platonism to form his strong dualism. For Philo regarded matter (ὕλη) as a distinct and self-existent principle apart from God—something which He did not create, and upon which He could only work, fashioning it into new forms of being.

But this dualistic view of things at once created a difficulty. How could God touch that mass of matter which is the source of evil without suffering loss in purity and perfection from the contact? Yet He is the Author of the world in its beauty and order. Philo met the difficulty by his doctrine of mediating beings, who represent God and act upon the world as His agents and messengers. Borrowing partly from the Stoic form of the Platonic 'idea,' partly from the Hebrew 'angel,' he seems at times to give a separate, personal existence to these intermediaries between God and the world.[2] Then, again, he allows them merely a life within the Life of God. This conflict of thought is hardly separable from the nature of his theory. It results from the double necessity of obtaining contact of God with matter, while preserving Him from all defilement in the process.[3]

The dualism of Philo's cosmology colours his view of Man. The spirit, as in the Mosaic account of creation, is due to the inbreathing of God. But the body is the source of evil, the prison house of the spirit. It is evil from birth. Its tendencies and affections must be resisted and overcome, not, as the Stoics had taught, by man's own unaided strength, but by yielding to the grace of God. Purity of life, the conquest of the body

[1] *v.* Bousset, *D. Religion des Judentums*, p. 522.
[2] *v.* Schürer, *op. cit.* iii. p. 552.
[3] *v.* Zeller, *Philos. der Griech.* iii. 2, p. 365.

by the spirit is, after all, not the highest end of life. There is something higher still. As man came from God, so is God his final home and destiny. The vision of God is for the pure and the wise, and it is attainable in this life. Here Philo seems to be influenced by Greek ideas of ecstasy.[1] Plato had conceived of a divine frenzy, in which, in spite of its enthusiasm, reason still held sway.[2] Philo goes farther. Intimate, as he seems to have been, with the mystic rites of the old Greek piety, he regarded the subject of ecstasy as a person so possessed by the sense of the Divine presence as to be transported out of himself and his rational life into pure contact with God.[3] Thus 'Philo is the first exponent of Mysticism and Ecstasy that we meet on the ground of definite monotheism. As such, he has his permanent significance in the history of Christian Mysticism.'[4]

Philo came too late upon the scene to contribute to the actual origin of Christianity: but his influence began to make itself felt before the close of the Apostolic age. Jew though he was and ever true to his faith, he had so steeped his mind in the study of the Greek literature and philosophy that he belongs as much to the realm of Greek thought[5] as to that of Hebrew. It was perhaps his mission to blend the two currents into one—to show the Greek world something of the majesty of the religion of his fathers, and to bring the Jewish world into touch with the wider and more progressive outlook of the Greek.[6] He was acquainted with Hebrew, as his writings show, but he was more familiar with Greek, and read his Bible in that language.[7]

If we try to specify in definite terms the contribution of Philo to the Christian religion, we are met by great difficulties. He was too eclectic a thinker to be a consistent one. His sympathies were so wide, and he drew his inspiration from so many and such different sources, that it is easy to present a formidable array of contradictions and of opposing views which appear in his

[1] *v.* Bousset, *D. Religion des Judentums*, p. 517.

[2] *v.* Zeller, *op. cit.* ii. p. 556.

[3] *v.* Phil. *Quis rer. divin. her.* 69.

[4] Bousset, *op. cit.* p. 520.

[5] 'He belongs to the series of Greek Philosophers.' Schürer, *op. cit.* iii. p. 545.

[6] 'Philo's dream of a reconciliation between Jewish and Hellenic culture remained a dream.' Bousset, *op. cit.* p. 502.

[7] 'By means of the Greek translation of the Bible, the Jew was enabled to entirely forget his own language without giving up his religion.' Bousset, *op. cit.* p. 498.

writings. To take his conception of the Logos, to which many have traced that of St. John in the Prologue to his Gospel, it is clear that he hovers between ideas borrowed from Platonic and Stoic philosophy and the beliefs of his own religion. From the first source he takes the thought of the Logos as the archetypal Idea on which God formed the visible creation out of the pre-existent material, or as the Reason of God energizing in the world. From Jewish beliefs he derives the doctrine that the Logos is the Wisdom of God, disposing and ordering all things according to His Will.[1] He is the chief of those mediating beings who stand between God and the world. In language which seems to anticipate the writer to the Hebrews, Philo declares the Logos to be the organ of creation,[2] the creative Word. Not only does He act for God upon the world, but as High Priest of the world, He intercedes for it before God.[3] Yet Philo cannot make clear to himself whether the Logos has an independent existence apart from God, or whether He is an attribute of the Divine Mind.[4]

When we come to estimate the debt of early Christian thought to Philo, we have to avoid being misled by similarities of expression. There is no doubt that 'For the young and growing Christian Theology there lay in Philo an inexhaustible mine of knowledge and power.'[5] But we may easily mistake coincidences of thought and expression for direct influence, where the general tone of mind is entirely different. The first New Testament writer to feel and respond to the influence of Philo is St. Paul. Although the word Λόγος is not used, the conception itself pervades Coloss. i. 15.[6] The whole passage is reminiscent of the language of Philo, and it is difficult

[1] In *De Profugis*, § 109 (Mang. i. 562) God is represented as the Father of the Logos, Wisdom as his Mother.

[2] Hebr. i. 2. δι' οὗ καὶ ἐποίησεν τοὺς αἰῶνας. Philo, *Leg. allegor.* i. 106; *De Cherubim*, i. 162. *v.* Schürer, *op. cit.* iii. p. 555.

[3] *De Gigantibus*, i. 269; *De Migratione Abrahami*, i. 452; *Quis rer. divin. her.* i. 501. *v.* Schürer, *op. cit.* p. 556.

[4] *v.* Zeller, *Philos. der Griech.* iii. 2, p. 324 f. Schürer, *op. cit.* p. 556.

[5] Bousset, *D. Religion des Judentums*, p. 196.

[6] *v.* Lightfoot *in loc.* Cf. 1 Pet. i. 23. J. Weiss compares St. Paul's idea of 'the Second Man, the Lord from heaven' (1 Cor. xv. 47) with Philo's interpretation of the two accounts of the creation of man in Genesis, and concludes that St. Paul was not dependent upon Philo. *Christus*, p. 39 f.

to avoid the conclusion that the writer had been a student of the Alexandrian Platonist.

The next writer who shows signs of being indebted to Philo for ideas or expressions is the author of the Epistle to the Hebrews. But while taking the language of Philo, he is by no means in agreement with his line of thought.[1] Perhaps the chief importance of indebtedness to Philo, on the part of St. Paul and the writer to the Hebrews, lies in their contribution to the thought of the Fourth Evangelist, and in the bridge which they thereby provide for the passage of Hellenistic thought and language into the mind of so Palestinian a writer as St. John. If St. John became acquainted at Ephesus with some of the speculations of Philo,[2] as may well have been the case, he may have been not unwilling to go to him for so expressive and elastic a term, and one so congenial to his Greek readers, as ὁ Λόγος. But, if so, in the Prologue to his Gospel he makes an entirely different use of it. The great proclamation of the Incarnation—'The Word was made flesh'—has no affinity with the thought of Philo. 'A Greek, an Alexandrian, a Jewish Doctor, would have equally refused to admit such a statement as a legitimate deduction from his principles.'[3] Even the use of the term Λόγος—the Word of the Fourth Gospel—is perhaps due rather to Palestine than to Alexandria. The oldest Targums show that, in all probability, the expression (Memra) was in use for the action of God before they were composed, and therefore in time for use by the writer of the Gospel. We may freely admit that he may have been led by Philo to the choice of the term: but in his hands it took a more precise and concrete meaning. It denoted the revelation of God to man in personal form. It

[1] Hebr. iv. 12, 13, is a typical passage. *v.* Westcott *in loc.*; H. Holtzmann, *Neutestamentliche Theologie*, ii. p. 334; H. Weinel, *Bibl. Theol. des N.T.* p. 530, 'The whole passage is only to be understood if one considers the Logos idea as its foundation.' Holtzmann remarks that if these words must be referred not to God but to the Logos, there is a parallel with Philo, but not with the 'Son of God.' *Ib.* p. 335. Yet in recognizing the origin of the idea in Philo, we are not thereby excluded from seeing in the N.T. writer's use of it the full Christian meaning.

[2] The language of the Prologue is so full of the terminology of Philo that it is difficult to avoid the impression of indebtedness. For detailed evidence, *v.* Weinel, *Bibl. Theologie des N.T.* p. 531.

[3] Westcott, *Gospel of St. John*, pp. xv, xvii. So too Pfleiderer, *Die Entstehung des Christentums*, p. 40; Inge, *Personal Idealism*, p. 47.

followed the Palestinian line of Jewish thought rather than that of Alexandria.[1]

Again, in many noble passages, Philo seems to anticipate and prepare for the Christian doctrine of faith. Faith was the strength and motive power of the Saints and Heroes of the old Covenant, but we find little expression given to it in the Old Testament Scriptures. Not until we come to Philo do we meet with its treatment as a chief and vital principle of the religious life. 'His disquisitions upon faith are the most beautiful portion of his writings, and assure him an honourable place in the history of Religion.'[2]

The importance of Philo, in the history of early Christianity, lies in the accumulations of idea and expression which his writings placed at the disposal of the framers of Christian doctrine. Fundamental conceptions, common to Judaism and Christianity alike, had been clothed by him in the flexible language which was the medium of communication between the primitive communities. So great was the use which early apologists and other writers made of the works of Philo, that it is hardly too much to say that they share with the Septuagint the task of moulding the forms in which the sub-Apostolic and immediately succeeding ages expressed their thoughts.[3]

[1] *v.* Westcott, *op. cit.* p. xviii.

[2] Bousset, *op. cit.* p. 224. Bousset remarks that 'the author of the Epistle to the Hebrews has passed through the School of Philo—not that of St. Paul.' *Ib.*

[3] *v.* Schürer, *op. cit.* iii. p. 562.

CHAPTER V

THE PREPARATION: GREEK THOUGHT

THE contribution of Greece to the preparation of the world for Christ was threefold: language, religion, philosophy. The Greek language, moulded as it was by the genius of the most cultivated people of antiquity, profoundly affected Jewish life and thought in the closing century of the pre-Christian era. The Aramaic tongue, spoken by Palestinian Jews and to some extent by the Jews of the Dispersion, was defective as a medium whether of literature or of communication. It was too concrete, too wanting in abstract forms of expression, to serve the purposes of Christianity. It was too little known to enable a people scattered over the world to maintain intercourse by its use.[1]

Greek, on the other hand, by its flexibility and by its capacity for the expression of thought in its most subtle modes, was the language best adapted to convey the truths of Christianity; while its possession of all the great centres of population made it the best possible medium for missionary purposes. It was perhaps not without reference to these facts that, as St. John[2] tells us, a visit of Greeks occasioned that prophetic allusion to the triumphs of His Gospel which our Lord uttered on the eve of His Passion. The sight of the men may have made Him think of the part their language would play in the victories of the Cross. Along with the language went the intellectual outfit of the Greek people—their rich philosophical inheritance, their facility of expression in the most profound subjects. Here, then,

[1] The Dispersion spoke Greek. Philo calls the Greek language 'our Dialect.' Bousset, *Die Religion des Judentums*, p. 498. But *v.* Bacher in Hastings' *D.B.* iv. p. 641.

[2] Jo. xii. 20 f.

at the very moment when it was required, there lay at the disposal of Christianity an instrument of the finest temper and of general adaptability for the expression of its living spirit. The Greek language, with its complement of Greek ideas and modes of thought, was at once enlisted in the service of the new religion.

But before the Greek tongue was employed by Christianity, it had begun to exercise great influence on Judaism. The translation of the Old Testament Scriptures into Greek was an event of the first importance. It kept the Jew, who in a far-off land and under strange circumstances might easily have lost all touch with the religion of his race, from becoming merged indistinguishably in the people with whom he lived. His native Aramaic, a dialect allied to the language in which his Scriptures were written, had ceased to be of use and was hardly spoken beyond the limits of Palestine.[1] What was there to preserve his allegiance to the old faith? It was here that the Greek version became of vital importance. Not only did it bring to him the old facts of his history, the warnings of his prophets, the songs of his home and of his exile, but it brought them with an authority which was not to be resisted. The translation was regarded as equal in value and accuracy to the original text. Philo[2] states that each of the translators employed the same words, and cites the fact as evidence of their inspiration.

The birthplace of the Septuagint was Alexandria, in the large community of Hellenistic Jews which had long been settled there. The process of translation was a lengthy one, carried out at various times and, as some think, in more than one centre of the Dispersion. The first part of the Bible to be translated was the Book of the Law, the Torah. This was in the reign of Ptolemy Philadelphus at Alexandria about 250 B.C. But nothing further was attempted for the present, for the Canon of the Prophetic

[1] Jülicher in *Encycl. Bibl.* ii. p. 2008, 'The Jews settled outside of Palestine lost almost completely their original tongue, and used Greek even in religious worship.'

[2] *De Vita Mosis*, ii. 7. *v.* Bousset, *D. Religion des Judentums*, p. 174. Cf. Irenaeus, iii. xxi. 4; Aug. *De Civ. Dei*, xviii. 43. *v.* Swete, *Introduction to the O.T. in Greek*, pt. iii. c. 5. Epiphanius, *De Mens. et Pond.* §§ 3, 6, gives the legendary story of the miraculous events which accompanied the work of translation, and guaranteed the divine inspiration of the new version.

writings was not yet fixed;[1] and it was only at the dawn of the Christian era that the Greek Old Testament was finally completed.[2]

If the Greek translation of his Scriptures served to keep the Jew of the Dispersion in touch with his faith, it also helped to make that faith known and respected in pagan circles. It revealed to heathen scholars and thinkers something of the intense religious earnestness, the purity of morals, the sublime and passionate devotion to God, which characterized the Jewish Faith. It powerfully supplemented and enforced the evidence of the good lives which were being lived in the pagan cities by the despised and often persecuted Jews.[3] Thus in no small degree it came to prepare the world for Christ.

The mere fact of a translation of the books of the sacred Canon was itself significant. The stricter and more conservative Jews viewed it with repugnance and apprehension. The books were thought to be too closely linked with the mind of God to admit of transference to the medium of another language, and that a profane one. Palestine had little sympathy with this new Egyptian enterprise; and later on, when the Septuagint came to be the Bible of the adherents of the new Faith, the prejudice against it was greatly increased.[4]

Here, however, at the opening of the Christian era, was a version of the Old Testament accessible to all the Greek-speaking world, both Jewish and pagan, furnishing, on the one hand, knowledge of God's dealings in the past, and on the other, a basis in thought and expression for the coming revelation of the Gospel.[5] It was a bridge between the old world and the new.

[1] Ryle, *Canon of the O.T.* pp. 113 and ix.

[2] Swete, *op. cit.* p. 27; O. Holtzmann, *Neutestamentliche Zeitgeschichte*, p. 59.

[3] Cf. Zech. viii. 23.

[4] The version of Aquila, a proselyte of Pontus, who lived in the reign of Hadrian and endeavoured by a more literal translation of the Hebrew to supersede the LXX, gradually took its place in the Greek-speaking Synagogues. Fragments of it remain and attest his zeal for accuracy at the expense of style. *v.* Swete, *op. cit.* p. 31 f. Although Aquila worked with a bias against Christianity, his version was regarded with great respect by scholars like Origen and Jerome, and was employed to supply deficiencies in the LXX. *v.* Swete, *ib.* p. 61.

[5] 'It created a language of religion which lent itself readily to the service of Christianity and became one of the most important allies of the Gospel. Swete, *ib.* p. 433.

While giving access to the best religious thought of the past, it provided a pattern for the formation of the religious thought of the future.[1] More than this, it provided an instrument for the expression of Hebrew conceptions, adapting them to the character of the Greek mind, modernizing them and facilitating their transference to the atmosphere which prevailed in the cultured centres of the Graeco-Roman world. What the Vulgate afterwards became to the language and thought of the whole Christian West, the Septuagint was to the more formative and critical period of the entrance of the Gospel upon the stage of history.

The Greek language was soon to render a new service to the cause of Christ. It became a medium of communication and a bond of union between the scattered congregations which formed the primitive Church.[2] Roughly speaking, it was the one universal language in common use among the first Christians. When the books were written which came by degrees to form the Canon of the New Testament, it was in Greek that they either made their appearance or took their final form. The only external evidence for an Aramaic version of any portion of our present New Testament, to which we can point, is the statement of Papias that Matthew, the Apostle, composed the Logia in the Hebrew dialect: and after all, that refers merely to the ancient source ('Q'), which forms the basis of the non-Marcan element common to the First and Third Gospels.[3]

But what was the general character of the Greek of the New

[1] A mere glance at the way in which the New Testament writers employ it in their citations from the Old Testament will show how very largely it helped to mould their thought.

'Without the Greek Bible, neither Moses nor the Prophets would have passed over the boundary of their own people, and Christianity too would perhaps have produced an obscure Aramaic literature, but no New Testament.' H. Holtzmann, *Neutest. Theologie*, i. p. 120. 'The Bible whose God is named Jehovah, is the Bible of a nation; the Bible whose God is named Lord (Κύριος), is the Bible of the world.' Deissmann, *Licht vom Osten*, E.T. p. 14. *v.* Holtzmann, *op. cit.* p. 127. 'The significance of this learned work for the history of religion lay in the fact that the thoughts of the Bible found expression in a world-language, and so became accessible to cultured heathen.' Oskar Holtzmann, *Neutestamentliche Zeitgeschichte*, p. 59. 'The Septuagint is the greatest work of translation produced by classical antiquity.' *Ib.* 'The holy Scripture of the Jews was incorporated in the world literature which was accessible to the Greeks.' *Ib.* p. 60.

[2] 'Official letters addressed to the Roman Church or proceeding from her during the first two centuries were written in Greek.' Swete, *op. cit.* p. 87.

[3] *v.* above, p. 18, n. 1. Cf. C. H. Turner in *J.T.S.* for Oct. 1909, p. 2.

Testament? That it differs widely from that of the classical period of Greek literature is evident. It has long been the custom to explain solecisms by attributing them to the Aramaic background of the writers; and it is necessary still to make allowance for that factor. We cannot decline to see the presence of Hebraisms of thought and expression in many passages, which arrest us by their contrast with ordinary Greek writing.[1] But the contrast is far from being accounted for on this theory alone. Through recent discovery of contemporary papyri, it has been found that many of the peculiarities of New Testament Greek, as distinct from classical, were common to the colloquial language of the time. The sacred writings are now seen to be no isolated productions standing in a class of their own.[2] They are the literary expression of the Greek of the period; and as fresh papyri are being discovered, fresh light is being thrown upon the Scriptures. They are seen to be written in the language of the Greek-speaking world in which they arose.

Closely connected with the influence of the Greek language upon the formation of Christian thought was that of Greek philosophy. The Greeks early manifested an unusual gift for abstract thinking, taking thereby a chief place among the intellectual peoples of the world. This faculty acted upon their language, which, by a natural law of reaction, helped to mould the lines of their thought. The Semitic mind could not come into contact with the Greek without receiving a large accession to its capabilities, and the use of the Greek language facilitated this acquisition. We should naturally expect to find traces of this influence in the Epistles, written as they were originally in Greek, rather than in the Synoptic Gospels, where Aramaic sources lay behind the Greek text. Perhaps we may say that it is the dogmatic passages of the Pauline Epistles and of the Hebrew Epistle which show the clearest signs of Greek abstract thinking. Yet, if the style is tinged with Graecisms, the contents are Semitic. It is Palestine, rather than Alexandria or Antioch, that furnishes the substance.

[1] *v* Milligan, *The New Testament Documents*, pp. 50, 52.

[2] One result of the change produced by comparison with the Greek of the papyri is the gradual reduction which is being effected in the list of the ἅπαξ λεγόμενα of the New Testament. *v.* Deissmann, *Licht vom Osten*, E.T. p. 73.

When we come to consider the material of Greek philosophic thought in the light of the Gospel, we find many anticipations of distinctive Christian belief, and much that seems preparatory to it. Clement of Alexandria does not hesitate to say that, as the law prepared the Hebrews, so philosophy trained the Greeks for Christ.[1] Ideas were suggested. Theories of God and the world and their mutual relation, attempts to reconcile the contradictions of life, to get at its purpose and to regulate its aims ; all these formed at least a preparatory mental and spiritual discipline for the reception of the Christian Revelation. 'We teach some things like the Greeks,' says Justin Martyr.[2] On the other hand, Celsus charges Christianity with borrowing from Greek philosophy and spoiling it in the act. Thus both the Christian and his opponents, from their contrasted points of view, admit the close connection between the two systems. They are not fortuitous atoms in the world of thought. They are in some way organically and logically connected.

For our present purpose it will suffice to point out the chief conceptions in which Greek philosophy and Christianity seem to come in contact.

The earliest formative influences of Greek thought, as applied to the mysteries of the world around us, are due to those profound thinkers of the sixth and fifth centuries B.C. who, in speculating on the origin of things, lighted upon truths which still form the very foundation of our knowledge of God and the world. Thus Xenophanes rises above the polytheism which surrounded him and conceives one supreme God, who is spirit, pervading all things, self-sufficing and omniscient.[3] Heraclitus sees in change the one constant factor of the universe. All *is* not, but is *becoming* ;[4] and in his theory of the spiritual reason of the world, we can trace the first indication of that doctrine of the Logos, which was afterwards to play so great a part in the theology of St. John.[5]

When we pass, in the latter part of the fifth century B.C., to Socrates and Plato, we at once find ourselves in a different region of thought. The mind has ceased to roam through the universe

[1] Clem. Alex. *Strom.* i. 5. [2] *Apol.* i. 20.

[3] οὖλος γὰρ ὁρᾷ, οὖλος δὲ νοεῖ, οὖλος δέ τ' ἀκούει. *ap.* Sext. Emp. ix. 144.

[4] πάντα χωρεῖ καὶ οὐδὲν μένει. *ap.* Plat. *Cratyl.* p. 402 A.

[5] *ap.* Sext. Emp. vii. 133. *v.* O. Pfleiderer, *Die Vorbereitung*, p. 9.

asking for the origin of things and trying to account for the world-force which is everywhere at work. The interest becomes centred in man himself. The philosophy of nature gives place to ethics. Man as a moral agent, with power to determine his conduct, is the supreme interest of Socrates. Unlike his predecessors, who submitted the current views of religion and the gods to severe criticism, and did much to purify them, Socrates had no quarrel with the prevailing religious beliefs of his time. The charge of atheism which was brought against him had no foundation in fact. It was said that he did not consider those to be gods whom the city so considered, but that he introduced new deities, corrupting the minds of the young.[1] What the philosopher really taught was the duty of investigating religious conceptions for oneself, instead of being content with traditional belief. In this he was a signal prototype of our Lord in His conflict with Jewish traditionalism. Like Christ, Socrates reminded men of their individual responsibility in matters of religious belief. They were not to take a thing on trust because it came to them with authority, however venerable and however strongly enforced. Behind and above the judgments of public opinion and tradition stood, for each man, conscience with its own claims, reason with its compelling demands. To Socrates, as afterwards to our Lord, a thing was not right because the popular verdict of the day pronounced it right. In each case, the attitude taken was considered dangerous to the public health.[2] It was the championship of responsibility and freedom of thought which, however mistakenly and unrighteously, led to the condemnation of the Greek. It was the attitude of Christ to the Jewish hierarchy and to its corruption of God's Word by tradition that led Him to the Cross. Socrates was the first great teacher to assert the rights of conscience and to insist on the necessity of informing it. This service to the cause of true religion is alone sufficient to entitle him to a high place among the religious geniuses of history. His stedfast resolve to continue the work, which he believed that God had entrusted to him, at the cost of life and freedom, was worthy of an Apostle, and indeed bears remarkable likeness to what we are told of

[1] Plat. *Apol. Socr.* p. 24; Xen. *Memor.* i. 1, ἕτερα δὲ καινὰ Δαιμόνια εἰσφέρων. Socrates was born B.C. 469, died B.C. 399.

[2] *v.* Plat. *Apol. Socr.* p. 18.

St. Peter and of St. Paul. When Socrates says to his accusers, 'I have respect and affection for you, but I must obey God rather than you,' are we not at once reminded how 'Peter and John answered and said unto them, Whether it be right in the sight of God to hearken unto you more than unto God, judge ye'?[1] And when he added, 'So long as I draw my breath and have the power, will I not cease to philosophize and to admonish you in my usual way. . . . For you must know that God has laid this upon me,' do we not hear St. Paul crying, 'Woe is unto me if I preach not the Gospel'?[2] If the Greek sage was convinced that for a good man nothing is amiss in life or in death, does he not anticipate the confidence of the Christian's faith—'all things work together for good to them that love God'?[3] When Xenophon says of Socrates,[4] 'He was so completely master of himself that he never chose what was pleasant in place of what was good,' we think how it was said by another disciple of *his* Master, 'Even Christ pleased not Himself.'

The contribution of Socrates to thought was less important than the example of his pure and noble life and of his constancy unto death. 'His personality was greater than his teaching.' Great indeed must have been the influence of this pagan saint upon the thought and life of the pre-Christian world; high is his place among the prophets and forerunners of the Gospel. In Socrates we see how the Spirit of God can work beyond the limits of His visible kingdom, and move at will in hearts and minds that know Him not by name.

The contribution of Socrates to the world's readiness for Christ is thus distinctly moral and spiritual. He set before men the highest aims—the will of God, the paramount claims of truth. His death was a martyrdom. He knew nothing of the Christian's sure and certain hope. Yet few of the white-robed host have surpassed in calmness and majesty the leave-taking of the Grecian sage: 'It is now time to depart; I to die, you

[1] Acts iv. 19; Plat. *Apol. Socr.* p. 29.

[2] Plat. *Apol. Socr.* pp. 29, 30.

[3] *Apol. Socr.* p. 41 (Jowett, vol. ii. p. 135). 'Wherefore, O Judges, be of good cheer about death and know of a certainty that no evil can happen to a good man, either in life or after death.' *v.* O. Pfleiderer, *D. Vorbereitung*, p. 15.

[4] *Memorab.* iv. 8, *ἐγκρατὴς δέ, ὥστε μηδέποτε προαιρεῖσθαι τὸ ἥδιον ἀντὶ τοῦ βελτίονος.*

to live. Whose is the better destiny is unknown to all save God.'[1]

Plato, the greatest of the pupils of Socrates, did much to carry on and extend his influence. His *Apology* is a noble vindication of his Master, and with the *Memorabilia* of Xenophon has set him for ever in the niche of fame which of right belongs to him. With Plato we pass into the world of theory. If Socrates was greatest in his life and in his death—in the realities of existence, Plato was supreme in thought and in its perfect expression.[2] To Plato rather than to Socrates we look for conceptions which herald many of the root-ideas of Christianity.

The philosophy of Plato may be said to culminate in his Theory of Ideas and in the consequences which he deduced from it. It is a question how far he was original in his conception. He apparently owed the first suggestion of his theory to the Socratic distinction between mere supposition and true knowledge.[3] Of these modes of the understanding, the former is concerned with the phenomenal, which is apparent to the senses; the latter with the original types or forms of things, which are eternal and are only to be apprehended by the reason. To these objects of thought Plato gave the name of 'idea' and assigned an existence of their own.[4] Chief among them is the idea of Good, which he identifies with God,[5] and which is the cause of the existence of the sensible world, as the ideas become realized in time and space.[6] Erroneous as was Plato's theory of the actual existence of ideas, it had the advantage of leading him to the thought of spirit as the principle of things. It is considered that he was partly influenced in this direction by Anaxagoras, who taught that reason is the governing and ordering principle of the world. But however Plato arrived at his conception, it at once gives him pre-eminence among the preparatory

[1] Plat. *Apol. Socr.* p. 42. Xenoph. *Apol. Socr.* § 33, ἱλαρῶς καὶ προσεδέχετο αὐτὸν (sc. τὸν θάνατον) καὶ ἐπετελέσατο. Plat. *Phaedo*, p. 115 *ad fin.* Cic. *Tusc. Quaest.* i. § 29.

[2] *v.* Arist. *Metaph.* i. vi. 2; Grant, *Eth. of Arist.* i. pp. 117, 137. Plato was born B.C. 427 at Athens; died B.C. 347.

[3] Pfleiderer, *Die Vorbereitung*, p. 16.

[4] R. Eucken, *Einführung in eine Philosophie des Geisterlebens*, p. 17.

[5] Ueberweg, *D. Gesch. der Philos.* E.T. i. p. 116.

[6] Pfleiderer, *D. Entstehung des Christentums*, p. 23.

influences of that religion which declares that 'God is Spirit.'[1] It places him among those thinkers who interpret the universe in the terms of the spiritual, and links him with the best thought of the present day.

Another great tenet of Christianity, and one which may be said to be specially due to the influence of Greek thought—the immortality of the soul—was suggested to Plato by his theory of ideas. In the *Phaedo* he says that all our learning of general truths, though effected through sense and perception, is not given by it. It is the recollection of ideas, seen by the soul in a former life, awakened here by reflection and thought.[2] This pre-existence of the soul requires as its counterpart a post-existence after the death of the body. The soul, as the invisible part of man, is closely related to the unseen being of the ideas. If the soul, in accordance with its divine nature, keeps itself unstained by the body and prepares for death by ceaseless striving after wisdom, it may hope for a life of happiness hereafter: if the soul, on the other hand, clings to the sensible and hates and avoids the spiritual, it becomes materialized and is again imprisoned in a body.[3] In reply to the objection that although it might survive the body, it would not necessarily be indestructible, Plato founded his theory on the idea of life. Since the soul participates in that idea, it cannot perish; for, as the moving principle both of itself and all else, it is the very principle of life.[4] After the close of the first earthly life, the soul comes to judgment and, according to its deserts, passes to happiness in heaven or to punishment beneath the earth.[5] In the *Phaedrus* the connection of the soul with a body is represented as due to an intellectual fall, through the weakness of its rational element.[6]

[1] Jo. iv. 24. *v.* Plat. *Laws*, x. p. 899, 'All things are full of Gods.' Cf. *New Sayings of Jesus from Oxyrynchus*, Logion 5, Grenfell and Hunt, *ἔγειρον τὸν λίθον κἀκεῖ εὑρήσεις με, σχίσον τὸν ξύλον κἀγω ἐκεῖ εἰμι.* On the relation of this saying to Matt. xviii. 20, and on its pantheistic Mysticism, *v.* Reitzenstein, *Poimandres*, p. 239.

[2] Plat. *Phaedo*, pp. 72, 76, 77. *v.* Grant, *Ethics of Arist.* i. p. 151.

[3] *v.* Pfleiderer, *Vorbereitung des Christentums*, p. 19. Cf. Rom. viii. 6, 'For to be carnally minded is death; but to be spiritually minded is life and peace.'

[4] *v.* Ueberweg, *D. Geschich. der Philos.* E.T. i. p. 127. Plat. *Phaedrus*, p. 245; *Laws*, 895, 896.

[5] *Laws*, 904, 905.

[6] *v.* Pfleiderer, *Die Entstehung des Christentums*, p. 22.

By his identification of the supreme Idea of the Good with God, the divine world-ordering Spirit, Plato laid the foundation for a theology in which metaphysics and ethics come together.[1] It was goodness that impelled the Creator to create.[2] But in the *Symposium*[3] we have a wonderful forecast of the 'One Mediator between God and men, the Man Christ Jesus,' of the fact that 'God was in Christ, reconciling the world unto Himself.'[4] 'What then is love?' I asked. . . . 'He is a great Spirit (δαίμων), and like all spirits he is intermediate between the divine and the mortal.' 'And what,' I said, 'is his power?' 'He interprets between gods and men, conveying and taking across to the gods the prayers and sacrifices of men, and to men the commands and replies of the gods; he is the mediator who spans the chasm which divides them, and therefore in him all is bound together. . . .'[5] Thus Love, the great Δαίμων, is represented as the power by which God has come into touch with the world and by which creation is made possible.[6] Here is the principle of mediation which was to play so great a part in Christian theology. If, with this gleam of prophetic vision, we combine what Plato says, in the *Theaetetus*,[7] of the striving of man after likeness to God, we have, as Pfleiderer remarks, 'the root conception of religious mysticism and speculation.'[8]

When we pass from Plato to his great pupil Aristotle, we find ourselves in a colder atmosphere of thought. Two great differences with his teacher become apparent. His analytic mind, while it laid the foundation for scientific study by separating

[1] *v.* Pfleiderer, *Die Vorbereitung des Christentums*, p. 25.

[2] Plat. *Timaeus*, p. 29, 'Let me tell you why the Creator made this world of generation. He was good and the good can never have jealousy of anything. And being free from jealousy, He desired that all things should be as like Himself as they could be.' *v. Phaedrus*, p. 247 A.

[3] *Sympos.* p. 202 D.E.; E.T. (Jowett), p. 573.

[4] 1 Tim. ii. 5; 2 Cor. v. 19.

[5] Cf. Col. i. 17.

[6] Cf. the Gnostic theory of emanations between God and the visible world.

[7] 'We ought to fly heavenward and to fly thither is to become like God as far as possible; holy and just and wise.' *Theaetetus*, p. 176. 'This is conversion . . . not implanting eyes for they exist already, but giving them a right direction which they have not.' *Republ.* p. 518. Cf. S. Aug. *Confess.* vii. 10, 16. *v.* Illingworth, *Divine Transcendence*, p. 34.

[8] *D. Vorbereitung*, p. 32 n. For the influence of Plato on Christian thought, see Holtzmann, *N.T. Theologie*, i. p. 111.

the various subjects of investigation and thought, and assigning to each its own province, proved its thorough-going character by drawing a hard and fast line between philosophy and morals. Thus his intellectualism is far more pronounced than that of Plato, and as a consequence he denies that God has any interest or concern with morality. His outlook is less religious than that of his master. His other disagreement with Plato was characteristic of his more practical mind. He denied reality to the Platonic Idea, and suggested Form (εἶδος or τὸ τί ἦν εἶναι) as the type according to which the phenomena of the sensible world were fashioned.

Like Plato, Aristotle arrived at the pure, spiritual being of God. He is the prime mover of all that is ; Himself unmoved, occupying the highest place in the scale of existence. It is not God who loves the world. The world loves God, and so is moved towards Him—'The object of desire and reason, though unmoved, is the cause of motion.'[1] When he comes to consider the Deity as a personal being, he represents Him as conscious of happiness, unbroken and everlasting. Then, regarding Him as thought, he seems almost to anticipate those later efforts to conceive of God, which illustrate the doctrine of the Trinity. Since the thinking subject must have an object of thought, and that from all eternity, it may be concluded that the Divine Being contains within Himself both subject and object.[2]

Plato, by his doctrine of Love the mediator between the spiritual and the sensible, had tried to find some kind of medium of intercourse between God and the world. Aristotle felt the difficulty. How did God, Who is pure thought, immaterial, spiritual, come into contact with and form the material world ?[3] He could give no answer, and his theology, embodied as it is in his *Metaphysics*, is not rounded off into a consistent whole. When to this failure, we add the fact that, with Aristotle, life and morality are regarded as standing in no vital and necessary connection with religion, and the Supreme Being is quite uncon-

[1] *Metaph.* xii. 7. κινεῖ δὲ ὧδε τὸ ὀρεκτὸν, καὶ τὸ νοητὸν κινεῖ οὐ κινούμενον. Cf. *Phys.* viii. 6, 'It is plain that there must be some one and eternal being which is the originator of all movement.' 'Something which, while itself changeless, is the source of all change, an eternal and essential energy.'

[2] 'He thinks Himself (as His own object) and His thought is thought of thought.' *Metaph.* xii. 9. Cf. 'God of God' (Nicene Creed).

[3] *v.* Grant, *Ethics of Arist.* i. p. 233 ; Pfleiderer, *D. Vorbereitung*, p. 42.

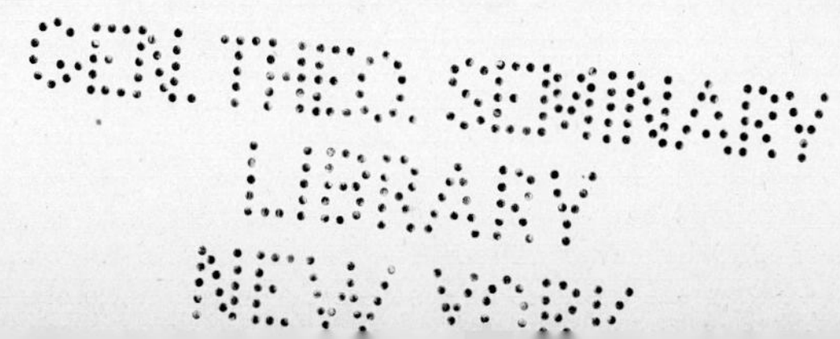

cerned with the question of right and wrong,[1] we can understand that his influence on early religious thought was less powerful than that of Plato, whose philosophy came to mould the thought of later Hellenism and to be thus a preparation for Christianity.

There is one other system of philosophy which forms a stage in the preparation for the Gospel of Christ. A shipwreck brought Zeno of Citium in Cyprus to the shore of Athens. There he came across the *Memorabilia* of Xenophon and read of Socrates. Becoming a pupil of Crates the Cynic, after some years he opened a school in the στοὰ ποικίλη, adorned with frescoes by Polygnotus, which gave its name of Stoicism to the system which he founded.[2] This was about B.C. 308.

The importance of Stoicism in the history of religious thought lies not in its coherence as a finished and complete system, for it presents difficulties and contradictions which it left to future ages unsolved and unreconciled. Rather is it weighty from the emphasis which it placed on life. It brought philosophy down from the skies, and gave it practical aims and objects. It turned attention to the individual. While not indifferent to the question of the origin of things, and going back for its cosmology to the pre-Socratic physicists, to Heraclitus and to the Pythagoreans, its chief interest lay in man, in his moral nature, in the end which he should have in view, in his destiny. So great indeed has been the influence of Stoicism on all subsequent thought, that we cannot exclude it from a share in the formation of the constituents of the Christian character. The very name has passed into a proverb for manly self-restraint, for a lofty sense of duty, for that carelessness of consequences which always attends action of the noblest sort. We must therefore inquire first into the theology and then into the moral system of the Stoic schools ; and this order will appear the right one when we recall the words attributed by Plutarch[3] to the Stoic Chrysippus: 'No ethical subject could be rightly approached except from the preconsideration of entire nature and the ordering of the whole.'

The 'soul of the world' is God or Zeus, and he is represented

[1] *Eth.* x. c. viii. 7. Cf. Pfleiderer, *D. Vorbereitung*, p. 43.

[2] *v.* Aeschin. *Adv. Ctesiph.* 186, 'the decorated porch.' His school was accordingly styled 'the men of the porch' *οἱ ἐκ τῆς στοᾶς, Στωϊκοί*, 'Stoics.'

[3] *De Repugnantiis Stoicis*, c. ix. *v.* Grant, *Ethics of Arist.* i. p. 264.

as fire. From him all things proceed; and when their cycle is completed they return to him. Here we have pantheism; for the world is part of the God from whom it proceeds and to whom it goes, and the spirit of man is an emanation from the world spirit; so that man in his spiritual life is divine and part of the great whole. It has been remarked [1] that this creed is tempered by the Stoic's strong sense of the personality of God and of the individuality of man. Nowhere do these conceptions come out more strongly than in the Hymn to Zeus, one of the most precious remains of Greek religious feeling, which we owe to Cleanthes, the pupil and successor of Zeno.[2]

With such a background of theology to the Stoic conception of morals, we are not surprised to find it a lofty one. Like the morality of the Cynic, it set virtue in the forefront of life as the only thing that mattered. But the virtue of the Stoic was more genial and humane than that of the Cynic. The latter withdrew from all active interest in life, holding aloof from the claims of society, looking down from his standpoint of isolation upon the employments and concerns of his fellow-men. The Cynic could never influence any but a few misanthropes like himself. The Stoic, on the other hand, however severe to himself, opened his heart to the claims of others, and looked not unkindly on the strivings and sorrows of mankind. His great rule of life was so to live as to accord with nature, meaning not the blind following of ungoverned instincts and affections, but the reference of all details of conduct to the standard of what was right for all; a standard which was to be ascertained by the use of reason.

This abstract conception of nature as a criterion of life could never become a popular standard of reference.[3] People are not influenced by abstract ideas. But the Stoic proceeded to exemplify his notion by a concrete instance. He sketched the portrait of the wise man who, virtuous and self-restrained, is never a slave to his affections, but is free to enjoy life under the guidance of his reason. This picture of the ideal wise man was indeed so highly coloured that it assumed an unreal, paradoxical

[1] By Grant, *ib.* pp. 265, 6.

[2] It is given by Ueberweg, *Geschichte der Philos.* E.T. i. p. 197. *v.* Grant, *Ethics of Arist.* i. p. 266.

[3] I find that K. Lake takes a similar view. 'The spiritual atmosphere of Seneca's religion was too rarefied to be breathed by the ordinary man; it dealt too much in abstractions.' *The Stewardship of Faith*, 1915, p. 68.

character. It made no allowance for the stern actualities of life. Dividing mankind into the wise and the foolish, and placing a stout barrier between them, it was too hard and fast a theory to be effective as a principle of conduct. None could claim the condition of the wise. Were all to be shut up in the hopeless category of the fools? The difficulty was met by the suggestion of progress, of a gradual advance from a lower to a higher standard of living, an idea which receives its full exposition in the requirements of the Christian life [1] and which, when it dawned upon the mind of the Stoic thinker, constituted a new and unheard-of step in the evolution of Greek morality.

Another original conception of the Stoics was that of duty, which, although it was only gradually formed out of the kindred notions of the 'suitable' and the 'right,' constitutes one of their chief claims to our respect and gratitude.[2] They held that the consciousness of duty was innate in man and was due to the Divine reason. Thus the moral law—Kant's categorical imperative—is referred to a direct revelation of the mind of God. It is difficult to rate too highly this deliberate assignment of the sense of morality to the influence of religion. It lays a foundation for Christian Ethics, finding as they do, its inspiration and sanction in the will of God. Duty is binding upon man because it answers to the Divine reason.

In his attitude to his fellow-men, the Stoic, strong individualist though he was, lifted his eyes beyond the limits of state or city. He knew no boundary to the brotherhood of men,[3] but imagined one universal country undisturbed by the rivalries of contending factions or the divisions of national politics. To the Stoic, his city was the world,[4] and if his ideas of the equality and kinship of men were not always carried out consistently in practice—as

[1] *v.* Grant, *Ethics of Arist.* i. p. 261; Pfleiderer, *D. Vorbereitung*, p. 49. Cf. Phil. iii. 13.

[2] Grant observes (*op. cit.* i. p. 262) that the idea belonged rather to the later (Roman) stage of Stoicism. But the elements of the conception were early recognized, and only wanted for a word to give them articulate expression. *v.* Pfleiderer, *D. Vorbereitung*, p. 46.

[3] Cf. P. Wendland, *D. Hellenistisch-Römische Kultur*, p. 231. After speaking of the unity and equality of mankind before God as taught by Christianity (Gal. iii. 28; 1 Cor. xii. 13), he says, 'This standpoint is closely allied to the Hellenistic, especially the Stoic conception of humanity, the general worth and the common rights of men.'

[4] Cf. Seneca's expression of this thought. *Ep. Mor.* xcv. 52.

witness the existence and toleration of slavery—yet we get a glimpse, in this wide outlook, of the theory of an universal Church, carrying the Gospel of Salvation to the ends of the earth and inviting all nations to come within its fold.

With the later developments of Stoicism in the Empire, we are not concerned. They come too late to be taken up into the preparation for Christianity. But no sketch of Stoicism, however brief, which failed to indicate the general effect of the thought of Seneca, of Epictetus and of Marcus Aurelius, would do it justice. So close is the resemblance of Stoic to Christian thought, that the attempt has often been made to trace a connection such as that of Master and Scholar between Apostle and Philosopher. Opinions differ as to the success of this endeavour. But it must be admitted that a great humanizing and deepening of thought and feeling passed over Stoicism in its later periods. Something of this result may have been contributed by the study of Platonism:[1] something too by knowledge of Judaism.[2] At any rate the change occurred and made itself felt in expressions of deep religious earnestness and of lofty feeling which might well have come from an Apostle.

There is greater sympathy and tenderness for man, and a real trust in the care and wisdom of God. How near this affinity to Christian thought appears in the writings of Seneca can be seen at a glance.[3] Indeed it is difficult to avoid the impression that the Spanish Philosopher and the Jew of Tarsus, although coming from the opposite ends of the Empire, may have looked upon one another in the justice hall of Nero; and that the bearing and demeanour of Christ's 'ambassador in chains'[4] may have drawn the moralist to the study of those Epistles, which were beginning to be circulated from town to town throughout the Empire.

We may at least acknowledge that, in enforcing a high standard of morality, a paramount law of duty, a sense of the claims of the weak and down-trodden, Stoicism, especially in the persons of its later upholders, has deserved well of mankind. It is easy

[1] *v.* Pfleiderer, *D. Vorbereitung*, p. 51.

[2] *v.* Lightfoot, *Philippians*, p. 299; Pfleiderer, *Urchristentum*, p. 30.

[3] Lightfoot has collected many resemblances, giving the corresponding New Testament passages in his dissertation in *Philippians*, p. 283 ff.

[4] Eph. vi. 20.

enough, when contrasting it with what became its successful rival, to point out its inferiority to Christianity in power over life and conduct, its materialistic identification of God with the world, its fatalism,[1] its cowardice in refusing to face at extreme moments the ills of life which it could not cure,[2] its contradictions between precept and performance, its inconsistencies, the isolation of its chief representatives from the interests and sorrows of mankind—in short, we may blame it for its want of the spirit of Christ. But after all, it was only the latest of its leading thinkers who lived within reach of that spirit. 'How should they believe in Him of Whom they had not heard?' We must not condemn it for its failure to produce those effects in life and conduct which can only be produced by living contact with the Person of Christ. Perhaps its chief gift to the world was the preparation which it made for Christian ethics, by its noble assertion of the will of a personal God and its firm grasp upon the claim of duty as binding upon all. Recognizing in these conceptions the hand of Him who is 'the Light of life,' we may claim Stoicism at its best and highest as one of the many ways in which 'God . . . spake in time past to the fathers,' in preparation for the Revelation of His Son.[3]

[1] *v.* Manil. *Astronom.* iv. 14, 'Fata regunt orbem, certa stant omnia lege.'

[2] Both Zeno and Cleanthes (the latter by wilfully continuing a prescribed fast of two days) put an end to their own lives.

[3] W. W. Fowler has remarked how Stoicism cleared the way for a new and universal religion by putting the old cults into the shade. *The Religious Experience of the Roman People*, p. 374. For a highly favourable estimate of the religious worth of Stoicism, see Dill, *Roman Society from Nero to Marcus Aurelius*, p. 331 f.

CHAPTER VI

THE PREPARATION: GREEK RELIGION

GREEK religion is almost too closely bound up with Greek philosophy to be capable of separate treatment. 'Plato is a religious genius in the mantle of a philosopher.'[1] Nevertheless, for our present purpose, some distinctively religious conceptions and practices seem to require separate handling.

Greek religion, like that of other races, has been characterized by a process of development. Beginning, so far as its literary expression is concerned, with the theogony of Hesiod and with the theology of the Homeric poems,[2] it passed, under the influence of Eastern religious importations, into the Orphic stage. Hesiod must be placed before 700 B.C. The Orphic theogony which, though based on Hesiod, made additions to his system, was supposed by the Greeks to belong to an earlier date, but this view is no longer held.[3] It gave special prominence to Zagreus Dionysos and Demeter rather than to the Zeus and Apollo of Hesiod and Homer. The ecstasy and frenzy which characterized

[1] Bousset, *Das Wesen der Religion*, p. 87. Cf. p. 152.

[2] P. Wendland, *Hellenistisch-Römische Kultur*, p. 96, 'A long religious development lies before Homer, but its history cannot be written.' Cf. Farnell, *The Higher Aspects of Greek Religion*, p. 18, 'I believe that the poems give us a partial picture of the Greek world of a period not far from 1000 B.C.'

[3] *v.* Grote, *Hist. of Greece*, i. p. 19. Cf. Farnell, *op. cit.* p. 139, '. . . the Orphic brotherhoods, based on certain mystic elements in the Dionysiac worship that were ultimately derived from Thrace. These sects were beginning to make themselves felt as a new force in the sixth century B.C., and in the fifth and fourth centuries were perhaps the strongest religious influence in the Hellenic world.'

'The Orphic brotherhoods preached to the whole world, Greek and barbarian, bond and free. Therefore the renown is theirs of being the first world-religion bearing a free message.' *Ib.*

the Orphic worship had little in common with the old Greek religious feeling.[1] It came from the East, from Lydia and Phrygia, while the god and goddess have been identified with the Osiris and Isis of Egypt. Along with these new practices came new religious conceptions, which embodied themselves in ritual. The need of purification made itself felt as never before in Greek religious thought, and thus the Orphic ceremonies were largely expiatory.[2] There was also the idea of the immortality of the soul.[3] To ourselves, perhaps the chief interest of the Orphic movement lies in the fact that Plato took over these two great conceptions into his religious philosophy and developed them by his creative genius.[4] But apart from this, it gave expression to higher and purer ideas of the gods, and led the way to those noble thoughts of the Godhead—the one almighty 'soul of the world'—which we also meet with in the writings of Plato and of the Stoics. In the sixth and fifth centuries B.C., men were ceasing to find satisfaction for their religious needs in the anthropomorphic myths of Hesiod. A deeper view of life was being taken. The worship of Dionysos, which seems to have been indigenous in Thrace, was set in opposition to the Olympian legends, and gradually a more or less monotheistic deity was evolved, who, sometimes called Zeus, sometimes Dionysos, gathered into himself, as the supreme being, the attributes and authority of the lesser deities.[5] And along with these higher views of deity came the Orphic doctrine of the heavenly origin of the soul of man, which became imprisoned on earth in the body, and for its fault needed redemption and purification.[6] It was this need of the guilty soul which lay at the root of the mystic rites, that characterized the solemn meetings of the Orphic

[1] 'In the enthusiastic religion of Dionysos, man found a deeper personal relation to the god who stands nearer to the hearts of the poor and wretched than the aristocratic Olympians, and who, in the thrill of ecstasy, raises him to himself and in the moments of exaltation and union with the godhead, allows him to forget the necessities of life.' Wendland, *ib.* p. 99.

[2] 'Orphism was the first form of a religion of redemption upon Greek soil.' Pfleiderer, *D. Vorbereitung*, p. 5.

[3] *v.* Grant, *op. cit.* i. p. 65; Farnell, *op. cit.* p. 139.

[4] *v.* above, p. 99.

[5] *v.* Pfleiderer, *D. Vorbereitung*, p. 4.

[6] *v.* P. Wendland, *op. cit.* p. 99; Farnell, *ib.* p. 139, '... the dogma that man is by origin half divine and is of the kindred of God; that even in this life man can attain to divine communion.'

worshippers, and found expression in ascetic practices and habits of life.

In the sixth century B.C., Pythagoras, emigrating from his native Samos to Croton in Magna Graecia, grafted upon the Orphic system his brotherhoods and associations, which aimed at a reformation of life through special doctrines and practices. In this, he only intensified the tendency to exclusiveness which had marked the Orphic life. Religion, as he conceived it, was not for the crowd, but for the few initiated. The life at which he aimed was that of a monastic community, owning strict obedience to its founder and sacrificing all lower pleasures and tastes to the supreme task of cultivating the spiritual life.[1]

About the same time, Xenophanes, driven by Persian invasion from Ionia, came into lower Italy and taught the worthlessness of the prevailing conceptions of the gods. In place of them he set before men the thought of one spiritual Being, pervading all things and knowing all things.[2]

The scientific thinking of the Ionic school of philosophers was already engaged in breaking down the mischievous teaching of the traditional mythology. Men were disposed to seek for answers to the riddles of the universe in nature, rather than in the region of pious fancy. Thereby, like Socrates, later on, they incurred the charge of atheism ; but unconsciously their speculations were preparing the way for some of the deepest truths of Christianity. The Λόγος of Heraclitus, the one immanent world-spirit of Xenophanes, the world-pervading Reason, which Anaxagoras conceived ; all these conceptions were in the direction of a higher unity of the deity than the old religious beliefs had ever contemplated. The movement is parallel to the gradual advance of monotheism among the Jewish people. What prophets had already done for Hebrew religious thought, the pre-Socratic philosophers were, in their way, doing for the Greek world. The ground was being cleared for truth and purity in religious thought and life.[3]

[1] Diog. Laert. viii. 3 ; Iambl. *Vita Pythag.* 81. *v.* Grote, *Hist. of Greece,* iii. p. 336 ff.

[2] Arist. *Metaph.* i. 5.

[3] Cf. Pfleiderer, *op. cit.* p. 3 ; Hamilton, *The People of God,* i. p. 169. 'The establishment of the Jewish national religion upon a definitely monotheistic basis was brought about prior to, and quite independently of, the philosophical activities of the Greeks.' *Ib.* p. 182. *v.* above, p. 63.

Side by side with the ordinary current of Greek religion ran an influence of quite unique character—the oracle of Apollo at Delphi. Rooted in an immemorial past, its fame as a holy place extended through every century of Hellenic history. It is uncertain when Delphi began to be connected with Apollo, but it was at a period previous to the Homeric poems.[1] The sanctity and authority, which were universally ascribed to the oracle and its sayings, would probably have been the same if the spot had not become a shrine of Apollo. The place itself was regarded as holy, and its integrity was safeguarded by decree of the Amphictyonic Council.

The oracle was a peculiarly Hellenic institution. There was nothing outside Hellenic lands with which it could be compared. In all times of danger to states or confederations, recourse was had to Delphi. There, the utterances of the priestess, as she spoke under the influence of ecstasy, real or simulated, were received by the 'holy ones,' the priests, and by them so amended as to suit their view of the actual circumstances. The vagueness of the final answer to the seeker was often a cloak which concealed their lack of grasp of the situation; and the saying would require further interpretation, or a second visit to the shrine, before its counsel could be acted upon.

In questions of morals or religion the influence of Delphi was on the whole salutary. In an answer addressed to 'Glaucus,' there is a forecast of our Lord's teaching in the Sermon on the Mount. The deity will punish the evil intention, even if it does not issue in action.[2] In one respect, Delphi was behind the average religious thought of the time. Human sacrifice was upheld by the guardians of the oracle after it had ceased to be practised in any Greek state. Yet, on the whole, the voice of the Delphian Apollo spoke on the side of righteousness, of truth and freedom, and while it helped to form the prevailing standard of religion and ethics, it reflected the best thought of the time.

If Greek philosophy and Greek religion played a considerable part in preparing the world for Christ, their influence had by no

[1] *v.* Farnell in Hastings' *D.B.* v. p. 145, and *The Higher Aspects of Greek Religion*, 1912, p. 97 f.

[2] Herod. vi. 86; Matt. v. 22, 28. *v.* Farnell in Hastings' *D.B.* v. p. 146.

means ceased to act, when He appeared upon the stage of history.

One of the most difficult problems in Christology is to explain the gradual recognition of the Godhead of our Lord. How did it come about that the Man Jesus of Nazareth, known to His neighbours and acquaintance as 'the carpenter,' reputed to be the son of Joseph and Mary, leading an ordinary village life up to the age of thirty, was within a short time—three years at the most—acknowledged to be the Messiah, the Lord, the Son of God? How is it that One, Who within that period was owned to have fulfilled in His Person the Messianic expectations of the chosen people, came to overstep the limits of that conception and to be recognized as standing within the circle of the Godhead, claiming the homage of Gentile as well as Jew, being 'over all, God blessed for ever'?

The main factor in creating this belief was undoubtedly the Personality of Christ Himself, as it became illumined by the light of His Resurrection-appearances and by the inspiring Gift of Pentecost. 'He shall teach you all things' was His own promise, and it was amply fulfilled. The primitive community, before St. Paul came upon the scene, worshipped Christ as God.[1]

But to acknowledge the part played by the Person and by the Spirit of Christ in producing this result is not to ignore the contribution made by other influences. To men who read the Old Testament in the Septuagint version, as several of the Apostles were probably in the habit of doing, the use of the title Κύριος in addressing Christ, or in reference to Him, would induce reflection. It is the Septuagint rendering for Jehovah. There is no evidence that Christ deprecated its application to Himself. When Hellenistic Jews and Greeks joined the community, the term commended itself to them, and for Greeks especially meant more than 'Messiah' could ever mean. As its employment increased, its connotation deepened,[2] and what, apart from its Septuagint use, had been little more than a title of respect, came to express, in an ever widening circle of converts, the highest view of

[1] Cf. Matt. xxviii. 17.

[2] 'The use of "Lord" was a long step towards the claim of divinity for Jesus.' K. Lake, *The Stewardship of Faith*, p. 93. As indicated above, the place of Christ in the Divine order was already recognized. The Greek title served to extend such recognition.

the Personality of Christ. Thus did Greek thought and language contribute to the development of the doctrine of His Person.

There was another service rendered by the Greek. His old religion permitted him to recognize various forms under which the Deity might manifest Himself. His philosophy had taught him that God was One, but it made concession to the popular mythology so far as to allow that the One God could and did reveal Himself in the person now of this deity and now of that. Zeus might be represented by Dionysos, by Hermes, by Apollo and yet retain his solitary supremacy.[1] The mere fact of this accommodating relation between philosophy and religion produced a tone of mind; and this tone of mind prepared the Graeco-Roman peoples to receive a religion, which, while it maintained the stern monotheism that it inherited from Judaism, was seeking to express its conception of the Godhead by the formula of the Trinity. The Greek did not create the Catholic doctrine of God. Its kernel was already in the possession of the primitive community. But he aided the process of its reception in the Western world, and prepared the way for the future conquests of the Catholic Faith.[2]

For the last service of the Greek to the cause of Christian truth which falls within our period we are indebted to the conception of the Λόγος. The Fourth Evangelist employs the term in the Prologue of his Gospel, when he speaks of the Eternity of Christ, of His creative work and of His appearance in time in the substance of our flesh. The history of the term begins, so far as we know, with Heraclitus, who taught that 'This Reason (or Word) existeth ever, yet men are unaware of It, not only before they hear but when they first listen to It.'[3] To the writer of the Gospel, in a Greek city such as Ephesus, the term would be quite familiar. There is no need to suggest knowledge of the writings of Philo.[4] But if St. John employs the expression, he puts it to a wholly new use, and after the Prologue he does

[1] *v.* above, p. 108.

[2] Hatch has greatly exaggerated the effect of Greek influence on the formation of dogma. *Hibbert Lectures*, 1888. For a criticism of his position *v.* Gore, *The Incarnation of the Son of God*, pp. 99, 100, 254.

[3] Heracl. in Hippolyt. *Refut. Haer.* ix. 9. *v.* Ritter et Preller, *Hist. Philos.* i. § 31; Inge, *Personal Idealism*, p. 40. *v.* above, pp. 95, 98.

[4] *v.* above, p. 88.

not employ it again. It has served his purpose, which was to bring before the Greek-speaking world the thought of our Lord, not as the Messiah of 'the Jews,' but as the pre-existent heavenly Reason, pervading and sustaining all things and in these last times coming to dwell with men as Man.[1]

[1] Cf. Case, *The Evolution of Early Christianity*, Chicago, 1914, p. 362; Harnack, *Dogmengesch.* i. pp. 109, 110, 'Greek theological conceptions do not operate in the Johannine Theology. Even his Logos has little more than the name in common with the Logos of the Porch (Stoicism), or even of Philo.... In spite of his anti-Judaism, we must regard the author as a born Jew.' Cf. H. Holtzmann, *Einleitung in das N.T.* p. 430, 'The Logos-conception has its ultimate roots partly in Old Testament representations (Gen. i. 3; Ps. xxxiii. 6...) with addition of the Apocrypha (Bar. iii. 28-38; Sir. i. 1-10; Wisd. vii. 22-30). The Palestinian theological expression Memra (Word) and earlier, the Alexandrian correlative—the Logos of Philo—...each range themselves along with it' (*i.e* the O.T.).

CHAPTER VII

THE PREPARATION: ROMAN RELIGION

THE chief contribution of Rome to the preparation for Christ lay in her genius for order, embodied and enforced in an Empire which marched with the confines of the civilized world. The effect of this reign of law upon the rise and early diffusion of Christianity was almost entirely external. It produced favourable conditions. It gave security to weak and struggling communities. It sheltered them from the attacks of a fanaticism, which would otherwise have crushed the movement at its very birth. It made travelling safe; and when disputes arose, it ensured a fair hearing to unknown and isolated representatives of the new religion.

Thus the influence of Rome was more apparent in the preparation for Christianity than for Christ Himself. Yet in a very real sense, it entered into the external conditions of His life, and can be traced from His cradle to His grave. Rome brought His Mother from her home to Bethlehem, and made it the scene of His birth.[1] It was the Roman Governor, with power over life and death, to whom the Jews turned to give effect to their hatred, and who set up the inscription over the Cross, to which at their bidding he had condemned the Redeemer. It was the Roman army which supplied the guard to the grave after it had nailed Him to the Cross.

It was a denarius, bearing the head of the Emperor, which Christ used to illustrate His teaching about paying tribute.[2] He upheld the authority and privileges of Caesar, although, at the time, they were in the hands of a Tiberius. Thus, from first to

[1] Lk. ii. 1-8. *v.* p. 144.

[2] *v.* Schürer, ii. pp. 53, 54. Swete on Mk. xii. 15.

last, the earthly life of Christ was in contact with Rome. It was at the climax of her world-power that the Saviour of the world appeared. Brute force, controlled and regulated though it was by a certain respect for law and order, stood face to face with incarnate love. What wonder that the former triumphed? The conflict was inevitable. We do not forget that Rome tried to save Christ, and if the effort had been less half-hearted, all the guilt, instead of the larger share of it, would have rested upon the Jews.[1] For the time force triumphed: but the power of love is stronger, and soon the Crucified began to conquer the conquerors.

It was chiefly by her powers of government and administration that Rome fulfilled her task in the preparation for Christ and His Gospel, by the assurance of a fair administration of law with its attendant security of order,[2] and by the provision of those noble roads which ran straight from one great military station to another throughout the Empire, affording a highway to the Gospel messengers. But there were other gifts which she was enabled to contribute—gifts of character and mind, ethical forces which only needed the transforming touch of the Gospel of Christ to call them into full employment.

In order to trace the development of these forces, we must take a brief view of the religious history of the Roman people.

The most masterful race of the ancient world were the most accommodating in the matter of religion. They readily permitted the incursion of alien faiths. The reason for this tolerance lay in the practical and mundane character of the people. The Roman was always more concerned with government and administration than with worship and rite. It was only at times, before Christianity appeared with its demand for supremacy and sole acknowledgment, that the Roman felt stirred to oppose any kind of religious observance.[3] He was tolerant of faiths which were

[1] Cf. Jo. xix. 11. [2] Cf. Acts xxi. 30 f.; xxiii. 23 f.

[3] For further detail, *v.* below, p. 122. Cf. P. Wendland, *Hellenistisch-Römische Kultur*, p. 230, 'Polytheism is generous and tolerant, for it makes room for other gods beside its own. Along with the incorporation of foreign races and peoples, Rome had to admit their gods. She preserved her tolerance, so long as it was a matter of polytheistic and national religions; even the oriental ones accommodated themselves easily to the state-religion as they pressed into it. Tolerance objected to the universalism and exclusiveness of Christianity.'

willing to live side by side with others. It became part of his policy and statesmanship to reject one which could only be received on condition that all else were to be cast out. As a man of affairs, regarding the question from the point of view of the official, he failed to understand the exclusive claim of Christianity.

The early religion of Rome was that of peasants and herdsmen, whose gods answered to the requirements and needs of their work. They did not worship the powers and phenomena of nature—sun and stars; nor did their gods embody ethical ideas, such as were to be found in later periods. The worship was as practical and ordinary as the pursuits of their everyday life.[1] The god of the house,[2] of the wood and the meadow, of harvest and fruitage, of the changing seasons,[3] of the birth and death of men; these were the deities of early Rome before she extended her dominion beyond the dwellings which clustered on the Palatine Hill. As yet Neptune is not a sea-god. The Tiber alone is furrowed by Roman keels. The trade of the merchant, which was placed under the protection of Minerva in early republican days, is unrepresented in worship; and the much honoured goddess of Fortune has not come into the circle of deities. The attempt has been made to connect the gods of early Rome with the legendary personalities of the kings. To Numa Pompilius especially has been assigned the work of ordering the cults and religious rites of the city. Whether the attempt is due to the natural desire to find a founder for the religion of the state, who can be set side by side with its political and military originators, or whether it is borne out by historic fact, we have no means of judging.[4] It has been shown that the growth of the city can be seen in the character of the early religious rites. Thus, the procession which encircled the Palatine at the Festival of the Lupercalia points to the origin of the feast at a time when all Rome was confined within those limits.[5] The spots connected

[1] *v.* Wissowa, *Religion und Kultur der Römer*, pp. 20, 21; P. Wendland, *Hellenistisch-Römische Kultur*, p. 137.

[2] *v.* W. W. Fowler, *The Religious Experience of the Roman People*, p. 73.

[3] Fowler, *op. cit.* pp. 92, 103, 116.

[4] *v.* Wissowa, *op. cit.* p. 25. The 'Calendar of Numa' belongs to a period before the Etruscan conquest of the city. *v.* Fowler, *ib.* p. 94.

[5] The Mundus, a dome-shaped building of tufa, regarded as the central spot of the original city as traced out by the ploughshare of Romulus, was discovered on Jan. 1, 1914, on the Palatine Hill. Wissowa, *ib.* p. 188 f., describes the

with the festivals of certain deities, as the Quirinal with the Quirinalia, mark steps in the gradual widening of the city boundaries. It is significant that as yet there is no trace of Greek influence.[1] Deities, which afterwards came to be co-ordinated with Greek gods or goddesses, are shown by their names to be of Italian origin.

'Janus was the first deity to be addressed in all prayers and invocations.'[2] Jupiter came next, the god of the sky, possessed by every branch of the Aryan race.[3] He was worshipped in Latium at Alba Longa before the foundation of Rome, and when the Temple on the Capitol had been founded by one of the Etruscan kings of Rome, he became the guardian deity of the city, with the title of Optimus Maximus.[4] Other deities, high in favour in primitive times, were Mars and Quirinus. The trinity of Jupiter, Mars and Quirinus[5] formed the representative deities of the state. Later, but still before republican times, Jupiter, Mars and Quirinus were replaced by a trinity which seems to have been received from Greece by way of Etruria—Jupiter, Juno, Minerva. With this new importation was connected the founding of the sanctuary of the Capitol. This religious upheaval, which displaced the gods of the country (*di indigetes*) in favour of the new deities (*di novensiles*) has been connected with the Tarquins:[6] it continued to mould the worship of Rome down to the time of the second Punic War, B.C. 218.[7]

It was in the dim twilight of the kingly period that the Latin goddess Diana was received into Roman worship from her ancient sanctuary at Aricia.[8] With the gradual extension of Roman

Mundus as 'a pit which was usually kept shut and only opened on the day of the Feast (of the "di manes") as, according to the Roman view, it was the place appropriated to the sacrifices offered to the "di inferi," since in a certain degree it exhibited the connection between the upper and lower world.'

[1] Unless we accept the legend of the purchase of the books of the Sibyl of Cumae by Tarquin. *v.* Wissowa, *ib.* p. 37.

[2] Fowler, *op. cit.* p. 126.

[3] *v.* Max Müller, *Introduction to the Science of Religion*, p. 106.

[4] *v.* Fowler, *op. cit.* pp. 128, 9.

[5] *v.* Wissowa, *ib.* p. 24.

[6] Cf. Wendland, *Hellenistisch-Römische Kultur*, p. 137. Tarquinius Superbus was banished 510 B.C.

[7] Wissowa, *ib.* p. 38.

[8] The modern Ariccia, 16 miles from Rome, on the Appian way. *v.* Wissowa, *ib.* pp. 42, 198.

lordship over the surrounding country followed, in regular course, the adoption of the deities of the subject peoples. But this practice had its limits. Beyond a certain point, the deities of the newly added peoples were merely received into the worship of private families, according to the dictates of individual taste and sentiment; but they were excluded from admission to the state religion;[1] possibly because a free and unchecked addition of festivals to the already crowded calendar of worship would leave too little space for the ordinary avocations of life.

Before passing from the time of the Kings, a brief summary of the religious character of primitive Rome will not be out of place. We have to bear in mind the agricultural and domestic life of the early settlers on the group of hills which rose out of the wide plain, between the Alban and Sabine Hills and the 'Great Sea.' They were an intensely god-fearing people. They regarded all life and force, whether of man or nature, as the direct result of divine or spiritual agency. Home-life and field work, war with neighbouring tribes, commerce by land or river, each department of activity had its own tutelary deity. The *Jus divinum*, ascribed to Numa Pompilius, regulated the system of sacrifices. They were of three kinds—those in honour of the god, those intended to atone for past offences or to propitiate his favour for the future, and those which ensured sacramental union with him. Thus, at the Latin festival on the Alban Mount, the tribes partook of a common meal, by which they entered into communion with Jupiter and with one another.[2]

Striking as these foreshadowings of Christian life and thought undoubtedly are, the spirit which inspired them is even more worthy of note. In the old Roman mind, two primal religious ideas were paramount. The feeling expressed by the word *pietas*—reverent devotion, the union of respect and affection—was deeply implanted. The other principle was that of awe—*religio*. Much of the Roman strength and uprightness may be traced to the religious influence of these two primary factors of the Roman character. Combined with them, was the sense that personal purity of life was essential to the worshipper who approached the divine altar.[3] Daily prayer was the custom

[1] Wissowa, *ib.* p. 44. [2] *v.* W. W. Fowler, *op. cit.* pp 172, 192.
[3] Tibullus, ii. 1. 11. Cf. W. W. Fowler, *op. cit.* p. 178.

in the old Roman household, while at certain seasons the blessing of heaven was invoked at the boundaries of the land.[1]

In the early years of the Republic, the state religion received a large accession of Grecian cults. This was due in part to the influence of the Greek cities of lower Italy; in part, to the effect produced upon men's minds by acquaintance with the oracles contained in the books of the Sibyl of Cumae. The questioning of the oracles resulted in the monition to adopt the worship of this or that deity. It was in this way that the cult of Apollo was introduced into Rome.[2] At first this Greek invasion was gradual. At the period of the second Punic War, it poured into Rome, penetrating and transforming the indigenous religion of the country.[3]

Before the Republic there was little or no attempt to represent the gods by statues. Simple chapels and altars were characteristic of the early time. Afterwards, regular temples began to be built and were regarded as the actual dwelling-places of the gods. In these, as time went on, were placed the figures of the gods to whom the temples were dedicated. Jupiter had a statue of clay in the Temple on the Capitol. Diana had a figure in her Temple on the Aventine moulded after the pattern of the great image at Ephesus.[4]

In studying early Roman religion, we have always to bear in mind the difference between the religion of the state—the official and recognized worship—and the various cults which were practised by guilds and other classes of the people, on the one hand, and by private families or households, on the other. It frequently happened that a day set apart in the calendar for the observance of the festival of a national deity would conflict with the feast of a guild. The people as a whole might be wending their way to the Temple of Jupiter on the Capitol, while the gardeners sought the shrine of their patroness, the goddess Venus. Minerva was receiving in her Temple on the Aventine the worship of the artificers and handiworkers of Rome, while on the same day the state, in the persons of her official representatives, visited the Temple of the old Roman god of war.

[1] *v.* Fowler, *ib.* p. 227.

[2] Wissowa, *ib.* pp. 45, 239; P. Wendland, *op. cit.* p. 137.

[3] Cf. Fowler, *op. cit.* p. 327. [4] Wissowa, *ib.* p. 50.

The simplicity and inwardness of the primitive worship began, in the early days of the Republic, to find expression in the public games which were held upon the feast days of the gods and were regarded as closely connected with the religious rites. Thus the *Ludi Romani* became a yearly festival upon the day of the foundation of the Temple of the Capitol. Times of public distress and trouble led to the curious custom of preparing in the streets banquets for the gods, who were represented by carved images; while the people privately made their houses free of access to all who cared to enter and receive their hospitality, prisoners even being for the time eased of their chains.[1]

The Rogation-tide processions of the early mediaeval church were in a way anticipated by the public 'supplications' which were inaugurated during the Republic, after consultation of the Sibylline books. A procession, starting from the Temple of Apollo before the Porta Carmentalis, passed through the Forum to the Temple of Juno Regina on the Aventine.[2] Offerings were brought to the goddess and supplication for deliverance from threatening danger was made as the procession moved along. It was on the advice of Greek oracular sayings that, for a short period before the second Punic War, human offerings were made in times of special need.[3]

It has been observed that B.C. 217, the second year of the war with Hannibal, was one of outstanding importance for the history of Roman religion.[4] Hitherto there had been a certain distinction between the worship paid to the gods of the country and that of the gods who had been introduced from abroad (*di indigetes* and *di novensiles*). Indigenous and foreign deities now become linked together in unity of worship (*di consentes*), and their statues are set up in the Forum.[5] Along with this movement, we can trace the constantly increasing influence of the Greek spirit. Not that new Hellenic deities were introduced into the Roman Pantheon; but old Roman gods and goddesses, while preserving their names, have become Hellenized and their cults modified accordingly. There was everywhere a transform-

[1] Liv. v. 13; Wissowa, *Religion u. Kultur der Römer*, pp. 52, 53, 356.

[2] Wissowa, *op. cit.* p. 360. [3] *Ib.* p. 54. [4] *Ib.* p. 54.

[5] Wissowa, *ib.* p. 55, and *De dis Romanis, indigetibus et novensidibus*, p. xii f.; P. Wendland, *Hellenistisch-Römische Kultur*, p. 137; W. Warde Fowler, *The Religious Experience of the Roman People*, p. 319.

ing tendency abroad. The times were anxious. The state was exposed to terrible danger. The war with Carthage was a life and death struggle. At such times the desire would be felt for a more concrete and visible presentation of the deities. As we have seen, this tendency was quite foreign to the genius of the old Roman religion, which was abstract and impersonal. It could now only be met by recourse to the expedients of Greek religious thought and art.

The introduction of Greek and, later on, of oriental cults naturally led to the gradual loss of interest in the forms and in the spirit of the old Roman worship. Offerings were still made, as in former days, and the festivals were officially observed: but the people generally ceased to regard those which failed to commend themselves by their special ceremonies. So much was this the case that, by the first century B.C., their meaning and significance had become lost. The old deities of birth and death, of seed time and harvest, gave way to Greek ones.[1] So far, the modification of the Roman worship, although destructive of the primitive beliefs, was not accompanied by any corresponding change in general morality. But the new movement did not stop with the introduction of Greek names and Greek forms of worship. 'In the next two centuries Rome gained the world and lost her own soul.'[2]

About the close of the second Punic War (B.C. 204), on the authority of the Sibylline books, the worship of the Asiatic goddess variously known as Magna Mater, Mater Deûm, or Cybele, was introduced into Rome. Her temple was dedicated on the Palatine and, for the first time in Roman history, the wild orgies of further Asia came to exercise their pernicious influence upon all classes of the people.[3] One has only to think of the stern sense of duty and the high moral tone of Roman life in the early Republic, to be able to form some estimate of the fatal effects of Eastern superstitions and practices upon the Roman citizen.[4] Following upon this momentous step, other

[1] *v.* Wissowa, *op. cit.* pp. 56, 57.

[2] W. W. Fowler, *op. cit.* p. 331.

[3] *v.* Wissowa, *op. cit.* pp. 57, 263 f.; F. Cumont, *Les Religions Orientales dans le Paganisme Romain*, pp. 58, 88; Fowler, *op. cit.* p. 330.

[4] About B.C. 140, the praetor C. Cornelius Hispallus banished Chaldaean astrologers as demoralising from Rome and Italy. Valer. Max. i. 3. 2.

cults were brought in from Asia and from Egypt. Campaigns in the East generally led to the adoption by soldiers of cults which they encountered in the course of their travels. Thus, the wars with Mithridates (B.C. 88-63) brought Romans in contact with the worship of Mithras,[1] which before long was to spread, largely through its attraction for soldiers, over every part of the Empire from York to India.[2] About the same time—the last century of the Republic—Mâ or Bellona, who was closely allied to the Magna Mater, began to be adored in Rome[3] and the worship of Isis was imported from Egypt. The authorities vainly tried to stem the tide of this invasion of Orientalism. In the third century A.D. it had well-nigh extinguished, not only the old Roman worship, but even its Hellenized forms, with the result that Christianity found its chief rival, not in the religions of Italy and Greece, but in the Oriental superstitions and practices by which those religions had been supplanted.

But there is another side to the question. There was a vein of personal piety in Oriental mysticism and a tendency to the worship of one eternal and universal deity which have to be taken into account. The Sun was thought to be the representative of the Divinity, and Sun-worship was largely spread over the East, coming at length to have its votaries in Rome. This cult tended to destroy polytheistic beliefs and thus to prepare the way for the pure monotheism of Christianity.[4] The supreme God was held to be of infinite power, and embodied in his person qualities which were associated in the Graeco-Roman world with Zeus or Jupiter Optimus Maximus.[5]

The influx of Oriental cults into the West brought with it the Persian doctrines of good and evil. Evil was deified and worshipped as well as the supreme God. Judaism itself was perhaps indebted to the Mazdeans for its conception of Satan as a personal enemy to God and goodness. Mithraism, with its Iranian dualism and its rigorous system of morality, introduced into the West principles which still exercise a

[1] It is remarked by F. Cumont that 'the Greeks never received the god of their hereditary foes, the Persians. Mithras passed directly from Asia into the Latin world.' *Op. cit.* p. 179.

[2] *v.* F. Cumont, *op. cit.* p. 169; Wissowa, *op. cit.* p. 58.

[3] *v.* Cumont, *op. cit.* p. 66.

[4] Cumont, *op. cit.* p. 161.

[5] *v.* Cumont, *op. cit.* p. 153.

certain influence.[1] Renan has said that, if Christianity had been arrested in its progress by some fatal malady, the world would have been Mithraistic.[2] Such a surmise cannot be checked or tested, for no such catastrophe occurred. The Christian religion held on its victorious way. But a cult or system which could offer the serious rivalry which Mithraism undoubtedly presented, must have had elements of high moral and spiritual value.

Such was the religious condition of Rome at the close of the Republican era. The old deities of the city and of Italy, which had long been overlaid by their Greek names, while their cults had been affected by Greek externalism in art and conception, have almost ceased to attract the worshipper. The East has come in like a flood. While games and orgies help to win the multitude, the educated and thoughtful are taken with the dreamy mysticism of the East, with its attempted solution of the standing problems of good and evil, with its astrology and fatalism, its rationalistic contempt for polytheism, and its steady tendency towards the thought of One Supreme Being over against the power of evil. There were one or two other influences which began to be felt as the Republic neared its close. The effort of the authorities to stem the Greek invasion could not hinder the progress of philosophical studies among the more cultivated classes.

About B.C. 181, Pythagorean doctrines seem to have been introduced from lower Italy, and to have obtained some acceptance among educated people.[3] A few years later, the teaching of Epicurus became known. In theory it denied divine interest in human affairs, although Epicurus was mindful of the danger of breaking down the religious habits of the people and sought to cast over public morality the sanction of religion. Cicero pointed out the inconsistency of his philosophic theory with its practical results. 'If they are right who deny that the gods have any interest in human affairs, where is there room for *pietas, sanctitas, religio*? . . . What is the use of worship, of honour,

[1] *v.* Cumont, p. 186. A colony of worshippers of Mithras was to be found in Rome as early as the time of Pompey. The cult was not diffused until the Flavian period. *v.* Cumont, *ib.* p. 169.

[2] *M. Aurèle*, p. 579, quoted by Cumont, *op. cit.* p. 194.

[3] Wissowa, *op. cit.* p. 61; Fowler, *op. cit.* p. 349.

of prayer ?'[1] It was perhaps the chief triumph of Epicureanism in Rome that it enlisted the enthusiasm of Lucretius and inspired his work. On Roman character generally, its influence could not be salutary.[2] Its ideal of self-pleasing as the greatest good was, both for nation and individual, the reverse of elevating. Whatever favour it gained was quickly to disappear before the stronger and healthier teaching of the Stoics.

Stoicism, as more nearly akin to Roman modes of thought and feeling, found a home in the circle of the younger Scipio, and thereby obtained a vantage ground for setting the tone of prevailing thought. Q. M. Scaevola, Pontifex Maximus, who died in B.C. 82, recognized the truth of the Stoic conception of the gods, but held it to be unsuited to the people at large. He and Varro were both opposed to the progress of conceptions which threw doubt upon the old Roman faith, and taught that the sacrifices and other external ordinances of religion were without significance.[3] In spite of their efforts to preserve the practice of religion in the state—a religion which, as virtuous and noble-minded men, they knew to be untrue to fact and without support in reason—the distrust in its observances spread far and wide. The last years of the Republic were marked by a general neglect of the sacrifices, and with it a decline in the character and zeal of the priesthood.[4]

The Christian era is about to dawn. Augustus had been fighting his way to supreme power. After his victory over M. Antony and Cleopatra at Actium in B.C. 31, he set to work to re-establish public worship and to restore the priesthood and the temples, which alike had suffered from the general decay of the old religious beliefs.[5] On the death of Lepidus, his former rival, in B.C. 12, Augustus assumed the office of Pontifex Maximus, which accordingly became united to the Imperial dignity. He had already taken measures to raise the worship of Apollo to a

[1] *De Nat. Deor.* i. 2. 3.

[2] Cf. Fowler, *op. cit.* p. 361.

[3] Wissowa, *op. cit.* p. 62 f. *v.* S. Aug. *De Civ. Dei,* iv. 27 ; vi. 5. For the origin of Stoicism, *v.* above, p. 102.

[4] Wissowa has traced the causes and progress of this decline. *Op. cit.* p. 63 f.

[5] Virg. *Aen.* viii. 714 f. ; Hor. *Carm.* iii. 6, 1 f. 'The revival of the State religion by Augustus is at once the most remarkable event in the history of Roman religion, and one almost unique in religious history.' Fowler, *op. cit.* p. 428.

place of eminence equal to that of Jupiter, bringing the Sibylline books from the vaults of the Temple on the Capitol to the house of Apollo on the Palatine,[1] which, with the Temple of Diana and his new Temple of Vesta, joined hard to his own palace. By so doing, he made it clear that the central sanctuary of the state (for that was what the Temple of Apollo had come to be) and his own personal and family shrine were one and the same thing.

But a more eventful step was taken when Augustus admitted and encouraged the cult of his own person. At first this was indirect. Homage was paid to the 'genius' of Augustus.[2] His qualities of justice and clemency were recorded in provincial inscriptions. The gratitude of an Empire at peace, after centuries of war and internal strife, found utterance in ecstatic expressions. So it came about that Caesar after death was placed upon a level with the old gods of the Roman state; and then, as though impatient of waiting for posthumous honours, he accepts in his lifetime the same kind of worship which had been regarded as due only to the gods.[3] Augustus had a Flamen and a Feast-day appointed in his honour. Loyalty to the person of Caesar thus became a matter of religion. How great a part in the experience of the early Church was played by this new deification of one, who, however exalted, was but a man among men, is shown clearly enough by the martyrologies and by the allusions of the Christian Apologists.

The idea was not new. It was Hellenic and Oriental in origin. From the time of Alexander the Great, and largely through the extraordinary influence of his attractive personality, the conception of a god present in the form of the sovereign came to be entertained, especially in Egypt and Syria.[4] The terms 'Saviour,' 'Deliverer' were applied to the Diadochi. It was only natural that, when world-power became concentrated in the figure of the

[1] Wissowa, *op. cit.* pp. 67, 68, 242; Virg. *Aen.* vi. 72 f.

[2] The 'genius' is a conception found in the primitive period of Roman religion. As every spot and every business had its own tutelary power, so had every individual. The 'genius' was to the man what Vesta was to the domestic hearth, or Saturn to the work of the sowing time. It was only at a later time that the notion of a 'genius' of the Roman people was formed. *v.* Wissowa, *op. cit.* p. 22.

[3] *v.* Wissowa, *op. cit.* pp. 71, 72, 284.

[4] *v.* Wendland, *Die Hellen.-Römische Kultur*, p. 124 f. Cf. the inscription found at Rosetta which styles Ptolemy Epiphanes (196 B.C.) *αἰωνόβιος θεὸς ἐπιφάνης, εἰκόνος ζώσης τοῦ Διός.* Wendland, *ib.* p. 406.

Roman Emperor, his Eastern subjects should at once show a willingness to revive the old, familiar conception of a *numen praesens*. From the East this tendency passed to the capital, and the Senate was not behindhand in giving it official recognition. 'Alas,' said Vespasian at the approach of death, 'I shall be a god!'[1]

With all his zeal for reform and for the re-establishment of the old Roman faiths, Augustus can hardly be said to have effected any permanent revival of the former worship.[2] The concentration of dignity and office in his own person as Caesar, combined with the admission of the flattering homage of the city and the provinces,[3] speedily marred the results of his early religious reforms, and led the way to a new order of divinities from which the self-respect and common sense of serious men were bound to recoil.[4]

If we try to sum up the influence of the religion of the Roman people upon the preparation of the world for Christ, we should lay emphasis upon two distinct and widely separated epochs of that religion. One was that in which the word *pietas* got its true meaning—the sense of reverent devotion to a higher Power

[1] Wendland remarks on the close connection of this cult of the sovereign with political necessities. 'The cult of the Ruler is the religion of the new monarchies.' It is often an expression of thankfulness for deliverance from the strife and turmoil which the state had been going through. 'Men saw in the leader of the army the divine helper and Saviour (σωτήρ) who had done what seemed impossible in all human reckoning. . . . Godhead has appeared bodily in his person (ἐναργὴς ἐπιφάνεια, praesens deus).' *Ib.* p. 126. Cf. Holtzmann *N.T. Theologie*, i. p. 117.

[2] Privately it went on until the fourth century A.D. Christian Fathers speak of it as actually existing in their day. 'It was Ambrose of Milan, who enforced the final sentence of condemnation against Paganism.' Milman, *Hist. of Latin Christianity*, i. p. 101. 'The type of religion introduced by Augustus was unable to effect an actual revival of deep religious life. The new cult of the sovereign alone proved quickening, but its establishment meant the increasing downfall of the old faith.' P. Wendland, *op. cit.* p. 150.

[3] It was not until after Augustus that Caesar-worship took its most pronounced form. Even Tiberius, in words recorded by Tacitus (*Annals*, iii.), refused to have Temples dedicated to him. 'Ego me, patres conscripti, mortalem esse fateor.'

[4] Since the above was written, I find that Mr. Warde Fowler remarks that the new Emperor-worship 'led to practices which are utterly repulsive to us, and repulsive, too, to an honest man even in that day.' *The Religious Experience of the Roman People*, p. 438. But he insists that the resuscitation of the old worship was real and adds, it 'continued to exist for at least three centuries in outward form, and to some extent in popular belief.' *Ib.* pp. 429, 456.

—the moving principle of all that was best in the old religious life of early Rome. It was a time in which prayer, though formal in expression, was full of the sense of dependence on that Power.[1] The other was when a tribute was laid at the feet of Christ by the Stoic conception of duty—the right use of the reason with which man is endowed by the reason which is God.[2]

From these two widely parted sources—the old religion of the primitive Roman family and state and the philosophic teaching of the Stoics—men like Virgil caught something of the ideals which were soon to find their perfect exponent in Christ, and to mould the thought of the following age.[3] The old words pass on into the use of the Christian Church. *Pietas, religio, sanctus, sacer, sacramentum* are got ready in Roman workshops for more spiritual employment.[4]

As the last years of growing readiness for Christ are trembling on the verge of fulfilment, and Roman religion, touched into a new seriousness by Stoicism, has unconsciously put forth its best efforts to prepare for Him, a breeze of healthy expectation seemed to be passing over the lands which bordered on the Mediterranean. The *pax deorum* which the Emperor had striven hard to restore was accompanied by peace among men. The gratitude of the provinces lives in the inscriptions which record it.[5] Hope was springing up in many a breast, and it was reflected in the pre-

[1] Cf. Fowler, *ib.* p. 468.

[2] 'With Stoicism, man as intellect is a member of the rational Kosmos.' P. Wendland, *D. Hellen.-Römische Kultur*, p. 232. Cf. Gwatkin, *The Early History of the Church to* A.D. 313, i. p. 24.

[3] 'Love and Duty are the essentials of Christian ethics; they are both to be found in this poet.' Fowler, p. 455.

[4] *v.* Fowler, *op. cit.* p. 459 f. 'There were words of real significance in the old religion which were destined to become of permanent and priceless value in the Christian speech of the Western nations.' *Ib.* pp. 465, 469.

[5] Cf. the inscription (in Wendland, *op. cit.* p. 410) discovered in Asia Minor in celebration of the birthday of Augustus, 'The Eternal God has brought us the Saviour of mankind. Prayers have not remained unanswered. Land and sea are at peace. . . . The Saviour is born : a greater there cannot be.' Such was the language in which Asiatic officials greeted the recurring birthdays of the first Emperor. Do we not see in these wistful thoughts of a better time the unconscious tribute of a weary world to its true King and Saviour—garlands of praise for the brow which was to be crowned with thorns ? Augustus sleeps in dust. Christ lives and reigns in earth and heaven. *v.* Ramsay, *The Teaching of Saint Paul in Terms of the Present Day*, 1913, p. 284 f.; K. Furrer, *D. Leben Jesu Christi*, p. 43.

vailing religions. It was not confined to the world of Judaism. It was to be found in the Greek cults. It stirred in the efforts made by Augustus to revive the influence of the old Roman religion.[1]

Expectation loves to fasten on a tangible form or embodiment of itself. To the Roman, the remarkable personality of the Emperor made strong appeal. Words and titles are applied to him which to our thinking fit none but the Saviour of a world wider far than Caesar's. Something may have unconsciously been borrowed from Jewish apocalyptic: for the hopes of Israel must have been known to many a Roman both of the capital and of the provinces. But such borrowing, if it occurred, does not suffice to explain the full current of hope which ran pulsating through the Empire. A better time had come, and with it higher conceptions of man's place in the world and of his relation to the Power above. A sense of duty to God was attended by that of duty to man. Materials were already brought together which only needed the fire from heaven to enkindle them into the flame of Christian tenderness and love.

At this point we leave the story of the world's preparation for its Saviour. We pass from the dim foreshadowings of expectation to its visible fulfilment. If Rome is the last resting place for the pinions of hope, a village among the hills of Judaea is the spot on which it folds them up.

We have seen that four lines of preparation, four highways of religious thought, pass down through the centuries to meet in Bethlehem. Each had its own part to play in bringing about 'the fulness of the time.'[2] Each could contribute something which the others lacked, and without which the required conditions of readiness for Christ would have not been found.

No doubt there are regions of thought and experience which had not been entered when 'God sent forth His Son.' We err if, as we look upon His perfect humanity and think of Him as the final stage, the goal of human completeness, we regard Him as the sum of the long evolutionary process; as though in His Person He embodied the result of all human endeavour. That

[1] 'The longing for deliverance from the curse of guilt and sin and for the dawn of a new era already dominates the age of Augustus.' P. Wendland, *Die Hellen.-Römische Kultur*, p. 235. Cf. Virg. *Ecl.* iv. 4-17.

[2] Gal. iv. 4.

is not the way to look at Christ. A full current of thought and action swept on past Bethlehem as though it did not heed Him. Mighty forces, unknown to the ancient world, were to open out to the eager grasp and control of mankind. These things were not the concern of the Redeemer. He came to reveal God, to disclose the spiritual heights and depths of which manhood is capable. Science, learning, art did not interest One Who knew the eternal issues from within, Who weighed the world in the balances of heaven.[1] That is why we have to look back to find 'a perfect man, . . . the measure of the stature of the fulness of Christ,' in all that belongs to the moral and spiritual life; while we look forward to the more complete development of the material and aesthetic capacities of our nature. Only at last, at 'the times of the restitution of all things,' will the two streams of the evolutionary process meet, when 'we shall be like Him, for we shall see Him as He is.'

[1] *v.* below, p. 265.

CHAPTER VIII

MIRACLES AND HISTORY

It is being very freely asserted that any explanation of the origin of the Christian religion which deals with the 'supernatural' and therefore requires for its reception the organ of faith, can make no claim to be scientific. It is at once removed from the province of history and from the sphere of knowledge in any true sense of the word. It has to take its place in the region of pious opinion. It can never attain to the quality of ascertained fact.

Now Christianity, according to the judgment of its greatest exponents and by the consent of every generation of its adherents, owes its rise to the direct and immediate interposition of God in human history. Christ is not, according to this belief, the highest point in a long and orderly process of development, between which and the next preceding stage there is no radical difference to be noted. He makes an irruption into time and place.[1] By an act above and beyond our knowledge, He, the Infinite and the Eternal, enters into human life. He does not proceed from the bosom of humanity as its flower and crown. He comes into it from above. Heaven meets earth. The Son of God takes flesh and blood and 'is made man.'

Such a view—the distinctively Christian view of the rise of

[1] 'The Incarnation is emphatically presented to us in the New Testament as an advent; no mere event in the ordinary line of evolution, but the coming of One from a transcendent sphere.' Illingworth, *Divine Transcendence*, 1911, p. 8. 'Religion implies not only a transcendence of time but also an entry into time.' R. Eucken, *Hauptprobleme der Religionsphilosophie der Gegenwart*, E.T. p. 49. 'The affirmations of religion always originate in a disclosure or revelation of the Divine.... The Divine, in all the fulness of its splendour, can enter into the human.' *Ib.* p. 79.

Christianity—has, they say, no right to claim acceptance as a statement of historic fact. It belongs to another plane of thought, sharply to be contrasted with, and held apart from, that of scientific knowledge.[1] The miraculous stands *ipso facto* outside the cognizance of our understanding. We cannot apprehend as a fact of history, with an objective existence of its own, any occurrence in which the supernatural plays a part. Our organs of perception cannot grasp that portion of a mixed event, composed partly of supernatural and partly of natural elements. All reasoned knowledge must proceed according to the usual rules of our experience. We are men. We can only reason and judge as men. We have no other standard to apply than that of our ordinary experience. We can note reports of supernatural occurrences. We can study the mental condition of those who vouch for them, and the effect which is produced in their life and conduct by what they conceive to have happened. But we are not to imagine that we are dealing with facts. The only element of an historic character which enters into such a process is the subjective impression, which, however it is to be accounted for, is borne witness to by the persons concerned. Their experience—not its contents—is matter for historical narration. It is merely a psychological phenomenon, which deserves to be recorded according to its value as a step in the development of thought.

Such we believe to be no unfair description of the attitude which is being frequently taken up towards the traditional explanation of the origin of Christianity. It is very plausible and is so fully in harmony with much of the prevailing methods of thought that it appeals to many with a force which is entirely disproportionate to its real value.

In the first place, the supernatural facts which, as it is alleged, marked the entrance into the world of the Christian Religion, are not so easily to be waved aside. They come to us on evidence which is admitted to be honestly reported. No one worth quoting doubts the good faith of the Apostolic writers. The age when resort could be had to such a method of criticism as that has passed away. We know too much of the men and their ideals to entertain such a thought. The picture of Jesus of Nazareth, as it is drawn in the Gospels, is not the work of

[1] *v.* Pfleiderer, *Die Entstehung des Christentums*, p. 1 f.

dishonest men. It conveys the impression made upon the writers' minds by their actual experience.

And that experience was of a most remarkable kind. They found themselves in touch with One Who, though a man like themselves in all that constitutes the truth of manhood, gave clear signs of being in touch with God, as no man had ever been. Their experience of Him agreed with His own self-witness, as we have it in undoubted portions of the earliest Gospel story. He had manifestly come from God and in every moment of His life so lived with God that His presence, to all who could in any way enter into sympathy with Him, was nothing short of heaven on earth. Again and again, they had to confess that He stood apart from them. We have only to think of the character of His teaching, of His attitude to the religious authorities of His day, of the inner meaning of His works of power and mercy, of the victories won in the world by faith in His Resurrection, to feel that here was One Who was not as other men; Who in His life on earth brought to men something of the life which was being lived in heaven. You cannot get rid of the conviction that more than natural forces appeared to operate in Him Who yet was so intensely human in His daily intercourse with men.

To pursue this line of thought no further at present, let it suffice to remind ourselves that these proofs of the impression produced on the New Testament writers by the Personality of Christ are freely admitted by all reasonable schools of thought, and that, like other facts of human experience, they require to be taken into account. They point to something transcendental in Him; something which to bystanders was not to be explained by any theory of unusual human genius.

There is, then, a great and consistent mass of evidence reported in all good faith, which assures us of the unique Personality of Christ. We cannot reject it without shutting our eyes to hard fact. Again and again, in the writings of the keenest and most unsparing critics, we find recognition of this characteristic of His Person. It would therefore appear that, when the Gospel narrative reports a transcendental element in the origin of the Christian religion, we cannot offhand refuse it a place in our conception of historic fact.

For, to take such an attitude consistently, we should have

to exclude from the province of scientific thought all phenomena which are concerned with the spiritual life of man. That which is deepest and most true in human nature belongs to the unseen world. It evades accurate definition and preciseness of statement. Yet it is just here that we feel we are dealing with realities. They have to be taken account of and reckoned with, however little we understand them.[1]

Besides, even in matters of a scientific character, a large part of their material can only be apprehended by faith. The bare, sensible phenomena themselves do not suffice for our purposes. At every point, we are reminded that they are not all with which we have to do. Completeness of data is not to be had without access to the unseen—to that which cannot be comprised in any series of scientific formulae. We must have recourse to faith. That alone can furnish us with the assumptions without which no scientific investigation can proceed. Science rests on faith. That fixity of the natural order which is its necessary presupposition can never be proved. The sequence of cause and effect is matter of pious belief. We cannot demonstrate it; and yet with all this absence of precision in the underlying truths which we have to posit, who would say that the results of an investigation, which depends upon them for its very existence, have no scientific value and cannot be chronicled as matters of fact? To make such an assertion would mean to admit the impossibility of attaining accurate knowledge on any subject whatever.

If we take any ascertained fact of physics and inquire into the history of its discovery; if we ask what are the fundamental principles on which it rests and then consider the presuppositions which had to be admitted before a single step could be taken in the inquiry, we find ourselves landed in the region of mystery. We have gone back into a realm in which ordinary human experience fails us. The nature of matter, the origin of force, the sequence of cause and effect—all these are as much mysteries, transcending the power of man to interpret and explain, as are the 'supernatural' elements which, in the view of the Christian Church, are involved in the entrance into the world of the Christian

[1] Cf. R. Eucken, *op. cit.* p. 12, 'He who denies the spiritual life and its independence should know ... that concepts such as truth and goodness have for him no shadow of validity.'

religion. If in the one case we do not exclude the result arrived at from the category of scientific knowledge and from the domain of history, we are not at liberty to exclude the other. Both are alike rooted in the supra-sensible lying altogether beyond the reach of human experience. Yet both alike enter into life, present themselves to our perception, figure on the ground of history, influence our decisions and are matters of practical moment. On what ground of reason and common sense can we deny to one, what we yield to the other—a place in our practical knowledge?

Is there not a fallacy common to much of the prevailing thought on this subject—the idea that directly you have recourse to faith as an instrument of perception, you pass out of the region of knowledge and experience, into that of mere opinion? Whereas the converse is the case. It is just where the deeper, primal faculties of our nature come into play, when we walk by faith and not by sight, that we are most true to ourselves and enter most fully into that which forms the true glory of humanity.

There can therefore be no ground for denying an historical character to that mode of explaining the origin of Christianity which attributes it to the direct interposition of God in human life, on the score that it requires the agency of faith. It is neither more nor less a matter of history and of accurate knowledge than any other conclusion, in which the necessary presuppositions depend on faith. Logically there is no distinction between them.[1] In each case we have to admit certain principles, which we cannot prove, but which are necessary for our purpose, and without which we can make no progress. They are arrived at by methods which fall short of mathematical certainty and yet the common sense of humanity requires our acceptance of them; and in religion it is common sense which is appealed to. If Christianity could not justify itself before the bar of the rational, sober judgment of men of open mind, it could never win its way, as it has done and is doing, to their allegiance.

But if the parity of circumstance attending the presuppositions of scientific inquiry and of religion be admitted, there remains the widespread reluctance to accept miraculous happenings. The spirit of the age, the tone of mind of the ordinary thinking man, is averse to receive an explanation of the origin of Christianity

[1] *v.* G. Hilbert, *Christentum u. Wissenschaft*, p. 172.

which is implicated in miraculous phenomena. A non-miraculous Christianity, we are told, is in line with the present character of thought and knowledge. Men want ethics rather than metaphysics—a guide to conduct, not an essay in speculation. Strip the Gospel of the story of the Virgin-birth, of the Resurrection and the Ascension, and you will have all that a man needs to guide him through time to the unknown future. A non-miraculous Christianity is the religion for the present day.

A widespread tone of mind requires investigation. To what are we to attribute this impatience of miraculous happenings ? [1]

There is little doubt that the scientific progress of the last fifty or sixty years has been a factor in this change of view. Every advance in science has widened the basis of our conviction of the reign of order and law. The belief itself is as old as human consciousness. Primitive man acted on the principle that similar causes are followed by similar results under similar conditions. The Old Testament is full of the recognition of the majestic order which pervades the world. But modern science has vastly widened and consolidated the foundation of this belief, with the result that men are inclined to be impatient of any apparent infringement of order.

I say apparent : for, strictly speaking, the root-principle of order, the fact that similar causes are followed under similar circumstances by the same results, is stedfast and runs through all nature in its widest sense. On this principle we base our freedom of action and our trust in God. It is a principle which necessarily follows from the conception of the universe as a cosmos pervaded by moral purpose, and not as chaos. We should have no security in bodily or in spiritual things if we could not rely upon it.

When a miracle occurs, it does not break this order.[2] That remains unaffected. It is the result which is changed by the

[1] 'Once regarded as the great bulwark of Christian faith, they are now regarded as its greatest burden.' Fairbairn, *Studies in the Life of Christ*, p. 149. 'If miracle was once an instrument of Apologetics, it has now become an object of apology.' K. Beth, *Das Wunder*, p. 13. There is some exaggeration in these statements, but they represent the attitude of many Christian people.

[2] It is a mistake to speak of the order of nature being 'suspended' by miracle, as, *e.g.* P. Gardner does. *Exploratio Evangelica*, p. 232. *v.* S. Aug. *De Civit. Dei*, xxi. 8, 'Portentum ergo fit, non contra naturam, sed contra quam est nota natura.' Dr. Sanday too speaks of 'alleged events that are contra

introduction of a fresh antecedent. If I raise my arm, the action of gravitation is not suspended; but a new factor, the effort of my will, comes in and produces a different result. When the dead were raised, the laws of life and death were not in abeyance. A new force entered the complex of antecedents, modifying their effect, and the dead were restored to life. Against the possibility of such an occurrence, science, as science, has nothing to say. 'Denying the possibility of miracles seems to me quite as unjustifiable as speculative Atheism,' wrote Professor Huxley long ago;[1] and Paulsen has said,[2] 'Should occasion demand, philosophy has a place for miracles.'

But from this position, a long step must be taken before a miracle is admitted as fact. Granted that nothing on the score of either science or philosophy can be said against it *à priori*, its occurrence has to be established. And for this purpose, two things have to be taken into account—the adequacy of the occasion; the nature of the specific evidence.

The adequacy of the occasion is to be considered from the side of God as well as from that of man. On what we know of the steady, even method of God's work in nature and in grace, we are justified in concluding that only an exceptional condition of things would lead Him to vary that method. At the rise of Christianity did such a condition obtain? Every Christian —one might even say every Theist—will admit that the beginning of our present era constituted an epoch in the relations of God and Man. Long prepared for in the history of the chosen race and by converging lines of thought and movement in other religions, the Incarnation marked a supreme effort and interposition for man on the part of God. Human need, human sin and human suffering were met within the limitations of humanity by One whose Person in its truth and fulness was Divine. Then, if ever, it might be anticipated that great things might come about. God had visited His people. Divine love manifested

naturam' as involving 'some definite reversal of the natural physical order.' *Bishop Gore's Challenge to Criticism*, p. 23. Cf. S. Aug. *Contra Faustum*, xxvi. 3, G, 'Sed contra naturam non incongrue dicimus aliquid Deum facere, quod facit contra id quod novimus in natura ... Contra illam vero summam naturae legem a notitia remotam, sive impiorum sive adhuc infirmorum, tam Deus nullo modo facit, quam contra se ipsum non facit.'

[1] *Spectator* for Feb. 10, 1866.

[2] *Einleitung in die Philosophie*, E.T. p. 297.

itself to mortal eye, as never before. The whole wealth of Divine grace appeared in active form. The war between good and evil came to a climax.[1] The salvation of mankind was being worked out by their Creator. Heaven touched earth. Is it likely that, at such a time, when such forces were at work, 'all things' would 'continue as they were'—that no sign of what was going on should be given, that the presence of the Redeemer among the objects of His redemption would remain unmarked, His passage through the world accompanied by no token that 'a greater than Solomon was here'? The probability lies all the other way: for the occasion was adequate. It was worth while—if we may so speak—for God to manifest His presence by signs, which, not by mere exhibition of bare power, but by acts of love in correspondence with His gracious purposes, might confirm the impression made upon men's minds by His Person.

But we are still in the region of preparatory, *à priori* argument. Many will be able to follow so far without dissent. We have yet to prove the actual occurrence of the miraculous. Its possibility is one thing; the adequate importance of the occasion is another. They each lead us to the crucial question and make it rational—did miracles actually take place?

It has been argued, by no one more forcibly than by Hume, that the evidence, furnished by those who have borne witness to them in the Gospels and other parts of the New Testament, does not suffice to counterbalance the weight of improbability presented by consideration of the ordinary course of nature. He declares that miracles are contrary to experience. But this is the very point in question.[2] We affirm that there *is* evidence of their occurrence in abundance, and that its peculiar strength lies in its connection with the historic ground-work of the Saviour's life.[3] They are not mere prodigies foisted upon Him with the view of colouring the narrative and heightening the effect of what He does or says. They form integral features in the Life, which becomes inexplicable if we remove them.[4] Besides, they are

[1] Cf. for different aspects of the same strife Lk. x. 18; xxii. 53.

[2] *v.* Fisher, *Grounds of Theistic and Christian Belief*, p. 110. For J. S. Mill's refutation of Hume's argument *v. Essays on Religion*, p. 221.

[3] 'In Mark,' says A. Schweitzer, 'the natural and the supernatural stand in equally good and sound historic connection.' *Von Reimarus zu Wrede*, p. 304.

[4] After the feeding of the 5000, such was the effect of the miracle upon the multitude that they proceeded 'to take Him by force, to make Him a

entirely congruous with His declared object in coming among us. They proclaim, in the form of acted parable, His love and care for the souls and bodies of men. They are always worked for others: never for Himself. Always to relieve or heal, to teach, or comfort others: never for self-preservation, never for display, never to win a victory in conflict. They always subserve the purpose of His love. They stand in the Gospel narratives, because they form part of the course of events. Any account of Christ from which they were absent would be misleading and incomplete.

Some who admit freely the restraint and the harmony with the general character of our Lord's life, which mark the Gospel narratives of His miracles, are withheld from belief in them by what they think is due to the highest conception of God's mode of working. They deem it a more reverent view to regard the settled, undeviating course of nature as the true expression of His will. Interruptions seem arbitrary and significant of caprice, or of a lack of foresight which needs repair. They think to honour God more by ascribing to Him equal perfection in design and issue, than by admitting intervention.

There would be force in this contention, if the matter was concerned with the Divine action alone. But the will of man and his sinful history have to be taken into account. By the gift of freedom God admitted the possibility that wills would be set against Him; and the possible has happened. Miracle is one aspect of the Divine effort towards restoration. The failure to which, according to the theory quoted, it bears witness, lies not in the incapacity of God, but in the sin of man. Freedom of will is dearly purchased. We pay a high price for our standing among God's creatures. 'But where sin abounded, grace did much more abound.' [1] And of that grace the miraculous element in our Lord's life—above all the miracle of His Self-Resurrection [2] —was a sign not to be mistaken. It pointed to the Creator's

king.' The miracle revealed *the Messiah.* This popular fervour was ill-timed. He withdrew (Jo. vi. 15). So, too, the events connected with the Entry into Jerusalem are closely bound up with the miracle of the raising of Lazarus (Jo. xii. 9 f.).

[1] Rom. v. 20.

[2] Jo. ii. 19; x. 18; Ignat. *Ad Smyrn.* (Ἰησοῦς Χριστός) ἀληθῶς ἔπαθεν, ὡς καὶ ἀληθῶς ἀνέστησεν ἑαυτόν. *v.* Pearson, *An Exposition of the Creed*, i. p. 302 f

redeeming action. It was of a piece with His purpose and with His method.

Arguing from the analogy of the modification of the results of natural law which can be effected by the action of the personal will, we conclude that the will of a transcendent, yet immanent, Divine Being may be reasonably expected to modify the ordinary course of things, if the occasion for His so doing is adequate. To gain this position places us in readiness to receive with open mind whatever evidence of such action is forthcoming.

But here again there will be some who will call a halt. Think, they say, of the change of outlook. To the New Testament writers, as to the first disciples, this earth was the centre of the universe. Many centuries were to roll by before Copernicus taught the insignificance of the earth and its place and movements in the solar system. On his statue at Thorn are the proud words, 'Stator solis, motor terrae.' But perhaps it is only within recent years that the full significance of his discoveries has come to be recognized. To an extended view of things as a whole, with its corollary of the smallness of our own world, has been added, through the general acceptance of the theory of evolution, the conviction that the world is very old. Extension in space has come to be met by extension in time. What is man, what are his interests amid the vastness of the universe?

When to this change of attitude towards the probability of the occurrence of a miracle, are added difficulties arising from the critical study of the documents, we find, in the case of many educated people, a certain unwillingness to commit themselves to the acceptance of a narrative in which miracle figures. They prefer to suspend their judgment. Or, moved by reverence for all God's handiwork, they decline to distinguish between the 'natural' and the 'supernatural,' still more between the 'natural' and the 'contranatural,' as banishing God from the world.[1]

In thus refusing to draw a distinction between the ordinary course of God's action and an extraordinary or 'supernatural' activity, men may appear more reverent in that they see God everywhere and at all times, not merely in occasional outbursts of energy. But after all, the distinction objected to is relative. From the point of view of God Himself, one kind of action is as

[1] *v.* Inge in *The Church Family Newspaper*, May 22, 1914.

normal as the other. It is from our own standpoint that the miraculous is removed poles apart from the ordinary, or 'natural,' as we call it. And when we draw the distinction, we are not 'handing over the natural order to some power which is not Divine,' [1] rather we are allowing to God the freedom to act in His own world in a manner which is not that of His ordinary working, and which may, on occasion, be something wholly unique, as in the Incarnation itself.[2]

It is therefore beside the mark to charge belief in the miraculous with a dualism which banishes God from the world. On the contrary, the belief implies a mind open to receive assurance that for an adequate end—the salvation of man, made in His image—He is willing to employ means which the ordinary course of His world-government does not require. Should we not welcome such activity in the spirit of Jacob at Bethel, 'Surely the Lord is in this place'? Everywhere, if we are wise, we trace God's presence and action. Yet here and there, can we not see that that presence is intensified, that action raised to higher levels of power and significance? To deny this, is to shut one's eyes to the Christian Revelation. It is not a question of attitude to a narrative of miracle; but to the fact of Christ Himself—Incarnate, Risen, Ascended, Glorified.

When we reach this stage, we are in a position to look at the question from the converse point of view. We are standing face to face with a Personality Who, even on the admission of men who do not accept the miraculous element in the Gospel, stood apart, solitary, unique among men.[3] Once has appeared on earth One Who is unapproachable in His likeness to God, in His summing up in His own Person of everything that befits a man. Such a Personality is instinct with Power: and if, on evidence which seems rooted in fact, we are assured that miracles followed upon His footsteps as the flowers at the call of spring, can we wonder? They seem the natural, proper works of such as He, the easy exercise of the Divine energy with which He was stored; so that, when occasion offered, 'power came forth from Him and healed them all.' [4] That at

[1] *v.* Inge, *op. cit.* [2] *v.* Illingworth, *The Gospel Miracles*, p. 142.

[3] For detailed evidence of this admission, see C. Nolloth, *The Person of Our Lord and Recent Thought*, p. 354 f. with notes.

[4] Lk. vi. 19.

least was the view of one who knew Him best. Speaking of the greatest of His miracles—His triumph over death—St. Peter said 'it was not possible that He should be holden of it.' [1] It was against the nature of things that the grave could hold the Lord of Life on Easter Day. The miracle of the Resurrection is bound up with His Person. Like His acts of power, when 'He went about doing good,' it belongs to an order far above our understanding. Looked at from below, it is supernatural. Looked at from the side of nature *as a whole*, as the sum of things, it is profoundly natural. It answers to the Person concerned.

No one, who realizes the greatness of God's purpose in the salvation of man, can say that if, in the Incarnation, God indeed came among us, the exceptional character of the means which He employed is too difficult to believe. Rather would it be strange, if so fresh and wonderful an incursion into the ordinary course of things did not bring with it a new and striking development, not from existing conditions, but out of the heart of the movement which He inaugurated. 'In Thee is the well of Life.'

To a merely humanitarian view of Christ, this line of thought makes no appeal. He is simply a link in a long chain of phenomena, exceptional perhaps in genius and in spiritual acquirement, but nothing more. On such a theory, it may seem more natural to impute delusion or error to the Christian witnesses than to admit such a break in the accustomed order as a wonder-working Christ implies. But then, questions of the greatest difficulty, going down to the heart not only of religion, but of morals, remain unanswered: questions that are not merely speculative, but to which we cannot remain silent and unresponsive. If the historic cross and grave of Christ have been succeeded by no Easter morning, it is not too much to say that we men still walk in darkness; a darkness deeper and more hopeless than that of the pre-Christian era. Then, there was anticipation that God would one day vindicate His ways to man; and One has come, whose life and character present, even to those who do not accept Him as their guide, a faultless example of holiness and goodness: yet men 'have done unto Him whatsoever they listed,' [2] and on this theory, God has made no sign. The Life, which has set

[1] Acts ii. 24.

[2] Matt. xvii. 12. Said of St. John the Baptist. But Christ applies the description, by anticipation, to His own case.

in motion the most beneficent work for the healing of the nations, has gone down to the grave by a violent and shameful death, and no message of hope has come from it. Nay more, that masterpiece of love, the Christian Church with all its agencies of uplifting for the souls and bodies of men, is founded on a cruel illusion. 'If Christ be not raised, your faith is vain: ye are yet in your sins.'[1]

On the other hand, the difficulties which attend belief in the occurrence of phenomena like the Gospel miracles, do not come to us weighted, as are the difficulties of unbelief, with considerations that play fast and loose with every principle of truth and justice. They are the difficulties which are to be met with in other fields of knowledge. They are concerned with disparities of evidence. They arise from the different points of view from which the facts are regarded; while, through every narrative run the clearest indications of sincerity and earnestness. He must indeed be untaught by the Spirit who does not note the presence of an inspiring touch, everywhere controlling and directing, illuminating and strengthening the hearts and minds of the Apostolic witnesses and writers.

Difficulties attend the investigation of every subject directly we get beneath the surface and try to see things as they are, to trace their antecedents, to bring them into harmony with other facts. We can afford, in most cases, to wait patiently for their solution. The march of knowledge tends to unity and simplicity. The supposed barriers between the spiritual and the material are breaking down.[2] There are signs that the conjunction and interaction of the 'natural' and the 'supernatural' will cease to present any serious obstacle to a reverent outlook upon the world. Every day the majesty of the moral order grows upon the mind. The progress of knowledge deepens our sense of the spiritual purpose which runs through creation. In Christ alone seems to be the safeguard that that purpose will one day be accomplished. But, as Christians hold, it is a Christ Who is God Incarnate, a 'Christ that died, yea rather, that is risen again, Who is even at the right hand of God.' In this belief and all that it means we think we have the key which will one day unlock 'all mysteries and all knowledge.'

[1] 1 Cor. xv. 17. [2] *v.* below, p. 365. [3] Rom. viii. 34.

CHAPTER IX

THE BIRTH OF JESUS CHRIST

THE world was ready for its Saviour. It was the hour. 'When the fulness of the time was come God sent forth His Son, made of a woman.'[1] The varied lines of preparation in the three great divisions of the world—Jewish, Greek, Roman—have drawn together. They started far apart. They had nothing in common. Yet they met at last; and their meeting-place was a village among the hills of Judaea.[2] Bethlehem had been designated by the prophet Micah in a passage well known to the Rabbis.[3] It was the city of David. Already in his day it was historic ground. There Jacob had buried Rachel. In its fields were enacted those idyllic scenes which make the pastoral beauty of the book of Ruth. It was well-named 'the House of Bread'; for plenty surrounded it, and within it was first to be seen 'the true bread . . . which cometh down from heaven.'[4]

The circumstances which led to the fulfilment of Micah's prophecy, and caused the 'greater Son' of David to be born within the walls of David's city, were so remarkable in their incongruity with the traditions of the race that they afford strong confirmation of the Gospel account. What brought the mother with her affianced husband to Bethlehem? At the moment when the hopes of the nation were to be fulfilled, when the promised Messiah and Redeemer was to appear in Person,

[1] Gal. iv. 4. 'The pre-Christian religions were the age-long prayer. The Incarnation was the answer.' Illingworth in *Lux Mundi*, p. 150.

[2] Micah v. 2. 'Thou, Bethlehem Ephrathah, which art little to be among the thousands of Judah, out of thee shall One come forth unto Me that is to be Ruler in Israel; whose goings forth are from of old, from everlasting.'

[3] Matt. ii. 4 f.

[4] Jo. vi. 32, 33.

when the Son of David was to be born, the place of His birth is dictated by a decree of the heathen Emperor of Rome. It was Caesar Augustus who fixed the birthplace of the Saviour. He was the last link in the chain of causes which fulfilled the prophecy of eight centuries ago, and gave to the city of Judah its deathless place among the cities of the world. But the strangeness of the interposition, the alien character of the determining factor, proves the truth of the story. When we consider the conflicting views which are held respecting the actual birthplace of Christ, and try to estimate the historic value of St. Luke's assurance that it was an imperial enrolment which brought Mary and Joseph from Nazareth to Bethlehem at the very moment of her expected deliverance—an assurance corroborated by the allusion of the First Gospel [1]—this consideration should have its weight. What brought the affianced pair to Bethlehem? Obedience—not to the well-remembered voice of prophecy, not to the call of ancestral feeling and to the claims of tradition, but—to the stern command of a hated ruler, whose every act served only to remind men of the height from which they had fallen, and of the tyranny to which their land was subject. Yet St. Luke, writing with accurate knowledge of all the events which he describes from the very first,[2] gives this reason for the journey. It is true that he is our sole informant of the fact, and his accuracy as an historian has been disputed on the ground that he confused the enrolment which took place in A.D. 6-7 with a supposed census in the time of Herod. But he refers elsewhere to the later census,[3] and it is wholly improbable that he would confound the two. The more momentous the occurrence which he has to chronicle, the greater would be his care for truth. Would he be likely, at the outset of his Gospel, after an earnest declaration of his power to confirm the instruction which was being given to catechumens, to prejudice his claim to accuracy by a mistake in a matter of common knowledge, which his readers would be at once in a position to refute? Taking us, as he does, into regions of fact and thought where faith alone can follow him, would he destroy our confidence in his guidance by a blunder in the history of the day? The Evangelist, in the course of his two great contributions to the New Testament Scriptures, has given us too many pledges of his truthfulness as an historian to make us

[1] Matt. ii. 1. [2] Lk. i. 3, ἄνωθεν. [3] Acts v. 37.

doubt him here. The narrative offers so much that surprises us—the journey of days by a woman at such a time of expectation, the outcast condition in which the pair found themselves on arrival—that we feel that a story told so circumstantially, so simply and under such a sense of responsibility as St. Luke must have felt, by its very strangeness appeals to us. An inventor would have taken another course. We have only to glance at the figments of the apocryphal writers to see what invention does. To turn from them to the Evangelist is to pass from the region of wanton fancy to that of soberness and truth. A careful historian, like St. Luke, would not assign the journey to Bethlehem to a great historic event if, as he knew,[1] that only took place twelve years afterwards. If invention and error are on such a point out of the question, our only reasonable attitude is to trust the historian's account of the main features of the event, giving due weight to the word πρώτη, with its implication of an earlier process of enrolment than the well-known one of A.D. 7, and to the indeterminate character of the hegemony of Quirinius at the time.[2]

[1] Acts v. 37.

[2] The whole question of the enrolment has been discussed again and again. The above considerations may tend to convince us that St. Luke was writing true history, when he gave the first carrying out of the edict of the Emperor as the direct cause of the birth of the Child of Mary of Nazareth at Bethlehem—the place assigned by St. Matthew. It is probable that Quirinius twice held office in Judaea. The word used is vague, ἡγεμονεύοντος. *v.* Plummer, *St. Luke*, p. 51. The first time, his hegemony may have been a post in connection with the enrolment, not the governorship; for the names of two other Romans cover the time from B.C. 9 down to the death of Herod.

Cf. Schürer, *op. cit.* i. p. 534; but *v.* Ramsay, below. Tertullian, *Adv. Marc.* iv. 19, gives the name of the official by whom the enrolment was carried out as Sentius Saturninus. It is possible that St. Luke, unconsciously influenced by the connection of Quirinius with the later census (*v.* Josephus, *Antiq.* xviii. 1. 1), and knowing that he had been engaged in administration in Judaea at an earlier date, may have been in error so far as to connect him, rather than his predecessor Saturninus, with the enrolment which brought the Holy Family to Bethlehem. So slight an error in a long-past detail does not render the general tenor of his account incredible. In its main outline, it definitely connects their presence so far from home at that time and in that place with the imperial enrolment. There is every ground for receiving it. No historian is rightly discredited, who, in a recital which bears all the marks of general truth, makes a slip—and that is all that could be alleged, in view of our present knowledge, against St. Luke—in connecting an event with one official rather than another, his predecessor by a short time. At any time, evidence may be discovered for the justification of St. Luke's statement as it stands. We

Both the First and Third Gospels, although differing in the point of view from which they regard the event, place the Nativity at Bethlehem. It is characteristic that, while the Gospel for the Gentiles connects it with the Roman edict, the Gospel for the Hebrews is content to link it with prophecy. But it is Bethlehem and not Nazareth to which they each point. When two such different testimonies agree in an historical affirmation and set it down at a time when error, if error there were, could at once be refuted, it is only reasonable to accept it. There is nothing more remarkable in the attitude of the 'advanced' representatives of German theology than their persistent refusal to receive this witness of the two Evangelists. We have again and again the dogmatic assertion that Jesus was born at Nazareth. The first two chapters of St. Matthew and St. Luke are either set on one side as no part of the original editions of their respective Gospels, and as reflecting a form of tradition which only grew up after the actors in the event described had all passed away, and which had no foundation in fact; or, as with J. Wellhausen, they are excluded, without a word of allusion, from their proper places in the forefront of the narrative. The reason of this attitude is not far to seek. Each recital is full of the 'supernatural.' That suffices to condemn it. Each aims at giving an account of the entrance into the world of the Son of God; and those who admit no divine element in His Personality, who see in Him but one constituent—if an eminent one—in the long process of the evolution of the human race, naturally turn from a narrative that clothes a merely human event in the garment of the supernatural. Thus the matter is foreclosed. Mystery is rejected. All must be on the level of ordinary, matter-of-fact life. There is no sign of any feeling that He Whom they confess to be unique among men, and to have known the mind of God as no one else has known it,[1] may perhaps have come into the world

already know that a similar enrolment was made in Egypt. *v.* P. Gardner in *Encycl. Bibl.* iv. col. 3995 ff.; Turner in Hastings' *D.B.* i. 404. Cf. Ramsay, *Expos.* Nov. 1912, 'We can now prove by indisputable contemporary evidence that Quirinius was governing Syria about the time of this first census' (B.C. 8). 'There was a system of periodical enrolments in the Roman Empire, at least in the Eastern Provinces, the first of which took place in 9-8 B.C.' Some of the census papers have been found in Egypt.

[1] For detailed evidence of these admissions of 'advanced' criticism, *v. The Person of Our Lord*, p. 354, n. 1.

in a manner corresponding with the strangeness and individuality of His Person.

The very fact that such things are said of Him by responsible writers, who in other portions of their narrative reveal their love of truth, should make us pause before rejecting them. If the Gospels were mere miracle-stories, employing incidents that touch earth solely to give a background to the miraculous, we might well suspect them. But the miraculous plays no such part in them. It is there, not for its own sake, but for the completeness of the story, which would be untrue and defective without it.[1]

What was the source of the Evangelists' knowledge? The compiler of the First Gospel must have had access to the mind of Joseph directly, or through an intermediary; for he gives us the processes of reasoning and consideration which led Joseph to act as he did.[2] St. Luke betrays no less clearly the guidance of the Blessed Virgin herself. When he was at Jerusalem with

[1] The two first chapters of the First and Third Gospels are of the same date of composition as the rest of their chapters. As regards the first, Burkitt remarks, 'I believe that Matt. i. ii. form an integral part of the First Gospel.' *Evangelion Da-Mepharreshe*, ii. p. 259. 'When we ask ourselves whether these chapters belong to the rest of the Gospel, or whether they are to be regarded as a later insertion, we find that the internal literary evidence is extraordinarily strong in their favour.' *Ib.*

With regard to Lk. i. ii., it has been shown that while the contents are strongly Hebraic and point not only in expression but in thought and feeling to very early sources of knowledge, they are the work of St. Luke and are of a piece with the rest of his Gospel. For instance, the Benedictus is more Jewish than Christian, and could only have been composed at the time and under the circumstances to which the Evangelist assigns it. The language of Elizabeth, and the Magnificat, which there seems no sufficient reason to cease ascribing to the Blessed Virgin (*v.* Burn in Hastings' *Dict. of Christ.* ii. art. 'Magnificat'; *v.* below, p. 166), are full of Jewish feeling and betray close familiarity with Old Testament models. But, with all this archaic material embedded in his narrative, the style of the writer of the Third Gospel and of the Acts is everywhere apparent. This has been clearly brought out by Hawkins, *Horae Synopticae*, p. 23; Harnack, *Lukas der Arzt*, p. 72 f., and others. The songs contained in Lk. i. ii. show signs of being the Evangelist's translations from written Aramaic sources, for while full of Old Testament terms and ideas, they also abound in Lucan phrases. *v.* Moffatt, *Introduction to the Liter. of the N.T.* p. 271; G. H. Box believes in Hebrew originals. *The Virgin Birth of Jesus*, 1916, p. 44 f.

[2] Matt. i. 19, 20. 'Joseph, her husband . . . was minded to put her away privily. But while he thought on these things, behold, the angel of the Lord appeared unto him in a dream.' Cf. also i. 25, ii. 22, 'he was afraid to go thither.'

St. Paul,[1] he would have had opportunity of intercourse 'with eye-witnesses and ministers of the word '[2] and men or women who had known the Blessed Virgin. If she herself had passed away,[3] St. John was living and somewhere the two may have met. But St. Luke must not only have conversed with those who could tell him of the events surrounding the Birth of the Saviour; he clearly had access to written records. The style of the two first chapters of his Gospel amply proves this. It points to the use of written Aramaic sources, which may have originated in memoranda of the Holy Family; for its Greek is full of Semitic terms of speech, as unlike as possible the Greek of the prologue, and yet, with all this colouring from the translated or adapted sources, it is the Greek of St. Luke.[4]

Here, then, in the *Vorgeschichte* of the two Gospels we have narratives which, if they are to be regarded as in any sense historical, go back for their data to the two most highly privileged of mankind—the Mother and the Guardian and Foster-Father of our Lord. Proceeding from such different sources, they naturally present great differences in point of view, in material, in setting. We have the secret communings of each of the Parents. They approach the one main object of their thought in quite different ways. They are each perplexed—the 'just man' and the pure Virgin. The same wondrous event comes before the mind of each. Differ as they must in the thoughts to which it gives rise, they are alike in their submission and obedience to the will of God, when it is made known to them. Intensely oriental is the method of its revelation in each case. To the man God's will is revealed in dreams. To the Virgin Mother an angel appears. Each mode of communication may be but a figurative description of the imparting of an impulse, which they each recognized as an utterance of the Divine will. But whether our interpretation of these parts of the narrative is figurative or literal, we have to own, if we accept it at all, that in some way God specially made known to these favoured ones what He

[1] Acts xxi. 15 f. St. Luke was in Palestine about A.D. 57 or 58.

[2] Lk. i. 2. Sanday in *Critical Questions*, p. 139, suggests that 'Joanna, the wife of Chuza, Herod's steward,' was the connecting link between the Blessed Virgin and St. Luke.

[3] But *v.* Ramsay, *Was Christ born at Bethlehem?* p. 85 ff., p. 74.

[4] For detailed proof of this *v.* Hawkins, *Horae Synopticae*, pp. 14 ff., 23. Cf. Plummer on *Lk.* i. 5; Sanday in *Critical Questions*, 1903, p. 134.

would have them do. They bow their heads in obedience and yield themselves each to that part in the great mystery that was appointed for them—the one to be the Mother of the Son of God, the other to be the protector of His childhood and His youth.

Another characteristic of the two narratives is their extreme simplicity and restraint. Their theme is the highest imaginable. It enters into the 'supernatural' and transcends our power to follow. Yet the story is told with a quiet beauty, a sense of reverence, an absence of all striving for effect, a conviction of its truth, which differentiates it from all other such narratives, whether apocryphal or legendary. If, as Renan says of St. Luke's Gospel as a whole, 'c'est le plus beau livre qu'il y ait,' its beauty culminates in its outset. There is nothing so supreme in loveliness in all the literature of the world. If, in forming our estimate of the trustworthiness of a person, we go largely by the manner of his speech, still more will the style and character of a written record attract or repel our confidence. Never, certainly, has tale been told that on the face of it bears the sign of its sincerity and truthfulness so clearly impressed. Those, who reject the first two chapters of the First and Third Gospels on *a priori* grounds, have to explain how it has come about that the narratives contain all the marks of being accounts of fact, and were received by the Christian communities who had the opportunity of testing a large proportion of their statements. Authentic and responsible writings are not to be waved aside because they run counter to certain presuppositions, which can appeal to nothing but subjective views of the world for their authority. Let it be remembered that science has no quarrel with the narratives of the Virgin-birth, while the writings which enshrine them bear all the marks of genuine history. They pass out of the sphere of science when they speak of the miraculous Conception, of the angel who announced it, of the chorus of angels on the night of the Nativity; just as in many a branch of scientific research the investigator quickly reaches a stage in his proceedings which his knowledge cannot penetrate. Certain phenomena elude his power to explain them. He is conscious of their presence in the point he is investigating, but he can give a scientific account neither of the phenomena themselves nor of their mode of acting upon the object of his research. This is especially true in such a phenomenon as electricity. Yet who would deny to its study and treatment the designation 'scientific'? In the same way, we can claim for narratives such as these which we are considering, that they are not to be excluded from the domain of scientific, historical knowledge, because at certain well-defined points they pass into a region where faith alone can come into touch with them. It is a mark of true science, as distinguished from charlatanism, to know its limitations. It is no less a mark to be able to recognize in its subject-matter the presence of a factor which, however inexplicable, is yet a very real element in the complex with which it is dealing, and to which it must give due importance in its description of the phenomena involved.

Now, it is just in this respect that so much of present criticism appears defective and inadequate to its task, when dealing with the Gospel narratives. Such an event as the entrance into human life of the Eternal Son of God might be expected to be linked with phenomena of an unusual kind. Unless we are prepared to surrender all conviction of His unique character, and to regard Him as but one of the most highly endowed among the leaders of mankind, we shall be prepared for events and conditions of a 'supernatural' order.[1] Only a thorough-going naturalistic conception of Christianity can warrant our feeling differently.

For the miraculous element is presented to us with such singular moderation, if we may so speak. It is nowhere assumed where ordinary instrumentality is adequate. Situations are not created for its exhibition. It is there because no other means would suffice;[2] and it is so serenely natural and germane to its surroundings and accompaniments that it never disturbs the even and quiet flow of the narrative. Read these chapters to an intelligent child, and he is not repelled as by the intrusion of a jarring element. He wonders, as well he may, but because he can wonder, he is able to understand and to adore. If the Birth of Jesus Christ were told in the Gospels as a bare fact with no hint of any connection with a higher order than the 'natural,' with no touch of mystery, no sign of any feeling that here was an event of the first magnitude, an epoch and a new starting-

[1] *v.* Stanton, *The Jewish and the Christian Messiah*, p. 359.

[2] A Divine Incarnation seems to require miracle. But we are not justified in saying that it could only have been effected in the way that the Gospels report.

point for the human race, we should be conscious of loss. It would at once be seen that, in the light of what we know of His life and His work, the narrators were ill-informed, or else that God had deliberately designed that His coming into the world should be unmarked by any departure from what ordinarily occurs in the birth of a child. If we could imagine that there was nothing to record and that, as other children, He came from God indeed, as they, and yet with no provision to separate His humanity from the entail of sinfulness which is the portion of every child of Adam, we should be in doubt as to the character of His life and work as the One Mediator between God and man.

We cannot say that without the Virgin-birth and all that it implied, He could not have stood in that relation, and that the resources of God would have failed to find for His Son another means of entrance upon His atoning and reconciling ministry on earth; but we *can* say that the Gospel narrative supplies us with a rationale of the Incarnation which, while it bears all the marks of an historical account, exactly suits the needs of the case. The requirement was two-fold. To be able to fulfil the righteousness of God in our nature and on our behalf, the Eternal Son must be one in race with ourselves. 'Forasmuch as the children are partakers of flesh and blood, He also Himself likewise took part of the same.'[1] But though one in flesh and blood with us through birth from His Mother, it was also needful that He should receive that nature without taint or spot; and this need was met by the character of His birth. There was no transmission of sin or of proneness to sin. In the words of the Angel of the Annunciation, the holiness of 'that holy thing' was secured by the overshadowing power of the Holy Ghost.[2] His agency—in place of that of human fatherhood—preserved the Child from the contamination which attends the birth of man from human parentage.[3] Thus the double requirement was fulfilled. He was of us and one with us; yet unlike us in His freedom from sin.

Much has been made of contradictions supposed to exist in the two narratives of the Birth of Christ. It is true that, pro-

[1] Hebr. ii. 14.

[2] Lk. i. 35, 'Wherefore, that which is to be born shall be called holy, the Son of God.' *v.* Plummer, *ad loc.*; Petersen, *D. wunderbare Geburt des Heilandes*, 1909, p. 17.

[3] *v.* Plummer, *The Gospel according to St. Matthew*, p. 7.

ceeding as they do from greatly differing sources of information, their descriptions correspond with their origin. But of contradiction in the sense that, if one version of the story is accurate, the other is untrue, we can see no trace whatever. There is no statement in either account which is negatived by a fair reading of the other; although, in more than one instance,[1] difficulties have been imported into the case by want of sympathy with the mind of the narrator, by an over-scrupulous insistence on details and by a perverse hypercriticism.[2] On the main facts both writers are at one. They alike convey the Divine, supernatural character of the Birth. Each places it at Bethlehem; the one as the fulfilment of prophecy, the other as the result of

[1] A constantly recurring defect in the historical methods of certain critics is the custom of assigning the ideas or sayings of the characters described by the writers to *the writers* themselves. An entirely wrong impression is thus conveyed. Indeed, it is one of the most fertile causes of misinterpretation with which we are acquainted. For instance, Usener in *Encycl. Bibl.* iii. col. 3344, observes that the remark has often been made that the Gospels know nothing of the miraculous birth of the Saviour. 'On the contrary, their knowledge of His natural filial relationship to Joseph the carpenter and to Mary his wife is still explicit.' Now the writers betray no such knowledge. What they do is to report what was said or believed by the people. Like faithful historians, they record the facts, however strongly those facts seem to tell against what they themselves believe and narrate in other parts of the Gospels. So Petersen (*D. wunderbare Geburt des Heilandes*, p. 24) asserts that in the Fourth Gospel, Jesus passes as the son of Joseph. He grounds this description of the mind of the Fourth Evangelist on the fact that he records the saying of Philip to Nathanael (Jo. i. 45), 'We have found . . . Jesus of Nazareth, the son of Joseph.' A faithful report of what was said by another in the first days of his discipleship is made to represent the feeling and belief of the reporter himself, and this without a shadow of proof! Holtzmann concludes that the absence of any contradiction of Philip's saying justifies critics such as Loisy and Réville in drawing the inference that the Fourth Evangelist makes no profession of belief in the Virgin-birth. *Evangelium des Johannes, in loc.*

It is surprising to find that P. Gardner, on the ground of the saying of Philip and even the belief of the Jews (Jo. vi. 42), declares that 'in more than one place, he (the Evangelist) speaks of Jesus as the son of Joseph.' *The Ephesian Gospel*, p. 287.

[2] Thus Usener, *Encycl. Bibl.* iii. col. 3343, says, 'Every unprejudiced eye will perceive that the nativity narratives of Matthew and Luke are mutually exclusive and irreconcilable.' As an instance of their contrast, he asserts that 'Joseph's home in Matthew is Bethlehem, in Luke Nazareth.' The assertion rests on an inference from Matt. ii. 23, that the Evangelist speaks of the Holy Family taking up their abode in Nazareth, as if it had not been their home before the visit to Bethlehem. It is quite possible that the source of information followed by the First Evangelist contained no mention of such

the Imperial edict. Each writer records the interposition of God—in dreams in the one case, by the ministry of angels in the other. In each account the faith and obedience of the Mother and her husband come into prominence. Now, if the narratives were identical in substance or so like one another as to suggest imitation, it might be felt that there was a want of independence, and our confidence would be proportionately weakened. But while they agree in their essential elements, they show that they are based on a variety of sources of knowledge, which, while they are required to supplement one another, if we are to obtain a complete picture, are yet never in discord, if we deal with them in all fairness.[1]

a previous residence, but his silence on that point is not to be quoted as a contradiction of St. Luke. Usener also draws attention to the fact that, whereas the visit of the Magi and the Flight into Egypt are in the First Gospel interposed between the birth at Bethlehem and the settlement at Nazareth, St. Luke speaks of a direct return to Nazareth after the performance of ceremonial duties at Jerusalem. Here again there is no contradiction. Lk. ii. 39 is not incompatible with the narrative of the First Gospel. Each speaks of a 'return' or of a 'coming' to Nazareth. But one narrates an intermediate series of events on which the other from ignorance, or from purpose, is silent.

[1] Usener (*Encycl. Bibl.* iii. col. 3349), by the pretext of interpolation in Lk. i. 34, 35, tries to eliminate the agreement of the Evangelist with the First Gospel in the matter of the Virgin-birth. But the plea cannot be entertained. The best authorities agree in recognizing the verses as part of the authentic text. *v.* Knowling in *Dict. of Christ.* i. p. 203. The ground of the exclusion of the passage from the text of our Gospel is stated (by Joh. Hillman in *Zeitschrift für Prot. Theol.* xvii. 221 ff., whom Usener follows) to be its incompatibility with the rest of the Lucan narrative. If passages are thus to be ruled out by such purely subjective considerations as this, the method might be pursued until little of the Gospel narratives would remain. The two verses *do* take us into a higher order of phenomena; but after all the whole recital of these early chapters of St. Luke passes again and again into that higher order. There is no special incongruity in this passage. It is in keeping with the rest, and its textual authority is complete. The Virgin-birth is not got rid of by this plea of interpolation. Not only does it appear in St. Matthew; but, apart from these suspected verses, the birth of an extraordinary Personage is implied in the context. The son is to be 'the Son of the Highest.' He is to have the throne of David. Elizabeth's condition is appealed to as confirming the promise of a birth extraordinary in itself. This appeal would be out of place if an ordinary birth in wedlock were contemplated. No doubt the question of Mary, at the message of the angel, 'How can this be, seeing that I know not a man?' surprises us, when we consider that she was looking forward to her marriage; but as Grützmacher (*D. Jungfrauengeburt*, pp. 9, 10) and others (*v.* Clemen, *Religionsgeschichtliche Erklärung des N.T.* p. 225) point out, she appears to consider that the angel's words, καὶ ἰδοὺ συλλήμψῃ ἐν γαστρί, are to be *at once* made good. We have also to consider the state of agitation and

A more subtle and formidable objection to the story of the Virgin-birth is raised by attributing its appearance in the Gospels to the suggestion of prophecy and to the imitation of Old Testament examples of unlooked-for birth. It is admitted that the two birth narratives are of Jewish-Christian origin in the ultimate sources that lie behind the text as we have it in our Gospels. It was in Jewish circles that the universally prevalent expectation of a Redeemer would find its focus. We observe it in the question put to our Lord at various times, 'Art Thou He that should come?', and in the requests for a sign. When the first generation of Christians began to reflect on the Person of Christ, when oral traditions began to take the form of written memoranda for the benefit of those who came after, the idea that our Lord was the fulfilment of prophecy and that Old Testament incidents were types of Him, began to exert its influence on the form which the story took and created the legend of the Virgin-birth.

To this theory there is a fatal objection. In the chief prophetic

perplexity which the visit and the words of the angel would naturally produce in a simple maiden; nor can we agree with Clemen (*ib.*) that her question is 'simply incomprehensible.' He indeed admits that the reference to Elizabeth suits vv. 34, 35 better than it would suit vv. 31 f. as a context if vv. 34, 35 were absent, and he considers the whole passage an addition by St. Luke himself to the original tradition and not a later gloss (*ib.* p. 226). To Clemen, the unhistorical character of the passage seems proved by Mary's judgment on her Son in Mk. iii. 21, 'He is beside Himself.' Whether, with Grützmacher (*ib.* p. 17), we attribute this startling saying to her impatience that One so highly endowed should be spending His days in lowly service, or whether we regard it as such a temporary lapse of faith as that which some see in the embassy from John the Baptist (Matt. xi. 2 f.), it affords no ground for the rejection of a passage which has such support as vv. 34, 35 possess. The wonderful experiences of the Blessed Virgin at the Birth of her Son would not preserve her from all failure in faith or temper during long subsequent years. It is one of the marks of the authentic character of the Gospel narrative that these psychological contrasts and inconsistencies (as some might think) are set down fearlessly. There is no paring down of awkward fact to gain credence. The story is told by men whose literary powers compel us to credit them with as keen a sense for disparity or incongruity as any of ourselves possess. You cannot negative a plain statement of fact by an appeal to consistency in so indeterminable a factor as the human mind. The Gospels furnish many an example of the futility of expecting a certain course of action or behaviour to follow invariably a certain set of circumstances. 'Have I been so long time with you, and yet hast thou not known Me, Philip?' was a reproach—perhaps not unmingled with surprise—from One Who 'knew what was in man' (Jo. xiv. 9; ii. 25). *v.* Weiss, *D. Leben Jesu*, i. p. 207.

forecast of the Saviour's birth,[1] as read in the Septuagint, the word παρθένος, 'maiden,' is an incorrect translation of the Hebrew. In the second century this fact was made use of by Jewish antagonists to Christianity, and was one of the causes which contributed to the Jewish dislike to the Septuagint version. But, whether this mistranslation was early recognized or not, the fact remains that Jewish thought never associated the idea of a Virgin-birth with the Messiah.[2] The foundation suggested for the story of the Virgin-birth is therefore insufficient to support it. A translation of the Hebrew original, which was known to be inaccurate, would not account for the creation of so startling a dogma. At the same time, given the fact of the Virgin-birth, the Christian narrator might well look back to the version of the passage, which was in current use, and see in its terms a forecast of what he knew to be historic fact.[3] It is entirely in the manner of the first Evangelist to link the leading facts of the Saviour's life with the past and to see in Him the one point on which the history of His people converged.

The theory that Old Testament examples of remarkable birth suggested a similar origin for Christ is as powerless as the prophetic theory to account for the Gospel narratives. There is no analogy between the late and unexpected birth of Isaac, of Samson, or of Samuel and the birth of Christ, except in the fact that each was of an unusual character and that the power of God was manifest in them all.[4] It is a far-fetched idea that a writer, dealing with what he plainly believes to be historical events, should go back to the twilight of his people's history to find something from which to create the central feature of his

[1] Is. vii. 14, עַלְמָה, young woman. *v.* Swete, *Introduction to the O.T. in Greek*, p. 30.

[2] 'The Old Testament affords no direct types of it.' Pfleiderer, *Urchristentum*, p. 418.

[3] Allen in *Matt.* i. 23, thinks that Isaiah hinted at a supernatural birth, and refers to Jeremias, *Babylonisches im Neuen Testament*, p. 47. *v.* Briggs, 'Criticism and Dogma' in *North Amer. Review*, June, 1906, p. 861 f. But Pfleiderer, *Urchristentum*, p. 419, takes a different view and adds, 'for the Christian readers of this passage, it was natural to explain this child by the Messiah in whom the "God with us" first received its true fulfilment.'

[4] The views of Philo as to the birth of Isaac and of Samuel (i. 215, 273, edit. Mangey) are not of course to be taken into account. They are entirely Greek in tone. There is nothing of Jewish exegesis in them. Cf. N. Schmidt, *The Prophet of Nazareth*, p. 249 ; Usener in *Encycl. Bibl.* iii. col. 3351.

story. But this does not militate against the eager recognition of points of similarity between the events, or the desire on the part of the Evangelist to find types and foreshadowings of the great reality to which he bears his witness.

Again, the attempt has been made to derive the narrative of the Virgin-birth from the New Testament itself. Pfleiderer sees its origin in the Pauline conceptions of the 'Man from heaven,' 'the Christ after the Spirit,' 'the Son of God according to the spirit of Holiness.'[1] In the working out of this idea in the Pauline Gentile communities he traces the source of the narrative of the Virgin-birth. But it has been pointed out that St. Paul never uses the manner of Christ's birth as an argument for the sinlessness which he imputes to Him. It is unlikely that he would have neglected to employ it for that purpose if it was known to him. The Divine origin of Christ is not ascribed in the New Testament to the character of His birth. Rather it is connected with His Resurrection and Ascension. 'The silence of the New Testament is a proof that in the circle of representation of the Apostolic age, there are not found the presuppositions out of which the origin of the narratives of the supernatural conception of Jesus could be explained.'[2]

In proportion as it is felt that Old Testament prophecy and types fail to account for the supernatural element in the Gospel narratives of the birth of Christ, there is a greater tendency among certain critics to seek for its origin on heathen and mythical ground. It has been remarked that, 'although much is still being said of Legend and Myth, the attempt of criticism to explain the origin of the Gospel History from the mythical standpoint has long been given up.' The writer defines a myth as 'the involuntary product of a consciousness which is so fully mastered by the force of an idea that it translates the ideal into the actual.'[3] There is here no intentional 'story-telling.' It is simply the creative play of fancy on ideas which are posited as facts because they seem so true.

No doubt this theory, in the form in which Strauss elaborated it, has been set aside by the action of historical criticism. The

[1] 1 Cor. xv. 47; Rom. i. 4. Cf. 2 Cor. v. 16. Pfleiderer, *Urchristentum*, p. 420.

[2] B. Weiss, *Leben Jesu*, i. pp. 212, 213.

[3] B. Weiss, *D. Leben Jesu*, i. p. 149.

events and their record were too near together for fancy to get to work. If there had been the disposition, there was not the time to weave the myth. Nor was the age when the Gospels were composed suitable for such processes. It was one of keen intellectual and commercial life, not one of dreaming twilight, in which truth and fiction could hardly preserve their separate characteristics, and would tend to pass imperceptibly into one another. If, then, there is any mythical element at all in the Gospel history, it does not come from within.

It must be imported. The process is deliberate, not as on the older theory, unconscious. It is not the working of an ecstatic fancy, but of a fixed purpose to intensify and exalt whatever is bound up with the life and work of One Who is thought to be Divine. But whence can the idea have originated? Not from Jewish sources for, as we have seen, apart from the Septuagint translation of Is. vii. 14, the Virgin-birth of the Messiah was not an article of Jewish faith. Therefore, they say, it can only have been brought into Jewish-Christian thought from some pagan source.

It should be stated beforehand that evidence of any such importation of pagan ideas into the early Christian conception of Christ must be very closely scrutinized. The probabilities of the case are all against such extraneous influence.[1] The associations connected with the sources themselves would be too abhorrent to the Christian sentiment to gain a hearing for them.

There is no doubt that heathen myth and legend were well known to Jews of the Dispersion. With Greek as their everyday language, Greek forms of thought, habits of life, religious ideas and customs quite familiar to them, we can hardly be surprised if, here and there, there were instances of syncretism; if now and again a Jew were found to be taking part in the worship of a heathen God. But, on the whole, the Jew remained faithful to the religion and life of his fathers; and whether his lot lay

[1] C. Clemen remarks on the fact that where borrowings can be detected (and their hypothetical character must be emphasized), the inner substance of Christianity is not affected; it is only the periphery which is concerned. *Religionsgesch. Erklärung des N.T.* p. 289. *v.* Harnack, *Beiträge*, iv. p. 99, 'A history of Jesus' birth freely invented on heathen-Christian soil about A.D. 50 or 80 or 100 would have looked very different from the *Vorgeschichte* of the First Gospel.'

in Alexandria or Rome or Ephesus, his bond with his brethren in Palestine remained unbroken.[1]

Yet the subtle influence of pagan ideas could not be entirely resisted, even where the old faith remained. The more cultivated the Jew of the Dispersion, the more sensitive would he be to the beauty and pathos of myth and legend as they came to him through the medium of an incomparable language, and perhaps recommended by the example of kindly friends. We have at least to admit that, during the centuries immediately preceding Christ, the Jew could easily become familiar with the beliefs and cults of the Greek-speaking world in which he lived. Thus he would become familiarized with Babylonian, Persian, Egyptian and Indian, besides Greek, modes of thought.[2] In each case the Greek language formed a medium for their reception ; and when Christianity dawned upon the world it found among its earliest adherents some to whom these Eastern and Greek beliefs were familiar. Did they pass into the current thought of the primitive Church, and so mould the form in which the birth-narratives were cast ?

Let us test some of the resemblances which give colour to this theory. Speaking generally, the tendency to attribute a Divine, or at least an abnormal, origin to kings, sages and heroes was to be met with all over the ancient East. In Egypt and in Babylonia, the kings were regarded as the offspring of their respective deities. Plato was said to be the son of Apollo.[3]

When we come to particular instances of resemblance, there is little to lead us to trace connection or indebtedness. It is surely far-fetched and gratuitous to see in the massacre of the Innocents a version of the Babylonian myth of the persecution of Marduk by the monster Tiâmat. Something of the influence of that

[1] *v.* Schürer, *D. Geschichte des Jüd. Volkes,* vol. iii. p. 90 ff. 'The Jews scattered about in the world maintained on the whole their religious peculiarities with remarkable tenacity. . . . Speaking generally, the restrained attitude of Judaism towards other religions was a characteristic mark of that faith. . . In the ground of their heart, the people remained Jews, feeling that in every essential they were one with their brethren in Palestine.' But Rev. ii. 9 points to a certain amount of degeneracy.

[2] Since the above was written, it has been remarked by Case that 'The influence of other national religions, if at all significant for the career of Christianity, was mediated mainly through Judaism or through the syncretistic life of the Gentile world.' *The Evolution of Early Christianity,* 1914, p. 192.

[3] So in the Roman legend, Romulus and Remus are sons of Mars.

myth is perhaps to be found in the curious imagery of Rev. xii. But that chapter will not explain how the incident at Bethlehem came to form part of the Gospel narrative. Still less can it be due to direct borrowing from the adventures of Marduk and his mother.[1] A writer disposed to derive his description from such a source would hardly be content to give us so simple a narrative as that of the Evangelist.

If Persian influence is suggested, we have to bear in mind the late period at which the *Avesta* was put together out of earlier materials.[2] The birth of the Saoshyant or Saviour from a maiden as there related is not to be seriously taken in connection with the Christian Birth-story.[3] At the same time, there is good reason to believe that Zoroastrianism, becoming known to the Jews through their residence in Babylon,[4] affected Jewish, and so indirectly Christian, thought in other directions.

But it is to India that some look for the closest resemblance to the Gospel of the Infancy. Here the question of date is of great importance. Scholars differ widely as to the side on which lies the debt of influence. The oldest Buddhist sources represent Buddha as the son of an Indian prince married to a wife from the hill country.[5] Only in later tradition do we begin to get ideas of abnormal happenings,[6] and then the contrasts with the

[1] Gunkel, *Schöpfung u. Chaos*, p. 386; Clemen, *Religionsgesch. Erklärung des N.T.* p. 236.

[2] *c.* A.D. 230, in the time of the Sassanide Empire of Persia. *v.* Bousset, *Die Religion des Judentums*, p. 547, who places its completion in A.D. 226-241 (*ib.* p. 549, n. 2). Zoroaster himself is assigned to a date varying between 600 and 500 B.C. His historical existence has been disputed, but on insufficient grounds.

[3] *v.* Clemen, *Religionsgesch. Erklärung des N.T.* p. 228; Petersen, *D. wunderbare Geburt des Heilandes*, p. 34.

[4] *v.* Bousset, *ib.* p. 548.

[5] *v.* Hackmann, *Der Ursprung des Buddhismus*, p. 6.

[6] See V. Hase, *Neutest. Paralellen zu Buddh^{n}. Quellen*, 1905, p. 12. It has been stated that 'belief in the Virgin birth of Buddha is completely contrary to the early Buddhist (Pāli) canonical works; it occurs first in the *Buddha-Caritra*, which was composed after Christian influence had made itself felt in India.' (*Record*, July 9, 1909). And Grützmacher points out that in *Lalita Vistara*, a work written, according to Seydel (*Die Buddhalegende*) *c.* 10-45 A.D., and therefore many centuries after the death of Buddha, and describing his life before he came forth to preach publicly in Benares, mention is made of strange accompaniments of his birth. It was not of a virgin, but of a married queen; not by a human father, but, according to one tradition, through a ray of light. The only point of connection with the Gospel account of the birth

Christian narratives are more striking than the resemblances. Fantastic and puerile descriptions remind us, not of the sober history of the Gospels, but of the apocryphal writings. The presence of slight parallels should not blind us to the points of difference; and these are vital and numerous. Where the Buddhist conception of its hero is that of a man, even before his appearance on earth, the Christian conception of Christ is of One Who was originally Divine.[1]

If none of the theories above referred to suffice to account for the form, still less for the material, of the Gospel narratives of the Birth,[2] we must either be content to leave them unexplained and unaccounted for, or we must take them as representing actual fact. The former alternative will never satisfy a serious thinker. He will not be content to let such a matter as the

of Christ is thus found to be in the absence of a human father. And Grützmacher goes on to say that 'for (Buddhist) influence on Jewish-Christian circles in the first two-thirds of the first century, not a shadow of proof has been brought.' *D. Jungfrauengeburt*, p. 28. *v.* Petersen, *D. wunderbare Geburt des Heilandes*, p. 33; von Hase, *ib.* p. 13. Oldenberg in *Theol. Literaturz.* for 1905, num. 3, admits the *possibility* of Buddhist influence penetrating to the circles in which the Gospels originated, but from the slight traces of any knowledge of Buddhism which have been found so far west of India, he considers it improbable. Cf. v. Hase, *op. cit.* p. 33.

[1] Cf. v. Hase, *Neutest. Parallelen zu Buddh^n. Quellen*, p. 30, 'No doubt points of contact and resemblances between Buddhism and Christianity are forthcoming, but in fact they are only ostensible, and quite misleading, while they are so over-balanced by the difference of the general view of the world and life, that the Christians of the first age, even if they came in touch with Buddhism, must have found this difference deep and repellent, and would certainly not have allowed themselves to be taken in by the apparent resemblances.' To mention but a few of the differences. The Buddhist believes in no God. Christianity is the full revelation of the Fatherhood of God. Buddhism is a religion of salvation, as is Christianity; but the redeemed and glorified life of the Christian is a totally different conception from the Nirvana —the extinction of individuality by absorption into the whole of things, as the bubble upon the surface of a stream—of the Buddhist hope. Buddhism is a system of pessimism carried to the most extreme point. Christianity is the source and guarantee of a living hope, a religion of cheerfulness—'Your joy no man taketh from you.' It is difficult to conceive how the primitive Christian writers could have cared to avail themselves of Buddhist legends (even supposing they were familiar with them) when putting upon record their knowledge of Jesus Christ. Cf. v. Hase, *ib.* p. 18.

[2] Harnack writes, 'Of the mythological, in the sense of Greek or oriental myths, nothing is found in these narratives ... Parallels to old stories of gods and heroes are more than scanty, and no one has been able to take them out of the domain of mere chance.' *Beiträge*, iv. p. 110.

entrance of Christ into the world hang suspended in mid-air, an insoluble problem, not merely in its details, but in the vital point of its origin. How came these sober, reverent narratives to find a place in the historical record of Christ's life on earth? Would the Evangelists prejudice the reception of their Gospels at the outset by advancing impossible and inconsistent claims, which could only be rejected by the thoughtful in time to come? Does not the barest admission of the guidance of the Holy Spirit in the selection and character of the Gospel narrative lead us to suppose that a restraining impulse would have intervened to prevent such a disaster? If we are dealing with the Word of God, if we recognize a Divine element in the composition of the Gospels, we shall expect to find traces of its presence in this particular part of those writings. In their entirety they put before us the idea of a more than human Personality. This is freely admitted by the best criticism. Judging from the general character of their representation, we should expect to find a corresponding uniqueness in the narratives of the Birth. And this is precisely what we do find. What is more, it pervades the Birth-stories so completely that you cannot sever it from them. Not only what is plainly stated, but what is implied, points to the presence of the transcendental. It forms the texture on which the narrative is woven. Tear it out and the whole fabric falls to pieces.

Adopt the other alternative and, if there is difficulty in bringing every detail in the two narratives into harmony with each other and into agreement with the facts of secular history, you have at any rate an explanation of the entrance of Christ into the world which suits the Gospel representation of His Person. It is the fitting opening of a career in which we have to recognize the presence of the Divine. Had it been a record of an ordinary birth, we could not have seen in it the character of verisimilitude: while at the same time the singular purity and restraint of the recital at once shows that we are treading, not on airy forms of legend and of speculative romance, but on the solid ground of actual history. In a question of this kind, men will, of course, be influenced by their standpoint. If their presuppositions forbid the theory of a miraculous intervention in bringing the Son of God into the world, they will reject, or at least pass by as unpractical, the opening chapters of the First and Third Gospels.

Divine things, they will say, cannot be proved by reference to human standards of truth or likelihood.[1] The two elements in the alleged fact do not mix. The 'supernatural' must always remain apart from the natural. However closely they may be conjoined in time and circumstance, they make entirely separate appeals to us—the one to faith, the other to reason and experience.

This is true, but only partially. For, we maintain that, if distinct in quality and character, the Divine can so penetrate the natural and human as to modify and affect it: so much so that its presence is thereby declared. The Gospels are written with that conviction. The Christian religion is founded on that assumption. If it be justified, then we have solid ground for believing in the historical value of the Birth-stories. We detect, in events taking place at a certain time and at a certain spot, the presence of a Divine factor, which we cannot comprehend but can mark in its effects. The same conditions are observable throughout our Lord's public ministry. Again and again men found themselves in the presence of a supernatural agency. They could not understand its mode of working, but the results were manifest to everyone. This is all that we claim for what lies behind the Birth-stories. God's hand is at work in the entrance of His Word into the world, and the Gospel records tell us what form this interposition took and how it affected the human instruments which were employed.

Against this position, science has nothing to say. Everything that is told us by the Evangelists is within the bounds of the possible. And if we come to the question of its probability, we have to remember that the cause for such Divine interposition was adequate. The salvation of mankind, their rescue from sin, their gain of eternal life, are surely reason sufficient to warrant modification of orderly processes and to justify the exceptional. If, to meet this antecedent probability, we have the assurance of happenings strange indeed, yet everywhere restrained and reverent; never betraying the slightest sign of exaggeration and, on the human side, life-like, pathetic and full of appeal to all that is best and deepest in our nature, then they demand a very respectful hearing. We shall ask ourselves whether, after admitting the possibility of a direct interposition of God in the course of human history, we have not here a record of its actual occurrence.

[1] *v.* Hutton, *Theological Essays*, p. 234.

The Birth of Christ is closely linked in time and circumstance with that of John the Baptist. The Annunciation takes place when Elizabeth's condition was becoming known. She had 'hidden herself' for the first five months after conception, unwilling to mix with her friends, who would still be thinking of her as childless and whom she would not care to undeceive. At the sixth month the coming event would be apparent. We seem to be led into some such train of thought by St. Luke.[1] He takes that condition of things as a fixed point from which to date the visit of the archangel Gabriel to the Virgin Mary.[2] Later on, we find him connecting the public life of Christ with the reigns of sovereigns, bringing it into touch with world-history. Here the spiritual and ethical connection is in his mind. He tells us that the Forerunner is six months older than He Whom he was to proclaim. And besides this fact, we get the assurance that the Saviour was to come in close touch with the prophecy that went before Him in the person of the greatest of the prophets.

Nothing can exceed the beauty of the Annunciation as it is narrated by St. Luke. A quiet home in a remote village of Galilee, the dwelling of a simple maiden, becomes the very antechamber of heaven. She is about her ordinary duties,[3] little recking of the destiny in store for her. One great change in her life is indeed full in view. She is betrothed to Joseph, a carpenter of the village and, as all knew, a member of the royal house of David. To every Jewish girl the prospect of marriage opened a greater—the possibility that she might become the Mother of the Messiah. In this case, the idea would be strengthened by the descent of the husband from the line to which prophecy had pointed with almost unvarying consistency as that in which the Christ was to appear. To this maiden not unmindful of such a hope, yet diligent in her home-life, the common round of the daily task is suddenly broken in upon. A form unseen before, human in outline,[4] but radiant with the light of heaven, appears in her presence. When he came before

[1] Cf. i. 24-27, and Plummer, *in loc.*

[2] The angel Gabriel employs the condition of Elizabeth as a re-assuring sign to the Blessed Virgin (Lk. i. 35, 36).

[3] At home. Lk. i. 28, *εἰσελθών*, shows this.

[4] Dan. ix. 21, 'the man Gabriel.' According to the Talmud, Gabriel is 'the man clothed with linen' of Ezek. ix. 3, x. 2. *v. The Jewish Encycl.* art. 'Gabriel.'

Zacharias, the priest was troubled at the sight. No such fear is ascribed to Mary. Only at what Gabriel said, at the manner of his salutation and the forebodings which it raised, was Mary troubled. In each case the angel speaks to calm the fear;[1] for in each case the message needed the full and undivided attention of the listener. Zacharias is assured that his prayer for a son is heard. Mary receives the news that her life is well-pleasing to God. Then comes the main burden of the message. To Zacharias, that his wife Elizabeth will bear him a son. To Mary, 'Thou shalt conceive in thy womb and bring forth a Son.' Thus the parallelism of the two Annunciations is preserved, with the differences required by the differing circumstances. In each case, too, the name is foretold, and the greatness of the destiny which will await these children of promise.[2] The Forerunner will be filled with the Spirit. The Son of Mary 'shall be called the Son of God.' John's work will be that of preparation. Jesus will reign a king upon the throne of David without end.

To Mary the accomplishment of the promise in her present condition as a maiden, betrothed indeed, but not wedded, seems impossible; 'How shall this be?' she asks.[3] The difficulty suggested by her question—for where is the improbability that she who was betrothed to Joseph should one day have a son?—is met by the fact that the announcement of Gabriel is in the present tense when translated into Hebrew, the language of the source underlying St. Luke's narrative:[4] 'Thou art now conceiving.' It was this which caused the surprised question of

[1] Lk. i. 28, 13, 30. [2] Lk. i. 13, 15, 31, 32.

[3] Some critics reject Lk. i. 34, 35, partly because the question appears out of place under Mary's circumstances as one looking forward to marriage; partly because they hope thereby to get rid of the miraculous birth from the story of the Nativity. But the apparent strangeness of her question disappears when we consider the probable effect of the surprise at the visit of the angel and his announcement, the confusion of mind it would cause, the likelihood that she would say the first thing that occurred to her. She seems, too, to imagine an immediate fulfilment of the promise and this, in her present maiden condition, she cannot understand. An invented rejoinder would have avoided this difficulty. Its presence is a proof that it represents the facts. *v.* above, p. 153, n. 1.

[4] Dalman, *D. Worte Jesu*, p. 31, 'The accumulated Hebraisms which Luke applies, especially in the first chapters of the Gospel, have led de Lagarde to the very just view that these chapters are throughout of Hebrew colouring, not Aramaic or Greek.' *v.* Zahn, *Einleitung in d. N.T.* ii. p. 406.

the maiden, for she was conscious of no cause of such a condition.[1] The conception was synchronous with the Annunciation.[2] Mary's question is not the expression of unworthy doubt, but of a natural perplexity, which would be all the greater in proportion to the purity of her mind. And therefore it is answered: answered by the most awe-inspiring tidings which ever fell on mortal ear. The Holy Spirit, Who at creation had brooded over the formless waste to prepare it for its new condition, to impart a predisposition to order and form, to fit it for the creative action of the Word of Life, He shall bring God's will to pass and thy child 'shall be called the Son of God.' It is God's way to grant signs to those who believe. Mary was such an one, and she receives a pledge of the truth of the tidings: 'Thy cousin Elizabeth, she hath also conceived a son in her old age. . . . For with God nothing shall be impossible.' This assurance completes the submission which was already waiting to be yielded to the angel's message. Never was obedience tendered with more devotion, more freedom from self-assertion, more meekness, than when Mary bowed her head, saying, 'Behold the handmaid of the Lord: be it unto me according to thy word.' The angel's task was ended, and his message delivered. He could go back to the Presence of God. The hope of all the ends of the earth is in process of fulfilment. A new day has begun to dawn.

And a proof of this is given in the beautiful episode which follows upon the departure of the angel. The mention of Elizabeth and the partial similarity of her experiences awake the natural desire of the Blessed Virgin to visit her cousin and to hold some communion with her. She had something to tell. Her secret was too great to keep wholly to herself, too solemn wholly to impart. But something could be communicated and received to ease the strain of thought and feeling, that might otherwise be too great for human endurance.

Her entrance into the presence of Elizabeth affords a fresh sign confirmatory of the reality of her experience at Nazareth.

[1] i. 34. Gunkel, *Zum religionsgeschicht. Verständnis des N.T.* pp. 67, 68. He adds, 'There is another positive argument for the genuineness of the verses (34, 35); why is the conception of Mary not narrated, while that of Elizabeth is expressly described (24)?' *Ib. n.* 1.

[2] The greeting of Elizabeth seems to imply that the Blessed Virgin was already 'great with child' on her visit, which took place immediately after the Annunciation (i. 39 f.).

No sooner had her word of salutation been spoken—the word of peace by the Mother of the Prince of Peace—than Elizabeth felt within herself as though the answer came from the life within her life. She rises to greet her cousin and, inspired with the gift of prophecy, felicitates the Mother and the Child that is to be. Filled with wonder at the privilege of the visit, she again pronounces Mary blessed, this time for her faith and trust,[1] which will receive in due time their assured reward.

Then Mary, carried away with prophetic fervour, like her cousin, and looking forward to the victories of her Divine Son all down the ages, sings, in answer to her, the Song of the Incarnation.[2] It bears all the marks of being what its contents suggest—her own song, not a composition of the Evangelist written for the occasion. 'Her Hymn was a native product of one particular moment of transition in sacred religious history, and of no other; when the twilight of the ancient dispensation was melting, but had not yet melted, into the full daylight of the new.'[3]

[1] Lk. i. 45, μακαρία ἡ πιστεύσασα. 'This is the first beatitude in the Gospel; and it is also the last: μακάριοι οἱ μὴ ἰδόντες καὶ πιστεύσαντες (Jo. xx. 29).' Plummer, *in loc.* On the sanctification of the Blessed Virgin, cf. S. Thom. Aquin. *Sum. Theol.* Quaest. xxvii. Art. I. Conclusio; Art. VI. Conclusio; Jerem. i. 5; Liddon, *The Magnificat*, p. 40.

[2] It is difficult to regard the attribution of the Magnificat to Elizabeth, in spite of the learning with which it has been urged by Burkitt, Harnack and others, as anything but pedantic and improbable. The salutation of Elizabeth surely required an answer. Would Mary be dumb at such a time, or if she spoke, would no echo of her words have reached the ear of the Evangelist? There is a good discussion of the subject by Burn in Hastings' *Dict. of Christ.* art. 'Magnificat.' Lk. i. 48, 'all generations shall call me blessed' seems to come as an answer to the beatitude pronounced by Elizabeth in verse 45, and it would be quite exaggerated and unsuitable in the mouth of Elizabeth. The other passages in St. Luke's Gospel in which Mary is beatified seem to point to the appropriation of this particular claim of blessedness to her. The doubtful condition of the text with the variety of patristic citation—Tertullian, for instance, differing from Irenaeus—renders certainty unattainable with our present knowledge. But, on the whole, the probability seems to rest with Mary. The text of i. 46 originally lacked a personal name. It has been supplied by various copyists, Μαριάμ or Ἐλισάβετ. We have to form our own conclusion as to which name is to be preferred.

[3] Liddon, *The Magnificat*, p. 14. In this and the other songs of this first chapter of St. Luke, we have 'the antiphonal morning psalmody of the Messianic day as it broke, of which the words were all of the Old dispensation, but their music of the New.' Edersheim, *The Life and Times of Jesus the Messiah*, i. p. 153.

For three months the kinswomen were together, more closely united by their expectations than by the tie of blood, the Mother of the Messiah with the Mother of the Forerunner; the elder woman destined to bear the last representative of the old order, the younger to bear the Founder of the new. Each was 'a handmaid of the Lord,' submissive and ready to do His will. To each, Christendom owes a debt of reverence and honour, for each played a noble part in its preparation. To Mary belongs the solitary privilege of giving to the Saviour all He possessed of the human nature which He came to save. She was His Mother. From her alone, through the creative power of the Holy Ghost, He took that vesture of His Deity which—except for the brief time of His redeeming death—He was never afterwards to lay aside. She was the Mother of Jesus, and as the Church came to think what this means, we can see that it was true to fact when it insisted that she was ἡ θεοτόκος.[1]

Mary returned to her home at Nazareth when her visit to Elizabeth was over. Soon her natural recourse to seclusion and privacy could no longer veil her condition. Nothing can exceed the feeling of delicacy and truth which characterizes the recital of St. Matthew. Joseph becomes aware of her state. We are told nothing of his surprise; but in his intention to sever his tie quietly we are asked to observe his justice—*facilis ac lenis, ut injustus severus.*[2]

How could he be enlightened as to the truth of what was happening? Mary, if she knew what he was meditating, could not speak. Elizabeth, who could have spoken, was far away. Therefore, 'while he thought on these things, behold the angel of the Lord appeared unto him in a dream.'

The Annunciation of Joseph was less direct than that of Mary. To her the angel came in the light of day and spoke face to face. The message came to Joseph in a dream, and the angel was no living being. No name is given him as in Mary's case. He is part of the dream,[3] in which Joseph is made, by the direction of his thoughts, to learn the will of God, and to receive—what Mary

[1] That is, the Mother of the manhood of Him, Who is both God and Man.

[2] Bengel, *in loc.*

[3] Such appears to be the interpretation of the narrative, in spite of the more direct visitation which seems implied in Matt. i. 24. What occurred may be represented thus. Joseph slept and dreamed. His dream was of an angel, who came from God with the announcement of the meaning of Mary's condition

had directly received, as the one more nearly concerned—the promise of the Saviour. 'Joseph, thou son of David,[1] fear not to take unto thee Mary thy wife: for that which is conceived in her is of the Holy Ghost. And she shall bring forth a Son and thou shalt call His name Jesus: for He shall save His people from their sins.' We see how the honour and the privileges of Joseph are preserved. He is reminded of his lineage. He comes of the house of David and is thus in touch with that expectation of the coming Messiah which was so deeply felt at the time. The reminder serves to prepare the sleeper for the message to which his thoughts are now to be led. The Redeemer is to be born of Mary his espoused wife, and he is not to turn from the marriage. His rights, as head of the home which the marriage would create, will be preserved for him. '*Thou* shalt call His name Jesus.'

Joseph was not disobedient to the heaven-sent dream and its message. 'He took unto him his wife.' Thus was formed the model of the homes of Christendom. It is significant of the privacy, the intimate relations and the seclusion of true family life that this—the type of all that is best in the home—should have been placed in a village of so little account as Nazareth. The name occurs neither in the Old Testament nor in the pages of Josephus. No great name or stirring event had ever been associated with it. But in the New Testament it leaps at once into fame. It is characteristic of certain critics, that the fact that it only emerges into public knowledge in connection with the birth of our Lord, at once renders its existence doubtful. The claim of trustworthiness, which they would not think of

and of the part which he was to play. The question is one of psychology. Sleep, that border-land of life and death, has often been the occasion of intercourse between God and man; and it is only in accordance with Jewish belief of the time that, to the mind of Joseph, an angel should appear as the medium of communication between God and himself. As sleep withdraws the mind from contact with the world and translates it into a condition in which spiritual impressions can the more readily be received, we cannot wonder that dreams have often been the occasion of momentous happenings; *v.* Myers, *Human Personality and its Survival of Bodily Death*, i. pp. 151, 152. In Matt. ii. 19, Joseph is again made aware of the will of God through a dream, and again to his thought an angel is the medium of communication. As, in i. 20, 24, the angel may be regarded as part of the dream, rather than, as in the case of the Annunciation of Mary, an actual person.

[1] *v.* K. Furrer, *D. Leben Jesu Christi*, p. 31.

refusing on such a ground to a third-rate chronicler, is denied to the serious and responsible writers of the Gospels. The obscurity of Nazareth previous to New Testament times is employed as a weapon against the historical setting of the life of Christ. A more unfortunate instance of the use of the argument of silence it would be difficult to find.[1] Were there no villages in Palestine but those mentioned in the Old Testament or in a writer like Josephus ? When we have specific evidence, not in one but in several writings, of the existence of a place, are we to reject it because it is not otherwise named ?

St. Matthew's account of the forming of the home at Nazareth is borne out by St. Luke. The two accounts taken together explain the latter's reference[2] to Mary as Joseph's 'espoused wife.' They had been but a short time together when the long arm of Imperial authority brought them, as David's descendants, to be enrolled in David's town.[3] They come to Bethlehem. The time of Mary's need was at hand. She was far from home, with no friends at hand to offer shelter. The one inn is filled with guests that appear of greater importance. She is obliged to seek the shelter of the stable, and there among the animals, who seemed kinder than man, 'she brought forth her first-born Son and wrapped Him in swaddling clothes, and laid Him in a manger.' Never was the dignity of poverty made more evident. The Son of Man, with life but flickering in His infant form, is cradled among the beasts. He takes from the world nothing but the humanity which was to redeem it. 'Though He was rich, yet for our sakes He became poor.' The simple recital bears within it the unmistakable proof of its truth to life. The Gospels are written with a purpose.

[1] 'The remoteness of Nazareth from intercourse with the world is unduly insisted upon. It had Zippori, the capital of Galilee, on one side and the cities of Japha and Kesalot in close proximity on the other. It lay on the important high road which led from Zippori to the plain of Megiddo and so on to Caesarea.' Dalman, *D. Worte Jesu*, p. 8. See K. Furrer, *D. Leben Jesu Christi*, p. 27 ; N. Schmidt, *The Prophet of Nazareth*, p. 243 ; *Jew. Encycl.* art. 'Nazareth.'

[2] Matt. i. 24 f. ; Lk. ii. 5.

[3] The Evangelist assumes that the cause of the journey was the Davidic descent of Joseph. Lk. ii. 4. This connection would not appeal to the Roman authorities. It is possible that Joseph lived at Bethlehem before his marriage. In that case, it was his proper place for enrolment apart from the question of his lineage. *v.* Box, *op. cit.* p. 56 f.

They mean to set forth Jesus as the Messiah, as Son of God. And yet this beginning—this entrance into the world! No invented tale would have thus begun. The risk of destroying at the outset all the impression which it was hoped to make would have been too great. The story indeed is beautiful to a degree which is not attained by any other record of a birth or a beginning. But its beauty is bound up with its adherence to truth. It were an incongruous situation, if it were not true. Its pathos lies in its deep significance. God comes in Person into the world that He made. 'He came to His own;' but not with the open tokens of majesty as once He will come again. He came to His own in the form and guise of one of them; 'and His own received Him not.' If we cannot see the sincerity and truth of St. Luke's picture of the scene of the Nativity, no amount of argument, no wealth of instance or of allegation would convince us. The height of the paradox is the measure of its truth.

But the stable and the manger are not all the wonders of that night. The Son of David, who before he reigned had kept his father's sheep, is visited by shepherds who in the same fields were keeping their flocks by night. How come they to leave them and go with haste into the town and seek Him there as He lies in the manger? The answer, if we will receive it, is not far to seek. Out there in the fields under the open sky, as all the stars look on, there has been another Annunciation. 'The angel of the Lord'—we are not told his name, but can imagine that it was Gabriel—'came upon them and the glory of the Lord shone round about them: and they were sore afraid.' For, like Mary, they were 'troubled' and needed, like her, the reassuring words that followed, 'Fear not.' Mary and Joseph, in their Annunciations, had each received the promise of a coming Blessing. The shepherds hear the Gospel of a Blessing already come. 'Behold, I bring you good tidings of great joy which shall be to all people. For unto you is born this day in the city of David a Saviour, which is Christ the Lord.'[1] Thus, by angelic lips, is preached for the first time in man's hearing the Gospel of the Incarnation. It is a Gospel, too, of the widest application, 'good tidings of great joy, which shall be to all people.' The words are spoken to Jews of David's city, but the message is for all the world. Thus, at its first publishing,

[1] Lk. ii 10.

the universal character of the Gospel is at once made known. 'Unto you He is born,' in the city of David. He is a Son of the House, of your people, but He belongs to the world.[1]

Another striking element of the angel's message is the assurance that the expectation of the ages was now fulfilled. The Christ had come. He 'is born this day.' The promise breathed in Paradise, and kept as a hope before the minds of people by every prophet, is now made good. Messiah has come, but not as men expected He would come. 'This shall be the sign unto you.' If the shepherds had gone to seek Him under the guidance of their own traditional views of the manner of His appearing, they would not have found Him. They needed a clue to lead them to Him. 'Ye shall find a babe wrapped in swaddling clothes, lying in a manger.' Other evidence of identity there would be none. This was the sign and it sufficed; for surely never was new-born child so strangely cradled. The angel ceases to speak and soon fades from view. But at once, so the shepherds afterwards assured the Virgin Mother,[2] there was with him a multitude of the heavenly host, praising God and saying, 'Glory to God in the highest, and on earth peace, goodwill toward men.'[3]

The shepherds stay to hear the song of heaven. Then they turn to one another, feeling that they are called to verify the announcement which has been made to them; 'Let us now go even unto Bethlehem, and see this thing which is come to pass, which the Lord hath made known unto us.' And every year, all who love their Saviour say the same words and walk in the shepherds' footsteps, bound on the same errand—once more to verify and see for themselves with the eye of faith, what can no longer be seen with the eye of flesh. 'They came with haste.' Such a message as they had had brooks no delay. They wonder,

[1] παντὶ τῷ λαῷ, 'to all the people' (R.V.) *i.e.* to Jews as opposed to Gentiles. But this limitation can hardly stand in view of Is. xlix. 6 and Lk. ii. 32, unless we adopt Bengel's suggestion (*in loc.*) that the angel did not yet know of the future extension of the Gospel message to the Gentiles—a mystery to be revealed διὰ τῆς ἐκκλησίας (Eph. iii. 10). '*Omni populo,* "all people," is the latitude or extent; *quod erit,* "that shall be," is the longitude or continuance of the joy.' Bp. Andrewes, *Sermons*, i. p. 71.

[2] Such was probably the source of the tradition.

[3] A.V., R.V. (margin), 'good pleasure among men,' ἐν ἀνθρώποις εὐδοκία. But the difficult reading εὐδοκίας, which divides the song into two clauses, instead of three, has the best MS. authority (ℵ* A, B, D, Latt.). *v.* H. Holtzmann, *D. Synoptiker*, p. 319.

as they run, if indeed the prophecies are fulfilled; if the expected Messiah has come, and they are to be the first to welcome Him. There is a singular fitness in the greeting of the Good Shepherd at His birth by the shepherds of Bethlehem. At once attention is drawn away from the political and kingly aspect of Messiah to His significance for the lowly and the humble. The ethical and spiritual meaning of His birth is enforced, and the keynote of His Ministry is struck as He receives the homage of the shepherds.

Entering the house, they find that the outward facts answer to the angel's words, and we gather that they have grasped the inner meaning of what they saw; for they return full of thankfulness, 'glorifying and praising God for all the things that they had heard and seen, as it was told unto them.'[1] They spoke to others of their strange and wonderful experiences, and for many a day in the hill country rumours of what had happened must have passed about among the people. But there is no sign that any stir was caused. The shepherds do not appear again in the Gospel history. Like the Magi, they seem to form no constructive part of the general preparation for the reception of the Messiah. They are merely an episode; and we can trace no special influence upon thought as resulting from it. Only in one case does the seed appear to have fallen upon good ground: 'Mary kept all these things and pondered them in her heart.'

[1] Lk. ii. 20.

CHAPTER X

THE CHILDHOOD OF CHRIST

AFTER the experiences which the Parents had gone through, it surprises us to read of the circumcising of the Holy Child. Yet, as was the custom, it took place on the eighth day. Through the teaching of the prophets, circumcision had come to be regarded as a symbol of the putting away of all impurity.[1] In the shedding of blood, which must always accompany it, the life was held to be rendered up to God as a sacrifice. A narrative which set out, not to relate facts, but to glorify and exalt a childhood which was that of an ordinary being, would not have admitted this incident. Set as it is in the midst of events that are full of the supernatural, it leads us to think that we are everywhere moving on historic ground. St. Luke's intention is to give us what he believes to have actually taken place.

From another point of view, the circumcision was a necessity for One who came primarily to redeem the House of Israel. An uncircumcised Messiah would have had no place within the family of the chosen people.[2] He 'came not to destroy the Law but to fulfil it.' The fact that He was submitted on the eighth day to this ordinance of the covenant of God's people is proof that the Parents were acting entirely according to the will of God. They were living at the time under the Divine guidance. Our Lord's own action in coming to the Baptist to be baptized by him gives a retrospective sanction to the circumcision; 'It becometh us to fulfil all righteousness.'[3] As St. Paul says, He was 'made under the Law.'[4]

[1] Jer. vi. 10; Ezek. xliv. 7. Cf. Col. ii. 11.

[2] *v.* B. Weiss, *Das Leben Jesu*, i. p. 235.

[3] Matt. iii. 15.

[4] Gal. iv. 4.

If we may judge from the fact that both the Baptist and Christ are said to have received their names on the day of their circumcision,[1] it was customary in Israel to make the rite of entrance into the chosen family of God the occasion of the naming of its new member. It was on the eighth day that the Holy Child was called by the name already designated 'by the angel before He was conceived in the womb,' Jesus, the 'Name which is above every name'[2]—the name which of all His titles is dearest to the heart of the Christian, recalling as it does every thought of help and salvation.[3]

Bethlehem was but six miles from Jerusalem and the Temple. Another custom was not difficult to carry out from the place of the Birth. The new-born Son must be presented to God for His service, according to the law by which the first-born of every family was regarded as dedicated to the Priesthood. The further law, which set apart the tribe of Levi exclusively for this office, did not abrogate God's claim on the eldest son of every family in Israel; but, while obliging his presentation, it released him from its duties on payment of redemption money.[4] But there was another reason for a visit to the Temple. For forty days after the birth of a son, a mother might not approach the sanctuary. When they were ended she came to God's house with an offering as atonement for whatever of ceremonial defilement she had contracted. Here, again, there is no trace of legendary accretion to the simple recital of actual happenings. If any tendency to exalt and glorify his subject had possessed the Evangelist, we should have had no such narrative as this.

The atonement-offering was legally determined according to the means of the mother. We note that Mary offered the gift of the very poor—'a pair of turtle doves or two young pigeons.'[5] It was all she could do; but her offering was a fitting emblem of herself, in her simplicity and purity.

The first entrance of the Son into the Father's House was not to pass unnoticed. Among those who at the time were waiting for the promised Messiah and 'for the consolation of Israel' was Simeon. He 'was righteous and devout.' God had marked the strength of his desire, and by an intimation which

[1] Lk. i. 59; ii. 21. [2] Phil. ii. 9.

[3] On the name 'Jesus' *v.* Nestle in Hastings' *Dict. of Christ.* i. p. 859 f.

[4] Ex. xiii. 12; Num. iii. 12. [5] Lk. ii. 24; Levit. xii. 2, 6, 8.

the Evangelist attributes to the Holy Spirit, he had been assured 'that he should not see death before he had seen the Lord's Christ.' 'The Holy Ghost was upon him,' and under His leading, he comes into the Temple at the moment of the Presentation. It was no mere coincidence. The conjunction was pre-arranged. The representative of the imperfect and incomplete, of that which was ready to vanish away, meets Him who is to bring in the new, the perfect, the final dispensation. The old man takes the young Child into his arms; the Gospel is cradled and nursed by the Law. Freedom can only live where there is restraint. Simeon utters for himself and many another saint, who has come like him to receive the Saviour, the dying song of satisfied desire. He had no more to live for. He could now go to his fathers in peace. In the Child, Who lay in his arms unconscious of what was passing, he was enabled by the Holy Spirit to see the glory of Israel and the Light of all the nations.[1] He was the first to realize what St. Paul long after taught, that 'no man can say that Jesus is Lord but by the Holy Ghost.'[2] Then, when Simeon's song of praise was ended, he turns to the Mother. In prophetic language he declares that the Holy Child will be the cause of stumbling and offence, as well as of hope and renewal, as all supreme gifts must be, according as they are received or rejected.[3] He will bring to light, by the attitude which they take, the inner history of those who come to know Him. Mary herself will not be without the trial which such relationship as hers must bring. 'A sword shall pierce through thy own soul also.'

The true Israelites who looked for redemption have another representative in the aged Anna. She is spoken of as a prophetess. Her life had been spent in the courts of God's House; and she too is blessed with the sight of His Christ.

The Parents have fulfilled their mission. Their own wonderful experiences have been met and confirmed by the words of Simeon and Anna. There is no more to do in Jerusalem. 'They returned into Galilee, to their own city Nazareth.'

But that return to Nazareth is only for a short period. Before long the Holy Family is in Bethlehem again, attracted by the

[1] Is. xlix. 6; 1 Enoch xlviii. 4.

[2] 1 Cor. xii. 3 Compare the visit of Asita, a Buddhist ascetic, to the new-born Buddha, *Lalita Vistara*, Foucaux, p. 91 f.; V. Hase, *op. cit.* p. 14.

[3] Matt. x. 34.

sacred associations of the place, or made aware that another presentation of the Saviour is to be made, not this time among His own people and in His Father's House, but to Gentiles. We should have expected the Visit of the Magi to find a place in the Gospel of St. Luke rather than in one so definitely addressed to the Jewish world as St. Matthew; especially if the incident had been devised in the interests of universalism. But St. Luke gives no hint of such a visit. His sources only inform him that 'when they had performed all things according to the law of the Lord,' the Holy Family 'returned into Galilee to their own city Nazareth.' He knows nothing of the sojourn in Bethlehem, of the Visit of the Magi or of the Flight into Egypt; or, if he knows, he does not speak of these things. Finding them in St. Matthew, where we should not have looked for them, we are at once disposed to receive them as historical. They are there because the writer believes them to belong to the Gospel as he knew it. He does not withhold them because they have little or no relation to the general purpose and drift of his Gospel. Their setting is thus a guarantee of their truth. And when we examine the literary peculiarities of this part of the Gospel, we find that they correspond with those of its other parts. The birth-chapters are the work of the author of the rest of the Gospel, if we may judge by similarities of expression and of style.[1]

At first sight the Visit of the Magi seems to hang in mid-air. We ask for some point of connection with the circumstances of the time in order to be able to account for it. Why should men leave their home and their occupations on so Quixotic an errand, as it would appear to all their friends? What was there in the birth of One destined, it was thought, to reign over the Jewish people, to draw to His cradle pilgrims of other race from a distant land? Why, too, should they bring costly gifts, and in presenting them, fall down and worship, yielding the adoration they would give to God? The answer is to be found partly in the condition of thought pervading the time; partly in a special form of guidance which was given to them; partly also in the teaching of Scripture as it was interpreted on their arrival in Jerusalem. We must examine each of these points.

In the first place, there was a general disposition among the thoughtful of non-Jewish peoples to anticipate an event of great

[1] Hawkins, *Horae Synopticae*, p. 4 ff. *v.* above, p. 147, n. 1.

significance. The origin of this feeling was due to various causes. There was profound dissatisfaction with the religions and philosophies current at the time. The craving of the heart of man for the knowledge of God and the desire to do His will, if only it could be ascertained, were unappeased. Crude and incomplete forms of belief and worship had been outgrown. The application of philosophic thought to religion had only exposed its weakness. There was no help in the importation of new cults and observances. They all suffered from their inherent defects, and failed to satisfy minds which had received some light and guidance from philosophy. But there was an additional cause of dissatisfaction. The Jews, dispersed over the East as far as India and southwards through Upper Egypt and Arabia, had everywhere brought with them their own pure monotheistic belief and its accompanying ethical system and practice. These became known to the peoples among whom they lived, and could not fail to have their influence on the higher minds. The hopes of Israel would be communicated. We have evidence that a feeling of expectancy was everywhere abroad.[1] There are inscriptions extant which show that great things were attributed to the reign of the First Emperor. He was hailed by many as a Saviour, and the era of peace, which the wide sway of his empire ensured, made many think that the golden age of the poets had begun.[2]

Such, roughly speaking, was the condition of the more refined and thoughtful of the pagan world at the moment of our Lord's birth—intense dissatisfaction with their religion and with the consolations which philosophy could afford them ; eager anticipation of what they thought was coming. There was a stir and movement in the air which boded they knew not what. It made them keen to notice changes. Anything new might be a portent. Especially would astrologers be quick to observe any conjunction of planets, or any star hitherto unknown. The Evangelist tells us that about that time there was an appearance in the heavens which attracted the attention of certain Magi. They connected it in their own minds with the birth of a King of the Jews ; and it is here that the influence of the Jew of the Dispersion seems to make itself felt. Otherwise, how could they have read the message of the sky and interpreted it thus ?

[1] Joseph. *Bell. Jud.* vi. 5. 4 ; Tacitus, *Hist.* v. 13 ; Sueton. *Vespas.* iv.
[2] *v.* above, p. 127.

Various suggestions have been made as to the identity of the star with any known to us, either singly or in conjunction with some other star. We have no means of determining what precisely was the astronomical fact. But we are assured that they saw a star which they were led to connect with the hopes referred to. When they arrive at Jerusalem, which they would naturally take to be the dwelling place of its people's king, they speak of the rise of this star upon their horizon.[1] It has brought them to the capital and they proclaim their belief in its meaning. But now they require more precise information: 'Where is He that is born King of the Jews?' 'Nuntiant et interrogant, credunt et quaerunt.'[2] The appearance of the Magi and their question cause excitement in the city. At any other time, we may imagine that little notice would be taken of what to many would seem a fantastic and unpractical mission, and the question would rouse little interest. But we are told that 'Herod the king . . . was troubled and all Jerusalem with him.'[3] Calling together the priests and scribes, he asked them what was to be the birthplace of the expected Messiah. They can at once tell him, in the words of the Prophet Micah,[4] that it will be Bethlehem in Judaea. Herod had apparently said nothing to the priests about the Magi. He now summons the latter secretly to ask the precise time of the first appearing of the star, for a cruel purpose was taking shape in his mind. Bidding them search diligently for the young Child and bring him word when He is found, he lets them depart on the last stage of their journey. The star, which they had seen at its rising, led them and seemed at length to stand motionless over the spot where the Holy Child was lying in His Mother's arms. They were filled with joy at this fresh proof of heavenly guidance; and entering into the house,[5] beheld the young Child—the one object of their long journey.

[1] Matt. ii. 2, ἐν τῇ ἀνατολῇ, 'at its rising.'

[2] Matt. ii 2; Aug. *Serm.* cxcix. § 2.

[3] Matt. ii. 3. 'Quid erit tribunal judicantis, quando superbos reges cunae terrebant infantis!' Aug. *Serm.* cc. § 2.

[4] 'Si Herodes timet, cur non quaerunt, cur non credunt Judaei?' Bengel, *in loc.* 'Sancta Scriptura, quam in ore, non in corde gestabant.' Aug. *Serm.* cxcix. § 2.

[5] Chrysostom and others think that the Saviour was still lying in the manger, but cf. Matt ii. 11, ἐλθόντες εἰς τὴν οἰκίαν. Maldonatus thinks not, but says that the opinion of the Fathers is not to be lightly rejected. *Comment. in IV. Evangel.* p. 55 E.

Prostrating themselves before Him with the homage which they would render to a king, they bring out their offerings—gold and frankincense and myrrh—the richest and most fragrant gifts that it was in their power to bestow.[1] Their adoration ended, the purpose of their journey was fulfilled. Warned in a dream, they disobey Herod's injunction to return to him, and depart to their Eastern home as mysteriously as they came.

It is only natural to see in this episode a fulfilment of Old Testament prophecy.[2] The access of the Gentiles, with their offerings, to the Church [3] is literally carried out by the Magi. But there is no indication that any supposed necessity for the fulfilment of prophecy, or any desire to fashion the life of Christ in accordance with accepted lines of thought, has had any influence upon the language of the Evangelist. His story is one of actual fact. It is placed upon historical ground and in connection with historical persons. It accurately reflects what we know to be the prevailing thought of the time, and is true to the life and circumstances of the age of which it speaks. Here, again, the Evangelist is indebted indirectly to the report of Joseph. How it reached him we cannot tell; but there is nothing improbable in the supposition that the memory of an event of such interest, and one so pregnant in consequences as the Visit of the Magi, would be treasured up in the community until it found a place in the Gospel.

The character of Herod, his ruthless cruelty, as proved by the murder of his sons,[4] his fears for his throne, would be known to Joseph. The dream of the Magi, accounting for the direction of their homeward journey, would be an additional warning. If he was already beginning to consider the safety of his precious charge, he had not long to wait for guidance. Once more in a dream he seems to see the form of an angel and to hear

[1] A symbolical reference has been found for each of their gifts and read into their thoughts. There is nothing to show this in the Evangelist's narrative.

[2] It is a mistake to see a reference to the star of the Magi in the prophecy of Balaam (Num. xxiv. 17). The star which was to 'come forth out of Jacob' points to the Messiah Himself, and was so understood in the Targums. Christian writers have wrongly seen in it the star of the Magi. *v.* Weiss, *Das Leben Jesu*, i. p. 245.

[3] Is. lx. 1 f.

[4] Joseph. *Antiq.* xvi. 11, § 7. For the saying of Augustus that it was better to be Herod's sow (ὗς) than his son (υἱός) *v.* Macrob. *Sat.* ii. 4.

a voice which bids him fly into Egypt and abide there until all is safe. Herod will seek to kill the young Child. Here, again, we are treading historic ground.[1] Judaea and Galilee were not safe as an abode for a Child of whom such things had been said, and round whose cradle such events had clustered as those which the Gospels report. In Egypt, which was near at hand, there would be a safe asylum among Jewish kinsmen and under another government. Our Lord might have been guarded anywhere by special intervention on the part of God. But no recourse is had to other than the ordinary means of preservation. The Holy Family simply retires before the threatened danger, remaining in Egypt until news is brought that the king is dead.

Joseph is about to return to Judaea. The associations of Bethlehem made it appear the most fitting home of the Son of David. But on the news that Archelaus [2] had succeeded his father, his former fears are aroused, and he is warned to turn aside into Galilee, and returns to Nazareth. St. Matthew had no knowledge of any previous residence there. He speaks of the Holy Family as coming to dwell 'in a city called Nazareth.' He was not aware that, in St. Luke's words, it was 'their own city.' When it becomes their home, and gives its name to Christ, he sees an allusion to prophecy.[3]

We do not know our Lord's age on the return from Egypt. He was a little boy, and may have brought away from that ancient asylum of His people hardly any recollections. Henceforth His home is in Nazareth. The only light thrown upon the early life there is that which St. Luke[4] affords: 'The child grew and waxed strong in spirit, filled with wisdom: and the grace of God was upon Him.'

Our desire to penetrate the obscurity which sheltered our Lord's home life for nearly thirty years is not gratified. Yet we

[1] The story receives a certain amount of corroboration from the statement which Origen imputes to Celsus, that our Lord had served for hire in Egypt and, coming to the knowledge that He possessed miraculous powers, returned to His own land and proclaimed that He was God. *Con. Cels.* i. 38.

[2] He may have heard of the character of Archelaus, who began his reign with the slaughter of 3000 people. Joseph. *Bell. Jud.* ii. vi. 2.

[3] Possibly Is. xi. 1. But no satisfactory explanation of Matt. ii. 23 has yet been found. *v.* Zahn, *Evangelium des Matt. in loc.* Cf. Is. iv. 2; Jer. xxiii. 5; Zech. iii. 8. *v.* Box, Hastings' *Dict. of Christ.* art. 'Nazarene,' and *The Virgin Birth of Jesus*, pp. 23, 28 f.

[4] ii. 40.

cannot help asking ourselves whether the truth of His Person—its origin and its destiny—stole gradually into His mind and coloured all His waking thoughts ; or whether it remained hidden from Him during those years of boyhood and early manhood, when He was first learning and then practising His trade as a carpenter.[1] We wonder if the Mother by questioning or instruction tried to understand His thoughts about Himself. In ordinary cases a habit of introspection is an unhealthy sign in young people. The objective interests of life are felt to be their more natural concern. A self-conscious person is apt to regard everything from his own point of view, and to become isolated from the interests of his kind. Of this we can at once say there is no trace in the case of our Lord. We know too much of His attitude—both towards Himself and His fellow-men—to imagine such a state of mind. He Who 'pleased not Himself' would take no pleasure in the analysis of His own thoughts and feelings from a personal point of view. Doubtless, He sought to realize to Himself His object and purpose in life. No one truly lives who has not made an attempt to do this. As His religious consciousness awakened, as He came to see that the family life of which He formed a part was lived in close communion with God, the prompting of the Spirit would direct His mind toward His Father in heaven ; His heart would open to His love ; new thoughts and surmisings would begin to stir within Him.

In the development of His mind and in the growth of His spiritual power, we must attach great weight to the reading and the study of the Scriptures. He knew the history of His people. He would be reminded that, like them, He Himself had gone down into Egypt and sojourned there for preservation of life. The persons of the patriarchs and their history were familiar to Him. In the birth and dedication of Samuel, He could see an example for Jewish youth. In the rise of David from obscurity to eminence, in his failings and in his devotion to God, He could take the more interest, as One whose family was descended from the king. His contemporary Philo tells us that the Jews made a point of instructing their children from their earliest years in the law of God and in a corresponding life. St. Paul, writing to Timothy,[2] remarks, 'From a child thou hast known

[1] Mk. vi. 3. [2] 2 Tim. iii. 15.

the Holy Scriptures.' Again and again during our Lord's ministry, we see evidence that the custom was faithfully observed in His own case. In all times of deep feeling, His thoughts move naturally in the forms of Old Testament speech. The Scriptures are the quarry from which He brings the fitting expression for what He wishes to say. He prefers their language to His own, partly, it may be, to show that they are His, that they express His own mind, and that He contemplated no reversal of their meaning and spirit; partly because, from old use and familiarity, their phrases came spontaneously upon His tongue.

We cannot say what effect upon His mind was caused by His becoming acquainted with the prophecies of the Messiah. How far did He realize in those quiet times when He was living the life of an ordinary man, that those prophecies, coming from such different periods, converged upon Himself? Who was the Suffering Servant of Jehovah? That picture of One who, by His own humiliation and suffering, would make atonement for the people of God, must have been often in His mind.[1] How far did He connect the expectations of the people, of which we have such ample testimony in the Birth-stories, with Himself? We cannot speak with certainty, but may be sure, from what we know of His sayings in after years,[2] that He knew that He stood in very close relation to God, and that a great work had been given Him to do.

But did He come to realize the mystery of His Person? Is there any indication that He knew Himself to stand in a relation to God solitary, alone? Before His entry upon His Ministry, and during those years of quiet, orderly work and seclusion, had He grasped His Divine Sonship?

If we follow the guidance of St. Luke, we shall have little doubt that the answer must be in the affirmative. It was an ordinance in Israel [3] that every father should teach his children to love and serve God, to keep His commandments and to walk in His fear. At the age of twelve, a Jewish boy became a 'Son of the Law.' He might worship in the synagogue and take part in pilgrimages to Jerusalem at the great Feasts. We can imagine the reverent delight with which this 'Son of the Law'

[1] Is. lii. 13 f. [2] K. Furrer, *Das Leben Jesu Christi*, p. 46.
[3] Deut. vi. 6 f.; 20 f.

would claim His right; how 'glad' He was when they said unto Him, 'Let us go unto the House of the Lord.'[1] But we are not left to form a picture for ourselves. St. Luke draws aside for a moment the veil that lies over the youth and early manhood of the Redeemer. We have one brief yet comprehensive view of Him at this critical moment of His life. We see Him passing from childhood to a responsible age; and the glimpse is very precious, for we are allowed to look not only at the outward facts, but into the working of His mind.

The people of the neighbourhood joined together, forming a large company of 'kinsfolk and acquaintance.'[2] As they journeyed they sang the Psalms of Ascent,[3] mingling strains of grief for exile and oppression, like the 'De profundis,' with those of rapturous delight in once more treading the courts of God's House. For those Psalms show the traces of the times of their composition, and contain the whole gamut of feeling, from the deepest affliction to the most radiant happiness. Thus attuned for their holy task, they shared the sacred joy of the Feast, and then turned homewards.

There was One, Who could not bring Himself thus to turn away and leave the hallowed spot. For Him, there lay in the sacrifices and in the historic associations of the Passover a meaning which no one else might fathom. The great deliverance of His people from the House of Bondage pointed through the Passover Feast to a new deliverance, greater far and from a sorer yoke, which was yet to come. And we gather from His recorded words that He knew that, in some way, the task was His; 'I must be about My Father's business.'[4] For His consciousness of the nature

[1] Ps. cxxii. 1. [2] Lk. ii. 44. [3] Ps. cxx.-cxxxiv.

[4] ἐν τοῖς τοῦ Πατρός μου δεῖ εἶναί με. 'I must be in the things of My Father,' *i.e.* the affairs, the business; certainly not the *house*, as in R.V. Cf. Matt. xvi. 23. There would have been no object in staying in the Temple after the Feast was over, because it was the Temple. It was the things of His Father that kept Him. He was hearing, and answering questions of, the accredited keepers of God's oracles. His parents, from their knowledge, should have understood the attraction of the place for Him. He asks, 'How is it that ye sought Me?' We may perhaps combine the two interpretations, when we remember that it was in God's House—in the halls surrounding the Forecourt—that the Teachers of the Law lectured and taught. That 'My Father's House' cannot have been His sole meaning is sufficiently shown by what St. Luke tells us of the effect of His words upon the parents; 'They understood not the saying which He spake unto them.' There would have

of His Person and of His Mission was already awakened. It is against reason to imagine that for thirty years our Lord had no clear conception on these points. The time was not wasted. He did not first come to realize Himself when His short Ministry began. He already knew that He was God's Son, called and sent to do His will.[1] How this consciousness awoke within Him with His growth in wisdom and in stature, we cannot tell. Some words may have been spoken by His Mother and by Joseph. They would not have left Him in ignorance of all the events that ushered in His birth. However guardedly they spoke, there was that within Him which met and corresponded with what they said, filling it out and deepening its content. We see this in the calm expression 'My Father's business,' set in contrast to the chiding saying of the anxious Mother, 'Thy father and I have sought Thee sorrowing.'[2]

However great was His longing to linger in the courts of the

been nothing mysterious in 'Wist ye not that I must be in My Father's House ?' But His 'Father's business' was a very different thing and opened out a train of questioning in their minds. What was this child, so wonderfully born, destined to be and to do ? What is this 'business' of which He speaks ?

[1] B. Weiss strongly refuses to see any allusion to unique Son-ship in Christ's words : 'A boy of twelve years, who speaks of His metaphysical oneness of being with God, or who merely hints at His supernatural birth, is no living human child, but an unnatural, ghostly form such as that which haunts us in the fantasies of the apocryphal Gospels.' *Das Leben Jesu*, i. p. 256.

This criticism would be just, if such thoughts lay behind Christ's words. Only, Weiss is belabouring a creation of his own fancy. So far from speaking of His 'metaphysical oneness of being with God,' or 'hinting at His supernatural birth' at the age of twelve, we find none of these assertions until a considerable time after His public Ministry had begun. There is nothing which contradicts the truth of boyhood in the words 'My Father's business.' But we maintain, to use Weiss's own words (*ib.* p. 257), that 'This Boy knows that He stands in an unique relation to God.' It is intended that we should be told something of the process of His awakening to the truth of His Personality. He is on the way to know Himself. We cannot dogmatize. But we may be thankful for the ray of light which shows the working of His mind. To use the phrase employed otherwise by Ignatius, *Ad Magn.* viii. 'The word comes out from silence' for a moment. It is the one saying of the Eternal Word which breaks the stillness that reigned over the thirty years of His life at Nazareth ; and it means—how much we do not know, but—far more than that He loved the House of God and fain would linger there.

[2] Dalman, *Die Worte Jesu*, p. 236 ; Garvie in *Expositor*, April, 1902. If some intimation of the events attending His birth and the destiny which they seemed to foreshadow had been made at the critical age which He had reached, there is reason for the reproach implied in His question (Lk. ii. 49). He recalls His Mother's thoughts to what she had told Him.

Temple, our Lord at once yielded to His Parents' wish, and returned home with them. Before the veil falls again upon the life of quiet industry which was being led at Nazareth, we are told that He was obedient to His Parents and that 'He increased in wisdom and stature and in favour with God and man.' Thus all the conditions of true human life are being fulfilled. There is no evidence of self-assertion ; no hint of any presuming on a knowledge or a condition of being which was not possessed by others. He develops as other young men develop. His character and disposition win the favour of all with whom He comes in contact. There is a grace and beauty in every act, which betray the simplicity and purity that reign within. And the conditions of His life and His occupation were natural and healthy. So He grows in stature [1] as in wisdom, and in favour with God, Who sees in Him with ever increasing joy the forming of what He intended man to be.

[1] Lk. ii. 52. In spite of appeals to the testimony of papyri (Milligan, *The N.T. Documents*, p. 74), the translation of ἡλικία by 'age' may be rejected both on the ground of the meaningless character of such an assertion and on the fact that elsewhere in St. Luke (xix. 3) it certainly means 'stature.' Cf. *Fragment of a Lost Gospel* from Oxyrhynchus (Grenfell and Hunt), p. 39 τίς ἂν προσθ(εί)η ἐπὶ τὴν ἡλικίαν ὑμῶν ;

CHAPTER XI

THE TWO NATURES

PERHAPS the chief problem which the Gospel presentation of Christ offers to thought is that of the meeting of the finite and the infinite in a single Personality with all that the conjunction involves. We have no experience to guide us; no data of our own consciousness on which to draw. Hedged in as we are on all sides by the limitations of a finite being, we can form no conception of what it must be to possess the character of infinitude. Let us see what are some of its qualities as disclosed in the Scripture representations of God.

But first, it is to be observed that even with God, infinitude does not imply absence of all restraint and limitation. A being totally without limitation would not be a Person. The essence of Personality consists in the possession of definite characteristics. An unlimited and unrestrained being is unthinkable metaphysically and morally. It would mean the co-existence at their fullest of mutually destructive elements. A Person requires the discipline of limitation of certain qualities and restraint from the opposites of others.[1] If God is good, He must be strictly limited, by a law of His own Being, from all evil: His character is bounded. Thus, Scripture tells us that He cannot lie. Neither can He repent. His nature is at harmony with itself. We can imagine no false step that has to be retraced; no mistaken course that has to be abandoned. There can be no regret where mind and heart are true to the highest aims.

[1] As Spinoza says, 'Omnis determinatio est negatio.' You cannot have a determinate being, such as is implied in personality, without resorting to negatives, if you wish to describe him. *v.* Wallace, *Logic of Hegel*, p. 147.

This consideration may help to remove the difficulty suggested by the Christian standpoint. God is not pure infinitude. Only under certain aspects can we conceive Him as unlimited. These are of two kinds, metaphysical and ethical. The first has to do with extension in time and space, and can only be expressed by negations. His being has no beginning or end. It is timeless. It is not bounded by any imaginable barrier in space.[1] It is all-pervading. There is truth in the higher Pantheism, if we take care to discriminate between the identity of God with the universe and His immanence therein. This conception has found no finer expression than that of Ps. cxxxix, and the advance of modern science, as it tends towards the unifying of phenomena, makes for its confirmation. An evenness runs through nature, which points to the presence of one will. The signs of discord which theology imputes to the presence of evil, difficult as they are to harmonize with this conception of unity, cannot hide from us the impression that a single mind has been at work and that law pervades the whole of being. The presence of God is without limit. It is all-pervading.

As in extension, so in certain qualities of His Being, God is patient of no limit. In love and in goodness He knows no bounds. If we could set a limit to the reach and intensity of His love, or could detect a flaw in the purity of His character, He would not be God. In these positive qualities of character, there need be no limitation for fear of their running counter to other necessary qualities. They can be infinitely extended, without contradicting any essential element of the Divine Being. It is perhaps impossible to give a more complete idea of the boundless character of the love of God than St. John has done in saying, 'God is love.' Here the predication of love amounts almost to a process of identification. God not merely *has* love among other qualities of His Being. He *is* love. Love in its supreme manifestation is something Divine, nay more, it is God Himself: and conversely, He is Love Personified; as we say of a man, 'He is kindness itself.'

In what, therefore, may be called positive characteristics, God, in His nature and in His qualities, is subject to no limit. But, as things are constituted, the exercise of certain qualities necessarily involves some adjustment in the exercise of other qualities.

[1] Cf. 'The Father incomprehensible . . .' Athan. Creed.

You cannot carry them to their furthest extent without imposing a restraint elsewhere. This is equally true in the relation of God and man. Take the qualities of love and justice. Justice stretched to its fullest is brought up against love. Love in its perfection modifies the exercise of justice, κατακαυχᾶται ἔλεος κρίσεως.[1]

This fact prepares us for the idea that, in view of the accomplishment of His purposes, God may consent to place restrictions on the exercise of powers and qualities, which find their complete fulfilment in Himself.

The fact of creation itself was one such purpose. As the calling into existence of the finite, of something which is not God, it involved a sacrifice on His part. It set a limit to the completeness of His self-expression. Perfect in Himself, in the mutual love of the Trinity, He had no need to go out of Himself for the satisfaction of His power and love. He was self-sufficing. All that constitutes the perfection of the Godhead could be and was completely fulfilled in what He was, from all eternity, in Himself. To give existence to a separate being—a creature which, coming in time and finite in capacity, is not God—must involve a Self-limitation, the nature of which is of course beyond our comprehension. It meant the finding room within the all-pervasiveness of the Divine Presence for something not Divine. It was the going out of Himself for the satisfaction of that Love and Goodness, which could yet be complete in Himself; and the amount of the satisfaction so obtained externally is the measure of the limitation of His own self-contained completeness, for it was incapable of being added to by reason of its existing perfection. Thus, in creation, God freely limits Himself. He makes room in the whole of things for what, however Divine its origin, is not itself Divine.[2]

Now, if God can bring Himself, in the overflow of His goodness, to create at the expense of the completeness of His own self-expression in the love of the Trinity, it is not hard to imagine that He might take a further step and, by the creation of separate

[1] James ii. 13.

[2] Cf. Martineau, *The Seat of Authority in Religion*, p. 36, 'The outward world is not God's characteristic sphere of self-expression. Rather it is His eternal act of self-limitation. . . . The finite universe is thus the stooping of the Infinite Will to an everlasting self-sacrifice.'

wills, permit other centres of determinate action to exist. The transition from existence separate from Himself to wills, not only separate, but possibly to be set against Him, as the power of self-determination implies, is not so great as at first sight appears. The great decisive step was taken in the primal act of creation. From God to other than God is the marvel.[1] From existence separate from God to wills independent of Him is not so complete a change. At any rate, it has been made. Man is a self-determining personality. He may will and has willed apart from God and in opposition to Him ; thus setting going action which is repugnant to Him.[2]

In all this we see the principle of limitation. God has in some way suffered a restraint upon the free and complete exercise of His sovereign powers.

If the Infinite and Almighty has thus, in the generosity of His love, tolerated limitations in His own action by the creation of an universe outside Himself and by bringing into being creatures with the power of self-determination, whose wills might conceivably be arrayed against Him, we have a background of probability for the fact of another and, from some points of view, a still greater mode of limitation.

The Incarnation of the Son of God, as taught in Scripture and as presented to faith in the creeds, implies that God, in the Person of His Son, has consented to subject Himself—the Infinite, Eternal God—to the conditions of a finite life in time.

Now, it is clear that the Incarnation of God involves an abasement, the extent of which is for us inconceivable. We can measure its depth as we take our stand before the Cross. We cannot gauge the height from which He stooped. The Incarnation itself is an act of humiliation. Had human nature remained sinless, the transition from the free, unfettered life of the Godhead to that of man would have been something wonderful : but 'to be made in the likeness of sinful flesh and for sin' implies a contrast which is beyond our understanding.

Yet, the previous act of self-limitation in the creation of a race of self-determining beings leads us up to the mystery of the

[1] I find that Du Bose takes the same view : 'To *other* Himself in others than Himself, that is the highest work, the divinest act of love, of which even God himself, or Love itself, is capable.' *The Gospel according to St. Paul*, p. 242.

[2] *v.* Illingworth, *The Gospel Miracles*, 1915, p. 143 f.

Incarnation. If we cannot understand, we can believe and adore. The way has been cleared for reason to assent to such an attitude. It is the function of reason to lay down the conditions on which faith can act, to impose certain limits within which faith may operate without degenerating into superstition. So here, a rational view of God and man permits the hope that the saving of man, the fulfilment of the purpose of his existence, the moral issues which are involved in his relation to God and the world, may lead to a revelation by which God, making Himself known to man, will lead man to find his end in Himself. It would be irrational to suppose that a being such as man, with his moral and spiritual equipment, with his instinctive feeling after and desire for God, with his sensibility to the profound impulses and cravings of the spiritual world, would be left with no clear guidance, a shipwrecked sailor on a desolate reef in mid-ocean. No theist could accept such a position as possible. May we not say that the creation of man in the image of God contains an implicit promise of the *humanizing* of God? By no other means—so far as we can see—could the gulf be bridged which separates us from Him. The pagan world attempted to resolve the discord by the apotheosis of man. Man has to scale the heavens. The Christian conception brings God down to earth. Rebellion, pride, self-assertion, is the method of the one. The self-humiliation of Him who 'pleased not Himself' was the self-chosen way of the other. And it is on the line of God's method in creation. Creation, as we have seen, is a going out of Himself in love, in order to bring into being something which is not Himself. In the Incarnation God unites Himself with the highest of His creatures to bring them to their destiny—union with and life in God. He goes out of His completeness—passes into a state of creaturely limitation—to raise the creature to the life for which He intended him.

And this state of limitation is real. The neglect to acknowledge its reality has led men to miss the message of the Incarnation. In every devout mind there is a more or less unconscious tendency towards Docetism. It seems more reverent to ascribe a lesser degree of 'self-emptying' than Scripture assigns to the Son of God, to regard language that implies it as symbolical, to see in the Carpenter of Nazareth a demi-god rather than a Jewish working man, to forget the human in the presence of the Divine. It is therefore well worth our while to recall the passionate vehemence with which the Apostle, who eagle-like soared higher than all his brethren into the region of the Divine, claimed for the Son of God that He has 'come in the flesh.' It was of the very spirit of the Anti-Christ to withhold that confession. Cerinthus lives in the pillory as one who taught that the heavenly Christ descended upon the man Jesus at His baptism; that 'He came in the water' only [1] and was not identical throughout His earthly life with the Son of Mary. Such a view cuts at the root of the Incarnation. It dissolves the union with our nature, on which depends the salvation of man and his restoration to that likeness to God for which he was created. Under the pretext that honour is being done to God, He is robbed of the glory of His greatest act of self-limitation, of that triumph of self-forgetting love which He exemplified when He stooped to take upon Himself our nature and 'though He were rich, yet for our sakes became poor.'

Yet we can hardly wonder that, when the Church at large came to realize the Divinity of Christ, there was a temptation to minimize His humanity. It is only what we should expect from the constitution of the human mind, that a great wave of enthusiastic belief in an august and awe-inspiring fact would be accompanied by a loose hold on any truth that, at first sight, seemed to run counter to it. There is always this tendency to merge what is true in what is thought to be of greater weight. We can never see things whole. We are always at the mercy of our imagination, and so it comes about that, as the ages pass, now one and now another aspect of the whole truth comes out prominently, to the exclusion of other sides which are perhaps of equal moment. This present age is one which answers to the appeal 'Ecce Homo.' Never has the truth of Christ's full and complete humanity been so strongly held; and one result has been the power to enter into the mind and heart of the Man Christ Jesus as at no other time. But along with this great gain—a gain largely due to the work of the historical critic—has come the danger of failure to realize the Godhead of Christ. The peril to faith nowadays is not Docetism.[2] It is rather such

[1] Iren. *Adv. Haer.* i. 21. *v.* Denney, *Jesus and the Gospel*, p. 84.

[2] The Docetism of the second century is indeed repeated by the eccentric and unhistorical movement represented by Kalthoff, J. M. Robertson, Smith and Drews, but its influence is slight. Cf. K. Lake, *The Stewardship of Faith*, p. 148.

an emphasis on the humanity as makes it cover the whole field of vision, and so hides from men's eyes the Divine lineaments that they seem to recede and fade. To borrow a metaphor from art, it is a question of values. The proportion of the faith is affected by the high colouring of one single element; and at the present time it is the humanity which is emphasized to the loss of the Divinity. Historic criticism has brought the Figure of Christ out into the full light of day, so that He lives and breathes before us with a sharpness of outline as never before; but great as is the gain, it has been dearly purchased. It was once said that, in the fourth century, 'the world woke up to find itself Arian.' It is to be feared that, nowadays in large sections of Christian thought, but a feeble grip is retained of the fact that Jesus of Nazareth is, in an unique sense, the Son of God.

Can we represent the effect of the Incarnation in such a way as to commend it to reason, while preserving the New Testament account of it?

We have seen that creation involved a process of self-limitation on the part of God, more especially when it issued in the production of creatures with the power of self-determination. In the first case, God tolerated the existence of something other than Himself, and went out of Himself in the exuberance of His love and goodness.

In the second case, God faced the possibility that the wills which He endowed would be turned against Himself. He not only limited His self-sufficedness by the act of creation. He endured to give existence to a possibly hostile element.

Here we touch on mysteries that we cannot penetrate. We can only say that the Love of God—the longing for the deliberate response of the love of His creatures to His own love, as well as the 'abandon' of a Love infinite and eternal on His part—moved Him to create and to endow as He has done. The Love of Father, Son and Holy Spirit, eternally sufficing, always fresh and always perfect, enters at creation into contact with the finite and the temporal, suffering the limitation which the act of creation demands and finding happiness and satisfaction outside Itself.

If God, foreseeing the result, could yet go on to create and still be love, He must also have foreseen the necessity of redemption. If His method is to correspond and harmonize with His action in creation, as we should expect, it will bear marks of the same self-chosen limitation and restraint. Some modification in the expression, if not in the essence, of His glory, some restraint on the fulness of His power and of its exercise, may be looked for. There is an inner harmony pervading the life and being of God which makes it possible to forecast His action under differing circumstances. What He was in creation, what He is in sustaining, that He is in restoring and redeeming. We found the note of sacrifice in His creative work. It will be found equally in the work of redemption.

And it is in this fact that we have to seek the explanation of the great principle of the Incarnation—the co-existence of the infinite and the finite in one Personality. To effect it, a check must be put upon the expression of the Godhead of the Eternal Son. Otherwise such a union with human nature as that created by the Nativity could not be. 'The glorious God that maketh the thunder,' 'dwelling in the light no man can approach unto,'[1] could not, as He is, be matched with human nature. He must abate something of His glory; something must be laid aside. Without ceasing to be what He ever was, He must set limits to the mode of His self-expression before He can 'take upon Him the form of a servant and be made in the likeness of men.'[2] Even then the distance bridged seems inconceivable. 'The Most High dwelleth not in temples made with hands.'[3] Yet, when the shepherds enter the cave on the night of the Nativity, they see before them in the Child of Mary the human tabernacle of the Godhead. They worship God robed in flesh.

Nor is such union of the Divine and the human unbecoming. God did not enter an alien order of being when He 'became man.' From the Gospel of the Incarnation we have repeatedly to recur to the Gospel of Creation, if it is not to remain an insoluble problem. There is a divinity in human nature which lasts on in its ruin. There is a correspondence between God and man which makes the way between them open and plain. There is access; and the approach does no violence to either. 'In the image of God made He man.' This likeness is intellectual. From it follows a possibility of mutual understanding. The mind of God, however it transcends the mind of man in reach

[1] Ps. xxix. 3; 1 Tim. vi. 16. [2] Phil. ii. 7. [3] Acts vii. 48.

and complexity, is of the same character.[1] There is likeness also between the ethical and spiritual nature of God and that of man, far as the one outsoars the other. Whatever the differences of ethical standards in various races, man at his best, in the highest stages of his moral development, thinks as God thinks. What is good or evil in God's sight is good or evil in the sight of the good man, so far as his knowledge goes. The conscience of a man who by right living has kept it true and keen is the voice of God within him. There is no discord. God and man understand one another. This consideration is of great weight as we approach the thought of the Incarnation. It does not remove the mystery, but it smooths the way for its acceptance. Man at his best, where the good in him reaches its zenith, is akin to God.[2] They belong to the same moral sphere. Their language is the same, for man has never lost the stamp of divinity which was impressed upon him at creation.

Therefore in the Incarnation God is not going out of His own sphere, He is not violating any principle of His being. Whatever had to be laid aside, and however deep the humiliation to which He stooped, no wrong was done to His essential nature. If this consideration were more generally kept in mind, it would not be so hard to receive the Gospel message. As in creating, the sacrifice which was entailed on the part of God brought no loss of His essential being, so we cannot imagine that the supreme exhibition of His love in redeeming caused Him loss. Rather it clothed Him with new glory.[3] In taking our nature, He remained what He had ever been—' God of God '—Himself and not another. If there was any change, it was not in essence,

[1] As an instance of this fact, it has been pointed out that the mathematical figure of the ellipse was worked out by the Greek Archimedes, (*ob.* B.C. 212), who traced it out in the sand of his study floor. When the telescope had been invented, Kepler found that the planets in their courses pursued the track which the ancient geometrician had evolved as a necessary result of the working of his own mind. God and man were at one in thought.

[2] Since the above was written, it has been said, 'Because humanity is not alien from God, but is spiritual as He is spiritual, God can be revealed in a human life.' *Foundations*, p. 255.

[3] Hebr. ii. 9. 'It may be as natural, so to speak, for God to become man, as for God to create man.' Illingworth, *The Divine Immanence*, p. 86. Cf. Athan. *De Incarnatione Verbi Dei*, p. 95, A-C.

but in the character of His self-manifestation.[1] St. Paul expresses this idea by saying 'He emptied Himself, taking the form of a servant.' [2]

What that expression is really intended to convey, we do not know. We can form no estimate of 'the glory which' He 'had with the Father before the world was.' [3] Therefore we cannot tell all that He laid aside. But at least we can say that no part of His essential being was touched by the Incarnation. It is a law of the Godhead that It can suffer no diminution. We cannot imagine that God could be greater at one time than at another. 'I the Lord change not.' [4] And this calm, unbroken peace and order, subsisting eternally, is claimed for the Incarnate Son Himself. 'Jesus Christ the same yesterday, to-day and for ever.' [5] When, then, He 'emptied Himself,' the process must have consisted in laying aside the manifestation or expression of His unchanging Deity.[6] 'God is Spirit.' We have no means of knowing the characteristics of an existence which is purely spiritual. But it must include various forms of power and knowledge, and the gifts which are implied by their possession. Certain of these, it would seem, were held back from their natural exercise. When the shepherds entered the cave of the Nativity, they saw God in the Person of the Holy Child: but every manifestation of God was absent. Instead of the power which set the planets on their courses, and which curbs the fury of the sea,

[1] *v.* Chrys. *Hom. in Joan.* i. 14. [2] Phil. ii. 7 (R.V.).

[3] Jo. xvii. 5. [4] Mal. iii. 6. [5] Hebr. xiii. 8.

[6] Cf. Westcott, *The Ep. to the Hebr.* p. 426, 'It (His humanity) did not limit His Divine nature in any way in itself; it limited only its manifestation.' Has not Loofs saddled the Kenotic theory with conclusions which its chief upholders would decline to draw? For instance, he says, 'The theory asserts that the Eternal Son of God, in the moment of His incarnation, emptied Himself more or less of His divinity, and so became the subject of a really human life, while His divine self-consciousness was changed into a human one.' *Op. cit. infra*, p. 224. No such implication lies in Phil. ii. 7. We are not to be deprived of the help which we can get from the passage by the fact that erroneous and unwarranted deductions have been made from it. On the line of thought which recognizes an ascending scale of self-restraint and self-limitation (certainly not self-extinguishment) in God's acts, first of creation of the physical universe, then of man as a self-determining creature and finally of the 'sending' of His Only-begotten Son, we can see something of the truth which St. Paul means to convey in the self-emptying of the Lord Jesus. It is the veiling and withholding of the full prerogatives of His Eternal Sonship, in concurrence with the Father's will, for an object dear to the Father's heart as to His own—the redemption of man.

they saw One who was subject to all the weakness and necessities of childhood: and yet in Him, as we are assured, dwelt 'all the fulness of the Godhead bodily.'[1]

In a recent work, Dr. Loofs, after testing ancient and modern attempts to solve the problem, comes to the conclusion that it is best met by St. Paul's saying, 'God was in Christ reconciling the world unto Himself.'[2] He had already[3] said that 'in the idea of the indwelling of God's Spirit in Jesus, we meet with the oldest formula which tries to explain the unique character of Jesus.' But although this expedient carries us some way towards a position in which faith and reason may well rest content, it is clear from what he says about the nature of our Lord's Personality that we are still far from the true Scriptural and Catholic solution. For he appears[4] to regard that Personality as a human one. In doing so, in order to render justice to the Scriptural account of our Lord's Manhood, he runs counter to the teaching of St. Paul, St. John and the writer to the Hebrews on the pre-existent, timeless Being of the Son of God—teaching, we must remember, which is found in the 'Q' element of the First and Third Gospels.[5] Now this conception of a pre-existent Son of God, which the New Testament undoubtedly presents to us, is not adequately met by the theory of a human Personality more fully dwelt in by the Holy Spirit than any other child of man has been or can be.[6] Even if it is not 'softened down,' the conception fails to answer to the Scriptural representation of His Person. We have therefore no alternative but to reject it; and with the feeling that it does not meet the needs of faith, a temporary and provisional formula is found in the words already quoted, 'God was in Christ reconciling the world unto Himself.'[7]

But, if we may gather from the course of his argument the sense in which Loofs is prepared to understand the passage, it goes no farther than the inadequate idea of the indwelling of the Spirit of God in Jesus; for in such a case the action of God and of His Spirit is inseparable. We cannot distinguish between them or their effects. Inasmuch as the indwelling of the Spirit

[1] Col. ii. 9.

[2] 2 Cor. v. 19. *What is the Truth about Jesus Christ?* 1914, p. 240.

[3] *Ib.* p. 237. [4] *Ib.* p. 236. [5] Matt. xi. 27 = Lk. x. 22.

[6] *v. op. cit.* p. 238. [7] *Op. cit.* p. 239 f.

may be predicated of any true servant of God, such a phrase, or its equivalent, does not suffice to express the truth of Christ's Person.[1] As a matter of fact, Loofs denies to the historic Jesus that pre-existence as the Son of God, which is implied in the Catholic doctrine of His Person. He regards His Sonship as dating from His Incarnation, not from Eternity. And yet he fully admits that the New Testament asserts the pre-existence of Jesus.[2] It must be supposed that he rejects its evidence; otherwise we cannot help asking what is the nature of a being, who is 'before all creation' and yet only becomes entitled to be called 'the Son of God' at the moment of His humiliation, when taking our flesh as 'Son of Man.' The passage which asserts the pre-existence of Jesus asserts His possession of cosmic functions, which are inconceivable as appertaining to a created existence.[3] In face of these considerations, it is beside the point to ask 'Where in the New Testament is this prehistoric, yea, this antemundane Christ called the Son of God?'[4] For it is the same Being who is thus styled in His earthly career; and if such a designation is fitting then, is it unbecoming in the midst of 'the glory which' He 'had with the Father before the world was'?

Loofs rightly insists on the fact of Christ's true and complete humanity. But he goes on to say, 'the assumption that the life of Jesus was a purely human one . . . is false.' In this conviction, he is also in agreement with St. John. Human, yet more than human; how are these positions to be reconciled without doing violence to one side or the other of the seeming antithesis? A true man, who is more than human, if we confine our representation within the limits proper to humanity, appears to possess the character of a monstrosity—an abnormal and therefore repellent object. But there is no indication of such a being in the Gospel portrait of Christ. His humanity, wherever it is disclosed, is normal, gracious and attractive. It has appealed to every following generation as the perfect type of what manhood was meant to be. No

[1] 'At no time, certainly not in the Apostolic age, were men satisfied by conceptions of His Person framed in accord with the category of Inspiration. *Journ. of Theol. Studies*, 1913, p. 109.

[2] *Op. cit.* p. 177.

[3] Col. i. 16, 17, 19, 20; Hebr. i 8 Cf. St. Ignat. *ad Rom.* 3, 6.

[4] *Op. cit.* p. 177.

discordant, inhuman feature appears. Where, then, are we to seek for the origin of that element in Christ's Person, which surpasses the measure of man and is not to be accounted for by any combination of human faculties? The step is a long one; it crosses a seemingly infinite gulf: but there is no other landing place for thought than God Himself. We can only explain the more than human element in Christ by having recourse to the language of the Fourth Gospel: 'The Word was God': but the Word entered into relations of time and space: 'The Word was made flesh.' Preserving His Divine Personality —we can imagine no change in the Ego of the Son of God—He took to Himself a perfect manhood; and henceforth that manhood becomes the mode of His manifestation. His action upon earth is mediated and conditioned by the self-chosen organ which He made His own.

But here we are met with a reluctance to follow St. John, St. Paul, and the writer to the Hebrews. Yet the plain, straightforward meaning of each is that a Divine, pre-existent Being came into the world in the substance of our flesh.[1] The

[1] 'All the rest of the New Testament (besides the Synoptic Gospels) with more or less of emphasis according to circumstances, θεολογεῖ τὸν Χριστόν, treats of Christ as God; and the Church universal has done the same from the time of the Apostles until now.' Sanday, *Christologies Ancient and Modern*, p. 120. It is strange that passages such as Rom. i. 7, 1 Cor. i. 3, 2 Cor. i. 2, should be quoted by Loofs, as making against the Godhead of Christ, and as implying the solitary unity of God the Father; and this 'without the shadow of a doubt.' *Op. cit.* p. 180. On the contrary, the co-ordination of the Father and the Son, as the sources of grace and love, has always been regarded as conveying the truth of their equality within the Godhead; and as showing that from the first the Church held the faith which was afterwards drawn out into the doctrine of the Holy Trinity. Loofs regards Christ's habit of prayer as fatal to the orthodox Christology. But what was the character of His prayer? It was the expression of His perfect and unbroken unity of will and mind with the Father—the mode in which He maintained His sense of communion with Him.

It was conceivable that He who 'was in all points tempted,' might have lost touch with the Father under the stress of His life of humiliation. Prayer was a safeguard; and for us it revealed the reality of the limitations to which He yielded in His earthly life. If prayer is fatal to His Divine Personality, hunger, thirst and many another condition of His human life are equally incongruous. But then, on that ground, we should have to abandon the idea of any true humiliation at all. And with it would go the Incarnation itself. Cf. Hebr. v. 7, 8. 'Though He were a Son, yet learned He obedience by the things which He suffered.' 'The title "Son" is here used of the eternal, divine relation of the Son to the Father' (Westcott, *in loc.*). Because he cannot (for who

position that God's Spirit dwelt in Christ, that 'God was in Christ' is inadequate.[1] It may be quite another thing from holding that in Christ *God became Man.* And nothing less than this position satisfies the full Christian conception of our Lord's Person.[2]

The mystery deepens when we try to grasp the fact revealed in Scripture, that the assumption of humanity by the Son of God involved not only the adoption of a new nature but of another will, while the Ego, the Personality, remained the same. Two natures had to live together: two centres of self-determination had to subsist within the confines of a single Personality. Our Lord had a will which was not necessarily in accord with the Divine will: which might conceivably assert itself in direct opposition to the will of God. The struggle in Gethsemane is an evidence of this fact. 'Father, if Thou be willing, remove this cup from Me: nevertheless, not My will, but Thine be done.'[3] The fact that the will of Christ could be opposed to

can ?) reconcile to his complete satisfaction the characteristics of Divinity and manhood, as they are imputed by the New Testament writers to the Person of our Lord, Loofs ignores one member of the supposed antinomy. Clinging, as we all must do, to the fact of complete humanity, he sees in it the contradiction of the Divinity. Such a position is fatal to any complete reception of the Gospel message. It is not Christianity as it has always been understood. To simplify, by surrender of what is vital, is not true science. Cf. Du Bose, *The Gospel According to St. Paul*, p. 302, 'We must, if only, hold on to and insist upon the opposite and complementary terms of our Lord's deity and His humanity, until we can better correlate them in our minds, and approve their coexistent and equal truth to our reason.'

[1] For a favourable opinion on this, the Ritschlian, view of Christ's Person, *v.* Sanday, *op. cit.* p. 104 f.

[2] K. Lake makes the assertion that although St. Paul freely calls Jesus 'Lord,' which, as he says, was a long step towards the claim of Divinity for Him, yet 'he never calls Jesus "God."' *The Stewardship of Faith*, pp. 93, 94. This assertion is hardly borne out by the best critical interpretation of such passages as Col. i. 15; ii. 9 (*v.* Lightfoot's notes); Rom. ix. 5. *v.* Sanday and Headlam, *ad loc.* Cf. Tit. ii. 13. The state of the case is as Dr. Sanday puts it. *v.* p. 198, n. 1. Cf. Clemen, *Religionsgesch. Erklärung des N.T.* p. 261, 'Paul has not only set Him (Jesus) along with God, but according to by far the most probable explanation of Rom. ix. 5, also named Him thus' (*i.e.* God). *v.* Du Bose, *The Gospel according to St. Paul*, p. 298, 'Christ is Θεός, but He is not ὁ Θεός. The Divine Word can never be other than personal, or less than God; but neither is He absolutely or exclusively God, in a monarchian or Sabellian sense.'

[3] Lk. xxii. 42. Unless we adopt the Monothelite heresy and deny to our Lord the possession of two wills, one human and one Divine, we must admit the

that of God in desire, though not carried into practice, shows that a very real obscuration of the Divinity must have taken place at His Incarnation. He did not cease to be God; but He entered into conditions which were not so permeated by the Godhead as to wholly exclude a view of life different from God's view. Such is the natural interpretation of the words 'not My will but Thine.' The two wills are not identical. They *may* conflict: and if the will of God is to triumph, it must be by the subjection of the will of the Man Christ Jesus whenever necessary. In this fact we cannot help seeing a very clear 'emptying' of the Divine—a real restraint put upon its manifestation when the Son of God assumed humanity.

And yet He was what He had ever been—the very and eternal Son of God, the Creator and Upholder of the Universe, One with the Father and the Holy Spirit. To some the contradiction which seems to be involved in this double nature existing within a single personality offers a problem which must remain insoluble. The thought of centuries, issuing in the suggestions which are connected with the names of Apollinaris, Nestorius, Eutyches, only succeeded in solving the difficulty at the expense of necessary truth. The revolt from Arianism had caused the humanity of Christ to pass into the background, to be explained away, or to be so merged in the Divinity as to lose its proper characteristics. At the council of Chalcedon, the Fathers were content to proclaim the co-existence in the Divine Person of each nature. They made no attempt to explain the fact.[1] In the present day, the tendency of thought is to seek for light, if any can be found, in our increased knowledge of the meaning of personality and of

possibility that He might make a decision contrary to the will of God. The Temptation is meaningless otherwise. The language of the Agony is inexplicable. There was no focus of rebellion within Himself. Temptation had to come from without. But it had a finite, human will, which was not the same as the will of God, to appeal to. And the appeal was made, not only on the occasions named, but again and again during the course of His Ministry. Being who He was, we cannot conceive that He would fall; but that He *could* fall was essential to the reality of the experience of One who 'was in all points tempted like as we are.' For a somewhat different view (but the passage is obscure), *v. Foundations*, p. 248. Exposure to the full force of Temptation seems to have been a chief element in the κένωσις. 'Human nature in its completeness carries with it the possession of a human will.' Strong, *Manual of Theology*, p. 130.

[1] *v.* below, p. 204.

the psychological considerations which are involved in it. It is a fact of very wide experience that personality is not the bare unit which it was supposed to be. Many persons are capable of leading a double life. They are conscious of two seemingly contradictory lines of thought and aim. A well-known novelist has illustrated this fact by the career of a singer, whose public and private life present such contrasts of experience, that she finds it hard to realize that she is one and the same person.[1] Who is not aware at times of a mental condition which is out of touch with that which he ordinarily recognizes as his own? There come glimpses of an actual experience, as it seems, upon which he knows that he has never entered. Places, which he has never before visited and scarcely heard of, wear a familiar aspect when he sees them. Ideas strike him as strangely congruous with what he has ever felt, though they had never emerged into his own conscious perception. He finds himself in them, becoming aware of a spiritual domain which is his own, though he had not dreamed of it. However we denote this fact of separate states of consciousness in a single subject, a fact it is, which at least suggests that personality in man is a richer and fuller thing than we had thought.

Now, if we take this enlarged conception of ordinary human personality with us when we study the Person of Christ, we may be able—not to explain the mode of the conjunction of the two natures therein, but—to imagine how the infinite and the finite, God and man, could harmoniously contribute to His one Personality—how the one Person of the Saviour could share an experience which comprised a life both human and Divine. The Gospels present Him to us as a Divine Being, the Eternal Son of God. As such, during His earthly life, He was performing His cosmic functions of upholding and sustaining as well as enlightening all things;[2] and, corresponding to the exercise of these functions, must have been His possession of a consciousness which was Divine in its power and range.[3] Yet, along with these indications of Godhead, we become aware of a life lived under the strict limitations of humanity. Even His miracles are more than once assigned to Him as man working by the power of God.[4] The divine reach and grasp of His consciousness

[1] *Soprano*, by F. M. Crawford.

[2] Col. i. 16, 17; Jo. i. 9; Hebr. i. 3.

[3] Matt. xi. 27.

[4] Jo. xi. 41; Lk. xi. 20.

does not exclude the signs of a limitation equally real and as clearly noted by the Evangelists.[1]

Although an explanation of the conjunction of these facts is impossible in our present state of knowledge, our enlarged conception of human personality should at least prepare our minds to receive it. The Personality of Christ is Divine. He is God, and at His Incarnation He has not ceased to be God. Yet the life on which He entered as man became a real experience. Thus, without any infringement of His original Personality, without ceasing to be what He had ever been, He allowed the restrictions of a limited sphere of being, on which He had voluntarily entered,[2] to impinge upon and to influence the manifestation of that 'glory which He had with the Father before the world was.'

At this point it is a help again [3] to remind ourselves that in thus joining a perfect human nature to His Divine Being, our Lord suffered no violence to His Person. The nature of man is akin to that of God. Even in his fallen state, glimpses of Divinity are to be seen; heroic acts of self-sacrifice, love and tenderness, patience towards the wayward and unruly, all show a likeness to the character of God, and reveal something of Him. And if this be so in fallen man—still more in the truth of human nature, in manhood as assumed by Jesus Christ, is this correspondence evident. If there is antithesis in the metaphysical qualities of God and man, the One being infinite, the other finite, there is none in those moral and spiritual qualities which constitute the supreme excellences of both. Love, whether in God or man, is

[1] When we compare the various aspects of our Lord's consciousness which are presented by the Gospels, we have to take the familiar dictum of His 'single consciousness' as a theoretical statement which, however correct logically, requires modification for practical accuracy. It was not a Divine but a very human consciousness which asked, 'Where have ye laid him?' (Jo. xi. 34). It was not a human, but a Divine consciousness of which He spoke when He said, 'No man knoweth the Father save the Son' (Matt. xi. 27). Yet, in each case, there was congruity between the two aspects of a consciousness, which in its depths was single as His Personality was single. Cf. Sanday, *Christologies, Ancient and Modern*, p. 167 f.; Mackintosh, *The Person of Jesus Christ*, pp. 294, 5.

[2] It was a single act of will at the moment of the Incarnation which effected this limitation; not a series of acts of self-restraint, undertaken for specific reasons during the course of His life on earth. No one has more strongly insisted on this view than Bp. Weston in *The One Christ*, *passim*.

[3] Cf. above, p. 193.

Divine, so are truth and sincerity. You have not to form different classifications when you speak of the highest characteristics of God and man. J. Stuart Mill [1] was right when he declined to call that good in God which offended his moral instincts as he saw it in man.

These considerations may make it easier to see how in the one Person of Jesus Christ, two whole and separate natures, that of God and that of man, could dwell together in unity: the Divine expressing itself in the language and manner of man, the manhood mediating for men the presence of the Divine. No formula of the schools has yet been found to set forth a theory that can logically account for the facts and bring them together in such a shape as to be completely satisfying. But we know enough of the two Natures to be able to see, in the light of a fuller knowledge of what is involved in Personality, that the Gospel picture of the Incarnate Son of God can claim not only the adherence of our faith but of our reason. Now, as in the stilling of the storm, we see the Godhead at work [2]: now, as in the rest of the weary traveller at the well-side, we see the man.[3] The economy by which this double mode of a single life was ordered, so that without infringing the reality of each nature, the one Divine Person spoke and wrought, is hidden from us.[4]

There is in the present day a certain discontent with the

[1] *Three Essays on Religion.* *v.* Kilpatrick in *Dict. of Christ.* i. p. 813[2].

[2] But in the manner and with the voice of man.

[3] And yet the manhood is hardly able to veil and restrain the Deity.

[4] Our Lord's earthly life was not, as it were, stored in two separate and watertight compartments. He never acted as God only or man only; always as the God-man. The two natures with their metaphysical distinctions were drawn upon by the one Ego, the one Personality, to which each belonged. Cf. Westcott on *Hebr.* p. 66, 'The two natures were inseparably combined in the unity of His Person.' Bp. Gore, *Dissertations*, pp. 165, 6, who quotes Westcott with approval, here seems to go too far when he says, 'His powerful works no less than His humiliations, are in the Gospels attributed to His manhood,' and his own admission that certain words and claims of Christ (Jo. x. 30; Matt. xi. 27), belong *per se* to His Divine nature, is against such a view. If, in His earthly life, Christ sometimes spoke as God only can speak, why should it be thought unlikely that He sometimes acted as God only can act? What we have to bear in mind is the inseparable presence in the one Personality of the two natures. His action as God was always mediated by His manhood. His manhood never acted in a manner unbecoming, or unrelated, to God. Cf. Illingworth, *The Gospel Miracles*, p. 58.

manner in which the decree of the Council of Chalcedon dealt with the Person of Christ. It is thought to constitute insoluble difficulties in the way of our obtaining a logical and consistent view; and that in the words 'one and the same Christ . . . to be acknowledged in two natures without confusion, change, division, or separation; the difference of the natures being in nowise taken away by reason of their union, but rather the property of each nature being preserved,'[1] there is presented a conception which is not borne out by the Gospel narratives. It is held that the Gospels convey the idea of a real modification of the Divine element of our Lord's Person in the interest of the purpose for which He became incarnate—a modification if not of essence, which is inconceivable, yet of expression. The principle of sacrifice, which we found running through all the relations of God to His creation, is thought to operate here. The Deity is shorn of some of its attributes temporarily through the economy of the Incarnation. Only on this ground is it possible to understand that God was in Christ as He walked among men. And may we not say that the Person of the Son was not only affected for time but for eternity by the experiences of His Incarnate Life on earth? He could not be the same after, that He was before, His Incarnation. There was something added to the sum of His experience; something, it may be, that was wanting to the former manifestation of His Divine excellences.

It is in the last words of the passage above quoted that the inadequacy of the formula of Chalcedon is most evident. Too much seems to be made of the difference of the two natures. That there is difference, there is no need to insist; but along with the difference is to be borne in mind the no less true likeness and correspondence between the Divine and the human, without which, we may safely say, an Incarnation would be impossible. In all that constitutes the reality of his spiritual and ethical being, man is like God. If it were not so, the two natures could never have come together. The Divine-human Personality of Christ would be a thing impossible. It is the close correspondence

[1] . . . *ἕνα καὶ τὸν αὐτὸν Χριστὸν, υἱὸν, κύριον, μονογενῆ, ἐν δύο φύσεσιν ἀσυγχύτως, ἀτρέπτως, ἀδιαιρέτως, ἀχωρίστως γνωριζόμενον, οὐδαμοῦ τῆς τῶν φύσεων διαφορᾶς ἀνῃρημένης διὰ τὴν ἕνωσιν, σωζομένης δὲ μᾶλλον τῆς ἰδιότητος ἑκατέρας φύσεως.* . . . *v.* von Hefele, *Conciliengeschichte*, ii. p. 464 f.

of man, in his best moments and in the higher aspirations which possess him, to the God Who made him, that renders the Incarnation, in the words of St. Athanasius,[1] 'not unbecoming.' It was perhaps too soon in the history of thought to expect this consideration to have the weight at Chalcedon which it would doubtless have at the present day, if a new attempt were made to formulate authoritatively the doctrine of the Person of the Redeemer. On the whole, it may be said that the Fathers who met together in A.D. 451 were in the main true to the great lines of Christian thought on the most profound subject which can exercise it.[2] Where they failed was in appreciation of the likeness and harmony which undoubtedly exist between God and man, and which it has been the province of later thought to bring into clearer light. 'He is, then, not so much God *and* man, as God in, and through, and as man. He is one indivisible personality throughout.' 'By looking for the Divine side by side with the human, instead of discerning the Divine within the human, we miss the significance of them both.'[3]

And along this line of thought there seem to open limitless possibilities for mankind. If the Eternal Son has become Man, if henceforth we are to see the Godhead united to manhood indivisibly—there must follow for us men results of which imagination can hardly dream. For what does it all mean? It means that in some very true sense the upholding of all things, the government of the world, the Lordship of things in heaven and things on earth, is shared by human nature; that God reigns as man: and if this be the case, the prospect for redeemed humanity, united for ever to the Godhead through the Incarnation, restored to the likeness for which it was intended and placed in the Person of Christ at the right hand of power, must be boundless in its reach. God has willed to be incomplete without man. Ever Self-sufficing within the perfect circle of His Tri-une Being, He went out of it to form creatures self-determining, spiritual, like Himself. These He willed so to unite

[1] *v.* above, p. 194.

[2] *v.* Mason, *The Chalcedonian Doctrine of the Incarnation*, 1913, p. 53 f. For a strong defence of the doctrine of Chalcedon, *v.* Warfield in *The American Journal of Theology* for July and Oct. 1911.

[3] Moberly, *Atonement and Personality*, pp. 96, 97.

to Himself in the fulness of time, that henceforth it should be impossible to think of God apart from man.[1]

[1] Such seems to be the teaching of Jo. i. 1, 14. The Incarnation was a new departure, not the exhibition of an existing factor, in the life of God. The *capacity* for a manifestation in humanity was ever present with God. The manifestation only took place 'when the fulness of the time was come.' For a different view, *v. Foundations*, pp. 250, 1. It seems to lend a certain air of unreality to the Incarnation, if it is regarded as an integral part of the Divine existence from all eternity.

CHAPTER XII

THE FORERUNNER

John the Baptist played a part in the coming of Christ's Kingdom which is not easy to describe. He stands upon its threshold, yet does not enter. He proclaims its nearness, and even points to the King Himself, but seems to have known little or nothing of its joy. He is the last of the long prophetic line of rock-hewn men, too stern of mould, too much filled with the seriousness of life for personal happiness. Fixed in principle and with one only motive in living—the preparation of himself and his fellows for the righteous judgment of God—he passes comet-like, a lurid and boding light, across the sky of Judaism as it was about to flush into the Messianic dawn.

He seems at first sight to be most concerned with himself and his own soul. Else why, if full of a message for his brother men, withdraw from the towns and villages to the desert? A man with a message to men goes where men may be found. John retires. Like the hermits of the Egyptian desert, Antony and his imitators, the Baptist seems to shun mankind and has to be sought out by those who would have intercourse with him. How men got to hear of him, we cannot say. A chance traveller may have noted a strangely clad and haggard form erect against the sky-line at morning or evening, with arms outstretched as in prayer; or resting at noon by a spring, shunning observation, seemingly intent on his own thoughts. What those thoughts were, we gather from the main burden of his preaching, when, as the traveller's report began to bring the curious out to look for him, he unfolded them to his hearers. The unreadiness of men and the certainty of judgment. The righteousness of God and man's need of repentance.

These formed the subject of his teaching—thoughts vital for every time, but acquiring a reality and force as never before, at the moment when he was speaking. In this conjunction of the man and the hour the greatness of the Baptist comes out. Others had preached judgment and repentance as strongly as he. Others had felt as deeply the needs of men. But none have so felt or spoken at the moment of the crisis. It was the glory of John that he could see within the already opening door. Salvation and Judgment, in the Person of the Messiah and in the fall of the city and the Temple, were at hand.

As he is preaching, Christ comes out to him. No Gospel narrative is more authentic than that of our Lord's presentation of Himself for Baptism. It runs so contrary to the line which would be taken by one who wanted to heighten the effect produced by the Saviour.[1] Nor need we doubt that we have true history in the saying which St. John puts into the mouth of the Baptist when, looking upon Jesus as He walked, he cried, 'Behold the Lamb of God which taketh away the sin of the world.'[2] It was in this power to point to the fulfilment of his prophecy, to grasp in one reach of inspired faith the promise and the substance, to look upon the end and goal of all former history and to say, 'Behold it,' that the true greatness of the Baptist lay.[3] No more majestic figure than that of Elijah dominates the early history of Israel. So great a spirit, passing deathless from earth to heaven, was not to be lost to earth. In a way he was to become re-incarnated. In his spirit and power, the Baptist was once more to show to men the great heights of spiritual and moral worth which might be attained by man. 'If ye will receive it, this is Elias which was for to come.'[4] Thus does our Lord apply to the Baptist the expectation, current among the people, that a return of Elijah was to precede the advent of Messiah. The origin of the idea is unknown, but its appearance in Malachi[5] would have given it currency. The praises of Elijah are set forth in glowing language by Jesus the

[1] We get a hint of this feeling in the fragment of the 'Gospel according to the Hebrews' preserved by Jerome, *Adv. Pelag.* iii. 2, 'Ecce mater Domini et fratres Ejus dicebant Ei: Johannes Baptista baptizat in remissionem peccatorum; eamus et baptizemur ab eo. Dixit autem eis: Quid peccavi ut vadam et baptizer ab eo? Nisi forte hoc ipsum, quod dixi, ignorantia est.'

[2] Jo. i. 29, 36. [3] Matt. xi. 11. [4] Matt. xi. 14.

[5] iii. 1; iv. 5.

Son of Sirach.[1] In a Jewish Sibylline prophecy, the coming of Elijah in his chariot from heaven is foretold.[2] The idea of the close connection of Elijah with the advent of the Messiah appears in the Gospel accounts of the Transfiguration.[3] Moses and Elijah talk with the glorified Christ of His coming death. The two witnesses, who prophesy during the time of the Gentile domination over the Holy City, seem to be Moses and Elijah.[4]

It was in the spirit and with the influence of the great Tishbite that John appeared at that critical moment by the Jordan. As Elijah confronted the weak and sinful Ahab and the brilliant and pagan Jezebel, so John came forth to call men to repentance, to warn them of the judgment to come, standing at length before Herod, as Elijah before the King of Israel, to rebuke him for his vice and to preach the righteousness of God.

For his earlier life, we are indebted to St. Luke alone. He had access to sources of information, which, if known to the other Evangelists, were not used by them. It lay outside the scheme of St. Mark to go back beyond the opening of Christ's public life. St. Matthew was probably ignorant of the special group of documents on which St. Luke seems to have drawn in his first two chapters. The interest of the narrative of the Third Gospel which relates to the Baptist culminates in his Nativity. With conspicuous differences it forms a fitting prelude to the story of the Saviour's Birth. The two accounts are fashioned on the same mould.[5] Each Nativity is the subject of promise, is announced by the same angel, is out of the common order in its origination and, above all, in the greatness of its consequences. This similarity is partly to be accounted for by the close connection of the two lives thus wonderfully begun. Both began their public career with the same end in view and the same

[1] Ecclesias. xlviii. 1-11.

[2] *v.* Bousset, *Die Religion des Judentums*, p. 267. He dates it *c.* 70 A.D.

[3] Mk. ix. 4, and parallel. *v.* Justin M. *Dial. cum Tryph.* § 49.

[4] Rev. xi. 3, 6. *v.* Bousset, *ib.* Cf. Swete, *The Apocalypse, ad loc.*

[5] The similarity to be observed here and there in the two narratives is not to be taken as casting doubt on the authentic character of either. Pfleiderer is right when he says that St. Luke 'puts forward an introductory history (*Vorgeschichte*) of the Birth of the Baptist and of Jesus, in order to show the significance of each and their relation to one another as already grounded in the divine pre-determination in, and even before, their earthly origins.' *Urchristentum*, 1887, p. 417. But when he goes on to speak of the Virgin-birth of Christ as required to outdo in miracle the miraculous element of the birth of the

proclamation of its meaning[1]—the preparation of a guilty world for the Kingdom of God. If One was the Bridegroom, the other was the Friend of the Bridegroom. Their one object was the marriage union between Christ and His people. And the likeness in the narratives is also due no doubt to the Aramaic mould in which the one—or the two—documents underlying the Evangelist's narrative was cast. The same spirit of early piety, the same tone of mind that we detect in what is told of Simeon and Anna, pervades the ancient source or sources of this part of the history.[2] This would lead—not indeed to the choice of the facts; that is determined by the historic circumstances of the case, but—to the shape and colour of the narrative.

The likeness between the birth narratives of Christ and the Baptist is continued in what St. Luke says of the boyhood of each, 'The Child grew and waxed strong in spirit.'[3] Afterwards the parallelism ceases. The Forerunner leaves home and kindred, at what age we do not know, 'and was in the deserts till the day of his shewing unto Israel.' Without the shelter and support of friends, driven by the impulse of the indwelling Spirit and early alive to the character of his mission,[4] he goes out to be alone with God. In this avoidance of human intercourse, John was not unique in his day. Other pious Jews sought the isolation and sternness of a desert life. Banus the master of Josephus was one

Baptist, he shows that disposition to make the Gospel history dependent for its motive rather on the desire to edify than to relate fact, which is so common a fault of some schools of criticism. Thus he says, 'Granted the superiority of Jesus to the Baptist, so that of the miraculous in His birth to the wonder of the Baptist's birth.' *Ib.* p. 418. 'If John is the God-given child wonderfully born of old, barren parents, and is filled from birth with the Holy Ghost, there remained, to intensify the miraculous in the case of Jesus, scarcely anything but the wonderful Birth in the strongest sense of the word—the Birth from the Virgin through the creative power of God, or of the Holy Ghost alone, without human fatherhood.' *Ib.*

[1] Matt. iii. 2; Mk. i. 15.

[2] 'In any case, we have here the earliest documentary evidence respecting the origins of Christianity which has come down to us,—evidence which may justly be called contemporary.' Plummer, *St. Luke, ad* i. 5.

[3] Lk. i. 80, of the Baptist; ii. 40, of Christ. Cf. ii. 52, and 1 Sam. ii. 26, which seems to have suggested the language employed. Ramsay draws attention to the touch of warm, motherly feeling in ii. 40 and 52, which is wanting in i. 80; another hint of the source of St. Luke's knowledge. *Was Christ born at Bethlehem?* p. 77.

[4] Cf. Lk. ii. 49, of Christ in the Temple at the age of 12.

such hermit, and the historian lived with him for three years in the desert.[1] At first sight, it seems natural to class such recluses as Essenes. But the vital distinction between that sect and the Baptist—that *their* life was in community and *his* in isolation—forbids such a view.[2] The Baptist and the other solitaries of his time were ascetics, and so were the Essenes. The Essenes went through ceremonial bathings and lustrations, and a large part of the work of John consisted in the administering of baptism: but these resemblances in life and practice fail to identify the Baptist with the sect.[3]

We have no means of knowing the duration of the Baptist's life in the desert before he entered upon his ministry.[4] The character and circumstances of that life would naturally lead him to think of those, who in the past had been prepared for their work by a similar experience. Their example may have helped to form the resolve which led him out into the desert, and he would have them often in his mind. Moses in the desert of Sinai, Elijah by the brook Cherith and at the Mount of Horeb, had each felt God to be near, to discipline and instruct them for the doing of His will. The frequent meditation of these episodes in the history of his people would prepare him for the direct call from God to begin the work of his ministry. Another factor would be the knowledge of the circumstances of his birth, which his father would have, at least in outline, communicated to him. Recalling the birth of Isaac, of Samson and of Samuel, they must have powerfully affected the direction of his thought and given him the certainty that, sooner or later, his own vocation would be made clear to him.

At length the time of silence and self-discipline was broken in upon. 'The Word of God came to John the son of Zacharias in the wilderness.' St. Luke's desire to connect this outstanding event with general as well as Jewish history is evident,[5] yet we do not get certainty as to the precise time. The fifteenth year

[1] *Vita Joseph.* § 2.

[2] *v.* Lightfoot, *Coloss.* p. 400. For a description of the Essenes, *v.* Joseph. ii. *Bell. Jud.* viii. 2-13; *Antiq.* xviii. i. 5. Lightfoot has quite disposed of the assertions of Ginsburg, *Essenes,* and Grätz, *Geschichte der Juden,* iii., which connect Essenism with Christianity. *v.* B. Weiss, *Leben Jesu,* i. p. 285. *v.* below, p. 231 f.

[3] *v.* Jülicher in *Encycl. Bibl.* ii. col. 1400.

[4] *v.* Sanday, *Sacred Sites of the Gospel,* p. 23.

[5] Lk. iii. 1, 2.

of Tiberius may be counted either from his association with Augustus in the Imperial dignity, or from the year of the death of Augustus, when he began to reign alone. It may be either A.D. 25-26 or A.D. 28-29. The latter date does not agree with other marks of time which are at our disposal; and reason has been shown for considering it very probable that St. Luke would count the reign of Tiberius from the time of his association with Augustus.[1]

St. Luke's description of the Baptist's call at once connects him with the order of Prophets. So Jeremiah,[2] Ezekiel and others received God's command to speak. 'The Word of the Lord came' to them: how, we are not told. Probably it was by some irresistible impulse that arose within them, due to no outward sign, a transaction wholly internal. 'The fire burned within; at the last they spake with their tongues.' At any rate, St. John felt that his period of seclusion was over. He remained in the wilderness, but moved into the district of the Jordan valley and there found opportunity to gather hearers about him.[3]

His practice was first to preach; then to baptize: first to awaken conscience to amendment of life in readiness for the coming Kingdom; then to fix and define the spiritual crisis by a rite which should commit him who received it to a new and higher life, and convey to him the assurance of the forgiveness of his sins.

In this call to repentance and its appeal to the conscience, the Baptist goes back to the teaching of the old prophets. It had been strangely neglected. The Jew had come to consider his descent from Abraham a security for his salvation.[4] Moral considerations had been lost sight of. The accident of birth sufficed to determine the future lot of the people. How opposed is this view to the language of Isaiah and of Ezekiel, it is easy to see: yet it seems to have acquired a great hold. Its effect on life and character must have been considerable. It could

[1] *v.* C. H. Turner in Hastings' *D.B.* i. pp. 405, 406; Ramsay, *Paul the Traveller*, p. 387. B. Weiss thinks that towards the end of A.D. 26, John appeared at the Jordan, and that St. John (ii. 20) confirms that date. *Leben Jesu*, i. p. 294.

[2] i. *passim*; Ezek. i. 3; Hosea i. 1.

[3] Lk. iii. 2, 3. Wernle makes the curious but characteristic remark, 'His preaching is reported to us only in Christian words and on that account is not accurately known.' *D. Anfänge unserer Religion*, p. 25.

[4] Cf. Plummer, *Gospel of St. Matt.* p. 21, 28. *v.* Rom. ii. 17-28.

never have been maintained by the most thoughtful people without serious misgivings. But the whole tendency of later Judaism, as influenced by the struggle with successive Gentile foes, was to increase their pride and respect for their own nationality, and to lead them to attribute to it a consecrating effect upon the individual. It was thus a strange summons that fell upon their ears. They had never been required so to humble themselves. Some among them, indeed, such as the Essenes, had become impressed with the need of purification from sin and had withdrawn themselves from ordinary society, the more unreservedly to give themselves over to a life of self-discipline. But it was to a people on the whole content and satisfied with their spiritual condition that the Baptist came.

How was this condition of things to be changed, this impenetrable cloak of complacency to be pierced? The first thing that struck the people who came out to St. John was the startling fact that a prophet had appeared among them. For centuries the prophetic order had been extinct.[1] The heavens were as brass. God had ceased to speak to men. 'There was neither voice nor any that answered.' But here was something new. A figure, gaunt and haggard, clad in rough camel's hair, a leathern girdle about his waist, cries aloud in a lonely land of coming judgment. Our Lord Himself was impressed with the unwonted sternness of His herald's appearance. 'What went ye out into the wilderness for to see?' At once, the people must have been reminded of the description of one of their old prophets. Here was a new Elijah. In those days of moral lassitude, of political unrest, of wickedness in high places, of scepticism and unfaithfulness in the Temple Courts, a solitary voice is heard proclaiming the nearness of the Kingdom of God and the certainty of impending judgment. God is once more speaking to them. The heavens, so long shut up, are opening. The excitement grows and spreads. The first to flock out to hear are the common people. But the stir and movement reach the ears of Pharisees and Sadducees. They also come, and are greeted with a sternness which must have startled and moved them.[2] But they

[1] That is as a separate and distinct order. Pathetic reference to this fact occurs in 1 Macc. iv. 46; ix. 27; xiv. 41. For the way in which the place of prophecy was partly supplied by the apocalyptic writers, *v.* p. 71

[2] In Lk. iii. 7, the terrible words, 'O generation of vipers, who hath warned you to flee from the wrath to come?' are addressed to the people generally. In

too are invited to repent, for 'The Kingdom of Heaven is at hand.'

The effect of the sight of St. John, of his speech and of his pronouncements, was immediate and extraordinary. He was at once recognized as a prophet. Some went so far as to raise the question whether he was the Messiah Himself.[1] The people submitted themselves to him as their guide and director. They set about ordering their lives in accordance with his teaching. One class after another—publicans and soldiers among the rest—came up to him with the question, 'Master, what shall we do?'[2] As a seal of their repentance and amendment, John enjoined baptism. It was a familiar rite. Proselytes were admitted into the fellowship of their religion by baptism.[3] It meant a complete breaking with the past and a birth into a new life. When Nicodemus expresses surprise at our Lord's teaching of regeneration as essential for entrance into His Kingdom, the question 'Art thou a master of Israel and knowest not these things?'[4] probably refers to the well-known practice of the baptism of proselytes and to the ideas of new birth that were commonly connected with it.

When, therefore, the Baptist required those who professed obedience to his call of repentance to submit themselves to immersion in the Jordan, he was merely adapting for his purpose something familiar, giving it a new application and a deeper meaning. Instead of a rite of admission of Gentiles into the fellowship of God's people, it was a seal of the consecration of the people themselves to a life purified and spiritualized, a pledge of their readiness to share in the coming Kingdom. Above all, it committed them to repentance for the sins of the past, and bound them to consistency of life for the time to come. It was a revolution within the limits of the people of God; but, at the same time, there is at least a hint that the coming Kingdom would not be dependent upon Israel for its members. 'Think not to say within yourselves, We have Abraham to our Father:

Matt. iii. 7, they are spoken to the Pharisees and Sadducees. There is little doubt that St. Matthew is right. Cf. Matt. xii. 34; xxiii. 33. *v.* Plummer in *Matt.* iii. 7.

[1] Lk. iii. 15. [2] Lk. iii. 12, 14.

[3] *v.* Schürer, *Geschichte des Jüd. Volkes*, iii. p. 129; Edersheim, *Life and Times of Messiah*, ii. Append. xii.

[4] Jo. iii. 10.

for I say unto you that God is able of these stones to raise up children unto Abraham.'[1] Already, in the message of the Forerunner, we get a glimpse of the wider outlook which is part of the glory of the Messianic kingdom, and receives its full sanction in the command of the risen Saviour, 'Go ye into all the world and make disciples of all nations.'[2]

What precisely did the baptism of John convey to a sincere recipient? If it ensured forgiveness, it could not impart the Holy Spirit; but it placed men in the position of being able to claim that blessing when the time of fulfilment should come.[3] 'I indeed,' said John, 'baptize you with water unto repentance ... He shall baptize you with the Holy Ghost and with fire.'[4]

Christian baptism would do what that of John could only hint at and not forestall—it would bring the baptized through the power of the Holy Spirit into living union with Christ, and therefore into a state of salvation. Yet, preparatory and incomplete as it necessarily was, the baptism of John was of heavenly origin.[5] He baptized on God's authority. All that he did and said was of Divine appointment.

The Baptist preached and baptized. He also gathered round him a band of disciples. This action pointed either to the permanence of the movement, or to its transformation into a permanent one. It has been suggested that St. John would require assistants in the work of baptizing his converts: but there was a deeper reason for collecting adherents. He wanted to form a school of repentance and hope, that when the Messiah stepped forth into the arena He might find a nucleus for His kingdom. There was no thought of self: 'He must increase; I must decrease.' Each of Christ's first disciples had been in the School of St. John. The fact that they were Galileans[6] (or at least had their avocation in Galilee) shows that the Baptist did not confine his operations to the wilderness of Judaea, but that he moved farther north, if not into the more populous districts round the lake, yet at least along the banks of the Jordan for a considerable distance. We hear of his baptizing at Bethabara or Bethany[7]

[1] Matt. iii. 9.

[2] Matt. xxviii. 19.

[3] *v.* below, p. 464, n. 2.

[4] Matt. iii. 11. Cf. Mk. i. 8.

[5] Mk. xi. 30 and parallels.

[6] *v.* Weiss, *D. Leben Jesu*, i. p. 291.

[7] Westcott in *Jo.* i. 28, calls Bethabara, 'the house of the ford,' a second century correction for Bethany in Peraea.

and at Ænon, places which have been problematically fixed about halfway between the Dead Sea and the Lake of Tiberias.

St. John's disciples were not only baptized on evidence of their repentance and faith. They observed something of his own strict rule of life.[1] He taught them a form of prayer.[2] It probably foreshadowed the Lord's prayer, petitions for the coming of the Kingdom and for forgiveness of sin forming part of it, just as the text of the Baptist's preaching, 'Repent, for the Kingdom of Heaven is at hand,' was taken up and repeated by Christ when He began to preach. These disciples had access to their Master in his prison; and when he was beheaded they came and gave burial to the headless body.[3]

Already, during the most active part of the Baptist's ministry, some of his disciples appear to have left him to follow Christ. This would be at his own wish. There is no trace of envy or of chagrin at the growing fame of our Lord. John was content to regard himself as the herald to bid men get ready for the King, as the pioneer, wielding the axe that is 'laid to the root of the trees,' levelling the rough places and smoothing the way of the royal progress. 'The friend of the bridegroom, which standeth and heareth him, rejoiceth greatly because of the bridegroom's voice: this my joy therefore is fulfilled.' John was no rival to Christ. The voice became silent when the Word Himself began to speak.

But if the master knew nothing of envy or rivalry, we are not to suppose that his disciples were equally large-hearted. Singleness of mind in a leader cannot always prevent partisanship in followers. We have no record of any large accession of the Baptist's disciples to the following of Christ at the death of their master. What we hear of them in later history leads us to believe that they made a more or less determined stand against merging their fortunes in the company of Christ. To some, the strictness and exclusiveness of the Baptist would present a more attractive example than the familiar consorting with publicans and sinners which caused so much comment among those who were watching the career of Christ.[4] The very fact that they were disciples of John marks them out as inclined to an ascetic view of life; and if they had little opportunity of understanding

[1] Mk. ii. 18. [2] Lk. v. 33; xi. 1. [3] Matt. xi. 2; xiv. 12.
[4] Matt. ix. 11.

the real, underlying motive of our Lord's intercourse with the lowest of the people, they might think that to cherish the memory of their master they must hold aloof from Christ.

Some of the Baptist's disciples come into view at Ephesus about twenty-five years later. They had evinced a certain leaning towards Christianity, for they are called 'disciples' by St. Luke. But they only 'knew' the baptism of John. They had never become incorporated into the body of Christ. When St. Paul pointed out to them the difference between the baptism of John and that of Christ, and the meaning and character of the two kinds of discipleship, they submitted themselves to the Christian sacrament with its completion in the laying on of hands.[1] Of these former followers of the Baptist, the most conspicuous was Apollos. It was at Ephesus that he too came to know 'the way of God more perfectly' through the kindly teaching of Priscilla and Aquila,[2] and became a mighty champion of the cause of Christ.

But there was a certain section of the Baptist's disciples who did not so readily give their allegiance to the Christian faith. Allusion to them seems to be implied in the emphatic distinction which St. John lays down, in his prologue, between Christ the true Light and His witness, the Baptist.[3] The Evangelist admits the heavenly origin of the Baptist's mission, but from his knowledge of later developments, he seems to find it necessary to remind men of the 'transient and subordinate character of John's ministry.'[4] The Fourth Gospel was written at Ephesus, and it was in proconsular Asia that men were to be found so late as the end of the first century, who clung to the memory of the Baptist and refused to take the logical step which led Apollos and others into full communion with the Church of Christ.

We have now to describe the chief event in the public life of St. John—his contact with the Person of Christ. There can be no doubt that in earlier life the two had often met. The close intimacy between their mothers would bring them together, and if Elizabeth, already advanced in years, lived but a short

[1] Acts xix. 1-8. *v.* Lightfoot, *Colossians*, p. 402.

[2] Acts xviii. 24 ff. [3] Jo. i. 6-10.

[4] *v.* Lightfoot, *Colossians*, pp. 402, 3, for the forms taken by what had now become a heresy.

time to watch the growth of her son in strength and wisdom, the blessed Virgin would not lose sight of one whose life and destiny had appeared to be linked so closely with that of her own Son. One passage seems to contradict this view. The Fourth Gospel tells us that the Baptist only became acquainted with our Lord after he had witnessed the descent of the Spirit upon Him; 'I knew Him not.'[1] But the phrase may well refer to ignorance of the Messiahship of Christ until the moment of His anointing with the Spirit; an ignorance quite compatible with full personal knowledge and intercourse. Besides, the Baptist had certainly been separated for some years previously by his desert life from familiar intercourse with our Lord. The Carpenter of Nazareth and the exile of the desert were not likely to meet, and the lapse of time might well have made them unrecognizable by one another.

It is St. Mark who tells us that 'it came to pass in those days that Jesus came from Nazareth of Galilee and was baptized of John in Jordan.'[2] 'Those days' were probably the early part of A.D. 27. If the Baptist began his open ministry in A.D. 26, as we have seen reason to think,[3] not many months could elapse before the news of the Forerunner reached Nazareth. As the tidings came to His ears, Christ would be deeply stirred. One after another coming into the Carpenter's shop tells how John the son of Zacharias, and His own kinsman, is preaching the advent of the Kingdom and baptizing all who come out to him and confess their sins. As He bent over His work, the thought must have again and again presented itself, I must leave this quiet home, this round of regular daily work. I must be about my Father's business. That voice from the wilderness is a call to Me. I must be up and doing. 'I must work the works of Him that sent Me while it is day: the night cometh.'[4] The impulse takes more definite shape. Seeking His mother, He speaks of the thoughts which are stirring within Him, and now seem to be met and answered by this far-off call. He will go and see and hear for Himself. 'The hour is come.'

[1] Jo. i. 31, 33.

[2] i. 9. Cf. Matt. iii. 13. St. Luke, who (ii. 39, 51) speaks of Nazareth as the home of Christ, makes no allusion to His leaving it for the Jordan. St. Matthew simply states that He came from Galilee.

[3] *v.* above, p. 212.

[4] Jo. ix. 4. *v.* above, p. 183 f.

It was the first prick of the sword that was to pierce the mother's heart. A widow probably by this time, the going forth of her Son leaves the home desolate, and as we gather from what is said of her at Cana and elsewhere, it is soon given up. Until the house of John the son of Zebedee becomes her second home, her life is a wandering one.

The Baptism of our Lord is one of the most certain facts in the early history of His ministry. The Baptist gives expression to the feeling to which all would own, that a rite which was only pressed upon those who had first confessed their sins and given proof of penitence was singularly unsuitable for the sinless Being who was the Christ of God.[1] The Gospel writers would be the last to give us such a narrative, if not impelled to do so by the stern facts of the case. How the Baptist came to draw a distinction between this newcomer and the people generally is not explained, when he tells us of the sign of the visible descent of the Spirit upon Christ, which he had been previously promised.[2] For this occurred, according to the Synoptic account, only after the baptism had taken place. It has been suggested[3] that, in the preliminary conversation, which the Baptist naturally had with his converts, the sinless character of Christ revealed itself. Here was One, Who, so far from needing the cleansing rite, might Himself administer it to a sinner such as John, notwithstanding his possession of the Spirit of God, felt himself to be. In that case, the Baptist was merely acknowledging that now at length he had come face to face with One Whose standing before God was on a wholly different plane from his own: and it might have crossed his mind that here possibly was the promised Messiah, the sign of whose advent he had already been taught by a special revelation to expect.

Our Lord quickly reassures him: not by disputing his acknowledgment of His surpassing holiness. That He admits. But in some way, as yet not fully disclosed, He was to range Himself by the side of those who had come out to the Baptist. He would not shrink, even at the cost of misunderstanding, from

[1] Matt. iii. 14. Cf. 'The Gospel according to the Hebrews' preserved by Jerome (*adv. Pelag.* iii. 2); Preuschen, *Antilegomena*, p. 4.

[2] Jo. i. 33.

[3] *E.g.* by Weiss, *D. Leben Jesu*, i. p. 296. Cf. Plummer in *Matt.* p. 30.

submitting to the same rite to which the sincere among them were admitted. He was willing in all points to be made like unto His brethren. For John to baptize Him would be 'to fulfil' for each 'all righteousness.' It would be in accordance with the will of God.[1] 'Then he suffered Him.'

Immediately after the Baptism, which seems to have followed that of a large number of people,[2] our Lord was praying. He had probably withdrawn with the Baptist from the throng. At this moment the sign was given for which John had been led to look.[3] To him and to our Lord Himself alone was it made evident. The Holy Spirit descended 'like a dove, lighting upon Him and lo, a voice from heaven saying, This is My beloved Son in whom I am well pleased.' To the Baptist it was the assurance that his work and ministry as the Forerunner of the Kingdom had not been in vain. To Christ Himself it was the solemn consecration of His life for the work which the Father had called Him to do. It gave no fresh accession of holiness. That He did not need. Rather, it was to His human spirit a sign of God's favour, and to His consciousness of Messiahship a confirming token. If we grasp the complete humanity of Christ, we shall see that some such confirmation of His belief about Himself was not unnecessary. He, Who was soon to be subjected to the trial of His motives and His methods, must have welcomed the assurance that He was in all things well-pleasing to the Father, and that His presence was with Him.

But it is not for a moment suggested that the Baptism with its attendant sign worked any change in our Lord's life. It did not constitute Him something that He was not before.[4]

[1] Cf. Ignat. *ad Smyrn.* 1. [2] Lk. iii. 21. [3] Jo. i. 33.

[4] It was the belief of certain Ebionite and Gnostic schools of thought that the Baptism of Christ marked not only His designation to the Messiahship but a change in His Person. According to them the Christ descended upon the man Jesus. This belief was due in part to the significant events that accompanied the Baptism—the descent of the Spirit and the voice of God. It was due also to the application to the moment of Baptism of the words of Ps. ii. 7. So precise was this reference considered that the text of St. Luke iii. 22 in some MSS. (D, a b c d ff[1] l) reads (instead of *ἐν σοὶ εὐδόκησα*) *ἐγὼ σήμερον γεγέννηκά σε.* Copies were evidently altered in certain circles to suit the prevailing idea and to bring the passage into connection with that of Ps. ii. 7. How entirely opposed to the main stream of the Christian thought of the period is this adoptionist view of the deity of Christ is at once apparent. *v.* Hippol. *Philos.* vii. 34; Iren. *adv. Haeres.* i. 26; Lambert, Art. 'Ebionism' in *Dict. of Christ and the Gospels*, i.

From His birth, Jesus was Messiah. In saying this, we do not lose sight of the subjective side of His office and its needs. In the Gospel of His boyhood, we have seen reason to think[1] that the consciousness of His coming task was already stirring within Him; that, in a special sense, He knew that He was the Son of God and that a career unlike that of ordinary men lay before Him. As time went on, this conviction—brooded over as He bent to His work in the carpenter's shop at Nazareth, compared with the Scriptures of which He was a devout student, quickened too by communications that His mother could not have withheld from Him as His manhood dawned—ripened into certainty. But it is a characteristic of the human mind to wish for confirmation of what is already regarded as certain; and He was truly man.

The voice of the Father was probably audible to Jesus only. The sight of the dove-like descent of the Spirit was given to the Baptist as well as to Himself. It enabled him to bear his witness that 'this is the Son of God.'[2] People had sent priests and Levites from Jerusalem to ask him 'Who art thou?' In his answer, the Baptist shows the entire loyalty of his nature. The way men had flocked out to him might well have stirred any tendency to personal ambition that he might have. But he rejects every suggestion of dignity that is made to him. Not only is he not the Christ, he will not claim to impersonate Elijah, although he must have been familiar with the expectation current in his day that, before the Messiah, Elijah would return as His Forerunner. Nor will he admit an identification with 'that prophet' of whom Moses spoke.[3] He sinks his personality in his office and his message. He will be only a voice—foretold indeed by Isaiah[4] but—heard for a moment and then to be stilled in the hush with which the world awaited the utterance of the Incarnate Word.[5]

The day after the incidents of the embassy, as we learn from the Fourth Gospel, and again on the following day, the Baptist bears his striking witness to the Personality and Work of the Messiah. He is 'the Son of God.' He is also 'the Lamb of God which taketh away the sin of the world.'[6] The Redeemer and His Person—this is the burden of the Baptist's testimony. It sounds like the witness of one who looks back on a finished

[1] *v.* above, p. 184. [2] Jo. i. 34. [3] Jo. i. 19-29; Deut. xviii. 15-18.
[4] xl. 3. [5] Cf. Ps. lxxvi. 8. [6] Jo. i. 29, 34, 36.

work, rather than of one who is thinking of a work which he will not live to see; and with the known difficulty of distinguishing at times the recital from the reflection of the writer of the Fourth Gospel, it is hardly to be wondered that some see in the words placed in the Baptist's mouth the mature belief of a disciple, who meditates on the past and colours his narrative with the hues of his own thought. But there are decided objections to such a view. The writer of the Gospel was himself a disciple of the Baptist. It was on hearing his master's testimony to Christ that he with Andrew followed Jesus[1] and, on His turning to ask them their business, inquired where He dwelt and, on His inviting them to enter, went in 'and abode with Him that day.' In a matter of such importance as that which transferred his allegiance from the Baptist to the Messiah, the writer would hardly be likely to forget the expressions used by his former master, and to supply their place by an afterthought of his own. It is to deal unfairly with a narrative which purports to be historical thus to amend it in the interest of a theory. If the words attributed to the Baptist seem an anachronism at such a period, it should not be forgotten that he was a prophet—the greatest of his line according to the mind of Christ—and such a reach of vision, as the words denote, may not be denied to such a man.[2]

Indeed, it was in this gift of insight, prepared for by his long solitary musings in the wilderness before his showing unto Israel, that much of the greatness of the Baptist consisted.

[1] This is clear from the characteristically allusive mode of narrative, Jo. i. 35. Cf. xiii. 23; xviii. 15; xix. 35; xx. 2; xxi. 20.

[2] It is a charge which is frequently brought against the Fourth Gospel that it fails to indicate the development in the knowledge and recognition of the Personality of Christ which is apparent in the Synoptics. Not only does the Baptist disclose a comprehension which, if reached at all by the Apostles during His earthly life, was not reached until a much later period, but Nathanael is alleged to have hailed Him Son of God and King of Israel (Messianic) at about the same time (Jo. i. 49). This early apprehension of the truth is thought to conflict so seriously with the Synoptic record as to discredit the historic character of the Fourth Gospel and to show that it is rather a meditation on, than a narrative of, the events to which it refers. We have indicated in the text reasons which give probability to the statement as regards the Baptist. The confession of Nathanael stands on a different footing. Yet from what we are told of Simeon and Anna and of the general feeling of expectation which was current at the time, it is not unreasonable to hold that historic ground lies under his confession as well as that of the Baptist. Here and there, true and pure-hearted men may well have been in advance of their time in insight and in its expression. *v.* above, p. 42

It was by this that he was specially enabled to act as the Forerunner of the Messiah. Some such forecast of the Messiah's office and work seems to be required, if the position consistently assigned to him in the Gospels is to be justified. We should expect that his comprehension of the true nature and purpose of the Messiah would be in advance of the knowledge of his contemporaries. According to the Fourth Gospel, this expectation is fulfilled. The historical narrative meets our sense of what is probable, and no theory of a gradual development in the recognition of Christ should prevent our accepting it. The full declaration of the Sonship of our Lord by the Baptist is made all the more probable by the fact that it was proclaimed by the voice from heaven. The fact became known to the Evangelists, as the Synoptic Gospels show.[1] His insight was met and confirmed by the voice of the Father, and fresh confirmation is given to his testimony, as related by St. John.

The question naturally arises: what precisely was the significance of the descent of the Holy Spirit upon Christ, which followed immediately upon His baptism? We have already been told that as a child He 'grew and waxed strong in spirit, filled with wisdom: and the grace of God was upon Him.'[2] We cannot deny to Him a full measure of the Spirit from His birth. Even of the Baptist, it was promised that 'he shall be filled with the Holy Ghost, even from his mother's womb.' Much more must this have been the case with our Lord Himself. The Spirit, Who created His humanity, would not have forsaken His work, but would have still possessed that choice and perfect shrine. And we can trace no development in the extent of this possession. The passages, which assure us of our Lord's increase of strength in spirit and of wisdom and stature,[3] refer to the development of His own human gifts and capacities, and of His receptiveness as regards the influence of the Spirit, which filled Him. They do not imply that at one time He had a larger measure of the Spirit than at another.[4] His endowment with the Holy

[1] Matt. iii. 17; Mk. i. 11; Lk. iii. 22. In this as in other questions of fact, the Synoptics and the Fourth Gospel meet and confirm one another. *v.* above, p. 33 f.

[2] Lk. ii. 40. [3] Lk. ii. 40, 52.

[4] Cf. Jo. iii. 34, 'He giveth not the Spirit by measure.' H. Holtzmann, *in loc.* p. 98, remarks that there can be little doubt of the correctness of the conception which supplies 'Christ' for the more remote object and 'God' for the subject.

Spirit was complete and perfect from His birth. It was His capacity to enjoy and use it which grew with the growth of His years.

When, therefore, we read that the Spirit descended upon Him after His baptism, it is clear that a special anointing for a definite purpose must be intended. It was official rather than personal. Following the analogy of Kings and Prophets under the Old Covenant, it implied the consecration and dedication of the Saviour for His work. The Spirit came *upon* Him—not within.[1] It was an external, verifying effusion of spiritual power, attesting His Messianic call, sealing and setting Him apart for His ministry.

We can observe the same distinctions of spiritual endowment in the life of the Apostles. Before His Ascension, the risen Saviour, who could already say,[2] 'All power is given unto Me in heaven and in earth,' imparted a gift of the Holy Spirit to them for the purposes of their ministry of binding and loosing.[3] But it was at Pentecost that the Spirit came to them as the power of their own life. The first occasion was official and answered to the descent upon our Lord at His baptism. The second was personal and answered to the primal gift at His birth. To Him and to them alike the personal gift was both a Pentecost and a Nativity.

For a time the Baptist continued his work of teaching and baptizing. At one period we find him at Aenon near Salim in Judaea, a place abounding in springs.[4] Our Lord came into the neighbourhood and taught and baptized. Thus there was a conjunction of the two teachers, a fact which not unnaturally led to some appearance of rivalry. The disciples of the Baptist are the first to take umbrage. They admit that their master had borne favourable witness to Christ. But they resent His baptizing and gathering the people to Himself. They feel the emulation which zealous disciples will often display if some other star appears in the firmament. They come to the Baptist and complain. Again that strong, heroic soul shows his superiority

[1] *ἐπ' αὐτόν*, Matt. Lk. and Mk. according to ℵ, A, L, etc.; *εἰς αὐτόν* according to B, D, etc. Cf. 'Ev. juxta Hebr.' Frag. 4 (preserved by Jerome, *Comment. in Is.* xi. 2) in Preuschen, *Antilegomena*, p. 4: 'Factum est autem cum ascendisset Dominus de aqua, descendit fons omnis Spiritus Sancti et requievit super eum.'

[2] Matt. xxviii. 18.

[3] Jo. xx. 22, 23.

[4] *ὅτι ὕδατα πολλὰ ἦν ἐκεῖ.* Jo. iii. 23.

to all self-interest. He will not be moved from his appointed station. He is nothing more than 'the friend of the Bridegroom.' He calls them to witness that he had before rejected the idea that he was the Christ. His joy is in the greatness of the Bridegroom. As He advances on His triumphal progress, the herald vanishes. As stars pale their light before the sun, so before the ever-increasing power and influence of Christ must the Forerunner fade into insignificance. 'He must increase, but I must decrease.'

But not only do the disciples of John show alarm at the growing fame of Christ. The Pharisees become aware of it and their knowledge of what is happening is reported to our Lord. He might have ignored the feeling of the disciples of John. He could trust to his power of preventing it from attaining any harmful dimensions. But the prospect of agitation among unfriendly and suspicious Pharisees was quite a different thing. It would have defeated His purposes, if anything of the nature of rivalry were known to exist between Himself and His Forerunner. He yields to circumstances. He will not incur the suspicion (however false and groundless) of acting in competition with the Baptist. Leaving Judaea with His disciples, He passes through Samaria into Galilee.

We do not know how the Baptist first came in contact with Herod—an experience which was to prove so fateful. The king may have desired to see him on the report of his work among the people, and may have sent for him to come to his castle of Machaerus. At any rate, however they came to meet, the Baptist lost no time in dealing as faithfully with the king as he had already dealt with the ordinary people. His adulterous life receives the plainest and fullest condemnation. He had taken to himself his brother Philip's wife. 'It is not lawful for thee to have her.' It is a state of things that admits of no compromise. Far from being offended at the boldness of John, Herod seems to have kept him near his person and to have 'heard him gladly.'[1] But 'that fox,' as our Lord called him, had merely an intellectual satisfaction in the intercourse. There was no repentance, no change of life. Herodias was still in the castle, hearing of the Baptist's words and seeking occasion to vent her hatred. It was probably at her solicitation that the

[1] Mk. vi. 20.

Baptist was cast into prison.[1] His confinement was not too close to allow access to him. He hears from his disciples of 'the works of Christ.' From his prison he sends an embassy of two of his disciples to ask, 'Art Thou He that should come, or do we look for another?'[2] It was of supreme importance that there should be no mistake as to our Lord's identity. 'The works' seemed to designate Him to Whom he had already borne witness. He will send his followers and let them hear for themselves. Our Lord receives them graciously, but He goes on with His work, teaching and healing, while the messengers are watching.[3] Then, after a time, He turns to them. They are to bear no special message. They are to report what they have seen and heard. That would suffice. Works of mercy, making the blind to see and the deaf to hear, are coupled with the stupendous act of the raising of the dead and—a specially Messianic work [4]—the preaching of the Gospel to the poor. But

[1] Josephus says that Herod was influenced also by fear of the excitement caused by his preaching. *Antiq.* xviii. v. 2.

[2] The real object of the dispatch of this embassy has been much disputed. 1. It was not for himself, but for the assurance of his disciples that John sent it. It may be said in support of this view that John must have known of the identity of Jesus with Him whom he had baptized and acknowledged as the Christ, and that had his own faith wavered, our Lord would not have spoken of him as He did after the embassy had departed. 2. It was for John's own assurance. The answer of Christ seems to imply this: 'Go and tell John the things, etc.' The strain of prison life to one whose existence had been spent in the open air may have induced a feeling of despondency or of impatience, as the news of the progress of Christ's ministry reached him. Besides, garbled reports of what He was doing may have reached the prisoner. *v.* Tertull. *adv. Marcion,* iv. 18. In a moment of irritation, fostered by the partisanship of his own devoted followers, he may have questioned the claim of this new Teacher, in whom he had once been led to see the chosen of God. Such a state of mind is quite possible. But in the case of St. John, it is very improbable. On the whole, we may take it that his object was to give his disciples practical proof that Jesus was the Christ. He himself was no 'reed shaken by the wind.' No doubt it was a comfort and support to his own conviction to receive on their return the report of his messengers. But nothing in the recorded character and attitude of the Baptist gives any hint of a weakening as his life, filled from his birth with the Holy Spirit, drew towards its end. The very form of the question, 'Art Thou He that should come, or do we look for another?' bears out this view. The alternative to Jesus being the Christ is represented as the appearance of one *still to be waited for,* one who had not yet appeared. After John's experience at the Baptism and the sign there given him, a *future* Christ such as this question implies, is not to be thought of as imagined by himself.

[3] Lk. vii. 21.

[4] Is. lxi. 1. Cf. Lk. iv. 18-21.

a solemn warning is added:[1] 'Blessed is he, whosoever shall not be offended in Me.' To stumble at the combined evidence of power and love would be to harden the heart and shut the eye to every sign of the coming of the Kingdom.

When the messengers had departed, our Lord breaks into a glowing eulogy of the captive of Machaerus. It stands apart among His sayings. The sorrows of the Baptist—alone in the power of Herod—seem to kindle the heart of Jesus till it glows, and He rises to an eloquence which He but seldom employs. With gaze turned back upon the long history of His people, calling to memory the prophets and kings, the patriarchs and heroes of the past, He sets them all, with one act of discrimination, at a level lower than that of His Forerunner: 'Among them that are born of women, there hath not risen a greater than John the Baptist.'[2] Praise can go no higher. Then, with a sudden, almost paradoxical turn of thought, as He looks forward to the immeasurable privileges of His coming reign of grace, to the 'things which prophets and kings have desired to see,' He adds, 'but he that is least in the kingdom of God is greater than he'—greater, not in personal gifts, but in opportunity and privilege, greater by the chance of time.

We are not told of the effect upon the Baptist of the return of his messengers. As, in the dispute of his disciples with the Jews on the question of purifying, he spoke of himself as 'the friend of the Bridegroom,' who rejoiceth greatly because of the Bridegroom's voice, so would he again feel, 'this my joy is fulfilled.'[3] The kingdom had indeed come in the person of its King; his own work was over.

Herod appears to have treated John with great consideration, sending for him out of the dungeon and not only listening to him gladly, but putting into practice much of what he heard.[4] Yet, the one thing that was needed—the surrender of Herodias—he failed to carry out.

Shortly afterwards came the woman's opportunity. Herod's

[1] Lk. vii. 23. The singular is no proof that the Baptist is meant. It has a general application, and must not be employed to support the view that it was *his* faith that failed. The meaning of the embassy has been strained both by those who think it required by the Baptist himself and those who oppose that interpretation. It was a perfectly legitimate endeavour to get open confirmation of the identity of the Worker and Teacher with the promised Messiah.

Matt. xi. 11; Lk. vii. 24. [3] Jo. iii. 29. [4] Mk. vi. 20.

rash promise, made under the excitement of a banquet to his lords, that the daughter of Herodias and Philip should have, for her dancing, whatever she asked—even to the half of the kingdom—is carried to the mother. The grim decision is instantly given—'the head of John the Baptist.' The promise is kept, and in the lonely vault of the castle the executioner does his work. Disciples are allowed to come and bear away the headless body of their master for his burial. Then they 'went and told Jesus.'

The Forerunner's task was over. The herald of the kingdom had sped his appointed course. The morning star must needs pale before the rising sun. It was the glory of the last and greatest of the prophets to seal his witness to the Son of God with the offering of his life—a last tribute to the cause of truth and righteousness, of repentance and hope, for which it had been the mission of his life to prepare.

CHAPTER XIII

JEWISH SECTS AND PARTIES

Our Lord's entrance upon public life at once brought Him into contact with the various parties into which the Jewish people were divided. Scribes and Pharisees, Sadducees and Herodians come into His presence, hear His teaching, listen to His claims, judge and are judged. Himself belonging to no party, a layman, careless of distinctions and differences, He turned men's thoughts to life and conduct, and made them the standard by which truth was to be ascertained.[1] A theory was only sound if it worked well. Life is the supreme test of doctrine.

In the Gospels, Scribes and Pharisees are constantly mentioned together, and as a rule formed one and the same party; although some Scribes were not Pharisees, and were either independent students of the Law or were connected with the Sadducees.[2] As a matter of fact, their origin was quite distinct. We may regard Ezra as the first Scribe.[3] On the return from the Captivity, he gathered round him men who quickly formed a party,[4] which set itself to the study of the Law, and to the maintenance of the purity and separateness of the Jewish race. The Pharisees, on the other hand, cannot be traced back farther than Maccabaean times. Whether or

[1] 'If any man will do His will, he shall know of the doctrine.' Jo. vii. 17.

[2] This seems to follow from such passages as Mk. ii. 16; Acts xxiii. 9.

[3] Ezra vii. 11, 'Ezra the priest, the scribe.' Cf. Nehem. viii. 13. *v.* Bousset, *Die Religion des Judentums*, p. 186. But as writers and copyists of the Law—if not as interpreters—they are found before the Exile. Jer. xxxvi. *v.* Oesterley, *The Books of the Apocrypha*, 1914, p. 114 f.

[4] 'It is difficult . . . to find words high enough to describe the work of the Scribes for after generations.' Burkitt, *Jewish and Christian Apocalypses*, p. 5.

not they are to be identified with the Assidaeans,[1] a sect of pious extremists among the Scribes, who had been bitterly opposed to the attempt of Antiochus Epiphanes to Hellenize the Jewish people, is doubtful: but from B.C. 135, the time of John Hyrcanus, they emerge as a distinct party and bearing their name of Pharisee, which is so constantly meeting us in the Gospels. Politically, their attitude was on the whole patriotic—first towards Hellenistic oppression, afterwards towards Roman interference. Religiously, they stood for the minute observance, not only of the Mosaic Law, but of the precepts deduced from it by its most rigorous interpreters. Thus they regarded religion as a matter of external observance, rather than an inward and spiritual thing; and exposed themselves to the full force of our Lord's invective, as men who made the Word of God of none effect through their tradition.[2]

In their zeal for the observance of the Law and in their opposition to the Sadducees, whose prescriptive claim to the High Priesthood had now become generally admitted, they were led to exalt the Law at the expense of the worship of the Temple. The Synagogue became more and more the rival of the Temple, and religion tended to find expression elsewhere—in the home and in the daily business of life.[3]

This change of feeling, brought about by Pharisaic insistence on the paramount importance of the Law, must have had its influence in circles far removed from that party, and helped to wean the minds of the nation generally from devotion to the worship of the Temple. The extraordinary multiplication of the Synagogue is one of the evidences of this influence. What was passing in the Dispersion went on in Palestine and even in

[1] 1 Mac. ii. 42. The Greek form of the sect of the Hasîdîm, or 'godly.' The Pharisees of the time of Herod and the N.T. were probably developed from the Hasîdîm of the age of the Maccabees. *v.* Bousset, *Die Religion des Judentums im neutestam*[n] *Zeitalter*, p. 213.

[2] Mk. vii. 13. 'No bridge leads from Pharisaism to the Gospel.' Friedländer, *D. religiösen Bewegungen des Judentums im Zeitalter Jesu*, p. 15.

[3] *v.* Holtzmann, *Neutest. Theologie*, i. p. 30. By the time of Herod the Great the Pharisees had practically secured that position of influence over the religious character of the people which appears in the Gospel narratives. *v.* Bousset, *Die Religion des Judentums*, p. 67. Cf. Jo. vii. 47, 48. Besides, the worldliness of Herod, who was but half a Jew, was less repulsive to the party of the pious than that of the aristocratic Sadducees of their own nation. *v.* Bousset, *ib.* p. 65.

Jerusalem. Things were preparing for the overthrow of the Temple and the end of the sacrifices.

It was from the Scribes and Pharisees that our Lord largely derived His acquaintance with the religious life of His people. Not only does He adopt their methods in argument, but He makes many of their principles the starting point of His own deep, spiritual teaching.[1] On the question of the Resurrection, He places Himself on the side of the Scribes rather than of the Sadducees. To one of the sect He gives the striking testimony, 'Thou art not far from the Kingdom of God.'[2] He admits their 'righteousness,'[3] their zeal and fervour: but motive and aim are wrong.[4] Religion had become a theology, divorced from life and action.[5] Few things in the history of religion are more sad to contemplate than the manner in which the Pharisees incurred the condemnation of the Saviour. The sternest language in all Scripture is addressed to them by the lips of Incarnate Love. A self-sufficing religiosity is more hateful to Him than any other wayward condition of sinful man. The woes on the Pharisees seem to be the counterpart to the Beatitudes. Thus the men who prided themselves on their separation,[6] from the Sadducee on the one hand and from the common people (Am-haaraz) on the other, stand apart in the view of their future Judge, as men almost beyond the reach of Divine Grace; while their name has passed into a proverb for all that is exclusive, self-satisfied and condemnatory of others, in the practice of religion or morality.[7]

Three other Jewish parties require brief notice. The Essenes

[1] Mk. xii. 28 f. Cf. Matt. xxiii. 2, 3. Cf. Holtzmann, *Neutestamentliche Theologie*, i. p. 37, 'What the people possessed of the knowledge of God's will, of recollections and possessions of faith and hope, was due solely to the instruction of the Scribes as their preachers and pastors.' Cf. Lk. ii. 46. *v.* Burkitt, *The Gospel History and its Transmission*, p. 169.

[2] Mk. xii. 34. *v.* Holtzmann, *Neutestamentliche Theologie*, i. p. 169 f.

[3] Matt. v. 20. *v.* Bousset, *Jesus*, pp. 63, 65.

[4] 'A greater hater of the Pharisees than Jesus, there has never been.' Friedländer, *op. cit.* p. 109.

[5] Cf. Bousset, *Die Religion des Judentums*, p. 194.

[6] Their name Pharisees, 'the separated ones' (*perusim*) marks their character of exclusiveness. But *v.* Oesterley, *The Books of the Apocrypha*, p. 130 f.

[7] *v.* the discussion in *Theologisch Tijdschrift* for 1914, p. 1, 'Farizeën en Sadduceën,' by Eerdmans; p. 214, 'Iets over Farizeën en Sadduceën,' by H. Oort; and p. 223, 'Nogeens: Farizeën en Sadduceën,' by Eerdmans.

are described by Josephus with a minute interest which is lacking in his accounts of Pharisees and Sadducees.[1] They, too, were in existence as a sect in Maccabaean times;[2] but were never of much importance in numbers[3] or influence. Ascetic in their mode of life, eschewing marriage, taking no part in the ordinary sacrifices of the Temple, but strict in their practice of lustrations, they appear to have lived very much in common after the manner of the primitive Church.[4] Strong in attachment to the Law and in their hope of the future life, their great desire was for purity and for conformity to the will of God. It has been thought by some that St. John the Baptist belonged to the sect: but there is no authority for the statement.[5] Essenes lived in community. The Baptist was a Solitary. But we may see in them true precursors of the Gospel;[6] for they were men who sought with all their heart to carry out in life and conduct the highest that they knew of love to God and man.[7]

For our knowledge of the Sadducees we are chiefly indebted to the Gospels. There is a strange uncertainty in Jewish sources

[1] *Bell. Jud.* ii. c. viii. 2-14; *Antiq.* xviii. c. i. 5.

[2] Joseph. *Antiq.* xiii. c. v. 9; speaking of the period *c.* B.C. 150. According to Zeller, *Philosophie der Griechen*, iii. t. 2, p. 334, the sect was not an offshoot of Jewish Alexandrian philosophy, but was developed independently on the soil of Palestine.

[3] 'There are about four thousand men that live in this way.' Joseph. *Antiq.* xviii. c. i. 5.

[4] 'That institution of theirs which will not suffer anything to hinder them from having everything in common; so that a rich man enjoys no more of his wealth than he who has nothing at all.' Joseph. *Antiq.* xviii. c. i. 5. Cf. Acts ii. 44; iv. 32, 34. 'Private property was excluded, everything flowed into a common chest.' Holtzmann, *Neutest. Theologie*, i. p. 140.

[5] Cf. above, p. 211. The fact that they prayed to the Sun and that they were inclined to Oriental speculations, would suffice to disprove any connection of the Baptist with the sect. Cf. Loofs, *Dogmengeschichte*, p. 44. Holtzmann remarks that their metaphysics were signalized by a strongly expressed Dualism according to which only good is derived from God, evil from matter. *Op. cit.* i. p. 141. Zeller, *op. cit. ib.* traces the Essenes to contact of Judaism with Pythagoraeanism, and refers to the Greek settlements in Galilee and the lively intercourse which was carried on with the Greeks in Egypt at that period.

[6] Jülicher, in *Encycl. Bibl.* ii. col. 1400.

[7] Philo, *Quod omnis probus liber*, 13. 'Essenism guarded like a holy fire in its bosom the noblest traditions of Jewish Hellenism against all Pharisaic attacks.' Friedländer, *op. cit.* p. 16. Holtzmann, while admitting that Christ may have become acquainted with the sect in villages of Galilee, rejects the idea suggested by some writers that He belonged to the order. *Neutestamentliche Theologie*, i. p. 167.

as to their origin and even the meaning of their name. It may have been given them by the Pharisees, or their precursors the Hasîdîm, to mark their sense of the degenerate love of the Sadducees for Hellenism. In that case it was ironical; for 'righteous'[1] in a Jewish sense, these worldly and ambitious Sadducees were certainly not.[2] The more probable derivation of the name is from Zadok, the High Priest of the time of David and Solomon. A Sadducee would thus be an adherent of the descendants of Zadok.[3] The High Priests of the Maccabaean family were mostly Sadducees; so were the High Priests in the time of Christ.

According to Josephus,[4] the sect was in existence in Maccabaean times, and both religiously and politically was in opposition to the Pharisees. In politics it favoured a friendly attitude to the foreigner, whether Greek or Roman, and in times of national danger could be charged with lack of patriotism. The Sadducees were thus a constant check upon the fierce, national temper of the Pharisees, while their worldly, careless tone of mind attracted to their party the aristocratic elements of the Jewish people. In religion they represented a school of thought which was essentially sceptical. For this the Pharisees had their own teaching and practices to thank. Sadducaeism was a natural recoil from unauthorized additions to the Law. We have only to read the trivial dogmatizings of Pharisaic teachers and the dishonest interpretations which they were wont to place upon plain questions of law, to understand that in the nature of things such a movement as that of the Sadducees was bound to be

[1] צדיק, righteous. Allusions to Sadducees as 'sinners' are found in *Ps. of Solomon*, i. 1; iv. 1-10.

[2] Josephus remarks that the Sadducees have none but the rich on their side. *Antiq.* xiii. 10, § 6.

[3] *v.* 1 Kings i. 34; ii. 35. Sadducees, Σαδδουκαῖοι from צדוקים. 'The party name was retained long after the Zadokite High Priests had made way for the Hasmonean house and the origin of the name had been forgotten.' Kohler in the *Jewish Encyclopaedia*, art. 'Sadducees.' Cf. Bp. H. E. Ryle, 'Their name denotes the claim of the Maccabee High Priestly family to the most holy office which their leaders have usurped.' *Guardian*, 1913, p. 1626.

[4] *Antiq.* xiii. c. v. 9. Friedländer traces their origin to opposition to the Hasîdîm or 'pious.' *D. religiösen Bewegungen des Judentums im Zeitalter Jesu*, p. 9. Cf. Joseph. *Antiq.* xiii. c. 10. 6, on the revolt of J. Hyrcanus from Pharisaism to the Sadducees.

forthcoming.[1] But in their reasonable dislike to Pharisaic hair-splitting, they went to an unwarrantable extent in the assertion of their freedom. Josephus is no doubt a prejudiced witness, but he may be trusted in the comparison which he draws between the teaching of the two parties. If Sadducees were right in denying that we live under the control of fate as Pharisaism taught, they went in complete opposition to the history of their people in denying also that God had any care for men's conduct, whether good or evil; and they displayed their materialistic, worldly spirit when they rejected an after-life of the soul with every thought of reward or punishment.[2] It was in keeping with their Greek sympathies that they denied the Resurrection of the body;[3] while the minute angelology and demonology of the Pharisees no doubt contributed to the sceptical position of the Sadducees on these questions.

For an answer to the question, what did a Sadducee profess to believe? we can only reply, the Torah. He took the Law of Moses as it stood and regarded it as his only guide of life and conduct. Traditionalism, apart from this central body of authoritative teaching, he entirely rejected.

This is to be borne in mind when we study our Lord's attitude towards the various sects and parties of His day. There is no vehement rebuke addressed to Sadducees like His reproof of Scribes and Pharisees. It is true that He tells them that they 'greatly err' in their disbelief of the Resurrection of the dead, and He stands silent before the accusations of the Sadducaean chief priests at His trial. But as a party, or school of thought, they do not incur the withering scorn with which He has for ever blasted the name of Pharisee. Cold, sceptical, supercilious they were: but they made no such claim to superior religiosity as the Pharisees boasted. They had not, like them, overlaid God's Word by their glosses. They had not corrupted it by their traditions. They sinned by default rather than by

[1] Cf. Friedländer, *op. cit.* p. 9.

[2] Joseph. *Bell. Jud.* ii. c. viii. 14; *Antiq.* xiii. c. v. 9. Cf. Mk. xii. 18 f. But in *Ps. of Sol.* ix. 7, the Pharisaic writer admits that 'Our works are subject to our own choice and power, To do right or wrong in the works of our hands.'

[3] Sirach, like Ecclesiastes, contains no reference to a Resurrection. Kohler supposes Ecclesiastes to have been written, at least in its original form, by a Sadducee in antagonism to the Hasîdîm. *v.* Eccl. vii. 16; ix. 2. Cf. *Jewish Encycl.* art. 'Sadducees.' *v.* below, p. 248, n. 2.

presumption. Unlike the Pharisees, they were not hypocrites. They were worldly, ambitious, materialistic. But at any rate, they were all this openly; and they did not make their religion the road to success and standing among their contemporaries. There is no woe pronounced upon them, as upon Scribes and Pharisees.[1]

Just before the Christian era, the Sadducees were compelled by adverse public opinion to adopt Pharisaic methods in the interpretation of the Law.[2] The Romans under Pompey deprived them of the princely power which, in Maccabaean times, had accompanied the High Priesthood.[3] Herod was severe in his treatment of them.[4] With the destruction of the Temple and the break-up of the state, they ceased to exist as a party and disappear from history.[5]

There was another party, entirely political, with which our Lord was brought in contact. Archelaus, who succeeded his father, Herod the Great, in his rule over Judaea and Samaria, had been deposed and banished by Augustus on account of his cruel abuse of power.[6] In his place a Roman Procurator was appointed. But the Herodian legend still lived. There was a party, small, yet of influence, which regarded the Herods as in some way embodying the national, patriotic cause in opposition to Rome. We find the Pharisees consorting with them in hostile approaches to our Lord. In one case, it is on the plea of Sabbath desecration. In the other, it is when they feel that the point of a Parable is directed against themselves. But in

[1] At the same time, it is to be observed that it was to a group of men largely composed of Sadducees—'the chief priests and elders'—that our Lord said, 'The publicans and harlots go into the Kingdom of God before you.' Matt. xxi. 31. *v.* Wellhausen, *Isr. u. Jüd. Geschichte*, p. 309.

[2] Joseph. *Antiq.* xviii. 1, § 3.

[3] Aristobulus I. in B.C. 104, took the title of king. *v. Ps. of Sol.* xvii. 7. When Pompey in B.C. 63 deposed Aristobulus II., he left the High-Priesthood to Hyrcanus. *v.* Gray in Charles, *Apocrypha and Pseudepigrapha of the O.T.* ii. p. 629.

[4] *v.* Bp. H. E. Ryle, *Guardian*, 1913, p. 1626.

[5] Kohler in *Jewish Encyl.* art. 'Sadducees.'

[6] It was by an afterthought that his father bequeathed Judaea to him. On getting to hear of the change of ruler—Archelaus instead of Antipas as had been anticipated—Joseph on returning from the Flight into Egypt, 'turned aside into the parts of Galilee' (Matt. ii. 22). The ill-fame of Archelaus had reached his ears.

each case, men must have marvelled at the strange fellowship of Pharisee and Herodian, which a common feeling of hatred and ill-will had brought about. Christ warned men on one occasion against the 'leaven of Herod' as well as 'the leaven of the Pharisees.' He had good ground for feeling that, discordant as they were, in their general aims and outlook, they were united in uncompromising hostility to Himself and the Kingdom which He had come to set up.[1]

[1] Mk. iii. 6; xii. 13=Matt. xxii. 16; Mk. viii. 15.

CHAPTER XIV

THE TEMPLE AND THE PRIESTHOOD

THE Jewish religion centred in the Temple. It was there that the piety of the people found its chief means of expression. Zeal for God's House was a characteristic mark of the true Israelite. Nothing so stirred the indignation of the people as the invasion of its sanctity by a conqueror such as Antiochus Epiphanes,[1] or Pompey.[2] Even the presence of a Gentile within the court reserved for Israelites was forbidden on pain of death.[3] Holiness was the law of God's House, and no one who was regarded as ceremonially unclean, or was uncircumcized, might enter. Our Lord, as a member of a pious and God-fearing family, may be said to have inherited this traditional feeling of reverence. From His presentation as a child of forty days up to the last few hours of His earthly life, He was in touch with the observances and the life of the Temple. Although, before the opening of His Ministry, we have but one account of His presence at a Feast, there is no reason to doubt that He frequently formed part of the group of relatives and friends who went up to keep their Passover in the Holy City. He would join in singing the Psalms of 'Degrees'[4] as the company wended their way to the House

[1] Joseph. *Antiq.* xii. 5, § 4.

[2] Joseph. *Antiq.* xiv. 4, § 2 f.

[3] *v.* the inscription discovered by M. Clermont-Ganneau (now at Constantinople), from the wall of the Court of the Israelites, in Benzinger, *Hebräische Archäologie*, p. 404, *μηθένα ἀλλογενῆ εἰσπορεύεσθαι ἐντὸς τοῦ περὶ τὸ ἱερὸν τρυφάκτου καὶ περιβόλου. ὃς δ' ἂν λήφθη ἑαυτῷ αἴτιος ἔσται διὰ τὸ ἐξακολουθεῖν θάνατον.* This warning throws a fresh light on Acts xxi. 28. The inscription itself is referred to by Josephus, *Antiq.* xv. 11, § 5; *Bell. Jud.* vi. 2, § 4, where in the siege, Titus refers to the inscription and reminds the Jews that he had upheld the prohibition, *οὐχ ἡμεῖς δὲ τοὺς ὑπερβάντας ὑμῖν ἀναιρεῖν ἐπετρέψαμεν, κἂν Ῥωμαίων τις ᾖ*; *v.* Schürer, *Geschichte des Jüd. Volkes*, ii. p. 209. *Τὸ μεσότοιχον τοῦ φραγμοῦ*, Eph. ii. 14, is probably an allusion.

[4] Ps. cxx.-cxxxiv.

of God. When arrived there, He would take His part in the offering of the daily Morning and Evening Sacrifice,[1] and in the intervals of worship would be found, as on the occasion mentioned by St. Luke,[2] sitting in one of the circles of listeners, as some Doctor of the Law taught the traditional view of the will of Jehovah. The Temple, whose magnificence His disciples once bade Him admire, was the third which had stood upon the spot consecrated by Abraham's great act of obedience, in the offering of his only son. The first, for which David had prepared and which Solomon had built, was swept away in B.C. 586 by the army of Nebuchadnezzar.[3] It fell with the monarchy of Judah. City, Temple and Throne perished together. In B.C. 520, sixty-six years later, the returning exiles commenced the rebuilding of God's House.[4] The work was finished four years later, in the reign of Darius.[5] This second Temple, after being plundered and desecrated by Antiochus Epiphanes, was restored and rededicated by Judas Maccabaeus.[6] The Feast of

[1] Our Lord's attitude to the Temple sacrifices is not easy to define. We have no ground for thinking that He would not take part in the sacrifices at the Passover. Cf. Lk. xxii. 7 ff. He paid the Temple tribute money (Matt. xvii. 24) and we cannot imagine that He was indifferent to the anticipatory character of the offerings and sacrifices which were celebrated there. On the other hand, His language shows that, with all His appreciation of the part played by the Temple in the long religious history of His people, He believed its work was well-nigh over. Mk. xiii. 1-3, and parallels. Cf. Jo. iv. 21. Moreover, He definitely ranged Himself with those prophets like Hosea and Micah, who had placed obedience to the ethical spirit of the Law above obedience to its ritual ordinances: 'If ye had known what this meaneth, I will have mercy and not sacrifice, ye would not have condemned the guiltless.' Matt. xii. 7; ix. 13; Hos. vi. 6; Mic. vi. 6-9. Nor can we account for this side of His attitude, as some have done, by alleging the influence of His expectation of the παρουσία. To do so would be to go with the extreme eschatologists in involving His deepest ethical teaching in a hopeless web of error and misconception. His attitude was determined by His clear view of the relative proportion of things; not by a mistaken outlook upon the course of history. It has been suggested that Christ's action in clearing the outer Temple court of the traffickers in doves and the money-changers was due to His vivid realization of the comparative unimportance of the sacrifices. Their presence in the outer court was not legally a profanation. Mk. xi. 15; Matt. xxi. 12. *v.* N. Schmidt, *The Prophet of Nazareth*, p. 281 f.; Oesterley in *Dict. of Christ.* ii. p. 712 f.

[2] ii. 46. [3] 2 Kings xxv. 8 f. [4] Ezra ii. 68; iii. 8 f.

[5] *v.* Benzinger, *Hebr. Archäologie*, p. 400. The Temple of which the prophet Ezekiel speaks, xl.-xliii. is a creation of his own fancy, an ideal construction, intended to represent certain views of his own as to what the Temple ought to be. *v.* Benzinger, *ib.* p. 393.

Dan. xii. 11; 1 Macc. i. 23 f.; iv. 43 f.

its Dedication became an annual event in Jerusalem, and we read of our Lord's presence at it.[1] To Herod, whose fondness for display and magnificence was a ruling passion, the Temple of the returning exiles seemed lacking in due splendour. In B.C. 20-19, he began to rebuild it, enlarging the ground-plan and making up for irregularities of the site by means of huge substructures. In our Lord's day, the spectacle which its white marble walls presented was magnificent; but even then, it was still unfinished, and remained so until eight or ten years before its destruction and the capture of the city in A.D. 70 by the army of Titus.[2] Up to the end, it was the central and hallowed place of Jewish religion. The round of its public and private [3] sacrifices filled the day. From apocalyptic sources and from the New Testament alike we get the same picture of its stated hours of prayer.[4] It had lost much of its sacredness in the course of time. The ark was no longer there. Even in the second Temple, the 'Holy of Holies,' the inner shrine,[5] was empty. But the whole building and its historic site to One so penetrated with the spirit and feeling of His people, were inexpressibly dear. He could say, 'Lord, I have loved the habitation of Thy House and the place where Thine honour dwelleth.'

Yet, we can well imagine that, as the time of His own perfect and all-sufficient sacrifice drew near, the sight of the vast apparatus of the daily offerings of the Temple must have been almost repellent. The number of animals which were sacrificed at the greater feasts was enormous.[6] When He set this lavish display

[1] Jo. x. 22, 23.

[2] *v.* Benzinger, *Hebr. Archäologie*, p. 403. For a description of it, see Joseph. *Antiq.* xv. 11, § 3; *Bell. Jud.* i. 21, § 1; v. 5.

[3] *v.* Bousset, *Die Religion des Judentums im neutest. Zeitalter*, p. 127. We must remember the distinction between the stated public offerings and the freewill and ceremonially obligatory offerings of individuals. *v.* Joseph. *Antiq.* iii. 9, § 1. *δύο μὲν γάρ εἰσιν ἱερουργίαι· τούτων δ' ἡ μὲν ὑπὸ τῶν ἰδιωτῶν, ἑτέρα δ' ὑπὸ τοῦ δήμου συντελούμεναι.* *v.* Schürer, *op. cit.* ii. p. 284.

[4] Cf. *The Book of the Secrets of Enoch* (Slavonic), li. 4, 'It is good to go morning, midday and evening into the Lord's dwelling for the glory of your creator.' Acts iii. 1. *v.* Schürer, *Geschichte des Jüdischen Volkes*, ii. pp. 290, 285. Bousset, *op. cit.* p. 127. Cf. Ps. lv. 17.

[5] דְּבִיר Pompey entered it, B.C. 63. 'At Cn. Pompejus, captis Hierosolymis, victor ex illo fano nihil attigit.' Cic. *Pro L. Flacco*, 28.

[6] Cf. 'The Letter of Aristeas,' § 89, in Charles, *Apocrypha and Pseudepigrapha of the O.T.* ii. written according to Andrews, *ib.* in B.C. 130-70, 'Many

of externalism, this stream of 'blood of bulls and of goats,' which could never 'take away sins,' [1] beside the formalism of the offerers, and thought how soon Temple and victims would together be things of the past, we can enter somewhat into the train of His thought. We can understand the sudden outburst of indignation which swept the traffickers from their seats. If a prophet, seven centuries earlier, was moved by the Holy Ghost, to cry in God's Name, 'Bring no more vain oblations; incense is an abomination to me,' [2] He, Who was so soon to offer in His own Person the one perfect and sufficient oblation and satisfaction for the sins of the whole world, might well have wearied of the sight.[3]

Before describing the daily service of the Temple, some account of its arrangement is necessary.[4] Everything took place within the inner court, which was divided into an eastern and a western half. The eastern part, which alone could be entered by women, was approached from the gate called 'beautiful.' [5] Only men might enter the western portion. Here stood the actual Temple, consisting, like the surrounding court, of two divisions, the larger one in front. Behind it was the small chamber called the 'Holy of Holies,' which the High Priest alone might enter on the Day of Atonement. Within the larger room stood the Altar of Incense, the Seven-branched Candlestick, and the Table of Shew Bread. Passing out into the court again, we find the chief centre of the daily service, the Altar of Burnt Offerings, standing under the open sky, built of unhewn stone and approached by stairs of unhewn stone. Close at hand was the brazen laver in which the priests washed their feet and hands before taking part in the service. Towards the northern side of the court was the place of slaughter, with pillars for hanging up the carcases of the victims.

thousand beasts are sacrificed there on the feast days.' *v.* Bousset, *D. Religion des Judentums*, p. 128.

[1] Hebr. x. 4, 11. Cf. Rom. iii. 25, 'For the passing by (or over) of sins that are past.' The sacrifices could not take away sins, but, in view of the One Sacrifice which was to be offered, God could 'pass over' them. *v.* Du Bose, *The Gospel according to St. Paul*, p. 101.

[2] Is. i. 13.

[3] Cf. Gore, *The Body of Christ*, p. 161.

[4] For a good description of the arrangement of the Temple as it was in the time of Christ, *v.* Schürer, *op. cit.* ii. p. 285 f.

[5] Acts iii. 2.

The priests of the 'course' which was on duty slept, the preceding night, in a chamber of the inner court.[1] Called before daybreak by an officer, lots were cast apportioning to each his special task in the day's service. The Altar of Burnt Offering had to be cleared of ashes and its fire replenished. It was determined who should act as slaughterer of the victims, who should bring the meat offering, who trim the lamps, with all the other details of the day's ministration. When the officiating priests have been chosen, one goes out to the eastern gate to watch for the first flush of dawn. When it appears, the ritual begins; the lamb is brought to the place of slaughter; the Altar of Incense and the Seven-branched Candlestick are tended and prepared for use. Then comes the slaughter of the lamb, the sprinkling of its blood upon the altar and its division among the priests.

After prayer lots are again cast, and this time for what was regarded as the most solemn part of the whole service, and its performance the greatest privilege that a priest could have. Who should bring the offering of Incense to the altar, present it there and with his fellow priests, each carrying out his own portion of the ritual, come forth and bless the people in the name of Jehovah, while from the altar within the Temple rises the symbolic cloud of smoke?[2] For it was at this point that the service culminated. Then followed the placing of the several parts of the lamb upon the Altar of Burnt Offering,[3] the presentation of the meat offering and of the wine of the drink offering; and as the priest bent forward to pour it out, the Levites burst into song, priests blew with their silver trumpets at every pause in the singing and, at each blast of the trumpet, the people

[1] *v.* Schürer, *op. cit.* ii. p. 294. Much of the following description of the daily service is based upon his work.

[2] *v.* Num. vi. 22 f. The moment of the offering of Incense, while the people waited without, was regarded as specially favourable for the reception of a Divine revelation. Josephus relates such an episode in the life of the High Priest John Hyrcanus. *Antiq.* xiii. 10, § 3. St. Luke tells of the revelation to Zacharias, i. 9-20. Philo attaches a greater sanctity to the thanksgiving at the oblation of Incense than to that which accompanied the offering of slaughtered victims. *De victimas offerentibus*, § 4. Cf. Box in *Encycl. Bibl.* iv. col. 4955.

[3] 'The original idea was that the Deity Himself partook of the offering, much as, in the same belief even later, food was placed in a grave. The burning is a more refined mode of presentation; for a spiritual being, the fragrance of the smoke is the least material form of enjoyment.' Benzinger, *Hebr. Archäologie*, p. 434. Cf. Gen. viii. 21; Ezek. xx. 41.

prostrated themselves in prayer.[1] In the words of the Chronicler,[2] 'When the burnt offering began, the song of the Lord began also with the trumpets.'[3] Such, in brief outline, was the daily morning service in the Temple, as our Lord must have frequently witnessed it. At evening, with one or two slight modifications, it was the same. On the Sabbath the number of victims was doubled.[4] On Feast Days it was still further multiplied.

On the Sabbath, the Table of the Shewbread was placed in the holy place before the entrance to the 'Holy of Holies' and the loaves were set upon it. 'Like the new moon, the Sabbath was a day of joy and festivity.' The rest, to which it was dedicated, resulted from the fact that the round of worship gave no time for work. Sabbath rest was only possible to a people of settled, agricultural, or town life. A nomad, pastoral people had their herds to attend to every day.[5] The rest was therefore a later, not a primitive, accompaniment of the Sabbath.[6]

The great feasts of the Jewish year were celebrated in, or in close connection with, the Temple. Of these, the Passover was

[1] Something analogous to the part taken by the people in the Temple worship may be seen at Constantinople by those who are fortunate enough to witness evening service during Ramadhan in the Mosque of St. Sophia.

As to other offerings, *v.* Benzinger, *Hebr. Archäologie*, p. 443.

On the Day of Atonement, the High Priest entered the Holy of Holies only after the offering of the Incense. Lev. xvi. 12 f.; Num. xvi. 46 f. *v.* Benzinger, *ib.* p. 445.

[2] 2 Chron. xxix. 27.

[3] After the burning of the flesh of the victim upon the altar, portions of it reserved for the priests were consumed in the holy place. *v.* Benzinger, *op. cit.* p. 456. He quotes with approval the view of Philo and others that the eating of the flesh of the offering was regarded as a proof of its acceptance by God as an atonement. 'God would not have called His servants to partake in such a meal, unless full forgiveness of sin had come about.' *Ib.* p. 457.

[4] ταῖς δὲ ἑβδόμαις διπλασιάζει τὸν τῶν ἱερείων ἀριθμόν. Philo, *De victimis*, § 3. Cf. Joseph. *Antiq.* iii. 10, § 1.

[5] 'The Israelites were originally shepherds.' Benzinger, *ib.* p. 205. Cf. Amos i. 1; 2 Chron. xxvi. 10.

[6] *v.* Benzinger, *Hebr. Archäologie*, p. 465 f. He considers that the motive derived from the Creation story is a late insertion into the decalogue, Ex. xx. 11 (*v.* Driver, *Introd*^{n} *to Liter. of O.T.* p. 35), and that the change of idea by which rest became legally obligatory was due to the exile, when the opportunity for the festal offerings ceased and rest from labour became the only possible method of keeping the day. *Ib.* p. 474. We remember that our Lord strongly opposed the idea of *mere rest* as a cast-iron, formal keeping of the Sabbath. The rule could always be overborne by an opportunity of well-doing or kindly action. Matt. xii. 12; Lk. xiii. 14 f.

bound up with the great national deliverance from Egypt. But not only is it reminiscent of the Exodus: it actually preceded it.[1] It is often spoken of as identical with the Feast of Unleavened Bread: but the two are distinct from one another. Each, at least in theory, goes back to the Exodus; but they point to different episodes of the deliverance, and were celebrated successively and not as one feast. First came the Passover. The lamb, sacrificed in the Temple, was eaten at home. Then, for seven days following unleavened bread was eaten in every household. But this latter feast, although so closely connected with the Passover and partaking of its historical associations, had quite a different reference. It was the occasion of the first of the three Harvest Festivals which marked the course of the Jewish year. The corn was beginning to be cut, and on the second day of the feast a sheaf of barley was brought into the Temple and 'waved' before the Lord.[2]

Fifty days after the Feast of Unleavened Bread came the Feast of Weeks.[3] It signalized the completion of the Wheat Harvest and lasted for one day only. As at the earlier feast the sheaf is presented as it is brought from the harvest field, so now there is a similar offering, but of the corn made up into loaves, while as at the Passover many lambs and oxen are offered. At first a purely agricultural feast, it became linked in late Judaism with the gift of the Law at Sinai.

The last of the old feasts was that of Tabernacles. It was kept in the seventh month. Two ideas were associated with it. Its name recalled the time when the people lived in booths or tents in the wilderness, before their entrance into settled homes. The time of year marked the completion of the harvest. It was the Feast of Ingathering.[4] It lasted for eight days and, as in the case of the other feasts, was celebrated with much slaughter of lambs and bulls.

[1] 'It was already instituted before the Exodus in order that Jehovah might spare the firstborn of Israel, not because He *had* spared them.' *v.* Ex. xii.; Benzinger, *ib.* p. 475.

[2] Lev. xxiii. 10 f.

[3] Pentecost, ἡ πεντηκόστη. Cf. 2 Macc. xii. 31, 32, 'They marched up to Jerusalem, as the feast of weeks was close at hand. After the feast called Pentecost, etc.' Cf. Acts ii. 1. *v.* Hastings' *D.B.* i. p. 861.

[4] Ex. xxiii. 16, 'The feast of ingathering which is in the end of the year.' Cf. xxxiv. 22.

One feast of quite recent origin remains to be mentioned. When Antiochus Epiphanes had captured Jerusalem B.C. 168, he profaned the Temple, robbing it of its treasures—the golden candlestick, the altars of incense and of burnt offering, the table of the shew bread—and setting up an altar to Jupiter.[1] Four years later, Judas Maccabaeus regained possession of the city, purified the Temple, destroyed the idolatrous altar and in its place reared again an altar to Jehovah. Then, in commemoration of this happy event, he founded the Feast of the Dedication to be kept with rejoicing for eight days from the twenty-fifth day of the month Chisleu.[2]

A religious institution so highly organized as the Temple requires a professional caste to keep and to serve it. But the religion that centred there dominated the whole life of the Jewish people. It was therefore to be expected that the caste which served it would have a corresponding influence in the nation at large. The existence of a separate order is traditionally referred to the Mosaic legislation. Its originator is the Lawgiver himself. He nominates his brother and confirms the succession in his brother's house. But he regards himself as possessing the power and authority which he bestows on Aaron.[3] Back to this high origin and sanction the people loved to point, when in later times the Temple had become the central home of the national worship. That Moses legislated for the religious life, as well as for the moral conduct of Israel, there can be no question. That the later priesthood of the Temple as a whole derived in clear and uninterrupted succession from the house of Aaron, or even from the tribe of Levi, is not borne out by the testimony of pre-exilic writers.[4] Whatever may have

[1] 'The abomination of desolation.' 1 Macc. i. 54; referred to by Daniel, xi. 31.

[2] Kislev (A.V. Chisleu) answers to our December. The day of profanation was that of the Dedication four years later. 1 Macc. iv. 54; i. 59; iv 59. Cf. Jo. x. 22. The feast was sometimes called the Feast of Lights, the ceremonial lighting of lamps forming a feature of its celebration. *v.* Joseph. *Antiq.* xii. 7, § 7, who calls it *φῶτα, lights.* Thus our Christmas Day, with its festivity and brightness in the midst of the darkest days of the year, corresponds to the Jewish Festival of Lights and like it recalls the memory of a great deliverance.

[3] *v.* Ex. xl. 29. Sacrificial acts are here attributed to Moses himself. McNeile does not admit this. *The Book of Exodus*, p. lxviii.

[4] 'It is impossible to trace the caste to the original stem; there exists no real connection between them. All connecting links are wanting. The stem disappeared early and the caste arose quite late, demonstrably from independent

been the enactments of the earliest (Mosaic) institution, we gather from Judges, 1 Samuel and other early historic books that there were periods when any layman might sacrifice,[1] when kings of Israel chose priests from any tribe and anything like a settled succession confined to a single tribe, or a single family, was quite unknown. What is true of the priesthood is true of the place of worship. There was no one exclusive sanctuary, as there was no one distinct priestly privilege of ministration. Not only were sacred places taken over from the Canaanite to be sanctuaries of Jehovah, but much of the worship and the practices which prevailed there were taken over with them.[2] In the time of the Judges and even subsequently, the task of the priesthood was to guard and care for the sanctuary with its images, and to consult the oracle connected with it. When we wonder at the manner in which the Temple became a slaughter-house, at the vast number of victims which day by day were sacrificed to propitiate Jehovah, we may think of the Canaanite origin of this exaggerated form of externalism which had crept into the national worship.[3] We can understand the repudiation

beginnings.' Wellhausen, *Prolegomena zur Geschichte Israels*, p. 150. This statement appears to represent the state of our knowledge. We cannot trace with any completeness the course of the Israelite priesthood through the ages; but we have at the same time to make all allowance for the existence of a persistent tradition which connects it with the house of Levi.

[1] Thus Samuel, of the tribe of Ephraim, sacrifices, 1 Sam. vii. 9. Gideon of the tribe of Manasseh and Manoah of the tribe of Dan offer sacrifice. Judges vi. 26; xiii. 19. Samuel wore the priestly linen coat (ephod bad) and the pallium. Both David and Solomon officiated as priests, 2 Sam. vi. 17, 18; 1 Kings viii. 5; ix. 25. David invested his sons with the priestly office, according to Buttenweiser's interpretation of 2 Sam. viii. 18, in *Jew. Encycl.* x. p. 192. Cf. Baudissin in Hastings' *D.B.* iv. p. 73. Wellhausen remarks on the change from the state of things which is said to have prevailed in the wilderness, when we turn to the Book of Judges. 'In place of the Church history of the Hexateuch, world history sets in at once with the Book of Judges.' *Prolegomena zur Geschichte Israels*, p. 131. 'Samuel, the Ephraimite, sleeps every night, because of his office, by the ark of Jehovah where, according to Levit. xvi., the high priest alone once in the year might enter, and then only after the most complete preparation and ceremonial use of atonement.' *Ib.* p. 136.

[2] 'The holy places of the Canaanites with all their paraphernalia, as well as other essential parts of their worship, were simply taken over by the Israelites.' Benzinger, *Hebr. Archäol.* p. 371. Cf. Deut. xii. 30.

[3] The 'High Places' (Bamoth) were originally Canaanite places of worship. Such were Shechem, Gibeon, Shiloh, Nob. *v.* Wellhausen, *Prolegomena zur Geschichte Israels*, p. 18. As to the ritual of Hebrew worship, 'The more complex sacrificial ritual which was now (about the time of Josiah) in force is

by prophet and psalmist of a formalism which left the life untouched, a repudiation which our Lord made His own, as with consuming zeal He swept the traffickers with their wares from the Temple and claimed it as a House of Prayer. Like all great historic institutions, the Temple with its worship tended to degenerate, to lose touch with its original purpose, to adopt new methods, to distract men's minds from what was fundamental, to admit a mercenary element which was foreign to its nature.

To say this is not to deny the divine sanction, which attached to offering and sacrifice, or their value as bringing the penitent into touch with the perfect and all-sufficing oblation, which was one day to be offered upon the Cross.[1] But our records contain allusions to a growth of mere formal observance that are not to be explained away. We have to note it, if we are to understand our Lord's attitude to the priesthood which confronted Him at Jerusalem.

The reforms in theory and practice which were brought about by the exile in the sixth century B.C. were of a far-reaching character. They took effect in several directions. The discipline of the Exile gave the death-blow to the idolatry which had prevailed to an extent which we hardly realize. It confirmed the centralization of all sacrificial worship in Jerusalem. Both of these reforms had already been enforced under Josiah in B.C. 624 ;[2] but it required the bitter experience of exile to establish them securely. On the return there was no more idolatry. The second Temple stood alone as the place of sacrifice and

manifestly not independent of the Phoenician ritual as we know it from the Marseilles tablet.' W. Robertson Smith in *Encycl. Bibl.* iii. col. 3844. The Hebrew name for Priest is the Canaanite or Phoenician word Kohen. *v.* Robertson Smith, *ib.* col. 3840. 'Without opposition, the Israelites claimed these sacrificial places for themselves and their worship of Jehovah ; Amos uses the word bâmâh as a general term for a sanctuary without any evil connotation (vii. 9). Samuel the man of God blessed the sacrifice which was offered on the bâmâh of Ramah (1 Sam. ix. 12 f. ; cf. 1 Sam. viii. 4) ; Solomon, the beloved of Jehovah, celebrated the beginning of his reign with huge sacrifices on the famous great Bâmâh of Gibeon ; Jehovah Himself appeared there and blessed him (1 Kings iii. 4 f.).' Benzinger, *Hebr. Archäol.* p. 373. Cf. 1 Kings xx. 23 ; Hos. iv. 13.

[1] 'With the misfortunes of the Captivity, the sense of national and personal sin had deepened and the need of pardon was keenly felt. Hence the sacrificial system received much attention.' F. J. Foakes Jackson, *The Parting of the Roads*, 1912, p. 34.

[2] 2 Kings xxiii.

the central home of worship. Only four out of the twenty-four courses of the priests came back from exile.[1] But 'what arose on the soil of Judaea was no people, but a community of the Temple . . . the whole common life of restored Judaism culminated in the worship of the Temple at Jerusalem.'[2] One consequence of this was the heightened dignity of the High Priest as time went on. Under the kings, he had been a subordinate; and after the exile he was for some time in a position inferior to that of leaders like Zerubbabel and Nehemiah. But in the later pre-Christian centuries we find him acquiring a status which can only be compared to that of prince,[3] until in B.C. 141, in the person of Simon Maccabaeus, the priesthood and the princedom were declared to be hereditary in his family;[4] and in B.C. 104, Aristobulus, the high priest, styled himself king.[5] The high-priesthood of Simon was dowered with a greater title than that of prince. The fervid expectations, which had been excited by the achievements of Judas Maccabaeus and his brothers, led some to see in that family the dawn of the Messianic kingdom. It is suggested that Psalm cx. refers to Simon. At any rate, it is singularly appropriate to the state of things at the time when Simon was high priest and prince.[6] Apocalyptic writers of the period, if they speak of a Messianic king, agree with few exceptions in tracing his descent, not to David and Judah but, to the tribe of Levi to which the Maccabaean family belonged.[7] Such a change of traditional conceptions is remarkable. It is a witness to the extraordinary position in their

[1] Ezra ii. 36 f. over 4000 in all. Of the Levites only 74 came back.

[2] Bousset, *Die Religion des Judentums im neutest. Zeitalter*, p. 111.

[3] 'The high priests of the pre-Maccabaean age as well as the Hasmonaean high priests, were also princes.' Benzinger, *op. cit.* p. 319.

[4] 'And the Jews and the Priests were well pleased that Simon should be their leader and high-priest for ever, until a faithful prophet should arise.' 1 Macc. xiv. 41.

[5] For parallels to this kingship of a priest in Palestine, *v.* Schürer, *Geschichte des Judentums*, ii. p. 215, n. 2.

[6] *v.* Driver, *Literature of the O.T.* p. 384 n.; Charles, *Between the O. and N. Testaments*, 1914, p. 78.

[7] *Test. of Reuben* vi. 7 f.; *Test. of Levi* viii. 14; *Test. of Dan.* v. 10. Other passages in the *Testaments of the Twelve Patriarchs* have been referred to a Messiah from the Tribe of Levi; but the reference is uncertain. This curious change in Messianic expectation, which displaced Judah for Levi as the favoured tribe, hardly lasted more than thirty years. The concentration of the offices

country of that great family, and to the extent of their achievements.[1] Nothing short of Messianic is the description applied to Simon's successor, John Hyrcanus. But the dream could not last. After Hyrcanus the family degenerated; and with their decline in character there gradually faded the thought of a Messiah from the tribe of Levi. The first century B.C. saw the revival of the old hope of a Messiah in the line of David. Meanwhile, the Maccabees had become Sadducees, and with the adoption of the cause of that sect had lost all hold upon the respect of the nation. Henceforth, the high-priesthood was involved in the worldly policy which characterized Sadduceeism at the opening of the Christian era; while the lack of faith in the spiritual aspect of religion, which distinguished the sect,[2] completed the unfitness of the holders of their great office for their task. Rich, haughty and exclusive, the Sadducean high priest stood apart from the people whom he served. Out of touch with the religious hopes of the nation, he became the willing tool of the prevailing power. If his voice made itself heard in the Sanhedrin, his personal tenure of office was no longer guaranteed and, as we gather from the Gospels, there was at one time quite a number of men who had once held it.[3]

of Priest, Prince and Prophet in Simon Maccabaeus and in John Hyrcanus was the direct cause of this revulsion of apocalyptic thought. With the adhesion of Hyrcanus to the Sadducees, the idea was dropped, and the traditional view reappeared. *v.* Charles, *Apocrypha and Pseudepigrapha of the O.T.* ii. p. 294; Burkitt, *Jewish and Christian Apocalypses*, p. 35. *v.* above, p. 70.

[1] The *Testaments of the Twelve Patriarchs* was written in the time of John Hyrcanus. 'For the first time since Solomon a Jewish Prince ruled all the promised land.' Burkitt, *op. cit.* p. 35. 'He it was who alone had three of the most desirable things in the world,—the government of his nation and the high-priesthood and the gift of prophecy.' Joseph. *Bell. Jud.* i. 2, § 8; *Antiq.* xiii. 10, § 7.

[2] The Sadducees rejected the doctrines of Resurrection and of a future life because they were not, as they held, in the written law. *v.* Joseph. *Antiq.* xviii. 1, § 4. Friedländer asserts that the Pharisees' doctrine of a Resurrection and future life is unknown to Biblical Scripture. *D. relig. Bewegungen innerhalb des Judentums*, p. 10. But cf. Dan. xii. 2, 3.

[3] *οἱ ἀρχιερεῖς*, Mk. xiv. 1; xv. 1; Matt. xxvii. 1. 'Herod and the Romans set up and deposed high priests at their pleasure. From these non-acting high priests arose the group known as ἀρχιερεῖς.' Baudissin in Hastings' *D.B.* iv. p. 96; Benzinger, *Hebräische Archäologie*, p. 319; Schürer, *op. cit.* ii. p. 221. O. Holtzmann *Neutestam. Zeitgeschichte*, p. 176, criticizes this view, considering that ἀρχιερεῖς refers to the family of the high priest. It is certainly true that there are passages both in the N.T. and in Josephus, which give this extended

In the time of Christ the supreme council of the Jewish people was the Sanhedrin.[1] Late tradition ascribes it to Moses and finds its original form in the body of Seventy Elders whom God bade him call together.[2] However that may be, a body answering to the later Sanhedrin appears to exist when the second Temple is being built.[3] In the reign of Antiochus the Great, B.C. 223-187, the senate (γερουσία) is distinctly mentioned.[4] At the head of this body stood the high priest. When the hereditary high-priesthood passed from the Zadokite line to the family of the Maccabees, the Sanhedrin maintained its position and is frequently referred to in the apocryphal books of the Maccabees.[5]

When Pompey had become master of Jerusalem in B.C. 63, he deprived the reigning Maccabaean high priest of his princely diadem, but allowed him to preside over the nation and made no attempt to destroy the Sanhedrin.[6] A remarkable episode of its history occurred a little later. Its rule extended to Galilee and on this ground it summoned the youthful Herod to appear before it and answer for certain actions of his in that region. He came, but with the protection of an armed force; and when he became king, one of the first acts of his reign was the murder of the members of the council which had sat in judgment upon him.[7]

interpretation of the term. *v.* Acts iv. 6; xix. 14; Joseph. *Bell. Jud.* vi. 2, § 2, υἱοὶ δ' ἀρχιερέων τρεῖς. Schürer himself is fully alive to this fact. *v. op. cit.* ii. p. 222 f.

[1] סַנְהֶדְרִין a translation into Hebrew from the Greek συνέδριον=βουλή, council or synod. *v.* Schürer, *Gesch. des Jüd. Volkes*, ii. p. 196. It is sometimes called in the N.T. πρεσβυτέριον, Lk. xxii. 66; Acts xxii. 5, or γερουσία, Acts v. 21, an assembly of Elders.

[2] Num. xi. 16.

[3] Ezra v. 5, 9. *v.* O. Holtzmann, *Neutestam. Zeitgeschichte*, p. 171; Schürer, *op. cit.* ii. p. 191, 'In Judaea, we find a γερουσία, *i.e.* an aristocratic senate in the Greek period. In all probability it rose out of the pre-Hellenistic, *i.e.* out of the Persian time.' Cf. Benzinger, *Hebr. Archäologie*, p. 320, 'An historical connection of the great council with that college of "the Elders of Judah" after the return from exile is not impossible.'

[4] Joseph. *Antiq.* xii. 3, § 3.

[5] 2 Macc. i. 10; iv. 44; 1 Macc. vii. 33. Cf. Judith xi. 14.

[6] *v.* Joseph. *Antiq.* xx. 10. Hyrcanus has the προστασία τοῦ ἔθνους. Schürer, *op. cit.* ii. p. 193, cites *Ps. of Solomon* iv. 1, as evidence for continuance of the Sanhedrin. *v.* Gray, *in loc.* (Charles, *Apocrypha and Pseudepigrapha of the O.T.* ii.).

[7] Joseph. *Antiq.* xiv. 9, §§ 3-5. According to Schürer, *op. cit.* ii. p. 193, this is the first occasion of the use of the word συνέδριον, Sanhedrin, for the council. So Benzinger, *Hebr. Archäologie*, p. 320, n. 1.

In the time of Herod's successor, Archelaus, the jurisdiction of the Sanhedrin was probably limited to Judaea. This limitation certainly obtained under the Roman procurators. Our Lord, as a Galilaean by residence, was not under its jurisdiction; and, as we learn from the Fourth Gospel,[1] it did not possess the power to inflict death. In Gospel times the Sanhedrin was an aristocratic assembly presided over by the high priest, himself a Sadducee, with a large admixture of Sadducees in its membership together with a certain number of learned Scribes.[2] Its influence in all matters of ordinary Jewish public life was very great.[3] With the break-up of the nation and the fall of the city and the Temple, it disappeared from history.[4] A pale reflection of it subsisted in the judgment court of Jamnia.

[1] Jo. xviii. 31. Schürer regards the stoning of Stephen, Acts vii. 57 f. as an act either exceeding jurisdiction or of popular fury. *Op. cit.* ii. p. 210, *v.* O. Holtzmann, *Neutest. Zeitgeschichte*, p. 174. Schürer, speaking of allusions to the Sanhedrin in the Mischna which he characterizes as merely theoretical, observes that 'what we derive from the N.T. is of more value.' *Op. cit.* ii. p. 208.

[2] 'Scribes often determined the judgment of the Sanhedrin, so Acts v. 34-39, Gamaliel.' O. Holtzmann, *op. cit.* p. 175. Cf. Lk. xxii. 66.

[3] The ordinary place of meeting of the Sanhedrin was a spot connected by a bridge with the Temple area. This explains the fact that, at night, the Sanhedrin met for the condemnation of our Lord in the palace of the high priest, because at night the Temple gates were always closed. *v.* Schürer, *op. cit.* ii. p. 212. But *v.* O. Holtzmann, *op. cit.* p. 177.

[4] *v.* Schürer, *op. cit.* ii. p. 196.

CHAPTER XV

THE PUBLIC MINISTRY (I.)

THE fact that Christ presented Himself as a candidate for Baptism among the crowd at the Jordan is a remarkable proof of the historical character of the Gospel narrative. The Baptism of repentance could hardly seem in keeping with the general character of a portrait of 'the Son of God.'[1] It is there because it actually occurred.

We may say the same when we come to study the story of the Temptation. Its presence in the Gospel narrative is sufficient proof of its truth to fact. No biographer who set out to draw an imaginative picture of the Son of God when He came among men, would willingly embarrass himself with so improbable an episode.

But how did the fact come to the knowledge of the Evangelists? It could only have been communicated; for no human companionship shared the strain of those Forty Days. 'He was with the wild beasts' indeed: otherwise He was alone with Satan. We can only conclude that an event so momentous in its bearing upon the whole course of the Public Ministry, and so typical of Christ's conception of His mission, was made known to disciples in some hour of retirement, and thus passed into the general store of knowledge which was open to the Evangelists.

In no other way can we account for its presence in the Gospel history; and of this we may be sure; it represents an actual occurrence. Deep, spiritual experience lies at the root of the narrative.

The First and Third Evangelists, who alone record the Temptation at length, are independent of the brief reference of St. Mark.

[1] Mk. i. 1.

The similarity of their accounts, combined with deviations of order and language, points to the use of a common source which is freely handled. It is only natural to identify it with the Logia (Q); while the brief summary of St. Mark is probably a reminiscence of the teaching of St. Peter, known to the First and Third Evangelists, but neglected by them for the more complete version which was at their disposal.

The Temptation is presented in the form of an interview between Christ and Satan. We are not told how the Tempter became aware that the Son of God had come among men. His knowledge of the fact was probably due to what had transpired at the Baptism; and when Christ, under the impulse of the Spirit, retired for thought and communion with God into the wilderness, Satan proceeded to test the stedfastness of One, Who had been publicly designated as the Son of God, and therefore his own adversary in his war against mankind. Will He do the work that God had laid upon Him in God's own way? Or can He be led to choose an easier method of bringing in His Kingdom? That appears to be the purpose of Satan's attempt and it reveals great knowledge of the issues involved.

Although the Temptation is presented pictorially with allusions to place and circumstance, we are under no obligation to conceive of its literal occurrence. Our Lord was not transported from the wilderness to a pinnacle of the Temple: nor for the purpose of the Temptation was He carried away to a mountain top.[1] But that the assault of the evil one was a reality, and that the thought of choosing for Himself a path of ease was presented to Him, we cannot doubt. The battle was spiritual, and it was fought within the recesses of His own mind. But it was a real temptation, and the experience left its mark upon Him to the end. His faithfulness and endurance had been put to the proof. His obedience to the will of God was henceforth rooted in victory. He had been innocent before: now His purity of life and purpose bears the sign of conquest. 'He Himself hath suffered being tempted.'[2]

[1] St. Mark distinctly says, 'He was there in the wilderness forty days, tempted of Satan.' If we take the event literally, the wilderness was the scene. If symbolically, there is no occasion to change the circumstances under which it was enacted.

[2] Hebr. ii. 18.

As in time, so in significance, the Temptation is in close connection with the Baptism. That had sealed the Messiah for His task of bringing in the Kingdom of God. The Father had acknowledged and designated Him as His Son. But He is not thereby exempt from the necessity of proving His Sonship by conformity to the Father's will. He might conceivably have preferred another course than the one which ended at the Cross. In vivid flashes of thought, the idea of employing the power and authority, with which He was invested, for His own relief, or to secure His own position, was presented to Him. The idea did not originate in His own mind. With Him there was no impulse of self-pleasing to suggest it. We are often our own tempters through our past history. There was no inheritance of former failure in His case. The suggestion came wholly from without; and He Himself directly attributed it to Satan. The form that it took proves its origin. Christ was now in a situation peculiarly favourable to assault. The exciting accompaniments of His Baptism had left Him in that state of mind which exposes human nature to all the distressing experiences of reaction. And He was alone. In that desolate waste, even the presence and companionship of the Father seemed for the time withheld. We gather this from the later remark that, when the stress was over, 'angels came and ministered to Him': but *not till then*. He has to fight His battle alone. There is no evidence of the interposition of Divine aid. His temptation was the occasion of real suffering: all the greater for the abhorrence which any thought of evil must cause to such a mind. And in addition there was the bodily strain of a long fast.

It was with an eye to this condition that the character of the Temptation was shaped by the Adversary. He began by the insidious suggestion of doubt. It was the old form, familiar to our Lord in His study of the story of the fall. It at once led Him to detect its author.[1] Can it be that One so placed as He was, alone and famished in such a spot, could claim Divine Sonship? 'If Thou be the Son of God,' use your prerogative. Failure to act will belie your pretension. How can you save others, if you cannot save yourself?

Again the source of the Temptation was betrayed by the view which the tempter took of the possession of power. It was for

[1] Matt. iv. 10.

self, to satisfy, to bring personal fame, to secure aggrandisement. Each temptation disclosed one or other of these motives for action. How they appeared to the Tempted we well know. 'Even Christ pleased not Himself' was the assurance of a disciple who knew Him.[1]

With the rejection of every advance was wrought the first of a series of victories over the powers of evil. The baffled tempter departed for a season. He could make no headway. He retired defeated, but not conquered. Yet the end is in sight and the victory of the wilderness gives the assurance of the final triumph of the Cross.

Our Lord's public ministry began shortly after His return from the wilderness of Judaea to Galilee.[2] But we learn from St. John that His first preparations for that ministry were made in the neighbourhood of the Baptist. Immediately after the Temptation, He returned to the scene of His Baptism. This return was marked by the Baptist's public proclamation, 'Behold the Lamb of God, which taketh away the sin of the world.'[3] Again, the next day, as the Baptist was standing with two of his disciples, our Lord passed by, and received from St. John the same testimony, 'Behold the Lamb of God.' As yet, He had neither said nor done anything to bring round Him any band of adherents. He was 'walking' alone, near His Forerunner, but silent, meditative, as one on the eve of a great enterprise, waiting for some clear token of the will of God, passive, rather than willing to take the first step; leaving it to others to make a forward movement. And here comes in the part of the 'Friend of the Bridegroom.' It was his testimony to Christ that stirred the interest of the two disciples.[4] Our Lord was walking on, as on the evening of His Resurrection when He had joined the two disciples in their walk to Emmaus. There, He waited for the invitation to enter their house. Here, He waits to be asked about His own dwelling-place, but when asked by

[1] Rom. xv. 3. [2] Lk. iv. 14. Cf. Weiss, *D. Leben Jesu*, i. p. 336.

[3] Jo. i. 29. *v.* Westcott, *in loc.* This sojourn in Judaea after the Temptation is not referred to by the Synoptic writers. Spitta, *Streitfragen der Geschichte Jesu*, p. 9, considers that St. Luke was aware of a period of activity in Judaea, and that it is hinted at in iv. 14. If so, the historical character of Jo. i. is confirmed. Cf. Jo. iii. 26; iv. 3.

[4] Jo. iii. 26; x. 41.

the two disciples of the Baptist, Himself invites them to enter. It was the first contact of the King with the citizens of His new kingdom, the laying of the first stone in the building of the Christian Church. The Saviour of men comes face to face, in the quiet of His temporary lodging by the banks of the Jordan,[1] with the first of those who were to be His Apostles and Evangelists. One was Andrew, the other the Evangelist himself who, minutely recording time and circumstance, shows his sense of the importance of the interview. Ever afterwards he would look back upon this day as the most eventful in his life.[2]

To Andrew belongs the imperishable fame of having been the first disciple to make known to others the news of the appearance of the expected Messiah. He was the first missionary. And he set for ever the example of the due order of Christian work—from within outwards. 'He first findeth his own brother.' St. John is with him: he has not yet gone off on his own quest: but it is implied that that was what he soon did.[3] Thus two pairs of brothers are the first to become members of Christ. The family relationship enters into the wide brotherhood of the household of God. It is not the formal beginning of the Christian Church. Much was to be done and suffered before that could be. But, as we look back upon it, the incident marks that beginning to all intents and purposes. Christ had drawn to Himself the interest, He was soon to draw the allegiance, of the best men of His time.

We do not know what passed during that first intercourse of Christ with the disciples of the Baptist, but we have clear evidence

[1] *v.* Zahn, *D. Evangelium des Johannes*, p. 116. The Baptist makes no attempt to detach his disciples from himself. He continues his work of preaching and baptizing. He would therefore still welcome their adherence. *v.* Weiss, *D. Leben Jesu*, i. p. 338.

[2] *v.* Zahn, *op. cit.* p. 132. Speaking of the anonymity preserved elsewhere in the Gospel, Zahn remarks that 'this nameless one was one of the twelve Apostles, and one who enjoyed the special friendship of Christ. This appears a probable suspicion in the present recital. For it is not a mere chance that, if we except Nathanael, the men who are named as in those days joining themselves to Jesus out of the band of scholars of the Baptist, Andrew, Peter and Philip, are found again in collective lists of the Apostles among the five first' (p. 131). 'The well known unnamed one, John the son of Zebedee.' Rüegg, in Herzog, *Real-Encycl. für prot. Theol. u. Kirche,* 3 Ausg. Art. 'Johannes der Täufer,' p. 325.

[3] *v.* Zahn in Jo. i. 41 (p. 131), 'We read between the lines, yet clearly enough, that in those days, just as Andrew lighted upon Peter, so his nameless companion (*i.e.* St. John) met with *his* brother and brought him to Jesus.'

of its effect upon them. They came to the conviction that here was the promised Messiah. Such, at least, was the announcement of Andrew, as he sought out his brother Simon and brought him to Jesus.

How essentially this early recognition of the Messiahship of Jesus appears to conflict with St. Matthew's account (if not St. Mark's) of what passed at Caesarea Philippi has been often pointed out. But we have evidence of its historic character in the fact that something about Him, either here or at the lake, must have attracted the disciples. What could it have been but a conviction of His Messiahship? What else could have led them to leave a great prophet like the Baptist to follow the Carpenter from Nazareth? If this reasoning is good, it makes little against the trustworthiness of the narrative that the disciples feel the influence of Jesus at this slightly earlier period. It is admitted that they feel it at Gennesareth and, as we shall see, some earlier experience such as this is required to account for what passed at the lake—for the sudden obedience to the call to leave all and follow Him.[1] Besides, we have to allow for the fact that, as we see clearly from the early chapters of St. Luke, the expectation of the Messiah was in the air. 'All men mused in their hearts of John whether he were the Christ';[2] and the Baptist himself had spoken of One who was to come after him, Whom, if he did not expressly call Messiah, he clothed with attributes which belonged to the Messianic idea. It was, therefore, no impossible effort of faith and insight if, after listening to the Baptist's testimony and following it up by their visit to Jesus, they already came to the conclusion that He must be the Christ. In forming such a conclusion, they would not necessarily mean all that they afterwards came to mean by the Messiahship of Jesus.[3] Crude and little removed from the ordinary ideas of the crowd would be their first reflections. They did not unlearn at the first interview the conceptions which they had always shared with the rest of the people. But there is nothing in the Evangelist's account, or in its relation to the Markan source, to lead us to doubt that here we have a true piece of history.[4]

[1] *v.* Weiss, *D. Leben Jesu*, i. p. 346.

[2] Lk. iii. 15.

[3] Cf. Weiss, *D. Leben Jesu*, i. p. 346.

[4] St. Matthew's account of what passed at Caesarea Philippi differs in several points from that of St. Mark on which it is based. In Mark there is no such

It was probably on the following day that Andrew brought his famous brother into touch with our Lord—a momentous interview only to be compared with the experience of Saul outside Damascus, or with that of the unnamed disciple on the previous day. With a look that pierced to the heart of Simon, Christ reads at once his character and his destiny: 'Thou shalt be called Cephas, a Stone.' But does this new name record our Lord's reading of the man's character? So, many have thought, notwithstanding the chequered nature of his after career. Or does it rather hint at the special character of his vocation, at the place he was to fill in the new kingdom? [1] We are not told what this new disciple, afterwards so forward to speak, said at this first meeting with his Lord. But to its effect upon him, all his subsequent history bears witness.

The time had now come for our Lord to leave the neighbourhood of the Baptist and to begin the ministry for which the Baptist had prepared. 'The day following Jesus would (ἠθέλησεν) go forth into Galilee.' He will return for a while to His old home and, as occasion serves, go out from there upon His new work. Among the Galileans who had come out attracted by the preaching of the Baptist, was a fellow-townsman of Andrew and Peter. Our Lord 'findeth him and saith unto him, Follow Me.' This is the first occasion on which Christ seeks out a disciple and lays on him the command of discipleship. Philip in turn, joyful at his own call, 'findeth Nathanael.' There can be little doubt

warm acknowledgment of St. Peter's confession as that which Matthew narrates. It is accepted as a matter of course. St. Peter has merely voiced the view of the disciples as distinct from that of the people generally. Our Lord gives him the opportunity of stating it, and remains quite unmoved. If we accept the narrative of the Fourth Gospel, this is to be explained by the fact that long before this, the disciples knew who their Master was. The heightened narrative of St. Matthew gives the impression that here was a new thing and that now for the first time Christ is acknowledged. When we reflect that although St. Matthew gives us a similar confession of St. Peter at an earlier date (xiv. 33), he now gives the impression that St. Peter has suddenly become the recipient of a direct revelation on the subject, are we not led to prefer the Johannine and Markan narratives as consistent with one another, to what bears trace of being an edited account with an ulterior purpose—the glorifying of St. Peter? Allen assigns Matt. xvi. 17-19 to the Logia. It is extremely doubtful if it comes from that ancient source. *v.* Nolloth, *The Person of Our Lord*, p. 351, n. 1. Cf. H. Holtzmann, *in loc.* 'The whole passage is precarious, and seems first to have taken its present form in the course of the second century.'

[1] So Westcott, *in loc.*; H. Holtzmann, *Hand-Kommentar*, *in loc.*

that he was the Bartholomew of the Apostolate.[1] Nathanael is inclined to withhold his assent to the didactic assurance of Philip [2] that he had found 'Him of whom Moses in the law and the prophets did write, Jesus of Nazareth, the Son of Joseph.' 'Can any good thing come out of Nazareth ?' Nathanael himself was of Cana and may have had a poor opinion of such a place as Nazareth; but Galilee generally was not regarded as a likely home of a prophet.[3] Philip, strong in his own conviction, does not stay to argue, but 'saith, Come and see.' The interview with our Lord is one of the most remarkable in the Gospels. Again He bends His scrutinizing look on the man before Him, reading his character and pronouncing it as His first word of greeting. Nathanael wonders at such a claim to knowledge. Our Lord replies that, even before Philip called him, He saw him under the dense foliage of the fig-tree, to which he had gone, like St. Augustine to the garden at Milan,[4] for prayer or meditation. The reply to this indication of a more than human knowledge shows that all Nathanael's doubt had passed. Loyal and sincere, with open heart and mind he owns, with a warmth not matched again until the Easter Confession of St. Thomas, the Divine Sonship and the Messianic rank of our Lord.[5] This good confession is rewarded with the promise of greater things than he had yet experienced. Our Lord uses, probably for the first time as a Self-designation, the expression Son of Man. Thinking of the opening of heaven to earth by His Incarnation, He promises Nathanael that he shall witness what Jacob had seen in vision, the ascent and descent of angels—prayers and the answers to prayers—upon the Son of Man.[6]

[1] 'No mention is made of Nathanael in the Synoptists or of Bartholomew in St. John.' Westcott, *in loc.* As Philip and Nathanael are together in their first experience of Christ, Philip and Bartholomew form a pair in all Synoptic lists of the Apostles. Only in Acts i. 13, are they separated by Thomas. Maldonatus, *Quatuor Evangelist. in loc.* though inclined to the identification, decides against it under pressure of all ancient authorities. Zahn, *Das Evang. des Johan. in loc.* considers that the identification amounts almost to certainty. H. Holtzmann, *Evangel. des Johannes*, i. 51, mentions other opinions as strange as that which identifies Nathanael with St. Paul!

[2] So Zahn, *in loc.* [3] Jo. vii. 52. [4] Aug. *Confess.* viii. 12. 28.

[5] On the significance to be attached to this confession of Nathanael, *v. The Person of Our Lord*, p. 273 ff.

[6] 'What the Patriarch saw but in a dream, the disciples should experience in very truth—continuous, living intercourse between heaven and earth, as it

With this group of adherents, Christ returns for a brief time to Nazareth.[1] He is invited with those who are now called His disciples [2] to a marriage feast at Cana. The two places were but ten miles apart. The marriage took place 'on the third day' after He set out from the spot where He had been with the Baptist. From Cana, when the feast had ended, He comes with His Mother and His disciples to Capernaum, which was to be the chief scene of His Galilean work. After a few days He goes up to Jerusalem for the first Passover of His ministry. At the close of this sojourn at Jerusalem, where He had opened His career of public preaching in the Temple and in the city, our Lord appears to have gone again into the neighbourhood where John was baptizing.[3] His disciples began to baptize, and for a time these two ministrations of baptism, that of Christ and that of St. John, went on side by side.

Not unnaturally some friction arose between the disciples on either side. The Baptist's followers appeal to their master and give him another opportunity to make a characteristic and loyal reference to Christ.[4] The Pharisees are not long in hearing of this new movement, which in dimensions and importance seemed likely to surpass that of the Baptist. Lest there should appear to be any rivalry between His Forerunner and Himself, and on hearing that the situation was being discussed by the Pharisees, our Lord withdrew from Judaea and went again into Galilee, passing through Samaria. At Sychar He holds a discourse with a Samaritan woman and stays in the city for two days. When He reaches Galilee, He is well received by the people. They had seen His action at Jerusalem, when present at the feast. It is at this point that the Synoptic narrative [5] appears to come into line with the recital of St. John, so far as concerns the return to Galilee and the effect of Christ's growing fame upon the Galileans.[6] Both St. Matthew and St. Mark connect the return with news of the imprisonment of the Baptist. Christ would not, at that early period in His ministry, expose Himself and His work to a similar danger. He avoids it by withdrawal.

began with the appearance of the Word of God in the flesh.' H. Holtzmann, *Evang. des Johannes, in loc.* *v.* Westcott, *in loc.*

[1] Jo. i. 43. *v.* Westcott, *in loc.*

[2] Jo. ii. 2.

[3] Jo. iii. 22.

[4] Jo. iii. 26 f.

[5] Mk. i. 14; Lk. iv. 14; Matt. iv. 12.

[6] *v.* Spitta, *Streitfragen der Geschichte Jesu*, p. 9.

'Jesus returned in the power of the Spirit into Galilee.'[1] It was there that the larger part of the teaching, which has come down to us in the Synoptic Gospels, was to be given. To their writers, the Ministry, until the closing week at Jerusalem, is almost exclusively Galilean. But this does not mean that a Judaean ministry is unknown to them. There is nothing, in a fair interpretation of the Synoptic narrative, to exclude such visits to Jerusalem as those which form part of the historical recital of the Fourth Gospel. If we had no such account, we should have to imagine one, in order to be just to the language of St. Matthew and St. Luke.[2] It is true that the Second Gospel gives no hint of work at Jerusalem before the last Passover; and the First and Third Gospels take the Galilean sketch of St. Mark as their chief basis in recording the Ministry. 'Accordingly we have *one authority*, and not three, *for this limitation to Galilee*.'[3] But where St. Matthew and St. Luke imply that there was a Ministry at Jerusalem, they are following another source than that Petrine one which forms the staple of St. Mark; and the Fourth Gospel comes in to give them independent support. With what fairness could 'the Just One'[4] upbraid Jerusalem for rejecting Him, if His Ministry had been confined to Galilee until its closing week? If the Gospel of the Kingdom was to be preached 'to the Jew first,' it would be only natural that the Jew at the centre of his religious life should have every chance

[1] Lk. iv. 14.

[2] Even Strauss regards the lament over Jerusalem (Matt. xxiii. 37; Lk. xiii. 34), if actually spoken by Christ (and there is no ground for its rejection), as proof that He must have worked in Jerusalem more often and for a longer time than the Synoptic accounts would lead us to think. *v. Leben Jesu*, 1864, p. 249; Plummer on Lk. xiii. 34. The passage is from the Logia, and perfectly attested. Spitta, *Streitfragen des Geschichte Jesu*, p. 63 ff. remarks that *v.* 35, 'I say unto you, Ye shall not see Me until the time come when ye shall say, Blessed is He that cometh in the Name of the Lord,' refers only to the entry for the last Passover, and was spoken not at Jerusalem but (*vv.* 31, 32) in the territory of Herod Antipas shortly before the journey to Jerusalem, but *v. ib.* p. 68. He adds that *v.* 34 implies repeated activity in Jerusalem. In reply to Wellhausen, who arbitrarily assigns the passage to early Christian sources after the destruction of Jerusalem, Spitta shows that the desolation of Jerusalem which is threatened by Christ is caused, not by the Roman army, but by His own withdrawal from the city. Such a departure is referred to by St. John x. 39, 40. Spitta remarks that, if He upbraids the city with killing and stoning God's messengers, He speaks from His own experience of its treatment. Cf. Jo. vii. 19, 25; viii. 59; x. 39. *v.* above, p. 40.

[3] Cf. Dean Robinson, *The Study of the Gospels*, p. 141.

[4] Acts iii. 14.

of hearing it. A ministry confined to Galilee until its closing week presents an insoluble problem.

In the course of our inquiry into the character of His teaching, we shall have to distinguish carefully between the mind of Christ, as manifested in His words and acts, and the comments and implications which are due to the reflection of the Apostolic Church; and this, notwithstanding the fact—as we believe it to be—that that reflection was guided and inspired by the Holy Spirit. It is of supreme importance to know how far the origin of the Christian religion corresponded with the intention of Christ, and whether it was modified in its early stages by the influence of its most illustrious adherents.

Accordingly, it will be necessary to endeavour to penetrate to the actual sayings of our Lord, and to trace His acts in the descriptive recitals of the Evangelists, stripping them of whatever literary accretions have gathered round them, and so bringing out their primitive force and meaning.

It is evident that such an analysis as this will be hypothetical. It is at times very difficult to distinguish the original saying from the form in which it is clothed, and our conclusions will be to some extent provisional. In the case of acts, there is less room for difference between the event itself and the report. Yet even here, it is not always possible to say that things occurred exactly as they are represented. The natural tendency to intensify the meaning of an action comes in and must be allowed for in certain cases. Only by admitting this condition of things can we hope to attain approximate certainty as to the mind of our Lord during His earthly career.

We have also to consider the effect upon His conduct and teaching of His desire to adapt Himself to the needs and capacities of men. The Incarnation itself is the great instance of such accommodation. Access to mankind is sought by restraining a manifestation of the Divine which would be intolerable. God can only consort with man by suiting His Self-revelation to their weakness. This must necessarily result in a certain compromise. A truth will be so expressed as to convey its meaning to the hearers in terms which they will understand; not necessarily in terms which would best express its full significance. 'He spake the word unto them, as they were able to hear it.' [1]

[1] Mk. iv. 33.

Thus it will sometimes be a question whether the actual words of Christ, as reported, convey His full meaning, or whether they represent the phase of thought which was best suited to the capacities and the requirements of His hearers. That He felt Himself restrained by this consideration is clear from such a saying as the following: 'I have yet many things to say unto you, but ye cannot bear them now.' [1]

A still more difficult problem arises when we ask—as we cannot help doing—if our Lord shared those ideas of His fellow country-men which have been superseded or modified by the advance of knowledge. In certain of His miracles He is reported as acting under assumptions which modern science would hesitate to recognize. He attributes the disease which He relieves to the agency of evil spirits. The modern man sees in it the action of natural causes, and is inclined to condemn as superstition the assignment of demoniacal influence. We cannot evade the question by saying that it is the report of the Evangelist which conveys that impression; not the actual words of Christ. For the evidence of His having used the mode of speech referred to is too circumstantial and too complete to be set aside. If, in our present state of knowledge, we cannot speak with certainty, we can at any rate detect a gradually increasing recognition of the number of cases which belong to natural conditions, although at one time they were supposed to point to other causes. But there remains a large class of phenomena which are obscure; and it may be that the attitude, which our Lord is said to have taken towards them, shows a far deeper knowledge of the real state of things than can be acquired by any amount of scientific research. In all these instances, we find the working of Satan, as the personification of evil, referred to as the malignant cause of trouble. He, 'Who knew what was in man,' may well be credited with a knowledge of the spiritual world to which no advance in human science can aspire.

If in this question our Lord shared the views of His age in their broader and more general aspect, He differed from them widely in certain directions. He distinguished between the powers of evil by which the sufferer was possessed and the man's own spiritual condition. If evil lay at the background as the original cause of the mischief, that did not mean that it was

[1] Jo. xvi. 12.

through the fault of the afflicted person. At times, indeed, our Lord shows that personal guilt is the immediate cause of suffering, but again He points out that individual misfortunes are not necessarily to be attributed to the person's own evil life.[1]

On the whole, it may be said that we are not at present in a position to say how far the advance of knowledge has affected the value of the judgments, which our Lord has pronounced on those obscure and mysterious ailments, which are among the most terrible that humanity has to endure. It is well to remember, too, that the presence of the Saviour upon earth, on becoming known to the powers of evil, would be likely to evoke an outburst of malignant influence, and that one of the results of His own healing and beneficent work was the curbing and restraining of their capacity to afflict mankind.[2]

In His literary judgments our Lord is apparently in agreement with the views prevalent at the time. He uses the Old Testament in the traditional way, both as to authorship and text. It has often been pointed out that, even if He held other opinions as to the authorship of books or passages which He quotes, He would not be likely to disclose His views, or to disturb the minds of His hearers and distract their attention from the main object of His teaching. We always find His interest centred in the spiritual and moral elements of His subject. He cares nothing for questions of taste or style. Literary problems as such do not attract His attention. But there is another reason for His attitude. In such questions as these, we have no warrant for assuming that His knowledge exceeded that of any well instructed man of His day. We are distinctly told that in His early years He had grown in wisdom. We find Him sitting at the age of twelve among the doctors, hearing them and asking them questions. If His knowledge was already complete on the ground of the Eternal Sonship which was His in youth as in maturity, such an attitude of respectful discipleship and pupillage would have been unreal; and we cannot admit that any part of His conduct could be charged with the least suspicion of insincerity. A wisdom and knowledge which were capable of growth, and were not at one time what they afterwards became, could not be described as perfect. It is therefore reasonable to suppose that, in matters of literary criticism, our Lord's knowledge was much like that

[1] Lk. xiii. 2, 4; Jo. ix. 2, 3. [2] Cf. Lk. x. 17, 18.

of men of His time; and that living as Man for our sakes, under the limitations of true humanity, He had no special knowledge on which to draw for judgments upon authorship or upon questions of date.[1]

In this connection, it may be observed that our Lord never sets out to disclose to us what may be discovered by the exercise of ordinary intelligence. He never forestalls the results of scientific research. It would have traversed the whole purpose of His coming to pronounce authoritative judgments on matters of merely human interest. To anticipate the findings of regular methods of investigation, by judgments based on His Divine knowledge, would have been to interfere with those laws of human development which form the foundation of all scientific progress.[2] He therefore leaves questions of historic criticism on one side. They do not concern His argument. Speaking, as He does, of what belongs to the moral and spiritual spheres, He will not complicate or lessen the force of His teaching by raising questions that belong to the province of ordinary investigation.

It is perhaps better to consider the question in this light than fruitlessly to raise the insoluble problem of the interaction of His Divine and His human intelligence. We have no data on which to go, when we try to represent to ourselves the mental phenomena of One Who is at the same time Divine and human. Some characteristics of His Divine Life were laid aside when He assumed humanity. There was distinct sacrifice and abnegation. In order that He might experience to the full all that belongs to the truth of manhood, some veiling of His Godhead, some forbearance to employ what Godhead can command, became a necessity. Otherwise, His manhood would have been unreal: He could not have been tried in all points as we are. If, among all that was voluntarily laid aside, the possession of knowledge which is usually gained by experience and research was included, we need not wonder. If, too, He forbore to disturb the orderly working of the laws which govern the acquirement of knowledge, and willingly submitted to them, we can trust Him all the

[1] On the whole question of Christ's participation in the modes of thought prevalent in His day, cf. H. Weinel, *Bibl. Theologie des N.T.* p. 42, 'That which is essential (in the religion of Jesus) is the new, the original. It is not what Jesus shares with His people and His time, but what transcended them, which possesses historical significance.'

[2] Dr. P. Gardner appears to take a similar view. *The Ephesian Gospel*, p. 264.

more, when He reveals to us the whole counsel of God in things which 'eye hath not seen nor ear heard.'

It has often been noticed that our Lord shows no interest in science or art. We occasionally see evidence of capacity for dealing with such subjects, but He does not actually deal with them. He Whose eye was open to the beauty of the fields in spring, Who saw in the lily a radiance of form and colour that eclipsed the raiment of Solomon, would have been quick to seize upon the principles of true art. But He had other ends in view and the time was short.[1] In matters of intellect, He seems almost deliberately to take a position, if not of hostility, yet of indifference. 'The wise and the prudent' know not things which are revealed to babes, and their disability is not unpleasing to Him. Yet with all this neglect of the pursuit of mere human learning, He combines profound knowledge and skill in reading that most complicated and abstruse of books—the heart of man.[2] Here, again, we see how entirely He is governed by the main object of His coming among us. He is like one who, in his eagerness to carry out the main purpose of his life, cannot brook the competition of other interests. Like the traveller on an errand of life and death, He will not stoop to gather flowers by the way. Had it been otherwise, the impression He has left on the minds of men would be weaker and less enduring. It was well that, in His own Person, He should live the lesson which He has taught us—'Seek ye first the Kingdom of God and His Righteousness.' The tremendous issues which hung upon His Ministry, the fulfilment of His Father's will, the glory of God in the salvation of man—these things possessed Him to the exclusion of all else. They filled His waking thoughts and must have shaped His dreams.

These considerations may help to counteract any reflection upon a want of universality in our Lord. Power owes more to intensity than to distribution. We see evidence of this in the character of St. Paul. He deliberately takes his line and will not be turned from it. It is the swift stream closely hemmed between its banks that drives the mill, not the quiet expansiveness of a still lagoon. Concentration is for man the prime requirement for effectiveness, and Jesus Christ was man.

It would be a mistake to see in His attitude to human

[1] Jo ix. 4. [2] Matt. ix. 4; Mk. ii. 8; Jo. ii. 24, 25; vi. 64.

learning any sign of hostility. The use and development of His own gifts, when carried out in accordance with the highest purposes of man's being, could never be repugnant to Him. All those powers which express themselves in the achievements of art and learning come from the creative energy of the Eternal Word.[1] We cannot imagine circumstances under which their cultivation could be displeasing to Him, so long as it was governed by true and noble purpose. The fact that He came to redeem all life is the assurance that no part of its rightly directed activities is withdrawn from the consecration of His approval. There is no Divine ban on intellectual effort. Only when it ministers to unworthy purposes, or where it is made an end in itself, instead of a means to a higher end, is it necessarily repugnant to Him.

It has been sometimes urged that our Lord shows want of originality in His recorded teaching, and that it will not bear comparison, from the point of view of intellectual force, with some of the utterances of other teachers. It may be replied, in the first place, that He made no effort to be original, that He never strove for effect, that He said what He said because it required to be spoken. It is also to be remembered that men's views of originality depend largely on their tastes and predilections. 'Spiritual things are spiritually discerned.' It is not to be expected that men of mere worldly wisdom would see the depth of sayings which touch the heart of the Kingdom of God. Yet, to any thoughtful mind, much of the teaching of Christ must wear an aspect quite different from anything else. If to be able to open out a whole vista of thought by the utterance of a single phrase, to stir the pulse of men of every race and nationality by a word, to touch the heart of the hardest by a loving appeal, is not originality, it would be hard to find it elsewhere.

This Christ has done. But it is perhaps in His actions, rather than in the substance of His teaching, that He is most original. The Sacrifice of the Cross is unique in its power and range, original and unparalleled among the events of history. And the principle which it embodied and carried to its highest point, that of life out of death, if it has parallels, has at any

[1] On the Holy Spirit, as potent in this way, *v.* Ex. xxxi. 3; xxxv. 31; 1 Cor. xii. 8.

rate no equal in other regions of thought. If we take the combined originality of deed and word, as seen in the historic life of Christ—the joint effect of His teaching and work, as seen in their highest efforts—we have to admit that He is supreme in the force of initiative and in the original character of His influence. Nor must we forget that, in at least one point, He makes a direct claim to originality. He is the fountain and well-spring of all true knowledge of God. What men know of the Father, they learn through Him.[1] And if we consider the way in which He invites trust and confidence in His own Person, in what He is, rather than in what He does, we have to admit that He comes before men in a manner unexampled. No one else has ever asked for the kind of personal faith and devotion for which He has asked. His claim on men's allegiance to His Person is without precedent and without a rival. And if we appeal to the experience of those who have responded to His claim and have learnt to know and love Him, we have a vast body of conviction that He—their Lord and Master—stands alone in speech and act as in Person: 'Lord to whom shall we go? Thou hast the words of eternal life.'[2]

[1] Matt. xi. 27. Cf. Jo. i. 18; x. 15. [2] Jo. vi. 68.

CHAPTER XVI

THE PUBLIC MINISTRY (II.)

THE subject of our Lord's preaching, on His return to Galilee, was that of the Baptist—the fulness of the time, the nearness of the Kingdom of God, together with a call to repent and believe the Gospel. As the return is made to depend to some extent on the Baptist's imprisonment, the correspondence with his teaching becomes the more significant. It is as if He would follow up the life-work of His Forerunner, and show His concurrence with it by framing His preaching on the same model. The Evangelist describes the contents of the preaching as a Gospel. What did our Lord mean when He called upon His hearers 'to believe the Gospel'? Was there at that time a Gospel to believe? The Baptist proclaimed Christ, and St. Mark speaks of his preaching as the beginning of the Gospel of Christ.[1] If that is the earliest conception of a Gospel, then it follows that Christ's first appeal to men was for *faith in Himself*, as realizing in His own Person the Kingdom of God. But how and when was this realization to take place? Two schools of thought find here their line of cleavage: that which makes the approaching end of the age the one subject, not only of the Baptist's preaching, but of Christ's,[2] and that which admits His purpose to found a Kingdom here on earth, to be perfected in the future. According to the first view, our Lord thought and spoke only of the end, when He would come in the clouds and close this present age. Nothing else was of any account in His sight. He had no interest in this present scheme of things. It was all to come to an end, and that speedily.

[1] Mk. i. 14, 15, 1.

[2] As Joh. Weiss does in *D. Predigt Jesu vom Reiche Gottes*, pp. 65, 71. Cf. A. Schweitzer, *Von Reimarus zu Wrede*, E.T. p. 252.

Others, while admitting that there is much to show for this view, decline to sum up Christ's attitude and teaching within such narrow limits, or to accept the alternative—either a Christ concerned only with the last things, or we know nothing of Him.[1]

Undoubtedly, the thorough-going eschatological interpretation of the Synoptic Gospels is attractive by reason of its simplicity. But to simplify by ignoring facts, which tell in another direction, is a method which soon brings its punishment. The only sound course is to proceed on an induction of all the available evidence, to take whatever is positive, unmindful of apparent inconsistencies, remembering that the sources of our knowledge are scanty and that the supposed contradictions would probably be resolved, if we knew more. What then are the facts?

In the first place, as we have seen, both our Lord and the Baptist began their ministries with the proclamation of the nearness of the Kingdom of God, and with the call to repentance and amendment as a preparation for it.[2] But when we look more closely into these announcements, we find that, with St. John, the coming of the Kingdom resolves itself into the personal appearing of the Messiah, Who will baptize men with the Holy Spirit. If we do not find the same impersonation of the Kingdom claimed by Christ, in so many words, at the outset of His preaching, we find it later on.[3] His own use of the term Gospel at once refers us for its meaning to St. Mark i. 1, where the beginning of that Gospel is stated to be the preaching of the Baptist—which preaching does contain such an impersonation. There was no conflict of view between our Lord and His Forerunner. Each was in possession of the mind of the other upon the central question. The knowledge that the Kingdom was near came to the Baptist in the course of his solitary meditations in the wilderness, before he came out to baptize. It was a divine illumination. On the day of his showing unto Israel, he came forth to put what

[1] Cf. J. Kaftan, *Jesus u. Paulus*, p. 24.

[2] After quoting the question of Wellhausen, 'How came it to pass that these two men came forward simultaneously with the same announcement?' J. Weiss remarks, 'The hour in which they became possessed of that conviction has good claim to be considered the birth-hour of the new Religion.' *Die Predigt Jesu vom Reiche Gottes*, p. 66.

[3] Cf. Mk. viii. 35. Matt. xvi. 25 and Lk. ix. 24 read ἕνεκεν ἐμοῦ, omitting reference to the Gospel. This shows that the Gospel and the Person of Christ are different expressions of the same idea.

he had learnt into practice by calling on the people to repent. To our Lord Himself, the meaning of His Person and His Ministry had become clear, at least by the time of His Baptism. There is nothing to hinder us from supposing that, related as they were, Christ and the Baptist had heard of one another before the time of the 'shewing unto Israel.' They may have never met since their boyhood. John was in the wilderness of Judaea; Christ at Nazareth in Galilee. 'I knew Him not,' said the Baptist.[1] But he had no doubt heard of the hopes and ideas which were being cherished within the circle of the Holy Family; and he may have wondered if this young kinsman of his own were not 'He that should come.' Yet he will not venture to give the sanction of his special office as Forerunner of the Messiah to any claim, however probable, until it has been divinely authenticated. This had been done at the Baptism. So, side by side, the double proclamation is made by the two Heralds of the Kingdom: 'It is near at hand. Repent and prepare for it.'

Now, we have seen that when the Baptist's announcement of the Kingdom is looked into, it resolves itself into the approach of One who will baptize men with the Holy Ghost. The actual setting up of His Kingdom will therefore be synchronous with an outpouring of the Holy Spirit upon all who by the preparation of repentance are found ready for the gift—the largesse of the new King to His new subjects. But such a gift is to be used and requires time and opportunity for its use. It would be meaningless if it only marked the close of opportunity, the end of the age, the passing of the state of probation. The Baptism of water might indeed be a rite of initiation preparatory to the Kingdom; and so we find it historically to have been. But the Baptism of the Spirit, to be inaugurated by the coming King, would be in itself a *dispensation*; and that, historically, we find it to be.

It is therefore difficult to assent to the view of those who regard the mission and preaching of the Baptist as wholly looking to the end. Rather it was a work of preparation for a new

[1] Jo. i. 31. Cf. Lk. i. 80. Weiss, *D. Leben Jesu*, i. p. 295, and Zahn, *D. Evangelium des Johannes*, p. 121, refer this statement of the Baptist, not to personal knowledge, but to knowledge of Christ's Messiahship. Cf. Chrys. *in loc.* p. 115 B; Sanday in Hastings' *D.B.* ii. p. 610. *v.* above, p. 217.

beginning—a fresh era for mankind. He does indeed speak of a judgment, and his words [1] have a meaning only to be exhausted by the events of the Last Day. But there is no note of time to fix their fulfilment within a certain period: and, in the fall of Jerusalem and the destruction of the Temple, there was enough of judgment to give a very real and terrible significance to the Baptist's words.

If, then, the proclamation of the Baptist was not wholly—or even chiefly—eschatological, what are we to say of the corresponding proclamation of Jesus Himself? The reasons which affect our interpretation of the Baptist's words are not without force here. The Baptism of the Spirit, which was to be a leading characteristic of the days of the Messiah, could never have been long out of the mind of Him Who was to administer it. Are we to imagine that our Lord contemplated no lengthened period of time for this new dispensation which He was to inaugurate? Was He so ignorant of the scope and character of the Kingdom of Grace which His coming was to set up, that He foresaw nothing but a speedy close, an entire shutting down, of all this present scene, so soon as His earthly career had ended; or, at any rate, within the life-time of His first disciples? The idea, when plainly stated, in view of what our Lord was and claimed to be, seems too preposterous to be seriously entertained. Yet, to be a 'thorough-going' eschatologist, one has to make it one's own. Schweitzer rebukes J. Weiss for having made some concession to those who tell us that, for all the eschatological element in Christ's early proclamation of His Gospel, He has something to say of the present time, some interest in what is passing, some idea of a Kingdom begun and continued here, if only to be perfected in the eternal world.[2]

And there is the course of intellectual development to be considered. Had the age closed within a generation or two

[1] Matt. iii. 7-10, 12; Lk. iii. 7-10, 17.

[2] *v.* J. Weiss, *op. cit.* p. 88 f. For a criticism on the too-ready appreciation of Schweitzer's views in England, *v.* V. Dobschütz, *The Eschatology of the Gospels*, p. 57. Cf. P. Wernle in *Theol. Literaturz.* 1906, p. 501 ff. The eschatological interpretation of His sayings first urged by Reimarus, *Von dem Zwecke Jesu u. seiner Jünger*, 1778, but almost lost sight of until J. Weiss revived it in his *D. Predigt Jesu vom Reiche Gottes* (1st edition in 1892, 2nd with considerable modifications in 1900), is quite inadequate for its task. It has received enthusiastic support from A. Schweitzer, *Von Reimarus zu Wrede*, but it attains

of Christ's life on earth, what a cutting short it would have meant in the realm of knowledge, of mastery of natural forces, of man's power in the world! The saying that 'there is nothing new under the sun' is often quoted with the respect due to an axiom. It was true in the main for the period when it was uttered and for many centuries afterwards—down in fact to the age of the Renaissance. The East did not change, and the West was but slowly emerging from a state in which all that was worthy in knowledge and achievement was but a reproduction of the thought of the ancient world. But with the Renaissance, came that awakening which was soon to take effect in scientific and intellectual achievements, which are making the modern world another from that of ancient and mediaeval times. It may be said that, apart from this extraordinary development in knowledge and in its application to life, man would not have attained his majority. The previous periods of history are the story of his childhood and youth. Only recently has he come of age, in his command of the world in which he lives.[1]

Was our Lord as ignorant of the capacity of the human mind, of its power of development, of its latent resources, as the eschatologists represent Him to have been in the case of the Kingdom of Grace? If He showed little interest in intellectual development, and subordinated everything to the one supreme question of man's relation to God, this insistence on and devotion to the one chief end of life did not, we may be sure, hide from Him all perception of man's place in the world. 'He knew what was in man.' He knew that man had not come to his full estate. The range of His fore-knowledge would include something of that conquest of the material world which man was yet to gain.[2] On this ground, therefore, we cannot attribute to our Lord the conviction that a few years were to see the close

consistency only by leaving unexplained passages which no less clearly indicate the present existence of the kingdom. So Harnack writes, 'The investigation of J. Weiss and Schweitzer's brilliantly written work, according to which the whole of Christ's preaching was determined by eschatology, have failed to convince me.' *Lehrbuch der Dogmengeschichte*, 4e Ausg. 1909, i. p. 68 n.

[1] This is, of course, only true in the sphere of practical knowledge—in its application to the purposes and uses of life. In the imaginative and abstract spheres, it is a question whether any solid advance has been made.

[2] *v.* above, p. 262.

of human affairs, the end of human development, so far as this world is concerned. To say so would be to deny to Him an insight and a range of vision of which we get glimpses in the thought of men like Aristotle,[1] as of other possessors of the prophetic gift. Our Lord was more than 'a religious genius.' His knowledge of the scope and possibilities of human life would not suffer Him to err in such a matter.[2]

Again, if we follow the Gospel record, we have to admit that one object of Christ's coming among us was to found a society of men like-minded with Himself—a Church to be the spiritual home of His people, with a ministry, with sacraments and a worship which, offered in His Name, would be acceptable to the Father. With such an intention, requiring for its fulfilment an ample space of time, it is difficult to imagine that His gaze was fixed only upon the end. The universal character of the Church is itself a plea for time. It is being more and more seen that the fulness of the Christian ideal can only be realized by the incorporation of every race within the bounds of the Christian Church. East and West, Black and White Races, with all their peculiarities, have their own special contribution to make to the full realization of the Body of Christ. The Indian can bring some gift which no Englishman possesses. In a Christian of China, or of some Pacific isle, the indwelling Christ will produce aspects of His own life which He could not effect in men of other race. But, for all these diverse contributions to the symmetry of the whole structure, time is needed. A Church, which was to know no distinction of race or privilege, embracing every kind of quality and gift, is no creature of a day ; and if Christ is the full and final Revelation of the Father, a Church less wide, a purpose less ambitious, He could not intend.

If we compare the passages of the Synoptic Gospels which

[1] I cannot, therefore, go with Streeter's observation, 'Doubtless had the Master explicitly contemplated the centuries of slow development still awaiting humanity, the actual form and phrasing of many a precept would have been different.' *Foundations*, p. 108.

[2] Since the above was written, Dr. Headlam has said, 'The thorough-going Eschatologist is prepared to accept a Christ who was not only limited in His human knowledge, but was hardly even intelligent and certainly had none of the foresight or intelligence of a great human mind.' *Church Quarterly Review* for April, 1913, p. 28.

deal with the Second Coming, we are at once struck with the indefinite character of the allusions to time. There is no fixed point to which we can appeal. Although He speaks of the Coming as certain within the experience of the generation which He was addressing, our Lord disclaims all knowledge of the day and hour.[1] He bids His disciples watch as for something which may come upon them at any moment;[2] and when they are sent out to preach, they are warned that they will not have gone over the 'cities of Israel until the Son of Man be come.'[3]

By the side of these indications of His speedy return, or as He expresses it, of a speedy coming of the Son of Man, we have to place passages which indicate a long process of growth and development before the great Day can dawn. We have to take care that we give to each conception its full value. If there is contrast amounting, as some think, even to contradiction, we must still do justice to each member of the antinomy.

The passages which require time are mostly in the form of parable—the tares,[4] the corn growing secretly, the leaven. Time is needed for that diffusion of the Gospel of which Christ speaks in the apocalyptic chapter of St. Mark and in extended form in St. Matthew: 'This Gospel of the Kingdom shall be preached in all the world for a witness unto all nations; and then shall the end come.'[5] There is the same wide field of work, requiring the same large allowance of time, in the command to the disciples 'to teach all nations' and 'baptize them in the Name of the Father and of the Son and of the Holy Ghost,' which forms the close of the First Gospel. Such teaching as this

[1] Matt. xvi. 28; Mk. ix. 1; Matt. xxiii. 36, xxiv. 34; Mk. xiii. 32.

[2] Lk. xii. 40; Mk. xiii. 35-37. [3] Matt. x. 23.

[4] Efforts have been made to take the parable out of Christ's mouth and to refer it to the Pauline theology of the early community. *v.* Jülicher, *Die Gleichnisreden*, ii. p. 540 ff. Cf. J. Weiss, *Die Predigt Jesu vom Reiche Gottes*, p. 40. With as much right, we could attribute our Lord's expectation of a speedy end of the age to the feeling of the primitive community as exemplified in 1 Thess. iv. v.; 1 Pet. iv. 7; 1 Cor. vii. 29-32; and allege that it was transferred to Him. This mode of reasoning cuts two ways. If expressions which point in one direction are to be refused assignment to Christ because we find traces of the same idea in the thought of the community, those which point in an opposite direction should be similarly treated, under the same circumstances. But the method is unjustifiable. It proceeds entirely upon subjective grounds, and no sure results can be obtained from its use.

[5] Mk. xiii. 10; Matt. xxiv. 14.

would be meaningless under the supposition that our Lord was convinced that a few years at most would see the end of all things.

We are, therefore, confronted with a problem which may be stated as follows. In Synoptic passages, the genuineness of which there is no reason to doubt, sayings are attributed to Christ which imply a conviction that the coming of the Son of Man is imminent. In other passages equally genuine, we have evidence that He took a wide and large view of the work which lay between His presence on earth and His second coming: work which would require time, and of which the result would appear as a process of long and slow development.

How is the problem to be sclved? We have seen that a fair exegesis demands that, if the fact that ideas purporting to be Christ's are to be found in the thought of the community excludes their attribution to Him in the one case, the same rule should be observed in the other. We cannot retain one member of the antinomy if we sacrifice the other on such a ground.

It will be admitted that our Lord's references to His second coming present several aspects. Now, it is the Final Judgment that He means; now, a presence of Himself with His people—a thought more fully expanded in the discourses of the Fourth Gospel. There the dispensation of the Spirit, to which indeed there is ample reference in the Synoptics, is regarded as a fulfilment of the Saviour's promised presence with His people. That presence is spiritual, and is effected by the Spirit. Now again, it is conceived as the break-up of the old *régime* concurrent with the destruction of Jerusalem and the Temple.

It is clear that with such a diversity of application, words which imply both imminence and delay of the end are not necessarily in conflict with one another. To be sure that there is contradiction, we should have to be certain that *the same aspect* of the question is thus diversely referred to. But it is not always easy to determine this point. The language employed is frequently symbolical. Our Lord was speaking to men whose thoughts naturally flowed in the channel of symbolism and imagery, and the form of His expression was determined by this fact. As the principle of the Incarnation involved such a veiling of the Divine in the things of time and sense as would enable men to grasp by their means the eternal reality that lay behind; so it was with our Lord's revelation of the future, of the course of the final dispensation which He came to inaugurate, of the close of the age. The eternal truths contained in these conceptions are projected in transitory forms. They are materialized to suit men whose habit of thought was essentially concrete. And with all this accommodation to human need and infirmity, there is the thought to be kept in mind that, after all, the facts that are being dealt with belong to a higher order; and that in such matters, questions of time, of imminence or delay, are out of place. They are attempts to capture what, of its very nature, refuses to be caught and imprisoned in a phrase.[1]

When, therefore, we are presented with alternatives which ignore these considerations, while we admit the difficulty of arriving at a certain conclusion on the data before us, we decline to be fixed on the horns of a dilemma. We reject the *entweder oder* of the 'thorough-going' eschatologist when he puts the question in this form: 'Our Lord foretold the speedy end of this world and His disciples understood Him in this sense. But He was mistaken, and His mistake on such a matter places Him in the category of fallible men.' Rather should we suspect our methods of interpretation, and see whether the supposed contradiction is not between *two erroneous explanations of our own*, rather than between two statements of Christ Himself.

Some allowance should no doubt be made for the possible importation of the views of His hearers into the Gospel reports of Christ's sayings. A subordinate and secondary phrase[2] may here and there have been pressed into a primary position. It is clear, too, that the order of our Lord's sayings is frequently neglected by the Evangelists. This is due in all probability to the didactic use of early records of

[1] 'To the man who sees through the existing frame of circumstance to the underlying realities, time is apt to stand still, or to appear as a mere unessential condition of human observation.' P. Gardner, *The Religious Experience of St. Paul*, 1911, p. 133.

[2] 'However strong Jesus' belief in eschatology might have been, it was only of secondary importance for His religious life and for His teaching. It was a misunderstanding on the part of primitive Christianity when they laid the greatest stress on this side of the Gospel.' V. Dobschütz, *The Eschatology of the Gospels*, p. 204.

His teaching, similar subjects being grouped together because of their similarity, not from any chronological connection. When these catechetical memoranda came to be used by the Evangelists, they would tend to be copied as they stood, for in many cases it must have been too late to seek for notes of time and arrangement. It is easy to see that some apparent inconsistencies in our Lord's way of speaking of the last things may be due to later arrangement of His words. For our part, we cannot admit that He was in error when He spoke of the close of the age. Still less can we believe that He gave an impression, knowing it to be incorrect.

It will perhaps be replied that those who heard Him understood Him to teach that the time was short and that He would quickly come.[1] The impression is not merely one that arose from textual considerations at a later date, as the Gospels were being put into their present shape. It was shared by His first disciples and formed the state of mind which we meet in the first years of the Church. Everywhere there is the same expectation of a speedy coming. St. Peter and St. Paul alike proclaim their belief that 'the time is short.' There are all the signs of a state of tension and of expectation. Men live in instant readiness for the heavens to open and for the Son of Man to appear upon the clouds. This fact, when taken with the literal meaning of many of Christ's own sayings, is thought to show that He knowingly gave the impression of an immediate return which—as a matter of fact—has not yet taken place, although nineteen centuries have rolled away.

Now, it may be granted that our Lord would not have been ignorant of the effect of His teaching. But it was not His usual practice to offer correction of misapprehension and mistake, unless He was directly asked. St. Luke tells us that, just before His Ascension, He was asked by the disciples, 'Lord, wilt Thou at this time restore again the Kingdom of Israel?'—a question which in its scope and bearing was certainly eschatological. Even here He gives no direct reply. He simply waves the inquiry aside. 'It is not for you to know the times or the seasons, which the Father hath put in His own power.' He leaves them to form their own conclusions and to be taught by events. It is all of a piece with His method that He gives out His teaching

[1] Cf. Feine, *Theologie des neuen Testaments*, p. 178.

in dramatic and often paradoxical form. Great principles, wide views, are opened out. He leaves their justification to the future. He is careless of their being crossed by other truths. The course of events, as illumined by His Spirit, will in time unfold the truth. When the first fervour of the Church's state of expectancy had passed, under the discipline of experience, into a calmer attitude and, under the later teaching of St. Paul and St. John, men realized that they were indeed living in the last time, but a time which was being measured, not by human divisions, but by the onward progress of the Kingdom of God, the present with all its duties and its interests asserted itself, and those who waited for the Saviour's return waited in confidence and hope.

The Christian community began to see that both the imminence of Christ's coming and its delay were being enacted among them, and were not contradictory, but different, aspects of the truth. Through the working of 'the Spirit of Christ' in their hearts, they were able to realize that, in accordance with His parting promise,[1] He was with them in Person, unseen, but closer far than when they saw Him. The *παρουσία* was already an accomplished fact. He had already returned. In the fall of the city and the Temple, in the ceasing of the daily sacrifice, in the judgment that overtook the ancient race, the sign of the Son of Man could already be seen in the clouds. If the language is still symbolical, it is the expression of actual fact.

'The culminating point of this development (of thought) is reached in the Gospel of John. The faith of this Evangelist sees already in the historical Jesus all that the oldest Christianity at one time expected from the Parousia.'[2] This historical Jesus was at the same time the risen and glorified Son of Man. 'Already in the likeness of the Incarnate, the full glory of God has become manifest.'[3]

Can we regard this identification of the spiritual presence of Christ with the *παρουσία* as being in accordance with His mind, and as resolving the difficulty which we have been considering? Or, are we forced to acknowledge that the mind of the Church in the latter half of the first century was not

[1] Matt. xxviii. 20. Cf. Jo. xiv. 16.

[2] J. Weiss, *D. Predigt Jesu vom Reiche Gottes*, p. 177. [3] *Ib*

the mind of Christ? As a matter of history, we have to note a complete change of idea. From the expectation of an immediate return in power, as expressed in 1 Thessalonians, and in 1 Peter, there comes about a gradual reassertion of the claims and duties of the present. In place of an apocalyptic Church, with gaze always directed upward, looking for the sign of the coming of the Son of Man, there gradually arises a Church filled with a sense of the presence of the Saviour, unseen, but real and vital. And this change of thought and attitude was due to the teaching of events, under the guidance and illumination of the Holy Spirit. An ecstatic, expectant Church, that lived only in the future, could never have carried out the purpose for which Christ came. That attitude enabled men to endure the first shock of conflict with the forces which, as soon as Jesus Christ was preached as the Lord from heaven, became arrayed against them. It had an economic value. It nerved them to stand against the persecution of reactionary Judaism and the contempt of the Roman authorities. But, as their numbers grew, and as they began to realize more fully that they had been called into the Church to leaven and to win the world for Christ, the importance and the interests of the present assumed different proportions. The call of to-day sounded more clearly in their ears. The end was still kept in view: but it was no longer allowed to dominate the whole field of vision.

And the course of history has proved that they were false neither to the mind nor will of our Lord, in this shifting of the focus through which they looked out on things. The greatest servants of the Cross have always felt the exceeding value of the present. They have looked forward to the end as the labourer watches for the lengthening shadows of the afternoon. But they have lived in and for the present; and in their Master's own words they have thought to find justification for their attitude—'I must work the works of Him that sent Me, while it is day: the night cometh.'[1] J. Weiss admits that this change of standpoint receives sanction from the practical, religious end which it has served.[2] But we cannot agree with him in thinking[3] that it in any way represents a condition of things

[1] Jo. ix. 4. [2] *D. Predigt Jesu vom Reiche Gottes*, p. 177.
[3] Cf. *ib.* p. 104.

foreign to Christ's own mind, and contrary to His own declarations.[1]

With all the emphasis which He placed upon the future, with all the value for eternity which He set upon the 'saving of the soul,' our Lord regarded the presence of His own Person on earth as already setting up the Kingdom of God. There is here a very distinct difference in the otherwise similar proclamations of Himself and the Baptist as to the approach of the Kingdom. While the Baptist announces its nearness, our Lord goes farther and proclaims that the time has already come.[2] In the clearest terms He conveys the idea that with Himself, living and working among men, the Kingdom is not merely near, it is already present. Thus, in speaking of the Baptist and his greatness, He adds 'the least in the kingdom of heaven is greater than he.' 'The kingdom of heaven suffereth violence and the violent take it by force.' 'If I by the Spirit of God cast out devils, then is the kingdom of God come upon you.'[3] 'The kingdom of God is within (or among) you.'[4] In all these cases there is no hint of the future. The Kingdom is present. Its organization and the details of its administration are no doubt far from His thoughts as yet. We date the Kingdom realized as a Church, not from the Baptism, but from Pentecost. Yet, in the Person of its Head it is already present.[5] The signs of

[1] 'We take the Johannine doctrine as an approximately good expression of Jesus' own views.' Von Dobschütz, *The Eschatology of the Gospels*, p. 204.

[2] Mk. i. 15, *πεπλήρωται ὁ καιρός*. Cf. Gal. iv. 4; Stanton, *The Jewish and the Christian Messiah*, p. 218. As he remarks, Christ does not again announce the nearness of the kingdom. (The Apostles are told, when sent forth, to make this proclamation, but it is with a view to His own coming. Cf. Lk. x. 1.) Bousset gives a wrong impression when he says, 'The thought that the kingdom of God is coming, remained the central point of His (our Lord's) teaching to the end.' *Jesus*, p. 35.

[3] 'Here one cannot speak of the break of the crimson dawn of God's kingdom; the kingdom is already a reality.' Feine, *Theol. des neuen Test.* p. 97. Cf. V. Dobschütz, *The Eschatology of the Gospels*, p. 126.

[4] Matt. xi. 11, 12; xii. 28; Lk. xvii. 21. Weiss admits that Matt. xii. 28 = Lk. xi. 20, is of great importance in determining the question. *D. Predigt Jesu vom Reiche Gottes*, p. 88, but is surely wrong in calling it 'the only clear and certain passage' in which Jesus speaks of the kingdom of God as present. Cf. V. Dobschütz, *op. cit.* p. 129 ff.

[5] Cf. Feine, *Theologie des neuen Testaments*, p. 148, 'Jesus did not organize His community, nor did He found His Church in the course of His work on earth. But the Christian Church is a necessary product of the sayings about the atoning power of His death.'

the Messianic Kingdom are open to all. When the Baptist sends his messengers to ask if Jesus is the Christ, the answer is to be the simple narration of what 'they do hear and see'—the opening of the eyes of the blind, the raising of the dead, the evangelizing of the poor.[1]

The parables which treat of the growth and development of the Kingdom—the mustard seed, the sower, the growing wheat, the leaven hidden in the lump—if they have any bearing at all upon its nature, require it to be understood as something already present. The signs of its growth are evident to all. It is a Kingdom which is even now expanding and progressing.[2]

On the return of the seventy disciples, when they announce with joy that even the devils are subject to them, our Lord says, 'I beheld Satan as lightning fall from heaven.' The victory of goodness over the forces of evil is a proof that the Kingdom is already set up.[3] To the Scribe, who had answered discreetly, Christ says, 'Thou art not far from the kingdom of God.'[4] It was therefore something attainable there and then which he might yet hope to gain. He upbraids the Scribes and Pharisees because they 'shut up the kingdom of heaven against men. Ye neither go in yourselves, neither suffer ye them that are entering to go in.'[5] It is impossible to separate from this passage the idea that the Kingdom is a present reality. There would otherwise be no point in the rebuke.[6]

How, then, are we to bring into line these various aspects of the Kingdom as both present and future? It has been pointed

[1] *v.* V. Dobschütz, *The Eschatology of the Gospels*, p. 138 ff.

[2] In these parables 'a process of development of the kingdom in the present and on earth up to its perfection is pre-supposed.' Feine, *ib.* p. 99.

[3] Lk. x. 17, 18. Cf. V. Dobschütz, *The Eschatology of the Gospels*, p. 128. The blessing on the disciples, who see and hear what prophets and kings desired, is 'a form of proclamation for the fact that in Christ's present actions all promises are fulfilled.' V. Dobschütz, *ib.* p. 143. *v.* Matt. xiii. 16; Lk. x. 23.

[4] Mk. xii. 34.

[5] Matt. xxiii. 13. There is a similar implication of a present kingdom in Mk. x. 15. *v.* V. Dobschütz, *The Eschatology of the Gospels*, p. 135.

[6] 'The kingdom of heaven is suffering violence and the violent are taking it by force.' Matt. xi. 12 refers to the present, to what is now—at the time of speaking—going on, not to the future. If there is any contrast, it is with the time prior to John the Baptist—the past. *v.* V. Dobschütz, *The Eschatology of the Gospels*, p. 134.

'In the teaching of Jesus there is a strong line of what I would call *transmuted eschatology*. I mean eschatology transmuted in the sense that what was spoken

out that the sources forbid us to explain the difficulty by assigning one view to the period of success and triumph, when our Lord seemed to be carrying all before Him, and the other view to the time when His prospects had begun to be clouded over. 'For both sides of the conception of the Kingdom run side by side and cross one another. Not only at the zenith of His work is the Kingdom present to Him, but also towards the end.'[1]

Unless the problem is to be given up as insoluble, we must find a solution which will do justice to each side of the antinomy and will at the same time contain a positive element. For the mind of Christ was too fully possessed of the idea of the Kingdom to warrant a conclusion which is simply negative or non-committal.

We think it is to be found in the idea of growth and expansion in the Kingdom itself; in the fact that in the line of its development moments of crisis occurred, which amounted in their essence and effects to nothing less than actual 'comings' of the Kingdom.

Our Lord, six days before the Transfiguration, said to His disciples, 'Verily I say unto you, that there be some of them that stand here, which shall not taste of death, till they have seen the kingdom of God come with power.'[2]

When was this promise made good? He seems to refer to it when asked, on the eve of His Ascension, 'Lord, wilt Thou at this time restore again the kingdom to Israel?' Ignoring the question of time, He answers 'Ye shall receive power, after that the Holy Ghost is come upon you.'[3] At the ensuing Feast of Pentecost, the promise, first made on the eve of His Transfiguration and renewed on the eve of His Ascension, is fulfilled. The Kingdom of God comes with power in the descent of the Holy Ghost. The Kingdom which had already come in the Person of the King, now through the inspiring presence of His Spirit comes afresh welded into a living whole and filled with a new power. Regarded in this light, other

of in Jewish eschatology as to come in the last days is taken here as already at hand in the lifetime of Jesus; transmuted at the same time in the other sense that what was expected as an external change is taken inwardly.... His disciples acknowledge Him to be the Messiah; and in His company they enjoy all the happiness of the Messianic time.' *Ib.* p. 150.

[1] Feine, *Theologie des neuen Testaments*, p. 99. Cf. Lk. xvii. 20.

[2] Mk. ix. 1.

[3] Acts i. 6-9.

passages which speak of an early coming fall into their place. On sending out the twelve, Christ says, 'Verily I say unto you, ye shall not have gone over the cities of Israel till the Son of Man be come.'[1]

There was one event still to come to pass which was to fulfil a double purpose and, in the tremendous consequences which it involved, was nothing less than a real coming of the Son of Man. The destruction of Jerusalem was a judgment on the Jews for their national rejection of Christ. That was one purpose. The other lay in the fact that, without the destruction of the Temple and its worship, the Christian Church as the visible embodiment of the Kingdom could not assume its universal character. It would have been tied to what was local and transitory. It could never have become, what its Founder intended it to be, the world-wide and age-long home of all who should call upon His Name. In this catastrophe, occurring soon after the death of St. James and St. Peter, and within the life-time of some to whom the words were spoken, Christ's

[1] Matt. x. 23. Considerable support is given to this view by the fact that the Fourth Gospel lays special emphasis on the spiritual coming of Christ. Sayings are reported which convey the idea that in the gift of the Holy Ghost the παρουσία is effected: 'I will not leave you comfortless, I will come unto you.' The mind of our Lord, as interpreted and reported by the Fourth Evangelist, is more concerned with the continued dispensation of the Spirit and His own presence which it effectuated, than with His glorious manifestation in Judgment at its close. Ought not this fact to be taken into account when we deal with the difficulties of the Synoptic apocalyptic discourse? By the time when St. John wrote, the expectation of the early, visible return of the Saviour had passed away. We can trace its passing in the Epistles of St. Paul. St. John's recollection of our Lord's promise of a spiritual presence following on His departure completes the process of change, and draws men's minds from a perpetual dwelling on the future to the mighty and practical tasks and issues of the present. *v.* H. Holtzmann, *Evang. des Johannes*, p. 268, who quotes Schenkel, *Christusbild*, p. 394, 'The Kingdom of the Holy Ghost is in the Fourth Gospel the future period of Christianity.' Holtzmann points out that in the discourses of our Lord in the Fourth Gospel, He speaks in a way that the first disciples could not understand, but which the advanced religious consciousness, of which the Evangelist was the interpreter, could enter into. *Ib.* p. 269. St. John certainly reports sayings of our Lord which were not reported by the earlier writers, probably because their significance was not apprehended and they were therefore not remembered. Holtzmann seems to imply that their source was not Christ but the Christian consciousness. We believe that it was the Christian consciousness, stirred by reflection and enlightened by the Holy Spirit, which was able in the person of the Fourth Evangelist to recall and fix in writing what had been actually spoken by our Lord. Cf. below, p. 400.

promise was again fulfilled: 'There be some of them that stand here, which shall not taste of death, till they have seen the kingdom of God come with power.' It has been noticed that in the apocalyptic discourse of St. Mark xiii. and parallels, the account of St. Mark is probably in closer correspondence with what was actually spoken than that of St. Matthew. The disciples ask the time and signs of the destruction of the Temple, not as St. Matthew has it, of the παρουσία. The First Evangelist, who alone of the Synoptics uses that expression, introduces a different subject—the end of the world, instead of the destruction of the Temple. It is true that St. Mark in *v.* 32 is (like St. Matthew) giving a wider application than a strict answer to the question would require. His words refer to the second coming. But his time reference in *v.* 30 may well apply to the destruction of the Temple.

There is little doubt that our Lord passed rapidly in thought from one aspect of His coming to another, and that the final scene (if it will surpass in intensity) was not more real to Him than those marked by such events as the gift of the Spirit or the destruction of the city and the Temple.

We have also to take into consideration the fact that in the apocalyptical discourse, of which the Markan version is the original one, there is no certainty that the words were all delivered at the same time. Papias observes[1] that while St. Mark

[1] On the authority of 'the elder.' Euseb. *H.E.* iii. 39. The view started by Colani and Weizsäcker in 1864 and adopted by many critics, that Mk. xiii. is an Apocalypse of Jewish or Jewish-Christian origin incorporated by the Evangelist in his Gospel, and not a discourse of Christ, is unsupported by any documentary proof. The circumstances of the case are better met by the theory of transposition to which the words of Papias lend colour. V. Dobschütz in *The Eschatology of the Gospels*, p. 85 ff., is inclined to adopt the apocalyptic idea, and quotes ὁ ἀναγινώσκων νοείτω, *v.* 14, and εἰ μὴ Κύριος, *v.* 20, as showing that it is not a sermon of Jesus. But does not ὁ ἀναγ. κ.τ.λ. refer to Daniel? If Mark xiii. contains an apocalyptic writing and is not a narrative of a discourse or discourses remembered to have been spoken by Christ Himself, we are face to face with a great difficulty. A Gospel which goes back to the preaching of St. Peter is weighted with the disadvantage that, in a subject of such gravity as the end of the world, words are falsely assigned to Christ—words, too, which, if we take them in the order assigned to them, are not borne out by the facts of history. It is admitted by those who regard the chapter as an apocalyptic insertion, that it contains 'genuine utterances' of Christ (so Streeter in *Oxford Studies*, p. 180). This makes the difficulty all the greater. Would the Evangelist, with his first-rate source in the preaching of St. Peter, confuse and perplex his readers by mixing the

wrote down accurately what he remembered of the teaching of St. Peter, he did not record Christ's words and deeds in order. Traces of this defective arrangement appear in this section. Words which clearly point to the close of the age (Mark xiii. 26, Matt. xxiv. 30, Luke xxi. 27), are embedded in a discourse which, as we most clearly gather from St. Mark, was spoken in reply to a question as to the sign and date of the destruction of the Temple, which Christ had just been foretelling. The very fact that He used expressions which speak of that event symbolically would easily lead the Evangelist (or rather his authority St. Peter) to pass from a clearly defined event, such as the overthrow of the Temple, to a mysterious one, such as the appearing of the Son of Man upon the clouds at the end of the age. In that case, we may assign the difficult verse, St. Mark xiii. 30, to the part of the discourse to which it seems properly to belong ; considering it to be an answer to the question as to when the Temple was to be destroyed, not a reference to the final coming.

We have also to remember that our Lord consistently set His face against the attempt to learn the time of His final coming. He deliberately leaves the question ambiguous. To Him, it is entirely beside the mark to try to penetrate what is even hidden from Himself.[1] It lies within the province of the Father

'genuine utterances' with an imaginative composition of no authority and no connection with the circumstances of the moment ? It is alleged (by Streeter, *ib.* p. 179) that 'a discourse thirty-seven verses long at once stands out as unique in Mark.' But the subject is of unique interest and importance, and might well receive special treatment. The very fact that the chapter contains material which is probably derived from 'Q' is a strong argument against the pseudonymous use of an Apocalypse. With the reminiscences of St. Peter and possibly the MS. of 'Q' before him, the Evangelist would hardly have recourse to an unauthoritative apocalyptic writing in order to convey the teaching of Christ. Streeter (*ib.* p. 183, n. 1) thinks that St. Mark accepted the Apocalypse 'as an authentic word of the Lord and inserted it whole.'

On the lack of orderly arrangement observable in St. Mark, see Wellhausen, *Einleitung in die drei ersten Evangelien*, p. 51.

[1] Yet in spite of this fact, the eschatologist insists upon imputing to Him the very intention—that of fixing the period of His return—which He repudiates. *v.* Mk. xiii. 32 ; Matt. xxiv. 36, one of the most surely attested of Christ's sayings. Cf. Acts i. 7, the correspondence of which with the passage in St. Mark is one of the many signs of the authenticity of the early chapters of Acts. It is the same Christ who is speaking. Cf. Jo. xxi. 23.

After the above was written, I find that V. Dobschütz insists upon the fact that although 'we cannot help agreeing that He was wrong regarding the

to determine times and seasons. Uncertainty is one of the elements of that probation which is the lot of humanity in this life. It is part of the discipline which is laid upon us, and which is intended to produce that spirit of watchfulness so characteristic of those who wait for their Lord.[1]

When, therefore, we are asked to consider the proclamation of the Kingdom of God with which our Lord opened His public ministry as an entirely eschatological announcement; and further, when we are told that the failure of His prediction to realize itself must cast serious doubt upon the authority of His teaching, we decline to accept the interpretation as a true statement of the facts, and are therefore not disturbed by the conclusion which is drawn from it.

In His Person and in His Presence with His people in the days of His Flesh, the Kingdom of Christ had already come. The Messianic feast was already spread. The Bridegroom was with

outward form of His predictions and especially the time of God's fulfilment, this does not involve any imperfection on His side.' This is a highly questionable position. If our Lord 'was wrong in His expectation,' and believed that the course of events, which for nearly 2000 years has been steadily pursuing its way, was at the time He spoke about to come to a sudden end; if, as that would imply, He was so destitute of every gift of foresight (prophecy) that the whole future course of the Christian centuries had no place in His thought, and an immediately impending close of the world's history alone filled His imagination, how could we regard Him as 'the Way, the Truth and the Life'—the guide and light of our souls? It will not help us to say that He Himself did not profess to know the day or hour. That is a very different thing from ignorance whether a long period was to elapse of slow development of His Kingdom, or whether it was to end presently and abruptly. But the difficulty *is* lightened when we regard the *παρουσία* not as a single act at the close of the age, marked by the coming of the Son of Man upon the clouds of Heaven, but as a process composed of various scenes and events—the Appearances of the Risen Lord (cf. Jo. xvi. 16), the coming of the Holy Ghost, the Judgment on Jerusalem, the crises of world-history—which culminate in the one final Return, to which eschatological ideas are often so exclusively applied.

The situation is not relieved by Streeter. After saying that 'it is impossible for candid criticism to doubt that He expected the consummation of the present course of this world to come at least within the life-time of those who heard Him,' he adds, 'Still, nineteen hundred years have passed and the end is not yet; nor will be, so far as science can foresee, for uncounted years to come.' He goes on to offer as partial fulfilments, the fall of Jerusalem, the fall of the Western Empire, the present power of the Spirit of Christianity in the world. Not one of these events, great and far-reaching as they were in themselves and in their results, can be regarded as fulfilling 'the consummation of the present course of this world.' *v. Foundations*, p. 141 f.

[1] Cf. Sanday and Headlam, *The Epistle to the Romans*, p. 379 ff.

His friends. 'Christianity is—and ever will be—the religion of sure salvation brought by Jesus, and to be experienced by His believers already during their present life.'[1] But His Kingdom is not yet assured. Its coming is to be a subject of our daily prayer. At present the issues are involved and confused. As in a long battle-line, victory at one point, defeat at another, mark the chequered course of events. It will not be always so: the time is coming when the Kingdom will be manifest, the victory decisive, the battle won. St. Paul especially insists upon this in the central group of his Epistles. He speaks of the 'manifestation of the Sons of God.' The tares will have been gathered from among the wheat. 'Every man's work shall be made manifest; for the day shall declare it'[2]—the 'day of the Lord,' the day of Judgment. The time of the secret working of the leaven, of the unobserved approach of the Kingdom will be past. No happening in the varied course of history, no return of Christ in the power of the Spirit, such as the Church enjoys in this, 'the last time,' can in any way fulfil all the promise to which the New Testament from end to end bears witness. 'We believe that Thou shalt come to be our Judge.'

When we proceed to inquire into the character and substance of our Lord's teaching, we have to remember the object which He had set before Himself in coming forward to attract the attention and thought of men. It was to reconcile the world to God, a work which He early recognized would require the sacrifice of His own life. It was to make this work known, and to show that it was laid upon Himself to do it by the will of His Father, that He came forth to preach. The preaching was entirely conditioned by this fact. It revolved round the one supreme object for which He had come into the world. Hence its limitations, which have been so freely commented upon. Hence its concentration upon one sole aspect of human life—man's relation to God, with all that flows from it.

This—as a general view of the object of His public ministry—will be conceded by most people. The love of God, the worth of the human soul, its eternal destiny, the need of its restoration—these are subjects of His preaching which will be generally admitted.

[1] V. Dobschütz, *op. cit.* p. 205.

[2] Rom. viii. 19; 1 Cor. iii. 13. *v.* Robertson and Plummer, *in loc.*

It is when we come to the mode of His presentation of the love of God that different views begin to make themselves felt. What was His Gospel? We at once reply—*Himself*. He offered to the acceptance of sinful humanity—a world dead in trespasses and sins—*His own Person* as the organ of its redemption and the object of its faith.

We thus in a word express our dissent from that mode of thought which regards our Lord solely as the *subject* of faith, the one supreme exemplar of man's right attitude to God. We assert that He is Himself the *object* of faith and that our attitude to Him determines our attitude to God. The difference between the two views is vital. The one ranges Christ upon the side of God, the other on the side of man—as the flower of manhood indeed, but no more than man. The one regards Him merely as the chief exponent of faith in God's Fatherhood and Love, as the highest example of the religious life, able as no one else to enter fully into communion with God, and so to set to all subsequent ages the pattern of a consecrated life. The other view goes beyond this, sees in Him the revelation of the Father, and is not content with less than the right to bring to Him all the faith and adoration to which the Father Himself is entitled.

When our Lord comes forward to proclaim the love of God to man, He so acts and speaks that attention becomes fixed upon Himself, as the perfect revelation and the actual embodiment of that love. It was in His own Person that the love of God was to be manifested. By the sacrifice of Himself for the sins of the whole world, men were to see the love of God at its height and climax. Any attempt to explain our Lord's teaching without reference to this fact must always fail. We cannot understand it unless we are on sure ground as to the part of the Teacher Himself in the subject-matter of His teaching.

Let us then endeavour to trace in the Synoptic report of our Lord's teaching the gradual unfolding of His redeeming purpose, supplementing it from time to time with what can be legitimately adduced from the Fourth Gospel.

It must first be stated that the teaching of our Lord cannot be understood in isolation from the active part of His life. His works, culminating in His death and Resurrection, must be considered in the closest connection with His words. He was altogether consistent. His life was of a piece. Never did His speech go beyond His action. Never did His action contravene the tenor of His words. There was no unreality traceable in His conduct. His enemies could bring no charge of inconsistency against Him.[1] We are therefore justified in having recourse to the expression of His mind in His works in order to interpret His verbal teaching. The two together convey His meaning and intention.

As already observed, our Lord began His Ministry with the same call to repentance which had formed the staple of the preaching of the Baptist. This means that He had sounded the depths of the human heart and knew its sinfulness. It means that the new life of the Kingdom which He had come to inaugurate is rooted in death—death to all that defiles and parts man from God. Thus at the very outset, He sounds the keynote of His death-song. His first utterance calls up the mystery of guilt and sin which reached its climax in the Cross. In that call to repentance, we have proof that our Lord had not only weighed and estimated the power and reality of sin, but was already thinking of the remedy which could alone make repentance efficacious. At least we may say that, whether or not the details of the Passion were known to Him, He was aware that, in calling men to repent, He had in His power that which could meet their repentance and make it acceptable to God.

And His preaching began with a call to faith; 'Believe the Gospel,' the good news which I bring to you. Our Lord asks for faith in what, as yet, is folded in the future—a Gospel which was only in the making. But He comes to men in the fulness of His loving heart, knowing that He alone has what they need. He asks for trust and confidence in His message. Who was He that they should believe in Him?[2] He invites faith in the tidings that He brought, before He expects faith in Himself. 'The Kingdom of God is at hand.' By quickening their expectation that

[1] In Jo. vii. 4, a charge of this kind is insinuated, due to want of faith and understanding on the part of His brethren, who brought it, as the Evangelist tells us. It took the form of a complaint that He was not so actively ambitious in a political sense, as His public career and expressed desires seemed to warrant them to expect. It was not so much inconsistency between profession and practice as lack of a self-assertion corresponding to His presumed intentions, which they objected to. But, as St. John remarks, 'Neither did His brethren believe in Him.'

[2] Cf. Jo. ix. 35, 36.

God would visit His people, by awakening the old Messianic hope, by the mere fact that He came out to them with a message, a claim to speak to them for God, He provoked inquiry, He roused their interest. He had something to tell them. He appeared as a Prophet. We see this in the way in which He appropriated to Himself the language of Isaiah,[1] when 'He stood up for to read' in the synagogue of Nazareth on the Sabbath Day. In the Messianic passage which He deliberately chose,[2] the Messiah claims to be entrusted with a Gospel for the poor, with power to bless and heal, and with the announcement of the acceptable year of the Lord. But all this, to His hearers' surprise, He refers to Himself. 'This day is this Scripture fulfilled in your ears.'[3] Thus He alludes to the teaching which, though St. Luke does not report it, He proceeded to give them; so that 'they wondered at the gracious words which proceeded out of His mouth,' and began to discuss His right so to speak.[4] He soon perceives that the proverbial prejudice against one who has been known from childhood will prevent their acceptance of His claim to teach; and a few striking instances of this feeling from the history of their people are all that they will listen to. Sacrilegious hands are stretched out against Him. 'Passing through their midst, He went His way.'

So far, we see that our Lord is keeping within the limits which are generally attributed to the Synoptic presentation of His claim. He speaks as a Prophet. Yet the incident at Nazareth certainly implies that He is conscious of being something more, and that the time had come to assert the fact. We cannot eliminate from the passage the distinct announcement of a more than prophetic claim. It is a striking fact that it was among His own people, with whom He had been brought up, that He advances it. His heart yearned for the highest good of His own countrymen of the despised Nazareth; and He will at least give them the opportunity of hearing from His lips that a time of grace was dawning for them, if they would have it. They,

[1] Is. lxi. 1. [2] Lk. iv. 17, *εὗρε τὸν τόπον*.

[3] *πεπλήρωται ἐν τοῖς ὠσὶν ὑμῶν*.

[4] Lk. iv. 22. The Evangelist records the latter part of His discourse, for it led to the outburst of wrath which made them lay hands upon Him. The earlier part, which moved their admiration, was apparently wanting in his source. It was not connected with so clearly defined an incident as the latter part.

and not the people of Jerusalem, should be the first to hear that One had come among them 'Whom,' though brought up with Him, 'they knew not,' Whom yet it concerned them to receive and know. For it may not be doubted that, in His interpretation of the Messianic passage of Isaiah and by its application to Himself, our Lord makes the first actual, if partly veiled, claim to be the chosen of God, the Christ.

If we follow the Synoptic account of our Saviour's teaching, we soon find that a distinction is made between that which is addressed to His disciples and that which is directed to the people at large. The distinction does not amount to what would be indicated by the terms esoteric and exoteric. Indeed, the more cryptic and veiled teaching is, as a matter of fact, addressed to the multitude. They are thus taught in order to stimulate their interest, to provoke inquiry, to get them to think. 'Without a parable spake He not unto them.' [1] He deals differently with His disciples; 'When they were alone He expounded all things to them.' [2] Thus the dark sayings are for the multitude; the explanation for the chosen few. 'To him that hath shall be given.' When Scribes came down from Jerusalem, 'He called them unto Him' and spoke in parables.[3] They had come with evil intention. He addresses them accordingly. But how are we to explain the reason for speaking in parables which St. Mark (followed by St. Luke, but modified by St. Matthew) assigns to Him, when asked by the disciples to interpret the parable of the sower? Quoting from Isaiah vi., He declares it is to prevent the people from understanding what is said.[4] The harsher version—that of St. Mark—is the original one. The attempts to reconcile the two have not been very successful. But it may be observed that it is against the whole tenor of the Gospel to

[1] Mk. iv. 11, 34. Once, moved with compassion for the shepherdless multitude in the desert place to which they had come in search of Him, we are told that 'He began to teach them many things,' a saying which implies a more direct mode of instruction and one less sifting than His usual parabolic method, Mk. vi. 34. But His general method with the multitude shows that He did not disdain the use of ways of attracting attention.

[2] *Ib.*

[3] Mk. iii. 23.

[4] ἵνα μή, Mk. iv. 12; Lk. viii. 10: ὅτι, Matt. xiii. 13. St. Matthew softens the idea of purpose, which St. Mark and St. Luke imply, into that of cause. Christ speaks in parables because (ὅτι) 'they seeing see not, etc.' He speaks in parables 'that (ἵνα ... μή) seeing they may see and not perceive' (Mk. Lk.). There is a similar change or softening of idea in the LXX of Is. vi. 10,

attribute deliberate and voluntary hardening of the heart of any one to Christ. His whole action and intention are grounded in love. But His words are double-edged. They harden when they do not touch and convert. We cannot be indifferent to them. If they do not heal, they wound—not from any baleful quality of their own; solely from the state of mind with which they are received. When, then, St. Mark represents Christ as saying that He speaks in parables to cause blindness and deafness to His message, the meaning is not that this is His primary intention, but that it is the natural result of the way in which His teaching was received, and, as such, the carrying out of an unfailing law of His kingdom. And He wills it so to be; He will not work a miracle to obviate the natural consequences. We have other instances of this Hebraic use of purpose for what is permitted under the circumstances, and is not of primary and absolute intention.[1] If there follows as a consequence of His parabolic language, an insensibility to His meaning, this result is due not to His own wish, but to the hard and unteachable attitude which they had taken up. It is a self-inflicted judgment on themselves.[2]

In distinction from His method in dealing with the multitude is our Lord's instruction of His disciples—of that body which, in its wider form as not confined to the twelve, was a fluctuating one.[3] 'To you it is given to know the mystery of the kingdom of God.' 'When they were alone (κατ' ἰδίαν) He expounded all things to His disciples.'[4] With those who had the hearing ear and the understanding heart, the parabolic form of teaching served several purposes. It aided memory by associating spiritual ideas with objects or facts of the natural world. The sight of these would afterwards call up unfailingly their religious counterpart. It provoked further inquiry. Ex-

as compared with the Hebrew. The hardening ascribed by the Hebrew to God is simply said to have taken place, ἐπαχύνθη γὰρ ἡ καρδία τοῦ λαοῦ τούτου, and the people closed their eyes, καὶ τοὺς ὀφθαλμοὺς ἐκάμμυσαν. St. Matt. in xiii. 15 follows the LXX. St. John (xii. 40) writing apparently with the Hebrew of Isaiah before him, ascribes the hardening and blinding, not as Isaiah does to the prophet acting on the bidding of God, but to God Himself. *v.* Lightfoot in *Expos.* 1890, i. p. 20.

[1] Matt. xxiii. 35, ὅπως ἔλθῃ. *v.* Winer, *Grammar of N.T.* (Moulton), p. 573. Cf. Jo. xii. 40, ἵνα μή.

[2] Cf. H. Holtzmann, *Die Synoptiker*, p. 72.

[3] Cf. Jo. vi. 66.

[4] Mk. iv. 11, 34.

planation was asked for. The disciples discussed the question among themselves. It roused their interest. Here was a link between what they saw going on every day under their eyes and the things unseen. Mystery has its attraction for almost every kind of mind; and although, from our familiarity with the parables and their application, few of them may seem to present any difficulty; yet when first heard they must have given rise to much speculation as to the precise lesson which our Lord intended them to teach. And they served to train the disciples in patience and teachableness. Their meaning was not obvious. It must be sought out and watched for. Thus the parable, while it was a sifting process for the indiscriminate crowd, became a school for those who chose to put themselves to it, and obey the Master's command, 'Learn of Me.'

From method we pass naturally to the subject of our Lord's teaching. A question which early presents itself is its relation to what had gone before. What was its connection, if any, with 'the Law and the Prophets'? Does it presuppose the Old Testament teaching or does it strike out a new line independently of the ancient Scriptures? Is it supplementary and confirmatory of them, or does it take its own way as something quite original?

It has been truly said that 'all Founders of Religion have been Reformers.' They have worked upon the material—the thought and customs—which they found to their hand. They have themselves belonged to the *régime* upon which they are innovating, and they make it their starting point.[1] But is this general fact true of our Lord and of Christianity? We may reply that it is, and more so than in the case of any other religion and its founder.

It is indeed impossible to state too strongly the inherence of the New Testament in the Old. Christ is rooted in the religion of His people and family. Brought up in it, observing its rites and customs,[2] joining in its worship,[3] He enforced its teaching and died with its prayers upon His lips and the music of its songs within His heart.[4]

The Old Testament was the Bible of our Lord. Its language

[1] *v.* 'Foundations,' p. 93.

[2] Our Lord regarded the ceremonial, as well as the moral law, as the ordinance of God and as binding upon men. Matt. v. 18, 19. *v.* B. Weiss, *Bibl. Theol. des N.T.* p. 83.

[3] Matt. xxiii. 21; cf. Mk. xi. 17.

[4] Lk. xxiii. 46; Ps. xxxi. 5.

was familiar to Him, as we see from the ease with which He quoted it on all occasions. It was His armoury whether against the temptations of Satan or the arguments of opponents.[1] He employs its incidents and its phraseology to illustrate His own teaching, and stands on its authority as conclusive of questions under dispute.[2] To Him, it is the Word of God.[3] He accepts the current views of the authorship of the several books. It is as mistaken an idea to expect critical judgments upon points of literary interest as to look for scientific accuracy of description in what He says of natural phenomena. He uses the language and ideas of His time, because He is speaking to contemporaries in the first instance. Had He done otherwise, His language would either have been incomprehensible, not only to His own age but to many a succeeding one, or it would have required re-adjustment to keep pace with the progress of knowledge and discovery.

To expect language suited to the requirements of scientific demonstration rather than to the understanding of His hearers is to miss the purpose of His appearance among men. He came, bathed in eternity, to speak to perishing men about the things which eternally matter; and He would not be drawn from His purpose. God and Man, Life and Death, Salvation and Loss. On and around these and kindred facts, His mind is always playing. And His language is chosen accordingly. Through His first hearers, in words that they could understand, He speaks to after ages. If it was comprehensible then, it can be understood now. There is continuity and homogeneousness in the successive ages of the human understanding. What was clear to the disciples will not be hidden from us. But to speak thus, *urbi et orbi*, to teach universally all quarters and all races, specialism must not be employed. As He willed 'all men to be saved and to come unto the knowledge of the truth,'[4] His speech was as wide and free as His desire.

Our Lord then took His stand upon the religion of His Fathers. He used its literature as His own, made it the material of His spiritual nourishment and found in it the Word of God.

[1] Matt. iv. 4 f.; xxii. 31. [2] Matt. xii. 3; Lk. x. 26.

[3] 'Out of it He hears His Father's voice; in it He lived.' Feine, *Theologie des N.T.* p. 35.

[4] 1 Tim. ii. 4.

But, with all this respect for it, He plainly asserts His own superiority.

He shows that it contains a transitory element, a lower stage of morality, because it corresponded to the time and the level of moral attainment[1]—not to the will of God. Thus, in the Sermon on the Mount, we read 'It hath been said, an eye for an eye, a tooth for a tooth: but I say unto you that ye resist not evil.' 'It hath been said, Thou shalt love thy neighbour and hate thine enemy. But I say unto you love your enemies.'[2]

The Sermon on the Mount has been compared with the Law given at Sinai. It has been called the code of the new kingdom: and, very naturally, men have thought to apply it to circumstances and occasions as they arise, in a literal sense. The temptation to do so is very great: for if an actual word of Christ meets the case which is in question, we seem to be saved from all further doubt. The Lord has spoken: we have but to obey. But on consideration it will be found that we may be coming to a conclusion too hastily, and that a literal application of a saying, however apposite it may seem, needs comparison with other teaching and possibly limitation in its use. Principles of wide and general application, rather than decisions upon special cases, form the staple of our Lord's teaching. He declined to adjudicate, when asked, in a matter between man and man. He would not step in to settle a dispute: but He uttered words which can create a basis of concord and agreement for men of every country and age, if they would receive them. Every passing theory, social and political, has claimed the direct sanction of some saying of Christ. Every new movement has thought to find support in His teaching. But when we come to examine the claim, we often find that it can be sustained only by exclusion of other parts of His teaching equally authoritative and equally binding upon the conscience. We therefore go to the Gospel records of Christ's sayings for principles of conduct rather than specific and detailed direction: for the spirit rather than the letter of the moral law.

The morality of the Old Testament could not suffice when Christ had appeared to reveal the whole mind of God and to elicit, as this revelation must, a corresponding standard of life

[1] Matt. xix. 8; Deut. xxiv. 1. [2] Matt. v. 38, 39; 43, 44.

among men.[1] Thus, the morality of the Gospel is on a higher plane than that of the Old Testament. Christ has set a pattern which can never be abandoned. When they have once seen the best and highest, nothing lower will meet the aspirations of men. It is impossible to go back. However often we fail in our endeavour, we are beckoned onward by the irresistible charm of what we know to be perfect. Nothing less can satisfy.

While, then, our Lord makes the religion and morals of the old dispensation His own, He declares Himself free to criticize and advance upon them. They were not the complete or absolute expression of the mind of God. They prepared for and awaited something better: better so far as depended on the spiritual receptivity of men; better, too, in that the developed flower is a more perfect thing than the bud. The appearance of Christ constituted an unfolding to man of what lay implicitly within the Godhead. The struggle of Judaism with the surrounding heathenism had required the clearest assertion and maintenance of henotheism and, when that conception was secured, of monotheism. It was no time for the drawing of distinctions. The struggles of the third and fourth centuries of the Christian Church show how hard it was for the Catholic party to uphold the distinctions of the Divine Being against the charge of Sabellianism. Still more vital was the necessity which was laid upon the elder Church to guard against the suspicion of a tri-theism which might easily be mistaken for, and pass into, an unlimited polytheism. Yet, with all its tenacity in upholding the Divine unity, the ancient Church, in the persons of its most spiritual thinkers, caught ever and anon a glimpse of the truth which lay as yet enfolded within its stern monotheism. The vision of Isaiah in the Temple, the frequent allusions to 'the Spirit of God,' the hint at the existence of a Creative Word, which seems at times to approach the conception of personality—these flashes of light from a world of higher thought forebode the coming of a day of greater knowledge. But they are not reflected from the consciousness of the people. The Messianic hope, with all the vicissitudes through which it passed, contributed nothing to the doctrine of God. At no time previous to the Christian era was it ever thought that the Messiah would be of the essence of the Deity. It is doubtful if His pre-existence as a heavenly being

[1] Cf. 1 Cor. xiii. 10.

before His appearance upon earth was widely held as a Jewish, as distinct from a Christian, idea.[1]

What was new in the revelation of God by Christ was not His ethical qualities. The Fatherhood and Love of God, His goodness to men, His Righteousness and Justice, are all as clearly taught in the Old Testament as in the New. Indeed, for the ethical character of God, it is to the Old Testament Scriptures rather than to those of the New Covenant that we resort for the fullest account. It is altogether a perversion of the facts to make the revelation of God's Fatherhood the main object of Christ's coming.[2] He did reveal it with a fulness and force with which it had never previously been revealed. But His characteristic contribution to the knowledge of God and of His relation to man lay in the work of redemption, by which became manifest the Love of the Father in the offering of the Eternal Son through the Holy Ghost. In the saving work of Christ there was seen the love of Father, Son and Holy Spirit in sacrifice; and in this ethical revelation the being of the Godhead was revealed. The Catholic doctrine of the Trinity, while it is a necessity of philosophical thought, became the possession of men through the manifestation of Divine love. It is the revelation of the Cross of Christ. And this, His dying gift, is His greatest contribution to religion—His chief advance upon Judaism, the pledge of a Church universal.

And corresponding to this amplified conception of the Godhead, seen in the climax of Divine love and sacrifice, was the other fresh element of Christ's teaching—an enlarged idea of the relation of man to man. 'I say unto you, love your enemies.' Here is the 'new commandment' in its most extreme form, a thing which humanly speaking is impossible. Yet nothing less could be accepted as the standard of human endeavour, when the truth about God is fully grasped. His unspeakable love in the redemption of man, so transcendent in the reach of its forgiveness, could claim nothing short of mutual forgiveness of injury between man and man. The height and depth of the love of God in Christ Jesus, as seen in the Passion and the Cross,

[1] *v.* Stanton, *The Jewish and the Christian Messiah*, p. 129 ff. But it had occurred to Apocalyptists. *v.* 1 Enoch xlvi. 1, 2; xlviii. 3; xlix. 2.

[2] *v.* Harnack, *D. Wesen des Christentums*, p. 91. But *v.* his Lecture, *The Two-fold Gospel in the N.T.* 1911, p. 5.

makes of necessity a new demand on the moral powers of mankind. The neighbour, who to the Jew always meant one of his own race, now means anyone with whom he may come in contact. The universal brotherhood, which is the root-conception of the Church of Christ, is the only possible ethical response to the love of God to man. In the parable of the Good Samaritan our Lord lays down the true principles of human relationship. St. John makes sympathy and kindliness a criterion of the reality of our love to God.[1]

[1] 1 Jo. iii. 17.

CHAPTER XVII

THE PURPOSE AND METHOD OF CHRIST

It is at this point in our course that we come upon great difference of opinion. When we try to penetrate to the inner mind of Christ—to what He thought about Himself and His Mission—we are at once confronted with very contentious matter. The view we take will largely depend on our estimate of His Person. If that estimate is an exalted one; if in a true sense we regard Him as Divine, we shall be prepared to take an exalted view of the purpose which He set Himself to accomplish, and shall not be surprised if we find in the earliest records of His life some allusion to such a purpose. If, on the other hand, our conception of Him is of one who was no more than man, we shall not look for any higher purpose than would fall within the measure of humanity: and when we find that the Gospels contain indications of a more exalted self-consciousness and of a wider purpose, perhaps we should be tempted—the thing is not unknown—to ascribe them to the idealizing tendency of too enthusiastic followers, or—as some have not shrunk from doing—to the fanaticism of an overwrought temperament.

In any case, the personal equation in a question of this kind has to be reckoned with. We, none of us, come to it without some prepossession. It is impossible to approach consideration of His work without first asking the question of ourselves and all who take part in it, 'What think ye of Christ?' Is He but one among the many whom God has sent to elevate, to enlighten and to instruct the world; or does He stand alone—the Only-begotten Son? As regards the present inquiry, it will already have been made clear[1] that we approach it with the conviction

[1] v. above, p. 189 f.

that it is the work of the Son of God which we have to investigate.

Had He a Mission ? Did He regard Himself as sent by God for any definite purpose ? A very hasty survey of the Gospels will enable us to answer that question in the affirmative. It is one of the most frequently occurring thoughts in the Fourth Gospel.[1] The idea of the Saviour as a Messenger of God is employed with curious iteration, so much so that it has helped to form the impression that a certain sameness of thought pervades the whole Gospel. In the Synoptics, the idea occurs, but sparingly. It is regarded rather from the point of view of the Saviour Himself than of God who sends Him. He says 'I am come' to do this or that.[2]

We may, therefore, conclude that our Lord believed that His presence on earth was due to a definite mission from His Father: that He had a work to do which He alone could carry out.

But, when we come to try to specify that work, we are at once upon debatable ground. We are often told that His object was to make known the Fatherhood of God to men, to mirror forth, by His own life of love and kindness, the compassion and tenderness of the Most High. Some will hardly admit any other specific purpose in our Lord's work than this. He was the revelation of the Love of the Father, and, as a practical corollary from that revelation, He enforced one all-embracing rule of life on His followers—that they should love one another.

There is no doubt that Christ *did* come to reveal the love of God; and His life of active benevolence was its best exemplification. But we may admit this to the full, and yet fail to grasp the purpose involved in His mission. St. John tells us[3] that our Lord's object was to awaken in men something which is presupposed by a revelation of love with its answering duties—that is, life itself. 'I am come that they might have life and that they might have it more abundantly.' He had a work to do at the very foundation of things. A dead thing can neither know nor respond to love. We must live to love. Christ came to quicken ; and the death from which He was to awake men was the death of sin : the life

[1] It occurs about thirty times.

[2] Matt. v. 17 ; ix. 13 ; x. 34, 35 = Lk. xii. 51. The same point of view occurs in St. John also. Cf. v. 43, vii. 28, ix. 39, etc.

[3] x. 10.

He came to bring is the life which 'is hid with Christ in God.' It requires freedom from the tyranny and the paralysing power of sin. Even the Psalmist caught a glimpse of this truth, 'I will run the way of Thy commandments, when Thou hast set my heart at liberty.' Job [1] sums up in a word the questioning and the longing of the ancient world, 'How can man be just before God?' Our Lord's own words are an assurance that He regarded His coming among men as an answer to that question, as it presents itself to every awakened conscience—'The Son of Man is come to seek and to save that which was lost.' [2] He came to be the Saviour from sin, the Quickener from the dead, the Mediator to reconcile man with God.

Again, the mission of Christ is represented as the exemplifying of a life of consummate faith and obedience. Thus, He is regarded as One in whom unity of feeling with God was so complete and extraordinary, that it placed Him at the head and, as the model, of all whose lives are in close communion with the Father. In that tie, maintained through all phases of fortune, was the ground of His Sonship. It differed in degree, but not in kind, from the sonship of any other member of the household of faith. It was purely an ethical relationship,[3] and was one of character and life, not of essential being.

The life of Christ on earth was, it is true, a life of faith in the Father. No one records this feature more fully than St. John. 'I knew that Thou hearest Me always.' [4] He lives as one who is in close union with God, spending nights in prayer, always in touch with the Father, referring to Him His power to work miracles, regarding them as an answer to His prayers.[5] 'The focus or centre of His being as man, was not in Himself as man, but in His Father, that is, God.' [6] And He ever remains the perfect example of a life of faith and obedience, of one whose will is always subject to the will of the Father.

But again, it must be said, the definition is inadequate. The purpose and object of His mission was more than the presentation to mankind of a life of perfect obedience and trust in

[1] ix. 2 (R.V.) and margin. [2] Lk. xix. 10.

[3] So, for instance, Pfleiderer, *Die Entstehung des Christentums*, p. 94. Cf. *The Person of our Lord*, p. 257.

[4] xi. 42; xvii. 25. Cf. Lk. x. 21, 22. [5] Jo. xi. 41.

[6] Moberly, *Atonement and Personality*, p. 104.

God. He Himself was *the object* of faith, and this, not only in the estimation of a few devoted adherents looking back through the medium of a grateful recollection, but according to His own judgment. Nothing is more untrue to fact than the idea that His own exaltation was a thought foreign to the mind of Jesus, and that He, Whose object was the sole glory of the Father, found Himself, against His will, placed by His followers on a height He had never dreamed of occupying.

It is no doubt true that there is a difference of proportion to be observed between our Lord's conception of His purpose, as recorded in the earliest stratum of the Gospels, and in the reflective and theologizing conceptions of the other Apostolic writings. The Christ of the Logia and of St. Mark does, we believe, make the highest possible demands upon the faith and obedience of His people, because the work He came to do for them was of transcendent importance for their present and eternal welfare. But, it was after the completion of the earthly portion of that work by His Death and Resurrection, that the significance of what are mere hints in the earliest Evangelic records was fully seized, and in the light of that unexampled sacrifice and that glorious triumph, found to contain the outline of His purpose.

For instance, if to St. Paul the atoning and mediating work of Christ is ever in the forefront of his conception of Christianity, he is not to be charged with departure from the mind of Christ. Not only have we clear references to the atonement in words which are placed by the Synoptic writers in the mouth of Christ, but we have to remember that, even more clearly than in His words, the crucified and risen Saviour declared His purpose by His acts. To St. Paul, that Death and Resurrection formed the central point of all his faith and hope. To him, it was not what Christ said or did during the course of His Ministry that formed the Gospel which he preached, and which he communicated to the Apostles who were in Christ before him, in order that he might not be charged with preaching another Gospel. It was those supreme acts of love and power in which the Ministry culminated—the sacrifice of the Cross and the victory of the Resurrection.

At the same time, it is well to remember that our Lord, in the clearest possible manner and in language fully attested as His own, declared the great purpose of His coming among men.

'The Son of Man came not to be ministered unto, but to minister and to give His life a ransom for many.'[1] 'This is My blood of the new testament, which is shed for many.'[2] 'This is My blood of the new testament, which is shed for many for the remission of sins.'[3] If these sayings stood alone, we might hesitate to place upon them a construction so far-reaching and vital as that of the redemption of man: but they are enforced and interpreted by what happened at the Cross. While, on the other hand, they show that the Crucifixion was no mere unfortunate and ill-omened termination to a life which was originally destined for a better ending; but that it formed part of a deliberate purpose. All along, the Saviour had in mind the probability that His witness for God could, among sinful men, terminate in only one way. He 'knew what was in man,' and in that knowledge lay His foreboding of the Cross.

This work of redemption looked Godward, not manward, in that it was the bringing back of man into peace with God, the presentation of the son to the Father--not the turning of the Father's face, which had been turned away, towards the son.

It was not needed by God. The Cross, though it was the supreme exhibition of the love of the Father, Who 'spared not His Only begotten Son,' did not effect any change of disposition on God's part. He had ever loved His creatures. 'Yea, I have loved thee with an everlasting love.'[4] The old, familiar conception of a God, angry with His people till appeased by the sacrifice of the Son and turned from wrath to love, satisfies neither the text of Scripture nor the moral sense of men. It was man who needed to be reconciled,[5] first 'coming to himself,' then returning to be met, while yet a long way off, by the ever loving and remembering Father. The guilt of man, not the anger of God, required dealing with; man's misunderstandings removed, his blindness cured. It was the world of sinful humanity that went astray, alienated and opposed to the Father's

[1] Mk. x. 45, included by v. Soden in the 'Petrine' portion of the Gospel, and taken over by St. Matthew (xx. 28) without change.

[2] Mk. xiv. 24. [3] Matt. xxvi. 28. [4] Jer. xxxi. 3.

[5] Cf. Westcott in *Hebr.* ii. 17. *v.* 2 Cor. v. 20 and Chrys. *Epist. II. ad Cor.* Hom. xi. § 3c, *καὶ οὐκ εἶπε καταλλάξατε ἑαυτοῖς τὸν Θεόν· οὐ γὰρ ἐκεῖνός ἐστιν ὁ ἐχθραίνων, ἀλλ' ὑμεῖς· Θεὸς γὰρ οὐδέποτε ἐχθραίνει.*

will. The reconciling power of the Cross is applied not to God, but to the world.

The work of Christ is, therefore, not to be looked upon as a mediating transaction between two parties who are estranged, but by the interposition of a third party agree to come to terms. The estrangement is entirely the act of one, and if it affects the attitude of God, it is man alone who is to blame. The love of the Father is ever going forth, wide and free as the sunlight. It is only a self-closed heart that bars its entrance. What is required is the bending of the stubborn will, the opening of the closed eyes, the turning of the heart estranged by sin and self. To this end is directed the whole force of the Gospel message. The appeal of the Saviour is to the heart and will of man. 'We pray you in Christ's stead,' says St. Paul, 'be ye reconciled to God.' [1]

Roughly speaking, there are two ways of getting intelligent, responsible persons to carry out our will. One way is that of force; it acts from without. The other is that of moral persuasion; it acts within. The one method respects the character and constitution of the person acted upon: the other treats him as a machine. In the present day, God's dealings with man are often criticized from the point of view that people should be compelled to be good and to act as their highest interests demand. It is complained that too much is left to their own will, and that a wise coercion might well be exercised, as upon children, who do not know what is good for them. This feeling is not unnatural and is shared at times by nearly everyone who is conscious of the discord which, at so many points, checks our spiritual advance. We sigh for a touch of tyranny. But we are not dealt with by God as though we were fit subjects for an inebriates' home, where, by free surrender of our will, we can be constrained into wiser courses. 'Then, must ye needs go out of the world.' We are treated as standing on an altogether higher plane. God respects us and the qualities with which He has endowed us. He never does violence to the primal facts of human nature. He is loyal to His own compact. If He has given us reason and a will, with its power of self-determination, He does not forget it. By no single act will He take from our responsibility. He never goes back on His purpose in our

[1] 2 Cor. v. 19.

creation. Made in His image, with characteristics that reflect His own, we are not treated as machines. 'Known unto God are all His works from the beginning of the world.' He keeps always before Him His original plan. Even when sin entered, and rough and strong measures might have seemed necessary to restore man, there is no departure from His method. During the waiting time, when the world was getting ready for its Redeemer, men were reasoned with,[1] taken aside and schooled. If one great object of the prophetic gift was to prepare the way for Christ by fixing men's hopes and setting their gaze upon Him, another was certainly the moral education of men—the production of a suitable environment into which, in due time, the Liberator might enter.

When Christ appeared, His action was on the same lines. It was always by correspondence with something in man, and not by external force, that He brought His saving grace to bear upon man's need. His first disciples had already shown their aptitude for higher things, their desire for truth and reality, by attaching themselves to the ministry of the Baptist. At their first meeting with Christ, they recognized in Him something akin to the character of their master, and He found in them that openness of mind and readiness to hear and learn, which always called forth His sympathy; and this mutual attraction led to their discipleship.

The same conditions are to be observed in our Lord's miracles. The power which He possessed to heal and to raise the dead was not to be exercised on mere stones, incapable of hope and feeling. What He required was trust; either personal or, when that was impossible, by representation.[2] If it be said that, if that be so, then the most necessitous cases—those who were dead to their actual condition—were left without remedy, we have to admit such a possibility. By opposing all good intuitions, a man may become incapable of the wish for higher things and put himself outside the reach of the arms that are stretched out from the Cross. There may come a time when the word has to be said, 'Behold, your house is left unto you desolate.' In this, as in all God's dealings with men, the power of self-determination is respected. Heart and will can be set

[1] Is. i. 18.

[2] Jo. xi. 25, 26. Before the raising of Lazarus, the faith of Martha is tested.

against the light. Such a condition of spiritual deadness may have one of two causes. The spiritual faculties may never have been awakened. No aspiration for higher things ever felt—a state which, it is to be feared, is only too common among large masses of people in the present day. Or, on the other hand, it may be due to the gradual atrophying of impulses which have been so constantly checked and thwarted that at last they have ceased to act. In the first case, there is hope that somewhere, if not here, undeveloped gifts may yet be quickened into action. In the other case, we can only say, 'Shall not the Judge of all the earth do right?'

If our Lord's miracles are examined, we find one unfailing law which governs their operation. They were not worked broadcast. He did not, like a returning conqueror, scatter His largesse indifferently among the crowd. Everything He did was individualistic. It had reference to separate needs and it depended on individual preparation. To let loose the powers which He had in His keeping, something had to be contributed by the object of His benevolence. 'To him that hath shall be given.' What that something was, we must try to find out. If we can do so, we shall see a principle which runs through all God's dealings with us. Take such a miracle as the healing of the two blind men.[1] 'Jesus saith unto them, Believe ye that I am able to do this? They said unto Him, Yea, Lord. Then touched He their eyes, saying, According to your faith, be it unto you.' Here our Lord's readiness to heal is made to depend on the trust which was forthcoming on the part of the men. The trust was partly in His power, that He was 'able to do this,' partly in His willingness to use it. It meant that they gave themselves into His hands without reserve. St. Luke speaks of the same disposition in the cripple at Lystra as conditioning the exercise of St. Paul's gift of healing; 'he had faith to be healed.'[2] With this contrast the behaviour of the people of Nazareth, whose attitude impeded the outflow of the Saviour's love and power and made Him marvel.[3] From these contrasted incidents we get a law of Divine action. The grace of God only effects its purpose under answering conditions. There must be surrender, confidence, complete trust. The will is always respected. God never acts in opposition to it. So Christ carried along with Him

[1] Matt. ix. 28, 29. [2] Acts xiv. 8, 9. [3] Lk. iv. 16 f.

those whom He healed. He admitted their faith and trust to a share in the forces which acted upon them. They were 'workers together with Him.'

But what are we to say of those from whom no personal trust was forthcoming, such as the man 'borne of four,' who was brought into His presence? The language of the Evangelist leads us to suppose that there was no faith on his part, for nothing is said of it, whereas something *is* said of the faith of the bearers. He may have made no actual resistance: but everything in the nature of hope or expectation was absent. The incident is profoundly significant. It for ever glorifies and commends the power of Christian sympathy, the ministry of intercession. It opens out vistas of what might be, if the Church realized the power of that ministry.

No response on the part of the sufferer, and yet the Saviour's power unlocked. Why? Because He transfers to the man the trust and willingness of his friends. On their hope and faith he is borne successfully into the Saviour's presence, and the co-operation between the agent and the sufferer is complete. There is the same acceptance of the faith of others in the case of the centurion's servant; and in the raising of Lazarus. In all these cases, the miracle is performed in an atmosphere of trust. The sufferer, or his friends, have cast themselves without reserve on the love and pity of the Saviour.

There is another small class of miracles which appear to have been worked independently of any contributing faith on the part of those who were benefited. Their need sufficed to move the Saviour to act. Such was the miracle of the feeding of the five thousand, with its analogous act of the feeding of the four thousand. The multitude, in each case, had been listening to the teaching of Christ: so far, we may attribute to them a ready, responsive attitude. But we can detect no such sign of faith as attended so many of the miracles of healing. Pity, deep, tender pity for sheep that had no shepherd, moved the Good Shepherd to act—to feed as well as teach.[1]

Another miracle of this class was the stilling of the storm on the Lake of Galilee. Here, again, we find direct action upon an inanimate object. Only here again there is a certain aptitude or readiness for trust and confidence on the part of

[1] Mk. vi. 34, 37.

those who were befriended by the miracle. We see this in the sudden awe which fell upon the disciples when they realized the mastery over the elements which Christ could wield.

The cursing of the fig-tree and its consequent withering away seems to stand in a class by itself, and to present difficulties peculiar to itself. Anger at a tree which was obeying the law of its own kind; condemnation to perpetual unfruitfulness at the bidding of His own sense of unsatisfied hunger; these seem strange and unwonted features in a Gospel portraiture of our Lord. Do they justify the attempt to explain away the miracle by the theory of an acted version of the parable of the unfruitful fig-tree? Only the clearest proof that the miracle-story is an unauthorized, *tendenziös* intrusion into the text can give colour to the theory. Some critics have no scruples against employing it.[1] But the account is circumstantial. The incident belongs to the last, holy week of the Ministry. The act itself and the recognition of its result fall upon two separate days. Everything points—not to the reflection of a former parable but—to an actual historical happening; full of symbolism indeed, full too of spiritual teaching, yet none the less for that, a concrete, definite fact. As with a lightning flash, the deadness of a life of mere pretence is revealed for all time. The withering of an insensate tree is a cheap price to pay for such a lesson against the dawn of that hour when fruit, not leaves, will be asked for by the Judge of all mankind.

It is significant that Christ only once designates His miracles by the word τέρατα, 'prodigies.'[2] They were never worked for their own sake as bare wonders. He Himself regarded them as 'signs.' Their true meaning and object lay not in the immediate relief or blessing which they effected for the individual concerned, but in the light which they cast upon His own redeeming office and work for the souls of men.[3] At the grave of Lazarus He stood confessed as Lord of life and death, quickening the body that had already passed to corruption, withdrawing the spirit

[1] Holtzmann, *D. Synoptiker*, p. 90; Wernle, *D. Quellen des Lebens Jesu*, p. 69. But *v.* Sanday, Hastings' *D.B.* ii. p. 627, 'It is just as possible that parable and miracle may stand side by side as a double enforcement of the same lesson.'

[2] Jo. iv. 39, and then in conjunction with the word σημεῖα, 'signs.'

[3] Mk. ii. 10, 'That ye may know that the Son of Man hath power on earth to forgive sins, then saith He to the sick of the palsy, etc.'

from Paradise: not surely that Lazarus might spend a few more years before again entering the gate of death; but that men might see in Himself, as we gather from His words to Martha, 'the Resurrection and the Life.'

Thus 'the point of a miracle lies, not in the process, but in the manifest token of "the Finger of God" which it bears. Its significance is in its aim.'[1] 'Miracula sine doctrina nihil valent.' The moral and spiritual context of a miracle is what distinguishes it as the work of God. Christ Himself applies this test to His own working: 'If I with the Finger of God cast out devils, no doubt the Kingdom of God is come upon you.' It was not mere power that constituted the sign: but its beneficent character.[2]

A great responsibility was thrown by this characteristic of miracles upon those who witnessed them. Their effect upon Christ's contemporaries was nothing less than a judgment. By their interpretation of them men were justified or condemned. Those who, failing to resist the miracle, attributed it to the working of Satan were in His own words guilty of the sin against the Holy Ghost. The beneficence of the act, taken in conjunction with its power, was a sign of Divine love. So to misunderstand it was to close the heart to every influence for good.

It is quite in keeping with this judgment-power of the Gospel miracles that our Lord never acceded to a hostile demand for a sign. It was a proof of the kind of temper which at once barred His action. Thus, to Pharisees who came 'seeking of Him a sign from heaven, tempting Him,' His refusal is peremptory, 'There shall no sign be given to this generation.'[3] To the people of Capernaum asking 'What sign shewest Thou that we

[1] R. Virchow in K. Beth, *Das Wunder*, p. 48, n. 1.

[2] Lk. xi. 20. Modern Jewish thought is in keeping with this view. Looking back to the Old Testament miracles, Rabbi Kohler says, 'The Torah itself lays down the principle that miracles are no test of the truth of the thing for which their testimony is invoked'; and he appeals to Deut. xiii. 2-4. 'Miracles are never,' he adds, 'adduced in support of the faith by Jewish writers.' Sometimes, like those of the magicians of Pharaoh, they are the work of Satan. *v. Jew. Encycl.* art. 'Miracle.' St. Paul warns the Thessalonians that the coming of Antichrist will be 'after the working of Satan with all power and signs and lying wonders.' 2 Thess. ii. 9. Cf. Matt. xxiv. 24.

[3] Mk. viii. 11, 12. On the parallel passage Matt. xii. 39, with its addition of 'the sign of the prophet Jonas,' *v.* McNeile in *Cambridge Biblical Essays*, p. 238; Holtzmann, *D. Synoptiker*, p. 245. Cf. Matt. xvi. 4 with Swete's note on Mk. viii. 12.

may see and believe Thee ?' He gave as answer the mystical teaching on the Bread of Life which forms the basis of the Eucharist.[1] Herod had long been 'desirous to see Him . . . and he hoped to have seen some miracle done by Him.' When He stood, a prisoner, before him and was questioned, 'He answered him nothing.'[2] Yet Renan could say, 'A miracle in Paris before competent *savants* would put an end to so many doubts.'[3] He is strangely forgetful of the teaching of history and as strangely ignorant of the human heart. 'If they hear not Moses and the Prophets, neither will they be persuaded, though one rose from the dead.'[4]

[1] Jo. vi. 30.
[2] Lk. xxiii. 8 ; ix. 9.
[3] *Les Apôtres*, p. xliv.
[4] Lk. xvi. 31.

CHAPTER XVIII

THE APOSTOLATE

God works through man for the salvation of man. Divine aid is ever at hand to prompt, to guide and enlighten; but its employment never takes the place of those natural means of knowledge and influence which God has put within our power.

The fact that our Lord chose for His purposes twelve men 'whom He named Apostles'[1] is an instance of this principle. It meant that for man He intended to use man; that the powers which dwelt within Him and which, by the outpouring of His Spirit, were to be liberated for wider and more effectual use, were not to supersede the necessity for human endeavour; that both in 'working out our own salvation' and in the saving of others, it is difficult to overestimate the part which man himself must play. It belongs to our very nature as self-determining beings, with life and death within our power of choice, that we should have much to do with the matter. The fact is fully recognized all through the Old Testament as well as in the New. God by His prophets in the one, by His Apostles in the other, above all by 'the Apostle and High Priest of our profession, Christ Jesus,'[2] appeals to man for the act of choice which shall fix his position for God, or against Him. We are not mere machines to be acted upon from without by magic or miracle.

[1] Lk. vi. 13. It has been remarked that discipleship, rather than Apostleship, is represented in the Gospels as the relation in which the Twelve stood to Christ during the period of His Ministry. The term Apostle is of very infrequent use. 'The Twelve' or 'The Disciples' is the more usual name employed. 'A far larger proportion of the Gospels is taken up with records of facts belonging to the discipleship than with records of facts belonging to the apostleship.' Hort, *The Christian Ecclesia*, p. 29; Lightfoot, *Galatians*, p. 94.

[2] Hebr. iii. 1.

We are moral beings, akin to God, most like Him when we rise to the height of some great decision, creative of our destiny and pregnant with our future; and it is therefore with, and not in spite of, our own co-operation, that the forces of Divine grace act upon our souls.

And this principle comes out in our Lord's choice and ordination of the Twelve. It also carries with it the further principle that much of the influence and circumstance which tend to men's salvation is in the hands of others.[1] It was the first murderer who first disputed the validity of this principle, when he asked, 'Am I my brother's keeper?' We *are* entrusted, to a far greater extent than we realize, with the keeping of our brother's soul. It was in view of this fact that Christ called men to His work.

The idea of an Apostle is of one sent forth on a special mission. He goes from the seat of authority, bearing the commission of that authority, to exercise it elsewhere.[2] The central thought in the case of the Twelve is that, as emissaries of Christ, they had been in close intercourse and companionship with Him and that this connection gave them their authority and their influence. 'He ordained twelve that they should be with Him.'[3] 'Men took knowledge of them that they had been with Jesus.' This was the effect of their intercourse. The secret of their power was their knowledge of His mind and the effect upon their character of His life and example. They had been to school with Him. The basis of their authority was moral. They went forth not only because sent, but because, from their intercourse with Christ, they were made capable of understanding His will and acting for Him. They were moral agents, not mere messengers. They knew the purport of their message. They did not convey it simply. Our Lord had this aspect of their office in view when He appointed them 'to be with Him.' They were to go forth and tell what they had themselves experienced.

The first step towards this object was to cast over them the spell of His Personality and win them to Himself. We can only trace it by combining the narrative of the Fourth Gospel with that of the Synoptics.[4] The adherence of the first disciples, if

[1] Cf. Wernle, *D. Anfänge unserer Religion*, p. 83.

[2] For the conception of an ἀπόστολος in classical Greek, *v.* Lightfoot, *Galatians*, p. 92. Cf. Mk. vi. 7.

[3] Mk. iii. 14.

[4] This is fully recognized by Schlatter, *D. Theologie des N.T.* i, p. 121.

we rely only on the latter recitals, remains inexplicable. Why should these men leave their work and their livelihood for the undefined following of One, of Whom apparently they had no previous knowledge? Turn to St. John and you find the necessary steps that led to their attaining such knowledge of Christ, of His claims and His purposes, that it was only reasonable that, when He called them, they 'straightway forsook their nets and followed Him.'[1] Three of these men, who form the first and innermost band of disciples, have already learnt to know Him.[2] As disciples of the Baptist, after hearing their first master's witness to Christ, they seek Him out and get to know Him. It is noteworthy that the first open step towards the discipleship which was to develop into the Apostolate was taken by the men themselves. Something in Christ attracted them when their attention was directed upon Him by the witness of the Baptist. He had silently drawn them to Himself. His spell was upon them. The first overt act was their own.

We are dependent partly upon St. John and partly upon the Synoptic Gospels for knowledge of the progress of the intercourse with Christ which resulted in the definite call to discipleship. Before leaving the Jordan, to return to Galilee, our Lord, by His own deliberate act, seeks out Philip and calls him to discipleship. Philip finds his own fellow-countryman, Nathanael, and brings him to Christ. Thus it was with a band of five that our Lord returns to His own country. The visit to Cana with the first miracle quickly follows. Then, with perhaps a brief stay at Nazareth, our Lord, accompanied by His mother, His brethren and His disciples, pays His first visit to Capernaum, where so many of His mighty works were to be wrought, and which was to be His home for a considerable part of His public ministry.[3] He 'continued there not many days. And the Jews' passover was nigh at hand.'[4] Again accompanied by His disciples,[5] He goes up to Jerusalem. The disciples witness the cleansing of the Temple, and they recall the passage in the Psalter which speaks of the consuming zeal of the Psalmist for the house of God. Long afterwards our

[1] Mk. i. 18; Matt. iv. 19; cf. Lk. v. 11.

[2] *v.* p. 254.

[3] Matt. ix. 1, ἰδία πόλις. iv. 13. *v.* Sanday in Hastings' *Dict. of Christ.* i. p. 270.

[4] Jo. ii. 12, 13.

[5] *Ib.* 17, 22.

Lord's answer to the Jews, who asked Him for a sign of His authority in what seemed to them a high-handed act, came back to their recollection, in the light of His resurrection.[1] This visit meant that for Christ the Temple and its worship were of Divine origin and obligation. It meant, too, that whatever His purpose might be, His own people should have the first cognizance of it. St. John's account is true to life. It narrates a step in His Ministry which was bound to be taken. From all that we know of our Lord's object in coming among us, we can be sure that an early visit to the central seat of the people and their worship would be a necessity. For the disciples, it meant that the leader, whom they were following, did not stand outside their own people and their own religion. It assured them that He was within the line of their ancestral covenant. At that period of their knowledge of Him, any departure from this position would have imperilled their immature allegiance.

On leaving Jerusalem our Lord 'came into the land of Judaea.'[2] But He leaves it after a period of teaching and baptizing in order, as St. John tells us, to avoid misunderstanding on the part of the Pharisees, who seem to have thought that there was a rivalry springing up between Himself and the Baptist. Passing through Samaria, He again comes into Galilee.[3] It is this return to Galilee to which St. Matthew and St. Mark refer as occurring soon after the imprisonment of the Baptist.[4]

It was in Galilee that our Lord laid upon Simon Peter and Andrew, and upon John and James the sons of Zebedee, the call of discipleship. As He walked by the Sea and saw them at their work, He called them from it to a new life and a new occupation.

The incident marks a definite stage in the formation of the Apostolic band. At this moment were laid—though at the time unseen and unnoticed—the first foundation stones of the future Church. Here was the root and germ of that primitive community which was to form the Kingdom of Christ. And it is characteristic of our Lord's approval of

[1] Jo. ii. 22. [2] Jo. iii. 22. The country parts.

[3] Jo. iv. 1-4. 'Again,' cf. i. 43.

[4] Lk. iv. 14, to which Holtzmann (*D. Synoptiker*, pp. ix, 330) alludes in this connection, narrates the *earlier* return to Galilee immediately after the Baptism, Jo. i. 43. St. Matthew connects this second return with the news of the Baptist's imprisonment (iv. 12). St. Mark i. 14 merely quotes the imprisonment as a note of time.

natural relationships and of family life that His choice fell upon two pairs of brothers. In following Him, they were not to become dead to the ties of family affection. Nor, as we find by their return at favourable opportunities to their old occupation, was there any incompatibility between the calling of an Apostle and the pursuance of a trade.[1]

On another day by the shore of the same sea, our Lord added another name to the four whom He had already called. Levi, son of Alphaeus, was sitting at the custom house of Capernaum. It was the point of the great trade route from Ptolemais to Damascus which formed the boundary between the jurisdictions of Herod Antipas and Philip. Its position made the business a lucrative one for the publican who farmed it. But Levi did not hesitate. With the same 'abandon' which marked the recipients of the earlier call, he rises from his counter; but, unlike them, he does not again return to his old work. He was henceforth to show himself 'a tried money-changer'[2] in coin of another kind. As Matthew[3] the Apostle and the recorder of the sayings of Christ which form one of the two staple elements of the First and Third Gospels, he hoarded up and handed on, to the lasting good of the Church to the end of time, the words of Him Who 'spake as never man spake.' We have no further account of any separate call to discipleship. The time was at hand when the five already called were, with seven others, to receive their Apostolic ordination at the Saviour's hand.[4]

It is significant of the importance of the event in our Lord's estimation that, before it took place, He withdrew into the heights behind Capernaum[5] and there, alone with His Father,

[1] Cf. Jo. xxi. 3.

[2] Cf. the extra-canonical saying attributed to our Lord, γίνεσθε τραπεζῖται δόκιμοι and the explanation of it contained in *Clem. Hom.* iii. 61. *v.* above, p. 22.

[3] The identification of Levi with Matthew, though often doubted, is proved by the expression 'Matthew the publican' in Matt. x. 3.

[4] Philip and Nathanael (Bartholomew) though brought into touch with Christ as disciples of the Baptist do not appear to have received another definite call like that of the five. *v.* Jo. i. 44. But that, either in that earlier intercourse with Him, or on some occasion unknown to us, they had received a call to discipleship as a preparation for the fuller charge which was to come, is plain from their position in all the three Synoptic lists of the Twelve. They stand in each immediately after the two pairs of brothers.

[5] *v.* Holtzmann, *D. Synoptiker*, p. 125.

spent the night in prayer.[1] In retirement from the world and in solitary communion with the Father, He brings into shape the purpose which had been slowly ripening in His mind. Self-limited in the range of His own action by the necessities of His human life, He takes to Himself a band of men who will spread the tidings of the kingdom. As His representatives they will be empowered to act and teach in His Name. Looking back upon this day, He exclaims in His high-priestly prayer, 'As Thou hast sent Me into the world, even so have I also sent them into the world.'[2] This mission gave them their title—'He chose twelve whom also He named Apostles.'[3] He is Himself the Arbiter of the choice; 'He calleth unto Him whom He would.' 'Ye have not chosen Me, but I have chosen you and ordained you,' is His own reflection on the events of this historic day.[4] It was this choice and appointment[5] by our Lord Himself that was the strength of the Apostles in their work. He had called them. They had not laid forward hands on the ark of God, or ventured into such an office unbidden. They had the sense of vocation to support them.

We gather from St. Mark's account that the first effect of the ordination of the Twelve was their admission to closer intimacy with their Master. 'He ordained them that they should be with Him.' The time for separate work of their own was to come later. They have to be filled and impressed with their message, and to acquire something of the Spirit of Christ, before they could go into the world and do and teach what He Himself had done and taught. Direct and close contact could impart this power. How long this intercourse lasted before the Twelve were regarded by our Lord as prepared to put their knowledge and experience to practical use, we cannot say. But we must follow St. Mark and St. Luke in placing a distinct interval of time between the ordination and the mission.[6] Then, on a certain day, 'He called unto Him the

[1] Lk. vi. 12.
[2] Jo. xvii. 18; cf. xx. 21.
[3] Lk. vi. 13; cf. Mk. iii. 14.
[4] Mk. iii. 13; Jo. xv. 16.

[5] The word employed for the act of ordination (A.V.) or appointment (R.V.) varies. In Mk. iii. 14, it is ἐποίησε. In the allusion in Jo. xv. 16, it is ἔθηκα, that is,' says Chrysostom, *Hom. ad loc.* ἐφύτευσα.

[6] Mk. vi. 7 ff.; Lk. ix. 1 ff. In each case the account of the mission starts from a state of things supposed as previously arrived at. The Twelve are already a college, a complete and definite body in themselves. St. Matthew,

Twelve and began to send them forth by two and two.'[1] They were 'to preach the Kingdom of God and to heal the sick.'[2] St. Matthew tells us that they were to take up and re-echo the cry of the Baptist and of Christ Himself, on beginning His Ministry in Galilee—'The Kingdom of heaven is at hand.'[3]

The motive that impelled our Lord to send out the Twelve was compassion. The multitude were like sheep which had no shepherd. 'They fainted and were scattered abroad.' There was no one to bring them into the fold, to lead them out to the pastures beside the still waters, to guard them from the beasts of the field.[4] He takes His disciples into His confidence and, in view of the extent of the work to be done, He bids them pray that God would send forth labourers. As yet they were few and the harvest was rich and abundant. It was waiting to be gathered.[5] This reference to God as the Lord of the Harvest, Who is to be supplicated for the means of reaping it, is entirely in harmony with Christ's words on the reception of His messengers.[6] There, too, He refers to God the Father as the ultimate Personality involved in that reception. It was not the two Galilean peasants, coming in at nightfall from some other village with their message of the nearness of the Kingdom, who offered themselves for acceptance or rejection, as the case might be. It was the Messiah—nay, it was the Father Himself.

The ministry of the word is to be attended by works of mercy and bodily healing. A time of grace was at hand both for soul

on the other hand, according to his usual habit of disregard for time and sequence, connects the mission directly with the ordination. He finds the ordination record a suitable place to introduce the discourse at the mission. 'Nothing is more self-evident than that the disciples acquired, through long intercourse with Jesus, the capacity to become His fellow workers.' H. Holtzmann, *Die Synoptiker*, p. 232. 'It is morally certain that (St. Mark) intended to represent the actual mission as *not* immediate.' Hort, *The Christian Ecclesia*, p. 23.

[1] Mk. vi. 7; Lk. ix. 1. [2] Lk ix. 2. [3] Matt. x. 7.

[4] Matt. ix. 36. St. Mark, vi. 34, speaks of the same compassion called forth by the same circumstances at a different time.

[5] Matt. ix. 37, 38. From the Logia. St. Luke places the saying in connection with the sending out of the Seventy disciples, x. 2. It is not unlikely that St. Matthew and St. Luke are both right in their assignment of the saying, and that our Lord used the same words on each occasion. B. Weiss considers that the saying was originally addressed only to the Twelve, but was applied by St. Luke to the larger circle of the Seventy. *D. Leben Jesu*, ii. p. 115.

[6] Matt. x. 40.

and body. No such opportunity had ever before dawned upon men. But full and comprehensive as the work would be in its effects upon those whom it reached, the mission was strictly limited to the chosen people. Israel alone was to enjoy this Messianic time of refreshing. No Gentile or Samaritan was to share it. It is characteristic of St. Matthew that this prohibition is mentioned solely by himself. And when our Lord had gone beyond the boundary of Galilee 'into the region of Tyre and Sidon,' St. Matthew omits the statement of St. Mark that 'He entered into a house.'[1] The healing of the Syro-Phoenician woman is regarded as a separate, exceptional event, not as something in the day's work.

Much has been made of this prohibition by those who try to limit the scope and range of our Lord's intentions. They say that He never contemplated the universal spread of His Kingdom; that nothing was further from His mind than the founding of the Catholic Church; that His objects were purely national and local and that, a Jew by birth, He remained one in feeling and thought; that to credit Him with wider views is to transfer to Him the ambitions and projects of a later time, for the earlier sources know nothing of plans extending beyond the boundaries of Israel.

It may be freely admitted that Christ's marching orders for the Apostles, on this their first missionary expedition, are strictly limited, and that the account in St. Matthew of His dealings with the Syro-Phoenician woman show the same limitation. St. Matthew alone puts into His mouth the very strong saying, 'I am not sent but unto the lost sheep of the house of Israel.' His source for the narrative—St. Mark—does not contain it. But there it stands, and there is nothing to show that it is not genuine.

Is there nothing to modify this exclusiveness? Is there no sign that the limitation is temporary, as belonging rather to the method than to the substance of Christ's propaganda? It may be replied that His own action in the healing of the child of the Syro-Phoenician is evidence that His grace could and did overflow the narrower limits of the Apostles' first commission; and we cannot leave out of calculation His dealings with the woman of Sychar and the result of His acceptance of the invitation to stay in the city.[2]

There were many reasons for restricting the first proclamation

[1] Cf. W. C. Allen, *St. Matthew, ad loc.*

[2] Jo. iv. 40-43.

of the Gospel to the Jews. 'Our Lord' Himself 'sprang out of Juda.'[1] It was not another religion that He came to found. Taking everything that was pure and true under the old Covenant, He developed and deepened and extended it. It was vital to His method that His own people, who had for so many centuries been the guardians of the Divine Revelation,[2] should receive the first presentation of the Gospel. And in this task the small band of His first adherents would find full scope for their powers.

But, that our Lord contemplated no wider flinging of the Gospel net is contradicted not only by His attitude to seekers after truth and suppliants of His grace from beyond the borders of the favoured race, but by His own express language. After the Gentile centurion had astonished Him by the intensity of his faith, Christ said to those who followed Him, 'Many shall come from the east and west and shall sit down with Abraham and Isaac and Jacob in the kingdom of heaven.'[3] Nothing less than the extension of the privileges of citizenship of the Kingdom to humanity as a whole could correspond with the plenary powers bestowed at His Resurrection on the Son of Man. No narrower a commission than the evangelization of all nations does the risen Saviour, on the eve of His Ascension, lay upon the disciples assembled on the mountain in Galilee.[4]

We have then His own action (at first no doubt exceptional) and His own express words, to assure us that our Lord's vision of the Kingdom travelled far beyond the boundaries set by Judaism. The great saying of St. John gives adequate expression to the fact: 'God so loved the world that He gave His only begotten Son, that whosoever believeth in Him should not perish, but have everlasting life.'[5]

Our Lord's instructions to the Twelve fall under two divisions: their manner of life and their work. The effect of their mission could easily be marred by inconsistency of living. They are to

[1] Hebr. vii. 14.

[2] Cf. Rom. ix. 4, 5; iii. 2.

[3] Matt. viii. 10, 11. Cf. Jo. xvii. 20. *v.* Hort, *The Christian Ecclesia*, p. 31.

[4] Matt. xxviii. 18, 19. 'The extension of the range of the apostolic mission takes place between the Resurrection and the Ascension.' Hort, *The Christian Ecclesia*, p. 36.

[5] Jo. iii. 16. 'Universality is a characteristic of the new apostolic mission.' *Ib.* p. 37.

go forth two by two. It was not good to be alone. In their conflict with the forces of evil, loneliness, while leaving the heart more open to subtle spiritual temptations, might also expose it to despair. Whereas, one might comfort and strengthen the other, and the consciousness of the presence of a witness would be a wholesome check.

They are to go forth as pilgrims, staff in hand, sandals on their feet, only wearing the barest necessary clothing. They are to take no money, no wallet for provisions, but to cast themselves on the hospitality which is unfailing in an eastern country, and on which, like any other honest travellers, they could live without care from day to day and place to place. Refusal of hospitality and neglect of their message would bode ill for the people among whom they went; and they are to signify their condemnation by shaking off the dust of their feet as they leave the city. They are to remain in the same house during their sojourn in a town. Their life is to be simple. Everything is to proclaim their mission. 'The King's business required haste.'[1] They are not to become dependent on bodily comfort.

Then, as to the work entrusted to them. Great stress is laid on the casting out of evil spirits. The coming of the Messiah marked a fresh stage in the age-long strife with evil. Our Lord's consciousness of this is clearly revealed. In His temptation He first finds Himself actually confronted by Satan and, though victorious in the encounter and unharmed in heart and conscience by it, He is aware that the Devil has only departed from Him for a season. When the time has come for the proclamation of the Kingdom, a definite onslaught upon Satan's possession of individual men at once forms a chief feature of the work. Again, when the Seventy have been sent forth and came back to Christ to report their success, 'He said unto them, I beheld Satan as lightning fall from heaven.'[2] The whole subject is wrapped in

[1] 1 Sam. xxi. 8. With our Lord's injunctions to the Apostles it is interesting to compare the rules laid down in the Didache for 'apostles and prophets' in their journeyings. An 'apostle' if he stay more than two days in the same place is a false prophet, and if he ask for money he is false (xi.).

[2] Lk. x. 17, 18. Our Lord says that He beheld the fall of Satan. He means, we may suppose, the fall which followed upon Satan's rebellion against God, and therefore far back in His own pre-existent state. Or, the expression may merely denote a symbolical view of the discomfiture of the Prince of Evil by the triumphant march of the Gospel. Cf. Is. xiv. 12; Rev. xii. 7-10. *v.* Trench, *Miracles*, p. 174; J. Weiss, *Die Predigt vom Reiche Gottes*, p. 92.

mystery. But that both our Lord and His first disciples encountered the powers of spiritual evil is a fact which is woven into the substance of the Gospel narrative; and there have not been wanting, in succeeding ages of the Church's history, indications that the conflict is still proceeding, and that the Christian has still to 'wrestle not against flesh and blood but against principalities, against powers . . . against the spiritual hosts of wickedness in the heavenly places.' [1]

Christ Himself is the stronger than the 'strong man armed' of the parable and, as He says to the Seventy on their return, He gives them 'power . . . over all the power of the enemy.' The fall of Satan from heaven is the loss of lordship. It was a double fall, far back in time from a position of eminence among his brother-spirits in God's presence and, again, when the influence of the Incarnation began to make itself felt at the proclamation of the Kingdom. It has been insisted that the expression θεωρεῖν in St. Luke x. 18 implies that Christ received an actual Divine revelation at some definite time, which brought Him the certainty that the power of Satan had passed and that the Kingdom of God had dawned upon the world.[2]

The healing of the sick is another charge laid upon the Twelve. The Gospel of the Kingdom is directed to the well-being of the whole man—body as well as soul. 'Heal the sick, cleanse the lepers.' So ran their Lord's commission. Accordingly we read that 'they anointed with oil many that were sick and healed them.'[3] In this they were carrying out their Master's practice: but, employing a symbolical rite in their work of healing, which He only resorted to on occasion, and then in a different form.[4] A Gospel, which took no account of the sufferings and infirmities of the body, would have had little power to heal the

[1] Eph. vi. 12. If Eastern legendary material is appealed to in explanation of these representations, we may admit that it may have contributed to their form, but it does not account for their substance. Their presence in the New Testament is due to experience. The knowledge of floating superstitions would never explain the conviction of actual contact with the forces of spiritual evil, which possessed the mind of Christ and played so large a part in the spiritual experience of a man like St. Paul.

[2] J. Weiss, *Die Predigt vom Reiche Gottes*, p. 93. Cf. Jo. xii. 29; 1 Jo. iii. 8.

[3] Matt. x. 8; Mk. vi. 13.

[4] Jo. ix. 6. We see traces of the continued use of unction of the sick in James v. 14.

sickness of the soul; while the close connection of pain and sickness with sin—though, as our Lord once pointed out, not necessarily to be imputed in every individual case[1]—made every act of healing a sign of what the Gospel could do for the soul.

St. Matthew alone, from his separate source, includes the raising of the dead in our Lord's charge to the Twelve. It is difficult to imagine that this power was actually exercised by the Apostles during the time of our Lord's Ministry. There is no reason to doubt that He gave the charge[2] and, if He gave it, we may be sure that power to fulfil it was conferred. But there is no record that any raising of the dead took place through the instrumentality of the Twelve. As with our Lord on more than one occasion,[3] the use of the power may have been checked by unbelief on the part of those to whom the dead belonged. Or, it may have happened that, during the short time that their mission lasted, no case of death was encountered which seemed to call for interposition. There is also the possibility that the writer, in accordance with his frequent custom, has brought together words which were spoken on different occasions. The charge to raise the dead, if given after the Resurrection, would seem to be better placed. 'Greater works than these shall ye do, because I go to the Father,' said our Lord; and the history of the Apostolic Church, in Acts, records the fulfilment of the promise. We also note that St. Mark has no mention of raising the dead in his report of the way in which the Apostles carried out our Lord's charge; an almost certain proof that none took place.[4]

To quicken their zeal in the use of the powers conferred upon them, Christ reminds His messengers of the obligation to impart to others what had been His gift to them. It was not for themselves, for their own glorification or advantage. They were but channels of His grace, through which without let or hindrance, if they were faithful, the healing and converting gifts would

[1] Jo. ix. 1-4.

[2] The MS. authority is ample. 'It is only with later copyists that a quite intelligible hesitation to insert the expression comes in.' H. Holtzmann, *Die Synoptiker*, p. 232.

[3] Mk. vi. 5; Matt. xiii. 58.

[4] Mk. vi. 12, 13. If their casting out of devils is named, still more would the raising of the dead—if it had occurred.

pass to all who needed them. 'Freely ye have received, freely give.'[1]

And if He lays upon them this obligation to make His cause their own, He assures them of His sanction, and promises that He will consider their reception as His own and that every act of kindness done to them—though but the gift of a cup of cold water—will have its reward.[2]

Rejection of His messengers will be visited by the Saviour with the sternest condemnation. The Twelve are to mark it at the moment with a truly oriental sign of reprobation, 'as a testimony against them.' This token of condemnation will be upheld in the day of Judgment. The sin of Sodom and Gomorrha was not so great as the sin of those who reject the apostolic messengers of the Saviour of the world. He speaks as Judge. It is He who thus apportions their guilt.[3]

The First Evangelist, according to his custom, has grouped together, under the dismissal of the Twelve on their first missionary journey, sayings which clearly bear upon a later stage of the proclamation of the Kingdom. The whole discourse from x. 16-40 is prophetic of times of persecution, such as that which saw the murder of St. James the son

[1] Matt. x. 8.

[2] Matt. x. 40, 42. Verse 42 seems to be a reflection or comment, not like *v.* 40 a direct address to the Twelve on their mission; but 'one of these little ones' refers to the same men to whom *v.* 40 is addressed. It is of the nature of a soliloquy overheard by the writer of 'Q' or of one of St. Matthew's other sources. There is no need to regard it as a confused recollection, by the writer of the First Gospel, of Mk. ix. 41, 42. We have no ground for imputing such carelessness to him, writing as he did, with our St. Mark before him.

[3] It is difficult to avoid the conclusion that here too the Evangelist is grouping together sayings which belong to a different connection. The sin of those who rejected the Apostles on their first mission is said to be more grievous than that for which Sodom and Gomorrha will have to give account at the day of judgment. Our difficulty would be lessened if we could regard these words as spoken by our Lord in reference to the post-Resurrection missionary work of His Apostles. The sin of rejection then would have less excuse, and the terrible words would be more fully justified. As they stand, in their present connection, they appear exaggerated. What a judgment for people who declined to see, in the ministry of these (as yet) untrained and simple Galilean peasants going about in pairs with the Name of their Master on their lips, messengers directly sent by God! After the Resurrection, with its astounding confirmation of the Messianic claim and work of Jesus, rejection was a much more serious thing. The words seem to belong to a stratum of teaching just before or after the Passion and Resurrection.

of Zebedee, of St. James the Just, or that of St. Peter and St. Paul.

On their return the Apostles reported their doings and their teaching to their Master. He called them to come apart in an uninhabited spot for rest, 'for there were many coming and going and they had no leisure so much as to eat.'[1] It was during such times of retirement that the Apostolic band received the teaching which, when brought home to them by the Holy Spirit, was to be their guide and support, when they came to preach Jesus and the Resurrection throughout the Graeco-Roman world. Along with the teaching went the personal influence that radiated from their Master. His mere presence was silently producing that effect upon their character to which men bore witness when 'they took knowledge of them that they had been with Jesus.' It was this discipleship that made, of fishermen and peasants, the men who were to revolutionize the world.[2]

[1] Mk. vi. 30, 31 ; Lk. ix. 10. [2] Acts. xvii. 6.

CHAPTER XIX

THE DEATH OF CHRIST

Every great event in the history of the world may be regarded, and is regarded, from very different points of view. As seen by one, it will appear to be full of benefit. Another will look upon it as a failure and a mistake. It takes time for judgments to ripen. Nothing can be seen in its true bearings at the moment. The process of time brings strange reversals. The trifling and insignificant gathers a seriousness of which no one dreamed. The conspicuous and imposing falls back into the obscurity to which it properly belongs. It is only here and there that men are found who have the gift of vision and see the worth of things at once. Two men possessed this gift on the day of the Crucifixion; the dying thief, who turned to Christ with the prayer, 'Lord remember me, when Thou comest into Thy Kingdom'; the centurion who said, 'Truly this Man was a Son of God.' To them, if to no one else, it was given that day to see, not the significance—that could only emerge to view in the course of time—but the majesty of the Sufferer, an indication that here was a Being of a higher order, and that this death of shame meant more than it appeared.

No event in history is more surely grounded than the death of Christ. We cannot conceive that it would have been taken up, as it has been, into the belief of Christendom, if the fact did not imperiously require it. What a task for the first preachers of the new religion—to commend to the belief and adoration of the Graeco-Roman world the Person of One Who had suffered death by crucifixion in the company of malefactors! Yet this is what they did, and that because the stern facts of the case obliged them. Could any presentation of a truth be more inauspiciously introduced? Their own traditional feeling that 'cursed is he that hangeth on a tree'; the contempt of cultivated hearers in the cities of the Empire for One who had been condemned to a death from which every ordinary freed man was exempt [1]—this double hindrance to the success of their message would have made them pause if they dared. But they could not. The thing was true. The death of Christ is fact and all we know of human thought and feeling goes to certify it. It is the last message they would have wished to carry to the world they wanted to convert, if they had had the framing of their Gospel. That this *was* the Gospel which they preached—Christ crucified—is one irresistible testimony to its historical truth.[2]

We get some idea of the weight which they assigned to the death of Christ from the space which it and its attendant circumstances take up in the Gospels. That consideration alone disposes of the theory which exalts the ethical teaching of Christ at the expense of His redeeming work. Why this minute and circumstantial description of the few last hours, when months and years of life itself pass with but meagre record in the narratives? Is it not because in those few hours the crowning work of the Ministry, the purpose of the Incarnate life was achieved? *The* work of His life was His death and what followed upon that death.

No doubt it may be said that the disproportionate amount of space appropriated to the Passion, as compared with the Ministry, is a reflex of the theology of the primitive community, and that we must not bring in the after-thought of the Church to fix the relative values of His life and of His death as they appeared to Christ Himself. It is maintained that in the Synoptic Gospels little importance is attached by Christ to His death. The thought that it would in any sense be an atonement for the sins of others stands outside the mind of Christ, and is quite foreign to His ideas. So far from His death being a chief part of the object of His entrance into the world, it only came upon Him as a surprise, as the penalty exacted by His bold freedom of speech and by His attitude to the hierarchy. It was an accident

[1] Cf. J. Weiss, *Jesus im Glauben des Urchristentums*, p. 10.

[2] I find that J. Weiss strongly emphasizes this view in *D. Urchristentum*, 1914, i. p. 76.

and not of the *esse* of His work. He bowed His head to it when it came, but it formed no part of His purpose for the world. It was on a line with the martyrdom of all, who have rebuked their generation and been rewarded as the world rewards those who condemn it; but like theirs, this too was an individual act, confined in its operation, except so far as its example might stimulate and incite to what is good and true. The thought of a redemption purchased for others is thus an addition to the mind of Christ as we study it in the earliest sources. He was not conscious that His death would work that change in the fortunes of mankind which is attributed to it by St. Paul and has become incorporated in the theology of the Catholic Church. The Gospel, in its simple form, is an announcement of the love of God as experienced and taught by Christ. It was a complete change, a distinct and all-important development when Christ, instead of being the highest exponent of faith in God, became the object of faith. This change, it is asserted, took place in the very beginning of the Gospel age, and the chief instrument to effect it was the religious experience and the preaching of St. Paul.[1] Through him the idea of Redemption effected by the Death and Resurrection of Christ became a system, which superseded the primitive Gospel of the Fatherly love of God for sinful men as proclaimed by Christ. An essential part of this theory is the contention that the idea of assuming the rôle of Redeemer of mankind was quite foreign to the mind of our Lord; our two earliest sources—the fabric of St. Mark and the Logia element of the First and Third Gospels—knowing nothing of it.

We must, therefore, inquire what was Christ's own view of His death and its results. Did He regard it as a supreme object of His coming into the world? How did He estimate its effect on the salvation of man?[2] When we have arrived at some idea of the mind of our Lord Himself, we have to consider how the primitive community understood the significance of His death.

It is impossible to determine at what point in Christ's life the

[1] Cf. Bousset, *Das Wesen der Religion*, pp. 180, 181 (Volksausgabe); Wrede, *Paulus*, pp. 94, 104.

[2] 'In the modern conception of the essence of Christianity, we miss satisfying investigations of the way in which Jesus has expressed Himself about His death and how He has understood the destiny of death which was determined for Him.' Feine, *Theologie des N.T.*[1] p. 121.

consciousness that He was to suffer and die first awoke in Him. We have to bear in mind that, as a student of Scripture, He must have reflected upon prophecies and intimations of an atonement for sin.[1] When did He come to the conviction that they met in Himself? Whether or not we accept the account of the words which the Fourth Gospel puts into the mouth of the Baptist, 'Behold the Lamb of God which taketh away the sin of the world,' we must admit that the Evangelist would not have attributed to him so significant an utterance so early in our Lord's public life, if the thought of redemption had never entered into His mind. The Fourth Gospel is the work of one who knew His mind as no one else had known it. He would not have commenced his Gospel with such a statement, if the idea of redemption had long remained foreign to Christ's thought.

Then, again, in the Baptism there was involved an allusion to sin[2] which, taken in conjunction with the expression of His Father's approval and acknowledgment, can only be understood as pointing to the Saviour as Redeemer. It was not for sin of His own that He was baptized. It was for some connection between Himself and the sins of men. This connection is only to be explained in terms of atonement. The consciousness of it led Christ to seek Baptism of the Baptist. It was the formal act of His identification with sinful humanity. In a sense, 'He was made sin for us, He who knew no sin,' when He stepped into the stream and the baptismal waters closed round

[1] There were two books to which He had access, and each of them spoke of death. One was the heart of man which lay open to Him day by day and in which He could read the signs of the hostility which was to result in His own condemnation. The conflict between the Divine and the human, between the kingdom of heaven and the world, between righteousness and sin, would be called out in its most intense form; and we can trace something of the progress of His increasing realization of these conditions. 'He is grieved,' 'astonished,' at people's hardness of heart. At times He withdraws from a rising conflict, careful not to embitter unnecessarily and before the hour came, the feeling against Him. Thus, from His complete knowledge of human nature and from His own experience of what was in man, He saw a probability that death would result.

But He was also learned in the Scriptures. He knew the fate of faithful prophets. Would *He* escape? The parable of the Husbandmen shows unmistakably His mind on the subject (Matt. xxi. 33 ff.).

[2] 'It is among the most assured facts of Gospel history that the baptism of John was a baptism for sinners.' Feine, *Theologie des N.T.* p. 121. Cf. *ib.* p. 89.

His sinless body. We cannot help coming to the conviction that already at the entrance upon His ministerial life He had dim forebodings of what the doing of His Father's will would mean to Him.[1]

At times, during the course of His Ministry, our Lord hints at a violent end which will one day come to it. He is speaking of the joyful time which the Bridegroom shares with his friends. It is not a time for fasting, and He defends His disciples from the reproaches of those who compared their conduct with what seemed to be the more edifying practice of the disciples of the Baptist. 'But,' He adds, 'the days will come when the bridegroom shall be taken from them and then shall they fast.'[2]

Once, after the Baptist's violent death, our Lord refers to it, and it is to draw a conclusion respecting Himself: 'Likewise shall also the Son of Man suffer of them.'[3] There is certainly at least a hint that the death is in His thoughts when He exclaims, 'I have a baptism to be baptized with; and how am I straitened till it be accomplished!'[4]

The first time recorded in the Gospels that our Lord distinctly spoke of His approaching death (and Resurrection) was at Caesarea Philippi after St. Peter's confession St. Mark expressly states that 'He began to teach them that the Son of Man must suffer many things . . . and be killed and after three days rise again.' But He attaches no special significance to His death at this time. Not until the end is almost in sight does He connect His death with redemption. The saying arose out of an incident related by two of the Synoptic writers—the request by the sons of Zebedee (or by their mother) for the places of honour in the coming Kingdom. Our Lord rebukes this spirit of ambition. It was of the world and had nothing in common with the methods of the Kingdom. It was not His own line of action, 'For even the Son of Man came not to be ministered unto, but to minister and to give His life a ransom for many.' Much depends on the

[1] *v.* Du Bose, *The Gospel in the Gospels*, p. 119.

[2] Matt. ix. 15. ἀπαρθῇ. 'By saying "be taken away," rather than "go away," He points for the first time to His violent death.' Plummer, *St. Matthew, in loc.*

[3] Matt. xvii. 12.

[4] Lk. xii. 50. Cf. Matt. xx. 22; Mk. x. 38, where our Lord uses together with the figure of baptism that of the drinking of a cup, in the same kind of allusion to His coming sufferings.

sense in which this 'ransom' (λύτρον) is understood. It is natural to see in it a reference to His death as a free-will (*to give*) offering up of the one life for the salvation of the many.[1] We have the same idea of the voluntary yielding up of His life in the sayings preserved in the Fourth Gospel, 'I lay down my life for the sheep,' 'I lay down my life that I might take it again. No man taketh it from me, but I lay it down of Myself.'[2] It is impossible to separate from these sayings of our Lord the thought of a vicarious sacrifice—an oblation of His own life for the life of others, an experience of suffering on His part for the deliverance of the many.[3]

But it is just this vicarious nature of the Atonement which to some has seemed foreign to our ideas of justice. No doubt the question is surrounded with difficulty. It leads us straight to theories which will never again be entertained by the thoughtful mind.[4] It seems to imply that God is only longing to strike some one, but careless as to who it may be. It appears to render nugatory and inoperative the law which runs through creation—the following of consequences upon acts; and thus to deal a blow at the morality of the Divine government. Without doubt, it has often been so stated as to sap the very foundation of our belief in the righteousness of God.

But the natural reaction to these perverted statements of the truth has gone too far, and has in turn lost sight of general principles of Divine government that are as well established as those with which the other view conflicted.

[1] Mk. x. 45; Matt. xx. 28. *v.* Feine, *Theol. des N.T.* p. 133. 'Following the analogy of the O.T. meaning, it is a price for which the many are liberated, a substitute which is provided for the many, that is spoken of.' It is remarkable that so Pauline an idea as that of redemption, as contained in these passages of the First and Second Gospels, is not found in St. Luke. From the absence of the saying in his Gospel, may we not argue to the genuineness of it as it stands in the Mk.-Matt. passage? At any rate, it is not there from Pauline influence—otherwise St. Luke would probably have had it. It belongs to the original Petrine stratum of St. Mark, and contains a recollection of Christ's own teaching.

[2] Jo. x. 15, 17, 18.

[3] 'The paradoxical expression, "He hath made Him to be sin for us, Who knew no sin," is only to be explained if, since real, ethical conversion of a sinless being into a sinner is unthinkable, substitution and imputation are being spoken of.' Holtzmann, *Neutest. Theologie*, ii. p. 118.

[4] Cf. Loofs, *What is the Truth about Jesus Christ?* p. 211.

All through nature the vicarial, redemptive, mediatorial principle is found at work. The child enters life at the cost of the pain and sometimes of the death of the mother. The death, or rather the dissolution, of the seed is needed for the liberation of the vital germ. The weak can only live by the self-sacrifice of the strong. Over and over again the guilty and sinful have been succoured by the self-surrender of the pure. Redemption is purchased at the cost of pain and the pain is suffered by the voluntary act of the redeemer. Knowledge is bought by sacrifice. To declaim against the vicarious aspect of Redemption is to repudiate a principle which runs through all life, and has called forth deeds of heroism and acts of unselfish service that have lit up the dim pathways of human history. Those, who are so anxious that the claims of justice should be safe-guarded, need to be reminded that the reconciliation of abstract justice with the supposed infringements caused by the action of a self-sacrificing love is a task which we are not capable of fulfilling. It may be that in another stage of existence it will be seen that there has never been anything to reconcile; and that God, Who is at the same time just and loving, has guarded against the breach of either principle—that, in short, His justice is always loving, and His love is always just.

We get further light on our Lord's own view of His approaching death from St. John's account of His interview with the Greeks who were introduced to His presence by Philip, at Jerusalem during the week of the Passion. 'I, if I be lifted up from the earth, will draw all men unto Me.' Thus does He foretell the effect of His crucifixion. It will have a constraining influence upon men. They will come and look and take their sides for, or against, Him. It is impossible to be wholly indifferent. We gather from this saying that the death of Christ is, in His own belief, a matter which profoundly affects all mankind. Even when they do not consciously respond to its appeal, it somehow touches them. It is an element in their spiritual history, though at the time they are not aware of its full significance.

A few days later, at the table of the Last Supper, the redemptive aspect of His death is again present to our Saviour's mind. It appears in the words, 'Take, eat, this is My Body which is given for you: this is My blood of the new testament, which is shed for many for the remission of sins.' [1] Here He is contemplating the effect of His death upon His people. His action in the breaking of the bread and the pouring out of the wine is symbolic. Each separate act portrays a moment in the sacrifice of the Cross. The breaking of the bread points to the parting asunder of soul and body; the outpoured wine to the effusion of the precious blood. St. Matthew alone records the object—'for the remission of sins.' From the action and the words attributed to Him, we see that our Lord's mind is running on the significance of His death. It will be for His people: for the remission of their sins. It will establish a new covenant with them. Thus 'the words spoken at the Last Supper stand in close connection with St. Mark x. 45.' [2]

When we pass in thought with our Lord from the Upper Room to Gethsemane, we are still under the shadow of His approaching death. He had already spoken of the baptism with which He was to be baptized and of the cup of which He must drink and, as if in foreboding of this hour, He had exclaimed, 'How am I straitened till it be accomplished.' [3] The natural Man in Him shrinks from the death which is now staring Him in the face. Hence the bitter cry, 'Father, if it be possible, let this cup pass from Me.' It is not merely a shrinking from the extremity of physical pain; although that must have been very real, when we think of the perfection of His sensitive and highly-strung organism. There is something deeper. He knew that, in some way, the sin of the world—its sinfulness and its actual sins—was to be so laid upon Him that, at the moment of death, He would be—though pure and innocent in His own Person—identified with it. 'He made Him to be sin for us.' It was from this contact with sin, in its reality, that He so shrank back as to pray that so bitter a cup might not have to be tasted; but with the agonized prayer yet upon His lips, the whole purpose of His coming into the world to do His Father's will rises in an instant before Him and He leaves the matter in the Father's hands. 'Not as I will, but as Thou wilt.' The cup which His Father had given Him, should He not drink it? Henceforward

[1] A conspectus of the words of institution according to the Synoptic Gospels and St. Paul (1 Cor. xi.) is given in Hastings' *Dict. of Christ.* ii. p. 67.

[2] Feine, *Theol. des N.T.* p. 143.

[3] Lk. xii. 50; cf. Matt. xx. 22; Mk. x. 38.

the struggle is over. All that is human within Him, after rising against what seemed its destruction, yields to the higher claim of the spiritual purpose. And He never looked back. The victory was already won.

Before we proceed, we must ask, Was the consciousness of Christ that He was to suffer for the sins of men reflected in the minds of His disciples ? The Gospels are conclusive in answering this question in the negative. As Jews, the first disciples had no conception of such a thing.[1] 'The notion of a "suffering Messiah" belongs exclusively to a late period.'[2] It is true that the servant of Jehovah in Isaiah, if identified at times with the people as a whole,[3] is elsewhere referred to an individual,[4] and that He is spoken of as vicariously bearing the sins of many. But this view was not adopted by the people generally. We see no trace of it in Jewish thought at the time of the rise of

[1] 'It is something incomprehensible to the Jews that the "King-Messiah" would die the death of a slave upon the Cross.' J. Weiss, *D. Urchristentum*, i. p. 80. Cf. 1 Cor. i. 23.

[2] Westcott, *Introduction to the Study of the Gospels*, p. 141, n. 6. Cf. Stanton, *The Jewish and the Christian Messiah*, p. 123, 'The idea of the Messiah's sufferings is not found in any Jewish document up to the close of the first century.' G. A. Smith sees in Is. liii. distinct allusion to an individual. Hastings' *D.B.* ii. p. 496. Who can this individual be but Messiah ? Stanton appears to modify his previous view, and admits that in the O.T. there are 'foreshadowings even of one pre-eminent vicarious sufferer.' On Messianic interpretation of Is. liii. and Hos. vi. 1, 2, *v.* J. Weiss, *D. Urchristentum*, i. p. 78. Weiss thinks that the proof-material, in the comparative scarcity of actual Old Testament references, was drawn from stores of private tradition which have not come down to us. This is hardly likely. Some traces of such a tradition would have survived. In apocalyptic writings which we possess, the only reference to the death of Messiah is in 4 Ezra vii. 29, 'And it shall be, after these years that My Son the Messiah shall die and all in whom there is human breath.' He will die after a reign of 400 years. 2 Baruch xl. 3, also implies that the Messianic kingdom will come to an end. *v.* Box in Charles, *Apocrypha and Pseudepigrapha of the O.T.* ii. p. 582. As Weiss remarks, the passage in 4 Ezra represents the Messiah as dying *after* fulfilling His Messianic task ; but 'that the Messiah will die at the beginning of His work and that His death will be a chief means of carrying out His work is nowhere declared.' *Ib.* p. 80. Cf. Schürer, *Geschichte des Jüd. Volkes*, ii. p. 554.

It is impossible to determine whether the widespread legend of the dying and rising God (Adonis, Tammuz, etc.) helped the primitive community to enter into the mystery of the crucified Messiah. J. Weiss considers it highly improbable ; but, as he goes on to say, the later Gentile converts may have been to some extent prepared by such a legend for the message of the Cross. *D. Urchristentum*, i. p. 81.

[3] Is. xli. 8 f.

[4] Is. xlii. 1-5 ; l. 4-10 ; lii. 13–liii. fin.

Christianity. Our Lord on the walk to Emmaus rebukes 'the slowness of heart' of His disciples to believe all that prophets have spoken. Nothing is more certain than the entire absence of any idea of a suffering Christ. St. Peter's bold chiding of the Saviour at Caesarea Philippi, following upon his confession, is in itself sufficient proof that the Christ Whom he had just acknowledged and the idea of suffering which our Lord had just given expression to were wholly incompatible in the eyes of Jews of that time. Yet our Lord says, 'Ought not Christ to have suffered these things?' Was there not in the preparation for Him, which in history and in prophecy had been going on through the ages, a *necessity*—not physical but moral and spiritual—that the Christ should suffer? In His own mind the thought had long been a fixed point. He is astounded that it was hidden from His disciples, notwithstanding its recurrence in the Old Testament and His own allusions to it. But in the strength of His rebuke, we have a complete assurance that the whole idea of a suffering Christ had been foreign to the thought of the disciples. They had gone with the rest of their countrymen in their apprehension of the political and triumphant aspect of the Messiah. They had made no response to His own warnings and hints of suffering. The idea was abhorrent to them. How could a suffering Messiah deliver a suffering people? Only in the light of events were they able to see the necessity of which our Lord speaks at Emmaus. Then the primitive community began to compare the facts with the Old Testament foreshadowings and to read the prophecies in a new sense; while St. Matthew makes diligent search for correspondences and analogies between the closing scenes in the Saviour's life and the language of prophecy, going so far as to say that such and such an event took place in order that the prophecy might be fulfilled.[1]

On the day of Pentecost, St. Peter preaches Christ crucified, and so far was the conception from hindering the effect of his message that, by the power of the Holy Spirit, three thousand people received the truth of a suffering Messiah and were added to the Church. So we find St. Paul borrowing almost the very

[1] *E.g.* Matt. xxvi. 56; xxvii. 35. Cf. xxvii. 9, 'Then was fulfilled that which was spoken by Jeremy the Prophet.' J. Weiss comments on this characteristic of St. Matthew: 'How much richer and more detailed (than in Mark) the proof has become!' *D. Urchristentum*, i. p. 81.

phraseology of our Lord at Emmaus, and 'opening and alleging that Christ must needs have suffered and risen again from the dead.'[1] As we gather from his Epistles, the Cross became the centre and pivot of his Gospel.[2]

The atoning death, with the Resurrection as its completion and explanation, formed the groundwork of the early Apostolic faith. There is no question that they were the elements of the primitive creed.[3]

Who shall say in what resided the necessity of Christ's atoning death as declared by Himself and as preached by His Apostles? The fact belongs to the eternal order. It was seen through the inspiration of the Spirit here and there during the course of prophecy; but not until it had taken place and its significance had been brought out by the operation of the same Spirit, was it grasped and realized.

It should be borne in mind that nowhere in the Bible do we find anything in the nature of a complete theory of the subject. All that we get are separate flashes of light which bring into view now one and now another aspect. But there is no attempt to combine these rays into one consistent and illuminating gleam. We know that sin is contradictory to the very being of God and that, if not checked and counteracted, it would hinder and effectually thwart His loving purposes for man. So hateful is it to Him, that His face was turned from His Son at the very moment when He was exhibiting the supreme act of obedience to the Father's will, because it required such an identification of the sin and the Sin Bearer that practically, though not ethically, the two were as one. 'He made Him to be sin.' We know, too, that this identification of the Saviour with the sin of humanity was possible because His Incarnation made Him not man only, but representative man, summing up in Himself the life and fortunes of every child of Adam. In taking whatever belonged to the propriety of human nature upon Himself, He took also

[1] Acts xvii. 3, ὅτι τὸν Χριστὸν ἔδει παθεῖν. Lk. xxiv. 26, οὐχὶ ταῦτα ἔδει παθεῖν τὸν Χριστόν. St. Paul may have derived the terms through St. Luke from the record employed afterwards by the Evangelist in the composition of his Gospel.

[2] H. Holtzmann, *Neutest. Theol.* ii. p. 120, quoting 1 Cor. i. 18; Rom. v. 10, etc., says, 'Accordingly the foundation of salvation is concentrated exclusively on the moment of death.' 'Only because and so far as He goes to death, does He pay the tribute of sin.' *Ib.* p. 121.

[3] Cf. Harnack, *Das Wesen des Christentums*, p. 98.

that in which man had become involved, but which was no proper part of him, his sin ; that which had come in upon him and had so tainted his nature as to become a part of it. 'In all things it behoved Him to be made like unto His brethren.' If He identified Himself with all that is good in man, He did not shrink from identifying Himself with what was evil. Only thus, so far as we can see, could He, from the depths of human sin and need, offer in and for human nature an acceptable offering—in His own words, a 'ransom.' This fusing of His own nature with ours involved the sharing of every experience of man except actual sin. That He could not share. It would have vitiated and negatived His oblation. What was required was an offering by sinful humanity which should yet itself be unstained, untouched by sin. And the sinless sufferer on the Cross, Who at the moment by deliberate act of His will identified Himself with sinful humanity, answered the requirement in His own Person. Sinless He was sin-laden, for 'the Lord hath laid on Him the iniquity of us all.'

But this offering by man to God, made in the Person of the Son of Man, did not mean that we are thereby exempted from making our own offering. Christ did not suffer vicariously in that sense. The vicariousness of His offering consisted in that which was beyond our power to render—in the purity, in the value, as of Himself who is above all price, in the representative character of the oblation. But besides those elements in it, which He alone—as the sinless Son of God—was able to offer, there is a whole world of sacrifice and penitence that the sinner, who claims his share and place in it, can present to God ; not as satisfaction—that is impossible to the sinful—but as the expression of concurrence in heart and will with the One perfect offering. It is in this sense that St. Paul speaks of filling up that which is lacking of the afflictions of Christ,[1] implying that there is room for the oblations of His people and that in a very true way they are united with Himself in the sacrifice which reached its culmination on the Cross. If this aspect of the subject is kept in mind, the morality of the Atonement is preserved. The suffering of the Sinless for the sinful is not the whole truth.

[1] Col. i. 24 (R.V.). Cf. *Letters of T. Erskine of Linlathen*, p. 220, 'Christ's sacrifice cannot be unlike anything else in the world—it is the very type of what must be done by the Spirit of Christ in every human being.'

The sinful as penitent suffer too and, in their penitence, join in the oblation.

If we ask, To whom was the sacrifice of the Cross presented? there is at least one answer. Certainly not to any abstract conception of righteousness, or to satisfy the justice of God as a separate element in His character, as a quality with which love and mercy could be in conflict. We may not thus divide the character of God, as though it consisted of elements so various and so much opposed to one another that they might be viewed as contending for the mastery. God is not divided. His love and His justice are never pitted against one another. His righteousness is His love discerning and acting accordingly. His love, if it is the one all-embracing quality which constitutes His being, is never weak. In face of sin, it is unbending in its justice. It always makes for the highest good of man, and therefore it can never tolerate sin, which is his destruction. It is more true to say that the Atonement was devised by love and presented to love. It was never meant to work a change in the mind of God.[1] God always loves and always, because He loves, hates evil. This hatred appeared in the death of Christ. The Cross was the occasion of the Divine sentence upon sin: 'God, sending His own Son in the likeness of sinful flesh and for sin, condemned sin in the flesh.'[2] While the death of Christ was the supreme manifestation of the power of sin, it revealed God's judgment upon sin. Sin stood condemned. Its sacrilege and its presumption were exposed. The hour of the triumph of sin and of the power of darkness was the hour of its defeat. The death of Christ was its destruction. He conquered sin and death by dying.

It is perhaps true to say that the efficacy of the Atonement lies not in the death itself but in that of which the death was the proof and manifestation—the full surrender, the complete obedience to the will of God, the sinless character of the Life offered. Self was crucified. All the oblation culminated in the death. It could go no farther. That was the supreme goal.

[1] Cf. Du Bose, *The Gospel according to St. Paul*, p. 293, 'Here and always God and Christ are so united and identified in the common act of divine reconciliation and human redemption that the act of each is the act of the other.' *v.* above, p. 303.

[2] Rom. viii. 3.

Thus the death came to be regarded as the central point of the sacrifice; whereas it was rather the sign and seal of the real offering—the Person of the Crucified. Christ Himself is the Atonement and He made this manifest by dying. The offering of the perfect Life was carried to its extreme point. The living Self died.[1]

What for us is the effect of the Death of Christ? It is important to point out clearly what it was not intended to do. It does not abolish death in the physical sense. Nor does it extinguish suffering. Death and pain are with us still. But they are not what they were before He died. 'The sting of death is sin.' Christ, by dying, has made forgiveness possible, and to the forgiven death is robbed of its terror. Pain is still hard to bear: but if borne under the shadow of the Cross and in union with the Crucified, its burden is less heavy. 'I can do all things through Christ which strengtheneth me.'

Sin, then, can be forgiven. God can 'be just and the justifier of him which believeth in Jesus.'[2] Sin can be forgiven, because the guilt of all the sinful was borne upon the shoulders of the crucified Saviour—the guilt, not all the consequences, but that which effectually barred the way to God, that which put man out of reach of His mercy and shut heaven against him. 'There is therefore now no condemnation to them which are in Christ Jesus.'[3] In Him hidden and included, because united to Him by faith, the guilty soul has made its offering. The sinless sacrifice becomes its own. 'I am crucified with Christ,' says St. Paul in the boldest of metaphors, which yet represents a fact; for the humanity of Christ is representative, and it touches and embraces the whole human family. Therefore in the sacrifice of the Cross all mankind have been offered up to God. The perfect obedience of the Son, Who is the elder brother, has been accepted by the Father, on behalf of all. And this is why all men are invited by the Gospel to come and take the full salvation provided for them. In Christ the offering has been made. Nothing is wanting but the will and the resolution to come.

But directly faith reaches forth and takes hold of the Cross, even if but dimly its significance is perceived, the way is open for all the ministrations of Divine Grace. Life and health flow

[1] Cf. Du Bose, *The Gospel in the Gospels*, p. 124.
[2] Rom. iii. 26. [3] Rom. viii. 1.

in. The heart expands and opens to the love of God and man. 'Old things are passed away, behold all things are become new.'

The effect of the Atonement appears in the life of the penitent. There is unceasing contrition for sin. The remembrance of it is not put away like a thing that is for ever done with. 'My sin is ever before me.' There is nothing morbid or unhealthy in this state of mind. It is one of the ways in which we may take part in that perpetual pleading of the Cross which alone enables us to stand before God. As, under the old Covenant, sacrifices which could 'never take away sins' were offered and accepted, so under the Gospel, oblations of a loving penitence, that have no power to atone, are yet received by God. They express the concurrence of our wills and help to fix our faith in the One offering. The theology of St. Paul is full of the idea. He speaks of dying and being 'buried with Christ,' of being 'crucified with Christ.' 'Ye are dead and your life is hid with Christ in God.' These are figures of speech, but they express facts of actual experience—the immolation of self, the abnegation of whatever is hateful in the sight of God, the taking sides with Christ in His war with evil.

CHAPTER XX

THE RESURRECTION

It is surely in the interests of faith that all the Evangelists minutely describe the deposition of the Sacred Body from the Cross and its reverent and loving bestowal in the grave. It is in reference to what followed that the significance of the burial comes into prominence and is erected into an article of the creed. The Evangelists have described the scene at the Cross. They have told us the last sayings of the dying Redeemer. They have solemnly averred that He died.

But they are about to tell us of the Resurrection, of the renewal of life, of the conquest of death, of the victory won by the Cross and soon to be manifested in glorious state. It is no mere artistic device to heighten the effect of the coming story that leads them to describe the burial. It is for the greater certainty of the Church. It is that we may be the more sure, not only of the reality of the death but, of the truth of the Resurrection, that the events of the evening of Good Friday are narrated.

The time was short. The Sabbath was coming on. What was to be done must be done quickly. A garden lay close to the place of the Cross.[1] A member of the Sanhedrin, already well affected towards the new movement and its Leader, acting on his own impulse or at the suggestion of a disciple, went boldly to Pilate and asked for the Body of Christ. St. Mark tells us that he was one who was waiting for the kingdom of God, one of that small band, who daily watched and waited for the redemption of Israel, and who seem to have been gifted with a keenness of spiritual perception, which we so often note to have been lacking among our Lord's more immediate followers. Some boldness was

[1] Jo xix. 41.

certainly required for a member of the Sanhedrin to show such interest in the body of One, Who had not only been condemned by the Council but had suffered a death which was so repugnant to Jewish feeling. But Joseph was not deterred by such considerations. Opening the cave hewn out of the side of a rock, which he had destined for his own burial, he placed within it the dead Body of the Saviour. The task was carried out by Joseph himself and his household. The disciples had fled. Only two or three brave women were lingering at the spot. They may have lent a loving hand to the reverent and tender removal of the Sacred Form. At least they 'beheld where He was laid'; [1] and as the last beams of the setting sun sloped redly over the spot and as the evening star began to shine in the western sky, they slowly turned and left the Saviour to His Sabbath rest.

'They that sow in tears shall reap in joy.' [2] Little did they think of the harvest which was soon to come from the sowing in which they had taken part, that evening of springtime in the garden of Joseph. We know how far it was from their thoughts, by the preparation which they made to embalm the Body. It meant that they had laid Him there to sleep on until the last Resurrection.[3] Never had it entered their mind that His rest was quickly to be broken, and at the very moment of the burial it was well nigh 'high time to awake out of sleep.' If we can say this of the women, as proved by their own action, still more strongly can we say it of the Eleven, who were trembling in sorrow and despair within the walls of their barred-up room in the city. Expectation of a triumphant issue, of an opening grave and of a risen Saviour, there was none.

We leave the great city to its Sabbath—surely the strangest it had ever spent—with the guilty satisfaction of its ruling classes, the uneasy feeling of the Roman Governor, to whom this miscarriage of justice seems to have brought more heart-searching than all the many acts of tyranny which he had yet committed, the foreboding of disaster in the minds of the crowd as they returned from the scene of the Crucifixion 'smiting

[1] Mk. xv. 47. [2] Ps. cxxvi. 5.

[3] 'On n'embaume pas un corps dont on attend la résurrection d'un moment à l'autre.' Réville, *Jésus de Nazareth,* ii. p. 433. 'Those who loved Him most devotedly came to embalm His corpse.' Westcott, *Gospel of the Resurrection,* p. 120.

their breasts,' knowing—the more thoughtful of them—that they had assisted at a great crime. We leave the city to its sleep, and led by the Evangelist our thoughts pass for the moment to where the Spirit of the Crucified had gone. He has told us in His promise to the dying thief, 'To-day shalt thou be with Me in Paradise.'[1] There, in the place of departed spirits—or perhaps to speak more truly, because less geographically—with, and under the condition of, the spirits of Patriarchs and Prophets and the whole company of those who had lived in the fear of God, the blessed Spirit of the crucified Man of Sorrows found its brief repose.[2] Such is the tradition which early won its way into the language of the Apostles' Creed. Its authority has been much disputed.[3] Against the passage in St. Luke's Gospel there is nothing to be said.[4] Reference in terms more or less clear is made to the Descent into hell in the Epistle to the Ephesians and by St. Peter.[5] On the day of Pentecost, he freely takes the language of the Psalmist, and applies it to the period between our Lord's Death and His Resurrection.[6]

It is upon the general result of these allusions to a place where the spirits of the faithful dead are at rest that the clause of the Apostles' Creed is founded. And the doctrine which it expresses has much to recommend it in the nature of things. A return of the Spirit of Christ to the Father, apart from His body, when the two had been sundered by death, is not to be thought of. No such incomplete entrance answers to the idea which the Church has always held of the triumphant return of the Son to the presence of God. A pale, disembodied human spirit which has just left the familiar tabernacle of the body, is not the King of Glory before Whom the Psalmist calls upon the everlasting gates to lift up their heads. God, Who 'giveth His beloved sleep,' has His own place of waiting and of rest in which, until joined by the risen body, the spirit lives in the repose of blissful expectation.

[1] Lk. xxiii. 43.

[2] In Lk. xvi. 22, 'Abraham's Bosom,' fellowship with the Father of the Faithful, conveys the same idea. Cf. 4 Macc. xiii. 17.

[3] *E.g.* by Harnack, *Das apostolische Glaubensbekenntniss*, 1892.

[4] *v.* B. Weiss, *Das Leben Jesu*, ii. p. 541, 'The notion that the episode (of the dying thief) was gratuitously invented in order to illustrate a dogma is contradicted by the general character of the Gospel narratives.'

[5] Eph. iv. 9; 1 Pet. iv. 6. But *v.* Swete, *The Apostles' Creed*, p. 58.

[6] Acts ii. 27; Ps. xvi. 10.

There the Spirit of our Lord, joined by the spirit of the repentant companion of His Crucifixion, kept its Sabbath, while unconscious of what had happened and little dreaming of what the dawn would bring, 'the whole earth . . . was still.'

Before we proceed, the alleged contradictions and inconsistencies of our Gospel narratives of the Resurrection must be considered, so far as they are supposed to bear upon the general trustworthiness of the story. It will be admitted by anyone who is acquainted with the nature of historical evidence that a well-attested fact loses nothing of its truth by a want of agreement in detail on the part of its witnesses. The case is quite the reverse. A mechanical, cast-iron rigidity of evidence is a sure sign that it is neither so wide nor so original as it seems. You at once get the impression of borrowed knowledge, of the parrot-like learning of a lesson, of servile imitation—indications which all point to a tendency, to a purpose to be served. There is no mark of spontaneity—of the telling of a story because it is true and *must* be told. Everyone who has the slightest knowledge of life is aware of this fact.

But when a story comes to me from various quarters with the central point as its unvarying burden, while the details are as complex and varied as the main topic is one, I feel that I am in touch with fact; for here is something which has impressed itself uniformly as to its kernel on a number of people, but as to its clothing and circumstance in ways that vary with the difference in character and the idiosyncrasies of each narrator. No one who has had experience of the sifting of evidence will deny that, in the relation of an episode, extraordinary differences will occur in the presentation of the facts, while all unite in their adhesion to the main point. Differences of mental training, of powers of perception, of judgment and discrimination, must affect the report of an occurrence. The greater the desire to convey the truth, the more marked will be the emphasis which is laid on an element of the story that appears essential to the narrator; and the laying of this emphasis will often obscure or even distort the impression which, to another witness, appears more vital.

Now these characteristics of historical evidence, which will be very generally admitted, are to be borne in mind when we approach the story of the Resurrection of our Lord. Here, in a remarkable way, we have identity combined with variety—identity in the report of the one transcendent fact, variety in its colouring and in its circumstance. Should these differences be allowed to prejudice the reception of the story? Must we refuse it our belief on the mere question of the character of the narrative apart from all other considerations? Its historic value is challenged by certain writers on this ground.[1] We must, therefore, consider the evidence as it comes before us in the Gospel narratives, in the allusions of the Pauline Epistles and in the speeches of the Acts. And in the first instance, let us take that nucleus of their story in which there is general agreement.

All the four Evangelists tell us that early on the first day of the week the grave of Christ was empty. There was no corpse there. The simplest statement is that of St. Mark. 'A young man,' who is found sitting, clothed in a long white garment, on the right side of the grave, tells the women, who have come with their spices to anoint the Body, 'He is risen; He is not here.' St. Luke makes them receive the same assurance, but from two men in shining garments. In St. Matthew, the same tidings are communicated by one whom he does not hesitate to call 'the angel of the Lord.' In the Fourth Gospel there is no mention of the angel. The writer is not dependent upon the information of the women. He was the loved disciple, who stepped into the grave and saw that the Body of the Saviour was not there.

Thus, we have the combined assurance of the Gospels that on Easter morning, the grave in the Garden of Joseph, in which three days ago the crucified Body had been laid, no longer contained it, and three of the Evangelists give as the reason that 'He is risen.'[2] St. Paul, writing when these facts, if not incorporated in Gospels, were the subject of oral teaching and had

[1] *E.g.* by Dr. Sanday, 'The accounts that have come down to us seem to be too conflicting and confused to prove this' (*i.e.* 'the actual resuscitation of the dead body of the Lord from the tomb'). *Bishop Gore's Challenge to Criticism*, p. 20.

[2] J. Weiss argues that the oldest Resurrection narrative—that of St. Paul (1 Cor. xv.)—contains no mention of the empty grave. In reply to this statement, it may be said (1) that the language, taken in accordance with the ordinary meaning of words (vv. 3, 4) most certainly implies that the grave was empty, *v.* below, p. 362; (2) that in the present state of criticism, we have no ground for regarding the substance of St. Mark xvi. 1-9 as a later source than 1 Cor. xv. *v.* above, p. 24. *D. Urchristentum*, i. p. 63 f. Weiss proceeds to trace various stages in the Resurrection narrative, making St. Matthew's contribution (xxviii. 11-16) form the transition to the narrative of the apocryphal

perhaps been committed to memoranda, tells the Corinthians that he had received, in the Gospel which he preached, the truth that 'Christ . . . rose again the third day.'[1]

It has lately been asked 'Does this statement rest on facts, on experiences of the disciples?'[2] We think that it does, and not on the desire to find confirmation for certain beliefs which, from one cause or another, had come to be held by them. For instance, the widely prevailing idea that the soul lingers near the body for three days after death, while the body itself is for that space of time preserved from corruption might, it is thought, have led to the statement of the Gospels and 1 Cor. xv. Or, it may be said, the statement merely embodies the conviction that Christ's own repeated prophecy of a Resurrection on the Third Day must surely have come to pass, especially when taken in connection with His appearances to the disciples. Others would see in such a belief the desire to find Old Testament sayings fulfilled.[3] Many students of comparative religion trace the origin of the belief to the changes of the seasons as embodied in the myth of Adonis among the Phoenicians, of Tammuz of the Babylonians, of Osiris in Egypt—a myth spread far and wide over the East, familiar to Jews of the Dispersion and through them to the Christian writers. Again, 'the Third Day' may be taken, in a merely conventional sense, for a short period; as the number 40 is often applied in Scripture as a rough indication of a considerable time.

Against all these suggestions, it is enough to point out the way in which a literal interpretation of the statement answers to the character of what, upon the face of it, purports to be an historical narrative. Thus, it was fitting that, at the earliest moment compatible with the end which He had in view—His disciples' assurance that the victory over death and sin was surely won—Christ should be raised to life again. When the Sabbath was past and the first day of the week began to dawn—that is, upon the 'Third Day'—the grave was left. 'It was not possible that He should be holden of it.' The Evangelists

Gospel of Peter. But a glance shows the gulf which parts that fantastic and legendary description from the sober and restrained narratives of our four Gospels. *v.* Weiss, *ibid.* p. 66. Cf. Headlam, *The Miracles of the New Testament*, p. 255.

[1] 1 Cor. xv. 4.

[2] By J. Weiss, *D. Urchristentum*, i. p. 67.

[3] *v.* below, p. 359, n. 2.

state the fact of the Resurrection on the Third Day simply and clearly as an actual occurrence. There is no occasion to cast about for an explanation of the terms of the narrative. It *was* a fulfilment of prophecy : it *did* correspond to certain phenomena of the natural world. It *was* a return of light and hope like the gifts of springtime. But analogies and prophetic intimations fail to account for the belief which prevailed in the primitive community, for the expression given to it in the New Testament and for its passing into the Christian Creed.[1]

Now, it is to be noted that in none of the Gospels and other New Testament writings is there any description of the Resurrection itself, or any claim that it was seen. It is shrouded in the mystery which naturally belongs to it and the Gospels gain in verisimilitude by that omission.[2] If the Resurrection story were the creation of pious fancy, some such description would hardly be lacking. But there is no trace of it, and the recital of the Evangelist who was an eye-witness of the state of the grave in the early morning is the simplest and barest account of all the four.

But although no narrative of the actual Resurrection—of the manner of our Lord's resumption of His crucified Body—is handed down in the Gospels, what for us is more important is related by all. The Saviour was seen by His disciples in bodily form. Here we have another great central fact, and this too is universally attested. In addition to the general Gospel report, we have an early and highly circumstantial account of the appearances in 1 Cor. xv. The empty grave and the bodily appearances of the Saviour, Whom the disciples had lost from their midst not forty-eight hours ago—here are facts forming that nucleus of the Resurrection story to which all our witnesses, whatever their variety in circumstance and mode of expression,[3] give consistent testimony.

[1] Cf. Harnack, *Mission und Ausbreitung des Christentums*, i. p. 64, n. 1, speaking of 1 Cor. xv. 4, 'the primitive Resurrection confession of the Christian community.'

[2] The so-called *Gospel of Peter* does attempt to give a description of the actual Resurrection. 'The disciples refrain from what belongs to God and speak of what they themselves have experienced.' Schlatter, *D. Theologie des N.T.* i. p. 569.

[3] 'The deviations of the texts from one another and the difficulty of piecing them together are proof that no apologetic skill has been applied to them.' Schlatter, *D. Theologie des N.T* i. p. 564.

That, around this coherent and unvaried nucleus are grouped narratives which are difficult to bring into complete harmony, is generally admitted. But does that fact negative the main fabric of the evidence? If this were conceded, a large amount of the world's history would have to be entirely rewritten, many settled historical judgments reversed, and there would be a general upheaval of the foundations on which our knowledge of the past is based. The examination of witnesses in a court of justice suffices to point this out. Independence and distinctness of information always produce variety in mode and in details of statement.

If it is suggested that, in a matter of so great moment, the inspired writers would have been preserved from error and guided in every particular of their narratives, we have to reply that so far as we know, the gift of divine illumination is never so bestowed as to supersede the necessity of ordinary research and accuracy of narration. Inspiration works where the meaning and significance of things has to be brought out. And, allowing for difference of scope and purpose, this is true of every individual Christian—'No man can say that Jesus is the Lord but by the Holy Ghost.'[1] If, then, the Gospel message is not dependent for its power and its authority upon the strictest accuracy of the men who convey it, and if, at the same time, we everywhere detect the signs of inspiration in their narratives, we are not to be prejudiced against the Resurrection story by the presence of conflicting detail.

That the grave was empty is placed beyond all doubt by the fact that when tidings of the Resurrection, and therefore of the failure of their plans, began to be talked about, the Jews did not at once produce the embalmed Body, as they might have done, if it were still in the grave; and that, being unable thus to controvert the proclamation of the Apostles that Christ was risen, they bribed the soldiers of the guard to state that, while they slept, the disciples came and stole the Body of the Lord. The fact that this report was started by the Jews (and St. Matthew refers to its continuance at the time of writing his Gospel[2])

[1] 1 Cor. xii. 3.

[2] xxviii. 15. Justin Martyr refers to this action of the Jews, *Dial. c. Tryph.* 108. *v.* also Tertull. *de Spec.* 30, who alludes to an explanation of the emptiness of the grave given by Jews in the second century; Joseph found the presence

is in itself strong proof that the grave was empty. But the alleged cause of its emptiness is at once disproved by the state of mind, into which the disciples confess that they were plunged at the time. The grave was empty for one only reason; the Saviour had taken to Himself the Body, safe and incorrupt, which for two nights had been lying there.[1]

This interpretation of the matter receives confirmation from what is an equally assured result of a critical handling of the sources—the conviction of the disciples that, on and after the Third Day, the Saviour appeared to them in Person.

If we attempt to draw up a complete account of the alleged appearances as they are reported in the Gospels, we at once encounter difficulties which are only to be anticipated in narratives based on sources originating in different branches of the community. Here, again, we have identity of representation in the central fact—that Christ was actually seen in bodily form—with variety of statement as to the place and manner of His appearing. In short, we have the usual characteristics observable in historical witnessing. A criticism, which ignores the force of the joint testimony to the central fact on the plea that certain details have to be reconciled, fails to do justice

of the disciples who flocked to the grave injurious to his garden and put an end to it by removing the body. It is little to the credit of a section of modern criticism that these theories of Jewish opponents of Christianity are being approved of and imitated. The conduct of Joseph in the burial of our Lord shows too stedfast and bold a nature for it to be imagined that he would so quickly go back upon his action and violate the sanctity of the grave which he had provided. But the empty grave is so stubborn a piece of evidence to refute that we can hardly wonder at the desperate shifts to which some have recourse.

[1] Harnack appears to admit the emptiness of the grave and this reason for its state when he says, 'This grave was the birthplace of the indestructible belief that death is vanquished, that there is a life eternal,' and again, 'the certainty of the Resurrection and of a life eternal which is bound up with the grave in Joseph's garden.' *D. Wesen des Christentums*, p. 102; E.T. p. 161. A. Meyer is inclined to think that the empty grave is a product of the reflex action of the 'Easter Faith.' *D. Auferstehung Christi*, pp. 124, 125. Cf. *Cambr. Theol. Essays*, p. 334; Wellhausen, *D. Evang. Matt.* p. 150. The emptiness of the grave is admitted by Streeter, *Foundations*, p. 134. Headlam speaks of the 'changed point of view with regard to the empty tomb. . . . It is recognized that the beginning of belief in the Resurrection was the fact that the tomb was empty, that that was why St. Paul spoke of the Resurrection on the third day, and why Christians kept the first day of the week.' *Church Quarterly Review* for April, 1913, p. 15.

to the ascertained principles of historical narrative both sacred and profane.[1]

That the disciples were fully convinced that Christ appeared to them in bodily form after His death and burial is a fact which no responsible critic disputes. But we can go further than this and maintain, with the advanced school of criticism, that these appearances actually occurred.[2] Much has been made of the different scenes assigned to them. St. Mark is the authority for the Galilean appearances, St. Matthew's account being in all probability founded on the lost ending of the Second Gospel.[3] St. Luke knows only of appearances in Jerusalem. He is supported in this by St. John xx. and by St. Matthew's account of the appearance of our Lord to the women on their return from the grave. But St. John xxi.—an integral part of his Gospel, with the exception of the attestation of the Ephesian elders which forms the two last verses—reports an appearance in Galilee. Now is there any necessary contradiction in the assignment of these different scenes? If we receive the appearances in Galilee, must we reject those at Jerusalem and *vice versa*? The evidence which points to a meeting of our Lord with His disciples in Galilee is early, probably going back to St. Peter. That Galilee, which had been the scene of so great a part of Christ's Ministry and of His intercourse with His disciples, should be chosen as a trysting place between them and the risen and glorified Lord, is eminently fitting. But the evidence of the Third and Fourth Gospels for the appearances at Jerusalem is of great strength. We have so many proofs of the accuracy of St. Luke in other matters of history, and of his 'perfect understanding of

[1] *v.* Langlois et Seignobos, *Introduction aux Études Historiques*, 1899, p. 173, 'La concordance vraiment concluante n'est pas, comme on l'imaginerait naturellement, une ressemblance complète entre deux récits, c'est un croisement entre deux récits différents qui ne se ressemblent qu'en quelques points. . . . Ce sont les points de concordance de ces affirmations divergentes qui constituent les faits historiques scientifiquement établis.'

[2] 'Appearances of the risen Jesus did actually occur; that is to say, the followers of Jesus really had the impression of having seen Him.' '. . the only fact that has emerged in the course of our examination—the fact that Jesus was seen, as we read in 1 Cor. xv. 5-8.' Schmiedel, *Encycl. Bibl.* vol. iv. art. 'Resurrection- and Ascension-Narratives,' cols. 4061, 4076. J. Weiss takes the same view. *D. Urchristentum*, i. p. 17 f.

[3] *v.* Rördam's article in *Hibbert Journal*, July, 1905.

The Gospel of Peter, vv. 59, 60, which gives Galilee as the scene, is dependent on St. Matthew.

all things from the very first,' that to reject his report would be an act of uncritical violence. And he is supported by the testimony of an eye-witness—the author of the Fourth Gospel. It is difficult to refuse assent, on any scientific ground, to this double stream of evidence.[1] One must admit that appearances at Jerusalem seem to be in contradiction to that express promise of Christ to the disciples that He would go before them into Galilee, of which the women at the grave are reminded by the angel.[2] But it has been acutely replied [3] that, as the disciples disbelieved the story of the women, they would not be likely to set out for Galilee. Even towards evening, when the two disciples went to Emmaus, there was doubt and hesitation in the minds of the Eleven.[4] Christ meets this state of mind by appearing in Jerusalem.

But if we accept the appearances in Jerusalem, must we abandon those in Galilee and, so doing, acknowledge that our Lord made an appointment with His disciples which He failed to keep? There is nothing to compel us to face such a dilemma. In fact, a dilemma can only arise through a false interpretation of a single passage of St. Luke. Time is needed for the explanation that there were appearances both in Jerusalem and in Galilee. St. Luke, according to some critics, tells us that the Ascension took place on the same day as the Resurrection.[5] If

[1] Cf. Loofs, *Die Auferstehungsberichte und ihr Wert*, pp. 26, 32, 36. As to St. Luke, cf. Ramsay, *Paul the Traveller*, pp. 4, 8, 12; and *Luke the Physician*, p. 55.

[2] Mk. xiv. 28; xvi. 7.

[3] By Rördam in *Hibbert Journal* for July, 1905, p. 778.

[4] Lk. xxiv. 11, 24. It is true that St. John 'believed' as he stood in the empty grave, but his faith does not seem to have affected the other disciples. *v.* Jo. xx. 8.

'John is right that the disciples remained over the festival week in the capital, and only returned with the rest of the pilgrims to their homes in Galilee.' B. Weiss, *D. Leben Jesu*, ii. p. 559, referring to Jo. xx. 26.

[5] Lk. xxiv. 50, 51. Thus Schmiedel says, 'In his Gospel the author of Acts has assigned the Ascension to a time late in the evening of the day of His Resurrection.' *Encycl. Bibl.* iv. col. 4059. Harnack, too, in *Das Apostol. Glaubensbekenntniss*, p. 25, regards the Resurrection and the Ascension as parts or aspects of the same event. In his *Die Apostelgeschichte*, 1908, p. 128, he says '(Luke) makes it (the Ascension) follow—not after forty days, but—on Easter Day.' Schmiedel cites the Epistle of Barnabas, xv. 9, in support of his view, but, as reference to the passage at once shows, the writer states that Christ both rose and ascended on a Sunday, not necessarily on the *same* Sunday. *v.* Swete, *The Apostles' Creed*, p. 69, and in *The Appearances of*

that interpretation holds good and we have no means of avoiding the testimony of St. Luke, the two sets of appearances become impossible.

But it is to be observed that St. Luke gives no note of time. 'The Ascension narrative of vv. 50-53 simply follows on the account of the Resurrection ; there is no time connection.' [1] In Acts i. St. Luke *does* assign a limit to the period of the appearances. Christ was 'seen of them forty days,' [2] and the expression leads us to think that, if not at the time of the writing of his Gospel, yet when writing the Acts, he was aware of the appearances in Galilee. If, therefore, there are forty days at least at our disposal for the assignment of the appearances, there is nothing to prevent our reception of the two apparently opposing streams of evidence which tend (original Mark, Matthew, 'Gospel of Peter') to Galilee, (Luke, John and Mark xvi. 9-20), to Jerusalem.[3] After the appearance to St. Thomas on the eighth day, the

Our Lord after the Passion, p. xvii ; Plummer in *St. Luke*, xxiv. 50 ; cf. the present writer in *The Hibbert Journal* for April, 1905, p. 537, and in *The Person of our Lord*, p. 252, n. 1. F. Loofs makes the same mistaken interpretation, quoting Jo. xx. 17 and Rom. x. 6, 7, as appearing 'to place the ascension immediately after the resurrection.' These passages convey no such meaning. *What is the Truth about Jesus Christ?* p. 123. Cf. Loisy, *Évang. Synoptiques*, ii. p. 742, 'Dans le troisième évangile, Jésus monte au ciel après sa dernière apparition, rattachée pour la perspective, au soir même de la résurrection.'

[1] Lk. xxiv. 50, Ἐξήγαγε δὲ αὐτοὺς κ.τ.λ. It is probable that *v.* 49—if not *vv.* 44 f.—was spoken not on the evening of Easter Day but on the return to Jerusalem just before the Ascension. *v.* Westcott in Jo. xxi. 1, and cf. Acts i. 4.

[2] Although the words ἀνεφέρετο εἰς τὸν οὐρανόν, Lk. xxiv. 51, may be an interpolation, yet, as Dr. Plummer observes, St. Luke considered that he had recorded the Ascension in his Gospel, for in Acts i. 1, 2, he states that ὁ πρῶτος λόγος (*i.e.* the Gospel) contained the work of Jesus 'until the day that He was taken up.' *St. Luke, in loc.*

[3] It has been shown by Rördam, *Hibb. Journ.* July, 1905, p. 776, that St. Luke by the time he wrote the Acts had become aware of other (Galilean) appearances than those which he records in the Gospel. Cf. Acts i. 3, δι' ἡμερῶν τεσσεράκοντα ὀπτανόμενος αὐτοῖς. Schmiedel states that 'there is no Gospel in which appearances to men (not women) are reported as having been made both in Galilee and in Jerusalem ; for Jo. xxi. is an appendix by another hand.' *Encycl. Bibl.* iv. col. 4064. Against this dogmatic assertion, we can set the words of Bp. Westcott, *in loc.* 'It is clear that xxi. 1-23 was written by the author of the Gospel. The style and the general character of the language alike lead to this conclusion.' Holtzmann, *Das Evang. des Johannes*, thinks that the chapter is by another hand, but 'we have no proof that the Gospel was ever published without c. xxi. The addition must have been very early.' Sanday thinks that xxi. 1-24 is by the writer of the Gospel. *Criticism of the Fourth*

disciples obey the instinct which leads them to return to their own country, enforced as it was by their recollection of Christ's own promise [1] and by the women's report of the words of the angel at the grave. Then once more they return to Jerusalem, where Christ bids them remain until the promised gift of the Holy Spirit has been bestowed.[2] There is nothing to be said against this arrangement of the two groups of appearances, each of which is too surely grounded in primitive sources of evidence to be lightly rejected. As Meyer remarks, both sources (Marcan and Lucan) lay before St. John.[3] With Acts also before him, he knew what had happened. He had himself been in the midst of the events. No such difficulty, as modern criticism finds, would have occurred to him, and he gives us what is evidently the true state of affairs, when he narrates appearances both at Jerusalem and in Galilee. For the return to Jerusalem, when the Galilean appearances had ended, we have not to imagine such dogmatic-historical reasons for again shifting the scene as present themselves to Meyer.[4] The Gospel writers do not do violence to their sources. It was fitting indeed that Christ should part with His disciples in the neighbourhood of the scene of His suffering, but there is no sign of any manipulation of the sources in order to bring this about. The Evangelists give us, out of their material, what they consider important for their representation of the events. They are not careful to harmonize their accounts with one another; and in this naïve, simple manner of writing there is a strong presumption of their truth. It is to be observed that the account of St. Paul in 1 Cor. xv. gives no information as to the scenes of the appearances.

Gospel, p. 81. Loofs remarks that 'among the Resurrection records, that of John and that of Luke with their purely Jerusalem appearances (Loofs thinks that Jo. xxi. is not by the Evangelist himself) deserve—according to critical considerations as to the sources—the preference to the record of the Mark—and Matthew—Gospel.' *D. Auferstehungsberichte u. ihr Wert*, p. 32. Meyer considers that the special source which St. Luke had at his disposal was perhaps older than our Mark and at least bore the stamp of antiquity. *D. Auferstehung Christi*, p. 34.

[1] Mk. xiv. 28. *The Gospel of Peter*, 58-60 ('verses of special importance,' according to Harnack, *Preuss. Jahrbücher*, 1893, p. 48) says that the disciples returned home when the feast was at an end, and at the point where the fragment breaks off, an account begins which resembles Jo. xxi. ff.

[2] *v.* Westcott in Jo. xxi. 1.

[3] *D. Auferstehung Christi*, p. 127.

[4] *Ib.* p. 128.

To pass from the scenes to the appearances themselves is to enter upon matter of still greater controversy. As observed above, it is admitted that Christ was seen, and in that admission the traditional position appears to be granted. But when we look more closely into the line of argument, it becomes clear that this admission only means that the disciples were quite sincere in their assertion that they saw their Lord, that they did indeed see Him, but as visionaries see—not the objective reality itself, but the self-created embodiment of their own thought. In other words, the risen Christ Whom they saw was His semblance, the effect of ardent longing upon minds stirred to their depths by the disappointment, the sorrow and the desire of the last few momentous days.

Now, this theory takes its stand upon history, in a way that the theory of mere legend or invention on the part of the disciples does not.[1] For it admits that certain strong impressions were produced, so strong that the whole outlook and character of the disciples became completely changed. Hope and energy succeeded despair. The Church was founded, and that course of the moral and spiritual regeneration of mankind began, which is renewing the world and preparing it for the Lord's return.

J. Weiss, admitting[2] the difficulty presented by a visionary, 'self-deceiving' explanation of so fundamental a fact in the Christian scheme as the Resurrection, asks, 'Who will maintain that the only fitting method was to work the miracle of the actual revelation of the exalted Christ?' No one would presume to say that it *was* the only way open to God in effecting the establishment of His Kingdom. But we do say that the only documentary evidence at our disposal reports that, as a matter of fact, it was the method which He adopted; and we add that the vision theory, which is suggested as an alternative, is not only contradictory to the reported mind of the witnesses of the event, but, while professing to be in harmony with modern science, is hopelessly at variance with the received principles of psychology.[3] Weiss, after extolling the value of a faith won by

[1] Schlatter, *D. Theologie des N.T.* i. p. 559. [2] *D. Urchristentum*, i. p. 20 f.

[3] By a vision, 'from a scientific point of view, we understand the process by which a picture comes into the field of sight to which no external object corresponds. The optic nerve is not set into vibration by waves of light or ether

effort and struggle over that of a faith produced by the external action of miracle, goes on to say, 'he who thus thinks can take the last step with us and affirm that the appearances did not come upon them (the disciples) from without, but were the conclusion of an inward struggle, in which faith triumphed over doubt . . . they are not the ground, but the effect of their faith.'[1] Here he is spinning a theory, attractive indeed and plausible, but one which is out of touch with historic fact—with all that is told us of the state of mind of the Apostles between the disillusionment of the Cross and the triumph of Easter.

But when the theory claims to assign the cause of the great historic change which is gradually altering the face of the world, it breaks down completely. It fails to account for the various elements of the case, and it proves itself inadequate for the task which it undertakes. A self-created representation of a fact cannot in the long run supply the place of the fact itself. Sooner or later the excitement dies down and leaves the soul disillusioned and cold. There is no trace of such disillusionment to be found in the history of the Christian Church; never a hint that converts find that they have been taught to 'follow cunningly devised fables.'

For the existence of a vision, or of the impression that a vision is experienced, certain conditions are essential. Visions are not fortuitous happenings. Law operates here as elsewhere. They

from without; it is excited by an inward psychological process.' *Ib.* p. 20. This psychological process—a tendency to believe, getting the better of doubt and materializing so far as to induce the impression of seeing external phenomena, is exactly what, according to all our evidence, was wanting in the case of the disciples. It is unscientific to posit a state of things of which the history knows nothing, in order to be able to withhold assent to a view which history offers us, on the ground that presuppositions (which by the way are in no sense demanded either by science or philosophy) forbid it. *v.* p. 136.

[1] J. Weiss, *ib.* p. 21. Weiss, after denying any reality or objectivity to the appearances of the risen Christ and attributing them to the faith of the disciples, proceeds to deal with them as though he had not already destroyed their basis in fact, and speaks of them as the experience of Easter (*Oster-Erlebnis*). But according to his theory there was no such experience. For the cross and the grave still held sway. There was no Easter. The disciples thought there was; for they believed that they had seen the risen Christ. But this belief was merely a hallucination, founded on their hopes and feelings. The foundation of Christianity therefore rests upon a process of credulity. The wish was father to the thought. Other origin of the creed of Christendom there was none. Such briefly is the logical conclusion of the theory.

are closely linked on to other phenomena, and may be said to be the pictorial reflection of mental processes which themselves are very real things. A vision does not come unbidden and unconnected. It has its history. It is not self-evolved. It has its roots in a state of mind, in a spiritual experience, which is closely connected with the particular form which it takes, and indeed is responsible for it.

If this be true, and illustrations of its truth can be found in such an historical sketch of visions as A. Meyer has given,[1] we should expect to find that the idea of Resurrection was present, in however crude a form, to the minds of the disciples; that they cherished, however dimly, the impression that the scene of shame and sorrow, from which they had so lately fled, was not final, and that soon God would work some great deliverance. This, supposing that the vision theory could be sustained, is what we should expect to find. Nothing could be farther from the truth. There was no such mental and spiritual preparation for a vision. The disciples witness against themselves. The Evangelists would not have taken from them the credit of the expectation, if they had possessed it. The hard fact remains as the disciples express it on the road to Emmaus. If the presence of an intuition were anywhere to be found, it would be in the faithful hearts of the women, who remained by the Cross when the disciples had fled, and who were the first at the grave when the Sabbath had ended, with the spices—signs of their utter abandonment of hope [2]—in their hands. There is the same absence of any expectation of relief from their sorrow as in the case of the disciples. There is no *material* of which a vision could be formed. To suggest a vision, as the dominating factor of the first Easter Day, is therefore to be indifferent to the historical position.[3] It ignores the patent facts of the case. It is untrue to the actual situation.[4]

[1] *D. Auferstehung Christi*, p. 217 f.

[2] *v.* p. 341.

[3] 'The decisive proof of the reality of the experience can be found only in the effect which it has produced. Out of doubt and prostration the disciples were constrained to victorious confession. The greater the contrast the clearer the fact that here an interposition has taken place which cannot be explained simply by psychological motives.' V. Dobschütz, *Probleme des apostol. Zeitalters*, p. 16.

[4] Maurenbrecher, *Von Nazareth nach Golgotha*, p. 262, has tried to explain the disciples' new faith and hope after Christ's death by the hereditary power of recovery to which the history of the Jewish people bears witness; but even if temperament were able to work such a wonder in the case of people like the

It has been acutely observed[1] that, if faith in Christ had suggested itself to the Apostles as the product of the inward movements of the soul, the Church would have become a community of mystics, whose sole occupation consisted in setting up such an ecstatic condition as would render Christ visible to them. But this conception is not in keeping with the history of the primitive community. Christianity on that hypothesis would be a religion by which man in some way brings himself to God. Whereas it is a religion which derives its foundation and its strength from an event which comes to it from without.[2]

But there are serious moral objections to the maintenance of the theory. If all that the disciples saw was a vision or a series of visions, they were the victims of a hallucination which became, when used as they proceeded to use it, a subtle and misleading deception. There can be no question that the disciples fully believed that they had seen their Lord alive in bodily form, and

first disciples, the theory does not explain how their trust came to be again placed upon Jesus, after the great disillusionment which was caused by His death. As J. Weiss asks, 'Why did not they abandon the idea of a personal Messiah ?... How comes it about that the revived hope turned back, in spite of everything, to Jesus ?' *D. Urchristentum*, i. pp. 15, 16. Weiss himself thinks that, while the fulfilment of Christ's warning of His passion cast them to the ground, recollection of His words and His Personality regained their influence. *Ib.* pp. 15, 22. But *v.* below, n. 2.

[1] Schlatter, *D. Theologie des N.T.* i. p. 563.

[2] 'Critical methods point ... to the conviction among the disciples that the Lord had appeared to them, and neither criticism nor philosophy can give any explanation of this fact without admitting that these appearances were dependent on the personality of Jesus.' K. Lake, *The Resurrection of Jesus Christ*, p. 275.

'All agree that an adequate explanation of the appearances cannot be furnished by psychological motives. One only attains thereby to the predisposition for the event, not the event itself.' V. Dobschütz, *op. cit.* p. 13. But there was not even a predisposition for the event. 'It remains a fact of history that the disciples first understood the meaning of Jesus and many of His sayings after Easter and Pentecost.... This lack of understanding is easily apprehended psychologically. Judaism expected the Resurrection at the end of the days along with the setting up of the Messianic Kingdom, Jo. xi. 24. But Easter morning broke over Jerusalem like every other morning. The disciples had no perception that day of the coming of the Messiah and the beginning of Judgment. Therefore they did not believe the tidings of the Resurrection of Jesus.' Feine, *Theologie des N.T.* p. 173. This meets the difficulty which many find in the complete misunderstanding of Christ's warnings of death and Resurrection which the Evangelists attribute to the disciples.

that He had risen from the grave to which He had been committed on the evening of the day of His crucifixion. Not only were they permitted to hold and proclaim this belief, but they proceeded to found the Christian Church upon the fact which, as they taught, lay behind it and inspired it. If they were wrong in their belief, if all that they saw was but the projection of their own thought and fancy into the semblance of a great historic process, then we have to face this insuperable difficulty—the foundation of the greatest institution of Divine beneficence that the world has seen upon a heartless and inexplicable delusion. It would mean that just where the hand of God seems most evident, where the finest flowers of love and mercy, of self-denial and pity, are to be seen, there lurk untruth, delusion, self-deception. In short, the vision theory, if it could be maintained, would be the death-blow to all moral certitude. But, if the Christian religion can be said in any sense to represent the mind of God in His dealings with men—nay, if there be at all in the universe a moral purpose at work among the complexities of human affairs—such a view cannot for a moment be held.

Now, it is useless, in reply to this moral difficulty, to say that the faith of the Apostles created the impression that Christ was living and victorious, and that in that impression was contained all that was needed for the Christian hope. Unless the Resurrection was an objective reality, there has been, so far as we can tell, no victory over death, no vindication of Christ, no triumph of good. Evil, in the supreme effort of Satan, has had the last word. To say that the Spirit of Christ survived the Cross and that this assurance suffices for all our needs, is futile. We believe in this survival of people generally: but the immortality of the soul is quite a different thing from the Resurrection. The Church is not built on what is true of others besides our Lord—the fact that His Spirit lived on after death. It is built upon the glorious resumption, on the third day, of the full, bodily, personal life, which He had laid down upon the Cross. Yet the two things are frequently confused, the Resurrection of the body and the Immortality of the soul—the former a Jewish conception, the latter Greek.[1] It was

[1] As, *e.g.* by K. Lake, who says, 'What we mean by resurrection is not resuscitation of the material body, but the unbroken survival of personal life.' v. *Hibbert Journ.* for Apr. 1908, p. 693. We mean nothing of the sort. Resur-

not without reference to Jewish thought[1] that the Apostles, by their experience of the risen Lord, created the Creed of Christendom.

The confusion of thought, which results from supplanting the idea of the Resurrection of the Body of Christ by that of the survival of His soul, should have been prevented by consideration of the Incarnation. A disembodied spirit is not Man. The Incarnation is an eternal fact; eternally foreseen[2] and, once it has occurred, eternally existing. The theory of a 'living Christ,' which finds no place for the Body which He took from His Virgin Mother, fails to meet the requirements of the Catholic doctrine of the Incarnation of the Son of God. The full humanity of Christ is essential to the truth of His Incarnation. We have no ground for the conception of perfect manhood apart from its

rection and the immortality of the soul are two entirely different things. Cf. Schmiedel, *Encycl. Bibl.* iv. p. 4059. A pious belief in the immortality of the soul of Christ is not the triumphant belief in His Resurrection, with which the Apostles went forth to convert the world.

It is worth noting that there is a similar movement of thought among Jews of the present day. 'In modern times,' says R. Kohler, 'the belief in Resurrection has been greatly shaken by natural philosophy, and the question has been raised by the Reform rabbis . . . whether the old liturgical formulas, expressing the belief in the resurrection, should not be so changed as to give clear expression to the hope of immortality of the soul instead. This was done in all the American Reform Prayer Books.' *Jew. Encyclopedia*, art. 'Resurrection,' p. 385.

[1] Cf. Acts xxiii. 6, where St. Paul confidently appeals, as a Pharisee, to the belief of the Pharisees, 'Of the hope and resurrection of the dead I am called in question.' As Kohler says, 'Both Pharisees and Essenes believed in resurrection of the body, notwithstanding the philosophical construction of their belief by Josephus to suit Roman readers.' It is a matter of dispute when this belief originated. It is sometimes said that in Dan. xii., written in the time of Antiochus Epiphanes, about B.C. 170, we have the first expression of the belief. It certainly is the clearest utterance on the subject that had yet appeared: but it is not the first. *v.* Is. xxvi. 19; Ezek. xxxvii. 1 f. 'This doctrine, which is first taught beyond possibility of doubt in Dan. xii. though a true exegesis will find many intimations of the doctrine in earlier books, was made a common-place of Jewish theology by 1 Enoch.' Charles, *Apocrypha and Pseudepigrapha of the O.T.* ii. p. 185. In Job xix. 25-27, a passage often cited as containing an allusion to resurrection, we have 'the thought that he (Job) will then himself *see* God. . . . The thought of a future beatific life is *nascent* in the Book of Job; it is expressed not as a generally accepted doctrine, but first as an aspiration, afterwards as a moral persuasion or conviction on the part of Job personally.' Driver, *Introd. to Liter. of O.T.* p. 418. Driver dates Job 'during or shortly after the Babylonian captivity.' *Ib.* p. 432.

[2] 1 Pet. i. 20.

adequate bodily expression.[1] When the King of Glory entered the presence of the Father, He entered 'like unto a Son of Man.' The failure to regard the Resurrection from the point of view of the Incarnation is natural enough in certain quarters: it is difficult to understand when we meet with it among men whose theology is based on the fact that 'the Word was made Flesh.'[2]

[1] *v.* S. Thom. Aquin. *Sum. Theol.* i. quaes. xc. art. 4, conclusio. 'Cùm . . . anima, quae est pars humanae naturae, non habeat naturalem perfectionem nisi secundùm quod est corpori unita.' 'Spiritual facts are not complete until they have expressed themselves; and matter as we call it is their language, the medium of their expression. And the risen body of Christ was to His disciples this expression.' Illingworth, *The Doctrine of the Trinity*, p. 228.

[2] As in *Foundations*, p. 127 f. It would seem that Manichaeanism persists still and that the danger of a false spirituality is a real one. *v.* J. A. Robinson in *J.T.S.* Jan. 1913.

'The doctrine of the Incarnation does not teach that Christ assumed human nature, body and spirit, only for the years of His visible Ministry, and then abandoned it like a discarded cloak.' J. H. Bernard in Hastings' *Encycl. of Religion and Ethics*, ii. p. 156.

J. Weiss seems to share the same confusion of ideas referred to above: 'The appearances to the disciples referred, not to a Resurrection at such and such a time after death, but to the fact that Jesus went to God at the moment of His death.' *Das Urchristentum*, i. p. 67. His view is that the appearances convinced the disciples that Christ must have risen again and that this conviction led to the thought of the empty grave and the third day. But the Gospels regard these as historic elements of the event. They show no sign of having been invented for the occasion, or of being merely the application of Old Testament prophecy or incident (Hos. vi. 1 f.; cf. Matt. xii. 40) to Christ. Still less are we justified in assigning them to the influence of oriental mythology. Weiss, *ib.* p. 69.

'According to which (the belief of the Christian Church) the Resurrection and the Ascension were the necessary completion of the Incarnation; the final stage of the taking of the manhood into God; and as such, a revelation to us of the ultimate destiny of matter and the material universe to be the adequate instrument and appropriate home of the sanctified and sinless spirit.' Illingworth, *The Gospel Miracles*, p. 38.

It was disconcerting to find that Dr. Sanday has found himself obliged, in the course of his study of the Gospel history, to raise the question of the bodily Resurrection of our Lord. 'Although I believe emphatically in a Supernatural Birth and a Supernatural Resurrection and in all that follows from these beliefs, I know that is not all that the Church of the past has believed' (*Bishop Gore's Challenge to Criticism*, p. 28). In his general treatment of the miraculous element in the Gospels, Dr. Sanday draws 'a distinction between events that are "supra naturam"—testifying to the presence of higher spiritual forces—and events . . . that are "contra naturam" or involve some definite reversal of the natural physical order' (p. 23). Only the latter class imply any breach in the order of nature. They are such miracles as the feeding of the 5000, the stilling of the sea, raising the dead, our Lord's own Birth and Resurrection. Here the action involved is regarded as unnatural: and this, on the ground

For, what is this denial of the Resurrection of Christ's Body but a fresh form of Docetism applied to His risen life, as once to the life of His public Ministry? He refutes it by anticipation in His words to the assembled disciples on the Evening of the Third Day. St. John has the Resurrection as

of general experience, he declares that the action of Divine Providence can never be. But can such a distinction be maintained? So far as we know nature, all the miracles attributed to our Lord in the Gospels appear to run counter to it: whether we say they are 'supra' or 'contra naturam,' in every case a force is at work which interferes with the ordinary sequence of cause and effect. But why regard one rather than another as contradicting nature? Here, surely, the maxim of St. Augustine should be borne in mind. 'No Divine action contradicts nature: for how can that be against nature which happens in accordance with His will? The portent is contrary to nature as we know it.' The Divine Agency in the Birth and the Resurrection of our Lord is certainly above our understanding, above all workings of nature, as we know nature; but not for that reason 'contra naturam.' *v.* above, p. 135. Cf. Swete, *The Ancient Creeds in Modern Life*, 1914, p. 24, 'No believer in the historical character of these two events will for a moment admit that they are in part or in whole *contra naturam*, or that any true miracle is such.'

In the feeding of the 5000, Dr. Sanday, while admitting the historical character of the narrative as a whole, excludes, like Schweitzer before him, what is the point of the story—the statement of the evangelists that 'they'—the multitude—'were all filled.' Apart from that fact of the satisfaction of the needs of the people in a desert place by the exercise of Christ's own power, the story is without meaning. But it is related, as of great importance, by all four Evangelists. According to Dr. Sanday, pp. 24, 25 (cf. p. 13), the miraculous element is an importation from Old Testament narratives of multiplied food; not a fact of Christ's Ministry, with its marvellous teaching for all time. 'The other nature-miracles are still easier,' we are assured (p. 26). Yet we remember that one consequence of the super-abundant provision for the needs of the famished people—the gathering up of a large quantity of remaining fragments—formed the subject of Christ's subsequent teaching on His disciples' lack of understanding (Mk. viii. 18, 19); while St. John tells of a definite, historical result of the miracle—the people's desire to seize upon our Lord's Person and there and then proclaim Him King-Messiah (vi. 15): an attempt which led to His withdrawal alone to the mountain from which (vi. 3) He seems to have descended for the feeding. Thus, to reject the miracle is to lacerate the Gospel narrative; not too, be it observed, at the bidding of a sound critical judgment on the text, but at the call of an *à priori* conception of the miracle itself. *v.* above, p. 133.

With regard to Old Testament analogies, cf. Webb, *Problem of the Relations of God and Man*, p. 242, n. 2, 'The fact of a story being told of several people does not of itself prove it true of none. Whether it be true in any particular case is a matter to be decided according to the evidence.' Long ago, Strauss accounted for the miraculous in the Gospels by supposing a mythology derived by the disciples out of the expectation (founded on O.T. narratives) that the Messiah would be a worker of miracles. This theory is refuted by replying that if there had been no *actual* miracles, the disciples themselves would not

well as the Incarnation in mind when he condemns those who deny that Christ has come in the flesh.[1] A vague, 'spiritual' Resurrection, as of a phantom appearing ghost-like and unsubstantial, would give no assurance that the Cross was not the final scene, that by dying the Saviour had destroyed death and had come victorious through the fight. There would be no 'power' in such a Resurrection as that. And yet, as all admit, a new strength did so possess believers that men spoke of them as 'those that have turned the world upside down.'[2] When St. Paul describes the essence of the Gospel as he had received and now preached it, he places the Resurrection in the closest relation to the death and burial. 'Christ died ... and was buried and ... He rose again.'[3] To die and to be buried requires a body. To 'rise again' is a meaningless expression if taken apart from this context. It is the same Body of Christ of which he asserts the three experiences of death, burial and Resurrection.[4] Even Schmiedel admits that St. Paul, 'When he first came to know of Jesus as risen, was still a Jew and therefore conceived of resurrection ... in no other way than as re-animation of the body.... As soon as he had become a believer ... he had no occasion to alter his conception.' And Schmiedel adds, 'That Jesus was buried and that "He has been raised" (1 Cor. xv. 4)

have believed in Christ. *v.* Fisher, *Grounds of Theistic and Christian Belief*, p. 163. Speaking of what he calls the legend of the feeding of the 5000, Bousset remarks, 'The slight parallels of the Old Testament and the allusions to the Christian Sacrament do not suffice to explain the origin of this narrative.' *Kyrios Christos*, 1913, p. 75.

[1] Lk. xxiv. 39 ; 1 Jo. iv. 2, 3. 'Scripture is wholly free from that Docetism—that teaching of an illusory manhood of Christ, which both within the Church and without it, tends to destroy the historic character of the Gospel.' Westcott in Jo. ii. 24.

[2] Acts xvii. 6.

[3] 1 Cor. xv. 3, 4. So, too, in his speech at Antioch, 'They took Him down from the tree and laid Him in a sepulchre. But God raised Him from the dead' (Acts xiii. 29, 30).

Here, the content of the 'Him' in the third member of the passage is identical with the content of the first and second 'Him.' We cannot dismember it when it refers to the risen Christ. Cf. Chase, *The Gospels in the Light of Historical Criticism*, 1914, p. xxi, 'There can be no doubt that the Apostle's conception of the Resurrection of Christ included as an essential element the empty grave and the Resurrection of the Lord's Body.'

[4] 'Words have a history behind them which needs to be reckoned with ; and they form sentences which are commonly intended to convey a definite meaning.' Gwatkin, *The Bishop of Oxford's Open Letter : a Reply*, 1914, p. 10.

cannot be affirmed by anyone who has not the re-animation of the body in mind.'[1] Yet we are told, 'The only question really at issue relates to a detail, the actual resuscitation of the dead body of the Lord from the tomb'; but, 'That the Risen Lord as Spirit still governed and inspired His Church is proved beyond question.'[2] If the assurance of a continued life of Christ as Spirit was all that the Resurrection afforded, one fails to see the reason for the access of fresh hope and courage, which enabled the disciples to go forth to the conquest of the world. *For the survival of the spirit through death to the future reunion with the body was a commonplace of the ordinary Jewish thought of the time,*[3] and the idea, when applied to our Lord, would have had no power to produce the results which all critics admit to have followed upon the Apostolic belief in the Resurrection.

Now the Gospels report that Christ manifested the reality of His risen life by actual, bodily appearances. 'Il est incontestable,' says Loisy, '... que les apôtres, même Saint Paul, n'ont pas eu l'idée d'une immortalité distincte de la résurrection corporelle.'[4] If it be said that St. Paul expressly states that flesh and blood cannot inherit the kingdom of God, we must go on to the rest of the verse to understand his meaning, 'neither doth corruption inherit incorruption.'[5] A change is needed before

[1] In *Encycl. Bibl.* iv. col. 4059. Cf. H. R. Mackintosh, *Expos.* June, 1914, p. 539, 'The total efficacy of a life, considered as a force acting on environment, is unmeaning apart from organism.' Yet J. Weiss says 'That Jesus is risen, they (the disciples) did not, as a matter of fact, experience; but only that He was living.' *D. Urchristentum*, i. p. 67.

[2] Sanday, *op. cit.* p. 20. So, too, in acquiescing in abandonment of the 'contra naturam' element in the two supreme miracles of the Birth and the Resurrection, Dr. Sanday speaks of it as 'only ... a small part of these great events.' p. 27. But v. *Form and Content in the Christian Tradition*, 1916, p. 150.

[3] 1 *Enoch* li. 1, 'Sheol also shall give back that which it has received.' *v.* the note of Charles, *The Book of Enoch*, p. 99. *Orac. Sibyl.* iv. 179 f. Cf. the Jewish morning Benediction, 'Blessed be Thou Who revivest the dead.'

[4] *L'Evangile et l'Église*, p. 120. J. Weiss is therefore beside the mark when he writes, 'In Paul no trace is to be found of the view familiar to us in the Gospels and Acts that Jesus returned at His Resurrection to earthly life; no trace that He ate and drank with His own; that He took again the body of flesh which He wore before.' *D. Urchristentum*, i. p. 61. On the contrary, St. Paul's deliberate and clear marshalling of the three concrete facts, 'died ... was buried ... rose again,' shows incontestably, to use Loisy's phrase, that he was at one with the Evangelists on the character of the Resurrection. *v.* above, p. 361.

[5] 1 Cor. xv. 50.

sinful man is fitted for God's presence. But no such impediment existed in the case of Christ. 'The sinless body of the incarnate Son of God had nothing to lay aside as unfit for God's presence. All it needed was to be "clothed upon," invested with new powers as a spiritual body.'[1] Nor does this difference between the conditions of Christ's Resurrection and our own destroy the connection between them. There is a similar difference between temptation in His case and in ours. He was 'in all points tempted like as we are, yet without sin.' But His sinlessness is no bar to His sympathy and help. 'He is able to succour them that are tempted.'[2] So, He Whose sinless body needed but the transfiguring of its material qualities to fit it for His Father's presence, will by the power of His Resurrection 'fashion anew the body of our humiliation, that it may be conformed to the body of His glory.' 'Christ risen from the dead' is 'become the first fruits of them that slept.'[3]

When, therefore, we are told that the whole argument of St. Paul in 1 Cor. xv. is 'vitiated if the Resurrection of Christ, on which he bases his conclusion, was after all a resurrection of flesh and blood,'[4] we reply that the lack of complete parallelism between the Resurrection of Christ and our own, which is due to the fact that while we are sinful He is sinless, does not destroy the causal connection between the two resurrections. In our case, the effects of a sinful nature will have to be so obliterated that personal identity has to be secured at the cost of the actual 'body of our humiliation'; for 'corruption doth not inherit incorruption.' Yet, even so, according to St. Paul's teaching,[5]

[1] *v.* article by the present writer, *Hibbert Journ.* Apr. 1905, p. 538. Cf. Westcott, *Gospel of the Resurrection*, p. 287, 'All that belonged to His humanity was preserved, and at the same time all was transfigured.' Ignat. *Ad Smyrn.* iii. ἐγὼ γὰρ καὶ μετὰ τὴν ἀνάστασιν ἐν σαρκὶ αὐτὸν οἶδα καὶ πιστεύω ὄντα.

[2] Hebr. iv. 15; ii. 18.

[3] Phil. iii. 21; 1 Cor. xv. 20. In view of the difference in the character of Christ's Resurrection and our own, there is much to be said for the opinion of H. R. Mackintosh, 'The term "Resurrection" is more wisely kept to denote Jesus' special victory over death.' *Expos.* 1914, p. 539.

[4] K. Lake in *The Guardian*, 1911, p. 1223. So too in his work, *The Resurrection of Jesus Christ*, 1907, p. 35, 'The whole of his (Paul's) argument in 1 Cor. xv. to the effect that flesh and blood cannot inherit the kingdom of heaven, is based on the parallelism between the Resurrection of Christ and the resurrection of Christians.' Lake draws the same parallel in his latest work, *The Stewardship of Faith*, 1915, p. 137 f.

[5] 1 Cor. xv. 38.

some element will remain to form the germ of the resurrection body and maintain the link of identity. The body will be no wholly new thing:[1] it will represent the old familiar 'tabernacle,' preserving that type which will fitly express the spirit. In the case of our Lord, the Body before and after Resurrection was identically the same.

When, therefore, we are asked to consider the nature of His risen Body as determined for us by the argument of St. Paul we decline to accept the exegesis which is offered. If we look into his words there is nothing to contradict St. Luke. St. Paul, in insisting on the change which will pass upon the bodies of the dead and of the living at the Resurrection, because 'Flesh and blood cannot inherit the Kingdom of God,' shows his meaning by adding, as an explanatory phrase, 'neither doth corruption inherit incorruption'; and again, 'For this corruptible must put on incorruption and this mortal must put on immortality.' To quote such expressions against the bodily Resurrection of Christ is to employ language which has nothing whatever to do with it. Certainly, in the case of sinful man, a change is necessary: 'we shall all be changed.'[2] A body, which has been the seat of sin and the instrument of sin, *must* undergo some process of purification before it can enter into the presence of God.[3] But with our Lord this necessity did not arise. The sacred Body of the sinless Sufferer upon the Cross had never experienced disease, much less corruption. The saying of the Psalmist, 'Neither wilt Thou suffer Thy Holy One to see corruption,' is applied to our Lord by St. Peter on the day of Pentecost and by St. Paul in his speech at

[1] I find that Robertson and Plummer appear to take this view: 'The new living organism . . . is neither identical with the former, nor is it a new creation.' *First Ep. to the Cor. ad* xv. 36.

[2] Lk. xxiv. 39; 1 Cor. xv. 50, 53, 51. Cf. Tertull. *De Resurr. Carnis*, L. Swete, *The Apostles' Creed*, p. 93.

Bousset makes the same mistaken application of 1 Cor. xv. 50 to the Resurrection of Christ. *Kyrios Christos*, 1913, p. 76.

[3] Cf. Orig. *c. Cels.* v. 18; Iren. *adv. Haeres*, v. 9, § 3, 'Caro sine Spiritu Dei mortua est, non habens vitam Regnum Dei possidere non potest'; Tertull. *adv. Marc.* v. 10, B, 'Operibus ergo carnis, non substantiae carnis, in nomine carnis denegatur Dei Regnum'; *De Resurr. Carnis*, L. 'Caro et Sanguis Regnum Dei hereditate possidere non possunt. Merito, sola et per semetipsa; ut ostenderet adhuc spiritum illis necessarium.' Cf. Rom. viii. 11. So too Chrys. *Hom. in* 1 *Cor. ad loc.*

Antioch. 'Nothing is taken away but something is added, by which all that was before present is transfigured.'[1] So far as we know, there is no barrier to the presence of God but sin. 'Flesh and blood' do not in themselves exclude from His Kingdom, but only as they are the seat of corruption. The humanity of Christ was pure, and it could at once lend itself to the transfiguring forces of the new life upon which He had entered. It was still true and complete humanity; but at the Resurrection it had done with time and had passed into the sphere of the eternal. The Evangelists give us the idea of a Being who belongs to two worlds, that of sense and that of spirit. There is the Christ Who speaks, Who eats, Who is touched. There is also the Christ Who enters closed rooms, moving at will without heed to material barriers. Now we mark the signs of true human nature. Now we are aware of a spiritual presence; 'the sensible hidden as within a veil of the supersensible, or shall I say, the supersensible veiled in a robe of the sensible?'[2]

It is worth while to observe how the march of scientific discovery is tending, not to remove all difficulty from this mystery, but to commend it to our reason. Matter, it is now said,[3] has almost certainly no actual existence. Experiment is refining it away and showing that it possesses no tangible base. Now, if the partition between the spiritual and the

[1] Westcott, *The Gospel of the Resurrection*, p. 164. Cf. J. A. Robinson in *J.T.S.* Jan. 1913; Gore, *The Body of Christ*, p. 127, 'Thus the risen body of Christ was spiritual in a very different sense; not because it was less than before material, but because in it matter was wholly and finally subjugated to spirit. . . . Matter no longer restricted Him or hindered. It had become the pure and transparent vehicle of spiritual purpose.'

[2] Loofs, *Die Auferstehungsberichte und ihr Wert*, p. 37. Cf. Weiss, *Das Leben Jesu*, ii. p. 553, 'It is not faith in a spiritual survival of Jesus which they (the disciples) express and strive to establish in others: it is the fact of His bodily resuscitation from the grave upon which they found their faith and hope.' Westcott, *The Revelation of the Risen Lord*, p. 68, 'The Risen Christ is . . . wholly changed while wholly the same; changed because He now belongs in His humanity to a new order. He can obey at His will the present laws of material being, but He is not bound by them.' *Ib.* p. xi, 'Jesus, alive after death for evermore, wholly changed and wholly the same.' *Ib.* pp. 7-9. Iren. *adv. Haer.* i. 10, § 1, *καὶ τὴν ἔνσαρκον εἰs τοὺs οὐρανοὺs ἀνάληψιν τοῦ ἠγαπήμενου Χριστοῦ 'Ιησοῦ τοῦ Κυρίου ἡμῶν.*

[3] *E.g.* by Sir W. Crookes. Herbert Spencer long ago observed that the ultimate nature of matter is a mystery as great as that of time and space. But in 1904, Mr. Balfour declared that 'Matter is not merely explained, but explained away.' Presidential Address to the British Association.

material, as regards physical qualities, is so slight as to be almost negligible, so that we can no longer place them in a true antithesis,[1] does not this help us to see that the seemingly opposite phases of our Lord's appearances are in no sense contradictory? If His Body has been transfigured and spiritualized at His Resurrection, and can yet manifest itself to touch and sight, can eat and drink and appear at will within the walls of a closed room, there follows no such contradiction as is often alleged. The sublimation of the material may, for all we know, make its conjunction with the spiritual perfectly natural. And when the sinlessness and freedom from corruptibility of our Lord's Body are borne in mind, the problem presented to us becomes far less formidable. His Body is completely subject to the requirements of its new condition. The Risen One is ready for His Ascension. The mortal has already put on immortality.

The contention[2] that the resuscitation of Christ's Body, as taught in St. Luke and St. John, was due to the anti-Docetic tendencies of those writers, whereas St. Paul represented the earliest tradition—that of the appearance of a spiritual being—is not borne out by the present critical position. In the first place, St. Luke and St. Paul, in view of their close religious connection, are not likely to have been in opposite camps on a question of such importance as the appearances of the risen Lord. Then, secondly, the date of the composition of the Third Gospel is too early for its writer to have to meet a condition of thought which confronted St. John. St. Luke, like St. Paul, would not have had to contend against Docetic tendencies, which were admittedly in evidence when the Fourth Gospel was written.

[1] There is no necessary antithesis between matter and spirit. Perhaps the relation of the material and the spiritual in our Lord's Resurrection Body is a mystery akin to that of the relation between the brain and thought—entities distinct, yet capable of united action. 'The theory of "psychophysical parallelism" recognizes that while there is correspondence between mental and material phenomena, changes in the mind and changes in the brain, the former cannot be explained by the latter, as the transition from one to the other is unthinkable.' O. Lodge, *Life and Matter*, p. 198.

Von Hartmann and others regard matter as energy, fixed and stationary in distinction from free energy. V. Hartmann speaks of the 'superstition of the substantiality of matter.' 'If the material part of our body is of a spiritual kind, what is there to prevent its further spiritualization and transfiguration?' Hilbert, *Christentum und Wissenschaft*, 1909, p. 162.

[2] K. Lake, *The Resurrection of Jesus Christ*, p. 265.

In their time there was no such view requiring notice: or we probably should find traces of it in the writings of St. Paul.[1] But one can hardly imagine that Docetism had so soon formulated its tenets respecting the Person of Christ. To find the reason for St. Luke's statement of the bodily Resurrection, not in the fact itself, but in the necessity to oppose a hypothetical Docetism in the primitive Church, is altogether too far-fetched an expedient. Besides, it means that St. Luke, a careful and conscientious historian, wrote with a view—not to the facts of the case, but—to combat a theology which was repugnant to him.

But how can the transfigured and spiritualized Body submit itself again to actions and requirements of the merely physical life, to eat and to drink, to present a tangible surface, as St. John tells us It did, to the inquiring finger of St. Thomas? If science helps us to understand the other side of the difficulty, by showing the probable immateriality of matter and its consequent fitness for conjunction with the spiritual, can it help us when we reverse the process of thought and try to imagine the manifestation of the spiritual under the conditions that ordinarily belong to the material? Here, the known influence of mind on body, of thought and feeling on physical conditions, may come to our aid. It is matter of experience that the mind unconsciously affects the bodily organism; that the body becomes sympathetic with the mind, and this apart from any deliberate intention in the thinking subject. If this be so, it appears but a short step to take when we admit the possibility of a highly spiritualized entity, such as the Body of the risen

[1] The only passage which seems to allude to a Docetic tendency, in Pauline writings, is that which speaks of the error of Hymenaeus and Philetus, who said 'that the resurrection is past already.' 2 Tim. ii. 17, 18. The Gnosticism, of which it was a form, was at work. *v.* Loofs, *Dogmengeschichte*, p. 107; Swete, *The Apostles' Creed*, p. 91. So far from the spiritual form of Christ's Resurrection representing the earliest tradition (K. Lake, *ib.*) the Resurrection of the Body was the form taken by late Jewish and primitive Christian thought. *v.* above, p. 362. Docetic Gnosticism came later, largely influenced by such teaching as that of St. Paul in 1 Cor. xv. 50. When this passage became so applied by the Docetists as to negative our Lord's bodily Resurrection—the very thing which our modern Docetists are doing—there was needed the anti-Docetic teaching of the Fourth Gospel (i. 14) and of 1 Jo. i. 1, in combination with such clear evidence of a bodily Resurrection as that of Jo. xx. *v.* Bousset, *Kyrios Christos*, p. 235, 'In the clear principle "Flesh and blood cannot inherit the kingdom of God" the Gnostics had a powerful weapon.'

Lord, manifesting its presence and its continued hold on human nature by eating and drinking, and by submitting to be seen and touched. After all, to be visible is as much a physical characteristic as to eat, or to be touched. If we reject these latter phenomena of the appearances, we should hardly be consistent in accepting the former.[1]

If we ask again, Could a Body which is now confessedly spiritual visualize itself to man? we have the analogy of the Transfiguration. There, although our Lord's human Body was changed so that it wore for the time the form and fashion of His heavenly life, it made itself perceptible to the Apostles' sight. It did not become invisible. The same power to render Himself visible was displayed after the Resurrection. But it required a certain capacity on the part of the disciples. We gather this from what St. Luke says of the disciples of Emmaus. 'Their eyes were holden that they should not know Him'; and again, 'Their eyes were opened and they knew Him.'[2] So at the conversion of St. Paul, 'the men which journeyed with him' saw 'no man,' but *he* saw.[3] To this extent the sight of the risen Lord was conditional. It needed an eye-opening of the seer. But the vision itself was an objective reality. It would be valueless if it were not.[4] Those who so magnify the subjective conditions under which the risen Christ was seen that actuality disappears, offer us a stone for bread, a fiction for a creative fact. The holiness and joy of the saints, the beauty of the Bride of Christ, cannot owe their origin to a cruel mistake.

The inadequacy of the vision theory to explain the facts before us is at once exposed when we confront it with the experience of St. Paul. He is convinced that he has seen visions, that revelations had again and again been granted to him. So carried away from contact with life and feeling was he, that he could not tell

[1] *v. Church Quarterly Review* for Jan. 1906, p. 334.

But the fact that Christ was visible to the disciples is admitted; *e.g.* by Schmiedel and lately by J. Weiss. *v.* above, p. 349, n. 2.

[2] Lk. xxiv. 16, 31.

[3] Acts ix. 7, 17; 1 Cor. xv. 8.

[4] Although the theory of Keim, which is substantially that which Streeter adopts (*Foundations*, p. 127 f.), posits an objective presentation of the living Christ to the Apostles, it offers neither in the hands of its originator nor of its latest exponent, any adequate account of the Resurrection. As the latter truly says, this conception of the appearances 'seems lacking in reality and substance.' Gwatkin describes it as 'seriously defective.' *The Bishop of Oxford's Open Letter*, p. 6.

if he were 'in the body or out of the body.' Lest the temptation to spiritual pride as a consequence of these visions should prove too strong, there was given him a thorn in the flesh, an emissary of Satan to buffet him.

But how profound the difference between these visions and that unique and separate one—so far as his experience went—which he saw at Damascus, in its objectivity and in its power of confronting him from without! It was no self-taught change of idea, no sudden inward conviction of a misdirected purpose in life, no loss of faith in his own religious position, which cast Saul to the ground. It was something which came to him from a region outside these conditions.[1] The living Christ manifested Himself to the persecutor,[2] and the prejudices and misconceptions, which had warped and marred his life, in an instant fell away. When, years hence, his Apostolate was challenged, he bases it on his having had an objective appearance of Christ granted to him.[3]

The weakness of the vision theory is further shown if we put ourselves into the position of the disciples when a few years have gone by. Lapse of time would have soon brought disillusionment. The work which they were doing—the preaching of One condemned and crucified before Jews and Greeks, with no certainty that the Divine sufferer had been vindicated, with no light in that grave and no word or appearance to explain the mystery of such a death in spite of such a life—would have been impossible. For we have to face one of two things, if

[1] 'The ὤφθη recurring six times (1 Cor. xv.) points to six definite processes of an historical kind . . . the first five of them could not have been thought by the apostle to be other than external Christophanies; wherefore also the sixth event—the Christophany before Damascus—must be understood in the same external sense.' Zöckler in *Real-Encycl. für Prot. Theol. u. Kirche*, 3 Aufl. art. 'Jesus-Christus,' p. 36. *v.* V. Dobschütz, *Probleme des apostol. Zeitalters*, p. 16.

[2] V. Dobschütz rejects Holsten's attempt to account for the conversion by analysis of the psychological condition of St. Paul, and remarks that here actual experiences are present in which very little admits of any psychological explanation. *Op. cit.* p. 13. So too K. Lake, speaking of the subjective vision theory of Christ's appearances to His disciples, says, 'The difficulty of this view is that it seems to fall to pieces against the experience of St. Paul. . . . Thus, to explain St. Paul's experience in this way demands the re-construction of an elaborate psychological process. . . .' *The Resurrection of Jesus Christ*, p. 267.

[3] 1 Cor. ix. 1.

the theory is maintained. Either a false impression was deliberately allowed. There were appearances as of One risen, whereas He had not risen. Or the disciples invented the idea to rehabilitate their fallen position. In any case, the result is the same—the founding of the Christian religion on, and by means of, a fact which turns out to be no fact, with the further consequence that our sense of moral values is confounded, and the position of the Theist—not to speak of the Christian—is rendered untenable. It is, perhaps, in the sphere of moral consequences that the chief strength of the argument against the vision theory will be found to lie. To hold it involves a complete reversal of our confidence in the moral government of the world; while the extent of its effect on our position as Christians is set forth in those words of St. Paul, 'If Christ be not raised, your faith is vain, ye are yet in your sins.'

We are dealing with a subject in which we are bound to be influenced by our *Weltanschauung*. With some persons no statement which involves the admission of miracle will be granted a hearing. Any interpretation of the Gospel records of the appearances of the risen Saviour would be welcomed, so long as a miraculous explanation is excluded. They are the victims of their own presuppositions. They come to judge the case with minds already made up. 'The decisive battles of Theology are fought beyond its frontiers. It is not over purely religious controversies that the cause of Religion is lost or won. The judgments we shall form upon its special problems are commonly settled for us by our general mode of looking at the universe.' [1]

It will be said that the Apostles came to the conclusion for which their outlook had prepared them. A credulous,[2] uncritical age will see miracles in ordinary processes of nature and life. Their intercourse with Christ would have predisposed them to

[1] A. J. Balfour, *The Foundations of Belief*, p. 2.

[2] When, after dealing with the other miracles which he regards as 'contra naturam,' Dr. Sanday comes to deal with 'the two great events, the Supernatural Beginning and the Supernatural Ending of the Lord's earthly career,' he assigns their origin—regarded as miracles—to the influence of the Old Testament. *Op. cit.* pp. 26, 27. The notion of such nature-contravening occurrences was derived by the disciples from their familiarity with Old Testament happenings. In fact miracles were in the air and it was only likely that they would be attributed to Christ, though no historic basis for them was in existence. That appears to be Dr. Sanday's position; for he speaks of the way that God has of bringing truth out of legend. In other words, the Birth and the Bodily

the acceptance of miraculous happenings. But the argument loses sight of the terrible disillusionment of the Cross. 'We trusted it had been He which should have redeemed Israel . . . but . . .' a whole world of disappointment and of shattered hopes lay in this utterance of the two disciples. There was as yet nothing to cause it to be otherwise.[1] But when the Form of the Crucified appeared before them and their eyes were

Resurrection are presented to us in the form of legends; 'I could not, as at present advised, commit myself to it (the Church's faith) as literal fact.' *Op. cit.* p. 28.

Now there is one well-attested fact which forbids the derivation of New Testament miracles from an atmosphere presumably favourable to such happenings, an atmosphere largely created by the recollection of Old Testament stories—the admission of his contemporaries that 'John did no miracle.' Jo. x. 41. If anyone might have been expected to show forth miraculous power, it was he. Standing, as he did, at a moment of crisis—the end of the old era, the dawn of the new—a man gifted once again with the voice of prophecy which, apart from apocalyptic utterances, had been silent for centuries, a new Elias; here was one who, by the strangeness of his life and habits and the tragedy of his death, might well have created for himself an atmosphere of prodigy and legend. Yet when they looked back on his career, the people own, as they come together to the Lord, 'John did no miracle, but all things that John spake of this man were true.' We can have no stronger evidence that the age which saw the rise of Christianity was not one in which 'miracles were in the air.' The man in whom prophecy was born again, the man whose character and action led people to flock out to him and ask if he were Messiah, was never credited even by the crowd with power to work miracles. When the miracles of Christ and, we may add, of St. Paul came to be reported, it was not to meet a desire for the miraculous: for such a state of mind does not appear to have existed. It was the simple proclamation of facts—facts too which, according to the Fourth Gospel, were freely admitted by enemies. Jo. ix. 16; xii. 19.

'It is remarkable that although there are allusions to signs and wonders in the Apostolic age . . . there is no allusion to miracles wrought by Christ. It cannot be said that, in the age in which the Gospels were being framed, there was a tendency to glorify Christ by attributing miracles to Him.' Robertson and Plummer, *The First Epistle to the Corinthians*, p. 266, note.

On this contrast between our Lord and the Baptist, see Weinel, *Bibl. Theologie des N.T.* p. 144, 'Our sources are quite agreed in contrasting His portrait with that of the Baptist, who did no miracle and show us Jesus so fully steeped in the miraculous that absolutely certain historical narratives and not semi-legends lie before us.'

As to the influence of the Old Testament on the New Testament narratives of miracles, see Du Bose, *The Gospel according to St. Paul*, p. 23, 'It is perfectly plain to see, with one and all the writers of the New Testament, that they are never trying to construct facts out of the material of the Old, but on the contrary are ever striving to find in the Old the meaning and interpretation of facts. . . .'

[1] 'We can hardly exaggerate the loss of courage and the despair of the disciples during those days.' J. Weiss quoted by V. Dobschütz, *op. cit.* p. 14.

no longer 'holden,' then indeed all that they had learned to know and love in Him came to incline them to receive and acknowledge Him. The Appearances of the Risen Saviour would have had no meaning to those who had not known Him in the days of His humiliation.[1] But granted, as they were, to men who had learned to see in Him the Son of God, the Messiah, the King, they matched the conception which they had formed of Him, rescued them from despair, renewed their hopes, set their feet on the way of life, and 'put a new song into their mouth.'

At the back of all the difficulties which beset the story of the Resurrection lies that of the apprehension of super-sensible phenomena by senses which are adapted to the reception of the sensible. Can we base any knowledge on such a foundation? And when the knowledge is communicated, as it professes to be in the Gospel narratives, does it come to us with an authority which can demand our acceptance? In other words, do the experiences of the first witnesses of events, which on their own showing transcend the capacity of human investigation, oblige us to believe them as an article of faith? Does our salvation, our hold on Jesus Christ as the Son of God, depend on our reception of phenomena witnessed, as it is said, by men whom we cannot question and whose testimony is concerned with subjects which could never appeal to men generally as matters of common understanding, because no scientific mode of verification is possible? Must our destiny rest on what was largely the pious belief of men who have passed away centuries ago?

Thus stated, the difficulty is indeed formidable; and yet the answer lies partly in the nature of historical evidence and in the conditions of its reception, partly in general considerations of God's dealing with mankind. The character and motives of the witnesses combined with their capacity of apprehension require investigation. It is admitted that they were sincere, that they had no *arrière pensée*, that they deliver that which presented itself to their minds. The further question as to their capacity for witnessing must now claim our attention. They

[1] If the case of St. Paul seems to negative this view, it is to be remembered that before his conversion, he had known of Christ and had fought against the idea of His Messiahship. 'He did it ignorantly, in unbelief.' The appearance of Christ at his conversion revealed to him in a moment the truth which he had conscientiously rejected and then all that he had heard of Christ came to enforce it.

knew their Master, as only they could know Him, who had been with Him under all circumstances and conditions for a considerable space of time. His voice, His features, His gestures, were to them the best known factors of their experience. They were engraven deeply on heart and mind. He suddenly leaves them for the grave. But while their hearts are full of their loss He as suddenly reappears. Have they forgotten Him? Does He come as a stranger? In touches, unpremeditated and spontaneous, fresh from the fountain of truth, we have the proof that it is the same Jesus who appears to them. We have only to refer to a writing like the apocryphal *Gospel of Peter*[1] to see what imagination and invention do when it is sought to heighten an effect, how grotesque and unlife-like the picture becomes. Indeed, the entire consistency of the description of the risen Lord with that of the Jesus of the public Ministry is one of the strongest internal marks of the truth of the Gospel records.

We may admit the capacity of the witnesses as well as their good faith, but something more is required for the reception of their testimony. Unless there is some preparation for it in our own character and in our spiritual condition, it will make no appeal, it will not get a hearing. Like the first disciples we must have got to know something of Christ, His claims and the facts of His Being which entitle Him to advance them. We must have been to school with Him and, however faintly, have won some true apprehension of the awful purity and holiness of His Person and His life; we must have seen that here indeed is something Divine in human form, and that all we hear and see reaches up out of the limitations of earthly things into the eternal order. It is only on such ground, prepared by thought and prayer for enlightenment, that the Easter message can take root and bud. It will be found that its rejection, when it is rejected, is due in most cases to the lack of such preparation.

And behind all there is often to be encountered in such cases a heedless and defective notion of God's general mode of dealing with us men. The presentation of truth always constitutes a challenge. It appeals to our higher nature, to our moral sense, to our power of spiritual insight. And we shall answer the appeal according to the character of our standpoint. If we believe that God loves us and desires our salvation; if we recognize in

[1] *Gospel of Peter*, vv. 39-42.

ourselves at times, in spite of sins and infirmities, some traces of the image of God in which we were made; if our mute aspirations, our dimly felt longings and restless seekings after light are felt to point towards a full revelation of God in the future, then we shall be prepared to believe that God has already spoken to us in the Person of His Son, and that the Gospel narratives contain the gist of that message. And as we read, we shall perceive their inherent truth, the absence of all inventive aims, their freedom from tendency. Men do not write thus except under the impulse of reality.[1]

With those who possess the historical sense, the course of Christian history is an argument which is well-nigh irresistible. To estimate the power of the Resurrection, we have only to try to imagine what that history would have been without it. The argument is negative: but none the less telling for that. It is not too much to say that if, after the third day, the grave still held the sacred Form of the Crucified, there would have been no Gospel to write, no Church to found. A story of a chequered life, much given to deeds of love, some sayings of lofty wisdom and deep spiritual meaning, might have been handed down in Galilean homes. But they would hardly have touched the great centres of civilization. They would probably have perished along with so much of the old world that has failed to reach us. Disciples, who after the catastrophe of the Cross, had returned to their homes, would not have come back to be filled with the grace of Pentecost. Jerusalem, Antioch, Rome would not have rung with the sacred Name. A great hope, flashing for a moment above the horizon, would have quickly faded. The ways of God had seemed more inscrutable than before. To disciples, as to unbelieving Jews and Greeks, the Cross would have been 'a stumbling-block' and 'foolishness.'

We can see what a knowledge of the Cross without conviction of the Resurrection actually meant, if we think for a moment of the infinitesimal effect produced by Christianity on contemporary and succeeding Jewish and pagan writers. Philo, our Lord's contemporary, is wholly silent. Of Josephus, a generation later, we have but scant reference. Pliny, as the second century is opening, has left us one priceless allusion to the Christian belief in the Deity of Christ. Tacitus soon afterwards tells of the

[1] Cf. Jo. xx. 27; Lk. xxiv. 39.

Crucifixion under Pontius Pilate. Suetonius makes bare mention of the sacred Name. Such was the fame of Christ crucified, *without the certainty of the Resurrection*, among the earliest Jewish and pagan writers and historians of the Christian era.[1]

With this comparative silence, this complete detachment and indifference, compare the inspired zeal of the Preachers of Jesus and the Resurrection, and one can form some estimate of the meaning of that Resurrection and the Resurrection Faith for Christianity.

Now, if the Resurrection was thus vital to the very being of Christianity, it must have been as concrete and actual an occurrence as the Death, as much a part of world-history as the Cross. Unless we do violence to every principle of psychology, we must own that a hope which was so shattered could not be revived without a cause equally definite and irresistible. No sane thinker doubts the story of the Cross. It is graven imperishably in the records of human experience. It stands before us, a fact that nothing can gainsay : and we have full proof that to the disciples it meant the ruin of their Master's cause. No one dreamt that such a death was the moment of victory. All was over. The form which devotion took proclaimed despair.[2] Then on 'the third day' there comes the stir and movement of a new hope—the conviction that the Dead is alive again. And unless we run counter to all we know of life and experience, we have to say that such a change in such men, under such conditions, was due to a cause external to themselves. It was not in them to produce the Easter Faith. The life that, since that day, has gone coursing through the veins of every servant of Christ is not the creation of a credulity struggling with despair. It springs out of truth and fact. It was of the risen Christ that St. John was thinking when he wrote, 'That which . . . we have seen with our eyes, which we have looked upon and our hands have handled of the Word of Life . . . declare we unto you.'[3]

[1] Cf. p. 6 f. [2] *v.* Lk. xxiii. 56 ; Mk. xvi. 1. [3] 1 Jo. i. 1.

CHAPTER XXI

THE ASCENSION

The Ascension of the risen Lord is rooted in His Incarnation. He came into the world, at His birth, a messenger from the Father. His task fulfilled, He goes back to Him, Who sent Him. The Ascension is the natural sequel to the Incarnate Life on earth. Even the law of circularity which runs through creation points to the return to heaven of Him who came from heaven.

But have we scriptural ground for what has passed into the Creed of Christendom, as one of the redeeming moments of our Saviour's Life as Son of Man? It is, perhaps, hardly to be expected that it would fill so large a place or be assigned such prominence as the Resurrection. The two events do not stand on quite the same plane. The one is a mighty achievement wrought in our midst. The other is a silent withdrawal from the scene. A departure can never compete in interest with a great event of present and abiding force like the Resurrection. Removal seems to take from the insistent, objective quality which can command attention. The Resurrection was a triumph, a great deliverance, a conquest. The Ascension marks its continuation, but in a sphere which is hidden from our sight.

And there is another circumstance which tends to lessen its individual significance. It is so closely bound up with the Resurrection.[1] As we have seen, the risen Lord, at the moment of His coming from the grave, belonged to that higher state of

[1] Yet it is a distinct event. The contention of Harnack, *Das apostolische Glaubensbekenntniss*, 1892, that in the primitive tradition the Ascension had no separate place, has been completely refuted by Dr. Swete, *The Apostles' Creed*, p. 64 f.

life which we call Heaven. His continuance here was purely for the purpose of manifesting to His disciples the reality of His return from the grave, and of laying upon them the commission which it involved. He was ready to ascend at that early hour when the crucified Body left the place of its brief rest. It was for economical reasons that He tarried. And so the Ascension is apt, in our minds, to be merged in and overshadowed by the Resurrection as the more critical event.

These minimizing considerations seem to be met by the small place assigned to the Ascension in the New Testament. There is much reference to the after-effects, but the narrative of the actual event is meagre; sufficient indeed for the purpose, but peremptory in its refusal to meet and satisfy our curiosity. A veil is drawn before the future of human life and destiny. 'A cloud received Him out of their sight.'

First as to the Gospels. St. Matthew has no narrative of the Ascension. He leaves us with our Lord and the disciples on the mountain in Galilee. St. Mark may have originally contained an account and the appendix contains one now.[1] St. Luke records that 'while He blessed them, He was parted from them and was carried up into heaven.'[2] The Fourth Gospel, while containing no actual account of the Ascension, has frequent allusions to it and explains its meaning.[3] The writer, who had the Synoptic Gospels before him, apparently was content with the description which he found there and saw no need to supplement it. In the words in which he records our Lord's high-priestly prayer, spoken aloud for the comfort of the disciples, St. John describes Him as speaking of His Ascension, 'And now I come to Thee.'[4] Though the way lay through the Cross and the grave, it was opening out before Him. In the discourse in which He prepared the disciples' minds for His

[1] Mk. xvi. 19.

[2] Lk. xxiv. 51. The words *καὶ ἀνεφέρετο εἰς τὸν οὐρανόν* are thought to be interpolated. *v.* Westcott and Hort. *Gr. Test.* ii. p. 73 (App.). But as Plummer remarks, St. Luke states that *ὁ πρῶτος λόγος* contained an account of the work of Jesus *ἄχρι ἧς ἡμέρας . . . ἀνελήμφθη*. Acts i. 1, 2. 'He therefore considered that he had recorded the Ascension in his Gospel.' *St. Luke, in loc.* The words *διέστη ἀπ' αὐτῶν* certainly imply such a withdrawal as the Ascension. Otherwise the joy of the disciples as they returned to Jerusalem is inexplicable.

[3] Jo. iii. 13; vi. 62; xiv. 2 f.; xvi. 5, 7.

[4] Jo. xvii. 13. *v.* Westcott, *in loc.*

departure, He seems to lift one corner of the veil and disclose more of the after-effects of His Ascension than is related in those Gospels which describe it.[1] We have, therefore, in the Fourth Gospel, if not a circumstantial account of the Ascension, allusions that confirm and illustrate what we read elsewhere; and the fact that the Evangelist sees no need to explain the allusions is proof that the Ascension had become part of the spiritual possessions of the primitive Church. It is taken for granted, and has its place in the drama of redemption.

But it is to St. Luke, to whom we owe so much of our knowledge of our Lord's entrance into the world, that we are indebted for the fullest narrative of His departure.

It forms the introduction to his history of the planting of the Church. There is a significance in this fact to which we must presently refer. When we turn back to the earlier account in his Gospel and to which he here alludes, we are conscious of nothing to be corrected, only of additions due to fuller knowledge. The Gospel speaks of no precise date for the event.[2] In the Acts we are told that the appearances of Christ to His disciples were spread over a period of forty days. We therefore infer that shortly after, if not at the very close of, that time the Ascension actually took place. In the Gospel we read that 'He led them out as far as to Bethany,' which lay on the slope of the Mount of Olives. In the Acts, when the Ascension had taken place, the disciples 'returned unto Jerusalem from the Mount called Olivet.' St. Luke had already spoken of the command not to depart from Jerusalem until they were endued with power from on high; but there is no precise indication of the occasion on which it was given. In the Acts he seems to connect it immediately with our Lord's departure; although the fresh start of the narrative in i. 6 makes it quite possible that this command was given on the occasion of one of the appearances. Once more Christ corrects the too mundane conceptions of the coming of His kingdom, to which the disciples give expression even at this moment and after such experiences as had been theirs. He promises the power of the Holy Ghost, and tells them that they shall be His witnesses unto the uttermost part of the earth.

The last words have been spoken—not in the failing accents

[1] Jo. xiv. 1-5. [2] *v.* above, p. 350.

of a dying friend, but with the force and hopefulness of a conqueror, who is looking into the future when He will reap the spoils of His victory. Their eyes are fastened upon Him. The time had come for Him to go. The centre of their interest, the supreme object of their affection, was to pass to another sphere. 'While they beheld, He was taken up.' It is a perverse adhesion to 'the letter which killeth' to find in these words a view of the Ascension which the state of scientific thought regards as untenable.[1] This was the exaltation of the risen Saviour, and His exaltation can only be represented to our minds in expressions which appear too physical for such a process. Yet they are not meant for one moment to chain our minds down to the necessities of language. The Ascension was a passing of the Saviour into the conditions of that life of blessedness in which the presence of God is experienced—into heaven itself. It is natural to the human mind to regard this change as involving upward movement. As the Master and the disciples stood together upon the Mount, He disappeared from their sight. It seemed, so they afterwards told their experiences, as if a cloud had enveloped His Form. There must have been some very clear and definite sign of His removal from them, for they were looking stedfastly after Him, and as they looked, two angels appeared.[2] From them the disciples learn the destination of their Lord. They are assured that He will return in like manner

[1] 'Since the appearances of the risen One were all intended to make the disciples sensibly certain of His bodily resurrection, it is quite conceivable that this, His definite departure from the earth, was demonstrated to their senses (*veranschaulicht wurde*) by His disappearance in a cloud and seeming to be raised up to heaven with it.' B. Weiss, *Das Leben Jesu*, ii. p. 577.

In the interest of his theory of a diversity between St. Luke's account of the Resurrection and 1 Cor. xv. Dr. K. Lake ingeniously employs the Ascension as a dividing line between two modes of appearance of the risen Christ. 'Those previous to it were of flesh and blood; those later than it were not.' *The Resurrection of Jesus Christ*, pp. 119, 233. *v.* above, p. 364.

It is beside the mark to try to discredit the narratives of the Ascension by appeal to the Copernican theory. Those narratives, it is true, belong to a time when the Ptolemaic view of the universe was prevalent. But the language of the inspired writers is in popular form, and the new light cast by science has no bearing upon the facts which the writers intended to convey. They do not set out to give a scientific account of what occurred; but in language which holds good for all time, they tell us the experiences of the disciples.

[2] Acts i. 10. St. Luke was a firm believer in the ministry of angels. Like the Acts, his Gospel opens with them. They play a great part in both of his writings.

as they had seen Him go into heaven ; and they are recalled to a sense of their duty and of the work which lay before them. In the Gospel, St. Luke makes no mention of the angels ; but he adds that the disciples worshipped our Lord, and 'returned to Jerusalem with great joy.'

The Ascension formed the necessary conclusion to the earthly life of the Son of God. To Himself it meant much. He had come forth from the Father's side to do His will. In the Temptation and in Gethsemane, and we may be sure at other times, He had experienced the full force of all that could be urged against the completion of His task. But He remained stedfast to His purpose ; and at His Ascension He returns with the proof of its accomplishment. At the same time He resumes the state that He had laid aside. He 'enters into His glory.' Once more the riches, abandoned when 'for our sakes He became poor,' are open to Him. A new adoration awaits Him. Hitherto the Son of God had been the object of worship, with the Father and the Spirit. Now He enters heaven as Son of Man as well as Son of God, and the unenvying powers bend in praise before Him in His new character as the Representative of Man. It is a marvellous thought that there, in the presence of God, are to be seen in fulness and perfection the nature and attributes of man, and that in that presence there is no shrinking, no confusion of face, no fear, as man might be thought to feel ; for the glorified Son of Mary wears His humanity as a robe which becomes Him and is endeared to Him by a thousand recollections of His life on earth.

At His Ascension, Christ entered upon a new phase of work. The Priesthood was already His when, 'Himself the Victim and Himself the Priest,' He made the oblation of the Cross. Now it is exercised in its proper place—the true Holy of Holies, the very presence-chamber of God. 'By His own blood, He entered in once into the holy place.'[1] Thus does the writer to the Hebrews declare the fulfilment, in the Person of the One Mediator, of all that had been prefigured throughout the ages of anticipation, in the offering of those sacrifices, which could never take away sin, yet became channels of the forgiveness and grace which were to flow from the 'one sacrifice for sins for ever.'[2] At His Ascension, the crucified and risen Saviour began to exercise to

[1] Hebr. ix. 12. [2] Hebr. x. 12.

the full His mediatorial office. The marks of His sacrifice, with their constraining power to move and melt, are shown to the Eternal Father. He had turned from them when they were bleeding upon the Cross, because of the guilt and sin with which they had become identified in Him Who 'was made sin for us.' Now He can behold them and, beholding, be touched with an unfathomable access of pity for all for whom they plead. We cannot measure the height or depth of the Father's love, as He is thus confronted with that irresistible spectacle of suffering and pity in the Person of 'the Son of His love.'[1] But it is a thought of unspeakable comfort to those who feel the need of pardon, that there, in the very home of love and power, 'He ever liveth to make intercession for them.'[2]

And the entrance of the ascended Christ to heaven was the entrance of a King. The Psalmist had already called through the ages to the watchmen at the gates to do their work and let the King of Glory in. There is given Him 'a Name which is above every name.' He is seated on His throne. We gather from St. Paul that the reign of the King, Who was crucified, is clearly defined by the time needed for the working out of the full salvation of mankind and for the destruction of His foes. But, 'when all things shall be subdued unto Him, then shall the Son also Himself be subject unto Him that put all things under Him, that God may be all in all.'[3] The Kingship of the Son will be merged in that of the Father, and 'He shall reign for ever and ever.'

Into these mysteries of the ascended life of Christ our Lord we can only peer, catching at times a glimpse of what, from our knowledge of Him, we are sure must be where He is reigning.

There are two considerations to which we can only allude as to things above our comprehension, which nevertheless seem to follow from our sense of His character. One is this. Although all suffering is passed and He, 'being raised from the dead, dieth no more,' although too He is at the source of all felicity and His manhood is bathed in the splendours of the Godhead, yet in the complexity of His heart there is a place for sorrow. He sees the

[1] How little this phase of our Redemption is regarded is only too clearly shown by the small importance attached to the Festival of the Ascension by the great majority of Christian people.

[2] Hebr. vii. 25.

[3] 1 Cor. xv. 24-27, 28.

sin and the suffering of the world—the cruelty of its dark places and the tragedies that are enacted there. He sees men go back from Him, He hears the fresh denials, He can measure 'the depths of Satan,' He can mark how slowly His mills are grinding and with what laggard steps the march of His Gospel is going forward. And if, from what we know of earthly joy and sorrow, the two are not incompatible in the same breast at the same moment;[1] and if, as we know it is, the heart of the ascended Jesus is a heart most truly human, we can see that even there and now He can, in St. Paul's strong figure, 'be crucified afresh.'

And along with experience of sorrow there must also be a certain sense of incompleteness. His Manhood is related to us all. As the Head, He is in vital union with the Members of His Body. How then can He be perfect and complete until the Body has attained its destined fulness?

One by one the separate members are being brought in. Coming from East and West, with all their varieties of character and capacity, they 'grow up into Him in all things which is the Head, even Christ.' But until this comes to pass, the blessedness of the Ever-Blessed One is incomplete. There is something lacking to the Head in the imperfection of the Body. What a prospect lies before the Church to stimulate and empower her missionary zeal—the completion of the felicity, and the rounding off of the wholeness, of her Lord! For He cannot be Himself in all His glory 'till we all come in the unity of the Faith and of the knowledge of the Son of God unto a perfect man, unto the measure of the stature of *the fulness of Christ.*'[2]

And the Ascension means much for ourselves. The passing of our Head and, with Him, of the seat of power from earth to heaven gives its peculiar character to the Christian religion. Its life and energy are sustained and moved from above. The Apostles quickly assert the true source of their miraculous gifts; 'The God of our fathers hath glorified His Son Jesus . . . and His Name through faith in His Name hath made this man strong whom ye see and know.'[3]

And this transference of the object of our interest and the source of all power from earth to heaven makes heaven our true

[1] Cf. 2 Cor. vi. 10. [2] Eph. iv. 13, 15.
[3] Acts iii. 13, 16; cf. ii. 33; iv. 10; v. 31.

home; for 'there Christ has for us entered.' It was a saying of Mahomet, 'Man has but one paradise and that is above.' Jesus, having passed within the veil which hides the life with God from the eye of sense, has given to our anticipations of the future a very definite stamp. What we see and what we touch is not that round which our hearts should entwine themselves. For a reason hardly dreamt of by the patriarchs of whom the words were first spoken, men of faith 'desire a better country, that is an heavenly.'[1]

The Ascension, like the Cross and the Resurrection, is intended to be a fact of experience in our own lives. Unless we know something of what it is to have moments of ascension when our 'life is hid with Christ in God,' we are not living as Christians in the New Testament sense of the word. These moments, with some of us, may be few and far between, but they form an element of spiritual experience with which we cannot dispense. The insistent pressure of material things and interests is always trying to chain us down to earth. Hence we need to cultivate communion with our ascended Lord, to find our happiness in following Him where He has gone, and in entering into the secret of His bliss. If we thus 'in heart and mind thither ascend and with Him continually dwell,' we shall know more and more of the joy of His presence with us, and shall be able to say with St. Bernard, 'Nunquam abs Te sine Te,' 'I never go from Thee without Thee.' In one of the oldest parts of our Liturgy, and one which is incorporated in that of every branch of the Catholic Church, the Priest cries to the people, 'Sursum corda,' and the people reply, 'habemus ad Dominum.' At the moment when the presence of our Ascended Lord is being invoked, it is recognized that, to have Him with us, we must pass in heart and mind to Him.[2]

According to St. John, our Lord said that His departure from the world was expedient for His disciples. Otherwise the Holy Ghost would not come to them.[3] But there was another reason. His continued bodily presence would have so engrossed their attention and so maintained their dependence upon Him,

[1] Hebr. xi. 16.

[2] With regard to the observance of the Feast of the Ascension, *v.* Aug. *Serm.* cclxii. § 3, 'Ecce celebratur hodiernus dies toto orbe terrarum.'

[3] *v.* below, p. 480.

that there would have been no opportunity for building up the Church and publishing the Gospel. They could hardly have endured the spiritual strain of His appearances. They would have passed their lives in expectation of His coming to them at any moment. They would also have failed to gain that power of initiative and that resourcefulness, which were required for the task that was before them. And only when He had passed from sight and touch could they have realized that God had been with them. He could only be fully 'manifested in remembrance.' [1]

It is one of the paradoxes which are so characteristic of Christianity that for Christ to go meant that, in a deeper and truer sense, He would stay. Just before His Ascension, at the meeting on the mountain in Galilee, with the prospect of His glory full in view, He said in words intended not to mock but to comfort His disciples, 'Lo, I am with you alway, even unto the end of the world.' [2] 'He departed from our sight to return to our hearts, that we might find Him. He departed and lo, He is here.' [3]

[1] *v.* Newman, *Paroch Serm.* vol. iv. p. 253; Aug. *Serm.* cclxiv. § 2; *In Johan. Evang.* Tract. xciv. § 4.

[2] *v.* Martensen, *Christian Dogmatics*, pp. 324-329.

[3] Aug. *Confess.* iv. 12, § 19 A.

CHAPTER XXII

PENTECOST

FROM end to end of the Old Testament, God has revealed Himself as Spirit. At times this conception has sunk into the background. It was long before anthropomorphic ideas lost their hold and gradually, under the influence of the prophets, gave place to a higher creed. In certain Psalms and in Ezekiel and Isaiah, the spiritual conception of God comes out in its fulness.[1] To this day, for depth of conviction and majesty of expression, we have to turn as much to the Old Testament as to the New for adequate utterance of the spiritual nature of God.

The importance of this fact in the history of Christian truth cannot be overestimated. At the outset there is handed on from the past the conception that, whatever in the development of religious truth is added by the appearance in the flesh of the Son of God, there can be nothing to conflict with the primal and outstanding principle of the spirituality of the Eternal Godhead. God, becoming manifest in the flesh, does not cease to be Spirit. Still, through the Spirit, takes place the closest intercourse between God and man. Nothing can be plainer than our Lord's insistence on the spiritual character of the Revelation of which He was the embodiment. It would not be too much to say that, all through His Ministry, He worked for the deepening and spiritualizing of men's thought of Himself, drawing away their minds from the temporal and visible to the unseen and eternal, preparing them for that full revelation of the Spirit which was to be the reward of His own perfect obedience in the flesh, and the crown of His own glorification at the right hand of God.

[1] Ps. li. 11; Is. xlviii. 16; lxi. 1; Ez. ii. 2; iii. 24.

As we should suppose, this insistence is more prominent in the Fourth Gospel than in the Synoptics.[1] It is true that in all three, the sin against the Holy Ghost is said by our Lord to be unpardonable, showing the great place which the Spirit occupied in His view.[2] But it is in the Fourth Gospel that the Person and Work of the Spirit of God appear in unmistakable clearness.[3] This may have been due in part to the character and bent of the Evangelist's mind; in part to experience of long years under the dispensation of the Spirit. Both factors would contribute to the selection of such remembered portions of Christ's teaching as bore upon the subject. Thus, 'inspired by the Spirit, John, last of all, composed a spiritual Gospel.'

But the Gospel of the Holy Spirit, historically considered, is naturally not to be found within the writings of the four Evangelists. It does not come within their scope. 'The Holy Spirit was not yet given; because Jesus was not yet glorified.' The gift of the Spirit and the earliest results of His Ministry belong to a later stage of Christian experience than that covered by the evangelic memorials of our Lord's life on earth. Even His departure is so briefly described and with such lacunae as seem to direct our thought to some subsequent narrative, and we cannot wonder if the gift which resulted from that departure belongs to quite a different stage of literature.

Linguistic indications, as well as direct statement, point to identity of authorship of the Acts and of the Third Gospel. Recent research has corroborated this view,[4] and there is a fairly general opinion that this author is St. Luke.[5]

[1] Cf. the tradition preserved by Clement of Alexandria that 'John last of all, perceiving that the bodily things had been presented in the (other) Gospels, and at the entreaty of his friends, inspired by the Spirit, composed a spiritual Gospel.' Euseb. *H.E.* vi. 14.

[2] Matt. xii. 31 f.; Mk. iii. 28 f.; Lk. xii. 10.

[3] vii. 39; xiv. 16, 26; xv. 26; xvi. 7 f.

[4] *E.g.* Hawkins in *Horae Synopticae*; Harnack, *Beiträge*, etc. iii. Cf. Headlam in Hastings' *D.B.* i. p. 29.

[5] J. Weiss (art. 'Acts' in Hastings' *Dict. of Christ.*) roundly states that 'we do not know the name of the author of the Book (of Acts), for St. Luke, or some other disciple of St. Paul, did not compose it, but merely supplied valuable materials for its composition.' He concurs in the view that the writer of the Third Gospel is the writer of the Acts. So too, Schmiedel, art. 'Acts' in *Encycl. Bibl.* col. 48. Renan is of the same opinion, *Les Apôtres*, p. x. *v.* above, p. 13, n. 1.

With a reference to the Gospel as his former treatise, the writer glides at once without further introduction into his subject. He connects it with the Ascension as the close of Christ's earthly Ministry, taking us so far back into strictly Gospel times that he gives us—what is omitted in all the Gospels [1]—the exact duration of our Lord's stay on earth after His Resurrection, and a conversation with the disciples which is not reported elsewhere.

It has been objected that the historical character of this narrative is affected by the statement that our Lord was seen for forty days. This period has been so frequently connected with probation and trial, or with preparation for some coming state of happiness and prosperity, that its presence is thought to cast suspicion on the recital of which it forms a part. But the didactic colouring of the passage is no bar to its historic value. Rather we may say that the period of our Lord's sojourn on earth after His Resurrection, if mainly determined by the necessities of the case, is only likely to have been affected by considerations of analogy. At any rate, the fact of analogy cannot be alleged as destructive of the historical character of a narrative.

The conversation that took place during this period between our Lord and His disciples turned largely on the coming Kingdom. Notwithstanding all that had happened, they strangely mistook His meaning. They were to wait for the promise of the Father of which He had already spoken. Not many days would elapse before they should be baptized with the Holy Spirit. But their thoughts of the Kingdom are still coloured by those old ideas of a temporal restoration of the glory of Israel, which all through our Lord's Ministry had hindered and thwarted His purposes. They ask, 'Lord, wilt Thou at this time restore again the kingdom to Israel?' His answer is indirect. It is no time, standing as He is on the eve of His departure to the right hand of God, to correct their misapprehensions. He had already told them that His 'kingdom is not of this world,' that it 'cometh not with observation.' Yet here again is the same dulness of apprehension—the same absorption in mundane considerations which had troubled Him before. While, therefore, He passes by this fresh proof of their want of understanding, He replies simply

[1] There is no note of time in the Gospel narratives of our Lord's departure from the earth, Mk. xvi. 19; Lk. xxiv. 51. *v.* above, p. 350.

to the part of the question which referred to time. 'It is not for you to know the times or the seasons which the Father hath put in His own power.' We are at once reminded of His saying, just before His Passion, in allusion to the time of His second coming; 'Of that day and that hour knoweth no man, no, not the angels which are in heaven, neither the Son, but the Father.'[1] The similarity here and in other sayings[2] to what He had said before His death shows the identity of the risen Christ with the Christ of the Passion and the Cross.

But no sooner has He turned their thoughts from the material and present to the supernatural and eschatological, than He tells them of a new work, which a new Power will enable them to do. They are to be His own witnesses from Jerusalem to the uttermost part of the earth; and the power to live and bear that witness will come upon them with the baptism of the Holy Spirit 'not many days hence'—as definite a prospect rooted in time, precise and clear, as the eschatological conception is indefinite and undetermined.

We have to deal with two distinct conceptions. Christ is here contemplating a sphere of active work for His witnesses which, though beginning at Jerusalem, will extend to the uttermost part of the earth; a sphere which will demand the co-operation of more than one generation, whether we take His outlook to be bounded by the known limits of the Empire, or to extend to the yet unknown spaces of the world at large. We are therefore safe in saying that the Apostolic witness to Christ, as here shadowed forth by Himself on the eve of His Ascension, is one which is entrusted to the Church at large, one which age after age will take up and pass on, one which will have an ever-growing reference, as race after race of mankind comes to hear the joyful sound. His Person, universal in its bearing and significance, demands this universal proclamation. He is not the Saviour of a nation or a race, but of the world. It is a narrow and (in face of the many proofs to the contrary) a perverse view, which allows the conception of the necessarily universal relation of Christ to be put out of sight by the few passages which seem to confine it to the bounds of the chosen people, or even of

[1] Acts i. 4 f.; Mk. xiii. 32; Matt. xxiv. 36.

[2] Cf. Jo. xx. 21-23 with xvii. 18 and Matt. xvi. 19 and xviii. 18; compare Matt. xxviii. 20 with Jo. xiv. 18.

the world as then known. He is the Son of Man; and nothing less than humanity as a whole offers scope for His influence and power.

If we adhere to Christ's confessed purpose and to His essential relationship to all mankind, rather than to a disputed interpretation of certain isolated passages, we get an extended range for the activities of the Spirit-bearing Body. The Church of Christ, as the home of the ministry of the Spirit, is entrusted with a world-wide mission. Even yet, after nineteen centuries of witness, there are races which it has hardly touched; races, nevertheless, which are necessary to the full revelation of what Christianity can do for man, necessary therefore to the fulfilment of the promise 'He shall see of the travail of His soul and shall be satisfied.' One of the worst errors in the interpretation of Scripture is that which loses hold of the broad general truths of Christianity out of respect to a certain pedantic adhesion to preconceived methods of interpretation. At times we have great difficulty in the reconciliation of conflicting statements. Now and again, if true to the demands of the widest conceptions, we must be content to give up all idea of reconciliation. One thing is certain, the leading and governing ideas of Christianity must never be lost sight of in the interest of ideas which neither belong to its essence nor are certain of proof.

Our Lord, then, in this conference with His disciples on the Mount of Olives, takes up the universal character of His Kingdom which He had already taught in His charge on the mountain in Galilee.[1] It is a Kingdom which requires time for its development and extension. It is to reach to the uttermost parts of the earth. It is to embrace all nations. The work of its adherents is that of witnesses to Christ. For that they are to be shortly empowered by an extraordinary effusion of the Holy Spirit. Its consummation will be at the end of all things. But here in Jerusalem, where the disciples are to wait for the promised gift, it is to begin.

Before we consider the historical character of the events of Pentecost, some reference to the presuppositions which the narrative implies appears to be necessary.

In the first place, Christianity is a spiritual religion. Although created by the visible appearance among men of the Word of

[1] Matt. xxviii. 19.

God and appealing for its confirmation partly to the sight and touch of its first witnesses, its life is that of the Spirit. As already observed, this fact was taken over by the new Faith from the old. Judaism at its highest and best moments was a spiritual religion. The attitude of the Sadducees towards spiritual phenomena, which is so clearly indicated both in the New Testament and by Josephus, does not detract from this view.[1] They were pure rationalists, and are not to be held representative of Jewish religious thought. That our Lord shared the convictions of the people as a whole as to the nature of their religion appears more than once during the course of His Ministry. He claimed to cast out devils by the 'Finger of God.'[2] After being anointed by the Holy Spirit at His Baptism for the work of His Ministry, He is urged by the Holy Spirit to betake Himself into the wilderness for temptation. He breathes on His Apostles and they receive the Holy Spirit for the work of their ministry. At Sychar He declares that God is Spirit and that only spiritual worship is acceptable to Him.[3] He promises, as the result of His return to the Father, that the Holy Spirit will come and abide with His people for ever. But, notwithstanding all these isolated references to the Holy Spirit and these claims of Christ to impart Him, we are told that 'the Holy Ghost was not yet given; because that Jesus was not yet glorified.'[4] The bestowal of the Spirit during His earthly Ministry was official, to empower for work. The true gift of the Spirit as the Spirit of Life 'was not yet.' Christ must 'enter into His glory.' The acceptance by the Father of the completed offering of the Eternal Son must first take effect.

[1] *v.* Matt. xxii. 23; Mk. xii. 18; Lk. xx. 27; Acts iv. 1-4; xxiii. 8. According to Josephus, the Sadducees 'deny the continued existence of the soul and the punishments and rewards of the underworld.' *Bell. Jud.* ii. 8, 14. 'Souls perish, according to their doctrine, simultaneously with bodies.' *Antiq.* xviii. 1. 4. In their denial of resurrection, they show their conservative adherence to the older teaching of the Old Testament. *v.* above, p. 358. But in denying (according to Josephus) the existence of the soul after death, they lose touch with the Old Testament entirely. Not only so, but they denied the Providence of God. 'They say that good and evil are in man's own choice and the doing of the one or the other according to his own inclination.' Joseph. *Bell. Jud.* ii. 8. 14. 'They maintained . . that God exercised no influence upon men's actions; that accordingly man is the architect of his own happiness or misery.' Schürer, *Geschichte des Jüd. Volkes*, ii. p. 415.

[2] Lk. xi. 20. Cf. Matt. xii. 28 and Jo. xiv. 10.

[3] Jo. iv. 24.

[4] Jo. vii. 39.

Only then 'will the Spirit be poured out upon all flesh.' But we cannot mistake the fact that from the first, Christianity, as we find it in the making, is like the old religion, spiritual. That, at any rate, is how the Gospels represent it. If, then, we come upon a narrative which reports a signal and unique outpouring of the Holy Spirit upon the disciples, we have no alien conception to deal with. It is in entire agreement with the Gospel representation of the character of the religion as Christ Himself exemplified it in His own Person. Himself, conceived, baptized, anointed, empowered by the Spirit, we should expect the continuance of His work in the world to be marked by the same spiritual character.

This becomes more evident when we consider how fully our Lord was dependent, during His earthly life, on the aid and strength of the Spirit. It is a matter on which we cannot dogmatize or speak with any precision. But we are constantly meeting with indications of this dependence.

The Spirit Who made possible His assumption of our nature did not quit the perfect humanity which He had created. Christ's growth 'in wisdom . . . and in favour with God and man' was due to His increased receptivity of the power of the Spirit.[1] He became more and more the organ of the Holy Spirit. At His victorious emergence from the Temptation, 'Jesus returned in the power of the Spirit into Galilee'—apparently invested with increased capacity for His work.[2] Fresh power is at His disposal and when at Nazareth, on the Sabbath Day, He stands up to take His turn to read the ancient Scriptures of His people, He is irresistibly led to choose the place in Isaiah which directly promises to the Servant of Jehovah the anointing of the Spirit for His Messianic work. He felt within Him the reality of the promised gift of power. In the enthusiasm of the moment—an enthusiasm patent to His hearers—He cannot refrain from communicating His thought, 'This day is this scripture fulfilled in your ears.'[3] It was apparently by the aid of the Spirit that He performed His miracles.[4] The Spirit was

[1] Lk. ii. 52, 40. Cf. the words of the Bishop at the laying on of hands in Confirmation, 'that he may daily increase in the Holy Spirit, etc.'

[2] Lk. iv. 14.

[3] Lk. iv. 16-22; Is. lxi. 1.

[4] Matt. xii. 28; Lk. xi. 20, v. 17. But we are also assured that He had intrinsic power to perform miracles. Cf. Lk. vi. 19; Mk. v. 30.

that form of the Divine power with which His humanity was charged. He was 'filled with the Spirit.'

Another presupposition, which is necessarily implied by the narrative, is the possibility of such a Divine interposition as it seems to convey. To a believer in the Incarnation, the miracle of Pentecost presents no difficulty. *That* was concerned with the appearance of the Son of God in visible form among men. *This* is the retranslation of the visible centre of religion into the spiritual world. For this purpose it was 'expedient' that our Lord should go away. The Incarnation, necessary as it was if man were ever to know God, was not the final expression of religion. It had to be completed by the manifestation of the Spirit. Thus Pentecost is the crown of that approach of God to man and of that drawing of man to God which was the object of the Incarnation. Without it, the Christian religion would lack the inward note which is its true glory. It would rest upon the visible and outward. It was necessary to show that, though the Incarnation is the source of power, and though it was the actual entrance of Christ in His glorified Humanity into the presence chamber of God that obtained for man the full outpouring of the Spirit, it is the possession of the Spirit which constitutes the essence of religion. 'It is the spirit which quickeneth: the flesh profiteth nothing.'

The narrative of Pentecost forms part of the material for which the writer of the Acts was dependent upon the information of others. There is nothing to justify any loss of confidence in the extreme care and accuracy which the writer of 'the former treatise' claims to have employed in his historical work. The Third Gospel and the Acts are not only generally admitted to be the work of the same writer,[1] but there is a consistency between the part of the Acts in which the writer speaks as eye-witness and the part for which he has to depend on the report of others which is very striking.[2] He must have had ample opportunity of intercourse with men who had

[1] Cf. above, p. 13.

[2] So Renan considers St. Luke to be the writer of the whole book. *Les Apôtres*, pp. xi, xii. Godet remarks, 'L'unité d'auteur et de composition de ce livre a été mise hors de contestation par Zeller lui-même,' *in Rom.* vol. i. p. 17. A. Meyer says that the trustworthiness of the Acts 'is at the present day increasingly winning respect.' *Wer hat das Christentum begründet, Jesus oder Paulus?* 1907, p. 10. Harnack after close examination concludes that the

experienced the doings of that historic Pentecost. With their narratives the reports of the speeches of St. Peter which refer to the events of that day are in thorough keeping. The whole recital of events and speeches is consistent.

We come, then, to the consideration of Acts ii. with the impression that we are dealing with an historic narrative, and that the events which it records are such as fit in with our conception of Christianity as a whole; that, in short, without this chapter, we should be at a loss to account for phenomena which form a vital part of the New Testament representation of the religion of Christ.

The college of the Twelve, broken by the fall of Judas, had been restored by the election of Matthias. All are now with the faithful women, the blessed Virgin Mother, the brethren of Jesus and others whose names we do not know.[1] There are no divisions

lexical and stylistic agreement of the first half of the Acts with the later ('We') section is much more pronounced than their disagreement. *Die Apostelgeschichte*, p. 131.

'Besides the four written Gospels, we possess a fifth, unwritten, and in many respects it speaks more clearly than the other four. I refer to the combined testimony of the primitive Christian community.' Harnack, *Das Christenthum und die Geschichte*, 1896, p. 16. It was this kind of direct knowledge of the events that was at the disposal of St. Luke in the early part of his work.

[1] Who were the actual recipients of the Pentecostal gift, the Twelve only or all the 120 disciples? Hamilton confidently says the Twelve, connecting it with Christ's parting promise, 'ye shall receive power after that the Holy Ghost is come upon you: and ye shall be witnesses unto Me ...' (Acts i. 8; 5), and with the election of Matthias in place of Judas 'to be a witness with us (in St. Peter's words) of His Resurrection.' But Acts i. 8 does not necessarily convey the idea of a causal connection between the gift of the Spirit and Apostolic witnessing. Moreover, the Eleven had already received the ministerial gift of the Spirit on the evening of the Resurrection (St. John xx. 22, 23). The gift at Pentecost was personal—a gift of life and power. That it was not confined to the Twelve seems to be deducible from St. Peter's application of the prophecy of Joel to the events of Pentecost. Acts ii. 16, 17, 18, 'all flesh,' 'your sons and your daughters.' Here clearly is a wider range of spiritual endowment. Besides, if we limit the gift to the Twelve, we exclude from it the Virgin-Mother herself, not to speak of Mary Magdalene and the other faithful ones. 'They were all filled with the Holy Ghost, and began to speak with other tongues' (ii. 4). The 'all' of this passage are the 120 of i. 15. Cf. Hamilton, *The People of God*, ii. p. 211 f.; A. Wright, *Some New Testament Problems*, p. 297.

Whether the sacramental signs—the fire and the tongues—accompanied the gift in every instance is not so certain. According to the straightforward interpretation of the text, the 120 manifested them; and there is nothing to

among them. When the great day dawned, they were all 'with one accord in one place,' possibly the Upper Room where they assembled on their return from Olivet, and where they seem to have continued in prayer and supplication during the time of waiting. But it may have been the Temple ; for, in the closing verse of St. Luke's Gospel, after the return to Jerusalem, we are told that 'they were continually in the Temple, praising and blessing God.' They could not have been 'continually' in both places. Although tradition points to the Upper Room as the scene of the Pentecostal outpouring of the Spirit,[1] there is much to be said for the Temple. There must have been room for the crowd of devout Jews of the Dispersion who came together on hearing the rumour of what was happening. The large number of converts added to the Church that day—'about three thousand souls'—shows that the scene of the preaching of St. Peter must have been wide. Perhaps we may gather from the statements in the Gospel and in the Acts that the election of St. Matthias was held in the Upper Room, and that it was during the disciples' continuance in prayer in the Temple that the subsequent events took place.[2]

The disciples are described as sitting as if in expectation. There was a stillness. Even the voice of prayer was silent. Suddenly they became conscious of an experience which, as they spoke of it afterwards, they could only describe as the sound of a rushing mighty wind with the appearance of tongues of lambent fire resting on every head. These were the outward and visible signs of the sacrament of Pentecost. They became conscious also of an inward experience. As they looked back upon it, they recognized the fulfilment of the promise for which they had been waiting. God the Holy Spirit had come and possessed them, according to the promise, 'I will dwell in them and walk in them.' As the first effect of this actual indwelling, they begin

be alleged against it. These 120 formed the life germ of the universal Church. They may well have shared with the Twelve every token and pledge of the reality of the Divine gift; while there is reason to believe that the words of the risen Lord (John xx. 22 f.) were addressed to a wider body than the Eleven. *v.* Sanday, *The Conception of Priesthood*, p. 49.

[1] *v.* Cyr. Hieros. *Catech.* xvi. 4.

[2] Bp. Chase thinks that the Temple was the scene of the Pentecostal gift. *Credibility of Acts*, p. 30 ; *Confirmation in the Apostolic Age*, p. 20. Dr. Swete argues for the Upper Room. *The Holy Spirit in the New Testament*, p. 69 f.

to speak in strange accents. It is the way of the Holy Spirit to deal with men as they neither imagine nor expect. God's action belongs to 'the secret things.' At the moment they only speak. They do not understand. But what sounded to some of those about them as a confused Babel of discordant voices, attracted Jews who had come up for the Feast, 'men out of every nation under heaven.' What to the chance bystander seemed a mere jingle of incoherent sounds wears another aspect to those who come together. As they listen, they recognize the languages of their parts of the Dispersion. First one and then another hears a message for himself, not in the Greek of his ordinary medium of communication, but in the language of his adopted country.[1]

The attempt has been made to explain the gift of tongues by reference solely to St. Paul's allusions to it in writing to the Corinthians.[2] Even supposing that the sounds emitted by those who were subject to spiritual ecstasy could not in every case

[1] vv. 8 f. 'That the disciples spoke in foreign languages is meaningless and incredible.' Denney in *Dict. of Christ.* i. 737. It is neither to one who considers the circumstances of the case and the evidence for the gift of tongues in the early Church. It was at once a sign of the universality of the new religion and a pledge of the reality of the gift which God had intrusted to it. The Church was to be world-wide. The Holy Spirit was actually given. It was no figment of an ecstatic imagination. The strangeness of the sign—not the gift of eloquence which would be unconvincing, but of a language never learned—was proof of real spiritual endowment. And the critical juncture itself makes some unique phenomenon probable. Christ had gone from sight. The inauguration of the dispensation of the Spirit might well give rise to new experiences. Cf. Aug. *Serm.* cclxvii. § 2, 'Ridebant et aliquid verum dicebant. Impleti enim utres erant novo vino.'

Then as to evidence of such a gift. Apart from that of St. Luke based, as we know from his method, on the report of eye and ear witnesses whom he must have met in his journeys, we have the allusions of St. Paul in 1 Cor. xii. xiv. The tongues must have been coherent, intelligible. They were capable of interpretation. They were not mere sounds. An interpreter would in such case be out of place. The gift does not appear to have been used for missionary purposes to supersede the learning of languages. In most parts of the Dispersion, Greek sufficed as a medium of communication. There was no need for the first evangelists to be great linguists. The gift was rather intended to point to the actual imparting of the Holy Spirit. 'If, according to the modern view, speaking with tongues consisted of incoherent cries, interpretation was impossible.' Wright, *Some New Testament Problems*, p. 299.

[2] So Schmiedel, *Encycl. Bibl.* art. 'Spiritual Gifts.' 'Either we must admit that diversity of language was employed, or we are forced to accept the contention of Meyer that St. Luke's account is "not historical."' A. Wright, *Some New Testament Problems*, p. 287. 'The Apostles spoke the praises of God in different languages.' Chase, *Credibility of Acts*, p. 39.

be assigned to any known language, we have still to reckon with the circumstantial narrative of St. Luke in Acts ii., and with St. Paul's own sayings, 'I thank my God, I speak with tongues more than ye all,' and 'ten thousand words in a tongue.'[1] It is out of the question that the Apostle is here alluding to the utterance of unintelligible sounds. The second saying, '*words* in a tongue,' excludes such a meaning. If the sounds formed words, as he implies, they must have belonged to some language. In that case the historic narrative of St. Luke receives confirmation from the experience of St. Paul.[2] In a fragment, preserved by Eusebius,[3] Irenaeus speaks of actually hearing many brethren in the Church who possessed gifts of prophecy and who through the Spirit spoke in various tongues. To accept the notion that incoherence in utterance, rather than intelligent speech in a foreign tongue, is a fitting gift of the Spirit shows a curious perversity of thought. 'There are so many kinds of voices in the world and none of them is without signification.'[4] It was so on the day of Pentecost, and the gathering Jews from remote parts of the Dispersion had experience of this truth.

The bystanders, who failed to understand what was passing and, knowing only their own Aramaic and perhaps a few words of Greek, could not recognize any of the languages which were being spoken on all sides, attributed the Spirit's gift to the

[1] 1 Cor. xiv. 18, 19. Besides, the argument of 1 Cor. xiii. 1, 'If I speak with the tongues of men and of angels,' *i.e.* if I am master of the highest forms of earthly and heavenly utterance, following, as it does, on xii. 30, 'do all speak with tongues?' could not apply to the jargon of mere incoherent sounds. It can only refer to ordered and intelligent speech. Otherwise, there is no meaning in the saying that language without charity is as sounding brass. 'Concrete languages are certainly implied in the eulogistic rhetorical description.' A. Wright, *Some New Testament Problems*, p. 285. Cf. 1 Cor. xii. 28, γένη γλωσσῶν, 'various kinds of tongues,' which surely points to distinctions in language, not merely in sound. How could an unbeliever possibly be induced to see the hand of God in an incoherent and unintelligible confusion of sounds? Yet St. Paul says, 'tongues are a sign . . . to the unbelieving. 1 Cor. xiv. 22. They reveal Divine working. They are evidence of the presence of the Holy Spirit.

[2] 1 Cor. xiv. 18, 19. The interpreter was one who understood the language. *v.* Wright, *Some New Testament Problems*, p. 299.

[3] *H.E.* v. 7. παντοδαπαῖς λαλούντων διὰ τοῦ Πνεύματος γλώσσαις. *Adv. Haer.* v. 6. 1.

[4] 1 Cor. xiv. 10.

effect of new wine. When St. Peter rises with the Eleven to explain what was happening, he directs his attention in the first place to this ridiculous charge.[1] The freshness of the morning hour, as he reminds the scoffers, sufficed to rebut it. Then, passing to the heart of the matter, he shows from their Scriptures and his that such a manifestation as they had been witnessing was to be looked for; 'This is that which was spoken by the prophet Joel; [2] And it shall come to pass in the last days, saith God, I will pour out of my Spirit upon all flesh: and your sons and your daughters shall prophesy and your young men shall see visions and your old men shall dream dreams: And on my servants and on my handmaidens I will pour out in those days of my Spirit; and they shall prophesy.' It is evident that this bold application of Old Testament prophecy was the result of meditation, on the part of St. Peter, upon our Lord's promises. During the days of waiting, it would be natural for the disciples to think whether the promised gift had been in any way foreshadowed. So, when the day came with its marvellous happenings, St. Peter could with assurance appeal to the ancient promise, and 'justify the ways of God to man.' It was a promise for 'the last days.' The coming of the Spirit marked the close of God's efforts for man's salvation. There was no further revelation to be expected. This view was in complete harmony with the prevailing belief that the end of all things was at hand. In the feeling of the primitive community these were the last days.[3]

St. Peter then proceeds to show the immediate cause of the descent of the Holy Spirit. It was consequent on the Death, Resurrection and Ascension of Jesus of Nazareth. He appeals to their personal experience of the way in which Christ was acknowledged by God. Yet they had crucified and slain Him. Their crime was not relieved by the fact that God, in His determinate counsel and foreknowledge, had delivered Him into their hands. Then, passing to the Resurrection and showing how it had been foretold in Psalm xvi., he proclaims its necessity. Death could have no power to retain Christ within its grasp.[4] And we, His Apostles, have seen Him. 'We all are witnesses.' But a further

[1] 'Quam stulta et calumniosa reprehensio! Homo ebrius non alienam linguam discit sed suam perdit.' Aug. *Serm.* cclxvi. § 2.

[2] Joel ii. 28 f.; Acts ii. 16, 17.

[3] 1 Jo. ii. 18; 1 Pet. i. 20.

[4] Acts ii. 24.

step in the triumphant progress of Jesus remains to be told. The risen Christ has passed to His throne. He has received the promise of the Father, and 'this which ye now see and hear'—the outpoured Spirit of God, manifest to your eye and ear in the flame and voices, and in the rushing wind—is the gift of God to His exalted Son.[1]

The effect of the Apostle's words, under the inspiration of the Spirit on the day of His outpouring, is very wonderful. There had been nothing like it during our Lord's Ministry. He had said of His own works, 'Greater things than these shall ye do because I go to the Father.' The power which He wielded from heaven exceeded far the power of His influence in the days of His flesh. No such result as that which followed on the words of St. Peter ever cheered Him as He moved and taught among men. The reason is not far to seek. He had Himself said that the Holy Spirit, 'when He is come, will convince the world of sin, of righteousness and of judgment.' And here we read, 'when they heard, they were pricked in their heart and said to Peter and to the rest of the apostles, Men and brethren, what shall we do?'

The answer is clear and direct. It goes back to the teaching of the Baptist. There is the same call to repentance, the same offer of baptism as the seal of repentance; but with the added qualification—'in the name of Jesus Christ,' and with the assurance, resultant upon it, of the forgiveness of sins and the gift of the Holy Spirit. For it was to these very people that the promise applied.[2] They had only in all sincerity to claim its fulfilment. Three thousand souls are at once added to the primitive company—the first great accession to the Church.

One of the most significant signs of a certain tendency of theological thought is the strange ignoring of the fact and meaning

[1] The Father is the primal Author of the spiritual endowment of the Church. 'God is always conceived as the actual Imparter of the Spirit, Jesus as the Medium of the gift.' Feine, *Theologie des Neuen Testaments*, p. 213.

[2] It had been announced by the Baptist: 'He shall baptize you with the Holy Ghost and with fire.' Matt. iii. 11. Thus the Gospel begins and ends with the baptism of the Spirit—first, with the promise from the lips of St. John the Baptist; lastly with its fulfilment at Pentecost. The Baptist foresaw in the Person of Christ the pledge of the gift. The Apostles looked back on the death and the risen glory of their Master as the cause of their experiences at Pentecost (Acts ii. 33). They recognised that He was Himself 'baptizing them with the Holy Ghost.'

of Pentecost. It is due to the increasing reluctance to admit the incursion of the spiritual into the world of sense. But it is a position which is not consistently maintained. The evidence for *geistigen Wirkungen*, as manifest in the early days of the Church and indeed up to the present moment, is too extensive and sure to be wholly set aside. In some cases, a purely psychological explanation is given for these phenomena. They are traced to a state of ecstasy or enthusiasm which at the moment carries the subject out of himself. The theory of a subliminal consciousness appears likely to be worked in the interest of such a purely natural way of accounting for them. But there are many theologians of liberal tendency whom a psychological interpretation of the facts fails to satisfy. They recognize the spiritual nature of what is alleged. They acknowledge that no explanation based on purely natural causes meets the circumstances of the case.[1] Yet they will not allow that the fact of Pentecost is an adequate reason for the phenomena in question. It infringes too much on their conception of God's method of work in His universe. It requires assent to a miraculous intervention of the first order; and this they are not prepared to give.[2]

How do the Scriptures represent the Holy Spirit's relation to Christ? It is sometimes said that He came to take the place of the Saviour, to fill the gap caused by His passing from earth to heaven. So far from this being the case, the converse conception is the true one. Christ was never so present with His people, as when—withdrawn from touch and sight—He was manifested to the deeper faculties of faith and love by the coming and the power of the Holy Spirit. The sight of Him had little effect on most of those who saw Him. They only saw Him to their good whose eyes were opened by the Spirit. 'No man can say that

[1] Cf. Eucken, *Hauptprobleme der Religionsphilosophie der Gegenwart*, E.T. p. 9, '(The spiritual life) cannot be a mere product of human reflection. . . . Our nature cannot in its present state give birth to the spiritual.'

[2] J. Weiss is a notable exception. 'How are we to take our stand in view of these phenomena and testimonies? In the first place, with regard to the facts, it is only complete prejudice that can deny the occurrence in this circle of extraordinary things. . . . We are far from denying the supernatural ground of these phenomena.' *D. Urchristentum*, i. p. 31. Unfortunately, Weiss proceeds to modify his view by comparing the experiences of Pentecost with the disciples' visionary apprehension of the Resurrection. But he admits that a psychological explanation fails to account for all that occurred. *Ib.* p. 32.

Jesus is the Lord but by the Holy Ghost.' He is not the supplanter of Christ, but His Revealer.

And, therefore, we are not to think that the gift of the Spirit takes the place of the Parousia.[1] Efforts have been made to evade the difficulty created by the non-fulfilment of the expectation of Christ's early return on the clouds of heaven by positing in its place the experiences of Pentecost. But we cannot thus account for the comparative absence of allusion to the Parousia in the Fourth Gospel. There is no ground for the exchange. The Third Person of the Godhead is not a mode of the Divine ὑπόστασις, which can be substituted for another. He is a distinct Revelation of the Godhead, with functions towards mankind which are all His own. Still less can we regard our Lord's promises of a personal return as in any way satisfied by what happened at Jerusalem ten days after His Ascension. It is Sabellianism of a particularly insidious type which thus confuses the distinctions of the Godhead under the pretext of getting rid of a difficulty in Scriptural exegesis. The outpouring of the Holy Spirit, as the result of the entrance into heaven of the glorified Christ, was a fresh and final revelation of the Godhead of another kind than that effected by the Incarnation, appealing to other faculties of man and with other modes of working, though it tended towards the same end—the glory of the Father in the redemption and perfecting of man.

For we cannot enclose the meaning of our Lord's return or exhaust its historical content by identifying it with any single event, however momentous. Although it is correct to speak of the outpouring of the Spirit, with its consequent result of ensuring the spiritual presence of Christ with His people, as an actual phase of His return, His promise is in no sense fulfilled by it. The secret and invisible presence of Christ, as He is made known to His Church through the ministry of His Spirit, is only a part of the Parousia. He must be seen and owned. He must 'be admired of all them that believe.' He must triumph over His enemies openly. That day has yet to dawn. Its earliest flush came at Pentecost. But the Church is still waiting for her Lord. 'The Spirit and the Bride say come.'

In this connection, the significance of the Fourth Gospel should be noticed. It appeared at a time when the general

[1] Cf. Inge, *Guardian*, May 13, 1910, p. 680. But *v.* above, p. 287.

expectation of Christ's speedy return and of the close of the age was fading away. The change of attitude can be traced if we read St. Paul's Epistles in their chronological order. By the time that the Gospel was written, the practical life of the Church, as realizing through the ministry of the Holy Spirit the actual presence of the Lord, came to supplant in men's minds the tension of an attitude of expectation, which might easily pass into morbid and unhealthy sensationalism. St. Paul himself had contributed to this result. 'Though we have known Christ after the flesh, yet now henceforth know we Him no more.' Through his influence, those recollections of St. John which brought back to him the spiritual significance of our Lord would have been sensibly quickened. Both the presence and the apprehension of Christ are made effectual for the believer only so far as the Holy Spirit operates upon his soul. The final gift of the aged Apostle to the Church was the assurance of the spiritual presence of his Lord. He received it from Him; and his memory, refreshed by meditation and by knowledge of the teaching of St. Paul, recalled words of Christ which had found no response, and therefore elicited no record from the earlier Evangelists. And this conception of Christ's spiritual presence with His people, when it became the property of the Church at large, was the final step in the universalizing of the Gospel. It gave its death-blow to the merely national, Messianic idea of Christ and prepared the way for His Lordship of the world. Thus 'it was expedient' that the bodily presence of Christ should be exchanged for a spiritual presence; that the sight and touch of Christ should be merged in those spiritual experiences which are the essence of true religion, and bring man into a communion with God far closer and more vital than any earthly intercourse can effect.

In this great task of spiritualizing Christianity, the part played by the Fourth Gospel was of supreme importance. It shows in our Lord's own words how entirely His mind was filled with the necessity of a spiritual appropriation of Himself. The Fourth Gospel is in a special sense the Gospel of the Holy Spirit. We have only to think of the discourse with Nicodemus, of the insistence that true communion is only attained through the quickening of the Spirit, of the application of the symbol of water in our Lord's discourse in the Temple, to see how close to

His mind, at every period of His Ministry, was the thought of the Comforter. But it is in the discourse at the Table of the Last Supper, when death is confronting Him and He is preparing His disciples' minds for His departure, that He reveals the relation of the Spirit to Himself, and the scope and character of the Spirit's energy.

His presence with His people is perpetuated by the Spirit. How we cannot say; but there are one or two lines of thought by which we can gain some light. Our Lord, in the first place, lays down the necessity of His own withdrawal. His visible, bodily presence, under the limitations imposed upon Him by taking our flesh and blood, is an obstacle to that diffuse, extended presence which is effected by the Holy Spirit. He must depart that He may be more truly with us: for His departure was not the passing to a remote, inaccessible heaven, but the entrance into the world of spirit. He so went that He remained; unseen, yet more truly present. Before His departure He showed, by the manner of His sudden comings and goings, how this could be. His disciples could feel more certain of His nearness and of the immediacy of His presence, during the forty days, than when they were with Him in the course of His Ministry. His life had already taken on a new and spiritual form of being, so that, in the later words of St. Paul, there is a closeness of relation which almost amounts to identification; 'the Lord is that Spirit.'[1]

As Spirit, God is everywhere. The exalted Saviour by His session at the right hand of God acquired the same freedom and independence. 'Where two or three are gathered together in My Name, there am I in the midst of them.' He who spoke thus was the man Christ Jesus, but He said it on the strength of that power of a spiritual presence, which would ensue upon the outpouring of the Holy Ghost. He Himself, in all the truth of His manhood and with all the power and efficacy which flowed from His finished work, would be with His people at all times and in all places when met together in His Name through the power of the Holy Ghost.

We may, therefore, regard the Spirit as deepening and extending the presence of Christ with His people. In this sense He is 'the Spirit of Christ.' If we may say so, His work is more

[1] 2 Cor. iii. 17.

closely bound up with the work of the Son than with that of the Father. In the inner life of the Godhead, the Spirit stands nearer to the Son. He 'proceedeth from the Father and the Son.' And this inner relationship is reflected in the character of the part which He takes in the redemption of man. His work revolves round the Person and the work of Christ.

We have seen [1] how the Holy Spirit was concerned in the creation of the Incarnate Life of our Lord: how fully He possessed and acted upon Him, so that every thought and act was in complete agreement with the mind of God.[2] But with the Ascension and the consequent gift at Pentecost, there came an endowment of the Church at large, which before was impossible. The Spirit, Who had possessed the Saviour, has now through His completed atonement become available for His Church. We have to trace the indications of this fact, as we find them in the scanty notices which have come down to us.

The influence of the Holy Spirit is always brought to bear upon men. It is personal, and acts upon persons, not upon things. When we speak of the inspiration of Scripture, we have to remember that it is the writers, not the writings, the men, not their penmanship, that are inspired. Indirectly, the Scriptures are said to be inspired; [3] but it is because they are the work of men who, themselves, have been *breathed into* by the Spirit. 'Men spake from God, being borne along by the Holy Spirit.' [4]

The belief that the Scriptures receive their authority from the Holy Spirit passed into Christendom from the Jewish Church. At first inspiration was claimed solely for what then constituted Scripture—the writings included in the Canon of the Old Testament, which was all that our Lord Himself possessed. But, as at the present day there is great difference of opinion as to what constitutes the Canon of Scripture—the Roman Church including the Apocrypha, while the English Church with the Protestant communities excludes it—so it was at the rise of the Christian Church; so it had been among the Jews themselves.

[1] *v.* above, p. 165.

[2] Cf. Acts i. 2. The injunctions given by our Lord to the Apostles immediately before His Ascension, are said to be διὰ Πνεύματος Ἁγίου.

[3] 2 Tim. iii. 16.

[4] 2 Pet. i. 21, ὑπὸ Πνεύματος Ἁγίου φερόμενοι. Cf. Hos. ix. 7 (LXX) πνευματόφορος. *v.* Gunkel, *D. Wirkungen des heil. Geistes*, 1909, p. 5.

Three periods mark distinct stages in the formation of the Jewish Canon. One was when 'the Book of the Law of Moses' was brought out by Ezra and publicly read after the return from the Captivity, as narrated in Nehemiah viii. ix.[1]

About B.C. 200 the book of the Prophets had been formally admitted into the Canon, which now consisted of 'the Law and the Prophets.'[2] But there was still a large portion of the sacred writings that had not yet received full canonical recognition. Among them were the Psalms, Job, Daniel, the Chronicles. They went by the general name of 'the Writings,' and were variously estimated by the people. In one or two cases, such as Psalms and Daniel, it is questionable whether they were fully completed by the time that the second Canon was fixed. Their inclusion in the list of Scripture was probably attempted about the middle of the second century B.C., but certain books, Esther, Chronicles, the Song of Solomon, were regarded with much suspicion, and it was not until the first or second century of the Christian era that the Jewish Canon—the Law, the Prophets and the Writings—could be considered as settled.[3]

But although the Jews differed widely at different times and among themselves as to what books constituted Scripture, they agreed in the view that 'the Holy Scripture arose through inspiration of the Holy Ghost and proceeds from God Who speaks in it.'[4] They distinguished degrees of inspiration, attributing to the books of the Law the primary position as a revelation. Then came the Prophets, while the Hagiographa stood at a lower grade of authority. The Jews held that the period of Revelation began in the time of the Patriarchs. 'The Patriarchs were Prophets and spoke through the Holy Ghost.'[5] The endowment of the Prophets with the Spirit closed in its strict sense with Malachi.[6] The factors which determined the degree of inspiration attributed to a book were partly external, but chiefly

[1] About B.C. 444. *v.* Ryle, *The Canon of the Old Testament*, p. 93. 'Substantially the same as our Pentateuch.' *Ib.* p. 83.

[2] *v.* Ryle, *Canon of the Old Testament*, pp. 119, 126.

[3] *v.* Ryle, *Canon of the Old Testament*, p. 182 ; F. H. Woods in Hastings' *D.B.* art. 'Old Testament Canon,' pp. 611, 607.

[4] Weber, *System der altsynagogalen Palästinischen Theologie*, pp. 80, 78.

[5] Weber, *ibid.* Cf. Jo. viii. 56. Our Lord shared to the full this belief of His people. Abraham foresaw the Gospel day.

[6] Weber, *ibid.*

internal. The authority assigned by tradition had weight; but the chief cause which led to the high or low estimation of a writing was its own evidence of inspiration. The detection of contradictions, or of doubtful teaching, would render a writing suspect. The appeal which it made to the conscience of the faithful Israelite was the measure of its inspiration.[1]

There is no reason to doubt the implicit belief in the inspiration of the Old Testament as a whole which was held by our Lord and His Apostles. Whatever doubts they may have shared with their contemporaries as to the authority of certain books of lesser importance, their trust in the Divine origin and sanction of the Scriptures is complete. We even find traces of discrimination as to the degree of authority possessed by different writings. Not only does our Lord begin to prove from 'Moses and all the prophets' the reference of the Scriptures to Himself, showing thereby at least a trace of a distinction in the authority of the several books; but we gather from His selection of quotations that 'the Law,' 'the Prophets' and 'the Psalms' appealed to Him as the very voice of God.[2] To the Apostolic writers, the 'Scriptures' are 'holy.' They express the mind of God.[3]

But a step was taken which was nothing less than revolutionary, when the peculiar sanctity ascribed to the writings of the Old Testament came to be imputed to other and later writings, and a *New Testament* was formed for which the same, if not a higher, degree of inspiration was claimed. Already within the New Testament itself we have an indication of this transition. The book of Enoch is quoted by St. Jude as an authority. The writer of the Epistle to the Hebrews borrows ideas and phrases from apocryphal books.[4] This does not, of course, mean that the writers in so quoting set any kind of *imprimatur* upon the books from which they borrowed. They had no thought, when they wrote, that the Church would ever come to regard their own Epistles as Scripture. But, looking back upon the historic process of the formation of the Canon, we can see that the mere fact that such quotations were made was in a sense preparatory to it.

[1] Cf. Woods, *ibid.* p. 606.

[2] Matt. iv. 4, 7, 10; Lk. iv. 18-22; Matt. xxi. 42; Jo. x. 35; Matt. xxii. 43. Cf. Lk. xxiv. 44.

[3] Cf. Rom. i. 2; 2 Tim. iii. 15, 16; Rom. ix. 25, 'He (God) saith in Hosea.'

[4] Jude 14; Hebr. i. 3. Cf. Wisd. vii. 26; Hebr. xi. 35. Cf. 2 Macc. xiv. 46.

The formation of the Canon of the New Testament only begins at the close of the Apostolic age; but within the writings, which afterwards came to be regarded as Scripture, we can already trace the signs of authority, of a sense that what is said goes back for sanction to nothing less than the will of God Himself. This is chiefly evident in the writings of St. Paul. He believes that he is expressing the mind of Christ.[1] He charges his correspondents to let his Epistle be read in another Church.[2] As he regards his Apostleship to be laid upon him by the will of God, so he considers that in his formal writing he is moved by what he holds to be the mind and purpose of God made known to him for his ministry. Thus to the Romans [3] he feels justified in sending, as a message, the assurance of 'grace and peace from God our Father and the Lord Jesus Christ.' To the Ephesians, he speaks of 'the dispensation of the grace of God given' him for them; and he refers to his 'knowledge in the mystery of Christ.'[4] To the Thessalonians he declares, 'Our Gospel came not unto you in word only, but also in power, and in the Holy Ghost, and in much assurance.' He reminds them of the commandments he gave them 'by the Lord Jesus.' He speaks 'by the word of the Lord,' and claims to know 'the will of God in Christ Jesus concerning' them.[5] What does all this mean but a conviction that what he writes comes with an authority greater than his own; that he is inspired so to write and that the breath which gives this character to his utterances is that of the Spirit of God? We can assent to such a view without fear that we are thereby putting into the mind of the Apostle anything like a doctrine of 'inspiration.' That would indeed be an anachronism. But, as a learned Pharisee, he was well aware of the singular authority and the Divine origin which were imputed to the Scriptures; and in the passages above quoted it is evident that he regards his own formal writings as invested with a similar sanction. In other words, he believes that God is speaking through him. And it is not presumption, it is not any exaggerated estimate of his own person, that leads him to take this view. He knows that God is 'working mightily' in him, that He has revealed His Son

[1] 1 Cor. ii. 16; vii. 40.
[2] Coloss. iv. 16.
[3] Rom. i. Cf. 1 Cor. i.; 2 Cor. i.; Gal. i., etc.
[4] Eph. iii. 2, 4.
[5] 1 Thess. i. 5; iv. 2; iv. 15; v. 18.

in him, and that he possesses, in a measure fitted to the needs of his ministry, the Spirit of Christ. How far this conviction was shared by his brother Apostles and by the other New Testament writers we cannot say. There is very little mention of any claim to speak with authority in any part of the New Testament, if we except the Pauline Epistles. Only in one or two passages in 1 St. John and elsewhere, do we notice any claim to the possession of special knowledge or illumination pointing for its source to a Divine gift.

Yet gradually there emerged in the mind of the Church the belief that the volume of Holy Scripture which had been received from the Fathers was not finally closed. Men began to recognize that God had again spoken through His servants, and that one result of Pentecost was a fresh gift of sacred writings worthy to take their place by the side of the Scriptures of the Old Covenant.[1]

Looking back, therefore, on the work of the Holy Spirit in the Apostolic age, in the light of the subsequent history of the reception of the New Testament Scriptures into the sacred Canon, we observe two distinct phenomena. One is that inbreathing which enabled Apostolic men to write in accordance with God's will. The other was a gradually awakened consciousness in the Christian community that God was enriching His people with fresh Scriptures, which were 'able to make them wise unto salvation'; that although there had been a pause of at least two centuries in the production of any work that made good its claim to be Scripture, yet God was indeed speaking to His people by inspired men in writings which, by their own inherent qualities, came to be acknowledged as of equal value to the Scriptures of the Old Testament. In each of these two quite distinct events we have to admit the operation of the Holy Spirit. In the one case He gives the power to write. In the other He opens the mind and the heart of the reader to perceive that it is He Who is speaking.

In later times, the discrimination, which we can already trace

[1] Cf. Wernle, *D. Anfänge unserer Religion*, p. 434, 'Christendom must have its N.T. as Judaism had its O.T. Derived from a book-religion, growing great in perpetual veneration for the sacred book, it cherished the determination to be a book-religion in its turn.'

It should be remembered that in the Apostolic age, the Canon of the Old Testament itself was only in process of being finally closed. This fact may have prepared men's minds for the conception of a fresh collection of writings which, like the old, laid claim to a measure of inspiration. *v.* above, p. 404.

in the creative period of the New Testament, makes itself felt in the separation of apocryphal writings from those which came to be regarded as forming the sacred Canon. All this lies outside the scope of the present work; but it is to be borne in mind if we are to take an intelligent view of the operation of the Holy Spirit in the first Christian age.[1]

We have already referred to the renewal of the gift of prophecy which appeared in the preaching of John the Baptist. Men found with wonder that there had risen a prophet in Israel. The marks of a prophet's calling were to be seen in the authoritative character of his spiritual and ethical teaching, and in his occasional glances into the future, that perhaps were only fully recognized in the light of subsequent events.

Nor was the Baptist the last of the prophetic order. He was the last in so far as his special gift belonged rather to the Old Covenant than to the New.[2] But the gift of the Spirit at Pentecost, which soon moved men to write, at once began to move them to speak. The latter phenomenon was the first in order of time. We shall never be able to enter into the spirit of the first age of the Gospel unless we try to realize the predominating influence of the spoken word. It was not a time of books. The living witnesses to Christ were the standard of reference and authority. Their teaching was constantly checked and compared with the Scriptures of the Old Testament. But as yet there was found no need for the formal committal to writing of the Gospel message. The living voice of men who had been face to face with our Lord came with a force and persuasiveness which would be lacking in the written narrative. And behind the prestige and the authority of the man lay the power of the Holy Spirit.

[1] We have a clear allusion to the idea, if not the name, of the New Testament Canon in 2 Pet. iii. 15, 16. We gather that the Epistles of St. Paul have been collected; that they have already attained the position of 'Scripture' (ὡς καὶ τὰς λοιπὰς γραφάς); that there was in existence a norm or canon in reference to which men were enabled to distinguish between what was inspired and what was apocryphal. From these facts, it has been concluded that the Second Epistle of St. Peter cannot be assigned to the Apostle of that name, and that its composition must be placed about the middle of the second century. *v.* Chase, in Hastings' *D.B.* art. 'Peter, Second Epistle,' p. 817. Cf. B. Weiss, *Der Erste Petrus-brief*, 1906, p. 4. But *v.* above, p. 57, *n.* 5.

[2] Christ Himself heads the line of prophets of the New Covenant, *v.* Lk. vii. 16. Much of His teaching was cast in the mould of prophecy. He answered to the promise attributed to Moses (Deut. xviii. 15).

St. Paul distinctly attributes to Him the prophetic gift which appeared in the first age.[1] If we attempt to distinguish between it and the prophecy which characterized the Old Covenant, we may say that the source of the inspiration was throughout the same—the inbreathing of God the Holy Spirit. If there was any difference, it was in the fact that, before Pentecost, the measure of that inspiration was limited. We see a sign of this incompleteness in the comment of the Fourth Evangelist—'The Holy Ghost was not yet (given) because Jesus was not yet glorified.'[2] The inspiration of the prophets and preachers of the Gospel was conditioned by that precise gift of the Spirit which was consequent on the finished work of Christ. We cannot specify or define the exact difference. But that there was a new outpouring of the Holy Spirit, due to the victory of the Redeemer, is made evident by the language of the Gospels and the Acts as well as that of St. Paul.[3]

Under the Gospel, as under the Old Dispensation, prophecy consisted of two elements. It possessed the power to forecast future events. But its chief work lay in spiritual teaching. In Acts we have instances of each.[4] It appears as a gift which belonged to the Apostles, and occasionally to men not otherwise known, such as Agabus and a band of men who with St. Barnabas formed at Antioch a prophetic college.[5] Judas and Silas, 'chief men among the brethren' in the Church of Jerusalem, were 'prophets also themselves';[6] while the Evangelist Philip, of Caesarea, 'had four daughters, virgins which did prophesy.'[7]

If we may judge from St. Paul's references to Christian prophecy, its chief value lay in its power to teach and edify. In 1 Cor. xiv. he extols prophecy as a means of building up the faith of the whole Church, and sets it before his converts as a thing to be desired far more than other gifts of the Spirit, such

[1] 1 Cor. xii. 10, 28, 29.

[2] Jo. vii. 39.

[3] Jo. vii. 39; Acts ii. 33 f.; 1 Cor. xii. 10.

[4] Agabus foretells the famine which occurred in the reign of Claudius (Acts xi. 28) and the fate of St. Paul at the hands of the Jews (Acts xxi. 10-12). The insight of the prophet, as distinct from foresight, is shown by St. Peter in his dealing with the lame beggar (Acts iii. 4 ff.); by St. Paul in the case of the impotent man at Lystra (Acts xiv. 8 ff.) and in dealing with Elymas the sorcerer (Acts xiii. 8 ff.).

[5] Acts xiii. 1. *v.* Sanday, *The Conception of Priesthood*, p. 65.

[6] Acts xv. 22, 32.

[7] Acts xxi. 8, 9.

as that of tongues. It was, indeed, open to abuse, like all good things. A man, feeling that he was being carried out of himself by the influence of the Spirit, would sometimes forget the need of self-discipline and of respect to others.[1] There is evidence that the gift was traded upon in the sub-apostolic age; and we find that it was considered necessary to scrutinize very closely the claims and the behaviour of those who gave themselves out to be endowed with it.[2]

But in the primitive community the influences of the Holy Spirit overflowed the bounds of the spiritual life and made themselves felt upon the bodies of believers. There were 'gifts of healing, by the same Spirit.'[3] We have many instances of the exercise of this gift in the Acts of the Apostles. Effects were wrought upon men's bodies which could not be explained by any known sequence of cause and result. It was clear that something new was in operation; and impressed by what they had already experienced of the working of the Holy Spirit, men did not hesitate to attribute this phenomenon to His influence.

Another gift, which was especially useful to the leaders of the Church, was that of 'discerning of spirits,'[4] the power to distinguish between the good or the evil origin of any movement which was going on within the Church, and to determine the nature of the motive which suggested an action. Some such gift was imperatively required at the moment that new forces of spiritual life were coursing through the infant Church. As at the time of the redemption of Israel from Egyptian bondage, the God-given powers of Moses and Aaron were parodied and imitated by the soothsayers of Pharaoh, it was only to be expected that the emissaries of Satan would travesty the operations of the Holy Spirit. Discernment was, therefore, a χαρίσμα which guarded the Apostles in their dealings with men. It kept them and their

[1] 1 Cor. xiv. 29, 31, 33, 40. [2] *v. Didachê*, xi.

[3] 1 Cor. xii. 9. This passage is a corrective of the curious idea of Wernle that, 'according to the popular view there is not one Spirit, but as many spirits as manifestations of power. One spirit effects speaking in tongues, another their interpretation.... Paul himself writes of *spirits* in three places in 1 Cor. (xii. 10; xiv. 12, 32).' Whatever the popular idea, one cannot attribute such a conception to St. Paul. *D. Anfänge unserer Religion*, p. 185 f.

[4] 1 Cor. xii. 10. In 1 Jo. iv. 1, the warning 'to try the spirits' is addressed to believers generally.

followers from being led astray on false issues, and from yielding to allurements which were not from above.[1]

These extraordinary manifestations of the Holy [illegible]irit were granted with a view to the founding and building of [illegible]tian Church as the home and scene of redemption. Roughly [illegible] they were designed to meet two main requirements of the primitive community. They proved the presence among and in God's people of His Spirit. They enabled them to triumph over every obstacle which lay, mountain-like, in the outset of their course. They were of entirely temporary nature. They served an immediate purpose. When the Church had become grounded and established, the need for extraordinary spiritual operations ceased; and, as a matter of fact, the phenomena themselves came to an end. Thus, when the sacred books of the New Covenant were completed, the special inspiration of writers can no longer be detected. As we look back upon the writings of the sub-apostolic age, we are struck with the measureless gulf which separates them from those which the inspired instinct of the Church has received into the Sacred Canon. The need was past. God had spoken and, as the stillness of the first Sabbath succeeded the work of creation, so upon the creative inbreathing by which the Spirit brought the Scriptures of the new world into being there followed silence. Henceforth, men could interpret, apply and adapt what was written, as the artist arranges and modifies the materials which are supplied to him; but in neither case can they create. The period of fresh beginnings, the creative epoch, has ended with its need.

To take another instance. The gift of tongues at once drew men's attention to what vitally concerned them, the presence of a new life-giving operation of the Spirit of God. Whether we take the view that the gift was that of intelligible speech in foreign tongues, as the story of the Day of Pentecost implies, or whether we understand the gift to manifest itself in incoherent cries, as allusions of St. Paul are thought by some to mean, there was, in any case, an appeal which was of the nature of a sign. The gift of speaking in tongues that had never been

[1] St. Peter detects the deception practised by Ananias and Sapphira (Acts v. 1-12). Cf. Nehem. vi. 12, 'And I discerned, and lo, God had not sent him: but he pronounced this prophecy against me: and Tobiah and Sanballat had hired him.'

learned was not intended to spare the heralds of the Gospel the labour of acquiring foreign languages ; nor, if the tongues were but the cries of an ecstasy too mystical for ordered utterance, could any lasting need be supplied by their continuance. They were for a sign that a fresh operation of the Divine Spirit was in progress, that God was fulfilling His promise, 'I will dwell in them and walk in them.'

It was well for the Church that extraordinary spiritual gifts lasted but for a time. They were not the 'best gifts.' Directly their primary function was forgotten and men began to pride themselves on their possession, they became a source of spiritual danger. The warnings against false apostles point in this direction.[1] Men became 'emulative of spirits.'[2] Envy, pride and jealousy, rather than mutual edification, were the result. And this, not from any defect in the gifts themselves, but solely as a consequence of human weakness.[3]

On the other hand, the work of the Holy Spirit as the Spirit of God and of Christ can never be dispensed with. If St. Paul has warned men against the misuse of what was transitory and occasional in His ministration, no one has been more urgent than he in impressing upon us the vital need of the Spirit for the truth and integrity of the Christian life. 'If any man have not the Spirit of Christ, he is none of His.'[4]

[1] 2 Cor xi. 13 ; 'false prophets,' 1 Jo. iv. 1 ; cf. *Didachê*, xi. 8. Cf. below, p. 444, and Gunkel, *op. cit.* p. 56.

[2] 1 Cor. xiv. 12, ζηλωταὶ πνευμάτων, *Eiferer nach Geistern* (Wernle). Here the whole is used for the part, πνευμάτων for χαρίσματα as in xii. 10.

[3] Wernle is not borne out by St. Paul's doctrine of the Holy Spirit when he asserts that 'the consequence of his (St. Paul's) work would have been the cancelling of the conception of the Spirit in the favour of the Person of Jesus. . . . What prevented him was mainly his own old-fashioned way of thinking, which led him to recognize something immediately divine in miracles and powers.' *D. Anfänge unserer Religion*, p. 191. Yet Wernle can say later on, 'All true Christian life that arose in after time has sprung finally from the Person of Jesus of Nazareth, or as Paul writes, from the Spirit of Christ.' *Ib.* p. 192.

[4] Rom. viii. 9.

CHAPTER XXIII

THE APOSTOLIC CHURCH

WHAT was the birthday of the Christian Church? The first Easter or the day of Pentecost? The question hardly admits of a simple, straightforward answer. Perhaps it is correct to say that by the Resurrection the redemption of God's people had been so fully accomplished that all was ready for their consolidation into a Church. The way was open. Sin had been atoned for, and the atonement had been accepted. But the power of life and movement had yet to be imparted to the new body. That was to come at Pentecost, when the Spirit should enter into the completed organism. 'I will . . . put breath in you and ye shall live.'[1]

We are told that the disciples returned from the scene of the Ascension to Jerusalem with great joy. In a few days, spent, it would seem, in prayer and expectation, the Feast of Pentecost would be at hand. The upper room, in which the Last Supper had been held, is still their place of meeting. They are joined by the women who had already proved so faithful and courageous, and by our Lord's Mother and His brethren. All the former unbelief and want of sympathy had passed, and the brethren of Christ are prepared to throw in their lot with the Apostles. In all the disciples numbered about 120. The acknowledged leader, notwithstanding his recent fall, is still St. Peter. The Apostolic college has lost one of its members. The motive for supplying his place shows the entirely Jewish and conservative character which pervaded the community at that early time. There had been twelve Patriarchs of Israel. The same number must be maintained by the Fathers of the

[1] Ezek. xxxvii. 6.

regenerated people. This incident of the substitution of St. Matthias for the fallen Judas, rounding off the company of the Apostles, is typical of their attitude.[1] They are conscious of no break in their connection with their people. They are full of an intense conviction that their risen Master is the long-expected Messiah, in Whom all prophecies meet and Who is the hope of Israel. As He was about to ascend, they had asked, 'Lord, wilt Thou at this time restore again the kingdom to Israel?' And His answer, while it waives the question of time, gives no hint that He rejected the idea that the Kingdom is to be restored. So we find them full of the thought that the Messianic reign is about to dawn. The speeches of St. Peter show this, partly by their frequent recourse to Old Testament prophecy and its Messianic interpretation, and partly in such sayings as Acts iii. 19-22. The Apostles were convinced that the glorious reign of the King-Messiah was the theme of prophecy from its beginning, and that it would be inaugurated by the return of their ascended Lord. Their identification of the Jesus of Nazareth, Whom they had followed as their Master, with the object of the brightest hopes of their historic race was a fixed point in the Gospel with which they were to set out to convert the world. And this fact accounts for the thoroughly Jewish mould in which the Hellenist, St. Luke, has cast the early speeches of the Acts. It points to the probability that his report is a representation of what was actually said, and not a creation of his own, in the manner of Thucydides.[2]

The election of Matthias is thus grounded on historic precedent of number, but its chief motive is explained by St. Peter in his speech to the assembled community; 'one must be ordained to be a witness with us of the Resurrection.' Thus early does the significance of the Resurrection appear in the Gospel outline. The Apostles conceive that they are to report the daily life and conversation of their Lord (i. 21), but above all, the fact that He was the same Jesus, in His Ministry and through death and Resurrection to the glory, to which they had seen Him pass but a few days ago.

[1] 'The number twelve is plainly of importance. One and only one of the disciples must be selected to make up the number and take the place of the traitor Judas (Acts i. 22).' Hamilton, *The People of God,* ii. p. 65.

[2] Thuc. i. 22. *v.* Lake in Hastings, *Dict. of the Apos. Ch.* i. p. 27.

The mode of the election is primitive, and may well have been suggested by the saying: 'The lot is cast into the lap; but the whole disposing thereof is of the Lord.' [1] They pray that the cast may be guided and, when the lot fell upon Matthias, they regarded him as designed for the office by Him who 'knoweth the hearts of all men,' and forthwith 'he was numbered with the eleven apostles.' With their number now complete and being all of one heart and mind, as they could not be while Judas was among them, they are ready, as an organic body, for the inbreathing of the Spirit of their Lord. They had already on the evening of the Resurrection received their commission to bind and loose—to apply the fruit of their Lord's redeeming work to the souls of men. With that commission He had imparted to them a gift of the Holy Spirit. This was ministerial and official. They had not yet received the Spirit as Life and Power. That gift they were to share with others who were not of the Apostolate and with those who should come after them, a personal gift to be the inspiration and strength of their own religious life, and to bring home to their hearers the Gospel of their salvation.

We may, therefore, regard Pentecost as the birthday of the Church. Its members had each separately become disciples. They each had their own spiritual experience; but with the gift of Pentecost they become a Church, the visible community within which the Spirit exercises His ministrations, to which is committed the cause of Christ on earth, the inspired home of His activity, the Body pulsating with the new life which is ever flowing from Himself the Head.

In view of later developments of the idea of the Church, we must inquire whether this conception of what took place at Pentecost corresponded with the mind and will of Christ. Are these first movements of the community, which He had gathered together during His Ministry, taking the course that He marked out for them? Did He mean to found a Church, a Kingdom upon earth; or is the long history of its development something which was far from His thoughts and, indeed, opposed to His purposes and methods? We find Wernle saying, 'Jesus did not found the Church; for institutions, the destroyer of Judaism had no mind.' [2] The eschatological school, of which J. Weiss is

[1] Prov. xvi. 33. [2] *D. Anfänge unserer Religion*, p. 83.

the leading spirit and Schweitzer the most popular exponent, will not hear of any intention to found a kingdom upon earth.[1] And there is no doubt that our Lord did set His face steadily against anything which tended to formalism or which stereotyped feeling. His work lay with the individual soul, and with the task of bringing it to face the great elemental realities. He had no liking for 'institutions.' And yet, now and again we can detect in His thought the emergence of corporate life, as the mode in which the grace of God and the gifts of His Spirit could best find a field of action; while we are distinctly assured by St. Luke that, during the Forty Days, when seen by the disciples, He was 'speaking of the things pertaining to the Kingdom of God.' St. John too relates how, in His High-Priestly prayer, our Lord supplicated for the unity of His followers with one another and with Himself.[2]

It would, therefore, be an entire misconception of His purposes to deny that He ever contemplated the existence of a body of believers and followers who should form His Kingdom upon earth. But so far as we can look into the 'economy' of the Divine ordering of things, our Lord did not regard it as part of His own work to set up the Church. He put in motion the vital forces and established the conditions necessary for the existence of such a thing. But He left its actual embodiment in fact to the creative energy of His Spirit.

Consciously endowed with the Spirit, Whose coming they recognize as the fulfilment of their Master's promise,[3] the disciples begin their work. They start with two convictions, and their object is to get others to share them. One was the Messianic [4] and Divine [5] character of Jesus. The other was the

[1] 'The founding of a religion lies outside the vision of Jesus because He feels that He is standing at the end of the age, as the summing up of all former prophecy, as God's final message to the world.' *Jesus von Nazareth, Mythus oder Geschichte*, p. 12.

[2] Acts i. 3; Jo. xvii. 21, 23. [3] Acts ii. 33.

[4] 'The belief that He was Messiah which the disciples held must have originated before His death. It could not have arisen after such a blow to all their expectations.' Wernle, *D. Anfänge unserer Religion*, p. 31.

[5] Much has been made of the restrained character of the speeches of St. Peter in the Acts. Christ is called 'a man approved of God' (ii. 22). The term 'servant' is applied to Him (iii. 13, 26). In a prayer of the disciples He is spoken of as God's 'holy Servant' (iv. 27). If His humanity comes out in these passages, it is also true that His Divine nature is acknowledged throughout

certainty of His Resurrection. We find these two facts rooted in their own minds and colouring all their teaching.

It is interesting to observe the way in which the actual work of the infant Church began. It came to the disciples. They did not require to go out and seek for it. At first they are alone in their place of meeting, but the rumour of what is happening at the descent of the Spirit—the rushing mighty wind, the tongues of fire, the speaking in other tongues—

the book. He is 'the Lord Jesus' (i. 21). It is He Who has poured forth the Holy Spirit (ii. 33). 'God hath made' Him 'both Lord and Christ' (ii. 36). The effect of the Resurrection was at this time so fresh and powerful upon the minds of the Apostles, that they speak as though the Lordship and the Sonship of Jesus dated from it and from His exaltation to the right hand of God. That this was not the case, but that His exaltation merely put the seal of certainty on what had long been their conviction, is apparent from the general tone of the speeches and their references to Christ. Men do not speak thus of one who is no more than human. 'This Divine Name (Lord) is very often applied in the Acts to God, but not infrequently also to Christ.' J. Weiss, art. 'Acts' in Hastings' *Dict. of Christ and the Gospels*, vol. i. The exaltation to heaven was indeed the coronation and glorifying of the Son of Man, but it would be quite unscientific to quote these passages, in which the Resurrection and Ascension are so vividly present to the Apostles' minds, in order to show that *then* our Lord became what He was not before; that, in other words, the Divine element of His being is regarded as an afterthought, a reward granted to Him, something grafted on to His humanity. To assert this, as J. Weiss seems to do in his article, is to run counter to what we know, from other sources, to be the mind of the primitive Church, and to what is evident in the very speeches which supply the expressions upon which he relies. It was only natural that the minds of the Apostles, which had but gradually been opening to the true Personality of their Master, should have been profoundly impressed by their recent experiences and, in the Resurrection and Ascension with the consequent outpouring of the Holy Spirit, seen the majesty of their Master revealed as never before. When J. Weiss speaks of Acts ii. 36 as 'a gem to the historian of primitive Christianity,' and as 'the principal extant proof passage for the *earliest Christology*,' he seems to lose sight of the fact that the primitive Church regarded Jesus Christ as essentially and originally the Divine Son of God. He quotes Rom. i. 4 as showing that St. Paul 'holds fast to the notion that Jesus became "Son of God in power," through His Resurrection.' But the passage says nothing of the kind. He did not then 'become,' but was 'defined,' 'marked out as Son of God,' ὁρισθέντος. What had all along been the case was now plainly declared by the Resurrection. Phil ii. 9, which Weiss also quotes, is equally inadequate to prove his point. Besides, we know from other parts of his writings what St. Paul really held on the Eternal Sonship of Christ, and that when he compared with St. Peter and the other primitive leaders the Gospel which he was preaching, he had no modification to make. It was the same. It is equally beside the mark to quote such passages as Acts ii. 22; x. 38, for the same minimizing purpose. We can bring verses as strongly worded even from the Fourth Gospel, in which our Lord expresses

gets abroad among the more devout pilgrims who have come up for the feast. They come together and see and hear for themselves. It is the first movement towards the general extension of the Gospel. Discipleship of Christ is not to be confined to those who saw and loved Him in the days of His flesh. 'I, if I be lifted up from the earth, will draw all men unto me.' The words get their first fulfilment on the day of Pentecost, as 'devout men out of every nation under heaven' betake themselves to the assembled Apostles.

When, in answer to the foolish charge of mockers that the Apostles' gift of tongues is the effect of their drinking new wine, St. Peter had preached Jesus and the Resurrection and shown that the outpouring of the Spirit had long been foretold by their prophets, the hearts of many were touched, their conscience aroused and they ask, 'Men and brethren, what shall we do?' It is remarkable that St. Peter's answer follows the line taken both by St. John the Baptist and by our Lord in the beginning of their public ministries. Like them, St. Peter calls for repentance. Like the Baptist, he offers baptism to those who profess it. Unlike both the Baptist and our Lord, he can impart something new. This baptism is not only efficacious for the remission of sins, but it conveys the Holy Spirit to be the seal and assurance

His entire unity with the Father and disclaims all initiative apart from Him. *v.* Jo. viii. 26, 28, 29. Schmiedel, who considers the Christology of the speeches of St. Peter 'historically important in the highest degree,' lays great emphasis, like J. Weiss, on the passages which seem to speak of Christ as merely a highly endowed servant of God, whom He crowned as Messiah at His Resurrection, and points to their agreement with 'the most genuine passages of the first three Gospels.' *Encycl. Bibl.* i. col. 48.

In his latest work, J. Weiss appears less inclined to minimize the homage which the primitive community paid to Christ. 'The relation of the disciple has become a religious connection.... There can be no doubt that... the disciples ventured to pray to the Exalted One. This is the most important step in the history of the development of Christendom, the step to Jesus-Religion.' *D. Urchristentum,* i. p. 26. Weiss lays stress on the effect of the exaltation of their Master upon their views of His Person: 'Jesus then became (to them) what He was not before.' But he also points out the great influence upon their belief which their knowledge of Him undoubtedly exercised. The recollection of His life and works, the wonderful experiences of Easter, all helped to form their heightened sense of His Personality. *Ib.* p. 28.

Loofs endeavours to prove from such passages as Rom. i. 7; 1 Cor. i. 2, that even to St. Paul, Christ stood in a different category from God the Father. It is easy to show by reference to other parts of his writings that this was not the view which he held. *v. What is the Truth about Jesus Christ?* p. 180.

of forgiveness. Christ could only hold out this new gift in prospect; for 'the Holy Ghost was not yet, because that Jesus was not yet glorified.'

Thus from the ancient Church, there passes over to the new Kingdom an initiatory rite which shows their continuity. In grace and privilege, the earlier type is but a shadow of the other: hence, when an Apostle comes across men who know no baptism but that of John, he at once calls upon them to offer themselves for the baptism of Christ. The old was obsolete: its day was over: the Kingdom of God had come. All who would might enter in.

Besides its function as a means of grace, baptism was a pledge of fellowship and a sign of unity. 'The same day there were added about 3000 souls. And they continued stedfastly in the apostles' doctrine and fellowship.' Thus began the answer to the prayer of our Lord, 'that they all may be one'; 'that they may be one, even as We are one.' This was from the first the ideal state of the Christian Church, visible unity (fellowship) and identity of doctrine. It was to last but for a short time. Too soon faction and self-will began to show themselves. But visible unity and the holding of the same faith are from the first regarded as the only conception at all answering to the mind of Christ.

Here, then, we see the Church fully equipped and started for its career of conquest. We must inquire into the nature of its normal life and practice. The Church of Jerusalem, as yet the only existing body of the primitive community, has an outer and an inner side. It is in a state of transition. The disciples were 'continuing daily with one accord in the Temple.' They still lived as Jews, as all of them were by race and by religion. But a new factor had entered into their lives, which was as yet unknown or unheeded by their brethren. The long-expected Messiah had, as they believed, already appeared in the Person of Jesus of Nazareth. He had come before them as the Son of God, as One with the Father, entitled to receive their worship and the homage of their lives. There was, therefore, an inner side to their religion which the world did not see and with which the hierarchy and the people at large had no sympathy. The characteristic expression of this inner side is given by St. Luke in the words, 'They continued . . . in the breaking of the bread and in the prayers.' All the fervour of their faith, all the new experience and knowledge which they had acquired during the last 'week of weeks,' are concentrated in these two modes of their worship—the Lord's Supper and the Lord's Prayer, with the other petitions which came to form in time the earliest Christian liturgy. And this 'life hid with Christ in God' is lived in their own place of assembly and in their own homes. Clearly it could not have been lived within the precincts of the Temple. 'No one thought of leaving the Jewish Church,' but 'private gatherings, meetings in the house of a friend with closed doors, these are the primitive services.' 'Christianity existed first as a sect.'[1] It was a guild of pious enthusiasts within the confines of the ancient Church. So far as we know, our Lord had given no command to His disciples to separate themselves from it. His own custom was to frequent the Temple when in Jerusalem and to take part in the worship of the Synagogue when in Galilee. So we find Peter and John going 'up together into the Temple at the hour of prayer.'[2] In the mind of the primitive community, whatever was new in their religion was in harmony with all they had been accustomed to. The Messiah was expected, and they knew that He had come. The Apostles are constantly appealing to the Old Testament Scriptures for confirmation of their preaching, and showing that what had happened at Jerusalem of late was only what God had already promised by the mouth of His prophets.

It is evident that this double strain in their religion would sooner or later produce conflict and division. The old and the new could not continue side by side. One element would prove

[1] Wernle, *D. Anfänge unserer Religion*, p. 92. Cf. Acts xii. 12; xxiv. 5. They are called the sect of the Nazarenes. *v.* V. Dobschütz, *Probleme des apostolischen Zeitalters*, p. 39, 'In Jewish Christianity of the first decades, we have to do, not with an independent form of Church or community, but with a form of brotherhood or union, which still remained entirely within the connections of the Jewish synagogue.'

[2] Acts iii. 1. 'The disciples were and remained Jews. As they took part in the Temple worship after as well as before they became disciples, so in the dispersion they shared in the divine worship of the Synagogue.' B. Weiss, *D. Leben Jesu*, i. p. 4. But we cannot think that they would share in the sacrifices after their experience of Christ. Even among strictly living Jews, the study of the Law had come to be regarded as a substitute for the offerings of the Temple. *v.* Weber, *System der altsynagog^{n} Palästin^{n} Theologie*, p. 39. *v.* above, p. 245.

to be the stronger or the more vitally necessary, and the other tend to 'vanish away.' This growing incompatibility within was accentuated by movements without. The preachers of the Gospel were met by the authorities of their country with resolute opposition. There was an uneasy feeling in the minds of the members of the Council that what they had done to Christ involved guilt from which they could not shake themselves free. 'Ye have filled Jerusalem with your doctrine, and intend to bring this man's blood upon us,' [1] they said to the preachers of the Resurrection and the workers of miracles in His Name. So long as the practices of their religion were carried on in their own houses, the disciples would be free to hold it. But this could not be their line of action, otherwise the primitive community would never have developed into the Church universal. The Master's parting command lay upon them : 'Go ye into all the world and make disciples of every nation.' And when bidden to be silent as to 'the Name of Jesus,' they can only reply, 'We cannot but speak the things which we have seen and heard,' and 'daily in the Temple and in every house, they ceased not to teach and preach Jesus Christ.' [2]

It is therefore not to be wondered at if antagonism soon arose. The rulers felt that the crucifixion of our Lord had been all in vain, if His deluded followers were to preach and proclaim Him as Messiah and as the risen and glorified Son of God. It was intolerable that such a state of things should go on unchecked.

And thus we get one leading factor in the life of the primitive Church—the deadly and unrelenting hostility of the chief men of the nation. It comes to the surface now and again, but it was always there and played a great part in the course of the development of Christianity. Without the check which it undoubtedly placed upon the accession of unworthy adherents to the fold of Christ, the community would have suffered grievous damage. The tone would have been lowered and the standard of Christian life affected wherever the Gospel came to be preached. Thus, we find Ananias and Sapphira joining the Church from unworthy motives. But persecution and the known opposition of the ruling classes had a restraining effect. Those who joined the Apostles did so, as a rule, with high intention. No thought of worldly advantage entered into their choice. The

[1] Acts v. 28. [2] Acts iv. 20 ; v. 42.

pressure of the ruling classes upon the primitive community kept it pure.

We must now inquire briefly[1] into the two specifically Christian practices which characterized the life of the disciples—'the breaking of the bread and the prayers.' 'The Breaking of the Bread' is clearly the distinctive name given to what became known in the Church as the Lord's Supper, the Eucharist, the Sacrament of Holy Communion. It was apparently chosen from its reference to the symbolical act by which our Lord prepared the bread at the Last Supper for distribution among the Apostles. The one loaf, signifying the unity of the whole number, was broken that each might partake. A deeper meaning was also involved. The Breaking of the Bread pointed to the dissolution of soul and body, which He Whom the bread symbolized was soon to undergo. Hence the term had a very special interest for the disciples. To their leaders it recalled the circumstances of that sacred evening. To the rest it indicated their participation in what was then inaugurated; as St. Paul asks, twenty years later, 'the bread which we break, is it not the communion of the body of Christ?'[2]

The rite took place within the house or houses in which the community met together.[3] At first it was celebrated weekly. This appears from Acts xx. 7, where it is distinctly said that on the first day of the week—the day of the Resurrection and of the gift of the Holy Spirit—'the disciples came together to break bread.'[4] Along with the Eucharistic Breaking of the Bread a social meal was partaken of, in which the poorer members of the community were regaled at the general expense. This ἀγάπη soon became the occasion of unseemly conduct.

[1] For fuller treatment of the subject, *v.* below, p. 474 f. [2] 1 Cor. x. 16.

[3] Acts ii. 46, κατ' οἶκον, 'Breaking bread at home,' or 'house by house.' Cf. κατ' ἄνδρα, Herod. vi. 79. *v.* J. Wordsworth, *The Ministry of Grace*, p. 310.

[4] *v.* below, p. 583. If Acts xx. 7 does not suffice to prove that 'the breaking of the bread' was only practised on the first day of the week, it should be noticed that in Acts ii. 46, we cannot extend the word 'daily' to the breaking of bread at home. The evidence of the *Didachê*, which belongs to the first or to the early part of the second century, is to a weekly practice of the rite. c. 14. Cf. Plummer in Hastings' *D.B.* iii. p. 144, n. I find that Dr. Swete takes the view that 'in the Apostolic Church, the Eucharist was celebrated at the weekly gathering of the faithful.' *The Holy Catholic Church*, 1915, pp. 88, 202. Bp. J. Wordsworth thinks that in the Church of Jerusalem and not elsewhere, daily communion was the practice. *The Ministry of Grace*,

St. Paul sternly reproves the Corinthian Church for their mode of celebrating the Eucharist, and although he does not command the separation of the social meal from the Eucharist proper, it was found fitting before long that the distinctively religious part of the rite should be entirely severed from the meal.[1]

What were the chief conceptions connected in the minds of the Apostles with 'the Breaking of the Bread'? The circumstances of its institution pointed clearly to an association of idea with Jewish worship and ritual. Whether we follow the Synoptic data for placing the Last Supper on the day of the Passover, or with St. John make it fall on the day before and the death of Christ on the Feast day itself, the connection of the Eucharist with the Passover is sufficiently close.[2] The words of institution refer to a covenant in Christ's blood and clearly go back to the saying of Moses, when, after reciting to the elders of Israel the commandments and ordinances of God, he took the blood of sacrificed oxen and sprinkled the people, saying, 'Behold the blood of the covenant which the Lord hath made with you.'[3] In any case, the Apostles would regard our Lord's words and acts as strongly reminiscent of ideas and practices which had always been familiar to them, and as in some way constituting an agreement binding them, as the Israelites had been bound, to a certain mode of life and conduct. It was the sign and seal of an undertaking on their part to live as He would have them live: while on His part, it assured them of every blessing which His death procured for them. Thus it was the sacred rite of a New Covenant between God and man, and that which sanctified and sealed it was 'the precious blood of Christ' shed once upon the Cross, but applied afresh every

p. 306. But we can hardly imagine that, if it had been the custom in the primitive Apostolic Church, other Churches would not have adopted it until nearly two centuries had passed. *Ib.* p. 332. Wordsworth himself calls such a daily breaking of bread 'a simple liturgical service,' as though he hardly assigned to it the full conception of an Eucharist. In their first fervour, every common meal, preceded by the blessing customary in Jewish families, was regarded by the primitive disciples as sacred. *v.* Rackham, *The Acts*, p. 38.

[1] *v.* Lightfoot on Ignat. *ad Smyrn.* 8.

[2] But *v.* Feine, *Theologie des N.T.*[1] p. 142, who points out that the words of St. Paul (1 Cor. v. 7) refer not to the Last Supper, but to the Death of Christ.

[3] Ex. xxiv. 6-8. *v.* J. A. Robinson, *Encycl. Bibl.* ii. col. 1420, and Wernle, *D. Anfänge unserer Religion*, p. 95, 'The death of Jesus, as the founding of the new Covenant, stands in the very centre of the rite.'

time His servants, by His own appointed rite, 'showed it forth.' [1]

The disciples also 'continued stedfastly . . . in the prayers.' The juxtaposition of this statement with 'the breaking of the bread' clearly points to the distinctively Christian prayers which they used 'at home.' The Apostles for a time, at any rate, frequented the services of the Temple. We find Peter and John going up there together 'at the hour of prayer being the ninth hour.' [2] When St. Peter was in Joppa, he went up to the housetop to pray at the sixth hour.[3] But in the prayers 'at home,' we have the germ of the Christian liturgies, the rudiments of the Divine offices of the universal Church. Can we form any clear idea of the nature and contents of these prayers? They were, doubtless, in harmony with, and partly suggested by, the prayers of the Temple; but they must have received much of their inspiration and been largely derived from our Lord's own habit and method of prayer as witnessed and overheard by the Twelve. The Gospels are full of reference to His custom. He prays at His Baptism; before the choice of the Twelve; when He went up to the Mount, 'and as He prayed' the celestial glory transfigured Him; in Gethsemane, as He entered upon His agony. He prays at the grave of Lazarus, and on the Cross makes intercession for His murderers. These intimations of His habit of prayer at momentous periods of His life show that prayer was one of the modes of intercourse by which He maintained His conscious communion with the Father. They reveal the atmosphere in which He lived, and the unbroken fellowship with the Father which was the joy and support of the time of His humiliation. At times, the Twelve or the chosen Three

[1] Cf. Wernle, *D. Anfänge unserer Religion*, p. 95, 'They proclaim His death, they thank Him for it, they partake of its blessings by sharing in the meal.'

[2] Acts iii. 1. It is interesting to see how the ancient worship serves as a connecting link between the two stages of the development of Christianity which are marked by personal discipleship and the community as a Church. In the Gospel, St. Luke ends his narrative with the continuance of the disciples in the Temple, praising and blessing God (xxiv. 53). In the Acts, as soon as they appear as an organized community, they are 'continuing daily with one accord in the Temple . . . praising God' (ii. 46, 47).

[3] Acts x. 9, cf. Ps. lv. 17. 'Communal prayer—that is, liturgy—is hardly found prior to the separation of Israel and Judah. The first ritual prayers are found in Deut. xxvi. 5-10, 13-15.' *The Jewish Encycl.* art. 'Prayer,' p. 164.

shared this experience with Him. They could mark the fervour of His approach to God, could sometimes hear His actual words; and the effect could be seen in the renewed calmness and majestic self-possession which characterized His bearing.

But the Apostles, while observant of their Master's practice of prayer, felt that they needed special guidance for the framing and method of their own prayers. John the Baptist had taught his disciples to pray, and one day, after Christ had been praying, a disciple came to Him with the request, 'Lord, teach us to pray, as John also taught his disciples,' [1] a momentous petition indeed, when we think of the way in which it was answered.

A fixed form of prayer was no unheard of thing when this request was made. The services of the Synagogue contained fixed forms of prayer in our Lord's time.[2] Indeed the attempt has been made to derive the petitions of the Lord's prayer entirely from Jewish sources, and to refuse to it all originality. In the prayer which Jews, old and young, in the time of Christ, prayed three times a day, are the words, 'Forgive us, our Father, for we have sinned much. Bring us back, our Father, to the Law.' [3] Thus the life of the pious Jew was lived in an atmosphere of prayer. Elijah, Hezekiah, Daniel exemplify this fact. In the public prayers of the Synagogue, it was the custom for a person to be designated by the Ruler of the Synagogue to pray, while the people generally merely joined in the responses.[4]

[1] Lk. xi. 1. St. Matthew gives the Lord's Prayer as part of the Sermon on the Mount; St. Luke, as the answer to this request, definitely made at a certain time, and therefore no doubt the actual historical occasion of its origin. St. Matthew, according to his usual custom of grouping similar material without reference to its historic connection, brings the prayer into use, when relating our Lord's teaching on the whole subject.

[2] *v.* Schürer, *Geschichte des Jüdischen Volkes*, ii. p. 452.

[3] *v.* K. Furrer, *D. Leben Jesu*, pp. 51, 52. The regular times of prayer were morning, 3 p.m. (the time of the evening sacrifice; cf. Acts iii. 1), and evening. *v.* Hamburger, *Real-Encycl. des Jüd.* 2, 'Morgen-, Mincha-, Abend-gebet.'

[4] *v.* Schürer, *ib.* p. 453, and note on 'Amen.' 'The belief in the objective efficacy of prayer is never questioned in the Bible.' *The Jewish Encycl.* art. 'Prayer,' p. 166. 'Prayer is in the O.T. considered so self-evident a form of expression of the religious life that it never appears there as a command.' *Real-Encycl. für prot. Theol. u. Kirche*, art. 'Gebet im A.T.' 'In the time of Ezra, public worship began with the call, "Bless ye the Lord," Nehem. ix. 5, each thanksgiving being followed by the congregational response, "Amen," Nehem. viii. 6.' *The Jewish Encycl.* art. 'Benedictions,' p. 8.

Our Lord brings one serious charge against the prayers of some of His contemporaries. 'They thought to be heard for their much speaking.' They used vain repetitions. They employed prayer as a means of credit with God. It was not an act of worship, or even a supplication for grace. It was rather of the nature of an *opus operatum*.

Against this abuse our Lord speaks vehemently; and to correct it He utters the prayer which has become the model and standard of Christian prayer for all time. For its foundation and sanction it rests upon the Fatherhood of God, that conception which, together with the doctrine of Monotheism, was the great spiritual gift of the Jewish world to the human race. As another root principle, it also bears witness to the fellowship and unity of those who call upon the Father. The Lord's Prayer knows nothing of selfish, isolated intercourse with God. Others are at once brought in. Whether the prayer is uttered by the solitary in the desert or by a great concourse of people, '*Our* Father' is supplicated. The Lord's Prayer thus became the distinguishing feature of the Christian liturgies. It is wide enough to embrace all needs, and must have at once become a chief element in 'the prayers' 'at home,' which were the beginning of the liturgical worship of the Christian Church. We may be certain that it would soon find a place in the ritual of 'the breaking of the bread.' The petition 'Give us this day our daily bread' would specially mark its appropriateness for such use.

From their familiarity with the Old Testament, and with the services of the Temple and the Synagogue, the Apostles would soon recognize the fitness of including the expression of adoration and thanksgiving in 'the prayers.' The great example of the wide range of supplication is to be found in the prayer of Solomon at the Dedication of the Temple. It embodies every form of prayer—adoration, thanksgiving, petition and confession.[1] Here, again, the close connection between 'the breaking of the bread' and 'the prayers' would be seen in the act of thanksgiving, adopted from our Lord's own procedure, which gave its name to the Eucharist. Thus the Eucharist, being the one service of our Lord's own appointment, became from the very first the chief expression of all the deepest religious feeling and the adoration of the infant Church. It was probably from its use

[1] 1 Kings viii. Cf. *The Jewish Encycl.* art. 'Prayer,' p. 164.

in that service that the Lord's Prayer very early obtained the doxology, which, although it stands in some ancient MSS., was not uttered by our Lord when He gave the Prayer to His disciples.[1]

If the religious fervour of the Church found its characteristic expression in the Eucharist and in 'the prayers,' it acquired its stability and was held together by unity of doctrine. For a brief time, which has never returned, it continued stedfastly in the Apostles' doctrine and fellowship. The Body of Christ was one—like the coat which had no seam. As yet, the pride and self-will of individual members were kept in check. There was 'no schism in the body.' The bond which united them was the teaching received from the Apostles. The men who had been with Christ could teach with an authority that at first was not resisted. We can gather 'the Apostles' doctrine' from the speeches of St. Peter. It began with Christ crucified, risen, ascended, but it did not end there. It held Him to be Messiah and Lord. It was gradually feeling its way towards the due expression of what that latter term really conveys. If there appears at times a restraint, a reluctance to face the truth, which it is clear was in their hearts and minds, we have to remember that the Godhead of Christ is not involved in Messiahship, as it was commonly held at the time; and apart from this, it would require much thought and meditation on all that their discipleship had taught them, before they could venture in so many words to formulate their belief. The passage from conviction to expression is not always quick. We can, at any rate, be sure that while their devotion to Christ found utterance in their worship, their belief in Him as Messiah and Lord was the connecting bond of their life as a Church.

And to consort with the Apostles, who thus gave their testimony to Christ, was another means of maintaining the unity of the Church. Oneness of mind and spirit, as it was then

[1] Had it formed an original part of the Prayer, it is quite unlikely that it would have been omitted, as is the case, by such MSS. as ℵ, B, D, and by the Vulgate. But a doxology was soon added, probably to supply the felt want of an act of adoration in a prayer so often used in the liturgy. A doxology is found attached to the Prayer in the *Didachê*, viii. 2, *ὅτι σοῦ ἐστὶν ἡ δύναμις καὶ ἡ δόξα εἰς τοὺς αἰῶνας*. It may be as early as the end of the first century. 'The Doxology is admittedly a liturgical addition.' H. J. Holtzmann, *D. Synoptiker*, p. 219.

conceived, involved bodily presence. Unity could not be preserved by voluntary absence. 'They continued stedfastly in the Apostles' . . . fellowship,' τῇ κοινωνίᾳ. The Church was one. No doubt the personal ascendancy of the Apostles, the interest which attached to men who had been in such close intimacy with the Saviour, would bind men to their company. In the new and perplexing situation in which the community found itself, recourse would constantly be had to the Twelve. Through them, men would feel they could best learn their attitude to the world, and to the old worship and its demands. If, as they were only beginning to realize,[1] Christ had superseded the sacrifices of the Temple; if the veil had been rent, would it not soon be impossible to find satisfaction for their spiritual needs within those walls? Could they be 'sons of the Law' and sons of God at the same time?

The whole attitude of the community to the religion of their fathers must have early presented itself as a problem of singular difficulty. The more it pressed itself upon them, the closer they would adhere to the fellowship of the men who had been with Christ and knew His mind. But fellowship with the Apostles necessarily involved persecution. From the very first the authorities had set themselves sternly against the preaching of the Gospel of the Resurrection; and it binds men the closer together when to seek each other's company brings peril. The unity of the Church has never been so great as in the ages of persecution. It was good for converts to the new faith thus to be driven in to the centre, and for the pressure of the world to bind them the closer in the fellowship of the Apostles.

Worship and Doctrine are intended to be carried out in life. We are given a brief glimpse of the character of the life which was being led by the Church in the dawn of its career. It was practical communism, a state of things which could only be temporary, as answering to a temporary need; not in any sense a model for the Church under altered circumstances. The spirit which pervaded it and led to the adoption of the system was altogether exemplary and a pattern for the Church of all time—the love and sympathy, the consideration and tenderness

[1] We gather this from the scanty allusions to the redemptive aspect of Christ's work. It took time to mould their conceptions and to make them see what Christ had done for them as sinful men.

which found their only possible expression, under existing circumstances, in the throwing of all means of sustenance, all abundance of wealth, into a common store. The pressure from without, the suspicion which was felt, the consequences of excommunication from the synagogues—all these external hardships forced the disciples together;[1] and in the common life which they were leading no one cared to take advantage of his own superior means of support. The weakest and poorest shared equally with the more fortunate. 'All that believed were together and had all things common; and sold their possessions and goods, and parted them to all men, as every man had need.'[2] And this was done from no constraint. It was not made a rule. No one was obliged thus to act. This is clearly enough pointed out by St. Peter to Ananias. Communistic life is not, as some have taught, the only practical realization of the principles of the Gospel of Christ. Under certain conditions it may become necessary, as in the case of the primitive Church.[3] But even then, when it was thought to be needful and was acted upon by large numbers of people, it was not compulsory as a rule of life. 'Whiles it remained, was it not thine own? and after it was sold, was it not in thine own power?'[4]

The spirit of love and goodwill which then led to the maintenance of a life in common, so that no one said 'that ought of the things which he possessed was his own,' might under different circumstances incline those who are 'of one heart and of one soul,' as these men were, to the sternest individualism. The communistic mode of life, human nature being what it is, would be full of spiritual danger to certain kinds of character; and love would lay on them the obligation, for their own good, of individual effort.

It cannot be too strongly urged that the common life of the primitive disciples was no example for Christians under different conditions. The spirit which inspired it, and the self-abnegation

[1] The transfer of their homes to Jerusalem by the Galilean disciples and the consequent abandonment of their ordinary means of livelihood contributed to the general need of support. *v.* Wernle, *D. Anfänge unserer Religion*, p. 91; V. Dobschütz, *Probleme des apost. Zeitalters*, p. 42.

[2] Acts ii. 44, 45.

[3] As among the garrison and people of a besieged city.

[4] Acts v. 4. *v.* J. Weiss, *D. Urchristentum*, i. p. 52.

with which it was carried out, are of perpetual value. The form which it took, like the conditions it was designed to meet, was transitory.

We must not forget that the indifference to personal possessions, which marked this stage of the Church's development, was in part due to the expectation of the end of the world and the return of Christ. The disciples were living in a condition of spiritual exaltation, caused by their own recent experiences at Easter and Pentecost, and by their daily looking for the 'Sign of the Son of Man.'[1]

The natural effect of these two strains of thought would be indifference to the attractions of wealth.

There is no doubt that St. Luke, in his description of the daily life of the primitive community, idealizes the picture of brotherly love which it presented.[2] He accurately portrays the general sentiment. It shows a singular want of imagination when we find the literary critic putting forth the theory of a number of conflicting sources for the narrative of St. Luke, because the pervading spirit of the community was not shared by every member of it.[3] The writer conveys his meaning by a few bold strokes, and the general effect is consistent and harmonious. He would have been as quick as the modern critic to distinguish contradictions, if any existed.

In their temporary adoption of the common life, the disciples were not influenced by any teaching of their Master. He nowhere enforces it; whereas care for the weak and suffering, help for the

[1] 'A cheerful, trustful, optimistic tone prevails; we notice nothing of the passion and bitterness of modern class differences.' J. Weiss, *D. Urchristentum*, i. p. 55.

[2] 'Neither said any of them that ought of the things which he possessed was his own.' As V. Dobschütz remarks, this is an ideal picture; all members of the community were not inspired by the same feeling. *Probleme des apost. Zeitalters*, p. 40. He points out that Pythagoras and his followers used to say that among friends everything is common property, *κοινὰ τὰ τῶν φίλων*, but they had no thought of communism. Weizsäcker has asserted that relief of the poor, not community of goods, was practised. *D. apost. Zeitalter*, p. 46. This is perhaps an overstatement of the case. There was certainly a measure of communism, which was voluntary and not in any way imposed by authority, in the earliest stage of the Christian Church. The necessity for it soon passed away, and was succeeded by the insistence of care for the poor as an obligation which rested upon everyone who had means. Acts iv. 32 is referred to in the *Didachê* iv. 8, and *Ep. Barn.* xix. 8.

[3] *v.* Schmiedel in *Encycl. Biblica*, art. 'Community of Goods.'

poor and distressed, are to be inferred from the whole spirit and tone of His teaching and example.[1] It would be contrary to His habit and method to lay down a specific rule of life in such matters. He was content to enunciate principles, leaving their application to the conscience and judgment of men under the guidance of His Spirit. He regarded riches as a dangerous foe to true discipleship, and one of His most solemn parables turns on a supposed instance of neglect of the claims of a poor man by a rich one ; but He never appears to contemplate community of goods as the normal way of life for His followers.

For ourselves, St. Luke's picture of the brotherly affection and concord of the primitive Church of Jerusalem is one which may well provoke self-examination as to our attitude towards our fellow Christians, and our concern for their wants and for their mode of life. In a very true sense, we are each of us our brother's keeper. We cannot shake off our responsibility. That is always pressing ; but in varying circumstances its fulfilment has to take very different forms. The communism of the primitive Church served its day, and has often been imitated among certain sections. The aims and purposes which gave rise to it are working still, but in different ways and under very different conditions. 'One good custom' would 'corrupt the world.' We may sum up this discussion in the words of von Dobschütz : 'The true picture of the primitive community shows fervent brotherly feeling and concern for the poor, on the ground of the right of the individual to his own property.'[2]

We pass from the worship of the infant Church and its mode of life to its action in the world, as a band of men with a mission.

The dictum of Wernle,[3] 'The Christian Church originated in enthusiasm,' mistakes an accompaniment for a cause. The spirit of joy and eagerness which pervaded the language and the work of the disciples is common to other beginnings than that of the Church. The cause lay deeper. As Wernle himself says,[4] 'The centre of the new community was nothing but the Person of Jesus.' Christ had become 'manifest to them in remembrance.' His Spirit, coming upon them in the fulness of His late

[1] Cf. V. Dobschütz's criticism of O. Holtzmann's interpretation of Mk. x. 28. *Probleme des apost. Zeitalters*, p. 42.

[2] *Probleme des apost. Zeitalters*, p. 41.

[3] *Die Anfänge unserer Religion*, p. 90. [4] *Ib.*

outpouring at Pentecost, gave to His Person a reality that they had never experienced during the hours of earthly companionship. Even the Death which had shocked and well-nigh overwhelmed them is now, in the light of His Resurrection, beginning to take its proper place in His redeeming work. They can see its necessity. His Ascension, which had brought the appearances to a close, is so far from being a withdrawal, that now they are conscious of His presence with them at all times, as they had not been before. He had gone from bodily sight to be with them for ever. And as a symbol of that abiding presence and its consequent power, they proclaim His Name,[1] invoking it as the very embodiment and guarantee of His action. It is not to be wondered, if exultation and enthusiasm accompanied the faith and the doings of the disciples, as they saw the proof of the presence of their Lord among them. Upon the people at large, the effect was a feeling of awe. 'Fear came upon every soul.' 'Of the rest durst no man join himself to them; but the people magnified them.'[2] Yet they stood high in favour with those who saw the wonders and signs which were done by them.[3] Like the miracles of their Lord on earth, these, His miracles from heaven, were all of them beneficent and health-giving, rescuing from pain and suffering, bringing hope and joy to the troubled and despairing. It was the springtime of the Church's year, and everywhere could be seen the signs of vitality and growth. The Spirit was moving in the hearts and consciences of men. The seeing of visions and the dreaming of dreams—those necessary preludes to all great enterprise—bore witness to His presence. What wonder that 'the Lord added to the Church day by day those that were being saved'![4]

Moreover, the time was one of transition. The Gospel as preached by Christ was now in the hands of His followers. 'As My Father hath sent Me, even so now send I you.'[5] How would it fare in their hands? Would it undergo a change? Would elements foreign to the mind of Christ be introduced into it, or

[1] Acts iii. 16, *τοῦτον, ὃν θεωρεῖτε καὶ οἴδατε, ἐστερέωσε τὸ ὄνομα αὐτοῦ.*

[2] Acts ii. 43; v. 13. [3] Acts ii. 47. Cf. iv. 33. [4] Acts ii. 47.

[5] 'The History of the Gospel contains two great transitional periods (*Uebergänge*) which both fall within the first century: from Christ to the first generation of His believers, including Paul, and from the first (Jewish-Christian) generation of these believers to the Gentile Christians.' Harnack, *Dogmengesch.* i. p. 81.

would it be simply the unfolding and expression of what was in His own mind, with the difference necessarily occasioned by the change of standpoint from Himself to them? These are questions the answers to which are vital to the right understanding of the rise of Christianity. It has been asserted that 'the Father alone and not the Son belongs to the Gospel as Jesus preached it,' [1] and that there is a marked distinction between the Gospel of Christ (*i.e.* which has Christ for its subject) and the Gospel which Christ preached. Now, if this contention is sound, it is perfectly clear that Christ, in His lifetime here, and His Apostles, after His departure, had two different Gospels. For Christ is the central thought, the one subject of the early apostolic preaching. If our Lord, in His own proclamation of the Gospel of the Kingdom, consciously stood outside of it, with His eyes directed only upon the Father, then we must admit that the Apostles have departed entirely from our Lord's own conception of His Gospel, and through them the Church as a whole has equally departed from the true Faith. For they have made that to be the core and object of their faith and preaching which Christ has not made. They move round a different centre. Christianity is not a necessary and true development of the teaching of Christ, but a side-issue, an abnormal growth, something which Christ did not contemplate or intend.

What are the facts? There is no doubt that our Lord, Who came to redeem the world, does very emphatically refer that purpose to the love of the Father. In the very Gospel which is full of His own Divine claims, Christ is represented as doing nothing apart from the Father. Even His miracles are regarded as done in virtue of power received from Him. There was good reason for this identification of His own action and teaching with that of God. All His plans and His object in coming among us would have been frustrated if, in anything that He said or did, it could be supposed that He was not one with the Father, and *that there existed another source of power than that which resided in the Godhead.* It would have been hazardous in the extreme to advance His own claims at the risk of encouraging that dualistic view which was familiar to the Jews at the time, from their con-

[1] Harnack, *D. Wesen des Christentums,* p. 91. The phrase is repeated, in slightly different form, in his *Lehrbuch der Dogmengeschichte,* i. p. 81. *v.* above, p. 297, n. 2.

tact with the East. But He forbears, as some have thought very strangely, to assert the truth about Himself in so many words. There is a reticence and restraint in His manner of speaking of Himself which has been much misunderstood. Yet all the time, men were noting and observing His life and conduct. They were listening to His words. They were watching His miracles. Now and again they catch a glimpse of the truth of His Personality; and then, as in the passing of a cloud across the face of the sun, the truth is hidden from them. With His own hand, He draws the veil; either by silence when a clear word would seem more natural, or by a strict injunction to the wondering and startled disciples 'not to make Him known.' And so the time passes. Those who loved and followed Him became more and more convinced that He was not as other men. The catastrophe of the Crucifixion comes; then the wonderful revulsion which followed on the Appearances, the Ascension and Pentecost; and we see that the effect of Christ's presence with His disciples has been their conviction that God has come among them, and that their message to the world must be the Gospel of Christ their Lord and Saviour. We see this from the opening words of the earliest of the written Gospels. It is 'the beginning of the Gospel of Jesus Christ, the Son of God'[1]—*the Gospel of which He is the subject.* And unless we conceive the Evangelist to have altogether mistaken the mind of Christ, we assert that this is the Gospel which Christ Himself preached; less by actual assertion than by act and bearing; and yet so effectually that, on the Gospel which He brought to the world, on His own Self-revelation, the Kingdom of Grace, the Church of Christ, has been founded.

It probably could not have been otherwise. The direct announcement that He was God, if it had been made at the outset of His Ministry, would have incapacitated the disciples

[1] Mk. i. 1. 'Αρχὴ τοῦ εὐαγγελίου 'Ιησοῦ Χριστοῦ, gen. objecti, as Wernle says. 'The whole Gospel of Mark is dominated by a leading idea—Jesus the Messiah, the Son of God.' *D. Quellen des Lebens Jesu*, p. 60. Cf. Mk. xv. 39. The confession of the Centurion was in accordance with his pagan faith, but was understood by the Evangelist answerably to the faith of his time in the sense of a metaphysical Sonship of God and in the sense of Mk. i. 1. *v.* Feine, *Theologie des N.T.* p. 41. If this view is correct, Harnack's theory implies that the Evangelist has quite mistaken the mind of Him whose Gospel he set out to write. To St. Mark, the Son, not the Father, is the main subject of his Gospel.

for that freedom of intercourse with our Lord which their training as Apostles and witnesses demanded. They would have been overwhelmed and oppressed. They would have failed to see in Him those traits of true humanity which are among the most precious possessions of His people's faith. The human eye cannot look upon the sun of summer at the height of noon. The full revelation of the Godhead of Christ in open majesty would have too much dazzled the spiritual sight of His disciples. But for all that, He did preach (*verkündigen*) Himself. His every act, with His sinless character and the perfection of His teaching, was every day proclaiming Him; and now and again the Divine was plainly revealed, as on the Mount of the Transfiguration, when He set out to die, and on occasions which St. John has been careful to record. Indeed, we may say that His very presence, whether He spoke or was silent, was and could not fail to be the presentation of Himself to the souls of men as their supreme possession; and thus the Son belongs to the Gospel as He Himself had preached it.

If we look through the Synoptic Gospels, to see what is the essence of Christ's teaching, and the Gospel which He preached, we find that the Father is not the distinguishing element that marks off His Gospel from all else and makes it unique. He speaks of the Father indeed—of His love and care: but so do the prophets. The Fatherhood of God was a familiar conception in Judaism. It did not need to form the heart of the Gospel of Christ. The new and the central thought in His Gospel, as we see from a broad view of His teaching and His life, is Himself as the revelation of the Father. The new thing is the fact that God, Who had 'spoken unto the fathers in the prophets . . . hath at the end of these days spoken to us in His Son.'[1] Christ coming among us, our Emmanuel—this is the essence of the Gospel. There is no sign that our Lord preached the Father alone. His own words, His admissions, the fact that He never corrected confessions of His Divine nature, all go to prove that, although from the reasons suggested above He chose to let His Personality reveal itself only in the course of time, the central core of His Gospel was Himself and the Revelation which He came to bring. Perhaps we see this most clearly in the scene at Nazareth, when in consequence of what He read and

[1] Hebr. i. 1, 2.

His bearing as He sat down, 'the eyes of all them that were in the synagogue were fastened on Him.' And He began to say unto them, 'This day is this Scripture fulfilled in your ears.'

Now it is to be allowed that, when the preaching of the Gospel passed, at the Ascension, from our Lord to His disciples, a transition of great moment took place. The point of view was changed. It was no longer, as it had been in His hands, a Self-Revelation, and therefore characterized by restraint and reserve. It was the adoring proclamation of a Person by men whose hearts and consciences He had won to Himself, who saw in Him the full revelation of God and called Him Lord. And this interpretation of the Gospel, apparent as it was already in the days of His Ministry, He had never checked. When He commanded silence, it was not because the confession was mistaken, but because it was inopportune. If He rebuked the evil spirits who acknowledged Him, it was for their presumption in breathing His Name, not for error.

But with the Ascension and the coming of the Holy Spirit, all need for restraint was at an end. Almost His last command was: 'Go ye into all the world and preach the Gospel to every creature.' What was the Apostolic interpretation of that Gospel? We are told in plain words. 'Philip went down to the city of Samaria and preached Christ unto them.' He 'preached unto him Jesus.' St. Paul 'straightway (on his conversion) preached Christ in the synagogues, that He is the Son of God.'[1] The burden of the Apostolic Gospel is Christ, the Son of God.

If, as some would persuade us, this is foreign to the mind of Christ, if it is an inference which cannot legitimately be drawn either from what He actually said or implied when He was upon earth—then the fabric of Christendom is wrongly named. It does not rest upon Christ. It is an invention of men who failed to grasp His mind. The transition from Christ to the Apostles has ended in disaster. Our religion is not that of Christ.[2]

[1] Mk. xvi. 15; Acts viii. 5, 35; ix. 20.

[2] Cf. Sanday, *Christologies, Ancient and Modern*, p. 119, 'No doctrine can hold good that can be proved to be inconsistent with what is revealed to us of the consciousness of Christ; our estimate of His Person cannot go beyond His own.' We may apply this to the Apostolic reading of the Gospel.

But the facts by no means require us to draw such a conclusion as this. It is to be remembered that very few of our Lord's statements about Himself have come down to us: yet, apart from what the Fourth Evangelist has preserved, we have clear and definite sayings which assign to Him equality with the Father.[1] He accepts from disciples confessions which place Him in the category of the Divine.[2] His Death and Resurrection, taken in conjunction with His Self-revelation, place the corner stone upon the fabric. He is Himself the central point of His Gospel. It is His position within it that makes it a Gospel. He is no mere prophet of God. He reveals God because He is the Son of God, and the Johannine phrases which are recorded of Him complete the testimony of the Synoptic representation; 'He that hath seen Me hath seen the Father'; 'I and My Father are one.' 'That Gospel really adds nothing fundamentally new.'[3] If this view is justified by the facts of the case, the Apostles, in taking up the Gospel torch as it fell from the hand of their ascended Lord, were kindling no strange fire. It was the same Gospel, although other lips than His had the framing of the message, and the perspective was changed. Instead of being the utterance of His own Self-consciousness, it was the proclamation by others of the result of their knowledge of Him, a knowledge gained partly by long intercourse and partly by deep religious experience. It was for this that He had chosen them, that on His departure they might tell men that He had been here, 'As My Father hath sent Me, even so send I you.'

And the first appeal of the Apostles was directed to the nation at large, calling upon it to acknowledge its crime, to confess its sin in rejecting its Messiah, and by repentance to get ready for Him when He will return at the 'restitution of all things.'[4] St. Peter declares that 'all the prophets from Samuel and those that follow after, as many as have spoken, have foretold of these days.' He reminds the people that they are the children of the prophets, and that to them first of all God had sent His Son Jesus. They take precedence of all nations in privilege. The

[1] Matt. xi. 27; Lk. x. 22.

[2] Mk. viii. 29; Matt. xiv. 33; xvi. 16, 17; Lk. ix. 20.

[3] John xiv. 9; x. 30. *v.* Sanday, *The Life of Christ in Recent Research*, p. 138.

[4] Acts iii. 19 f.

great choice is offered first to them. We find the same view taken by the man who was destined to be the Apostle of the Gentiles. St. Paul and St. Peter are at one in recognizing the prior claim of the Jews to be evangelized. They are naturally the eldest sons of the Church if they will only see it. 'It was necessary that the word of God should first have been spoken to you.'[1]

We know the issue. The nation at large turned a deaf ear to the Gospel message.[2] The ingrained prejudice and pride of centuries refused to see a crime in the rejection of Jesus of Nazareth. The attitude of Jerusalem is repeated at Antioch.[3] The preaching of the Gospel is met by general opposition. The Jews become the most active opponents of the Church. Had the case been different, had the people as a whole recognized their sin and looked upon Him Whom they had pierced, we cannot doubt that as a city and a nation they would have been spared. The course of history would have run in a different channel. The Church Catholic would have borne the stamp of that Judaistic Christianity which, after a brief and ineffectual struggle to maintain its character and independence, became merged in the common life and creed of the whole body. What would have been the effect of this upon the future fortunes of the Church cannot be imagined. Sooner or later, as Gentiles entered the Church, bringing with them the culture and breadth of the Graeco-Roman world, a struggle for the supremacy of their respective characteristics would have arisen, and a harder fight been needed than that which St. Paul encountered, to vindicate 'the liberty with which Christ has made us free.'

As a matter of fact, the Jews as a whole, the hierarchy and the Scribes, the leaders of the religious sects of Pharisees and Essenes, of political parties like the Sadducees and Herodians, set their faces as a flint against the call to repentance and faith. Notwithstanding this formal rejection of their message, the disciples, who are still Jews, remain for a few years in close touch with their hereditary faith. As we have seen, they

[1] Acts iii. 26; xiii. 46.

[2] 'According to Justin, who must have known the facts, Jesus was rejected by the whole Jewish nation "with a few exceptions."' Inge, *Quar. Rev.* Jan. 1914, p. 62.

[3] Acts xiii. 45.

frequented the Temple and observed the customs. In the towns they attended the synagogues.[1] But all the time they are preaching Christ, baptizing converts, celebrating the Lord's Supper and waiting in eager expectation for the advent of His Kingdom.

It is impossible to speak with certainty of the progress of the Church during these early years. The number of actual disciples, who formed its nucleus and the germ of its future development, amounted at the dawn of the Pentecostal morning to 120.[2] The preaching of St. Peter quickly multiplied this little band and the Church was numbered by thousands. The Apostles were at first in great favour with the people generally.[3] They were eagerly listened to, and the power of healing which they possessed [4] would commend them to many. Their fame spread to neighbouring cities and, as when Christ was upon earth, people brought their sick folk to be healed. St. Luke uses a similar expression to express the effect produced, 'They were healed every one.' [5] The miracles of healing acted as signs of God's favour and presence. Not only were the people at large touched with the power of the Gospel, but 'a great company of the priests were obedient to the faith.' [6]

The Apostles held a position of unique authority in the

[1] While the Temple was still standing, there were said to be 480 synagogues with schools of the Law in Jerusalem itself. Weber, *System der altsynagog*[n]. *Paläst*[n]. *Theologie*, p. 38.

[2] This was the traditional number of the members of 'The great Synagogue' —the school of Scribes said to be founded by Ezra. *v.* Taylor, *Pirke Aboth*, p. 110. We can hardly avoid seeing in St. Luke's employment of the round number 120 a more or less conscious reference to that tradition.

[3] Acts ii. 47.

[4] There is no reason to doubt the accounts given by St. Luke. He must have had many opportunities of verifying the statements of his sources on this point, and of questioning people who in their own persons had received benefit.

[5] Acts v. 16 ; Lk. iv. 40.

[6] Acts vi. 7. There were also 'certain of the sect of the Pharisees which believed' (xv. 5). There is no ground for the contention of Bousset, *Kyrios Christos*, that Acts is at variance with the Pauline Epistles in representing the Pharisees as friendly to the primitive community. J. Weiss, too, charges the writer of Acts with the 'formal (*schematischen*) and unhistorical conception' that the Pharisees on the whole were friendly inclined to the Christians. The leaders as a whole are not so represented. It is only here and there that 'certain' members of the great parties are influenced, such, for instance, as Joseph of Arimathaea, or Levites like Barnabas. *D. Urchristentum*, pp. 37, 38.

constitution of the community as men who had consorted with the Lord and had received from Him the Gospel which they were now to publish to the world. This state of things lasted until Agrippa I. made a blank in the circle of the Twelve by killing 'James, the brother of John, with the sword.' One who was not an original Apostle is soon seen in a place of authority, and seems to take precedence of Apostles like St. Peter and St. John. James, the Lord's brother, stands at the head of the community in Jerusalem. When, immediately after the martyrdom of James the son of Zebedee, St. Peter is imprisoned by Agrippa, this other James is found in the leadership. On his release from prison, the Apostle tells the people who are assembled in the house of Mary the mother of Mark to go and 'shew these things unto James and to the brethren.'[1] When, some years later, St. Paul goes to Jerusalem to see St. Peter, he tells us that the only 'other Apostle' whom he saw was James. When St. Paul is again at Jerusalem, fourteen years later, James is mentioned with Peter and John as a pillar of the Church and he is the first-named of the three. To what is the eminent position of this James to be attributed? He had not been a believer in Christ during the time of His Ministry, and is therefore certainly not to be identified with the James, son of Alphaeus, who appears in the lists of the Twelve.[2] For he is called 'the Lord's brother,' and we are expressly told that our Lord's brethren did not believe in Him. Yet, after the Ascension, they are assembled with the Apostles. They have come to receive the claims that He made and to own Him as Lord. This change was apparently brought about by an incident to which St. Paul refers in 1 Cor. xv. 7. Christ appeared specially to James. The James referred to could only be the Lord's brother. At the time when St. Paul wrote, he was the James who would at once be recognized.[3] May not his rank and eminence in the Church of Jerusalem have

[1] Acts xii. 17. The retirement of St. Peter from Jerusalem for a time left the guidance of the Church in the hands of St. James. *v.* B. Weiss, *Bibl. Theol. des N.T.* p. 125. *v.* below, p. 445.

[2] *v.* Sieffert in Herzog, *Real-Encycl.* art. 'Jakobus im N.T.'

[3] *v.* Lightfoot, *Galatians*, pp. 265, 274; B. Weiss, *D. Leben Jesu*, ii. 574, 'This appearance mentioned only by Paul... evidently brought the still unbelieving brother to faith.' The *Gospel according to the Hebrews* had a version of this incident. It has been preserved by Jerome, *De Vir. Illustr.* ii. *v.* Preuschen, *Antilegomena*, p. 8.

been due partly to the fact of his relationship [1] to our Lord and partly to his having been singled out to receive this special appearance of his Divine kinsman? [2] His own character and gifts doubtless contributed their share in placing him in his new position of authority.[3] He stands at the head of the Mother Church of Jerusalem and Apostles such as Peter and John acknowledge this supremacy. Yet he was not one of the original Twelve. His Apostleship was not due to his choice by our Lord. He had never been an actual disciple of the Master. What precisely was his position? We have to distinguish between Apostles who were of the original college of the Twelve and Apostles who received the title and office owing to special circumstances. Thus Matthias was chosen to fill the rounded number in which the fall of Judas had left an ill-omened blank. That the original Apostleship implied a direct call from Christ, is proved by the prayer of the assembled Apostles that He would 'dispose' of the lot which they cast. St. Matthias is at once regarded as the chosen of Christ.[4] The choice of St. Paul is held to be equally direct. He is himself very emphatic in his

[1] For the much-debated character of this relationship, *v.* Lightfoot's essay, 'The Brethren of the Lord' in *Galatians*. He takes the view that the relationship is that of half-brother, the son of Joseph by a former wife. B. Weiss speaks of St. James as 'our Lord's own (*leiblichen*) brother, the son of Mary and Joseph.' *Bibl. Theologie des N.T.* p. 125. Zahn, who takes the same view, says, 'It is easy to see that originally it was not historical but dogmatic and sentimental considerations which have prevented the general acknowledgment of the situation presented by the Bible and by the oldest tradition of the Church of Jerusalem.' *Einleitung in d. N.T.* i. p. 73. Mayor takes the same view in his edition of the *Epistle of St. James* and in Hastings' *D.B.* art. 'Brethren of the Lord.'

[2] Cf. V. Dobschütz, *Probleme des apostol. Zeitalters*, p. 45.

[3] We see his influence on St. Peter (Gal. ii. 12). *v.* Sieffert in Herzog, *Real-Encycl.* art. 'Jakobus,' p. 578.

[4] There is no ground for the theory of J. Weiss that the narrative of the election of St. Matthias is a legend of the Church. *D. Urchristentum*, i. p. 34. He regards the number Twelve in its connection with the Apostles as resting on no actual historical tradition, but as an embodiment (*Verkörperung*) of the idea contained in Christ's saying to the disciples, 'Ye shall sit on thrones judging the twelve tribes of Israel' (Lk. xxii. 30; Matt. xix. 28). On this theory, not only is the sober history of Acts reduced to fiction, but that of the Evangelists is discredited. Imagine the confusion which would be introduced into all historical narratives, whether sacred or profane, if any analogy or resemblance that could be brought forward were held to disqualify a serious historical account from being received as such!

assertion of this.[1] James, the Lord's brother, appears to come into the same category of Apostleship, but in his case there is no evidence of any direct call. If one was given, it was probably at the moment of our Lord's appearance to him; but we do not know. The contributing *facta* in his election as an Apostle were no doubt to be found in his kinsmanship to Christ and in the force of his character. The one without the other would not have given him such eminence in the Church. He was called 'the Just,' and his murder was regarded as the immediate cause of the troubles which culminated in the fall of Jerusalem.[2]

Another condition of Apostleship, and one which is specially emphasized in the election of Matthias, is personal knowledge of Christ and the power to bear witness to His Resurrection. St. Paul claims to have fulfilled this condition.[3] The question of its fulfilment by other men, who are apparently admitted to apostolic rank, is not easily answered.[4] St. Barnabas was set apart as an Apostle at the time of the election of St. Paul. Andronicus and Junias are said by St. Paul 'to be of note among the Apostles.' But we cannot say what had been their oppor-

[1] Gal. i. 1.

[2] Euseb. *H.E.* ii. 23. James is said to have been put to death by the high priest Ananos during the time of anarchy which ensued between the death of the procurator Festus, 62 A.D. and the arrival of his successor. Origen, *Comment. in Matt.* xiii. 55, quotes Josephus, *Antiq.* xx. 9, 1, for the opinion that the murder of James and the fall of Jerusalem were connected with one another. But this thought is not in our MSS. of Josephus, and Origen probably got it from Hegesippus, as reported in Euseb. *H.E.* ii. 23, forgetting at the moment the source of the quotation. Origen read the words 'James, the brother of Jesus, who was called Christ,' in his own copy of Josephus, but the passage is generally regarded with suspicion as an interpolation. Batiffol defends its genuineness, *Orpheus et l'Évangile*, p. 16, n. 2. *v.* Schürer, *op. cit.* i. pp. 548, 581, n. 45; Sieffert in Herzog, *Real-Encycl.* art. 'Jakobus.' But *v.* above, p. 7, n. 1.

In 1 Cor. xv. 7, St. James is spoken of as an Apostle.

[3] 1 Cor. ix. 1.

[4] The term ἀποστόλος is applied to men as messengers from one Church to another (2 Cor. viii. 23). *v.* Lightfoot on *Phil.* ii. 25. It is possible that their employment on missions of importance may have led to their being characterized by a term which came to mean that they belonged to the apostolic college. Strictly speaking, besides 'the Twelve,' only St. James the Just and St. Paul are to be considered as Apostles in the full meaning of the word. Cf. Hamilton, *The People of God*, ii. pp. 70, 71; Gwatkin, art. 'Apostle' in Hastings' *Dict. of the Bible*, i.

tunities of personal knowledge of our Lord.[1] The function of an Apostle seems to have been to hand on to the Church the knowledge of the Revelation of God in Christ, and to lay the foundation of Christian certainty. They stand between Christ and His Church, guaranteeing that the Church is the fulfilment of His will and purpose. Their position is thus unique, and in this respect there is no question of any appointment of men to succeed them. They could not hand on to others the privileges of personal knowledge and opportunity which gave them their office.

We speak of the Church of the first days as 'Apostolic,' and rightly, for the direct government of the primitive body lay in the hands of the first witnesses to Christ. But we often fail to recollect another order to which great authority is assigned in the New Testament; so much so that St. Paul declares that, along with the Apostolate, it forms the foundation of the Church of Christ.[2] The reason for attaching so great an importance to the 'prophets' forms one of the problems of the early history of the Church. Nothing that we are told of their action or influence in any way justifies this position. St. Paul and St. Barnabas, when together at Antioch, are called 'prophets'; but this was before their ordination to the Apostolate. Their gift of prophecy seems henceforth merged in the wider and greater task of Apostleship. They cease to be called 'prophets'; and so quickly does the title come to lose significance in the growing life of the Church that, when writers of the second century speak of the prophets, they invariably mean those of the Old Testament.[3] The prophetic gift lingered on for a time. Justin Martyr speaks of its exercise in his day: [4] but the prophets

[1] The title of these disciples to be called Apostles is discussed by Lightfoot, *Ep. to the Galatians*, p. 95 f. St. Barnabas is not only said (Acts xiii. 1, 2) to have been ordained an Apostle along with Saul, but he is specially associated with St. Paul in the Apostleship to the Gentiles (Gal. ii. 9; cf. 1 Cor. ix. 5, 6).

[2] Eph. ii. 20. *v.* Lightfoot, *Gal.* p. 97, n. 3; Turner, *Studies in Early Church History*, 1912, p. 15. So too Ellicott, *Eph. ad loc.*; H. Holtzmann, *Neutestamentliche Theologie*, i. p. 575. Cf. Eph. iii. 5; iv. 11, with Ellicott's notes. Chrys. *ad Eph. Hom.* vi. 1, takes προφητῶν in Eph. ii. 20 to be Old Testament prophets. The way in which prophets are mentioned with Apostles in the *Didachê* (xi.) points to the fact that in Eph. ii. 20 they are New Testament prophets.

[3] *v.* Turner, *op. cit.* p. 16.

[4] Παρὰ γὰρ ἡμῖν καὶ μέχρι νῦν προφητικὰ χαρίσματα ἐστιν. *Dial. cum Tryph.* p. 179 c.

as an order of recognized and almost Apostolic authority clearly belong to the formative age of the Christian Church. Like the Apostles, whose special office as witnesses to the Person of Christ could not be handed on, the prophets were living exponents and proofs of the new dispensation of the Spirit. Their special gift was needed at the first. When the settled government of a local and permanent ministry was set up, the order of the prophets ceased to exist. There was something in the nature of their office which made it unsuited to the requirements of orderly Church life. Many failed to resist the temptations to which the prophetic gift exposed its possessor; and as we learn from the *Didaché*, it soon became necessary to discriminate between those who used and those who abused it.[1]

Another form of the earliest ministry is named by St. Paul in close conjunction with Apostles and Prophets. 'Teachers' appear to have been men with a special gift for conveying instruction.[2] Like the 'evangelists,' with whom they are coupled in Ephes. iv. 11, it is probable that they formed part of the general or missionary ministry of the apostolic age; although every considerable Church would soon come to number among its leading men some who were 'apt to teach.' Philip, the deacon, is called 'the evangelist.'[3] The title seems to belong to a class of 'teachers' who specially concerned themselves with proclaiming the 'good news' of salvation, not where anything of the nature of a settled ministry was beginning to come about—'not where Christ was named'[4]—but rather as pioneers, as mission preachers preparing the ground for the occupation of the Gospel. It was only later that the title 'evangelist' became attached to the actual writers—or supposed writers—of the Gospels. It is an instance of the fact that, in the rise of the Christian religion, the spoken word of the living agent played the chief part in spreading the knowledge of Christ. The written word came later. With our present knowledge it is impossible to fix the exact status of the 'teacher' and the 'evangelist' in the early ministry. On the whole, we may assign to them a

[1] Dr. Armitage Robinson has pointed out the contributing causes of the extinction of prophecy in the true sense. *Encycl. Bibl.* iii. col. 3887. *v. Didaché*, xi.

[2] 1 Cor. xii. 28. *v.* Robertson and Plummer, *ad loc.*

[3] Acts xxi. 8.

[4] Rom. xv. 20.

roving commission, a place somewhere between Apostles and Prophets on the one hand, and the presbyter-bishop and deacon of the local ministry.[1]

It is easy to see that no date can be assigned to the passing of the missionary and travelling ministry into the local and settled hierarchy. The change came about earlier in one place than in another.[2] Two main causes were responsible for it: the gradual loss of the Apostles as, one by one, they were taken away by the hand of death; and the gradual cessation of the prophetic gift. Of these causes, the first was especially effective.

When the men who had seen Christ had passed away, another era opened. A leadership arises which has not the same undisputed claim to authority. There is not the actual, historic contact with Christ which formed the chief sanction of Apostolic rule. When St. James, the Lord's brother, was at the head of the primitive community in Jerusalem, the Apostles Peter and John appear to have retired from the city for a time. The brother of St. John had been slain by Herod. St. Peter had been imprisoned and, on his miraculous deliverance, would still, if remaining in the city, be in danger of his life. The Church was therefore left in the care of the Lord's brother and we read of 'elders' who are associated with him.[3] His position was that of a bishop surrounded by his priests.[4] Here in rudiment and germ we have—hardly as yet an order but—a body of men who in time develop into the two higher ranks of the Christian ministry —that of bishop and that of priest.[5] The elders of the primitive community are, no doubt, rooted in the elders of the Synagogue —the men who, from their age or their standing in the general

[1] *v.* Plumptre in Smith's *D.B.* i. art. 'Evangelist.'

[2] It 'was not only practically complete by the year 150 A.D. but can be traced in germ nearly 100 years before.' Turner, *Studies in Early Church History*, p. 22. *v.* Watson, *Life of Bishop John Wordsworth*, 1915, p. 336.

[3] Acts xii. 17; xxi. 18; xi. 30.

[4] *v.* V. Dobschütz, *Probleme des apostol. Zeitalters*, p. 44; Lightfoot, *Philipp.* p. 208, 'As early as the middle of the second century, all parties concur in representing him as a bishop in the strict sense of the term.' *v.* Hegesippus in Euseb. *H.E.* ii. 23, *Διαδέχεται δὲ τὴν ἐκκλησίαν μετὰ τῶν ἀποστόλων ὁ ἀδελφὸς τοῦ Κυρίου Ἰάκωβος.* Clement of Alexandria in a passage quoted by Eusebius, *H.E.* ii. 1, states that 'Peter, James and John . . . elected James the Just Bishop of Jerusalem.'

[5] Bp. Lightfoot has proved conclusively the identity of the bishop and elder during the Apostolic age. *v.* *Philippians*, pp. 96, 97. *v.* below, p. 447, n. 1.

respect, were chosen to interpret the Scriptures and to pronounce the benedictions and the prayers.[1] This respect for age and experience, to which Jews had always been accustomed, would naturally assert itself in the entirely Jewish community of Jerusalem; and the term 'elder' passes into a title of authority in the Christian Church.

The first instance of its actual use occurs in connection with the help sent by the Church at Antioch to the poor brethren in Judaea in a time of famine. Saul and Barnabas bring the money to the elders.[2] A few years afterwards, the Apostles were in Jerusalem. On the question of the circumcision of Gentile converts arising in the Church of Antioch, St. Paul and St. Barnabas were unable to get their views accepted. It was determined to send a deputation of the brethren to Jerusalem to the Apostles and elders. These two orders accordingly receive the brethren and consider the matter. A letter is written to Antioch in the name of 'the Apostles and elders and brethren.'[3] Again, after the lapse of several years, we find St. Paul, on his last visit to Jerusalem, communicating to James the result of his ministry to the Gentiles, and with James 'all the elders were present.'[4]

So far, there is no distinct assignment of duties or even of position to these elders. They have hardly become crystallized into a separate order. But the title has already been adopted elsewhere. It is not in Jerusalem but in Antioch and other towns that something of a distinct order of officer seems to attach itself to the name. We read that Paul and Barnabas 'ordained elders in every Church.'[5] This means a solemn setting apart by the laying on of hands, with prayer and fasting. And when St. Paul was on the journey to Jerusalem which led to his apprehension and imprisonment, he sent from Miletus to Ephesus for 'the elders of the Church.'[6] In his parting address to them, he makes use of an expression which shows a distinct development of function in their office. 'Take heed unto yourselves and to all the flock over the which the Holy Ghost hath made you overseers to feed the Church of God.' Here we have a position of authority assigned to them. It includes general

[1] *v.* Sanday, *The Conception of Priesthood*, p. 59.
[2] Acts xi. 30. [3] Acts xv. 23. [4] Acts xxi. 18.
[5] Acts xiv. 23. [6] Acts xx. 17.

oversight and care, and the supply of the spiritual necessities of the Church by sacrament and teaching. They have been made ἐπίσκοποι by the Holy Ghost. We see an indication of the office which was afterwards to play so great a part in the fortunes of the Church. But as yet every elder is an ἐπίσκοπος.[1] We are still far away from the concentration of authority and office in the person of one man. The monarchical episcopate is a thing of the future.[2]

As we have seen, it is not in Jerusalem, but at Antioch and neighbouring cities, that we first find elders 'ordained'—set apart by consecration—for their office. Yet it is in Jerusalem, the Mother Church, that we can watch the process by which the general body of the elders was afterwards to become differentiated into the two orders of 'bishop' and 'priest.' St. James, the Lord's brother, on the departure of the older Apostles on their missionary work, himself an Apostle and an elder, is seen to occupy a position which answers very closely to the subsequent monarchical episcopate. Eusebius[3] tells us that when this position was vacated by his martyrdom, Symeon, his cousin, was chosen to succeed him by the general assent of the surviving Apostles and disciples of the Lord. The example of what was happening at Jerusalem—the separation of one eminent elder to sole authority—became a model and incentive for the future action of the Gentile communities.[4]

[1] 'That the "bishops" in the New Testament were not what we call bishops is proved by the single fact that there were sundry of them at Philippi. . . . The elders of Ephesus are reminded that they are bishops.' Gwatkin, *Early Church History to* A.D. 313, i. p. 69. 'The titles Presbyters and Bishops seem to be interchangeable, as in the Epistle to Titus.' Wordsworth, *The Ministry of Grace*, p. 125. 'St. Irenaeus, writing *c.* A.D. 180, still uses the terms Presbyter and Bishop as interchangeable.' *Ib.* p. 127. So Darwell Stone in Hastings' *Encycl. of Religion and Ethics*, v. p. 332, and Maclean, *ib.* viii. p. 660.

[2] 'Upon the whole, we meet with elders quite early in the Apostolic age, and deacons rather later, but we find no trace of bishops in the New Testament.' Gwatkin, *op. cit.* p. 72. But *v.* above, p. 445; and Dean Robinson in *Encycl. Bibl.* i. col. 582, 'The development of the monarchical episcopate lies outside the limits of the New Testament; but even within the Canon we find indications of a tendency which the later history enables us to interpret as moving in this direction.'

[3] *H.E.* iii. 11. He does not give his authority, but quotes Hegesippus for Symeon's relationship to St. James.

[4] Cf. Bp. Lightfoot, *Philippians*, p. 197; Bp. J. Wordsworth, *The Ministry of Grace*, p. 124, 'In Jerusalem, which was a sort of ideal community, a Symeon naturally took the place of his brother James, and so the succession of bishops

It would thus appear that the Episcopate is not to be regarded as a continuation of the Apostolate, but rather as a development from within an order which existed contemporaneously with the Apostles; and that this development was directly caused by the Apostles ceasing to reside in Jerusalem and entering upon the missionary work which was implied in their very name. The persecution which scattered them among the cities of Judaea led to the quasi-episcopal and *local* position of St. James. That the bishop exercises certain functions of the Apostolic office is true. But if we study the origin of the Episcopate, as it is seen in the dim foreshadowings presented by Acts and the Epistles, the office takes its rise not from the Apostolate but from the Presbyterate, not by derivation from a higher source, but by elevation and distinction from below.[1]

was established. So it was in Asia Minor where St. John lived and laboured ... for perhaps thirty years. So it was in Antioch and its neighbourhood where tradition went back nearly as far as it did at Jerusalem. It is evidence from these three centres, particularly the explicit evidence of St. Ignatius of Antioch, that enables us to accept without reserve the statement of the Preface to our Ordinal that "from the Apostles' time there have been these Orders of Ministers in Christ's Church; Bishops, Priests and Deacons."' On the other hand, Gwatkin observes that there is 'no serious evidence that he (St. James, the Lord's Brother) held the office of Bishop of Jerusalem.' *Early Church History to* A.D. 313, i. p. 70. Probably the truth lies between these positive assertions, and we may consider that St. James held, by common consent, a position to which the nearest parallel is the subsequent monarchical Episcopate, and for which it formed a model that was soon copied elsewhere. *v.* Clem. Alex. *Quis dives Salvatur,* xlii.; Tertul. *Adv. Marcion.* iv. 5, 'Ordo tamen episcoporum ad originem recensus in Joannem stabit auctorem.'

There was no contemporaneous choice of one elder, as bishop, from his peers in the various churches. The monarchical episcopate did not come about by common consent, but by force of local needs and circumstances. If early at Jerusalem, Antioch and Smyrna, it was late in Rome. 'It is clear that from the middle of the second century onwards, the settled system of the Church was episcopal and the episcopacy that of a single bishop everywhere.' D. Stone in Hastings' *Encycl. of Religion and Ethics,* v. p. 335.

Hort regards ἐπίσκοπος in the New Testament as descriptive of function, not of office. Thus in Philip. i. 1 σὺν ἐπισκόποις καὶ διακόνοις, 'such as oversee and such as minister.' *The Christian Ecclesia,* p. 190. So Loofs before him in *Studien u. Kritiken.* *v.* Sanday, *The Conception of Priesthood,* p. 90.

[1] Since the above was written, Mr. C. H. Turner has emphasized the great distinction which existed in the first century between the 'missionary ministry' (Apostles, prophets, teachers, etc., 1 Cor. xii. 28) and the local presbyters or bishops and deacons. 'When we have explained how the supreme powers of the general ministry were made to devolve on an individual who belonged to the local ministry, we have explained the origin of episcopacy.' *Cambridge*

The Apostles were, from the very nature of their calling and their experience, a transitory and passing body of men. They were men 'sent forth' to tell the world of the Christ with Whom they had lived, and of Whose Resurrection they had each been personally assured by 'many infallible proofs.' One by one they were removed by death. No one could succeed them in this peculiar feature of their office.[1] Their name is kept for them, and the office, which in time came most nearly to resemble theirs, emerges from the ranks of a lower order.

There was another kind of ministry, 'the College of the Seven,' often spoken of as the Deacons, which, like the Apostolate, was of a temporary character, passing away and leaving no direct

Mediaeval History, vol. i. pp. 144, 5. As stated above, we see something of this transfer of function in the position acquired by St. James in the Church of Jerusalem. But the solitary glory of the Apostolic order as eye-witnesses of Christ could not be handed to others. The truth seems to be that, as local needs increased with the growth of churches, the presbyter-bishop acquired an Apostolic character, which he did not possess when his church was being visited from time to time by Apostles and other members of the 'missionary ministry,' as Turner calls it. As the office of bishop emerged from the presbyterate in response to local needs of administration, it became more and more identified with the special work of the pastor (Acts xx. 28; 1 Pet. v. 1, 2), so that churches were regarded as bound by the tie of Shepherd and Flock. Cf. Turner, *ib.* p. 148; and in *Studies in Early Church History*, 1912, pp. 13, 22. *Encycl. Bibl.* i. col. 581, 'One member (of the class of Elders) comes to stand out above his fellows.'

[1] Acts i. 3. But in the task of ruling, in transmission of authority to minister the Word and the Sacraments, indeed, in much that concerned the maintenance of the Christian life, they were succeeded by the historic Episcopate. *v.* Mason, *The Relation of Confirmation to Baptism*, p. 474; Headlam in *The Prayer Book Dict.* art. 'Apostolic Succession.'

Apostolical Succession is to be regarded rather in the light of an historical fact than as a doctrine. Can we say that the Bishops and clergy of our Church are in a true sense the direct successors of the Apostles? As we have seen, the Apostles could have no successors in the primary task to which our Lord appointed them—that of bearing witness to Him, as He was seen in His earthly life, and to the reality of His Resurrection. But in the work of ruling and teaching, of feeding and guiding all who should believe in Him through their preaching, they had successors, appointed by themselves with prayer and the laying on of hands. Nor is there any doubt that this succession has been unbroken, reaching from Apostolic times to our own day. But in saying this, it is not implied that the authority of the clergy and their right to minister have been handed down like some heirloom passed from hand to hand in a family. Every priest or bishop receives his mission from God. His ordination, by which he is set apart for his office, is the act of the Church as a whole, through her appointed ministers, the Bishops. The grace of orders is a fresh gift of the Holy Spirit. It is not transmitted from one to another, as though it were

succession.[1] In neither case is there any organic connection, although in each there are functions and ministries which connect the past order with the present. The need for the 'seven men' and the cause of their choice was secular. It had no religious or ceremonial purpose.[2] It arose through a state of discontent due to the presence within the congregation of two classes of disciples, Jews of Palestine and Jews of the Greek dispersion,[3] who, being less at home in Jerusalem, felt

something which a man could pass on to his neighbour. The saying, 'As My Father hath sent Me, even so send I you' holds good to-day as when it was first spoken. Thus, two considerations have to be kept in view, when we speak of Apostolical Succession. Ministerial power and authority come fresh from the living and exalted Christ. The security that what takes place in ordination is in historical connection with our Lord Himself and His first disciples is guaranteed by the fact that the three orders of the Christian ministry can be traced back to Apostolic times. Grace has been made effectual in orderly and regular manner, according to the Apostolic precept, 'Let all things be done decently and in order.'

[1] 'That in these seven men the origin of the Diaconate is to be sought has certainly been maintained since the time of Cyprian (*Ep.* iii. 3), but the idea has only the similarity of the name to prove it.' V. Dobschütz, *Probleme des apostolischen Zeitalters*, p. 43. Yet the name is not given to them. It is hinted at by the verb which expresses their work, and the noun is applied to the ministry of the Apostles (Acts vi. 4). Irenaeus is perhaps the first to connect the Seven with the Diaconate of the Church, 'Nicolaum unum, ex vii, qui primi ad Diaconium ab Apostolis ordinati sunt' (I. xxvi. 3, and elsewhere). Lightfoot assumes 'that the office represents the later diaconate.' *Philip.* p. 188. Gwatkin considers that the evidence on the whole is against their identification. Hastings' *D.B.* art. 'Deacon.' Wernle speaks of the 'somewhat enigmatical Seven Men.' *D. Anfänge unserer Religion*, p. 89. *v.* Hort, *The Christian Ecclesia*, p. 50, 'The appointment of the Seven, answering to a great extent to those who were later called deacons.' *Ib.* p. 209, 'There is, of course, no evidence for historical continuity between the Seven and either the Ephesian διακόνοι or the developed order of Deacons of later times. The New Testament gives not the slightest indication of any connection.'

Remembering that the Seven are nowhere in Scripture called Deacons, and that their appointment to a ministry in the Church was due to a temporary state of affairs, we probably keep more close to the historical situation if we see in them, not the actual beginning of the subsequent Diaconate, but an order whose functions devolved later on upon the inferior rank of the clergy, and suggested their name. As with the Episcopate, the tendency was to connect it with the Apostles in a directness of succession which history does not warrant, so with the Diaconate. There was an early inclination to trace its lineage in unbroken sequence from the College of the Seven.

[2] 'It was only an institution for the care of the poor and was of merely temporary significance.' V. Dobschütz, *op. cit.* p. 43.

[3] Ἑλληνιστῶν, Acts vi. 1, Greek-speaking Jews. *v.* Hort, *The Christian Ecclesia*, p. 206; Heinrici, *Das Urchristentum*, p. 54.

themselves aggrieved by what they considered to be partiality shown to the former in the administration of relief. Thus, from a misunderstanding somewhat sordid and personal, there came about a series of incidents which form one of the brightest chapters in the history of the Apostolic Church; and a short-lived, but glorious order of sainted men arises among whom, small as was their number, are found the first of the Martyrs and the first of the Evangelists[1]

Now, the object of appointing the Seven was the fair and regular distribution of the alms of the congregation among the necessitous widows. The course taken by the Apostles, when they found that it was time to take action in the matter, was marked by great wisdom. They first represented to the assembled community the impropriety of neglecting their own proper religious work—the ministry of God's Word—in order to become relieving officers. They saw that, if they once departed from their own peculiar domain to attend to the everyday requirements of ordinary life, the Church, and the world which the Church was to win, would suffer in the long run. The glowing enthusiasm of Apostle and Missionary would be stifled by the petty cares and details of daily ministration to bodily wants. Then, having pointed out the need for choosing responsible persons for the work, they left the selection of them to the whole congregation, 'Wherefore, brethren, look ye out among you seven men . . . whom we may appoint over this business.' To secure a general feeling of confidence, the choice is left in the hands of the people, Jews and Hellenists; but the authority to appoint is retained by the Apostles themselves. The special character of the office and order thus created is shown by the qualities which the Apostles specify as requisite in the men who are to be chosen. They are to be 'of honest report, full of the Holy Ghost and wisdom.' To meet the complaints which had been made, the strictly Hebrew portion of the community join with the rest in choosing none but Hellenists, as we gather from their names. They are set before the Apostles, and after prayer receive from them the solemn laying on of hands. Thus, to meet a temporary necessity, an order was established which became a precedent for a permanent kind of ministry

[1] Philip. Acts vi. 5; xxi. 8. Εὐαγγελιστής in the N.T. always refers to a preacher, not a writer, of the Gospel. Eph. iv. 11; 2 Tim. iv. 5.

in the Church—the care and service of the poor and defenceless—a truly Christ-like work, for He 'came not to receive the ministrations of others, but to be a deacon to them.'[1] If the Seven were the pattern of the subsequent Diaconate, the prototype and example of all such ministries of love and service was the 'Son of Man,' 'the Servant of Jehovah.'

We have traced in three classes of ministry in the earliest days of the primitive Church—Apostles, Elders, the Seven—the first indications of a settled order of hierarchy. If our reading of history is correct, we find elements of a temporary character in the Apostles and in the Seven, which confine those two orders to the period of the first days and do not allow of their continuance. The Apostles were called and sent by Christ Himself, or had been in personal touch with Him during His Ministry; while the Seven were men of high standing and repute for sanctity and wisdom set apart for a particular purpose. It is in the other body, the 'elders,' that we can trace elements of a permanent character which the Church would always need. It is from their ranks that the two higher orders of the Church's ministry were destined to take their rise. Within their body were the qualifications which were to find their field of exercise in the future Episcopate and Priesthood of the Catholic Church.

But when we ask for the source of their authority and for the sanction which attaches to the exercise of their ministerial functions, the universal belief of the primitive Church is met and confirmed by what we can ascertain from the Acts and the Epistles. Whatever the course of the historical development of the Christian Ministry, however determined by the pressure of events, there is the clearest indication that its powers and its gifts are received through the Apostles from their Lord. In this sense, the Christian Ministry is in succession to the Apostles. All that is of permanent value and concern in the Apostolate and the Presbyterate of the first days has continued to the present time.[2] The grace of orders is a fresh gift of the risen Lord to each recipient of His call. The Apostolic

[1] οὐκ ἦλθε διακονηθῆναι, ἀλλὰ διακονῆσαι. Matt. xx. 28; Mk. x. 45.

[2] I find that Bp. J. Wordsworth took a similar view. 'If we are to speak of a doctrine of Apostolical Succession, it must include both Bishops and Presbyters as partakers in it. Their office is fundamentally the same.' *Life* by E. W. Watson, p. 338.

Episcopate is the guarantee that the ordination is lawful and regular. The spiritual gift is direct. The channel of its bestowal is historical. Only Christ can empower through His Spirit. But He works through the lawful and orderly succession of an Apostolic ministry.

The Bible of the first Christians was the Old Testament. They had no other. There is nothing to show that they felt the want of any further written authority. Their first preachers, on going forth to tell of Jesus and the Resurrection, always referred their hearers to the Old Testament for confirmation of their words.[1] Our Lord Himself, on the evening of His Resurrection, had already shown them how to use their Scriptures.[2] It was at once recognized that the Gospel had no claim upon the Jew if it could not take its stand upon the Law and the Prophets, and if its message was foreign to the teaching of the Old Testament. The Gospel was implicit in the Old Testament. It was the utterance of the same God; it followed in an orderly and logical sequence.[3]

Such was the chief literary equipment of the Apostolic Church. The disciples had nothing to place on a level of authority with the Old Testament. They had received no direction from our Lord Himself to write. Their standing orders were to go forth and preach. The Synagogue, the open-air, the courts of the Temple, not the study, were the field of their enterprise. And in this they were following His example as well as His command. Like Socrates, Christ wrote no book.[4] The living voice conveyed the message and searched the hearts and consciences of men. Writing needs spaces of leisure and our Lord had none. Days of work and teaching, followed often by nights spent in prayer, allowed no room for it, and the

[1] Acts ii. *passim*; iii. 21 f.; iv. 11, 25; vii.; viii. 35; xviii. 28.

[2] Lk. xxiv. 25-28, 44-48. In the latter passage, Christ shows His adhesion to the Jews' threefold division of the Canon—the Law, the Prophets, the Hagiographa (Psalms, etc.).

[3] Hebr. i. 1.

[4] Cf. P. Wendland, *D. Hellenistisch-Römische Kultur*, p. 226, 'Socrates and Epictetus wrote nothing, they had something more important to do, and even Plato, the greatest master of style, in the *Phaedrus* regards a writing as a sorry make-shift for the living word.'

'time was short.' His course through the world was quickly over and, after all, it was in the close of His life, in the last weeks of the Passion and the Resurrection, that the substance of His message was contained. Without it there could be no Gospel; and we cannot imagine the risen Lord sitting down to write that story, when in the glory of His new life, ready for Ascension, He still lingered to confirm the faith of His chosen witnesses.

And when He had finally passed from their sight, there was for a time the same lack of any felt desire for written records. While men could speak face to face with an Apostle, and question him on the appearance and manner, as well as the language of the Master, there seemed little need for books. Even so late as 100 A.D. Papias sets a higher store by oral tradition than by writings. 'I did not think that I could get so much profit from the contents of books as from the utterances of a living and abiding voice.' [1]

But this state of things was not to last. As time went on, and the first witnesses of Christ began to pass away, the need for some permanent record of His words and acts began to make itself felt. The sayings of Christ would, in the estimation of believers, possess a sanctity and an authority which nothing could surpass. Along with the sayings there would naturally be a connecting narrative of time and place, and we have good ground for thinking that, even during the Ministry, some such record was attempted.[2]

The year A.D. 44 may well have been a critical one in the history of Gospel-writing. The murder of St. James, the son of Zebedee, and the imprisonment of St. Peter brought home to men's minds the possibility that ere long the Church would be without the presence of the eye-witnesses of the Saviour. There is little doubt that about this time some beginning was made with those sketches of the Gospel history to which St. Luke refers in his preface. Evangelists and teachers required summaries of 'those things which are most surely believed,' and thus the incipient attempts at Gospel writing were accompanied by rudimentary efforts to define a creed. We have to remember

[1] In Euseb. *H.E.* iii. 39. There was the same feeling in the sixth century B.C. when great prophets were living. Ryle, *The Canon of the O.T.* p. 67.

[2] *v.* p. 22 f.

that the period was instinct with creative energy. A religion was in the making. Rooted though it was in the past of a single people, and ever pointing to that past for the justification of its claims, it was a new creation. Springing from the open grave of the crucified Redeemer and baptized at Pentecost with the fulness of His Spirit, it was the 'new thing' of prophetic promise.[1] The men in whom the Spirit moved were conscious of the urgency and the meaning of their task. We see this in hints dropped from time to time in the Pauline Epistles. They are not only to be read in the Churches to which they are addressed, but an exchange is to be made with Epistles sent to other communities.[2] Here is, perhaps, the first step towards a claim of general authority for this kind of writing: but anything in the nature of the general recognition which is implied by canonization is not yet thought of.

The Canon of the Old Testament itself had not long been finally settled.[3] Any proposal to assert Divine sanction for a new series of writings was a challenge of equality with the earlier series. In the time of which we are speaking, it was the practice to read portions of the Law and of the Prophets in the weekly service of the Synagogue.[4] When was the corresponding step taken, and writings of Apostles or their companions made to form part of the weekly devotions of the Christian assembly? We cannot say; for the practice was probably of far earlier date than the first mention of it would lead us to suppose. Indeed, there is good reason to think that the monition of St. Paul to read his Epistles in various Churches led to their admission into the services of those Churches and, at a later date, to their co-ordination with the writings of the Old Testament. If this view is correct, we may go on to suppose a similar recognition for the Second Gospel at a date within the first century.[5]

[1] Is. xliii. 19; Jerem. xxxi. 22. [2] Col. iv. 16. *v.* below, pp. 539 f.

[3] Probably by the year B.C. 105. *v.* Ryle, *The Canon of the O.T.* p. 184 f. But even then, the claims of certain books, such as Esther, were regarded with hesitation and their inclusion in the third division of the Canon was only ratified as late as A.D. 90 and 118 at the Council of Jamnia. Ryle, *ib.* pp. 149, 182 f. *v.* above, p. 404.

[4] Lk. iv. 16, 17.

[5] Since the above was written, I find that Gwatkin takes a similar view. 'The Epistles obtained a canonical position even earlier than the Gospels. They were read from the first in public meetings like the Old Testament.' *Early Church History to* A.D. 313, i. p. 281.

The distinctive character of the meetings of the Christian communities in Jerusalem and elsewhere suggests this view. Why did Christians come to meet in their own assemblies and no longer, as at first, among the worshippers of the Synagogue ? [1] Because they had now a new Faith, with new experiences and new hopes, which needed new forms of expression, and found utterance in prayers and hymns to which the ordinary worshipper of the Synagogue was still a stranger.[2] No better expression for these new religious needs could be found than the writings of Apostolic men, as from time to time they came into general recognition, and were acknowledged to be 'given from the Spirit.'[3] There is evidence that writings which failed to gain a permanent place in the Canon were early read in the Church for edification.[4] It stands to reason that Gospel writings and Epistles of St. Paul would not be excluded. Thus the distinctively Christian character of the Sunday assembly of the various communities led to the gradual adoption of the Apostolic records and epistles as writings conveying the word of God, and as inspired in a special sense, because they were the work of men who were known to be filled with the Holy Spirit.[5] It was believed that, as once 'holy men of God spake as they were moved by the Holy Ghost,' the same inspiring Power was at work in the Church. Everything shows that people lived in the persuasion that the Spirit of God was directly energizing in their midst, and that the writings of Apostles and Evangelists were as fully charged with His influence as were the books of the Old Covenant.

But time was needed for the full recognition of these facts, especially among the Jewish members of the Church. So long a period had elapsed since anything was written which could make good its claim to be regarded as Scripture, that a certain hesitation to receive new writings, so different from the old in form and style as were the Gospels and Epistles, can easily be understood. Besides, the period was prolific in the production of Gospel writings and the greatest care was needed in dis-

[1] Cf. Acts ii. 46, *κλῶντές τε κατ' οἶκον ἄρτον*. Rom. xvi. 5 ; 1 Cor. xvi. 19 ; Col. iv. 15 ; Philem. 2.

[2] Cf. the distinction involved in Hebr. xiii. 10.

[3] Cf. Harnack, *Dogmengeschichte*, i. p. 110.

[4] *v.* Dionysius of Corinth in Euseb. *H.E.* iv. 23 on the use of St. Clement of Rome, *Ep. ad Cor.* in the Church of Corinth in the Sunday service.

[5] Cf. Acts ii. 4 ; iv. 31 ; vii. 55.

criminating between them. It was not long before a love of the marvellous for its own sake, and a tendency to magnify the Divine element of Christ's personality at the cost of His true humanity, made themselves felt in such works as the Gospel and Apocalypse of Peter, and other apocryphal fragments which have come down to us. They heighten the value and suggest the inspiration of the Canonical Gospels by the contrast which they present to them. They help to show that, in the selection as well as in the actual composition of the received books, the Church was guided by the Holy Spirit. Nineteen centuries of Christian experience have set their seal to the decisive judgments which were being slowly formed. The Church has never gone back upon them.

We can trace one or two of the steps which were taken towards the formation of a New Testament Canon by noting the attitude of the Apostolic Fathers to the Gospels and Epistles. There is profound reverence for the person and the writings of St. Paul.[1] If the language of the Gospels is reproduced, it is perhaps indirectly derived from the common Christian tradition rather than from an actual Gospel: but the similarity of the expressions employed to the actual phraseology of this or that Gospel seems to show that the Gospels themselves were well known, and that their language had entered into the familiar Christian thought and speech of the time.[2] Yet, 'there could not be any occasion for an appeal to the testimony of the Gospels when the history of the faith was still within the memory of many.'[3] St. Clement himself and his Epistle belong to the Apostolic Age: Saints Ignatius and Polycarp had been in touch with St. John. It is only reasonable that the memory of intercourse with the first witnesses of Christ should outweigh, in their estimation, the Gospel writings of various degrees of authority and value which were passing from hand to hand in the Christian communities, and which had not yet received the general assent of the Christian Church as a whole. We cannot enter into the character of men's attitude to the New Testament Scriptures during this transitional period, unless we remember that at present there was no provision for the expression of a general

[1] Clem. Rom. c. xlvii.; Polycarp, *Ep.* c. iii.; Ignatius, *ad Rom.* iv.

[2] *v.* Westcott, *History of the Canon of the New Testament*, pp. 49, 52.

[3] *Ib.* p. 55.

authoritative agreement on the subject. Certain writings of Apostolic men and their companions were being circulated in the various Churches, and were winning or losing their way to acceptance. The idea of a New Testament of equal standing and authority to the Old Testament, if it had occurred to some far-seeing mind, was unknown to Christians generally. The collection of Scriptures to form a New Testament Canon belongs to the history of the Catholic Church. Tendencies and indications are already apparent. The work itself lies in the future.

CHAPTER XXIV

THE SACRAMENTS

THE sacramental principle is of the essence of the Christian Religion. Other religions possess rites and ceremonial acts which bear a certain resemblance to the Sacraments of the Church, but Christianity stands alone in attributing a character of fundamental importance and value to the two Sacraments which tradition has traced back to the direct initiative of Christ Himself. Christianity, being the Religion of the Incarnation, is itself sacramental as a whole. In Christ the Invisible God presented Himself to man under the outward and visible sign of His perfect humanity. Christ used sacramental language when He said, 'He that hath seen Me hath seen the Father.' The action of sacrament is the conveyance of inward and spiritual reality through the medium of what is apparent to the senses. 'The Word was made flesh and dwelt among us.' In this fact the whole system of Sacrament is contained. Every separate ministration of the rite is a fresh manifestation of that historic event—the greatest the world has known—in which the Eternal Son came among men, in order to reveal in ways that man can understand the presence and the mind of God.

Ideally, the sacramental principle permeates all religious life. Actually, and as a matter of practical moment, it is exhibited under two forms, which are vital for the existence and continuance of that life.

Theoretically, the contact of God and man which results in salvation requires no intermediary operation. God can save with a word. Practically, He does not thus act. It is His tribute to the reality of human nature and to the independence of the human will that He requires a medium by which His grace may pass to us. He takes that medium of communication from man and makes it the channel by which His gifts are received. It is the principle of the Incarnation ; and it is on the foundation of the Incarnation and on nothing else that the whole structure of sacramental grace is placed.[1]

If, as we believe is the case, the Sacraments can be referred for their origin to the action of our Lord Himself, it must be admitted that they constitute an exception to His ordinary procedure. As a rule, He dealt with principles that underlie conduct rather than with specific rules of practice. He spoke and acted on a large scale, with every succeeding age, and with every race of mankind in view. He left the working out and application of those principles to the enlightened understanding and practical wisdom of His people. But in the matter of the Sacraments He makes an exception. Very briefly, but very definitely, He lays down in each case the species and its administration ; Bread and Wine in the one case, Water in the other. And to each Sacrament He assigns its own attendant grace—His own Body and Blood in Holy Communion ; regeneration and initiation to discipleship in Baptism.[2]

[1] Nothing can be more untrue to the Gospel conception of salvation than to maintain an opposition between the ministry of the Word and the ministry of the Sacraments, as though the former was in accordance with the mind of Christ and the latter an intrusion of ecclesiastical presumption upon the simplicity of the Gospel message. To attack Sacraments is to criticize the Incarnation itself—to impugn the principle on which the salvation of man is effected. 1 Cor. i. 14 has actually been quoted in support of the theory that Baptism was not directly instituted by our Lord, it being thought that St. Paul would not have spoken thus, if He had ordained it. Whereas the context shows that St. Paul, far from depreciating Baptism, was merely thankful that he had not added to the existing strife by giving occasion to the suspicion that he baptized in his own name. In a similar manner Weizsäcker quotes 1 Cor. i. 14-17 as proving that St. Paul knew nothing of any imparting of the Spirit at Baptism by means of certain persons specially qualified for the purpose. *D. Apost. Zeitalter*, pp. 572, 3. Cf. Case, *The Evolution of Early Christianity*, p. 348.

[2] Matt. xxviii. 19. Christ seems to regard the Baptism which He enjoins as going along with discipleship, or, more accurately, introducing men to discipleship. Thus, the grace attendant on Baptism may be regarded as that of discipleship—the following of Himself as the core and kernel of the Christian life ; involving nothing less than that new birth of which He spoke to Nicodemus (Jo. iii.), for it meant a change of nature and with it a deliberate entering upon another course. The command itself centres in the making of disciples ; the Baptism is the formal initiation into discipleship. The stress of the passage is in the first sentence. Heitmüller in *Taufe und Abendmahl im Urchristentum*, 1911, p. 3, speaks of the passage as solitary in the Gospels, and one 'which

It may be admitted that our direct evidence for the institution of the Holy Communion by Christ is fuller than that for Holy Baptism. There are certain phenomena in the New Testament evidence which at once arrest the attention. The Apostle, who alone records our Lord's discourse on the principles and facts which underlie the Eucharist, makes no allusion to its actual institution. The Gospels which record it report no preparatory teaching on the subject; while the account in St. Luke is in close connection with St. Paul's narrative in 1 Cor. xi. For St. Luke alone contains by implication [1] that command to repeat the Sacrament which forms so prominent a feature in the Pauline account. If it could be proved that St. Luke borrowed from St. Paul,[2] we should have to admit that the Sacrament, as an institution of the Church of perpetual

cannot be reconciled with what we know of Christ Himself and the actual relations of the Apostolic age.' But Mk. xiii. 10 supports the wide-world conception of Christ's mission; and it has been shown that Matthew who, as A. Meyer says (*Die Auferstehung Christi*, p. 28), 'follows Mark in his narrative in everything essential step by step, often almost word for word . . . *and goes right on where our Mark ceases*' (*i.e.* at xvi. 8), found the command in the original ending of the Second Gospel. *v.* Rördam in *Hibbert Journal*, July, 1905, p. 781; Chase in *Journal of Theological Studies*, July, 1905, p. 482, who at the same time arrived independently at the same view, that from the last chapter of St. Matthew we can reproduce the lost ending of St. Mark.

In that case we have the assurance of a double Synoptic attestation of the joint command to make disciples of all nations and to baptize them in the Name of the Holy Trinity. The argument of Feine, *Theologie des N.T.* p. 220 and Heitmüller, *Taufe u. Abendmahl im Urchristentum*, p. 3, that the command (Matt. xxviii. 19) is unauthentic because St. Paul does not refer to it in the dispute about the mission to the heathen, is beside the mark. We do not know what were all the arguments used in the course of the Apostles' deliberations. It may have been employed, just as the vision of St. Peter may have been referred to—an equally clear intimation of God's will and purpose—which was probably known to the other assembled Apostles. The fact that evident signs of God's good pleasure accompanied St. Paul's work, is said to have played a part in recommending it to the Church of Jerusalem (Gal. ii. 7 ff.). But that does not exclude the force of other considerations such as the command of our Lord in Matt. xxviii. 19, or the vision of St. Peter at Joppa. To say that an argument which would seem to us convincing *must* have been used if it were possible to use it, and that its non-occurrence in a short account of lengthened deliberations proves that it was not used, is to make statements which are incapable of proof and have no bearing upon the authentic character of Matt. xxviii. 19.

[1] Lk. xxii. 19. As Plummer points out, ποιεῖτε is the present imperative, 'continually do this to bring Me to mind.' *St. Luke, in loc.*

[2] Cf. Feine, *op. cit.* p. 136.

obligation, depends for its sanction on a record which is not the original account of our Lord's acts and words at the Last Supper. St. Paul received his own information on the subject 'from the Lord':[1] but the earliest form of the tradition is that which is contained in the two first Gospels, and it proceeds from the preaching of St. Peter as recorded by St. Mark. This account contains no command of perpetuation.[2] How did it come about that, from the first days of the Pentecostal Church, the Sacrament was an integral part of the life of the disciples? There was never any hesitation as to its being an ordinance of continual obligation. The meetings of the First Day of the week were held for the purpose of its celebration. The Church of the Holy Spirit was never without its Eucharist. The omission of the command of perpetual observance in St. Mark and through him in St. Matthew is one of the most difficult problems which the New Testament presents to us. But parallel with this omission we have, through St. Paul and St. Luke, the assurance that the primitive community had authority 'from the Lord' to practise the rite.

When we turn to Baptism, we are struck in much the same way by the character of the evidence. The command to baptize rests on one passage, itself derived from an original source which has perished, and which can only be hypothetically reproduced from the other.[3] Nor is the command the main clause of the passage, but is rather complementary to the main clause—'the making disciples of all nations.' As in the case of Holy

[1] 1 Cor. xi. 23. The information reached him from the Lord through the original community. Feine, *Jesus Christus und Paulus*, p. 228. 'Paul ascertained his historical information about the Supper by a way which opened directly to the Lord and proceeded from Him.' Id. *Theologie des N.T.* p. 139.

[2] Feine remarks that the repetition of the Sacrament is implied by Matthew and Mark, and we see it carried out in Acts. *Theologie des N.T.* p. 138. He says 'Mark and Matthew clearly mean to hand down the institution of the Supper which the community of their time celebrated; to neither Evangelist can be imputed any doubt that Jesus Himself ordained the repetition of it which was actually in use.' *Ib.*

[3] Cf. B. Weiss, *Bibl. Theologie des N.T.* p. 105, 'The oldest tradition contains no express command of Jesus to perform the Baptismal Rite in the case of disciples who have been won by the preaching of the Apostles.' This statement is only true on the understanding that Matt. xxviii. 19 remains alone and unsupported. But as we have seen, there is no doubt that it is here following a lost portion of its original source, St. Mark; and we may therefore regard

Communion, we get from the Fourth Gospel alone our Lord's statement of the principles which underlie the necessity of Baptism—the need for birth into a new nature, the change of condition which is vital to entrance into the Kingdom. Yet, again, as in the case of the other Sacrament, from the first moments of the Church's corporate existence we find Baptism enjoined and practised as an essential constituent of salvation. Not only so, but two blessings are associated with it, the remission of sins and the gift of the Holy Spirit, for neither of which have we any recorded word of Christ.[1]

These facts, both of omission and of statement, point to the conclusion that our Lord must have spoken clearly and definitely on the subject of the Sacraments, their meaning and their obligation on occasions which have not been recorded, and in words which, if they have not come down to us, are reflected in the earliest practice and life of the Church. Each Sacrament can be traced back as a rite of actual observance to the first days. The only conclusion to which we can come, when we compare the records of their institution with the clear evidence of their celebration that at once meets us on the threshold of the Church's life, is that the primitive Church was fully acquainted with her Lord's will, and assured of His express sanction for all that was done. The instinct of Christendom has not erred in tracing the two great Sacraments of our Redemption to the institution of our Lord Himself.

The appointment of Baptism as the sacrament of initiation into the fellowship of Christ's Church is one of many indications

Matt. xxviii. 19 as Apostolic (Petrine) evidence of our Lord's words. Weiss adds, 'But the command to baptize unmistakably shows . . . that the earliest community arrived, under the guidance of the Spirit, at the consciousness that in the carrying out of the command, it was only fulfilling the will of its exalted Lord.' *Ib.* n. 4.

It may be remarked that the very early substitute for the lost ending of St. Mark (xvi. 9 *ad fin.*) contains in v. 16 a passing allusion to Baptism, which points to the probability that the original ending contained a reference to it. If the writer knew something of the scope and contents of the original ending from hearsay, it is only likely that he would endeavour to keep as closely as possible to what he had heard.

[1] Acts ii. 38. *v.* B. Weiss, *Der erste Petrusbrief*, p. 52. It is only reasonable, on the ground of this dogmatic teaching of St. Peter on the day of Pentecost, and therefore at the very outset of the Church's corporate life, to conclude that he knew he was carrying out his Master's own teaching in baptizing, and that he had heard Him speak definitely about the actual effects of Baptism.

that our Lord, so far as possible, continued and thereby upheld, practices and beliefs of the old religion. It had long been the custom to baptize proselytes on their admission to Judaism. The idea of purification and separation from former defilements was the governing principle. Frequent washings and 'baptisms' were practised by ascetic sects of Jewish faith who, like the Essenes and, later on, the hermits of Christendom, had fled from the world and made their homes in the solitary regions that stretched beyond the Jordan eastwards. The principle of these baptisms, whether single, on initiation to Judaism, or repeated as in the case of the ascetics, was wholly negative. It regarded the past; it was for the putting away of sin and defilement. It was not held to convey grace. Yet, there was much in the serious and earnest purpose implied by it that appealed to our Lord. It was something that men should sternly face the fact of sin and, in however halting and inadequate a manner, set themselves to deal with it. It was His way to take the common and insufficient, the poor and inadequate methods and expressions of what men truly felt and, with a touch, fill them with new meaning and set them in another light.

And it was an advantage in the inauguration of Baptism as an initiatory rite of universal obligation that it was already known far and wide over the world, through the Jewish Dispersion. It did not come upon people, when they heard of it in the Apostolic preaching, as something wholly unfamiliar. There was no hesitation at receiving it, among those who were being touched by the message of the Gospel.[1]

And there was another kind of Baptism which served to prepare men for that of Christ. The Forerunner, from the use which he made of it to seal the effects of his preaching of the Kingdom, is called 'the Baptist,' as if to sum up, by that title, the whole scope and purpose of his mission. Here, again, was a Baptism which regarded the past, confirming the putting away of sin by a voluntary act of renunciation; yet a rite which brought no new gift of strength.[2]

[1] Cf. Acts ii. 41; viii. 12.

[2] Jo. vii. 39. Josephus, *Antiq.* xviii. v. 2, denies that the Baptism of John conferred remission of sins. But *v.* Mk. i. 4, Lk. iii. 3, 'the baptism of repentance for the remission of sins.' Cf. Heitmüller, *Taufe u. Abendmahl im Urchristentum*,

In seeking to explain the origin of Christian Baptism, there is no need to travel far. It is sometimes said that Hellenic lustrations furnished the point of departure for it. There is no doubt

p. 7. Tertullian understands Mk. i. 4 to mean that the remission was future, only to be conferred when Christ had completed His atonement for sin. *De Bapt.* c. x. Plummer (Hastings' *D.B.* 'Baptism,' i. p. 240) remarks that 'it may be doubted whether, if John's baptism had conferred remission of sins, Jesus would have submitted to it.' But as Christ submitted to the death of a malefactor and was on the cross numbered among the transgressors, and as God 'made Him Who knew no sin to be sin for us' (2 Cor. v. 21) it was not unfitting that He, the sinless and therefore unrepentant, should accept the Baptism of the repentant who had sinned, being thus 'in all things made like unto His brethren.'

If the Baptism of John was preparatory and the blessings attendant on it were due to the coming work of Christ, yet it was not an idle ceremony, it sealed the penitence of those who came to it; and the penitent are (for Christ's sake) forgiven. To deny forgiveness to those baptized by John is to run counter to the general teaching of the O.T. and of the N.T. on the efficacy of repentance. *v.* Swete, *The Forgiveness of Sins*, 1916, pp. 28, 78. There is a sense in which Christ Himself was a penitent when He submitted to the Baptism of John. His complete identification with us led Him to accept the consequences, though He could not share the guilt, of our sins. In that sense He was the Great Penitent. He 'bore the sins of many.' In regarding the Baptism of John as conferring (by anticipation of the Cross) the remission of sins, and remembering that our Lord Himself accepted the Baptism with full knowledge of its meaning, we see the fittingness of the Baptist's prophetic cry, as he looked upon 'Jesus coming unto him and saith, Behold the Lamb of God, who is bearing (taking away, ὁ αἴρων) the sin of the world' (Jo. i. 29). The Baptism of the Sinless One consecrated the preparatory Baptism of John for the remission of sins. Those who deny that it had that efficacy have to account for the fact that under the O.T. sin was forgiven on penitence (cf. Ps. li. 1, 2, 9; 2 Sam. xii. 13; Ps. ciii. 3; 2 Chron. vii. 14), but that forgiveness was withheld when, on the eve of the Atonement which made sin pardonable under the Old Covenant, and the Redeemer Himself was here, men sealed their penitence by confession and Baptism at the preaching of John the Baptist (*v.* Matt. iii. 6).

Dr Mason remarks 'John's Baptism was for others (than Christ) only a baptism of repentance and not a sacrament of grace, not even conveying (though some in old days believed that it conveyed) forgiveness of sins.' *The Relation of Confirmation to Baptism*, p. 16. If John's Baptism conveyed no grace—not even forgiveness of sins—if it was merely 'symbolical,' it is hard to see that it was anything but an idle ceremony. *v.* Plummer in Hastings' *D.B.* art. 'Baptism.' If, as Tertullian, *de Bapt.* x. maintains, 'the remission of sins' in Mk. i. 4 was wholly in the future, how are we to explain the meaning of the same phrase, εἰς ἄφεσιν ἁμαρτιῶν in Acts ii. 38? It is contrary to sound exegesis to insert a future reference in one case and not in the other. Cf. Hastings' *Dict. of Christ. and the Gospels*, 'Baptism,' i. p. 169. Zahn, speaking of the feet-washing of the disciples, says, 'They already had forgiveness of sins through the baptism of John, which in any case the first six Apostles, but probably all of them had received.' *Das Evangelium des Johannes*, p. 530. *v.* Feine, *Theologie des N.T.* p. 121.

that the use of water as a symbolic means of purification was widely spread over the Graeco-Roman world. It would naturally commend itself to men who felt the strain of moral disquiet. Its use among the Jews in the larger cities would become known and, like other practices and ideas of Judaism, be borrowed by Greeks. But it is not only unnecessary, it is unhistorical, to trace any direct connection between Hellenic lustrations and the institution of Christian Baptism. The principle lies nearer home. When a likeness can be traced between a Jewish and a Christian custom, it is practically certain that *there, and not in any alien counterpart,* is to be found the historic connection which we are seeking.[1]

Our Lord, then, took the Jewish conception of Baptism as He found it in use and as it had been adopted for his purpose by the Baptist, and left it to His disciples to be applied with a new meaning under the inspiration of His Spirit. As He gave it to His people with His parting command, it conveyed forgiveness of past sin and the presence of the Holy Spirit. We see this partly from what is said of the preparatory Baptism of John the Baptist, which was a 'Baptism unto repentance with a view to the remission of sins,' coupled with the Baptist's own prophecy that Christ would 'baptize with the Holy

[1] *v.* A. Schweitzer, *Geschichte der Paulinischen Forschung*, p. 150. Heitmüller (*Taufe u. Abendmahl im Urchristentum*) and others have traced dependence of St. Paul upon the Greek mysteries for his teaching on Baptism. Heitmüller (p. 24) disclaims the idea of conscious and direct dependence—'the Jewish and Christian Paul could not entertain the idea of it'—but he considers that indirectly and imperceptibly the practices which surrounded him influenced his action and teaching. Schweitzer entirely rejects any Hellenic influence on St. Paul and thinks that the theory has had a disastrous effect upon the study of Pauline theology. Heitmüller, it should be noticed, speaks of the vast difference between the mystic Hellenic rites and the Pauline teaching on Baptism, in their ethical significance. If St. Paul borrowed, he put the whole question on a higher plane. *Ib.* p. 26. Schweitzer reminds us that analogies do not necessarily imply dependence. *Op. cit.* p. 152. Jacoby, who considers that mystery religions invaded Christianity in the form of Gnosticism, remarks that 'its inheritance of monotheistic Judaism and still more the superior strength of the new Gospel gave to Christianity its exclusive character unharmed by dependence on tendencies of the time. . . . The inclination towards tolerance of other faiths was sharply met and rejected by the Church in the conflict with Gnosticism.' *D. Antiken Mysterienreligionen und das Christentum*, 1910, p. 25. 'Il ne faut pas se hâter de conclure d'une analogie à une influence.' Cumont, *Les Religions Orientales dans le Paganisme Romain*, p. xii.

Ghost and with fire,' and partly from the words of St. Peter on the Day of Pentecost to those who asked for guidance: 'Repent and be baptized every one of you in the Name of Jesus Christ for the remission of sins, and ye shall receive the gift of the Holy Ghost.'

But there is another effect of Baptism, which, as we gather from the Fourth Gospel and from certain expressions of St. Paul, came to be attached to it by our Lord Himself. In the discourse with Nicodemus, which bears much the same relation to the Sacrament of Baptism as the discourse at Capernaum bears to the Lord's Supper, regeneration is assigned to Baptism as its normal effect. Entrance to the Kingdom requires the new birth.[1] 'Flesh and blood cannot inherit the kingdom of heaven.' This new birth is effected by the Holy Spirit, and He employs the outward, visible means of water in carrying it out. Here again, as in the other discourse, we have the foundation principles and truths underlying the Sacrament, which it symbolizes and applies to the individual case.

The chief emphasis is laid upon the necessity of an entire change, not of character or disposition, but of nature. The candidate for the Kingdom—the Church on earth which is to be perfected in heaven—cannot enter it as he is. A change, vital though imperceptible, must pass upon him—nothing less than what St. Paul calls a 'new creation.' This is what our Lord teaches in His reply to the courteous and discerning address of the member of the Sanhedrin. The requirement is universal (τις). No station or position of esteem, no reputation for piety or learning dispenses with it. In the new kingdom to be set up on earth as the Kingdom of the Messiah, only the regenerate, the twice-born may enter. When the ruler expresses surprise at a demand which seems to do violence to every principle of nature, Christ, without modifying or qualifying it, goes on to specify the manner in which it is carried out. The second birth is spiritual and it is of water.[2] The Holy Spirit is the creator of the new life and He uses water

[1] Another birth of one who is born again, ἄνωθεν, not, as has often been thought, with reference to other Johannine passages such as i. 13; 1 Jo. iii. 9, etc., 'from God' or 'from above.' Nicodemus shows by his question in *v.* 4 (*γέρων ὤν . . . δεύτερον*) that the idea is of a second birth, not of its origin (from God).

[2] The attempt which has frequently been made to eliminate the allusion to Baptism by saying that water is only mentioned as a symbol of the purifying

as the symbol and instrument of His action. There is profound reason for the necessity of this new birth. 'That which is born of the flesh is flesh: and that which is born of the Spirit is spirit.'[1] The Kingdom of God is a spiritual thing. 'The Kingdom of God is not meat and drink; but righteousness and peace and joy in the Holy Ghost.'[2] The Holy Spirit is the power by which all its activities are carried on. There must be correspondence of nature with this life, in those who enter upon it. Hence the need of the new birth.

The movements of the Spirit are viewless as the winds. They cannot be watched or measured as He acts upon the spirit of man. But He has taken Baptism as the instrument and expression of His hidden operations, and made it the occasion of His manifested power. With this view, as we find it in our Lord's discourse with Nicodemus, the earliest account of Christian Baptism, on the Day of Pentecost, entirely agrees. St. Peter filled with the Spirit promises to repentance and Baptism the gift of His presence. Thus the Church started on her way with a solemn rite of initiation to which was attached, for every believing and repentant adherent, the forgiveness of past sin and the gift of the Holy Spirit.

In His parting command, our Lord ordained that Baptism should be administered 'in the Name of the Father, the Son, and the Holy Ghost.' It has been shown that the expression 'in the Name' meant, to the Greek-speaking world of that day, much more than it means to us. It conveyed the idea of the person to whom the name belonged. Baptism in His name implied the transference of the baptized into Christ's possession;[3]

action of the Spirit, and that the spiritual birth alone is in our Lord's mind, implies His use of an unnecessary and disturbing expression. As a matter of fact, the phrase has been interpreted in reference to Baptism by the unvarying consent of writers down to the Reformation, as well as by critical scholars of the present day.

[1] Jo. iii. 6. [2] Rom. xiv. 17.

[3] 'The name is connected in the closest way with its bearer. It is a part of his being and yet at the same time has an existence independent of him.' Heitmüller, *Taufe und Abendmahl im Urchristentum*, p. 12. Cf. Feine, *Theologie des N.T.* p. 224, 'The formula (εἰς τὸ ὄνομα) expresses the fact that the baptized is placed in a relation of dependence upon the Person concerned.' Harnack, *Dogmengeschichte*, i. p. 88, n. 3. Cf. the significance attributed by St. Peter to the Name of Christ in the healing of the man at the Beautiful Gate of the Temple (Acts iii. 16). *v.* Jam. ii. 7, 'that worthy name which was pronounced over you,' τὸ ἐπικληθὲν ἐφ' ὑμᾶς. Cf. the discussion in *J.T.S.* for 1905-7.

he became His property, and Baptism was the sealing of the deed of transference.

The act of Baptism thus became the occasion of a confession of faith. If we may judge from St. Philip's dealing with the Eunuch, the baptizer questioned the candidate for Baptism as to his belief. He suggested a statement of doctrine to which he asked assent.[1] It is clear that in the first years of the Church this confession was brief, direct and simple. This consideration helps us to understand the apparent contradiction between the Trinitarian formula of St. Matt. xxviii. 19 and the universal use of the single name of Christ, which occurs in the narratives of Baptism in the Acts. Instruction of a convert in so profound a subject as that which is suggested by the use of the Threefold Name was at the time a thing unheard of. The systemization of its beliefs, their co-ordination into formulated doctrines, was not the task of the primitive Church. One great work lay before it, the preaching of redemption through Jesus of Nazareth, 'declared to be the Son of God through the resurrection from the dead.' The emphasis and weight of the earliest teaching, the core of the profession of faith required from the convert, was thus confined to simple but definite belief in Jesus Christ.[2] There was no need

[1] Acts viii. 37. But the verse is perhaps an early interpolation, suggested by marginal reference to a formula in general use. It is quoted by Irenaeus as part of the text. *Haer.* iii. 12, 8; iv. 23, 2. *v.* Rackham, *The Acts*, p. 123.

[2] The naming of Christ in the baptismal confession was its distinctive mark. It was that which made it Christian Baptism as contrasted with that of John the Baptist. And with the naming of Christ came the thought of the Spirit, as the Baptist said, 'He shall baptize you with the Holy Ghost and with fire' (Matt. iii. 11). In the *Didachê*, we have directions to baptize with the full Trinitarian Formula (c. 7). Lightfoot places the treatise in the first or beginning of the second century. If we may judge from the picture of Church life which it presents, it appears to fall within the Apostolic age. Apostles are named. The order of prophets, who travelled about from place to place, is still in existence (c. 11). Bishops and Deacons are mentioned. The former are not yet differentiated as a separate class from the elders (c. 15). The writing may well have come from a decade close upon the death of St. Paul. The Church life of its period resembles that of the Apostle in so many of its outward features. It is therefore of great significance for the question of the primitive baptismal confession that this ancient treatise lays down the rule of baptizing with the Trinitarian formula, without considering it necessary to explain or interpret it, or even to allege authority for the direction. Again we cannot help thinking that a definite, express command of our Lord Himself, such as that which St. Matthew gives (xxviii. 19), is required to account for this condition of things. The reasoning of Harnack is very unconvincing. He declines to allow that Baptism as a Sacrament can be traced back to our

to require confession of belief in the Father. That was already the possession of every Jew who approached Christianity, as it was of those Gentiles, who, as proselytes of Judaism, formed a

Lord, or that its necessity can be referred to any ordinance on His part. *Dogmengeschichte*, i. p. 88, n. 3. Yet, as we have seen, not only have we the passage in Matt. xxviii. 19, which is in all MSS. and versions and can only be removed by the employment of subjective and unverified assumptions (for we know too little of the early Apostolic age to be able to say that such an expression is certainly of a later date), but St. Mark's lost ending, on which it has been shown to be based, contained in all probability a similar passage; while in St. John's discourse of Christ with Nicodemus, we have the necessity of Baptism laid down. When Harnack disputes the historical character of the sending out of the disciples into all the world with which St. Matthew connects the command to baptize, he is setting aside those passages of St. Mark and St. Matthew which refer to the same world-wide casting of the Gospel net (Mk. xiii. 10; Matt. xxiv. 14). Harnack dogmatically asserts 'that the risen Christ made speeches and gave commands belongs to a later stage of the tradition.' When we inquire the grounds of this assertion, all that he can allege is that 'Paul knows nothing of such things'; as though from his extant Epistles we had complete knowledge of all the Apostle's information of our Lord's sayings and doings. *Dogmengeschichte*, ib.

Another plea against the genuineness of Matt. xxviii. 19 is that, had the command been given, 'the contention of the Apostle Paul about the right of the mission to the Gentiles would be historically inexplicable.' 'For this solemn command of Jesus to baptize would have removed all hesitation which arose in Jerusalem against the mission of Paul.' Feine, *Theologie des N.T.* p. 221. As Wendt points out, 'In the disputes between Paul and the primitive community, the question was not as to whether the Messianic salvation was accessible to non-Israelite people, but as to the conditions under which Gentiles might be received into the Messianic community.' *Die Lehre Jesu*, p. 584. Feine, who admits that the essence of Christianity can only be fully grasped in the form of the Trinitarian revelation of God, says that 'the formal authenticity of the passage (Matt. xxviii. 19) is to be challenged and that it is to be admitted that the later community recognized its experience of the effect of Christian Baptism as being in accordance with the will of the Lord and referred it to a direct saying of Jesus.' *Ib.* p. 222. Kirsopp Lake (*Encycl. of Religion and Ethics*, art. 'Baptism (Early Christian)') holds that the fact of the passage standing in every version of Matt. xxviii. does not prove that it was an original saying of Christ, as it might be due to an editorial insertion. This kind of argument is most unsatisfactory and could be equally fairly applied to any other Gospel passage. The probability that a saying comes from Christ, when it is referred to Him and when some such saying seems required to account for conditions which are known to exist (cf. Matt. xxiv. 14; Mk. xiii. 10; 2 Cor. xiii. 14; Rom. xv. 16, 30; Eph. ii. 20 f.; 1 Pet. i. 2), far outweighs the probability that it is due to the falsifying activity of an 'editor.' The way in which recourse is had to the theory of editorial interpolations is one of the most disquieting characteristics of a certain kind of criticism. The fact that in a writing otherwise shown to be trustworthy a statement not inconsistent with known facts is attributed to a certain speaker, is in itself a strong recommendation of its truth and fitness, as so attributed.

half-way house to the Faith of Christ.[1] It was only at a later time—how much later we cannot say—that the widening of the basis of instruction of catechumens, and the greater care which experience proved necessary to ensure good faith on the part of would-be adherents, led to the fuller and more specified confession of Father, Son and Holy Ghost.[2] It is not improbable that confession of Christ continued still to be the usual mode of allusion to the baptismal profession long after the use of the full formula had been adopted; as at the present day, we speak of Baptism in the name of the Holy Trinity as 'Christian' Baptism.[3]

The use of a brief form of confession at Baptism was a necessity at the first. Men were received into the community after the shortest possible instruction as to what they were pledging themselves; but the requirement meant much: allegiance to Jesus as

[1] Cf. Feine, *Theologie des N.T.* p. 221; Holtzmann, *Neutest. Theologie*, i. p. 454.

[2] Weizsäcker, after speaking of allusions in the Acts to Baptism in the Name of Jesus, remarks that 'at the same period, the formula of Matt. xxviii. 19, which finds its explanation in 2 Cor. xiii. 14, was already in use.' *Apost. Zeitalter der Christⁿ. Kirche*, p. 573.

Cf. Holtzmann, *Neutest. Theologie*, i. p. 453, 'So long as a Jew became a Christian simply through believing reception of the Messiahship of Jesus, Baptism needed no lengthy preparation.' Holtzmann refers to the immediate Baptism of the Ethiopian chamberlain, of the 3000 on the Day of Pentecost and of Saul, who was baptized without any previous instruction. He adds, 'The matter could not end there on heathen ground. As in the case of the monotheistic Jews, it concerned the Messiahship of Jesus; with polytheistic heathen, belief in God Himself had first to be dealt with.' *Ib.* p. 454.

Heitmüller rejects Matt. xxviii. 19 as a saying of our Lord on the ground that Baptism in the Apostolic and sub-Apostolic ages, and indeed up to the third century, was only practised *in the Name of Jesus Christ*, and he quotes (after citing passages from St. Paul and the Acts), *Ep. Barn.* xvi. 6; *Hermas, Vis.* iii. 7. 3; and *Simil.* viii. 6. 4; ix. 12. 5. Now, we may allow that the passages from Hermas point to Baptism in Christ's name. But in *Ep. Barn.* the writer is quoting from the book of Daniel as a sanction for his teaching and there the reference is undoubtedly to God. While, at the same time, Heitmüller omits to mention the full Trinitarian formula which is twice given in the *Didachê* (c. vii.), a treatise which belongs, at the latest, to sub-Apostolic times.

[3] So Irenaeus regards the Name of Christ as conveying the idea of the Holy Trinity. *Haer.* iii. 18. 3. In the *Didachê* (ix.), baptism εἰς ὄνομα κυρίου appears as the equivalent of the full Trinitarian formula of c. vii. 'In early times, the formula Te baptizo in Nomine Domini Jesu Christi was usually admitted with the proviso that a baptism in the Name of Jesus was to be regarded as having been also in the Name of the Father and of the Holy Spirit.' G. L. Hahn, *D. Lehre von den Sakramenten*, 1864, p. 147.

Lord, risen again. It meant much, for it carried with it the taking of a decided stand and the pledge of a whole-hearted service. It was to range oneself on the side of the crucified One. It was a 'going forth without the gate, bearing His reproach.' We find this confession in Rom. x. 9. Those who had thus pledged themselves to faith in the Lordship of Christ and in His Resurrection had committed themselves to His cause. The brevity of the confession made its terms more telling. Only two things; but a world of meaning lay within them. For instance, there is no mention of the atoning death. It is covered by the words that speak of the Resurrection. The death was notorious. All knew the shame of the Cross. Faith comes in when the Resurrection is confessed. When we think in this way of the circumstances under which the early baptismal professions were made and what they meant to the baptized, we can better understand how it came to pass that Baptism in the Name of Christ covered the ground sufficiently, and that Baptism in the Threefold Name would have led to difficulties and questionings, which at so early a stage of Christian experience would have been undesirable. After Baptism, as opportunity offered, would come the catechetical instruction in the principles of the Faith to which St. Luke alludes in the preface to his Gospel.

We have seen that the effect of Baptism was at first held to consist of two supreme blessings, remission of sin and the gift of the Holy Spirit—forgiveness and the power of holiness, the cancelling of the past and new life for the time to come. Very soon we detect a change. St. Peter and St. John 'laid their hands' on the baptized Samaritans and 'they received the Holy Ghost.' We find St. Paul asking disciples at Ephesus 'Have ye received the Holy Ghost since ye believed?' that is, since they made their act of faith at their Baptism.[1] From this we perceive that a process of development has taken place since the day when St. Peter promised the gift of the Holy Spirit as an accompaniment of Baptism. He is now held to be given, not at Baptism, but at the rite of Laying on of Hands, which had come to be regarded as the completion and perfecting of the baptismal rite. This at once creates a difficult problem, which, owing to our scanty knowledge of what passed during the Apostolic age, we have no means of solving. According to St. Peter, converts at their Baptism

[1] Acts xix. 1 f.

received the Holy Spirit.[1] According to St. Peter and St. Paul, later on, the Holy Spirit was not necessarily given at Baptism. The laying on of hands of an Apostle was required; and when the Epistle to the Hebrews was written, Laying on of Hands was regarded as one of the 'principles of the Doctrine of Christ.'[2]

Can we reconcile these accounts of divergent practice? At one time we have the gift of the Spirit associated with Baptism, no further rite being named. But at the visit of St. Peter and St. John to Samaria,[3] and afterwards in the practice of St. Paul, the gift is said to accompany an act which took place after the Baptism of water—the laying on of the hands of the Apostles, with prayer. If a special rite had been set on foot by our Lord Himself for the imparting of His Spirit, we may be sure it would have been practised by the Apostles from the first. But the Laying on of Hands was not thus instituted, and our own Church does not regard it as a Sacrament due to our Lord's own initiative. It appears rather to be an adjunct to Baptism, which commended itself to the Church as a solemn and fitting means for the conferring of spiritual strength upon the baptized: not, as though in their Baptism, they had not been touched by the Spirit; but in order to concentrate the grace of that particular gift on what was a complementary part of the great Sacrament itself. So it came to pass that, in the Laying on of Hands, and not in the Sacrament of Baptism itself, was to be found the ordinary occasion for the full outpouring of the Spirit.

At the same time, in the face of what we are told in the Book of Acts, we are justified in regarding Baptism as securing to the sincere recipient the promised gift of the Holy Spirit. If a distinction came soon to be made between the two parts of the Sacrament—Baptism proper and the Laying on of Hands—there was no such distinction at the first. There is nothing to show that the three thousand converts of the Day of Pentecost, to whom on condition of their repentance and Baptism, St. Peter promised the gift of the Holy Spirit, received the Laying on of Hands. Its origin as a rite especially connected with the illapse of the Holy Spirit upon the baptized can only be traced

[1] Acts ii. 38. There was no rite of laying on of hands when the 3000 people were baptized on the Day of Pentecost. Cornelius first received the Holy Ghost and afterwards was baptized (Acts x. 46 f.).

[2] Hebr. vi. 1.

[3] Acts viii. 14 f.

problematically. We have no means of knowing how or when it came to take its place as a recognized custom of the primitive Church. We find it there; whereas at the first there is no mention of it.[1]

But all through sacred history, the laying on of the hand had been a symbolical act of benediction. Thus, Jacob in blessing the sons of Joseph, before his death, laid his hand upon the head of each. Moses laid his hand upon the head of Joshua to set him apart as the leader of the people. That the custom was more frequently employed than we should conclude from the scarcity of references to it, is clear from the words of the ruler when he asked our Lord to come and lay His hand upon his daughter, who was at the point of death. In the appendix to St. Mark, our Lord is stated to have said to the disciples, on giving them their mission to evangelize the world, 'they shall lay hands on the sick and they shall recover.'[2]

It is in the Eucharist that the distinctive characteristics of a sacrament are most clearly seen. The bread and the wine become the effectual symbols of the body and blood of Christ.

It is remarkable that the root idea of the Eucharist was only made known to the Church in writing as the first century was closing. Our Lord's discourse at Capernaum is contained only

[1] It was an ordinance of the Apostles, and its administration was confined to them, during the Apostolic age. If it was among 'the things pertaining to the kingdom of God' on which our Lord spoke to the Eleven during the forty days, we are not told so (Acts i. 3). If it had been, we can hardly imagine that it would not have been practised from the first. *v.* Rackham, *Acts of the Apostles*, p. 117; Chase, *Confirmation in the Apostolic Age*, pp. 24, 34; Swete, *The Holy Spirit in the New Testament*, p. 92.

[2] Gen. xlviii. 14; Num. xxvii. 18 f.; cf. Deut. xxxiv. 9; Matt. ix. 18; Mk. xvi. 18.

The relation of Confirmation to Baptism is further complicated by the fact that it was not always held to be the completion of that Sacrament. In the primitive Churches of Syria, it was sometimes administered before, and not after, Baptism. With this we may compare, as indeed likely to give rise to the practice, the laying on of the hands of Ananias upon Saul, that he 'might receive his sight and be filled with the Holy Ghost' *before* he was baptized. It was also the custom in Syria to administer unction before the baptismal immersion. *v. Encycl. of Religion and Ethics*, art. 'Confirmation.' It seems reasonable, therefore, to suppose that at first there was no fixed order or method in the various constituents of the rite of the reception of the Holy Spirit. Baptism itself was always and everywhere the chief part of the sacramental rite. Laying on of hands and unction, though closely associated with it, took varying relations to it and were not originally of its organic content.

in the Fourth Gospel. It had been spoken in the hearing of the Twelve; but the fact that no mention of it occurs before that late period shows that it was imperfectly understood, and that it made no great impression upon the disciples generally. It was reserved for the one man who grasped its significance to preserve it for the Church. His memory, stimulated and quickened by the promised gift of the Spirit,[1] reproduced the teaching of that eventful day long past; and we have in St. John vi. the great principles which underlie the Eucharist, and find in it their expression and their application to the needs of men.

Our Lord could not have so spoken of Himself and of His relation to man, if He had not already formed the highest possible view of His own Person. In His Self-consciousness, He stood in a position to mankind which was indistinguishable from that of God. All humanity are concerned in His relation to them. He is universal in His bearing upon the salvation of man. And it is in virtue of His human nature that He can stand in this relation. It is His flesh and blood that form the point of contact between Himself and man. He is vitally necessary to man, and must be received by one who is spiritually alive. The normal mode of reception is effected by the eating of His flesh and the drinking of His blood.

The Evangelist does not hesitate to tell us that this idea, as put forth by Christ, met with no acceptance on the part of the people. To many it gave great offence. And when He turned to the Twelve and said 'Will ye also go away?' the answer of St. Peter shows loyalty still, but no great perception of the truth which he had heard: 'Lord, to whom shall we go?' as though the existence of an alternative source of truth than Christ was at least imaginable.

We may say, then, that the thought of feeding upon Himself—a partaking of His flesh and blood—was an idea quite foreign to the mind of His hearers when our Lord presented it to them. There was nothing in their religion to throw light upon it or to make it acceptable. 'How can this man give us his flesh to eat?' There is a tone of aversion to be heard in the question. And as there was nothing in Judaism to help them to His meaning, their attitude points to the fact that there was also nothing in their knowledge of other religions to be their

[1] Jo. xiv. 26.

guide. This consideration makes strongly against the widely prevalent assumption of syncretic influences, through Judaism, on the formation of Christian thought.[1]

It was only by coming to realize the significance of our Lord's Person, and the relation to man effected by His human nature, that the eating of His flesh and drinking of His blood became so far intelligible that men could take an understanding part in the Eucharist. For a year after the discourse at Capernaum, no allusion was made to the subject by Christ. The great words were left to sink into men's hearts, where there was any intelligence to receive them. Not until the last Passover was there any further attempt to re-assert their meaning and to press them upon the active co-operation of the disciples.

But, if there was no preparation in Judaism, or elsewhere, for the peculiar sacramental teaching of St. John vi., there were certain analogies to it, derived from God's dealing with the people in the past. Our Lord used them in enforcing the need of such communion with Him as could be best expressed by feeding upon His flesh and blood. They were analogies; nothing more. The chief of these analogies—the manna—was adopted by our Lord on the suggestion of the people. They had asked Him to show a sign which should warrant their belief in Him, implying that the great miracle of the multiplying of the loaves and fishes, a day or two previously, was not of sufficiently striking a character to win their faith in view of what God had done in past time through Moses. 'Our fathers,' they said, 'did eat manna in the desert; as it is written, He gave them bread from heaven to eat.' Taking that suggestion of heaven-sent food, our Lord applies it to Himself. It is just what He Himself designed to be to the Israel of God. 'Man doth not live by bread alone, but by every word that proceedeth out of the mouth of God.' Had they known it, a living Word had now proceeded from the Father and was in process of becoming, through Death and Resurrection, the food of all who would receive Him. 'I am the Bread of Life.' At this they begin to murmur. When He had spoken in general terms, saying that

[1] Cf. Bartlet in *Encycl. of Religion and Ethics*, art. 'Baptism in the N.T.' p. 377. 'The peculiar New Testament doctrine of the Lord's Supper is independent of these (heathenish) influences.' C. Clemen, *Religionsgeschichtliche Erklärung des N.T.* p. 288.

it was God Who had given of the manna, and that 'the bread of God is He which cometh down from heaven and giveth life unto the world,' they had responded gladly to what they thought to be a covert assurance of some bountiful supply of their needs. When He plainly connects it with His own Person, they draw back. 'The Jews then murmured at Him, because He said, I am the bread which cometh down from heaven.' They knew His family and thought they knew His origin, 'Is not this Jesus the son of Joseph?' He plainly states the whole truth, 'I am that Bread of Life'; and He specifies its precise nature: 'The bread that I will give is My flesh, which I will give for the life of the world.' When there is again a murmuring at language so unheard of, our Lord presses the matter home and, insisting upon the binding character of His offer to mankind, He declares that its acceptance is essential to the possession of life (*v.* 53). In some way, He does not say how, there must be such communion with Him, such vital contact as is best expressed by the metaphors of eating His flesh and drinking His blood. But after He had become aware of murmuring, even among His disciples, at the astonishing character of His language, our Lord is careful to guard against the thought of any mere *opus operatum*, any magical property of His flesh and blood as such. The flesh, though it be His, taken by itself, received as a mere charm, apart from all ethical connection, would be powerless to profit. It could not give life. The mere performance of a rite, a literal observance, a punctilious carrying out of the command, can never result in the living communion with Him which He makes a necessity for all who would enter into life. 'It is the Spirit that quickeneth. . . . The words that I speak unto you, they are spirit and they are life.'[1] The gifts of God are never merely dynamic, bare exhibitions of power apart from spiritual and moral connection. They are bound up with the Spirit, and for their reception they require the co-operation of man's best

[1] 'In this passage, He does not mean to cancel or weaken the previous paradoxical saying that we must appropriate to ourselves His Flesh and Blood in order to attain to life; but He furnishes an explanation which shows the truth of the saying.' Wendt, *D. Lehre Jesu*, p. 463. '(The Evangelist) thinks that it is degrading to attach an excessive or magical significance to the Sacraments, yet he declares them essential to the Church.' P. Gardner, *The Ephesian Gospel*, p. 253. For 'the Evangelist,' we should rather say Christ, as reported by the Evangelist.

spiritual and ethical faculties. They are spiritual things. And 'spiritual things are spiritually discerned,' and, we may add, spiritually received.

The analogy of the heavenly bread which our Lord employs in this discourse is only a slight help towards our grasp of His meaning; have we any other saying or incident to throw further light on the mystical feeding upon His flesh and blood? St. Paul says that the fathers of Israel 'did all eat the same spiritual food,' making the manna, as our Lord had done, the symbol of the living bread that came down from heaven. He goes on to speak of another symbol. They 'did all drink the same spiritual drink.' If the manna was an analogy of the bread, 'the spiritual drink,' which came from the smitten rock, was a symbol of the precious blood. 'For they drank of that spiritual Rock that followed them; and that Rock was Christ.'[1] But here again there was nothing in the analogy—as it was afterwards noticed and applied in the Christian Church—to throw any light on our Lord's meaning. His hearers would have been far from connecting the water from the rock with the drinking of His blood, as they had been far from perceiving any analogy between the manna and the eating of His flesh.

There was one other custom in their religious life which was afterwards seen to furnish a parallel to His teaching in St. John vi. The Passover, according to the Synoptic account, formed the occasion of the first institution of the Eucharist. Here, again, there was nothing in its detail or ceremonial to explain the eating of the flesh and drinking of the blood of One Who claimed to have come down from heaven to give life to the world. The Passover, with the eating of the lamb and the drinking of the cup of wine, commemorated a great national deliverance. But, as we gather from St. Paul's words, it looked forward to a greater deliverance still. 'Christ our Passover is sacrificed for us. Therefore let us keep the Feast.'[2]

It was only in the light of the completed work of Christ that the fitness of the sayings in St. John vi. was realized. They fell on ears unprepared by any similar teaching of word or symbol

[1] 1 Cor. x. 3, 4. For the legend of the following rock *v.* Driver in *Expositor*, Ser. III. ix.

[2] 1 Cor. v. 7. According to Feine, 'Christ as the Passover Lamb refers to His sacrificial death, not to the Last Supper.' *Theologie des N.T.* p. 142. *v.* Robertson and Plummer, *ad loc.*; Burkitt and Brooke in *J.T.S.* for 1908, p. 569 f.

to receive them; and we read that 'From that time many of His disciples went back and walked no more with Him.'[1] Thus, at the first unfolding of the principles which lie at the root of our mystical union with Christ in His Sacrament, men were scattered and divided: a foreshadowing of what would come about in after years, when that which was intended for a bond—*a communion*—of God's people with Christ and each other became the source of strife and division.

It could hardly have been otherwise. What was there to suggest that the religious life of His hearers could only be maintained by the eating of the flesh and the drinking of the blood of the Jesus, Who stood before them—one of themselves as He seemed to many, acquainted as they were with His bringing up, His home and family ties? But it seemed as though He were unprepared for this rejection of His teaching and the forsaking to which it led. It was a sad and almost despairing question with which He turned to the Twelve, 'Will ye also go away?' St. Peter, as usual their spokesman,[2] answered, 'Lord, to whom shall we go? Thou hast the words of eternal life.' And then in a confession closely akin to that at Caesarea Philippi, as we have it in St. Matthew's account, he adds, 'And we believe and confess that Thou art that Christ, the Son of the Living God.'

The discourse at Capernaum dealt with principles—the necessity of union with God through the sacred humanity of His Son, the fact that all true spiritual life in man is an imparted life. It comes from heaven, as the living bread which sustains it is from heaven. For a year these truths were left to do their silent work in the minds of the disciples.

But just one year afterwards, the hour of His departure was at hand. 'Having loved His own that were in the world He loved them unto the end.' The Passover drew nigh. The feast of the old national deliverance is once more to be kept by faithful Israelites. He will link with it a feast of a new deliverance, world-wide and of deeper meaning—the feast of a redemption from spiritual bondage and sin into the glorious liberty of the children of God. By a consecrating act of

[1] Jo. vi. 66.

[2] One of the many instances which show that the writer of the Fourth Gospel and the Synoptic writers have had the same direct knowledge of the daily life of Christ and His disciples. In each group of writings, St. Peter plays the same leading part, and is the first to speak and act.

His will, He will make that new feast the Sacrament of the new relation into which, by His coming Death and Resurrection, He will enter with His people. Like the old Passover, it will be the sign of a covenant.[1] That marked a deliverance from blood, from the death which fell upon the first-born of the world-power. This, a deliverance through blood, the death of the First-born of God. The issue of what the Passover commemorated was life. The same issue is celebrated by the new feast—life through real, sacramental union with the dying and rising source of all life, the Eternal Son of God.

Here we must not forget the mystical conception which lies beneath the actual Sacrament. Christ having died has risen in a glorious body, which has passed into the heavens. He can 'fill all things.' The properties of His Manhood received the extension which belongs of nature to His Godhead. It is in virtue of this glorified and thus extended Manhood that 'the mystical union which is betwixt Christ and His Church' is effected. He can now be the life of His people, because He has entered on a new relation to them, a relation which enables Him to come into that close contact of which He speaks in His discourse at Capernaum. No one has realized this fact more fully than St. Paul.[2] In this respect he is the greatest of the mystics. He pictures the Christian life as that of Christ in the Christian, as though the man himself had passed out of being, that Christ might take his place. And it is true that 'the old man' has died, the man whose one end was self; otherwise there would be no room for 'the new man, which after God is created in righteousness and true holiness.' He can still say 'I live.' The will is there, the character, the nature, but each renewed, converted, regenerated. Once, as in the inn at Bethlehem, there was no room for Christ. Now 'Christ liveth in' him.

This is the foundation fact—the mystical presence of the glorified manhood of Christ the Lord—which gives reality and life to the Sacrament; and conversely, the Sacrament is a dead letter, an empty rite, if it does not act as a means of ensuring and perpetuating that presence.

[1] I find that F. Loofs draws attention to this, remarking that such passages as Exodus xxiv. 5, 6, 8 and Jerem. xxxi. 31 f. were in Christ's mind on the eve of His death. *What is the Truth about Jesus Christ?* p. 135.

[2] Cf. Gal. ii. 20.

The Evangelist, who records the discourse which lays down the principle of the Sacrament, has left no account of its institution; we may think this strange. He brings us into the upper chamber and tells us, as the other Evangelists fail to do, of the symbolic foot-washing, by which our Lord taught His disciples the need of a cleansing from all defilement contracted in daily life, for those who would have part in Him.[1] Thus St. John seems to have the supper in mind and its deeper meaning, as a sacramental bond of union with Christ, although he does not mention it. With good reason, for as he wrote, the Synoptic Gospels lay open before him, not to speak of his acquaintance with the account of St. Paul. His silence is the confirmation of what was already said.[2] The writer of the Gospel of the Sacrament might well leave to others the record of its institution. So would he the more emphasize the reality, which alone makes of the Sacrament a means of saving grace. It is to St. John that we turn when, as we watch with the Twelve in the upper room the acts of consecration and listen to the words, 'Take, eat, this is My Body,' 'Drink ye all of this: for this is My Blood,' we wonder afresh and ask, 'what mean ye by this service?'

And it is in complete correspondence with the teaching of St. John vi. that our Lord proceeds to utter His mystic words of blessing on the unleavened bread of the Passover and the cup of Passover wine. He calls them His body and His blood, of which all must partake who would have life.[3] Thus He converts the elements of the old feast into the sacramental material of

[1] Jo. xiii. 8.

[2] St. John's residence at Ephesus makes it probable that his acquaintance with the mind of St. Paul was extensive; and by the time he wrote his Gospel, the circulation of 1 Cor. throughout the countries in which St. Paul had laboured must have made the Evangelist familiar with his teaching on the Sacrament. If this is admitted, we have the silent attestation of the last of the Evangelists to the Pauline, as well as the Synoptic, version of the institution of the Eucharist, for St. John does not hesitate to give his own account of an event, by way of correction, where he thinks that other writers have been in error.

[3] In Jo. vi. 51, 53 f. the word 'flesh' is used. In the Synoptic and Pauline accounts of the Institution, its place is taken by 'body.' The difference answers to the scope and occasion of each narrative. The 'flesh' is the more abstract, general term and is more fitting in the discourse in which it is found—a discourse laying down the necessity of communion with the humanity of Christ. The more concrete, particular term 'body' was in accordance with the circumstances of the moment, when 'in His own Body' our Lord was about 'to bear our sins upon the Tree.' 1 Pet. ii. 24.

the new. He links the central act of the worship of Christendom on to the memorial of the old national deliverance, Himself the cause and the life of both.

Much has been written upon the words of institution—what our Lord said and what He meant. It is possible [1] that the first account to be written down is that of St. Paul, who tells us that he 'received of the Lord that which' he delivered to the Corinthians when he was with them.[2] When we compare his narrative with that of the Synoptic Gospels, we are at once struck by remarkable differences of detail combined with similarity in leading characteristics. There is in each case the solemn taking of the bread, then the blessing (εὐχαριστήσας, Paul, Luke; εὐλογήσας, Mk., Matt.), then the breaking of the bread. In each account Christ says, 'This is My body.' The cup 'is My blood of the new testament' (Matt. Mk.), or 'the new testament in My blood' (Lk. Paul). All the accounts agree in these main features. The chief disparity is concerned with the command of continuance. Was this solemn, symbolical proceeding of Christ a farewell feast which ended in itself? Farewell banquets are not usually repeated. We do not willingly perpetuate a mournful occasion, unless there is something morbid and unwholesome in our disposition. No one cares to linger over the saying of a good-bye. And the shadow of death hung heavily upon the company in the upper room. 'With desire I have desired to eat this Passover with you before I die.' Certainly it was a feast of leave-taking. It brought the companionship of three years to an end. It was the last episode of a close and familiar

[1] 'Possible' only: no longer certain, in view of the early date now assigned by many critics to the composition of St. Mark's Gospel.

[2] 1 Cor. xi. 23. He is speaking of his instruction upon the subject when he was at Corinth. He refers to our Lord Himself as his authority. Was it directly given by revelation to the Apostle, or indirectly through communication with the original Apostles? We have no means of giving a certain answer to this question. The literal meaning is that of a direct communication from Christ by revelation, although it is asserted that in that case παρά or ὑπό would have been used instead of ἀπό (*v.* Schmiedel, *Hand-Comment.* ii. p. 133). But there are many instances of ἀπό being used to express the direct source of information, especially in the Fourth Gospel. Feine remarks, 'The information proceeded from the Lord through the primitive community.' *Jesus Christus und Paulus*, p. 228. 'It is not Christ's way to impart by revelation what can be learnt historically.' 'Paul ascertained his historical information about the Supper by a way which opened directly to the Lord and proceeded from Him.' Id. *Theologie des N.T.* p. 139.

intercourse which could never be renewed on the same terms. What was there in such a meal, under such circumstances, that admitted of repetition? The central Figure would no longer be there as He was to-day. And if He were absent, the object of their gathering together would be gone. The question must be answered from the narratives before us. Can we find any hint at continuance of such a character as to command assent?

We at once see that there is no clearly expressed command of continuance in the Gospel narratives. St. Luke follows St. Paul in the words spoken after the giving of the bread, 'This do in remembrance of Me.'[1] In St. Paul alone Christ speaks of what is taking place as a thing to be often repeated, 'This do, as often as ye drink it, in remembrance of Me.' And even here the words are less an actual command than an implication contained within

[1] Lk. xxii. 19. τοῦτο ποιεῖτε εἰς τὴν ἐμὴν ἀνάμνησιν (*v.* above, p. 461, n. 1). Placed within brackets by Westcott and Hort, who consider (ii. p. 64) that 'the words were absent from the original text of Luke,' and that they were supplied from 1 Cor. xi. 24. Holtzmann cites them as an instance of dependence upon Paul. *v.* Feine, *Theologie des N.T.* p. 136, 'It is natural that Luke, who was used to celebrate Holy Communion in Pauline circles, now adhered to the Pauline record of it, conscious that he was recurring to the original Apostolic traditions.' According to this view, the insertion of the words may be assigned to the Evangelist himself, and not to some later copyist. Cf. Salmon, *Introduction to the N.T.* p. 337; Hastings' *D.B.* ii. pp. 636, 638. It is to be noted that St. Paul alone says that our Lord, after giving the cup, repeated the words τοῦτο ποιεῖτε εἰς τὴν ἐμὴν ἀνάμνησιν (inserting after ποιεῖτε, ὁσάκις ἐὰν πίνητε). The words τοῦτο ποιεῖτε mean 'carry out this thing'—'this whole proceeding.' They are not to be taken to mean 'sacrifice this.' If such were the thought intended, we may be certain that it would have been expressed in much clearer language and in a more extended form. As Robertson and Plummer say (on 1 Cor. xi. 24 in *Inter. Crit. Com.*), 'the proposal to give to τοῦτο ποιεῖτε the meaning "sacrifice this" must be abandoned.' The marvel is that the idea was ever conceived. It is quite meaningless under the circumstances, and would have conveyed nothing intelligible to the assembled Apostles. *v.* Darwell Stone in Hastings' *Dict. of Christ.* ii. p. 74, 'The truth appears to be that in itself ποιέω is simply negative as to this point. Apart from other indications of sacrifice it would not suggest any such thing, since in the very large number of instances in which it is used in LXX and N.T. it is in a merely general sense.' When Stone says, 'the word . . . is in itself wholly negative and does not suggest or deny the idea of sacrifice' (*ib.*), we should hardly expect a denial of an idea which was not likely to occur to the disciples at such a time. The endeavour which has often been made to place a forced interpretation on these words has done much to hinder the reception of that sacrificial character which was attributed to the Sacrament by the Fathers of the first four centuries, and is taught in the Office of our own Church. 'I have not the least doubt that τοῦτο ποιεῖτε, *do this,* can only mean *do this act* (including the whole action of

another command, 'this do . . . in remembrance of Me.' Verse 26 is clearly a remark of the Apostle, not a saying of our Lord.

We are thus faced with the fact that an Epistle, written nearly thirty years after the event, is our only authority for any expression of our Lord's will that the Last Supper should be perpetuated in the Church. And this expression comes incidentally. It is not a direct command.

We have now to ask, Do the Gospel narratives, if not actually in so many words supporting the Pauline account, lend any kind of confirmation to it? In St. Mark we read that our Lord said, 'I will drink no more of the fruit of the vine until that day that I drink it new in the Kingdom of God'; and St. Matthew inserts 'with you' and replaces the Kingdom of God by 'My Father's Kingdom.' Here is a reference to other drinking of the wine than that in which they were now taking part. St. Matthew makes the joint act clear, which St. Mark from custom had taken for granted. Each Evangelist in his own way records that it will be part of the practice of the Church—the Kingdom of God.[1] We have to remember, too, that the Evangelists, writing with the knowledge that everywhere, from the first days of the Pentecostal Church, the Sacrament was celebrated as an ordinance of Christ, would be less careful to record any command of continuance than we should wish or expect. Everywhere throughout the Church it was regarded from the first as an ordinance of our Lord of perpetual obligation. Every Christian as such was a

hands and lips) and not *sacrifice this*; and that the Latin also can only have this meaning.' Bp. Westcott, *Life and Letters*, ii. p. 353. Bp. Gore, after investigating the Old Testament use of ποιεῖν, comes to the conclusion that 'there is not sufficient evidence to entitle us to say that ποιεῖν bears the sacrificial sense in the New Testament.' *The Body of Christ*, p. 318.

[1] *v.* Feine, *Theologie des N.T.* p. 138. 'It is perceived that Mark and Matthew apparently wish to hand down the founding of the Supper of the Community as it took place in their time, and that to neither of the Evangelists can be imputed any doubt that Jesus Himself ordained the repetition of it which was then in use.' Feine remarks that if Volkmar's theory that the original text and tradition of the Last Supper merely contained the words 'This is My Body—This is My Blood,' we should be in doubt as to the way in which the Christian rite originated immediately after Christ's death. *Ib.* 'It is an instance of the practical wisdom of the teaching of Jesus that in this situation, He gave His disciples not a piece of theoretical instruction, which they could not have understood at the time, but that He spoke to them by a transaction which must have stamped itself ineffaceably upon their memory.' Wendt, *D. Lehre Jesu*, p. 568. *v.* Swete on Mk. xiv. 25.

'communicant';[1] and in what is perhaps the first written narrative of the event that has come down to us, we have a statement which embodies the idea of the continuance of the feast in our Lord's own words.[2]

St. Mark and St. Matthew say that Christ blessed the bread, thus setting it apart, consecrating it. St. Luke and St. Paul interpret His action and words as a giving of thanks, εὐχαριστήσας. It is probable that He did both. He would be following the custom of His people in offering thanksgiving to God before food; and in doing so at this particular point, notwithstanding His having given thanks at the beginning of the Passover meal, He marked the division and let the Apostles see that He was inaugurating something new. At the giving of the cup, St. Mark and St. Matthew record that—as, according to St. Luke and St. Paul, He had done in the case of the bread—He gave thanks. Each authority therefore agrees that, during the course of the meal, He gave thanks. St. Peter (St. Mark and St. Matthew) is clearly the authority for the blessing or consecration of the bread. By that formal act, the great High Priest inaugurated that solemn setting apart of bread, to become in the faithful His own flesh, which forms so vital an element of the Canon of the Eucharist. We are told that it was only the bread which He thus consecrated. The wine may be regarded as blessed in the other element, as the blood is contained in the flesh.[3]

To all our authorities the cup represents the sealing of a covenant in Christ's blood. All three Evangelists—but not St. Paul [4]—say that the blood 'is shed for many' (Mk., Matt.) or 'for you' (Lk.). St. Matthew alone further explains the benefit imparted by the blood-shedding as 'for the remission of sins.' Thus the blessing of forgiveness of sin, as the consequence

[1] *v.* Falconer in Hastings' *Dict. of Christ.* ii. p. 68. The restriction of the Eucharist to the baptized is laid down in the *Didaché*, Μηδεὶς δὲ φαγέτο μηδὲ πιέτω ἀπὸ τῆς εὐχαριστίας ὑμῶν, ἀλλ' οἱ βαπτισθέντες εἰς ὄνομα Κυρίου (ix. 5). From this Weiss draws the conclusion that the rule had previously been less strictly preserved, and that in certain cases unbaptized adherents had been admitted to communion. *D. Urchristentum*, i. p. 49.

[2] 'The Rite rests on Jesus' own ordinance.' Feine, *op. cit.* p. 139. Cf. Harnack, *D. Wesen des Christentums*, p. 101, 'I see no ground for doubting the fact that Jesus founded a perpetual memorial of His death by a solemn rite.'

[3] On mediaeval use of this idea *v.* Gore, *The Body of Christ*, p. 279.

[4] But the body is broken ὑπὲρ ὑμῶν, 1 Cor. xi. 24.

of the outpouring of His blood upon the Cross, is connected by our Lord with the reception of the sacramental cup.[1] St. Paul is in agreement with this great truth, when he says by way of comment on his report of our Lord's words and acts, 'For as often as ye eat this Bread and drink this Cup, ye do shew the Lord's death till He come.' It is the Sacrament of the atoning Death, and therefore to those who worthily partake of it, it is the Sacrament of Life—of Life through Death—the Life of the 'many' by the Death of One.

The idea of a covenant was a familiar one to the assembled Apostles. The 'bow in the cloud' was the 'token of the covenant' which God made with Noah on the morrow of the Flood. The blood sprinkled upon the door-posts of the Israelites, on the night of the slaying of the first-born of Egypt, was 'a token' of a covenant of safety, of the passing of the Lord 'over the door' of every house of His own people.[2] When our Lord, holding the sacramental cup, said, 'This is My Blood of the Covenant,' or, as St. Paul and St. Luke say, 'This cup is the new Covenant in My Blood,'[3] there must have flashed upon the disciples' minds the thought of a great deliverance.[4] And the Church has

[1] *v.* Bousset, *Kyrios Christos*, p. 288. J. Weiss, drawing attention to the striking fact that the words εἰς ἄφεσιν ἁμαρτιῶν are found only in the First Gospel and not, as one would expect from his knowledge of St. Paul's teaching, in St. Luke, concludes that Luke possessed older sources, and that not only the Marcan form of the words of institution (expanded by St. Matthew) but the passage Mk. x. 45 go considerably beyond what we learn from that older tradition. Weiss thinks it possible that certain circles of the primitive community, such as that connected with St. Stephen, had laid greater emphasis upon the atoning death of Christ than St. Peter had done. *D. Urchristentum*, i. pp. 83, 84. 'That "Christ died for our sins" is a thought that is already possible for the early community; only it would be Paul's explanation, if out of his own experience he has added "for our sins."' *Ib.* p. 85.

[2] Gen. ix. 12; Ex. xii. 21 f.; cf. xxiv. 3 f.

[3] Cf. Jer. xxxi. 31-34. *v.* Wendt, *D. Lehre Jesu*, p. 502.

[4] But at the time they were not in a condition of mind to be able to connect any deliverance with the thought of their Master's death. This is apparent from their state of gloom and perplexity during the Last Supper and their despair after the Crucifixion. 'It should be considered how little the disciples were disposed on the last evening that they were with Jesus to enter into the thought of His approaching Death by violence, not to speak of their being able to form an estimate of the inner necessity and the healing virtue of the Death.' Wendt, *D. Lehre Jesu*, p. 568. J. Weiss regards the institution itself and the earliest repetitions of the Supper as wanting in direct allusion to the death of Christ, and he cites the fact that the oldest Eucharistic prayers which

always regarded it as the new covenant of God with His spiritual Israel, sealed in the blood of His Son shed upon the Cross.

Our Lord then looks forward. 'Verily I say unto you, I will drink no more of the fruit of the vine until that day that I drink it new in the Kingdom of God.' All three Gospels agree in this anticipation, with immaterial differences of expression. St. Paul is silent. The Marcan (Petrine) tradition lies at the root of the saying. St. Luke here keeps to it, having nothing to draw upon in the Pauline tradition. To what future drinking of the fruit of the vine does our Lord refer? There is one certain, if partial, interpretation of the words. He speaks of the Eucharists of the Church. The drinking of the fruit of the vine in the Kingdom of God, when it 'shall come' means, according to all analogy, and in its primary application, the Eucharistic Feast with the promised presence of Himself.[1] Light is thrown on this interpretation by the beautiful saying of one who sat at meat with Jesus in the house of a Pharisee on the Sabbath Day, as he listened to the Saviour's teaching and was touched for the moment with prophetic impulse

we know, those of the *Didachê*, contain no mention of it. He also emphasizes the constant use of the term 'breaking of the bread' for the Supper, in the Book of Acts, considering that, while mystical and symbolical ideas soon began to creep in, the bread and the breaking of it was the main substance of the feast. The oldest form was without the wine. 'When Jesus ate with His disciples, often enough there was no wine (*e.g.* at the feeding of the 5000). Besides, there was not so clear and impressive a gesture at the handing round of the cup. Therefore only the breaking of the bread stamped itself upon the minds of the Disciples and was adopted by them.' *D. Urchristentum*, i. p. 42. Now, it may well be that the more significant action of the breaking of the bread appealed more forcibly to the disciples in the first instance; hence the title given to the feast in the earliest celebrations of it. But we are hardly justified, on these grounds, in drawing the conclusion that the cup was an afterthought. Our Lord's own action and example would have been too well remembered: bread and wine were the common and universal constituents of a meal. Weiss seems to imply that the addition of the cup formed a notable innovation upon early practice (p. 44) and that St. Paul may have had a hand in bringing it about: but he adds, 'Unfortunately we cannot observe the process by which the change of views came about, we can only recognise that it occurred very quickly' (p. 45). It is also against Weiss' view of the cup that in the *Didachê*, which, as he says, contains prayers uninfluenced by Pauline teaching, and standing near to the oldest ideas, there is a special thanksgiving for the cup.

[1] Mk. xiv. 25, with Swete's note; Matt. xxvi. 29; Lk. xxii. 18.

—'Blessed is he that shall eat bread in the kingdom of God.' In reply our Lord spoke the parable of the Gospel Feast, with the message, 'Come, for all things are now ready.' [1] But as in the parable, so in these words at the Last Supper, the primary sense, as so often in our Lord's sayings, is far from exhausting His meaning. Beyond the Eucharists of the Church 'the marriage supper of the Lamb' awaits the Saviour's guests. The Beatitude will only be fulfilled then in His unveiled Presence. The 'True Vine' will Himself impart the fruit.[2] He will drink it new with His people in His Father's Kingdom. There is reason to believe that eternal life will only be eternal as sustained by that which is its support here—the flesh and blood of the crucified, but now glorified, Son of God. Something of this is conveyed in the complete fulfilment of the promise of drinking the fruit of the vine in the Kingdom of God. Our Lord, at the institution of the Eucharist, was founding no temporary rite. He had in view the perpetuation of that eternal life, which must be begun here in the dispensation of grace, if it is to be lived there, where the Life Himself dwells for ever with the Father and the Holy Spirit.

Having thus considered the salient features of the inauguration of the Eucharist, we must inquire more particularly into the meaning of certain expressions which occur in the course of it. When our Lord said, 'This is My body,' 'This is My blood,' are the words to receive a bare literal interpretation, such as is at once suggested by their use, or are they to be interpreted with reference to other sayings and in accordance with the context in which they appear? Round this point has circled for ages the keenest of theological controversies. Taken by itself, the literal meaning of the word 'is' seems to express identity. The bread and the wine are actually what He says—His body and His blood; and there is an end of the matter.

But there are considerations which forbid this short and summary conclusion. One is the reflection that language, however clear and expressive, is after all descriptive and symbolic, pictorial rather than precise, presenting an image of the truth and not the truth itself. And our Lord, as part of the requirements of His Incarnate Life, accommodated Himself to the restrictions of language and employed it under the limitations which affect its use by ordinary men. He clothed His thoughts in terms

[1] Lk. xiv. 15. [2] Cf. Rev. vii. 17.

that would find an entrance into the minds of men. Otherwise, His words would have found no acceptance.

In trying to get at His meaning, we therefore have to interpret Him in accordance with those canons of language and interpretation which held good among His hearers. He spoke to be understood, and He therefore spoke as men speak, although beneath the language are the Divine realities into the meaning of which He alone could enter.

Another thing to be considered is the light thrown on His words by other corresponding sayings. Using the first person of the same verb 'to be' instead of, as here, the third person of the present tense, He says, 'I am the door of the sheepfold'; 'I am the True Vine.' Here identity is out of the question, yet the meaning is perfectly plain. The verb applies a description. It does not assert identity between the two members of the sentence.

Then we have to take into account the circumstances of the moment. When our Lord called the bread which He was handing to the Apostles His body and the wine His blood, there was no likelihood that they would think for one instant that He had performed a miracle, constituting the elements which He was giving them parts of Himself. The bread and the wine were and remained distinct from the hand which held and conveyed them. Failing such a thought, as something entirely out of the range of their conception, they would at once see that, in accordance with Eastern usage, symbol and fact are so intertwined in His language that the one is said *to be* the other; and that in so speaking He intended the symbol to convey the reality which it symbolized. The narratives of St. Paul and St. Luke in the delivery of the cup should alone have prevented the thought of identification. In each our Lord is represented as saying, 'This cup is the New Testament in My Blood.' Clearly there could be no question of identity here. A cup of wine, whatever its significance on consecration, and a testament or covenant can never be one and the same thing. This consideration must govern our interpretation of the words we have been considering.[1]

Such pictorial, representative language abounds in Eastern

[1] *v. Life of Bp. Westcott,* ii. p. 354. In Aramaic, the language of Christ at the Last Supper, no equivalent of the ἐστίν of the Greek Gospel occurred. *v.* Allen on St. Matt. xxvi. 26.

speech. Our own linguistic methods afford many analogies. I sell a house or a piece of land. When the purchase is completed and I hand the title-deed to the purchaser, saying 'here is your house or land,' my meaning is unmistakable. Receiving the deed, he becomes possessor of the property. But the two things are never identical. The Church of Rome from the eleventh century onwards has taught that the elements of the Eucharist become, on consecration, the actual body and blood of Christ. As bread and wine they have ceased to be, and are now that which our Lord said they represented and conveyed. While they retain the qualities or 'accidents' which belong to their kind, their 'substance' is said to be changed: if not in appearance, yet in reality, they are now His body and blood.[1] With that branch of the Church, therefore, the Eucharist is no longer a Sacrament. Its representative, symbolical character has gone. A miracle has taken place to which our Lord's action here on earth offers no parallel. The effect of such a conception on the Sacrament is like that of the Docetic view of the Incarnation upon the doctrine of the Person of Christ. To secure the Deity, the reality of the Manhood was sacrificed with disastrous results. In the same way, the sacramental value of the Eucharist is marred by the effort to obtain a literal fulfilment of Christ's words.

A literal meaning is excluded also by the fact that, at the time of the institution, the offering of which the Eucharist is the memorial was not yet made, the body not yet yielded to death upon the Cross, the blood not yet shed. It is the body so offered and the blood so shed that the Sacrament is the assured means of imparting.[2] Hence the institution was not so much an actual Sacrament as the exhibition of what was to be in the time to come. Our Lord founded it indeed, but rather as a pattern and example of the Eucharists of the Church. The time was not ripe for its full celebration. It belonged to the Kingdom of God, and the Kingdom could not be until Christ

[1] The theory of transubstantiation violates a recognized principle of metaphysics, by drawing a distinction between the substance of an entity and its apparent qualities. For, we have no knowledge of a substance apart from the qualities or 'accidents' which constitute it. The qualities *are* the substance.

[2] 1 Cor. xi. 24, 'This is My Body which is broken for you.' Mk. xiv. 24, 'This is My Blood of the New Testament which is shed for many.'

had suffered and risen.[1] One great object of the Sacrament is the solemn showing or proclamation of the Saviour's death before God. 'As often as ye eat this bread and drink this cup, ye show the Lord's death till He come.' And this could not be done before the Cross was reared on Calvary.

But there was another reason. 'The Body and Blood of Christ, which are verily and indeed taken and received by the faithful in the Lord's Supper,'[2] are the body and blood of One Who has passed through death, but is now the risen and glorified Lord; and His presence is mediated by the Holy Spirit. St. Paul in one place speaks of Him as 'that Spirit,'[3] so entirely is His glorified life conditioned by the Spirit, Who is His organ and minister, manifesting His glory, preparing men to receive Him and making the Eucharist itself an effectual means of imparting Him. Thus, strictly speaking, it was not until the Holy Spirit was given at Pentecost that the full efficacy of the Sacrament could be experienced; not until He came, as the reward and consequence of the Death and Resurrection of our Lord, that the Saviour's presence with all its grace and power could become the possession of the faithful communicant.[4]

From all this it is clear that a bare, literal meaning of the words of institution is not to be thought of. But in saying that, we do not deny that they have a very true, if far higher, meaning. The faithful reception of the Sacrament ensures that communion with Christ of which He spoke at Capernaum. Our own branch of the Church fully expresses this truth in the Prayer of Humble

[1] Cf. A. Schweitzer, *Geschichte der Paulin^{n}. Forschung*, p. 159, 'The naïve and unhistorical representation as though Jesus has instituted the Sacraments is not recognised by the Gnosis of the Johannine Theology. According to that He did not found them but He created and foretold them.' 'Jesus came into the world to bring about the time of efficacious (*wirkungskräftiger*) Sacraments.' *Ib.*

[2] The Church Catechism. [3] 2 Cor. iii. 17.

[4] Cf. A. Schweitzer, *Geschichte der Paul^{n}. Forschung*, p. 157, 'Without the Spirit there is in the Supper no Body and no Blood of Christ.' The Sacrament was thus, at its institution, an anticipation, 'a shadow of things to come' (Col. ii. 17). It could not be more while Christ was bodily present. It was 'expedient' that He 'should go away' for its accomplishment. For then the Spirit would come, Who alone can vitalize what would else be a lifeless ceremony. 'The flesh (alone) profiteth nothing.'

It has been pointed out by Bp. Gore that 'if there be a real communication to us of the flesh and blood of Christ, it must be the flesh and blood of the glorified Christ, for no other exists' (*The Body of Christ*, p. 66). And he asks

Access.[1] The mystery of the *manner* must not blind our eyes to the *fact* of the real Presence of our Lord in the Sacrament.

Closely connected with the question of the real Presence is that of the object of Eucharistic worship. The one service of Divine appointment is confessedly the chief occasion of worship which the Church possesses. Who or what is the

(*ib.* p. 315), 'how then could it be instituted before the passion? How could Christ, while yet in His mortal body, give His disciples His flesh and blood to eat and drink?'

These considerations make it apparent that a literal construction of the words of institution is impossible. And with that construction goes the local, materializing view of the presence in the elements which lies at the root of the heresy of transubstantiation. Bp. Gore, after alluding to the belief of the early Church in the real, objective presence of Christ in the Eucharist, observes that the Fathers would have shrunk from speaking of Christ 'made present on the Altar under the forms of bread and wine' (*ib.* p. 91). 'Primarily, the gift of Christ's Body and Blood is a spiritual gift for the spirit. Faith alone is the instrument which can receive it and not the mouth of the body. The gift accompanies the material bread and wine, but is to be distinguished from it' (*ib.* p. 64). Cf. *Life of Bp. Westcott*, ii. p. 351, who says in a letter, 'The Lord offers His Body given and His Blood shed. But these gifts are not either separately (as the Council of Trent) or in combination Himself (*v.* Freeman, *Principles of Divine Service*). . . . It seems to me to be vital to guard against the thought of the Presence of the Lord "in or under the forms of bread and wine." From this the greatest practical errors follow.' Cf. *ib.* ii. p. 79. *v.* B. Weiss, *Leben Jesu*, ii. p. 477, 'For the disciples, in whose midst Jesus sat in bodily form, every possibility was excluded of understanding His words otherwise than that His action with the bread symbolically represented what must happen to His Body.'

[1] The fact itself is taken for granted, the prayer is for the right reception of the flesh and blood of Christ, 'Grant us therefore, gracious Lord, *so* to eat, etc.' Cf. 'Then we spiritually eat the Flesh of Christ and drink His Blood' in the second exhortation, and the words of administration, 'The Body of our Lord Jesus Christ,' 'The Blood of our Lord Jesus Christ'; also the thanksgiving of the second prayer after reception for the feeding 'with the spiritual food of the most precious Body and Blood of Thy Son our Saviour Jesus Christ.' Nothing is clearer than the intention of our Church to insist upon the real, spiritual Presence of our Lord; while, at the same time, nothing is said as to the precise mode in which that Presence is effected.

On the confusion of the *real* Presence with a *material* Presence of Christ in the Eucharist, see Strong, *Manual of Theology*, p. 371. 'Ignatius calls the thankoffering the Flesh of Christ, but the conception "Flesh of Christ" is with him a spiritual one; Justin, on the other hand, sees the actual Flesh of Christ in the Bread, but he does not refer the idea of an offering to it. Both writers are still far from sharing the later conception.' Harnack, *Dogmengeschichte*,[4] i. p. 235, n. 1. Bp. Jer. Taylor points out that it is the spiritual presence of Christ which 'is the most true, real and effective.' *The Real Presence and Spiritual of Christ in the Blessed Sacrament*, sect. i. 6, 7.

object to which her worship is to be directed? We are not left without guidance here. The supreme object of worship is the Source of all Being and Power, the Father of our Lord Jesus Christ. Our Lord's own example directs our attitude. In no Gospel is His practice shown more clearly than in that which is pre-eminently the Gospel of His own Divinity.[1] He is ever looking up to the eternal Source of His own Divine Being. He always leads us to infer in that respect His own position of subordination; for the Father and not the Son is the *Fons et Origo* of all that is.[2] And in the most solemn moments of our worship we have this attitude of our Lord to point us to its true and proper object.

We have other guidance in the practice of the primitive Church, which was at one with the mind of Christ. If we look through the early liturgies, we find that worship is seldom directed to our Lord. 'The mind of the ancient Church in general is represented in the Canon of the African council of Hippo, A.D. 393, "When we stand at the altar, let the prayer always be directed to the Father."' Our own liturgy shows its strict adherence both to Scripture and to the practice of the primitive Church. Our Lord is worshipped, but the Prayer for the Church Militant, the General Confession, the Prayer of Humble Access and, more significant still, the 'Prayer of Consecration,' are all directed to the Father, not to speak of the prayers following upon the administration of the Sacrament.[3] It is clear that a liturgy so framed has no place for the worship of Christ *under the forms of the consecrated bread and wine.* We are called to worship the Father through His risen and glorified Son, Whose presence in

[1] *v.* Jo. xiv. 28.

[2] Cf. Bull, *Def. Fid. Nicen.* iv. 1, § 1, 'Proinde Pater, Divinitatis quae in Filio est, fons, origo ac principium sit.'

This is fully maintained by the Father to whom more than to any other teacher the Church owes the preservation of the truth of our Lord's Divinity. *v.* Athan. *Contra Ar.* ii. p. 365 B. 'The very name of Son and the very idea of derivation imply a certain subordination of the Son to the Father so far forth as we view Him as distinct from the Father, or in His personality.' Newman, *The Arians of the Fourth Century*, p. 168.

[3] *v.* Gore, *The Body of Christ*, pp. 100, 103, 106. 'The official prayer of the community remains lastingly directed to God.' Bousset, *Kyrios Christos*, p. 285. Cf. the Lord's Prayer; *Didachê*, 9-10; Justin M. *Apol.* 67, *'Επὶ πᾶσι τε οἷς προσφερόμεθα, εὐλογοῦμεν τὸν ποιητὴν τῶν πάντων διὰ τοῦ Υἱοῦ αὐτοῦ 'Ιησοῦ Χριστοῦ καὶ διὰ Πνεύματος τοῦ ἁγίου.* But *v.* the Gloria in Excelsis; below, p. 586; Keble, *Eucharistical Adoration*, p, 116.

His Eucharist is assured to us by His own words and action. But we do wrong to that presence when we try to tie it down to the symbols and types which are the appointed means of its fulfilment. We incur the risk of destroying the Sacrament and the still greater risk of setting up, in the midst of the most sacred act of worship possible here on earth, a rival object of devotion to the God Who made and redeemed us.[1]

In the belief of the primitive Church and the express language of our own formularies, the Eucharist is the occasion of sacrifice.[2] But the precise character of the sacrifice must be defined. It is in no sense a propitiatory offering, repeating the sacrifice of the Cross. Christ made there 'a full, perfect and sufficient oblation and satisfaction for the sins of the whole world.' Any conception of the Eucharist as propitiatory is a dishonour done to Him Whose offering is thereby declared to be incomplete. Whereas, being the offering of the Eternal Son of God, it had an

[1] Cf. Liddon, *Bampton Lectures*, pp. 199, 422; Bp. Talbot, *The Holding of the Truth*, p. 10; Westcott, *Social Aspects of Christianity*, p. 111.

[2] For evidence of the belief of the early Church *v. Didachê*, xiv. *κατὰ κυριακὴν δὲ Κυρίου συναχθέντες κλάσατε ἄρτον καὶ εὐχαριστήσατε προεξομολογησάμενοι τὰ παραπτώματα ὑμῶν ὅπως καθαρὰ ἡ θυσία ὑμῶν ᾖ.* Cf. Justin M. *Apol.* i. 67; id. *Contra Tryph.* 41. 117. Irenaeus, *Adv. Haeres.* iv. 17. 5, writes, '(Dominus) novi Testamenti novam docuit oblationem; quam Ecclesia ab Apostolis accipiens, in universo mundo offert Deo.' Later on the evidence broadens into a stream.

In our own Church the idea of sacrifice is plainly conveyed in the first of the alternative prayers following the administration, 'this our sacrifice of praise and thanksgiving,' 'a reasonable, holy and lively sacrifice unto Thee.'

This sacrificial character of the Eucharist answers to the same element in the offerings of the Old Covenant. The central and controlling sacrifice of the Cross is the object to which the one group of sacrifices looks forward and the other looks back. Scripture itself guards against the claim of intrinsic efficacy in the Jewish sacrifices (Hebr. x. *passim*). They served to connect the penitence of the worshipper with the one perfect offering which was to come; and in so far as they expressed the faith and penitence of the offerer, they made him a sharer of the virtue of the Cross. But in themselves, they could never take away sin. They were legitimate because the perfect sacrifice was not yet offered. They performed their part, and that was to point forward to it, to prepare men for Christ. His offering for ever abrogated them. The destruction of the Temple after a probationary period of forty years completed that abrogation; and the Temple has never been rebuilt.

To regard the Eucharist as a sacrifice of intrinsic virtue, as is done in the Church of Rome, is to set that abrogation at defiance, to go back on the processes of history, 'to build again the things which are destroyed,' to assign to a memorial and a representation the actual qualities of the thing which it represents.

universal and an eternal efficacy, and needed no supplementary or additional offerings to make it good. We have, therefore, to guard most carefully against any view of the sacrificial aspect of the Eucharist which infringes the completeness of the one offering. Christ, and Christ alone, by the one historical sacrifice of the Cross, has made full atonement for every sin, by fulfilling in His own perfect and sinless obedience the whole law of the righteousness of God. Nothing is clearer than the teaching of the New Testament on this point; and no expressions of late writers should be allowed in any way to weaken or modify our hold on this fundamental truth.[1]

We must, accordingly, consider in what sense the Eucharist can be said to be a sacrifice, or more strictly, the occasion of a sacrifice and what it is which is offered therein.

Our own Church names two distinct offerings in the Eucharist—the oblations of bread and wine, which are to form the material of the Sacrament together with offerings made to God for the benefit of His people in the shape of alms, and the presentation of the communicant himself, body, soul and spirit 'to be a reasonable, holy and lively sacrifice unto' Him. In respect of these two oblations, ourselves and our goods, presented in faith of the one sacrifice and in union with it, the Eucharist is rightly called a sacrifice.

It is also a solemn commemoration; the showing of the sacrifice of Christ—the proclamation of it before men and the representation of it before God. For as often as it is celebrated, the offering upon the Cross is pleaded once again for the forgiveness of sin. But here again, we need to distinguish carefully between a repetition of the sacrifice—which the Eucharist can never be—and the memorial or presentation of the sacrifice—which the Eucharist always is; 'For as often as ye eat this bread and drink this cup, ye do shew the Lord's death till He come.'[2]

[1] As Bp. Gore points out, consecration does not effect any renewal of the sacrifice of the Cross. 'The death is commemorated only, not renewed or repeated.' *The Body of Christ*, pp. 174, 175. *v. Foundations*, p. 303.

[2] 1 Cor. xi. 26. 'The conception of the Table as an Altar is later than the middle of the second century. . . . It is used by Ignatius in a Christian sense, but always metaphorically. It may be noted that though the Apostolic Constitutions (Bk. II.) speak of a θυσία, they do not speak of a θυσιαστήριον. This use of θυσιαστήριον is probably not earlier than Eusebius (*H.E.* x. 4).' Hatch,

The Eucharist is a feast of communion and fellowship. This was recognized at the first. It was part of the common life of the primitive community. Very early, a feast of good fellowship (ἀγάπη) became attached to it, how soon, or where, we do not know; but it was the custom at Corinth, when St. Paul addressed his First Epistle to that Church. Intended to promote kindness and harmony between the brethren, it speedily degenerated into a mere festivity. The sanctity of the Eucharist became imperilled, and the Apostle uses the sharpest language of rebuke. From that time the association of the Ἀγάπη with the Eucharist began to appear undesirable and gradually ceased.[1]

The Eucharist is a communion in a double sense—with Christ, with fellow-Christians. 'Ye are all one in Christ Jesus.' The closest union with Him is secured by spiritual feeding upon His body and blood. In Him is the source of our life. And it is through this united communion with Him that our fellowship with one another is secured. Approach to the altar is barred, by the express language of our Church, to those who are living in wilful enmity against others. The fact that in the Eucharist all are partakers of one bread makes it a sacrament of unity.[2]

The Eucharist is a communion in another sense. It is something to be shared, not a rite to be enacted without the participation of the worshipper. Our Lord intended it for reception by His people, and no subsequent consideration, arising from a heightened sense of its sanctity and its significance, has any authority to set aside that intention. He meant it for all who belonged to Him; and the actual eating and drinking of the bread and wine are essential for its proper fulfilment.[3] That this was not only Christ's intention, but the practice of the primitive Church, is apparent from statements of what occurred when the Eucharist was celebrated.[4]

Hibbert Lectures, p. 302. On θυσιαστήριον *v.* Westcott, *Ep. to the Hebr.* p. 453 f. In late ecclesiastical Greek (Socrates) it means the sanctuary of a Church, while the altar is τραπέζα. For mod. Greek *v.* Hépitès, *Dict. Grec-Français*.

[1] See Dean J. A. Robinson in *Encycl. Bibl.* art. 'Eucharist,' col. 1424, 5.

[2] Cf. *Didachê*, c. 14.

[3] 1 Cor. xi. 26, makes this clear.

[4] Justin M. *Apol.* i. 67, giving an account of a Sunday service, says, *παυσαμένων ἡμῶν τῆς εὐχῆς ἄρτος προσφέρεται καὶ οἶνος καὶ ὕδωρ . . . καὶ ἡ διάδοσις καὶ ἡ μετάληψις ἀπὸ τῶν εὐχαριστθέντων ἑκάστῳ γίνεται.* 'Distribution is made to each.' All communicate. Only the unbaptized (cf. *Didachê*, c. 9) or the excommunicate were prohibited from receiving.

They only receive the virtue of the Sacrament who communicate. Attendance at the celebration of the Eucharist without communion in no sense fulfils the purpose for which our Lord intended it.[1]

It must also be observed that nothing is more opposed to the primary intention and meaning of the Sacrament than the reservation of the consecrated elements for the purpose of securing the presence of our Lord in the Church.[2] The practice savours of magic and superstition, and has nothing in Scripture or early tradition to recommend it.[3]

It is one of the saddest paradoxes presented by the history of Christian thought that the chief means of unity with our Lord and with His people has formed the material of strife and disunion. That which should have been for our health has been an occasion of falling. Prejudice on the one hand and self-will on the other have combined to mar the gracious purposes of the Redeemer.

Yet, notwithstanding this strange misuse of a Divine gift, the blessings of its faithful reception are borne witness to in the lives of every generation of the saints of God. They eat and drink at the table of their Lord. They know that in that sacred feast they come in touch, body, soul and spirit, with the Person of their Saviour. Nourished and supported, 'they go from strength to strength,' until they are ripe for the heavenly vision and come to appear before God.

[1] *v.* Gore, *The Body of Christ*, pp. 196, 276.

[2] 'The Sacrament was instituted in order to be eaten. It was not "by Christ's ordinance," or in accordance with any expressed intention of His, "reserved" (except so far as the reserving is necessary for the communion of sick or absent brethren), "lifted up or worshipped"—constituted, that is to say, an external object or centre of worship here on earth.' Gore, *ib.* p. 134.

[3] The fact that the presence of the risen and glorified Saviour is mediated by His Spirit is alone sufficient to show that the practice is untenable. The end and object of the Eucharist is spiritual communion with Christ, not the setting up of a novel means of securing that presence of Himself which is always granted to those who seek it in accordance with His will. Matt. xviii. 20. Cf. Gore, *ib.* p. 141.

CHAPTER XXV

DOCTRINE. ST. PETER

Three creative personalities are conspicuous in the rise of Christianity—Saints Peter, Paul and John. Each had his own natural gifts transformed by the operation of the Holy Spirit; yet each retained, through that transformation, the qualities of his gifts. The zeal of St. John burned still, but with the lambent flame of charity. The warm-hearted impetuosity of St. Peter came out in the courage that withstood earthly authority at the call of God. The rigid obedience and the logical and philosophic gifts of Saul found full opportunity for their exercise in the apostolate of St. Paul. The identity of the man—his strong type of character, his individualism—was maintained; but everything was transmuted, fired by the purifying flames of Pentecost, lifted to a higher plane, put to nobler uses, consecrated by his new vocation. Each felt the transforming power of a new affection. The 'love of Christ constrained' him.

We have to remember this in studying the contributions of these three creative forces to the moulding of the Christian religion. It at once prepares us for the entrance of a diversity of elements—a diversity which seems at times almost to amount to contradiction, so varied is the impression which we receive, as we turn from one Apostle's conception of Christianity to that of another. In this primitive diversity of apprehension and of teaching, we have a microcosm of the subsequent variety of thought which was to characterize the Church at large. Repression of the individuality of the primitive Apostles would have maimed their witness and crushed out their life; and if at times we are inclined to deplore our lack of unity and the bewildering variety of men's opinions, we are reassured on looking back to the differences observable in its first founders. Life is variety. Sameness in nature and in grace is a sure sign of obscuration and weakness.

But while we note the differences, we must not let them hide from us the essential unity of faith and practice which underlay them. One object of devotion was ever before the Apostles. One purpose inspired them. They were the servants of Christ, and they lived to make men know Him as Son of God and Saviour of the world.

Two of the three men had been disciples of Christ from the first. St. Peter and St. John were followers of the Baptist and were among the first to transfer their allegiance from him to Christ. St. John himself recounts the circumstances which led to this change of discipleship. The Baptist had borne his witness to Christ in terms which seemed to some of his disciples to leave no doubt as to what they should do. If we do not accept the narrative as historical, we shall find it difficult to account for this facile abandonment of one master for another. Take St. John i. as substantially giving us history, and the matter is readily explained. The two men were impressed with the conviction that One of Messianic character had appeared in the Person of Jesus. The Baptist's cry, 'Behold the Lamb of God, which taketh away the sin of the world,' would have conveyed little meaning at the time. Subsequent events recalled to the Evangelist's mind the cryptic words and filled them with significance. But the two disciples understood enough to assure them that they were right in leaving the Baptist for our Lord, and that in so doing they were not guilty of desertion, but were only following the wish of him who had said, 'He must increase, but I must decrease.'

The effect of this early entrance upon discipleship made itself felt in the character which their discipleship assumed. They each became profoundly impressed with the significance of the historical life of our Lord. The scenes through which they passed remained an ineffaceable memory, and the result appears in the realistic hold which they each maintained upon the facts of our Lord's life and ministry, and upon the identity of His glorified and exalted Person with the Jesus of Nazareth, Whom they had known and loved in the days of His humiliation. In the case of St. Peter, this comes out in the speeches of the early chapters of Acts. So impressed is he with the vital necessity of proving that the risen and exalted Christ, Whose gift of the Spirit was evident at Pentecost, was none other than the Messiah of prophecy; and that this foretold and glorified Being was the Jesus Whom all knew as the crucified Galilean of a few weeks ago, that for the moment he does not care to assert the Divine Personality of our Lord.[1] We have the impression that the glory of Christ began at His Resurrection. 'God raised Him from the dead.' 'God hath made that same Jesus whom ye have crucified both Lord and Christ.' 'Jesus of Nazareth, a man approved of God among you.' As we read, we feel that the Christology of these early chapters is in a transitional stage—a strong evidence of their trustworthiness; for the language of St. Peter is true to the circumstances and the apprehension of the time.[2] The Apostles had had experience of a wonderful life terminated by a violent and shameful death. They had now, but a few days ago, come to see in the appearances of their risen Master a confirmation of what some of them at least had been suspecting, although the crucifixion had shattered and confounded their hopes and their surmises. The Jesus Whom they loved and followed was 'made' Lord and Christ. In the overwhelming effect of the Resurrection they have no thought, and at the moment no need for thought, of His original Deity. Besides, at that early time, we find no trace of any

[1] 'For the moment' perhaps; but only for the moment. We remember the character of his confession at Caesarea Philippi. The emphasis laid upon the human aspects of His Personality was not of such significance as to prove, at any rate in the case of the leading Apostles, that all the effect of former experiences was forgotten. They had stood with Him on the Mount of the Transfiguration. They had been present at the feeding of the 5000.

[2] When J. Weiss (Hastings' *Dict. of Christ.* art. 'Acts') characterizes these early chapters of Acts as highly significant for the earliest Christology, we have to bear in mind the period of thought which they represent. If we look in them for an authoritative statement of the full mind of the primitive community on the Person of our Lord, we shall be lacking in our sense of historical perspective. Other elements were awaiting recognition, and were very soon to receive it. It would be against reason to expect a complete doctrinal apprehension of the subject at a moment of such startling and overpowering transitions of thought and feeling as those that characterized the first days. I do not know of any satisfactory account of this chapter of early Church history. Psychologically and sympathetically treated, it would throw great light upon the early history of Christian doctrine. At present it is often regarded as affording a complete view of the mind of the primitive community on the most vital of all questions that could engage its attention.

knowledge among the disciples generally of the story of His birth. The secret was still locked in the bosom of two or three women. It had not yet come out into the consciousness of the Church. There was, therefore, no opportunity for that adjustment of conceptions, which, after taking shape in the minds of St. Paul and St. John, was to receive doctrinal expression at the hands of the Fathers at Nicaea.

There is the same insistence on the historical reality of our Lord and on the identity of the Jesus of the public Ministry with the exalted Christ, in the theology of St. John. He, who soars the highest of all New Testament writers into the empyrean of mysticism, in his treatment of the communion between God and man as mediated by Christ, is the most passionate in his insistence upon the reality of our Lord's manhood, and upon the life of actual experience which He led on earth. Docetism found its strongest opponent in St. John. The fervour of his opposition may have been partly due to the thought that his own mystical interpretation of certain facts of our Lord's Personality may have led unbalanced minds astray. However that may be, in the loved disciple, who, of all the companions of His ministry, stood closest to the human heart of Jesus, we have the stoutest upholder of the historic reality of His life on earth. Like St. Peter, he is filled with the sense of the exceeding significance of that life. 'Every spirit that confesseth not that Jesus Christ is come in the flesh is not of God: and this is that spirit of anti-christ.' [1]

When we try to estimate the part played by St. Peter in the formation of Christian doctrine, we must go back to the great scene at Caesarea Philippi. There we find the root of his teaching at and after Pentecost. It was his merit to give, if not the first, yet a formal and definite, expression to the truth that Jesus was the Christ; and it is this great truth which is the basis of his teaching when he stands out to lead the primitive community in the first days of its life as a Church. Isolated sayings pointing in the same direction there had indeed already been; [2] but the

[1] 1 Jo. iv. 3. *v.* Burkitt, *The Gospel History and its Transmission*, p. 233.

[2] Jo. i. 29, 50; Matt. xiv. 33 (cf. Dalman, *D. Worte Jesu*, p. 225). Holtzmann, *Einleitung in d. N.T.* p. 348, thinks that St. Mark's well-ordered account of the progressive recognition of Christ is disturbed by Matt. ix. 27, xiv. 33, xv. 22, xii. 23. But compare the Messianic references in Mk. ii. 10, 19, and *v.* Bousset, *Jesus*, p. 84.

force and fervour of this confession went to the heart of Christ and called forth His warmest acknowledgment. It implied a great step in advance, when the disciples passed from appreciation of a Master to open faith in the Messiah. No more than this is expressed in the doubtless Petrine communication which St. Mark has preserved. St. Luke forms an intermediate step between St. Mark and St. Matthew, 'the Christ of God'; while St. Matthew alone attributes to the Apostle the full confession of Sonship, 'Thou art the Christ, the Son of the living God.'[1]

The conception which St. Peter had formed of Christ during His Ministry had been interrupted for the brief period of the crucifixion and the grave. It asserted itself afresh on the Resurrection and Ascension, and received new meaning under the influence of the Holy Spirit. We may be sure that he did not go back upon it when engaged in showing the identity of Jesus of Nazareth with the 'Christ of God,' 'the Son of the living God.' We may, therefore, with some certainty assign to the influence of St. Peter a large share in the formation of the Christology of the primitive community, and regard him as a leading upholder of the belief, which was held from the first age, that Jesus Christ was the only Son of God. And if this con-

[1] Mk. viii. 29; Lk. ix. 20; Matt. xvi. 16. 'There is no difference in meaning between the three reports of the reply.' Plummer, *ad loc.* 'Matthew's ὁ υἱὸς τοῦ Θεοῦ ζῶντος is explanatory.' Allen, *ad loc.* But surely there is considerable difference of meaning, and a difference which is more than merely explanatory, in the addition of Sonship to Messiahship. As Dalman remarks, it is this designation of Christ as Son of God which calls forth the saying of our Lord that Peter's knowledge was imparted by God (Matt. xvi. 17). *D. Worte Jesu*, p. 209; although Dalman himself considers that the phrase is an enlargement (*Erweiterung*) of the original text of St. Matthew. *Ib.* pp. 224, 5. But may we not rather see in it an instance of the departure of the writer of the First Gospel from his dependence on St. Mark in favour of the ancient source (Q), which he had at his command? In that case, we have the written memoranda of St. Matthew to set against the remembered (by Mark) oral teaching of St. Peter, who might also have been disposed, from humility, to minimize, instead of intensifying, the full compass of his confession. Cf. Sanday, *D.B.* iv. art. 'Son of God,' p. 572. Besides, the version of the confession in St. Luke, ὁ Χριστὸς τοῦ Θεοῦ, carries one very far on the road to the full Matthaean form, and is probably dependent on what was to be found in Q. It was something deeper and more vital than a confession of the Messiahship of Christ which called forth the eulogium of Matt. xvi. 17-19. Cf. *The Person of our Lord and Recent Thought*, p. 254, n. 2, for the conception of Messiah as Son of God in Jewish thought.

clusion is well-founded, we have to attribute to him the most important and vital part in the guidance of Christian thought at its most critical period. Humanly speaking, it meant everything for the future of Christianity that, when St. Paul and the other new adherents of the Faith were coming into the life and work of the Church, the Divine Personality of our Lord was already held in the primitive community of Jerusalem. To no one more than to St. Peter does the glory of this achievement belong. Thus the faith, which he confessed at Caesarea Philippi, became the very rock-bed of the future thought and worship of the Church. It was St. Peter, who, inspired by the Spirit and nerved by his own recollection of the life and words of Christ, led the Church safely through the dangers and difficulties of the first days. In a short time the significance of Christ's Person became a settled possession of His people; and, however opposed and denied in certain quarters, it has never ceased to be a fundamental part of their creed, and the core and mainspring of their spiritual life.

Closely connected with the substance of the Faith is the question of its propagation; and here again St. Peter takes an unique position. It had been our Lord's consistent method to confine His own Ministry to the race to which He Himself belonged.[1] His instructions to the Apostles, on sending them forth, are in accordance with it.[2] Here and there an isolated act of mercy beyond these limits only throws into stronger relief the force of His determination. So much for His action. What of His ultimate aims and His purpose for His Church? His mind is as clearly to be discovered here, as in the principles which guided Him during His Ministry. Race, country, language, custom are now all alike to be disregarded in the widened outlook of an universal Kingdom of righteousness. The chosen people are the microcosm of the Church of the future. Within them had lain in His own Person the seed of the coming Kingdom. For many reasons, ethnic, historical, moral and spiritual, it was expedient that, during the earliest stage in the process of the world's new creation, the Gospel should first be preached to Jews.[3] To them the world owed its monotheistic preparation for the Christian religion. 'Unto them were committed the oracles of God.' Among them arose the Scriptures of the Old Covenant. It was

[1] Matt. xv. 24; Mk. vii. 27. [2] Matt. x. 5, 6. [3] Cf. Acts xiii. 4, 6

only reasonable that they should have the chance of assuming to the New Covenant and the wider Faith the position which they had held to the Old. Therefore, with a firmness which seems to border on severity, the Saviour curbs the impulses of His heart, and restricts His mission to the narrow limits of His own race. It is a purblind view of His purpose to make the restricted activity of His Ministry the measure of His attitude to the world. The preaching of the Kingdom followed the law of development observed in His own personal life on earth. He deliberately chose a secluded part of Western Asia, and in the most rural of its provinces grew up to manhood. With a few brief visits to Jerusalem, He exercised His Ministry within that narrow range. It was wholly in keeping with His method to pass by the world of men and cities, and to choose the humble, the remote, the simple as the field of His enterprise. But all the time He had the world in view, and no suspicion of isolated interpolations in the text [1] can destroy the impression which an honest reading of the sources is bound to convey. We do not need the Fourth Gospel to assure us that Christ's love for man and His purposes for man were wide as humanity itself. The modern attempt to confine His aspirations to a single race fails on every ground of history and philosophy. Christ remains an enigma so long as He is conceived as a local reformer of a faith which had seen its day. If we follow the Synoptic record of His mind, we shall come to the conclusion that the limitations of His Ministry were economic and provisional. His outlook went far beyond them; and in nothing is the Fourth Gospel more consistent with the Synoptics than in its clear witness to this fact.[2]

When we inquire into the attitude of St. Peter to this question, we find that, as in his Christology, so here, his position is transitional. He clearly takes the exclusive view which seemed to follow logically from our Lord's own practice. As a Jew, he regards the Kingdom as the destined inheritance of his own people and of those who join themselves to it as proselytes by circumcision.[3] It required a special revelation to assure him

[1] Such as that of Harnack on Matt. xxviii. 19, *Dogmengesch.* i. p. 88.

[2] *v.* Matt. viii. 11; xxi. 43; xxii. 9; xxiv. 14; xxviii. 19. Cf. Jo. iii. 16; x. 16; xii. 32.

[3] Cf. Acts x. 28.

that he was wrong. While observing our Lord's practice, conditioned as it was by present circumstances, he had failed to notice the wider outlook which His teaching had contained.[1] The vision at Joppa, and its sequel in the reception and baptism of Cornelius, marks the opening of St. Peter's eyes to the fitness of the Gentiles for the Church of Christ. But even then, he had not been able to dismiss from his mind the traditions and prejudices of a lifetime. Notwithstanding his action in the admission of Cornelius, St. Paul regards him as being still in a special sense 'the apostle of the circumcision'; and when St. Peter, from fear of Judaistic Christian opinion, withdrew from social and religious intercourse with the Gentile Christians of Antioch, St. Paul 'withstood him to the face.' A man like St. Paul was unable to enter sympathetically into the difficulties and scruples of St. Peter. Having, under the influence of an unique religious experience, seen once and for all the universal character of the Personality of Christ, he had no patience with one who had been only partly emancipated from the old views. We can now look back more impartially upon the services rendered by St. Peter to the Church universal. Vacillations, blameworthy at the time, are almost lost sight of in the splendid action by which he opened the doors of the Kingdom to the Gentile world, and by so doing prepared the way for the future conquest of the nations of the West. It was a good omen that Cornelius, a soldier of the empire that dominated the world, should be the first Gentile adherent of the new world-wide Kingdom.

Thus in practice, as in doctrine, it is hard to estimate too highly the epoch-making work of St. Peter. If, when we place him by the side of St. Paul, he is at once overshadowed, both in achievement and in authority, he loses nothing of his eminence in the earliest formative period of Christian life and doctrine. His career was less striking and less active than that of the Apostle to the Gentiles; but he performed the inestimable service of guiding the first tottering steps of the primitive Church as it came out of the cradle of Judaism into its destined world-position. It was St. Peter who presented to men the crucified Jesus of Nazareth, proclaiming His glory as Lord and Christ

[1] So the Second Gospel (reminiscences of St. Peter's preaching) is without allusions to the wider view.

through the Resurrection from the dead. It was in the state of things created by the stedfastness and spiritual power of St. Peter, that men like St. Paul and St. Barnabas found at once a field prepared for their action. When they gave in their allegiance to the Cross, the Church was already equipped for its world-wide mission.

CHAPTER XXVI

DOCTRINE. ST. PAUL

WHAT would have happened to Christianity in the course of its development if St. Paul had not come upon the scene, it is impossible to say. We may be sure that sooner or later it would have arrived at that parting of the ways of which we get some intimation in the Council of Jerusalem and its decisions ; but we cannot be so sure that the results would have been equally favourable. Great issues are mostly determined by great leaders of thought. And in spite of the stand made by St. Peter at the admission of Cornelius to the Church, that Apostle had neither the natural gifts nor the kind of disposition to be a fitting instrument in God's hand for the momentous task of the Apostolate to the Gentiles. His sympathies were wholly with his own people. It required a man of larger heart and more original force to effect that widening of the Church's mission, which was the chief event of the fourth and fifth decades of the first century. Besides, near at hand St. Peter had to reckon with a reactionary influence of much strength. St. James, 'the Lord's Brother,' a man of the highest character and standing both among Jews and Christians, held firmly to the exclusive side of the Faith. As nearly related to the Lord, he would naturally be a commanding figure in the community ; but his love for his people and the stern uprightness of his character, which was acknowledged by all, lent additional weight to his influence. A fragment of Hegesippus preserved by Eusebius [1] tells of his yearning anxiety for the salvation of his race. His knees had become 'hard as a camel's' through his long-continued habit of inter-

[1] *H.E.* ii. 23. Hegesippus *flor.* c. 150 A.D.

cessory prayer for Israel. He had a reputation for sanctity from his birth, and his mode of life was as austere as that of the Baptist. But he held fast to the privileges and customs of his nation, and had no heart for carrying the message of the Cross beyond its borders.[1] Against this powerful spirit of exclusiveness and reaction St. Peter found it hard to struggle. It was fortunate for himself and also for the peace and prosperity of the Church at large that he came in contact with one who, while he was as passionately devoted to his nation as St. James,[2] could yet look beyond it; and when by repeated rejection he was forced to turn to the Gentiles, could throw into the new field of his work all that ardour and energy which his own people might have claimed.

In considering the part played by St. Paul in the formation of Christian doctrine, we have to guard against exaggeration. From two contrary directions he is being credited with an influence, which is not borne out by the evidence at our disposal. On the one hand, he is charged with corrupting the Gospel—with teaching a religion which was altogether foreign to the mind of Christ. On the other hand, so great are thought to be his services to the Christian religion that he is spoken of as its second founder, and as occupying a place not inferior to that of our Lord Himself. Without him, it is said, the Faith would have dwindled away into a mere sect on the confines of Judaism; it could never have won its way to be the religion of the nations of the modern world. St. Paul is therefore responsible for the Christian religion as we know it to-day.[3]

The best refutation of these, as we think, erroneous estimates of the influence of the most commanding personality which the religion of Christ has produced, is an account of the man and his mind as it stands in the sources at our disposal. What was the secret of his power? What did he aim at? What were the ruling motives of his life? What his ambitions? On all these

[1] *v.* Gal. ii. 12.

[2] Cf. Rom. x. 1; Acts xxviii. 17.

[3] I find that J. Weiss protests against an exaggerated estimate of the influence of St. Paul: 'We underrate the fact that the essential foundations of general Christianity . . . were laid by the primitive community and were to a certain degree ready to the hand of Paul.' *D. Urchristentum,* i. p. 2. 'The primitive community has contributed important foundation stones for the erection of Paulinism, *e.g.* in Christology and Ethics.' *Ib.* p. 3.

points the evidence is perfectly clear. The actual life and ruling principles of the man himself are before us. The character of his influence is not to be judged from the illogical developments which it has undergone in its course through history. We must consider his own aims and motives. No man is to be condemned because, in the course of time, a one-sided use has been made of his example and teaching. It is easy to exaggerate responsibility; but we have no reason to think that St. Paul was gifted with any vision of the influence which his teaching would assume in the future, or of the use which after ages would make of isolated sayings. He lived his life to the full; he loved his Lord with a whole heart; he spoke and wrote out of the deepest conviction, believing that he was in accord with the mind of Christ. If we wish to estimate the contribution of St. Paul to the development of Christianity, we must go back to the only means at our disposal for forming a judgment—the evidence of his own writings and of the Acts of the Apostles.[1]

He started in life with a character of intense earnestness. He could do nothing by halves. A Pharisee by birth and conviction, no man of his time was more zealous for the law or more devoted to the faith of his fathers. This note of character comes out in his own words, as well as in what is recorded of his early life.[2] His intensity of conviction and of purpose never left him. It was ever a ruling feature of his life. When, at his conversion, the direction of his energies was changed, there was the same passionate zeal. The character of the man remained the same. Only, his eyes were opened to the fact that he was mistaken; that his zeal for God's service was leading him wrong. The sight of Christ revealed this in a moment. He had served God 'ignorantly and in unbelief.' The conversion of St. Paul was thus a conversion in the truest sense—a change of direction took place, a complete turning round. He had always been a deeply religious man. His one object and aim in living was the glory of God. It made him a persecutor of Christ and His people.

[1] Harnack now thinks that both the Third Gospel and the Acts were written during the lifetime of St. Paul. *Beiträge*, iv. 1911, p. 86. We shall return to the question of St. Paul's alleged departure from the Gospel as preached by our Lord Himself, later on. We must first trace the steps by which he became an Apostle.

[2] Phil. iii. 4 f.

His mistake was intellectual rather than moral. His conversion made him see things differently.[1]

How are we to account for the slowness of his apprehension? He must have been well acquainted with the circumstances of our Lord's life and ministry. As a disciple of Gamaliel, he was no stranger to Jerusalem, and if, as is probable, he was never there during the period of Christ's ministry, on his return from Tarsus he would inform himself of what had been happening. His energy as a persecutor of the Christians shows that he formed the strongest possible opinion of the dangerous character of the new sect. He was aware that Christ claimed to work miracles, and that He had said and done much to set the minds of the people against that particular form of Judaism which St. Paul himself regarded as the truest embodiment of the ancient faith.

But the greatest obstacle to St. Paul's reception of the Faith of Christ lay in His death. To a Pharisee, more than to any other Jew, the crucifixion of the promised Messiah seemed a contradiction in terms, an impossibility. Nothing in life or character could resolve such a dilemma. Was this to be the fate of the long-looked-for Christ, the hope of all the ends of the earth—a death, in early prime, such as the stern and cruel law of Rome reserved for slaves and moral outcasts? And the stories of a Resurrection, spread abroad by disciples who seemed to be clutching at some straw in hope of rehabilitating their Master, availed him nothing in the face of a fact which all Jerusalem had seen. Yes, that death was a fact. He had heard all about it on his return. Then the sufferer, the crucified, could not be the Christ!

Hence while others were being won over to Christianity by the preaching of the Apostles, this man burned the more fiercely in his zeal against it. When he afterwards thought of this slowness to be convinced, and as he compared his own experience with that of men who 'were in Christ before him,' he sorrowfully speaks of himself as 'one born out of due time.'[2]

[1] Cf. Wrede, *Paulus*, p. 8, 'The root of his fanaticism is love for his religion; to make war upon false belief a duty to God.' *v. ib.* p. 10, 'Here lies the ground of the fact that Paul the Christian and Paul the Pharisee are not two different persons. The direction of his energy was fully changed. . . . Yet it also remains true that the whole man became another.'

[2] 1 Cor. xv. 8.

Yet, as he looks back upon his career, he cannot charge himself with moral blame. 'I did it ignorantly, in unbelief.'[1] His rejection of the claim of Christ was due to want of knowledge. When the Saviour appeared to him, outside Damascus, he knew at once who He was. His question shows this, 'Who art thou, Lord?'[2] The sight of the risen and glorified Lord neutralized the effect of the crucifixion on his mind. That had seemed to render impossible the claim which the disciples had asserted for their Master. Yet in a moment, the persecutor yields assent to the identity of the crucified with the promised Messiah. The Being Who addresses him he had already called Lord, in the question which reveals the final struggle with old prejudice. Then he bows his head to the announcement that this Lord and Jesus of Nazareth are one and the same Person—'I am Jesus whom thou persecutest.'

It is quite likely that the previous workings of his mind prepared him for this sudden change. The fury which animated him as a persecutor can hardly be accounted for by the anger of a zealot against men whom he thought to be the enemies of his religion. There are signs of a deeper and more personal cause. Weinel[3] has well described the mental anguish and the inward conflict which presumably raged within the man. With his strong sensibility and clearness of judgment, he must have seen, in the death of Stephen, that the Christians at least knew how to die nobly for their Master and His cause. Then, too, what of his own spiritual condition? Had he peace, goaded on the one hand by the exigencies of a law which he could not fulfil, and on the other by a passionate desire to stand right with God? It is probable that, when the vision came, he was already somewhat prepared for it.

[1] 1 Tim. i. 13. Cf. Wrede, *Paulus*, p. 10, 'The fault of his life he sees to be in misunderstanding Jesus, in the error which had driven him to persecute the cause of God. . . . His conversion was therefore a change of conviction.'

[2] He *knew*, as the terms of his question imply: but still he asked. A touch true to life. People are very apt, in their unwillingness to yield to what runs counter to them, and the truth of which they cannot dispute, to soften their submission by a question. This is one of those pieces of accurate psychology which abound in St. Luke's narrative of the conversion and go far to substantiate its authentic character.

[3] *Paulus*, p. 57 f.

But if, like Weinel,[1] we see in St. Paul's own mental and spiritual history the entire and adequate cause of his experiences before Damascus, we do violence to the only positive sources of information which we possess—his own and St. Luke's account of what happened and their interpretation of it. According to the sources, St. Paul saw and conversed with the glorified Christ. There was an objective Presence which manifested itself to eye and ear. It is certain that ever afterwards St. Paul had the conviction that he had been face to face with the living Christ. He himself and the original Apostles believed that they had seen the risen Lord, and this faith enabled them to found the Christian Church. St. Paul believed that he was vouchsafed an appearance, *which was in all respects as real and objective as theirs.*[2] His words can mean no less, 'Last of all He was seen of me also, as of one born out of due time.'[3] He dates his entrance into the life of discipleship from that appearance. It was the hour of his 'birth.' He became another man; identically the same, yet wholly different; the same in his devotion to God and to what he believed to be His will; yet another by reason of the change of method and direction forced upon him by the sight of Christ and all that it meant for him.[4]

But not only are the narratives of the conversion decisive as to the objective reality of St. Paul's vision; all the circumstances point to the same interpretation of what occurred. The hour was midday, the farthest removed from a time of meditation or

[1] *Ib.* p. 66. So too Wrede, 'It was a vision and visions are processes within the spirit of man and are products of his spirit.' *Paulus*, p. 9.

[2] Weinel considers that St. Paul regarded the other visions vouchsafed to him (2 Cor. xii. 2 f.) as equally objective and real as that before Damascus, describing them in similar language; and that if we allow our view of the world (*Weltbild*) to affect our judgment and regard them as merely subjective visions, we must come to the same conclusion as to that before Damascus. *Paulus*, p. 64. But, as Weizsäcker remarks, 'the raptures into the third heaven . . . belong to another period and to a different kind of revelations, among which he certainly does not reckon the vision which made him an Apostle.' *Das apostolische Zeitalter*, p. 6. *v.* A. Sabatier, *L'Apôtre Paul*, p. 46; Godet, *L'Épître aux Romains*, i. p. 17. Baur even says, 'We can see nothing short of a miracle.' *D. Christenthum der* 3 *ersten Jahrhun*^{n}. p. 45. Keim, too, affirms the objectivity of what happened.

[3] 1 Cor. xv. 8. *v.* Behm, *D. Bekehrung des Paulus*, 1914, p. 20.

[4] *v.* Wrede, *Paulus*, p. 10. Cf. Plato, *Repub.* vii. pp. 518, 519, 'This is conversion . . . its object is not to produce the power of sight; that he has already, but to give it the right direction.'

of dreams. A man like St. Paul, fervid in pursuit of his one object, and when about to enter the city for which he was making, would not become the prey of hallucination, or be so mastered by his secret doubts and questionings as to let them take a visible shape, which itself would pass sentence of condemnation on his whole enterprise and upon all that he lived for. The conditions are altogether too prosaic for such a state of mind to be psychologically possible. Midday in Syria is no mystic hour conducive to the seeing of visions or the materializing of inward thoughts and imaginings.[1] Saul's object was to reach his journey's end and get shelter from the burning sun as soon as might be. The weariness and discomfort of the way would only inflame his mind the more against the objects of his avenging zeal.

It is generally admitted that the person immediately concerned in the occurrence had no doubt about its objective character. Ever afterwards he believed that he had been face to face with the crucified Jesus of Nazareth now living and glorified. It is against all reason to imagine that one so fully in earnest as Saul would allow himself to be put off his purpose, have his whole life transformed, abjure his most intense convictions, on the strength of a mere phantasm.

If his thoughts were creative at that moment and capable of producing a vision—which the circumstances render very unlikely—they would have materialized into something akin, not opposed, to them. St. Paul's own subsequent reflection upon what happened made him clear upon this point. If his mind was already full of foreboding whether, after all, he was wrong and men like Stephen right; if the figure of the Crucified was already taking visible shape within his thoughts, he would afterwards have wondered whether, after all, he was not the victim of his own fancy. But no, as he looks back, he sees no sign of

[1] 'A quiet stillness, strongly speaking to the soul, lay at this mysterious (!) hour of the southern day over the face of nature.' Weinel, *ib.* p. 65; an instance of far-fetched reasons and of special pleading brought to prove a conclusion arrived at on *a priori* grounds; and an instructive example of the writing of history to prove a theory rather than to relate fact. Dr. Inge remarks: 'The Vision came in the desert where men see visions and hear voices to this day.' *Quar. Rev.* Jan. 1914, p. 57; but he goes on to say 'the form of Jesus flashed before his eyes. Stephen had been right; the crucified was indeed the Lord from heaven.' *Ib.*

wavering or hesitation : 'I thought with myself that I ought to do many things contrary to the name of Jesus of Nazareth.'[1] And this determination he kept until he was close to the gates of Damascus. Then came a great change, an entire reversal, a complete conversion. *Was it self-produced?* Did the man's own conscience convert him ?[2] It is against reason, as well as contrary to the narratives, to say so. A subjective vision of Christ

[1] Acts xxvi. 9. We can test psychological explanations of the event by the ample description of his state of mind before and after his conversion, which St. Paul has given us in his Epistles. Nothing is clearer than the entire absence of any doubt as to the rightness of his action as a persecutor during the period in which he was playing that rôle. If he had had misgivings and had lost confidence in himself, we may be sure that he would have told us. For he keeps nothing back. His past life in its spiritual aspect lies open to us. We know more of his religious history than of that of any other personage of the time. From his own self-revelations we can refute the psychological explanations of his conversion which have been worked out by modern writers. Cf. B. Weiss, *Leben Jesu*, ii. p. 581.

Ramsay has lately taken a similar view: 'Paul states in the strongest way that he was in the full course of unhesitating and fanatical persecution. He had no doubt. . . . There was in the mind of Paul no preparation for the great change in his life.' *Expos.* 1911, p. 300. Cf. P. Gardner, 'Paul himself claims with perfect confidence that he has seen the risen Lord.' *Hibbert Journ.* Supplement, 1909, p. 51. Olschewski, *D. Wurzeln der paul*^{n} *Christologie*, pp. 162, 168.

[2] Weinel says, 'It is an evil conscience which cries out of Paul "Saul, Saul, why persecutest thou Me ?"' *Paulus*, p. 64. In order to support this theory, Weinel proceeds, in defiance of the evidence, to imagine Saul's state of mind as that of one who is in doubt of the Law and of its authority and righteousness, thus imputing to him a state of mind before his conversion which came to him only after that eye-opening event. *Ib.* p. 65. So, too, J. Weiss, who, admitting that *a vision* could not have taken place without considerable mental preparation, proceeds to specify certain experiences of Saul, of which, unfortunately for Weiss's argument, we have no knowledge. *Paulus und Jesus*, 1909, p. 17. He goes farther. Unless St. Paul had had personal knowledge of Christ during His life on earth, Weiss considers that the materials of a psychological preparation and the power to recognize Christ in a vision would have been alike wanting. He therefore stakes his argument on an interpretation of 2 Cor. v. 16 *εἰ καὶ ἐγνώκαμεν κατὰ σάρκα Χριστόν*. He regards the passage not—as most people do—in the light of a supposition inserted for the sake of argument, but as conveying the assertion that St. Paul actually 'knew Christ after the flesh.' Thus we see that Weiss's subjective vision-hypothesis is ultimately made to rest upon a reading of a passage which is generally discredited—hardly a safe foundation for a theory which has also to meet the difficulty of being opposed by all the narratives in which the event is recorded. Cf. *ib.* p. 23 ff. *v.* Vischer, *Der Apostel Paulus*, 1910, p. 22 f., 'We nowhere have a trace of his having known and heard Jesus. . . . In 2 Cor. v. 16 he says nothing of having known Jesus during His lifetime.' As Vischer points out (p. 23), 'it is not personal knowledge of the man Jesus that St. Paul means,

existing only in the mind of Saul is, from all we know of the circumstances of the occurrence and *its after effects*, a psychological impossibility.[1]

If, then, all attempts to explain the occurrence naturally fail to convince us, we have to choose between two alternatives: either to abandon the thought of an explanation, or to attribute what happened to a supernatural intervention of Christ; in other words, to adopt the explanation given by St. Paul himself and by his companion and biographer, St. Luke, on the Apostle's authority.[2]

If, to take the first alternative, we resign ourselves to dispense with an explanation, we leave suspended in mid-air the most influential fact in all the history of Christendom, if we except the chief events in our Lord's own life. On the other hand, a supernatural explanation is supported not only by the belief of the man himself, but by the historical significance of the event in which he was the chief actor. The fashioning of the vessel chosen to bear Christ's 'Name before the Gentiles and kings and the children of Israel' was a task in which, if anywhere, Divine interposition might be expected.

The terms in which, according to St. Luke, St. Paul describes his experiences point unmistakably to actual phenomena presented externally and in no sense created from within the workings of his own mind. A great light shines from heaven round about

but such a knowledge of the Christ, which was common to the ordinary Jew of the time, and which he himself possessed prior to his conversion. It is to this defective, political and national knowledge of the Messiah that St. Paul opposes the true spiritual knowledge in which he now lives.' J. Weiss's reasoning is an instructive instance of the way in which a hypothetical position is pressed into service, as though it were a statement of actual fact. Cf. P. Gardner, *The Religious Experience of St. Paul*, 1911, p. 25, 'It seems certain that he had not seen Jesus'; and p. 200, 'This reference is not to the human life of Jesus, which Paul had probably not witnessed, but to the kind of knowledge which is only of the senses, and has not become a process of the spirit.' So Deissmann in *St. Paul*, 1912, p. 122; Inge, *Quar. Rev.* Jan. 1914, p. 56, 'It is very unlikely (in spite of Johannes Weiss) that St. Paul ever saw Jesus in the flesh. But he had come in contact with the little Christian community in Jerusalem'; Wernle, *D. Anfänge unserer Religion*, p. 113, 'Paul did not know Jesus during His lifetime'; Wellhausen, *Isr. u. Jüd. Geschichte*, p. 319.

[1] It is also quite contrary to the evidence to say that subsequent reflection had anything to do with creating the event of Damascus. *v.* H. Holtzmann, *Lehrbuch der neutest[n]. Theologie*, ii. p. 59, n. 4.

[2] 'Paul had probably never doubted that he actually saw Jesus. . . . The vision had the full effect upon him of an objective fact.' Wrede, *Paulus*, p. 9.

him; he falls to the ground. He hears a voice. His companions see the light and are terrified. The blinding effect of the light upon himself is noted.[1] This was what St. Paul said of his experiences; and on the whole the description tallies with St. Luke's own narrative in Acts.[2] Unless, therefore, we reject these incidents as entirely unhistorical—and this we have no ground for doing—we must admit that they completely exclude the hypothesis of visionary happenings produced by St. Paul's own spiritual condition, and having no relation to any actual objective fact. The occasion for Divine intervention was adequate; the evidence is good. Only on the presupposition that so miraculous an occurrence is not to be thought of as coming within the bounds of human experience, are we at liberty to reject it. But, then, to be consistent, we must decline to admit the possibility of our experiencing any penetration of the conditions of our mundane life by the action of Divine power; and this means the negation of Theism, not to speak of Christianity. All revelation becomes impossible.

[1] Acts xxii. 6 ff.; xxvi. 13 ff.

[2] ix. 3 ff. No one possessed of historical sense will make it an objection to the authentic character of the narratives that in Acts ix. 7 the men 'hear a voice,' but in xxii. 9, 'they heard not the voice of him that spake.' The sound as of one speaking, whose words and meaning are not caught, answers to each description sufficiently to remove suspicion of error in one case or the other. It is also to be noted that in ix. 7, ἀκούοντες is used with the genitive. In xxii. 9, οὐκ ἤκουσαν is used with the accusative. Among recent writers, P. Gardner seems to exaggerate the differences in the several narratives. *The Religious Experience of St. Paul*, p. 29. He says, 'To our modern criticism . . . it is naturally suggested that the bright light, the heavenly vision, the articulate words, may, in part at least, be due to the Evangelist' (St. Luke). Now, there is little doubt that Acts was written in the close companionship of St. Paul and finished during his lifetime (*v.* Harnack, *Neue Untersuchungen zur Apostelgeschichte*, 1911, pp. 86, 114). Would not St. Paul himself have prevented the publication of such a narrative as fact if its contents originated in the mind of St. Luke? Those who attempt to depreciate the value of the recital of St. Luke must reckon with this consideration. They allow that St. Paul permitted the promulgation of a story which was false in important points. When criticism directly leads to such a position, it is clear that its methods need revision. Cf. Godet, *L'Épître aux Romains*, i. p. 17, 'Les nuances mêmes que l'on remarque entre les trois narrations du fait que donne ce livre, prouvent qu'un phénomène mystérieux fut perçu par ceux qui accompagnaient Saul, et que l'apparition appartenait par conséquent en quelque manière au monde du sens . . . ils ne comprirent pas distinctement les paroles qui lui furent adressées (Act. xxii. 9), mais ils entendirent le son d'une voix (Act. ix. 7) . . . s'il en est ainsi, l'objectivité de l'apparition est garantie.'

It is instructive to note the tortuous expedients adopted by scholars who are unable to reject the evidence for an objective intervention of the Divine at Damascus, and yet cling to the consequences of their own philosophic standpoint. They are impressed by the indications of a Divine working, and in the subsequent life of the Apostle they detect the signs of his having passed through an unique experience. But their *Weltanschauung* forbids them to admit the logical outcome of the evidence that lies before them.[1]

It was upon his experience at Damascus that the religious life of St. Paul was henceforth to rest. Once for all, he had gained certainty. God had revealed Himself in the Person of His Son; for to St. Paul, the Jesus Who appeared to him by the way was not only the expected Messiah, but the Son of God, the Saviour of the world. This entire revulsion of thought and feeling brought with it, as a necessary consequence, a change of standpoint, an expansion of St. Paul's conception of God. Henceforth his approach to the throne of grace was mediated by his faith in Christ. He worshipped God as the Father of the crucified and risen Jesus. He could not think of God apart from his thought of Christ. To that extent his religion had become

[1] Cf. Wrede, *Paulus*, pp. 8, 9; Weinel, *Paulus*, p. 60 f.; Jülicher, *Paulus und Jesus*, p. 28 f. H. Holtzmann refers the great change in St. Paul to his experiences at Damascus, but in his account of the *Christophanie* he takes the view that the body of the risen Christ who appeared to St. Paul was not one of flesh and blood, and that it therefore was not visible to the organ of sight. *Lehrbuch der neutest*[n]. *Theologie*, ii. p. 63. Weinel's notion of the ordinary *Weltanschauung* is wanting in scientific accuracy. He puts as alternatives the appearance of a person from another world made visible to our eyes and the admission that the world is subject to the law of uniformity. There is no necessary opposition between these two positions. In each alternative, in the sphere of the supernatural, as well as in the ordinary course of nature, we can find no reason to doubt that law obtains. The appearance of Christ to St. Paul was not an event outside the sphere of law. It followed laws which indeed are above our understanding; but here, as throughout nature conceived as the sum of things, an adequate antecedent was followed by an appropriate consequent. It is not scientific to limit the range of that uniformity of sequence which permeates nature, as we can observe it, to the world of sense. On the contrary, when we cast our eyes upon the moral and spiritual order so far as it appears to us, we detect the same nexus of sequence, which is manifest in our experience of sensible things. It is, therefore, a mistaken mode of reasoning to set the objective appearance of the glorified Christ to St. Paul in opposition to the uniformity of nature, taken as a whole. *v.* J. Wendland, *Der Wunderglaube*, 1910, p. 124.

Christocentric. Not that the Father was dethroned or set aside, but that God was only rightly to be thought of as Father, one with the Son in the bond of the Spirit. St. Paul could never lose sight of the fact that it was the appearance at Damascus which revealed the true nature of the God Whom he had always from childhood loved and worshipped, however ignorantly.[1] And as a consequence of this revelation, it is henceforth God in Christ, God made known in the Person of His Son, who appears as the central and peculiar object of the Apostle's adoration. We see this in the principles and maxims which crystallize the contents of his religion and present it in a form that no one can mistake : 'To me to live is Christ' ; 'I determined not to know anything among you save Jesus Christ and Him crucified.' But is this a new religion ? Have we here a Gospel unknown and undreamed of by Christ Himself and, more than this, a Gospel which, in its content and its results, contradicts and defeats all that He lived and died to proclaim ?

That at least was not St. Paul's own conception of his work, if it is the view of a certain school of thought in the present day. It is impossible to study his attitude and not see that, if in any particular his Gospel differed from what he believed to be the mind of Christ, he was entirely unconscious of the difference and that it was the last thing he would wish for. If there is the radical difference which some would have us believe, it must, therefore, have been due to misunderstanding of the mind of Christ by the greatest of all His followers and, in consequence, to a haziness and uncertainty as to the vital elements of the Christian Faith, which would render the Apostle the least trustworthy as a guide, of all who have claimed to speak in Christ's Name. We should be clear upon this point. If St. Paul parodies the Gospel of Christ, the glowing eulogies pronounced upon him by many of those who say so are entirely misplaced. We cannot have it all ways. Unless our Lord is to be dethroned from His place as the head and source of Christianity, we are not entitled

[1] V. Dobschütz has lately published a similar view. There is not a double Gospel in the N.T. as Harnack contends. The main difference between the preaching of Christ and His Apostles was the change in the historical situation. It was to be expected that our Lord Himself would seldom speak of His death and of the benefits (redemption, etc.) to be obtained thereby : but for all these conceptions we have starting points in Jesus. *Theol. Studien u. Kritiken*, 1912, pp. 331 f. 364 f.

to give our trust to a professed follower, who has only succeeded in presenting us with a garbled version of what He taught. This dilemma, as so often happens in the case of extreme theorists, is never squarely faced. The opposition between the Apostle and his Master is eagerly maintained and, in spite of it, the Apostle is lauded to the skies.

Can we orientate ourselves upon this difficult problem by tracing what was the probable course of development, which the thought of St. Paul pursued as a consequence of the experiences at Damascus? We have, to begin with, a mind which was far from being a *tabula rasa* in respect of his knowledge of Christ and Christians. Much that has been written on this point by the critics to whom we have been referring is true and forcible. The very fury of the persecutor is proof of a considerable knowledge of the objects of his rage. Men do not lend themselves—not merely to a passing outburst of passion, but as he did—to a determined course of hostility, unless they have *some* conception of the person or the cause which they oppose. It may be a mistaken conception, but at least there is acquaintance with the subject. A man of the mental acumen of St. Paul would have a very complete knowledge of the grounds on which he set out to act. All that he tells us goes to show that he was fully convinced of the character and religious significance of the claims of Jesus of Nazareth. The circumstances were known to him; what he did not yet apprehend was the solid ground of fact and reason on which those claims rested. In that respect, he acted 'ignorantly and in unbelief.' But he knew much of Christ, and of His life and teaching; and as he stood among the throng which listened to the last speech of the first martyr, he heard the case for Christ stated in the clearest language. Indeed, if it were not so, how are we to explain the fact to which St. Paul himself pointedly refers, that after his conversion he deliberately abstained from access to those Apostles 'who were in Christ before' him, and who could have given him the fullest information on the life and character and teaching of the Lord to Whom he had now yielded himself in full self-surrender?[1]

Starting, then, from Saul's knowledge that the Jesus of

[1] Cf. J. Weiss, *Paulus und Jesus*, p. 30. Weiss rightly argues that this neglect to seek an interview with the Apostles at Jerusalem proves that St. Paul was already well informed.

Nazareth Who was crucified, and Who was believed by His followers to have risen from the dead, had claimed (or, at least, never repudiated the claim when made by His disciples) to be the promised Messiah, we have to consider what contribution was made to this knowledge by the events of Damascus. In the first place, Saul was at once convinced that the claim was justified. In the Jesus Who appeared to him by the way, he saw and recognized the Messiah. What it was that brought about this conviction, we cannot tell. But we may reverently imagine that one sign was that of the sacred wounds still visible in the exalted Figure; and that the solemn yet loving gaze of the glorified Lord smote upon his heart and conveyed a certainty to which he could not but yield, though he might never be able, or even willing, to put it into language. Then the words of the heavenly Visitant, showing knowledge not only of his outward acts but of his inward struggles against the light that was ready to break in upon him, revealed the Searcher of hearts. Saul knew enough to feel the force of all that was converging upon him, breaking down his will and calling him 'to burn what he had adored and to adore what he had burned.'[1]

It was the challenge which, at moments of crisis, God hurls at those whom, in spite of themselves, He will claim for His service; when the chains of habit break and the prisoner is released; when the false and distorted judgment is revealed by the lightning flash of truth, and the heart and will are won for ever.

Saul's surrender was instantaneous and complete. Instantaneous because the man was cast in a mould which does not suffer paltering with conviction. To be assured was, with him, to act. He did not put off the decision. 'Lord, what wilt Thou have me to do?' And there were no half-measures in his submission, no looking back. While life lasted, his allegiance was whole.

But there was a further and a long step to be taken before the acknowledgment that Jesus of Nazareth was the Christ could ripen into the developed estimate of His Person which we find in the Pauline Epistles—a long step not in time, but in the extent of its significance. The submission of will, which is at

[1] The words of St. Remigius to Clovis at his baptism. *v.* Greg. Turon. ii. 30; Milman, *Latin Christianity*, i. p. 352 (edit. 4).

once yielded, will not explain the process. St. Paul might well have promised obedience to the Messiah, as one sent from God to do His will, without making the admission that Christ was Divine. There was no consistent body of teaching in the Jewish Church which implied that the Messiah would stand in such relation to God that he could only be regarded as a Divine Being. When Saul accepted the Messiahship, there was nothing in the traditional interpretation to lead him to think of Christ as within the circle of the Godhead.

And yet, that he came to that belief is no less certain. We shall not, perhaps, be far wrong if we conclude that the momentous step was taken during the following days of blindness, when it was said of him, 'behold he prayeth.' St. Paul has himself told us that 'No man can say that Jesus is Lord but by the Holy Ghost.' His heart and mind were open to receive the Spirit's ministration during that time of isolation from the world of sense. Shut up within the circle of his own thoughts and experiences, he could work out for himself, under the guidance of the Spirit, the meaning of what had befallen him. He who appeared to him, though crucified, was now living and glorified. What could this mean? He tells us in his own words what it meant to him: 'Jesus Christ our Lord which was . . . declared to be the Son of God with power, according to the Spirit of holiness, by the resurrection from the dead.'[1] That he came to this conclusion during the time of his stay in Damascus, and probably during the first days of blindness and seclusion which preceded his baptism, is definitely asserted by St. Luke: 'Straightway he preached Christ in the synagogues, that He is the Son of God.'[2] Thus early were the main outlines of his Christology drawn. He never departed from them; though subsequent reflection enabled him to fill up and complete the picture.

That St. Paul meant much when he designated Christ 'the Son of God' is shown by passages in which his conception of Him is expanded and illustrated. In Phil. ii. 5, 6, both the Divinity and the pre-existence of our Lord are plainly conveyed.[3]

[1] Rom. i. 3, 4. [2] Acts ix. 20.

[3] See Lightfoot, *ad loc.* 'The possession of the μορφή involves participation in the οὐσία also: for μορφή implies not the external accidents but the essential attributes.'

Christ is One in essential nature with the Father and One with Him in eternity of being. He is the eternal Son, as God the Father is always Father. The Godhead is not to be thought of apart from this eternal relationship. The Incarnation can only be rightly considered in the light of the everlasting connection of Fatherhood and Sonship, within the life of the Godhead, as St. Paul represents it in this great passage. The appearance of our Lord in time and in the flesh is an episode in a history which spans the ages of eternity. It is a new departure, an assumption of fresh conditions, a novel experience in the life of God. *But it is not a beginning.* Nothing less than this view will satisfy the requirements of the passage.[1] St. Paul's conception of the Sonship of Christ is that of an unique, an eternal, relationship with the Father.

Another passage which illustrates his doctrine of the Sonship of our Lord is Col. i. 15-18. He is 'the Firstborn of all creation,' or, to be more explicit, 'He was born before all creation.'[2] The passage expresses the immanence of Christ in the world which He made, and, at the same time, His transcendence of it.

Now this exalted conception of the Person of Christ, to which the writings of St. Paul and the record of his sayings in the Acts bear witness, is not disputed. But it is said to be something new. And this novelty is not only in respect of our Lord's own estimate of Himself, but of the estimate which was formed of Him by the primitive disciples.[3]

Does St. Paul present a Gospel which was unknown and uncon-

[1] So in Rom. viii. 3, ὁ Θεὸς τὸν ἑαυτοῦ Υἱὸν πέμψας, the sending of His own Son implies that the Son was with God before His Incarnation. Cf. Gal. iv. 4.

[2] *v.* Lightfoot, *in loc.* Πρωτότοκος πάσης κτίσεως implies the absolute pre-existence of the Son. *v. The Person of our Lord*, p. 316, n. 4.

[3] *v.* A. Meyer, *Wer hat das Christentum begründet, Jesus oder Paulus?* p. 95. Wrede goes so far as to say that 'with Paul both the origin and the Being of Christ have become heavenly,' thus alleging an entire disagreement with the doctrine of the primitive Church, and making St. Paul the originator of a new religion, for that is what Wrede's position implies. *Paulus*, p. 96. Meyer, too, declares that 'for the Jewish primitive community, Jesus was still a human Messiah.' Human He certainly was, but what does St. Peter say in the house of Cornelius? '. . . Jesus Christ, He is Lord of all.' 'It is He which was ordained to be the Judge of quick and dead.' Acts x. 36, 42, 43. What does St. Stephen mean by addressing the Saviour Whom he saw in glory in terms which, *mutatis mutandis*, that Saviour Himself had used, as He resigned His own spirit into the hands of God the Father? Thus from the heart of the

templated by our Lord Himself, and one which was quite outside the mind of the primitive Church? In answering this question, we must consider the historical conditions of our Lord's proclamation of His Gospel. We may not draw up tables of their respective teaching and, without reference to the circumstances, find contradiction in the fact that the Apostle speaks where the Master is silent. It is wholly contrary to what we know to be our Lord's method in presenting Himself to the world, to expect from Him the language of a forward and insistent Self-assertion. His language makes one thing supremely clear. He came not to do His own will, not to set up, apart from the Father, a standard or an object of worship. His great endeavour was to avoid the least possibility that men would imagine any rivalry with the God of their fathers, or any separate centre of Deity. This fact is seldom taken account of in considering our Lord's assertion of His claims. His frequent silences, His refusal to take the place and attitude which men held to be fitting for One Who admitted His Messiahship, are misunderstood. It is forgotten that no progress could be made in the proclamation of the Kingdom, if it were thought that He stood over against God in the assertion of His claims. The preservation of the unity of the Godhead was all-important at such a time. Hence His silence, His strange reluctance, as it has been thought, to come forward openly before the world, proclaiming Himself in His true character as the Eternal Son, the Lord of Angels and of men. Rather would He wait and let the secret of His Person gradually disclose itself to the humble-minded and the teachable.[1] This

earliest community, while St. Paul was still the persecutor, comes the language of adoring confession of the Godhead of Christ. As Lépin says, 'The Christ of the first days of the Church is the Son of God, sharing in the powers and privileges of God, the Christ all Divine.' *Jésus, Messie et Fils de Dieu*, p. 341.

If there was any change in the Pauline conception of religion from that of Christ, it was not St. Paul who was responsible for it. *v.* Schweitzer, *Geschichte der Paulinischen Forschung*, p. 125; Harnack, *Dogmengeschichte*, i. p. 107; Jülicher, *Paulus und Jesus*, p. 34.

v. Loofs, *What is the Truth about Jesus Christ?* p. 149, 'How is the faith of the primitive Christian community to be accounted for if the life of Jesus was only a purely human one?' p. 98, 'The Gospel of John really throws insurmountable obstacles in the way of describing a purely human life of Jesus.'

[1] Cf. Origen, *Contra Cels.* i. 48, 'The whole life of Jesus proves that He avoided speaking of Himself. . . . He would rather make known that He was Messiah through His works than through His words.'

restraint was in His day misinterpreted, as it is now. 'If Thou do these things, shew Thyself to the world.' Men could not understand how One, Who was performing Messianic deeds and raising hopes of the good time that was to come, could wish to remain in the obscurity of a country province, when the capital was open to Him.[1] Our Lord's way was first to let men see the entire loyalty—if one may so speak—with which He went about doing the will of the Father, the oneness of feeling and purpose with God which lay at the root of all He said and did. Nowhere does this unity come out more clearly than in the Fourth Gospel. So much so that men have mistaken the loyalty for the sign of a consciousness of essential difference between Himself and the Father.[2] That there is one sole fountain of Deity, and that in manifesting the Father to the world, He can and will do nothing which has the least trace of rivalry or competition, is the fixed point in our Lord's attitude during the whole of His Ministry.

But this is not all. If He is often silent as to His Person and claims, when it would seem natural that He should speak, and if the fact of that silence has been misinterpreted, we have already seen that, when challenged or when conjured to declare Himself, He does not hesitate. And even when there has been no such provocative occasion of speech, our Lord again and again used language, of which the only fair interpretation is that He considered Himself One with the Father in His essential nature, that He stands within the circle of Deity and that He has a right to the adoration of mankind.

But not only is St. Paul's language said to be an innovation upon Christ's own estimate of His Person and significance, it is also said to be in excess of the conception which was formed by the primitive community in several vital points. Now, in order to form a fair judgment in such a question, we have to distinguish between the introduction of essential differences of belief and the deduction of the consequences which follow from a belief already held. In other words, we have to ask, Did St. Paul bring in new doctrine about the Person of Christ, or did he simply develop the implications which rightly belonged to the body of

[1] Jo. vii. 3, 4.

[2] For instance, Jo. v. 19, 30; vii. 28, 29; viii. 42, 54; xii. 49; xvii. 4, 8.

doctrine that was already held by the primitive Church? If it can be shown that he struck out a new line of thought and teaching, involving essential differences of belief, then indeed he was an innovator upon the Faith once delivered to the saints. Then we must take him at his word when he says: 'If any man preach any other Gospel unto you than that ye have received, let him be accursed.'[1]

But if his teaching is, on all essential points, one with that of the Apostles 'who were in Christ before' him; and if we find on examination that the same principles of belief and practice animated himself and the primitive community, we have no ground to dispute his loyalty to Christ and to the original Apostles.

We will accordingly take elements of our Lord's Self-consciousness from Synoptic narratives of His own words, together with their resultant effect in the thought and the confessions of His earliest disciples. Side by side with them we will place the estimate which St. Paul formed of Him and expressed in his Epistles.

The great passage, St. Matthew xi. 27 = St. Luke x. 22, stands beyond the reach of doubt as an actual saying of our Lord.[2] It means that, in His own mind as here revealed, He was conscious of standing in an unique relationship to the Father as the Divine and only Son; that this relationship is from eternity, for with it goes a knowledge which He places on the same plane as that of the Father, and so we have the great fact of the pre-existence of the Son, which is so strongly insisted upon by St. Paul as the necessary presupposition of all that is meant by the Incarnation. Then, to pass to the invitation of the following verse, 'Come unto Me all ye that labour and are heavy laden and I will give you rest.' Who can He be Who confronts every sorrow-laden child of man with such an utterance as this, and such a promise of relief? Nowhere is the Divine all-sufficingness of the Saviour more strongly asserted. It is the sufficiency of God which thus meets all human need. There is the same mark of Divinity in the calm authority with which, in

[1] Gal. i. 9.

[2] For evidence of this, cf. *The Person of Our Lord and Recent Thought*, p. 163, n. 2. *v.* Plummer, *Saint Matthew, ad loc.*; Dom J. Chapman in *J.T.S.* for 1909, p. 552 f.

the Sermon on the Mount, He deals with the acknowledged precepts of the Mosaic law.[1]

And this estimate of His own place within the Godhead—for that is what His claims imply—is reflected in the answering attitude and in the confessions of His disciples. No straightforward system of interpretation can take from St. Matthew xvi. 16 the conviction of St. Peter that the Sonship which he imputed to our Lord placed Him in the category of Divinity. Nathanael too had long before this declared, 'Thou art the Son of God,' and St. Peter himself had already confessed, 'Thou art that Christ the Son of the living God.'[2]

When we come to place the teaching of St. Paul beside these claims of Christ as we find them asserted and acknowledged in the Gospels, and ask wherein does the Apostle innovate, and what fundamental difference can be detected in his teaching, we are at a loss for an answer.

But St. Paul does draw out the logical consequences. He shows the effect, in belief and in practice, of that which more or less distinctly hovered before the mind of the primitive Apostles. What had previously been held in solution was precipitated by passing through the alembic of a mind singularly fitted for seeing the true bearing and significance of any matter presented to it. He fixed in imperishable language and erected into dogma the experiences and ideas that had been floating in the atmosphere of the first age.[3] There is no sign of discord or conflict between St. Paul and the Church of Jerusalem in any matter of belief or doctrine. The practical questions connected with the admission of Gentiles to the Church threatened for a time to rend the Church in twain. But we have the strongest evidence for the fact that, whatever St. Paul may have effected for the consolidation and systematizing of the Faith, and for the extension

[1] Matt. v. 20, 22, etc.

[2] Jo. i. 49; vi. 69. It is significant that Spitta includes both of these remarkable confessions of Christ in the *Grundschrift*—the original and fundamental element of the Fourth Gospel, to which he assigns an anthenticity and value for the life of Christ surpassing all other narratives. *Das Johannes-Evangelium*, pp. xi, xxiv.

[3] P. Gardner takes a different view of St. Paul's doctrinal influence: 'With the Apostle, all doctrine is in a fluid state; it could not coagulate into regular dogma until the heat of the first Christian inspiration was dying down.' *The Religious Experience of St. Paul*, p. 196.

of its message throughout the world, he was no revolutionary speculator, no 'bringer in of strange doctrines.' The primitive community was at one with him in every detail of the Faith.[1] St. Paul's own words suffice to remove all doubt that his Gospel was that of the first disciples, not merely at the outset of his Apostolic career, when it might be thought that his grasp of the essential elements of the Faith was still weak, but after years of thought and experience. Fourteen years after the first visit which he paid to Jerusalem as an Apostle, he says that he 'went up by revelation and communicated unto them that Gospel which' he was preaching among the Gentiles. The result of this frank communication was complete mutual confidence between the new and the older members of the Apostolic college. 'When James, Cephas and John, who seemed to be pillars, perceived the grace that was given unto me, they gave to me and Barnabas the right hands of fellowship.'[2]

Whether, therefore, we test it by its internal content or by the evidence of history, the modern theory of St. Paul as an innovator and a new source of Christian theology, as the preacher of a Gospel undreamt of by Christ and His first disciples, appears wholly inadequate to meet the circumstances of the case. There was no such division, as Wrede and his

[1] Wernle remarks, 'It never came to be any difference between Paul and the primitive community as to the vital question, who is Jesus?'; but he adds somewhat inconsequently and, as we think, unhistorically, 'Yet under the hand of Paul arose what was almost a new creation.' *D. Anfänge uns. Religion*, p. 177. Cf. Loisy, *Jésus et la Tradition Évangélique*, 1910, p. 35, 'Paul et les apôtres de Jérusalem s'accordaient sur le point essentiel de leur foi, à savoir que Jésus le Crucifié, maintenant Jésus le Ressuscité, était le Christ promis à Israel.'

Bousset remarks that 'for Paul faith is of the same meaning and content when directed on Christ Jesus as on God.' And he refers to Rom. x. 9 as a formula of faith which St. Paul had received by tradition from the primitive community. *Kyrios Christos*, pp. 123, 179. 'The effect of his conversion was to make him receive Jesus as the primary apostles declared Him.' Mackenzie, art. 'Jesus Christ,' Hastings' *Encycl. of Religion and Ethics*, vii. p. 529. 'There is no sign that he had any controversy with the original group in the field of Christology.' *Ib.* 'The doctrine of the Exalted Christ of which he (St. Paul) was the great champion, arose early out of the Christian consciousness.' Gardner, *The Ephesian Gospel*, p. 33. J. Weiss attributes to Ps. viii. 6, and to passages in 1 Enoch, such as xlviii. 2, 3, St. Paul's belief in the pre-existence and heavenly rank of Christ. *Christus*, pp. 42, 43.

[2] Gal. ii. 2, 9.

followers have contended,[1] between the place and significance of our Lord as taught by St. Paul and the conception which He Himself, by His own words and bearing, impressed upon the minds of those who knew Him in the days of His flesh.

If the Christology of St. Paul is not, as we maintain, out of harmony with the impression made upon the primitive disciples by the Person of our Lord, what are we to say for his teaching on redemption? Have we not here something foreign to the Gospel? Where, in the teaching of Christ and in its reflection in the mind and attitude of the first Apostles, can we find that particular doctrine of satisfaction and atonement which enters so largely into the Gospel of St. Paul? [2]

The question is difficult, and in its discussion we find, as a rule, that little allowance is made for difference of circumstance and for the lapse of time which, if rightly accounted for, demand a certain difference of perspective. Indeed, there are considerations which need to be given their full value if we are to form any just estimate of the problem. Let it at once be freely admitted that, in the writings of St. Paul, there is an insistence upon the death of Christ as a redeeming and justifying act, which is out of all proportion to the place which it occupies in our Lord's own references to it,[3] and with its treatment in the recorded language of the first Apostles.

[1] Cf. P. W. Schmidt, *D. Geschichte Jesu*, 1904, ii. p. 74, 'The Gospel of Jesus is thoroughly Theocentric; the Faith of Paul entirely Christocentric.' Quoted by H. Holtzmann, *Neutest. Theologie*, ii. p. 74, n. 1. *v.* Harnack, *Dogmengeschichte*, i. p. 107, 'No one who reads attentively the Epistles of the Apostle and the Acts could come to the conclusion that we must consider him as the second Founder of the Christian Religion or even merely as the Founder of the Church. But the question whether he has not made something different out of the religion of Jesus (Wrede) requires serious consideration. Before all it is to be remarked that, if something different has come about from the religion of Jesus in the first generation, it is not Paul who bears the chief responsibility, but the primitive community.'

[2] 'Jesus, not Lawgiver or Teacher of wisdom, but Redeemer, that is the central point of the Pauline preaching, as later that of the Reformation. By this Paul proves that he is the first interpreter of Jesus.' Wernle, *D. Anfänge*, p. 125.

[3] 'His (Paul's) Gospel, in speaking contrast with that of Jesus, is essentially a "word of reconciliation."' H. Holtzmann, *Neutest. Theologie*, ii. p. 119. But for criticism of attempts by Pfleiderer, etc., to trace Marcan references to the Cross and Redemption to Paul, *v.* Feine, *Jesus Christus und Paulus*, p. 144 f. He says, 'If one recognizes, as is generally the case in the present day, in Mk. viii. 31–ix. 1 an historical narrative untouched by Paulinism, one cannot separate

But is this to be wondered at? Our Lord's words, whenever He alluded to His coming death, fell on heedless or insensate ears. The death of their Master was the last thing His followers cared to contemplate. Their picture of the Christ was of a living and victorious Lord. So far from expecting redeeming consequences from such an event, the whole idea was abhorrent; and when, on the evening of His Resurrection, He meets disciples plunged in gloom and uncertainty by what had happened, He exclaims in wonder and sadness, 'O fools and slow of heart to believe all that the prophets have spoken.' They had not grasped those hopes of salvation, which had stood before the minds of ancient seers, and here and there had found a welcome with lowly and pious souls like Simeon and Anna, who 'waited for the consolation of Israel.' Such was the state of men's minds before the event. The event itself brought with it new conditions. It had happened. They could but ask themselves what it meant. And already we can detect the change of attitude in men like St. Peter, when the Cross and the Resurrection, that unparalleled and close-linked pair of events, had struck conviction into their minds. As yet, it takes the form of a glorying in the victory over death, in the triumph of righteousness, in the joyful return of the living Lord from the depths of suffering. There is little or nothing of a *doctrine* of redemption in the speeches of St. Peter in the early chapters of the Acts. Reflection was needed: and a man, who stands half-stunned before an

the scene of the Transfiguration from the history of Jesus without causing a gap.' *Ib.* p. 146. 'The parallel between the Transfiguration and 2 Cor. iii. 7–iv. 6 does exist, but Paul is not the original and the Gospel narrative the copy; the Apostle is there dependent upon the Gospel tradition. In those pictures in which he reveals the depth of his own Christian experience, the narrative of the Transfiguration hovers before him in the light which fell upon it from the Resurrection. . . . The Gospel of Mark therefore does not stand under the influence of the Pauline Theology.' *Ib.* p. 149. Much has been made (by Wendt, *D. Lehre Jesu*, p. 508, and others) of the teaching of the Parable of the Prodigal Son, as if the free forgiveness by the Father on the penitent's return implies that God forgives the repentant unconditionally and quite irrespectively of any mediation. This method of interpretation treats a parable, which has a certain definite aim in view, as though it authoritatively excluded everything which it does not mention. Wendt also considers that in our Lord's sayings in the Fourth Gospel, as in the Synoptic Gospels, there is no mention of the thought that Jesus by His obedience has set up a foundation for God's good-will in the forgiveness of sin. *Ib.* p. 520. Wendt attributes the saying of the Baptist (Jo. i. 29, 36) to an editor who has used the Johannine source of the sayings of Christ. *Ib.*

overwhelming experience such as he had been passing through, can hardly be expected to do more than think of the events themselves. Later, as we see by turning to his first Epistle, we get to know what he thinks it all means; and his mature thoughts are in thorough harmony with the constructive teaching of St. Paul.[1]

When, after these necessary preliminaries, we turn to the Gospels for correspondence with the teaching of St. Paul, we are not disappointed. Unless we lay violent hands upon the text, we have to admit that our Lord does contemplate His death as an atoning, redemptive act; and that the salvation of man can be effected by no other means. There is no doubt that our Lord believed that He stood in such relation to mankind that His death would be an act of transcendent value and significance, 'a full, perfect and sufficient sacrifice, oblation and satisfaction for the sins of the whole world.'[2] And the evidence comes from a wide field. It is not only to be found in St. Mark[3]

[1] *v.* 1 Pet. i. 2, 11, 18, 19; ii. 24; iii. 18; iv. 1. If St. Paul preaches a Gospel of redemption which was foreign to the mind and will of Christ, his fault, as these passages show, is fully shared by St. Peter. Each deduces from the Cross and the Resurrection hope, salvation, victory over sin and death. Each shares in the glory of proclaiming the Gospel of Christ. Each shares, if the critics are right, in the shame of its perversion. The mind of St. Paul is the mind of the first disciples. Christianity is the religion of redemption. It started with that message, and in so doing it believed it had 'the mind of Christ.' *v.* Wendt, *D. Lehre Jesu*, p. 505, 'Paul has expressed this conception of the saving worth of the Death of Christ with special emphasis and made it the foundation of his whole Gospel. But according to his own remark in 1 Cor. xv. 3, the proclamation of the Death of Christ for our sins was not a doctrine peculiar to himself, which he held in distinction from the original Apostles, but a doctrine which he had received from the community.' Bousset, *Kyrios Christos*, p. 160, 'It is possible that the thought of sacrifice in all its consequences is a conviction of the community which was simply taken over by Paul.'

For traces of the mind of the primitive disciples, *v.* Acts v. 29-32 (St. Peter); viii. 32 f. (St. Philip). The awful nature of the crime of the Crucifixion, rather than its atoning results, seems to have dominated St. Peter's mind in the first days.

[2] Office of Holy Communion. 'In the Synoptic, as in the Pauline narrative, lies the tradition that Christ understood the death that lay before Him as an offering for His people.' Feine, *Theol. des N.T.* p. 138. Cf. Wendt, *D. Lehre Jesu*, p. 561, 502, 'Through the application of the conception of a covenant is implied the special relation in which Jesus has regarded the saving meaning of His death for others.'

[3] Mk. x. 45 = Matt. xx. 28; Mk. xiv. 24 = Matt. xxvi. 28. In this addition by St. Matthew to the Marcan report of Christ's words, 'is merely explicitly defined what was implicitly said in adjudging the Blood as the Blood of the

and its parallels in the First Gospel, but in passages of St. John which are embedded in what has been held to be the fundamental element of the Gospel.[1]

If, then, the circumstances of the case are taken into consideration, there is clear and definite evidence that, in his view of the propitiatory character of Christ's death, St. Paul was in line with the mind of his Master; that his Gospel was that of Christ Himself, and that it agreed in this vital particular with the Gospel of the primitive community.

There is another subject on which the teaching and the practice of St. Paul are said to show a marked departure from the purpose and teaching of our Lord. St. Paul was an universalist in his conception of the scope and object of the Gospel message. The Ministry of Christ was, with one or two exceptions, confined within the limits of the chosen people. Besides rigidly

New Covenant shed for many.' Wendt, *D. Lehre Jesu*, p. 506. Cf. *Ep. of Barnabas*, v. 1, *εἰς τοῦτο γὰρ ὑπέμεινεν ὁ Κύριος παραδοῦναι τὴν σάρκα εἰς καταφθοράν, ἵνα τῇ ἀφέσει τῶν ἁμαρτιῶν ἁγνισθῶμεν, ὅ ἐστιν ἐν τῷ αἵματι τοῦ ῥαντίσματος αὐτοῦ.*

'This belief' (that Christ died for our sins, 1 Cor. xv. 3) 'must date from the earliest times.' Loofs, *What is the Truth about Jesus Christ?* p. 150. Cf. Moffatt, *Introduction to the Literature of the N.T.* p. 502, 'The redemptive function of the Lamb . . . was widespread in primitive Christendom.'

[1] As, for instance, Jo. x. 15; xii. 24, 32. *v.* Spitta, *Das Johannes Evangelium*, pp. xxviii, xxxiii, xxxiv. It is one of the indications that the Synoptic Gospels give us history and that they record what was actually said—not something inserted afterwards as being likely to correspond with the actual state of things—that so little has been reported of what Christ said of the meaning of His death, as apart from the death itself. The feeling of His hearers was against the idea. They took little heed of what He said upon the subject. At the time when the underlying fabric of our present Gospels was committed to writing, the propitiatory significance of His death was only beginning to be understood. St. John, on the other hand, possessed an insight into the meaning and effect of Christ's sayings which was not attained by the rest. It is increasingly felt that, for the deepest and most characteristic elements of His teaching, the Fourth Gospel is our surest witness. Thus the poverty of the record of our Lord's teaching about the effect of His death points to the early committal of His sayings to writing. The reporters put down what they realized and understood. On the other hand, the disproportionate amount of space assigned in the Gospels to the actual circumstances of the Passion and the Death shows that the fact itself, illumined by the Resurrection, produced a profound impression upon them. Only the writer of the Fourth Gospel appears to have grasped, not only the momentousness of the event, but the teaching which preceded it. The other Evangelists, keeping close to their sources, report sayings of our Lord in which, with the exception of those already named, He speaks of His death without reference to its meaning.

defining His own activities, He charged the Twelve to circumscribe their movements and their work in the same way. What is more, He said that they would not have gone over the cities of Israel—the glad tidings of the Kingdom would not have been fully preached within the bounds of the ancient race—till the Son of Man be come.

What justification, therefore, could St. Paul have had to go beyond these limitations and say, as he said in the Synagogue of the Pisidian Antioch, 'Lo, we turn to the Gentiles'? Certainly, he could quote Isaiah for a sanction; and he proceeded to do so; but in the practice of our Lord Himself, apart from His ultimate aims, there was little or no authority for the wider field of Gospel ministry which St. Paul set out to occupy.[1]

When, however, we try to get at our Lord's mind on the range and scope of the Gospel message, we find a distinct enlargement of what we should gather from His own action and His commands during the time of His Ministry. Here and there appear indications of a wider outlook. This is again especially noticeable in the Fourth Gospel. As in the references to the efficacy of His death, it is the memory of St. John which recalls sayings and hints that passed unnoticed by the earlier Evangelists.[2] Yet in the Synoptics, there are indications of a purpose wider than the confines of Israel.[3]

[1] Cf. Loisy, *Jésus et la Tradition Évangélique*, p. 66, 'Jésus ne s'adressait qu'aux Juifs, et il ne semble pas avoir jamais eu la pensée de porter l'Évangile aux Païens.' But, as the wider hope existed in Jewish circles in His day (Lk. ii. 32, cf. 1 Enoch xlviii. 4), He could not fail to share it.

[2] See, for instance, the general invitation on the last day of the Feast of Tabernacles, Jo. vii. 37; 'other sheep I have which are not of this fold: them also I must bring,' x. 16, a saying which certainly contemplates a wider mission; 'I, if I be lifted up from the earth, will draw all men unto Me,' xii. 32, 46. All these passages belong, according to Spitta, to the original substance of the Fourth Gospel, and are therefore of the highest authority for the mind of Christ. *Das Johannes-Evangelium, in loc.* Cf. Gardner, *The Ephesian Gospel*, p. 232, 'The Fourth Evangelist . . . advances towards the universalism which was from the first implicitly present in his Master's teaching.'

[3] Luke vii. 9; Matt. xiii. 38, 'The Field is the world'; Matt. viii. 11 = Luke xiii. 29. If Christ said to the woman of Canaan, 'I am not sent but to the lost sheep of the house of Israel,' an oriental way of saying Israel is my first and chief object, yet He does not refuse her plea, Matt. xv. 24 f. He does overstep the boundary. Matt. x. 18, τοῖς ἔθνεσιν implies mission work beyond the borders of Palestine. *v.* McNeile, *ad loc.*

Not until He is risen and about to ascend, does He openly claim the whole world and all its peoples as the field of His enterprise. He has come forth triumphant and, as the risen God-Man, the kingdoms of the world are open to Him for conquest.[1] His universal rank and position, so to speak, is a consequence of the victory over death and sin declared at His Resurrection. Such seems to be the meaning of His saying, 'All power is given unto Me in heaven and earth.' His Manhood has been ennobled. 'God hath highly exalted Him.' Through His obedience unto death, with its limitations, its narrow grave, its silence, its passing out of sight, He has won a place and 'a Name which is above every name.' Thus a relation to all the world, a Gospel for every creature—nothing narrower—does our Lord claim as His by right.[2] And the first to see this in all its bearings was St. Paul.[3] But to acknowledge this service to the cause of Christendom is one thing. To speak as though he were its second founder is quite another. It is true that, apart from St. Paul, there was little apparent likelihood that Christianity would have passed beyond the frontiers of Judaism and, leaving the East, have captured the nations of the West. The evidences of reaction are so many and so convincing, that we cannot shut our eyes to the critical state in which Christianity found itself on the very threshold of its expansion. The figure of James, the Lord's brother, is a noble and inspiring one, but he had no wide outlook. His heart was absorbed by the interests and the hopes of his own people. The courage of St. Peter was high, and at times he appears capable of larger views than St. James. But he was easily influenced and had not the intellectual or

[1] Matt. xxviii. 18 f. On the authenticity of this passage *v. The Person of our Lord and Recent Thought*, pp. 218, n. 1, and 259, n. 1.

[2] 'The preaching of Jesus was universalistic in spite of the Jewish covering, His consciousness of God was universalistic in spite of its Messianic clothing; His Mission has become universalistic, although Jesus Himself knew that it was limited, so far as He was concerned, to His own people.' Harnack, *Dogmengeschichte*, i. p. 79.

[3] *v.* Jülicher, *Paulus und Jesus*, p. 34. St. Peter had partly grasped the truth, but he had a relapse into Judaistic exclusiveness, notwithstanding his experiences and his action in the case of Cornelius. Loisy runs counter to the evidence when he says, 'In this conflict (between St. Paul and the Apostles at Jerusalem), what is significant is that the authority of Jesus cannot be alleged by either of the contending parties. . . . He had not conceived the idea of organizing within Judaism a religion which was to become distinct from it, still less of organizing such a religion outside Judaism.' *Jésus et la Tradition Évangélique*, p. 34.

moral force which was required at such a time. 'Even Barnabas was carried away by dissimulation.' It is impossible to doubt that St. Paul felt strongly about the lack of determination and even of complete straightforwardness, which characterized the attitude of the Church of Jerusalem and infected those who came into touch with it. It is therefore difficult to rate his services too highly, so long as we keep on the actual plane of his Apostolic ministry. It is false to history to place him in a position in which he is to compete with his Master Himself for the central place in Christianity. Nothing could be further from his own wish or thought. He is 'the slave of Jesus Christ.' His 'life is hid with Christ in God.' To St. Paul the idea of rivalry with our Lord, of placing himself at the source of religion by His side, would have been blasphemy.[1]

In estimating the influence of a man who comes to the front in a great movement, we are apt to consider him indispensable and to say that, but for him, the movement would have collapsed. Whereas, for all we know, there were other men, overshadowed no doubt but, if the field were empty, ready to step into the front rank. Opportunity brings out the strength and resources which lie hidden in the womb of time. To St. Paul belongs the glory of giving that liberating touch to Christianity which rescued it from narrowing and reactionary conditions, and gave it the comprehensiveness which was in the mind of Christ and accorded with His purpose. But we cannot imagine that, failing a St. Paul, no other champion of Catholicity would have been forthcoming. To say so is to limit the resources of the Providence which guided the destinies of the Faith and to make the purposes of God dependent on a creature. All honour to the man of the hour who rises, as St. Paul rose, to the height of his opportunity; but the ideal had long ago taken shape within the mind of Christ, and could not fail for lack of an instrument to bring it to pass.

Closely connected with St. Paul's grasp of the universal mission of Christianity and following from it, was his attitude to the Jewish Law. Here, again, we have his practice placed in sharp contrast with that of Christ. The two are said to be irreconcilable. Our Lord stands forth as a pious and circumspect Jew; punctilious

[1] Bousset puts St. Paul's relation to Christ forcibly in *Kyrios Christos*, p. 126.

in attendance at the feasts, from His circumcision onwards submitting to every rite and ordinance, declaring that the fulfilment of the Law was the object of His coming into the world. Living as a Rabbi and regarded as such, He seems to give the impression that He is content with Judaism if only men would faithfully carry out its real spirit; as though it were God's final and complete revelation of His will, and as though no further Gospel were waiting to break forth.

Over against this picture stands the destroyer of the Law, the passionate declaimer against its shackles; the man who has freed the religion of Christ from its bondage and who asserts for our Lord, as though he knew His mind better than He Himself knew it, a freedom from the Law which He neither taught nor practised. It is difficult to emphasize too strongly this glaring contrast between the language and the action of our Lord and that of His Apostle. Can we explain it fairly without special pleading?

Our Lord's practice was conditioned by His birth and position. 'He sprang out of Judah.' He was 'the Son of David.' The Jews were His own people. To have ostentatiously severed Himself from their religious life would have cast doubt on their whole religious past and on the certainty that, in their obedience to the Law and in their worship, they were following Divine guidance. It would have destroyed confidence in the sacred and preparatory office, which the nation was of old called to discharge—the getting ready of the world for the final and complete revelation of God in the Person of His Son. Yet, along with the steady adhesion to the full round of Jewish life and observance which every page of the Gospels shows our Lord to have maintained, we cannot help noticing that, in His conception of the complete fulfilment of the Law, there is involved a wider reach, a more spiritual element than the Judaism of His day could recognize. For parallels with Christ's view of the Law we require to go back to the Prophets. From their elevated standpoint we get a view of what the Jewish religion meant for Christ. That He fell behind the noblest conceptions of Isaiah and Ezekiel and certain of the minor prophets, it is impossible to conceive. At the same time, He felt that His liberty of expression must be curtailed. Nothing that would shake men's confidence in the Divine mission of the Law, and in the sacred character of the religion which encircled it, could be allowed.

But between the ministry of Christ and that of St. Paul mighty events had intervened. The Cross and the Resurrection had given practical effect to those anticipations of a wider casting of the Gospel net, which our Lord certainly cherished. No less wide was the field of work which was claimed for the Holy Spirit. The gift of Pentecost was for 'all flesh' who would appropriate it.[1] St. Peter sees and proclaims this at once, taught thus to interpret the prophet Joel, in all probability, by Christ Himself before His departure. What wonder, then, if an Apostle with St. Paul's consummate gifts of mind and spirit drew the boldest conclusions from his conception of the significance of Christ, and came to think that in accomplishing the Law, He had abolished it? St. Paul saw that, if 'the law was our schoolmaster to bring us unto Christ,' 'after faith is come we are no longer under a schoolmaster.'[2] So far is the teaching of St. Paul from being an unauthorized addition to the plan and purpose of Christ, it is rather the logical conclusion of His work.

But we must look more closely into the supposed opposition between the attitude of St. Paul towards the Law and that of Christ. We have admitted that, on the face of the narrative, we have no choice but to acknowledge that they move in different spheres. Christ is a Son of the Law. He does not give the idea of one who expects to be anything else. Its practices and its worship suffice. If He is in Jerusalem, He frequents the Temple. Nothing so roused His indignation as its profanation. He regards it as the central seat of worship for all nations.[3] If He is in the country at Nazareth or Capernaum, the Synagogue is His constant place of resort and He naturally takes part in its services and rites.[4] 'I came,' He said, 'not to destroy the Law but to fulfil it.' Not only is this His own personal standpoint, but He appears to have no other view for the religious future of His disciples. When one comes to Him to know the secret of eternal life, He refers him to his reading of the Law.[5] He gives no hint that a new factor has come into operation, or 'that life and immortality' are about to be 'brought to light through the Gospel.' And the force of this restrained and conservative attitude is

[1] Acts ii. 17. [2] Gal. iii. 24, 25. [3] Mk. xi. 17.
[4] Lk. iv. 16. [5] Lk. x. 25, 26.

not to be explained away by appeal to the acknowledged intimations of a wider and a revolutionary outlook. It stands in the records as we have received them, and we have to face the fact.

To turn again to St. Paul. It is true that to the end of his life he was full of love and devotion to his own kindred. Our last glimpse of him in history, apart from the evidence of his Epistles, shows him conversing with the Jews, who came to his lodgings in Rome. We find, too, that everywhere he offers his Gospel to the Jews before he preaches to the Gentiles.[1] He regards the Jews as first in religious privilege. It was contrary to the nature of things to put them in the second place. Only on their rejection of the Gospel were they passed over in favour of the Gentiles.

But when all this is allowed for, we cannot shut our eyes to the fact that, according to St. Paul, the centre of gravity has been removed; that, if the Jew is the privileged person, it is only out of respect to his past. Salvation is no longer to be found in his religion, as he had always practised it. There had been a development, a growth, logical and consistent so far that whatever is new lay hidden within the folds of the old; yet a very real development, so momentous and critical, that he who apprehended it could not remain within the conditions of the past. The true light had come. The full truth had been revealed. The whole mind of God had been declared. The Messiah had appeared. He had died, yea had risen again and was at the right hand of God. To remain in, or to go back to, the old state of things was to reject God. It was apostasy. 'If I build again the things which I destroyed, I make myself a transgressor.'[2] It was the full Messianic salvation for which the faithful hoped, who were 'waiting for the consolation of Israel' and 'looked for redemption in Jerusalem.' They had not got it. They were waiting for it. But now it had come and St. Paul cannot live as one who had not received it. He turns his back on the Law. It is superseded. Its day is over. The Christ has come.

It is this change of circumstance, this entirely new state of things, which accounts for the contrast between the attitude of St. Paul to the Law and that of our Lord. Christ lived

[1] Acts xiii. 46. *v.* Vischer, *Der Apostel Paulus und sein Werk*, p. 34.
[2] Gal. ii. 18.

within the old conditions. Nothing had occurred to remove their sanction. St. Paul lived in a new world. Everything had changed.[1] But in saying this, it is not meant that any opposition is implied. Had St. Paul acquiesced in the retrograde policy of the Judaisers in the Church of Jerusalem, he would have been untrue to Christ. But he followed Him by taking a different course to that which He took. For the times were different. 'When that which is perfect is come, that which is in part is done away.' 'Christ is the end of the Law.' When the goal is reached, the journey does not need to be retraced.

This difference of situation—the death of the Cross lying between our Lord's Ministry and the work of His Apostle—explains the contrast between the Gospel of Jesus and that of St. Paul. Our Lord said little about His death during His Ministry, significant as His sayings about it were. We cannot say that it was the central point of His Gospel. He was content to let it speak for itself, and find its justification in the Resurrection. It belonged to the majesty of His patience to let the offering up of Himself upon the Cross work its own way into the hearts and consciences of men. But, when we turn to St. Paul, the case is altogether different. Convinced of the Messiahship of the crucified Jesus of Nazareth and of the significance of His death and Resurrection, St. Paul makes it the pivot and the burden of his Gospel. He sees in it the cause of the world's redemption and he brings to the preaching of Christ crucified and risen all the force and energy of which he is capable. Nothing is farther from the truth than to say that he has distorted or travestied the Gospel of Christ, or designed to supplant it with a Gospel of his own. Rather, to its application to the needs of men, to the unfolding of its eternal significance, to its justification as the supreme gift of God, he has devoted a zeal and love which have never been equalled by any other servant of God. To St. Paul, more than to any other of the builders of Christendom, the world owes whatever it has learnt of the Gospel of Christ. He 'understood Jesus better than all his predecessors.'[2]

[1] So Jülicher, *Paulus und Jesus*, p. 62, 'The difference in the situation which Paul found from that in which Jesus had taken up His work.'

[2] Wernle, *D. Anfänge unserer Religion*, p. 192. Wellhausen says, 'Paul is the one who has understood the Gospel and drawn its logical consequences.' *Isr. und Jüd. Geschichte*, p. 319. *v.* Schweitzer, *Geschichte der Paulin. Forschung*, p. 124.

St. Paul, by one of the most remarkable turns of fortune in all literary history, became, without in the least intending it, the most influential and, by reason of that influence, the greatest of all writers. His works are among the first, and at the same time the most voluminous, of the writings which form the New Testament. 'In striking contrast to Jesus, Paul without his wish or purpose became a literary force and thereby was the first to aid Christianity to acquire a literary existence.'[1] It is true that he became conscious that his letters were considered effective, although his rhetorical powers were thought very poorly of:[2] but he could have had no suspicion that Epistles which, as he wrote them, were meant solely for direction to specific bodies of disciples on occasional difficulties, or to meet certain definite local needs, would ever be placed on a par with the greatest examples of inspiration. Only once does he direct an interchange of his letters between two neighbouring Churches.[3] There is no hint that the writer intends them for the use of the Church at large. He could never have imagined that, within a generation of his death, they would be read as Scripture in the services of the Church, and quoted as authoritative on equal terms with the books of the Old Testament.

Yet so it was. It became recognized that those Epistles, if dictated by the pressure of circumstances in isolated communities, belonged to the Church as a whole. It was seen that, with all their individual characteristics, they dealt with matters of general concern and that they plainly bore marks of the inspiration, which, however men expressed it, was traced to the direct working of the Spirit of God.[4] The various steps,

[1] H. Holtzmann, *Lehrbuch der N.T^{n}. Theologie*, ii. p. 236. Wrede, *Paulus*, p. 97, 'Paul, without any action on his part, after his death became a literary force.' Wernle, *D. Anfänge unserer Religion*, p. 435, 'Paul, the founder of ecclesiastical science, is the father of the N.T., though nothing else was farther from his thoughts.'

[2] 2 Cor. x. 10.

[3] Col. iv. 16. Lightfoot has shown (additional note *in loc.*) that 'the Epistle from Laodicea' is not a letter addressed to that Church—certainly not the forged one which obtained credence here and there down to the time of the Reformation—but the Epistle to the Ephesians.

[4] In 2 Pet. iii. 16, the writer refers to them as Scripture. This has been considered to point to the late composition of 2 Pet. But *v.* Harnack, *Dogmengeschichte*, 1909, i. p. 110, 'Every writing had to be recognized as an authority which proved itself to be given from the Spirit, and every

by which this process of recognition was effected, are lost in the obscurity which lies over the last thirty or forty years of the first century. But that they were taken both in the East and the West is clear from the position in which we find the Epistles of St. Paul, as soon as we come into possession of reliable data. There is no doubt that the Apostle's own injunction that his First Epistle to the Thessalonians should be read to all the brethren in the Church of Thessalonica was the first thing to direct men's minds to the importance attached by the writer himself to his work. In the Second Epistle, he claims obedience to his will, as expressed in it.[1] But these signs of the Apostle's own consciousness that he stood in a special relation of authority towards a certain Church are far from stamping the writings themselves with Divine authority. Between the wish of the Apostle that his views should be known and acted upon, and the admission of the writings that embodied them into the category of Scripture, there was much to be done.

The first reference to any Epistle of St. Paul, outside the New Testament itself, is by St. Clement of Rome about A.D. 95. He is writing to the Corinthians, and he bids them 'take up the Epistle of the blessed Paul the Apostle. What wrote he first unto you in the beginning of the Gospel ? ' and then he refers to the passage in 1 Cor. i. 12 f., in which the Apostle charges the Corinthians with party spirit.[2] Thus it is implied that the Epistle was kept ready to hand, and was regarded as a standard of Christian teaching and practice. We learn from a statement of Dionysius of Corinth [3] that it had been an ancient custom there to read the letter of St. Clement of Rome on Sundays. It would be all the more likely that letters of St. Paul would be read in the services.[4] The extreme reverence in which writings

tested Christian Prophet, Apostle and Teacher could claim respect and reception of his solemn words as the words of God. Accordingly the Twelve chosen by Jesus stood in special reverence and Paul claimed the same authority.' If this view of Apostolic authority and teaching was taken as early as the lifetime of the Apostles, there is no need to place 2 Peter so late that it could not have been written by him, on the ground that the writings of St. Paul are there called 'Scripture.' It is highly probable that it was so taken ; for the Apostles showed such clear signs of inspiration in all that they said and did, that their writings would at once be regarded as 'given from the Spirit.' *v.* above p. 57, n. 5.

[1] 1 Thess. v. 27 ; 2 Thess. iii. 14.

[2] Clem. Rom. *ad Cor.* xlvii.

[3] In Euseb. *H.E.* iv. 23.

[4] Cf. Sanday, *Inspiration*, p. 361.

of an Apostle were held, as we see from the language of St. Clement, will have led to their authority being regarded as parallel to that of the Old Testament. The subsequent steps in the process of canonization belong to a later period than that with which we are dealing.

In reading the Epistles of St. Paul, one is struck with the way in which his thoughts crowd upon one another, fresh ideas pressing tumultuously into the current of his argument, interrupting it, and themselves in turn interrupted by ever fresh ideas. Meanwhile, there is little concern for strict grammatical construction. The new phrase is hurled into the sentence, and has to find its own place and connection as best it can. There was a cause for this peculiarity of style, apart from mere exuberance of thought. Many of the anomalies of construction in the Pauline Epistles are due to the fact that St. Paul himself wrote little. He was in the habit of dictating, perhaps while at work, or while pacing up and down. As parenthesis followed parenthesis in the breathless rush of thought, the speaker would forget the construction of the first members of a sentence and his amanuensis, if he noticed, would not wish to interrupt the inspired speaker. The style is that of a man who is dictating, and is too full of the subject itself to be careful of the niceties of grammar.[1] Nor does he care, when the finished Epistle is read out to him, to amend or simplify his language.

The reason for this indifference to form and style may, for ought we know, lie deeper than in any necessities of composition. The Apostle was profoundly convinced that he wrote according to the mind of Christ.[2] He believed in his inspiration ; and with this belief he would feel that 'first thoughts are best,' and that revision would remove from his words their original sharpness

[1] Cf. Rom. xvi. 22 ; 1 Cor. xvi. 21 ; Col. iv. 18 ; 2 Thess. iii. 17. 'Apparently he wrote only Galatians and Philemon with his own hand.' Holtzmann, *Einleitung in das N.T.* p. 225. Cf. Gal. vi. 11 ; Philem. 19. For the view that Gal. vi. 11 *ad fin.* only was in St. Paul's own hand and the rest of the Epistle by an amanuensis, *v.* Lightfoot, *ad loc.* On the practice of dictation in the first century, *v.* Milligan, *The New Testament Documents*, p. 21 f.

[2] Cf. Robertson and Plummer on 1 Cor. xv. 20-28, p. 351. von Dobschütz, *Probleme des apost. Zeitalters*, p. 64, St. Paul 'had the most complete authority over the communities in the first place as the possessor of the Spirit.' Cf. 1 Cor. vii. 40. Fairbairn, *Christ in Modern Theology*, p. 496, quoted by Sanday, *Inspiration*, p. 124, n. 1 ; '. . . il gran vasello Dello Spirito Santo.' Dante, *Par.* xxi. 127.

of outline, and something of their power to represent what he knew was the will of God—something of their correspondence with the Divine inbreathing. It is a familiar experience of literary work that strength and vigour are lost by excess of polish. The *bite* of a saying is weakened, and its power to influence goes. It was because he dictated under sense of a force that was acting upon him and giving life to his utterance, that St. Paul declined—if the thought ever suggested itself—to remould his sentences and bring them into closer touch with literary form. For we cannot for a moment admit that he was insensible to grace of style or beauty of expression. In many parts of his Epistles, his language rises to heights of pure eloquence unmatched in the New Testament, and unsurpassed by any other literature. Such passages at once occur to us.[1] He who could so speak and write was initiated into the secrets of language. It is not failure of power to wield his weapon, if at times he seems uncouth or halting in his speech. Rather, he is being carried away by the fervour of his faith and by the urgency of his message.[2]

No one of the spiritual and mental force of St. Paul could fail profoundly to influence the future course of the work to which

[1] *E.g.* Rom. viii. 37 f.; 1 Cor. xiii.; the Ep. to Philemon, a masterpiece of style and good taste, one of the choicest gems in the whole range of literature.

[2] The eccentricities of St. Paul's style make him very difficult to interpret. It is often hard to trace the logical connection of sentences. His use of particles is peculiar. At times we are conscious that he finds his command of language inadequate to the needs of his thought. Already in the New Testament itself, we meet with criticism of his writings. It is couched in friendly terms, but it is none the less criticism for all that. In 2 Pet. iii. 16, the writer says of St. Paul's Epistles, 'in which are some things hard to be understood, which they that are unlearned and unstable wrest.' The difficulty of grasping his teaching and of reconciling apparent contradictions in a series of writings which, owing to their various objects and the differences existing in the Churches to which they were addressed, had no close logical cohesion, was no doubt a chief cause of their neglect in early times. 'Only one Gentile Christian, Marcion, has understood St. Paul, and he profoundly misunderstood him.' Harnack, *Dogmengeschichte*, i. p. 100. In later times it was the work of the Reformation to rediscover the Apostle of Faith, and to assert for his teaching a place in the Christian religion which had been denied him through whole periods of the Church's life. He has been called 'the great Protestant,' but it is significant that one of the cleverest studies of his writings which has appeared in modern times charges Protestantism generally with having grievously misunderstood him (M. Arnold, *St. Paul and Protestantism*). Cf Wernle, *D. Anfänge unserer Religion*, p. 459.

he had devoted his life. He appeared upon the scene at a critical moment. In spite of the effect produced upon the minds of the primitive community by the conversion and admission of Cornelius, the habits and prejudices of a thousand years had still kept their grip of the leading spirits of the Church. Christianity was Messianism. It was the peculiar privilege of the Jewish people. If here and there the work of grace manifested itself outside these limits, the phenomenon was exceptional. The leaders of the Church had not grasped the theory of an universal Kingdom. Then came St. Paul with his wide outlook, his generous heart overflowing with love for mankind, his claim that 'there is no difference,' that all may be one in Christ Jesus. And the dreams of a reformed Judaism, of a Messianic Kingdom as narrow and as exclusive as would please the most bigoted Pharisee, vanish before his logic and the fire of his zeal. We owe it to St. Paul that the world-wide commission of the risen Saviour was rescued from becoming a dead letter. Through him it was inscribed ineffaceably upon the order-book of the Church and emblazoned upon her banners. The Catholicity of the Christian Church owes more to St. Paul than to any other servant of the Cross.[1]

[1] 'It is too strong a statement to say, with Renan and others, that to Paul alone belongs the honour of having brought Christianity out of Judaism. Certainly the great Apostle could explain in reference to this, *περισσότερον αὐτῶν πάντων ἐκοπίασα*, but besides himself, nay before him, there were those (men of Cyprus and Cyrene) who in the power of the Gospel surmounted the barriers of Judaism. We may now regard it as certain that Christian communities had arisen in the Empire (in Rome for example) which were essentially free from the Law, without having been influenced in that direction by the preaching of Paul. It was his merit to have sharply defined the question, to have laid the actual foundations of the universalism of the Christian religion; and in thus founding it, to have retained the character of Christianity as a religion, in distinction from Philosophy and Morals.' Harnack, *Dogmengeschichte*, i. p. 99.

CHAPTER XXVII

DOCTRINE: PAULINE INFLUENCE: ST. JOHN

The influence of St. Paul on the thought and writing of other New Testament writers is not easy to determine. There is a tendency to attribute any passage, which bears a resemblance to the chief elements of Pauline teaching, to direct borrowing from his Epistles. An Evangelist is charged with toning his narrative to suit the character of Paulinism. Even words which a Gospel places in the mouth of Christ Himself are denied their authenticity, if they happen to correspond closely with sayings of St. Paul. They at once become suspect. This is especially the case with St. Luke, although it is not absent from much of the criticism of the Second Gospel.[1] Pauline influence is asserted to account, not merely for supposed insertions in the original narrative, but for the narrative itself as it came from the Evangelist. Now, such influence is incapable of proof. It is always most precarious to refuse to a writer, who in every part of his narrative gives evidence

[1] There is no reason for excluding the influence of St. Paul's personality upon a man like St. Mark. We know that he was in the Apostle's company towards the close of his life. But that influence is not distinguishable in the Second Gospel. St. Mark had been too much in the companionship of St. Peter to be forgetful of him, or to pass under the intellectual sway of St. Paul. The attempt has often been made to detect Pauline ideas in the Second Gospel. von Soden, *Die wichtigsten Fragen im Leben Jesu*, p. 38; J. Weiss, *Das älteste Evangelium*, p. 95; Pfleiderer, *Die Entstehung des Christentums*, p. 188 ff. But as A. Schweitzer remarks, 'It is about time that, instead of constantly asserting Pauline influences on Mark, people would prove them.' *Von Reimarus zu Wrede*, p. 302. Close intimacy with St. Peter, who had been conversant with our Lord's daily life, is shown by the minute descriptions, as of an eye-witness, which characterize the Second Gospel. There is no indication that the writer was likely to be dominated by the influence and character of an Apostle, who, however great, had not been (like St. Peter) an eye-witness of Christ. The Second Gospel is more concerned with the

of a sincere desire for accuracy of statement—and this is freely allowed for the Synoptic writers—belief in the seriousness and the truth of what he states. We have no right to take the words 'to give His life a ransom for many' out of the mouth of the Divine Speaker, as He is reported by St. Mark, and ascribe them to the Evangelist, or to an interpolator writing under the influence of St. Paul. As a rule, it will be found that this transference of origin for a saying is due to a theory. In the present case, the theory is the contrast between the Pauline Gospel and the teaching of our Lord. But, when we examine it, we can find no proof of any such borrowing. The words correspond to what we know, from other sources, to be ideas of Christ Himself; and we are justified in regarding them as His until definite evidence can be produced to the contrary. In the case of St. Luke, his known contact and intimacy with St. Paul would predispose us to trace the influence of the Apostle in the choice of subjects, if not in their handling. He seems to have been impressed by the large-heartedness of St. Paul, and by his strong sense of responsibility for the preaching of the Gospel to the Gentile world. It is not unreasonable to assign the mention of certain names and certain incidents of the Third Gospel to the Evangelist's close association with the ministry of St. Paul. It is, perhaps, more in the choice of topics from among the mass of materials at his disposal, than in actual correspondence of phrase,[1] that we can detect this influence. The predominating interests of the two men are similar. The Third Gospel is pre-eminently Catholic. Jesus Christ is not so much the Messiah as the Saviour

narrative of facts than with inferences drawn from them. Hence its extreme value as a Gospel which sprang from the heart of the community that had seen Christ during His Ministry and was, perhaps, entirely untouched by Paulinism. Feine, *Jesus Christus und Paulus*, p. 139, remarks on 'the one decisive point in which the Christology of Mark deviates from that of Paul. With him, the most frequent Self-designation of Jesus is "Son of Man." . . . That is true historical tradition which has experienced no influence of Paul, since the Apostle, though he is aware of this designation of Jesus, has given it no place in his theology. The attitude of Mark to the tradition to which he had access shows . . . that he went to school anywhere but in Pauline circles, when he had to collect material for his Gospel. It comes from the primitive community. The tradition of Peter here receives honour.' *Ib.* Feine attributes certain apparent 'Paulinisms' not to the theological, but merely the linguistic influence of St. Paul. *Ib.* p. 141.

[1] For a list of passages in St. Luke to which there are parallels in the Pauline Epistles, *v.* Plummer, *St. Luke*, pp. xliv, xlv.

of the world. The Judaistic spirit is absent. There is less reference to the Old Testament than—for instance—in St. Matthew. Parables of Christ, in which appears His yearning for the salvation of men beyond the frontiers of Israel, are narrated. In all this it is easy to detect the influence of the great personality who was for certain periods at St. Luke's side. The Third Gospel is full of the spirit of St. Paul.[1] When we reckon up our debt to the writer of the most beautiful book in the world, as the Third Gospel has been truly called by one who was himself a master of style,[2] we must not forget that we owe something to the influence of the Apostle.[3]

The writer of the First Gospel does not appear to owe anything to St. Paul. His interest is almost entirely absorbed by the needs of the Jews. He is concerned to show that our Lord is the fulfilment of prophecy. The references to the Old Testament are constant. He seems to say that certain things took place in order that prophecy might be fulfilled. In this, both his mode of thought and his style are thoroughly Jewish. We should rather regard the occurrence or event as corresponding with what had been foretold, not as occasioned by its utterance. And if cause and effect are alleged at all, we should say that the Messianic life and its events, as seen through the inspired vision of the Prophets, gave rise to their prophecies; not that the Messianic life was due to the requirements of prophecy and that Christ did or said this or that 'in order that prophecy might be fulfilled.' No doubt St. Paul himself loved to trace the connection between Old Testament prophecy and its fulfilment in the Person of our Lord. But his tone of thought and style of reference are entirely distinct from the intensely Jewish manner in which the writer of the First Gospel deals with prophecy.

The Epistle to the Hebrews marks a stage of transition, when the Church of Christ was passing from its close connection with Judaism to Catholicism. It thus serves as a connecting link between St. Paul and the writer of the Fourth Gospel. With

[1] Cf. Tertul. *Adv. Marcion*, iv. 2; Iren. *Adv. Haer.* iii. 1. 1. [2] Renan.

[3] The probability of this indebtedness is much heightened by the fact that critical opinion is now inclined to place the composition of the Third Gospel well within the lifetime of St. Paul. *v.* Harnack, *Beiträge zur Einleitung in das N.T.* iv. p. 86.

its many indications of the influence of Pauline language and thought,[1] it shows affinity with the Christology of St. John.[2] Indeed, it is easy to see that it plays no small part in the preparation of the Evangelist for his task. The fact that the worship of the Tabernacle is described as though its representative the Temple were still standing, has led to the theory of the composition of the Epistle before A.D. 70. But it is now generally felt that a later date must be assigned, and that the present tense is descriptive rather than chronological.

The great object of the Epistle, or Homily, is to settle and reassure the minds of believing Jews in view of the break-up of the old religion. It is difficult to place ourselves in their position. It was one of the chief turning points in all religious history. The Temple had been destroyed ; the sacrifices had ceased. Did this mean that the religion itself had lost all significance, and that the Scriptures, as well as the worship, of the Old Covenant had lost their Divine sanction ? Was it all a delusion that Israel was God's peculiar people ? Had their past, with its deliverances and its signs of God's presence and favour, no real and lasting meaning ?

In answer to the doubts and questionings which would be felt by every thoughtful mind, the writer brings out the educational and anticipatory character of the old religion. He shows that the offerings and sacrifices only availed in so far as they found their perfect fulfilment in Christ.[3] The first few verses of the Epistle, like the prologue of the Fourth Gospel, sketch the outline of the treatise that follows, and give the keynote to the meaning of the whole. God *had* spoken to the Fathers by the Prophets, and the perfect revelation which He has given by His Son is not the negation, but the completion of the revelation of the past. The same God, Who was worshipped in the services of the Tabernacle and Temple, commands allegiance now. In accepting the new conditions, in coming over to Christ, they are not false to their past. They fulfil it. As St. Paul had said, 'Christ is the end of the Law for righteousness to every one that believeth.'[4]

But, along with reassurance as to the position in which their conversion had placed them, the writer distinctly warns

[1] *v.* Westcott, *Epistle to the Hebrews*, p. 427.
[2] *v.* Hebr. i. 2, 3.
[3] c. ix.
[4] Rom. x. 4.

believers who had passed from the preparatory to the completed Faith, that there must be no going back, no dallying with the old state of things. He reminds them that Christians 'have an altar, whereof they have no right to eat which serve the Tabernacle.' Christ was a stone of stumbling and a rock of offence to those who were disobedient to His appeal.[1] But 'let us go forth unto Him without the camp, bearing His reproach.'[2] He makes a similar demand to that of St. Paul to Judaisers in their attitude to the Law. When the hour has struck and the time of the old dispensation is over, it is not obedience, but rebellion, that permits a believer to linger in the observance of an obsolete worship. 'That which decayeth and waxeth old is ready to vanish away.'[3] We may suppose that the unknown writer of the Epistle felt himself justified in persuading believing Jews thus to cut themselves loose from old habits and associations, not only by the momentous cleavage with the past which was brought about by the Fall of Jerusalem, but by the authority of St. Paul, who warns the Galatians 'to stand fast in the liberty wherewith Christ has made us free.'

When the Epistle was written, the expectation of an immediate return of Christ was passing into the background. The prospect of a national deliverance and of the restoration of the throne of Israel had faded away. The Parousia is referred to,[4] indeed, but as a certainty of the future, not as an object of instant concern. Here, again, we can trace the influence of St. Paul. In his later writings there is a gradual lessening of the insistence with which, in his earlier Epistles, he presented the immediate prospect of the return. The writer to the Hebrews urges upon his readers the fact that, in virtue of their religion, they are already 'come to Mount Sion, to the city of the living God, . . . and to God the Judge of all.' The παρουσία is an accomplished fact as far as its essentials are concerned. The approach of man to God in the way of faith has taken place. The open vision will yet be granted. Christ will come again; but His redeemed have already come, and are coming, to Him.

While it owes much to the genius and inspiration of St. Paul, the Epistle has exercised a certain influence in its turn upon the

[1] 1 Pet. ii. 8.

[2] Hebr. xiii. 13. *v.* Zahn, *Einleitung in d. N.T.* ii. p. 133.

[3] Hebr. viii. 13.

[4] Hebr. ix. 28; x. 25.

writer of the Fourth Gospel. In each, in the first chapter, there is definite assignment of Godhead to the Son. In Hebrews, God creates through Him. In St. John, His direct work in creation is emphasized,[1] and this is a further stage in the development of the cosmic place of the Eternal Son. At the same time, the writer reaches a hand back to St. Paul in his description of the relation of the Son to the Father as 'the brightness of His glory and the express image of His Person,' and as the sustaining as well as creating power of the universe.[2]

The importance of these links in the history of the development of doctrine is obvious. It means that writers of different schools of thought are at one on the most vital truths of the Christian religion. Christ is God, the Creator, alike for St. Paul, for the writer to the Hebrews, for St. John.

The writer of the Fourth Gospel has been thought to be largely influenced by St. Paul. During his residence at Ephesus, he may well have been familiar with the Epistles to the Colossians and the Ephesians. There is, at any rate, a remarkable similarity between St. Paul's conception of the cosmic place of our Lord in those Epistles and the teaching of the prologue of the Gospel. They 'form the connecting link between the writings of St. Paul and St. John.'[3]

But are we justified in taking the view that the Johannine doctrines of salvation, of the Sacraments, and above all, of the Person of our Lord, are derived from St. Paul? Wernle declares that 'the whole Johannine theology has grown out of the theology of Paul and is Paulinism modified to suit the needs of the post-

[1] Hebr. i. 8. Cf. Jo. i. 1, 8; Hebr. i. 2. Cf. Jo. i. 3.

[2] Hebr. i. 3; Col. i. 15-18.

[3] Westcott, *St. John*, on i. 16. Cf. Col. i. 15 with Jo. i. 18; Col. i. 16, 17 with Jo. i. 1, 2, 3; Col. ii. 9 with Jo. i. 1; Eph. i. 23, iii. 19, iv. 13 with Jo. i. 14. The influence of St. Paul helps to account for the development of thought which enabled a fisherman of Galilee to write the prologue of the Fourth Gospel. Yet apart from such influence, there is no difficulty in understanding that St. John had become acquainted with Greek speculative thought during his residence in so Greek a city as Ephesus. The same philosophic ideas which affected St. Paul may have acted directly upon the mind of St. John. But it seems only reasonable to allow that St. John, from his knowledge of St. Paul's writings, would be aided in the expression of his own thought on such a subject as the Person and cosmic place of our Lord. As to his supposed Alexandrianisms see Allen in *Encycl. of Religion and Ethics*, iv. p. 321.

Apostolic age . . . there is no Johannine theology independent of the Pauline . . . John and Paul are not two theological forces, but one . . . Paul only is original and John is not.'[1] But, further, Wernle considers that the effect of the Fourth Gospel is to place a Pauline interpretation on the Synoptic Gospels, to which the Fourth was added in order to complete them; thereby hiding Jesus behind Paul and the Church.[2] In fact, he charges St. John with making a true, historical understanding of Christ impossible through his Paulinism.

To such lengths does a one-sided method of criticism lead. Now, whence did the writer of the Fourth Gospel derive his conceptions of the Person and work of Christ? We do not hesitate to say that his ideas were, in the main, fully formed before the teaching and influence of St. Paul had begun to make themselves felt in the Christian community. Wernle himself admits that St. John's conception of Christ as the Saviour of the world was in no sense new. 'Every Christian in the Church at large believed it.'[3] St. John had nothing for which to thank St. Paul, in the possession of this primary faith. The chief points of the Christian doctrine of the Person of Christ, His Divine Sonship, His sole power to save, were the common property of the Church before it received, in the adhesion of St. Paul, the greatest exponent of its faith and practice. The attempt to prove that St. Paul and St. John between them have perverted the Gospel of Jesus, by making it a religion of which He is the centre, whereas He ever made the Fatherhood of God and the love of man the core of His teaching, is the natural result of low views of our Lord's Person and significance. Our knowledge of the dimly lighted period which extended from the conversion of St. Paul to the publication of his first Epistles is but slight. But we know enough to be able to say that in regarding Christ as the revelation of the Father, as summing up in Himself God's redeeming power, and as the object of the faith which saves, St. Paul was entirely in accord with the mind of

[1] *Die Anfänge unserer Religion*, p. 455.

[2] *Ib.* pp. 457, 446.

[3] *Ib.* p. 449. Wernle would say that St. John's doctrine was not new simply because St. Paul had already preached it. We should rather say that it was not new because, independently of St. Paul, it was already contained in the faith which was held by the primitive community, by St. John himself, by St. Peter and the rest.

the primitive Apostles.[1] From the Day of Pentecost onwards, the central place of Jesus Christ in the Christian religion was assured. It was St. Paul who, so far as we know, first set this belief into something of a system and who first treated it philosophically.[2] To St. John belongs the merit of perceiving that the teaching of St. Paul was true to the facts of Christ's life and mind. So it befell that he was able, as the first century was closing, to confirm the faith which was common to the Synoptic Evangelists and to St. Paul.

It was through his writings, rather than by his life, that St. John became a formative power in the history of Christian doctrine.

The Evangelist begins his Gospel with a preface in which he sets out the main lines of the conception which he has formed of the Person and significance of Christ. At once he makes it clear that He is God, One from all eternity with the Father ; but that He became flesh and as Man was seen by man. Those are the two main strains of St. John's theology—the truth of the Godhead, the reality of the Manhood, of Christ. And everything that follows is chosen, from the sum of his knowledge, for its bearing on one or other of these two sublime facts. The Gospel deals with the relation of the Son to the Father in virtue of His Godhead, and with His relation to man in virtue of His Incarnation. St. John does not manipulate facts or incidents to bring them into touch with his subject and make them serve the purpose of his Gospel ; but he chooses from his ample store of recollections just those incidents in event or speech which bear upon it. For it is true that he writes with a purpose.

Can we trace with any certainty the course of the evolution by which a Galilean fisherman became the author of the Fourth Gospel ? A Jew by birth and religion,[3] he was one of the first to be attracted by the preaching of the Baptist and may, therefore, be presumed to have shared to the full the Messianic expectation of his countrymen. Yet in his Gospel he can speak of 'the

[1] Speaking of St. Paul's part in bringing faith into its central position in the Christian life, Bousset remarks, 'He seems to presuppose a formulated confession of the faith of the community, Rom. x. 9.' *Kyrios Christos*, p. 123. Cf. *ib.* p. 179.

[2] For the influence of St. Paul upon Gnostic speculation, see the able criticism of Bousset, *Kyrios Christos*, p. 262 f.

[3] Harnack, *Dogmengeschichte*, i. p. 110, 'In spite of his antijudaism, we must regard the author as a born Jew.'

Jews' in a detached manner as though he now had no part or lot in them; and one of the most distinctive marks of his Gospel is the absence of Messianic ideas.[1] He has left far behind him the narrow circle of Jewish thought which in its Messiah saw the end and object of its merely national hopes. He has passed beyond the confining horizon of legalism. He has lifted his eyes to a wider prospect. In the Person of the Messiah, he has been able to see Him Who made the worlds and Who is Himself 'both Lord and God.' How did he get to this faith? It has been said that 'no way leads from the Old Testament and from Rabbinism up to the doctrine of the Divinity of Christ'; that 'the Jew has simply no place for a Second Being, who is named God in the strong sense.'[2] The thought is said to be forbidden even by Jewish Christianity. If that be the case, we should have to seek for the root of the Johannine doctrine of Christ's Person in some other field of religious thought than that which has preserved for us the vital truth that there is one God. If the Divinity of Christ is an idea hostile to that solitary Being of God, which is the great dogmatic contribution of Judaism to the thought of mankind, we must look for its origin elsewhere. But is it hostile? Do we not rather meet again and again with indications of a plurality of life within the Godhead in the various strata of thought which form the Scriptures of the Old Testament? The Spirit who moves upon the face of the waters at creation seems to point to an interpretation of Gen. i. 26 which hints at it. The song of praise which Isaiah heard in the Temple seems to symbolize it. The personification of wisdom in the book of Proverbs, and the 'One like unto a Son of Man' in Daniel, show that Jewish thought was feeling after a conception of God which, while maintaining His unity, yet recognizes distinctions of manifestation in the Divine life. When, along with this reappearing note of plurality in the Scriptures, the Apocalyptic writings[3] drew special attention to the Person of the

[1] I find that Bousset takes a similar view: 'There can be no doubt that this title "Son of God" has here (in St. John) a metaphysical meaning which is quite foreign to all Jewish Messianic doctrine.' *Kyrios Christos*, p. 188.

[2] *v.* also Wernle, *D. Anfänge*, p. 304.

[3] Especially 1 (Ethiopian) Enoch xc. 37 about 200-175 B.C., and in the *Sibylline Oracles*, iii. 652, about 150-100 B.C. In the *Psalms of Solomon*, 70-40 B.C., the Messiah is styled Χριστὸς Κύριος. In 1 Enoch xlvi. 1-6, more than human power is assigned to Him.

Messiah, the way was further prepared for Christian thought. As a disciple of the Baptist, St. John must have been early initiated into the ideas which characterized the time of waiting for the Messiah, and was at once drawn to Him, when He appeared.

On a mind thus prepared by training and reflection, the impression made by our Lord was deep and immediate. From his first meeting with Him, St. John appears to have at once devoted himself to His service as a disciple ; and in his gradually expanding recognition of the Divine nature of our Lord, he entered upon an inheritance of faith which was the rightful product of the best Jewish thought.

But the rejection of their Messiah by the Jewish people and the following catastrophe of the destruction of their city and their Temple, together with their more complete subjection to Rome, could not but have a great effect upon the Apostle's attitude to his own race. It confirmed for him what he had already begun to realize—the end of the national conception of Messiah. His mind expanded to the reception of wider views. And two factors no doubt had great weight in producing this result. One was the influence and teaching of St. Paul ; the other was his own long residence in so typically a Greek city as Ephesus. Each of these influences strengthened the conception which St. John had already formed of the Saviour—that His field of work, the width of His redemption, could be nothing short of the whole wide world. The rejection of Christ by the Jewish nation as a whole, led St. John, as it had led St. Paul, to see that the triumphs of the Gospel would henceforth be won in the regions where Greek thought prevailed ; and that was practically the whole world. If it was St. Paul, who by 'turning to the Gentiles,' set the Church on the way to Catholicism, it was St. John who carried the task to completion. St. Paul had long stayed and taught at Ephesus, and St. John must have come into close contact there with friends and disciples of the Apostle of the Gentiles. His influence thus gained gave the final blow to the reactionary spirit of Judaistic Christianity, which had at one time threatened to stifle the progress of the Kingdom. His Gospel has been described as forming the most important turning point in Christianity. It identified the new religion with the hopes and aspirations of the nations which were destined to rule the modern world: 'Asia was lost, but Europe was won.'[1]

[1] P. Gardner is right in saying, 'For the Fourth Gospel he (Paul) paves the way.' But he surely exaggerates when he adds, 'It may be said with perfect confidence that but for the Pauline School of Christianity, the Fourth Gospel could never have been written.' *The Religious Experience of St. Paul*, pp. 181, 182. For fuller consideration of the Johannine literature, *v.* above, p. 24 f.

CHAPTER XXVIII

EARLY CHRISTIANITY AND ETHICS

It has been warmly disputed whether Christ introduced, as an effect of His work and teaching, a new standard of ethical values.[1] That He gave great impetus to the acknowledgment and diffusion of existing principles of right conduct, by the force of His own character and example, will be generally admitted. But did He originate conceptions of life and conduct? Was there anything new in His teaching or in His method of practice? Did He innovate upon the highest reach of prophecy among His own people, or upon the loftiest morality of pagan philosophy?

Christ Himself certainly claims originality for His teaching. He regards love of others, *as He teaches it*, as something quite new,[2] notwithstanding the fact that it was a binding precept of the Law which was recognized by all instructed people in His day.[3] In the Sermon on the Mount, He declares Himself to be an innovator on the standard of morality which was laid down for 'them of old time.'[4] The old, outworn forms of Judaism are, in His view, incapable of holding the new wine of the Gospel. A new revelation requires new vehicles for its reception and diffusion.[5] He regards His death as the seal of a New Covenant between God and man, of which the Eucharistic cup is to be the perpetual symbol and pledge.[6]

[1] Weinel roundly declares that 'Jesus had no intention of announcing a new principle of morality.' *Bibl. Theol. des N.T.* p. 76.

[2] Jo. xiii. 34; Lk. x. 27. [3] Levit. xix. 18; Lk. x. 27.

[4] Matt. v. 21, 22; 27, 28; 33, 34 f.; 38, 39 f.; 43, 44.

[5] Mk. ii. 22; Matt. ix. 17; Lk. v. 38.

[6] Lk. xxii. 20; 1 Cor. xi. 25.

This claim of Christ Himself is reasserted, at least in regard to its consequences, by the Apostolic writers. To be 'in Christ' is to be 'a new creation.'[1] This 'new creation' is all that matters.[2] Christ, says the writer to the Hebrews, is the 'Mediator of a new Covenant.'[3] Thus, if we deny originality to the teaching of Christ, an originality which was subversive of existing theories of life and conduct, we have against us the combined views of our Lord Himself and of those who stood nearest to Him and best interpreted His mind. Christianity does profess to impart a fresh view of life and, what is more, to have the secret of carrying it out. It enables as well as teaches.

It is not enough for those who deny originality to Christ to allege parallels to His teaching from the Old Testament or from pagan writers. It is not a question of a saying or a phrase. The freshness of Christ's teaching springs from the nature of His Personality and from the character of His work. It was not so much what He said, but who it was that said it, and what He was doing when He said it, that gave to His views on life and conduct the colours of the dawn, the light of a new day. It was because He was the supreme revelation of the Love of God, in His Person and on the Cross, that His teaching has a meaning and a depth unknown before. His death manifested, as nothing else could do, the power and guilt of sin; while it revealed, as nothing else could do, the love of God. All that Christ said and did during His Ministry was conditioned by these facts. It took its meaning from the Personality and the purpose of the Speaker. Life and death, sin and holiness gathered a new significance. He made all things new. Match His sayings as we may, we cannot find in their analogies the meaning that lies within His own. When people wondered at 'the new doctrine,' as they called His dealing with the possessed, it was the 'authority' of His action, His mastery of the situation, which

[1] 2 Cor. v. 17.

[2] Gal. vi. 15; cf. Eph. iv. 24.

[3] ix. 15; cf. viii. 8; viii. 13. When St. John says, 'I write no new commandment unto you, but an old commandment,' he is not denying the newness of the Gospel; for he adds, 'which ye had from the beginning (ἀπ' ἀρχῆς),' *i.e.* from the beginning of your Christian life and experience. *v.* Westcott, *ad loc.* It was old because it had been given at the dawn of Christianity. It was new because it was unknown before then, except in the secret counsels of God. Cf. 1 Pet. i. 20; Rev. xiii. 8. Cf. Church, *The Discipline of the Christian Character*, pp. 137, 86.

called forth their amazement.[1] He moved in the world of spirit, as in the world of sense, with equal ease. And there was the same note of authority in all that He said. With a word He amended the teaching of the Fathers, or revised the law that had been current for centuries. It was recognized that He spoke magisterially; not as an interpreter, who has to feel his way, but with the certainty of one to whom all truth lay open.[2] The freshness and originality of Christ's teaching proceed from the Personality and the work of the Speaker, which give new power to His words and fill them with a life unknown before.

But in order to see this, we have to study His teaching, not merely in the sense in which it was spoken, or with reference to the immediate circumstances which occasioned it, but in the light thrown back upon it by the Cross and the Resurrection.

If we do this, two considerations will appear which at once stamp Christian ethics with a character to which all previous systems of morals bear no resemblance.

One is the exceeding sinfulness of sin as shown in the crucifixion of the Incarnate Son of God. The other is the exceeding love of God in His Self-sacrifice for man. From these two considerations there follows an entirely new conception of ethical values and sanctions. A brief comparison will demonstrate it.

Under the Old Covenant, the ordering of a man's life was determined by what was known of the revealed will of God. That will was made clear by prophet and psalmist. But it is in the priestly code that we find the command to love, not only one's neighbour, one of the same race, as oneself, but even the stranger who is sojourning in the land.[3] It is true that the idea of what constitutes a neighbour was not generally held to embrace a stranger living in the country; for there is a prohibition against the slavery of Israelites which does not extend to persons of another race. We cannot love as ourselves a person whom we hold in durance. We must, therefore, regard the love of a neighbour, under the Law, as conditioned by the question of race. That this was the view held by instructed people in our Lord's day, we gather from the question of the lawyer, who asked, Who is my neighbour? and from the tenor

[1] Mk. i. 27.
[2] Mk. i. 22.
[3] Levit. xix. 18, 33, 34. *v.* Kautzsch in Hastings' *D.B.* v. p. 722 *b*.

of Christ's answer.[1] We may, accordingly, conclude that the idea of what constituted nearness and neighbourliness was very limited. Race meant everything. 'The Jews have no dealings with the Samaritans' bluntly expresses the prevailing attitude. It was thought that God did not require a man to love one of another race. He must be just, and might be generous in his treatment, but farther than that he was not required to go.

The pagan standard of ethical relations was frankly selfish. It was dictated by self-interest and expediency directly the boundaries of family or friendship were passed. Men acknowledged no claim on their kindness or forbearance, still less on their affections, where strangers were concerned.

To what is this imperfect conception of duty traceable in the case of Jew and pagan? The Jew acted in accordance with what he believed to be the will of God. It was his habit to refer everything to the Divine sanction. 'I am the Lord your God' stands as the authority for every direct command, and enforces every prophetic message. His life was lived under constant reference to the immediate care of God. But although he believed in His Fatherhood, he had never grasped the fact that 'God made of one blood all nations of men to dwell on the face of the earth.' The privileges of Israel were so cherished as to exclude concern for all who stood outside the chosen race, and to bar the thought of their being objects of the love of God. This appears in the contempt with which Scribe and Pharisee regarded the common people even of their own nation.[2] We may say, therefore, that brotherly love, although enforced in their law, was not realized in practice.

Still less was it an active principle in the pagan world. It is true that the Stoic held and taught the brotherhood of man;[3] but the conception never got beyond the stage of academic theory. It found no response in the mind or practice of any but a few thinkers.

The reason why Jewish and pagan standards of duty towards others failed, when put to the test, was the absence of an adequate sense of sin on the one hand[4] and of the love of God

[1] Lk. x. 29, 36 f. [2] Jo. vii. 49. [3] *v.* p. 104.

[4] Judaism and paganism are not, of course, on the same plane as regards sense of sin. The Jew was profoundly conscious of personal sin. The pagan, while alive to the presence of discord in his life, had no such consciousness of

on the other. The Christian, if he is awake to the realities of his calling, is mindful of both these facts of his spiritual experience. Hence his outlook on life and his mode of dealing with it. Conscious of sin in himself, he can be forbearing and forgiving towards others. Knowing the love of God in Christ, as revealed in the Cross and as crowning the Incarnate life with the principle of self-sacrifice, he sees in his fellow-man the object of redeeming love, and he dares not hinder the outflow of that love by any hardness or ill-will of his own. His love to God compels him to love his brother also.

Thus the whole system of ethics is placed by the Cross upon a new foundation. One touch of the wounded hands has effected a revolution in morality which ages of development could never have brought about. We see our neighbour in a new light. Our fellow-man is a sinner like ourselves. He is the object of the redeeming love of the Incarnate Saviour, as we are. Hatred, ill-will, revenge, are put out of court on each ground. We fellow-sinners have no right to deal hardly with one who, if in the wrong, is but frail and sinful as we are. Love to God in Christ, if sincere, must embrace those who with ourselves are, in turn, the objects of His redeeming love.

When we compare the Christian standard of ethics with those which have preceded it, we come upon another contrast. The Mosaic law was chiefly prohibitive. It forbade wrong actions. It set a hedge round a man's life. It cramped his movements by warning him of trespass. It was mainly negative. Where it was positive, it inculcated particular acts or habits.

The moral standard of the Gospel, on the other hand, is positive. It is far less concerned with forbidding sin than with commending goodness. It holds up before the Christian the example of a life of perfect and complete achievement, the life of One 'Who went about doing good.' It says 'Thou shalt' rather than 'Thou shalt not.' In the great parable that reveals the principle on which the awards of the Last Judgment will be given, those who have shown love and kindness by definite, concrete actions will be accepted. Their neglect so to do will be the condemnation of the lost. The religion of Christ is an affirmation—an active,

evil as sin, which was one of the leading endowments of the Jew. Jew and pagan alike came short of the knowledge of sin as it was afterwards revealed by the life and death of Christ.

positive, vital thing. Its morality is of the same character. It contemplates a life so fully charged with good as to admit of no evil. It therefore incites to good rather than dissuades from evil. Entirely of a piece with this character is our Lord's own attitude to Pharisees and Scribes, as compared with His treatment of 'publicans and sinners.' His anger is stirred, not so much by positive sin, as by spiritual pride; by complacency, by the self-sufficiency which, content with its own condition, presents an impenetrable barrier to every approach of grace and every desire of amendment.

Another contrast between the ethics of Judaism and of Christ is seen in the particular injunctions and prohibitions in which the former delighted, as compared with the care which Christian morality displays for the character of the man as a whole. Our Lord set Himself to redeem and purify the whole man; not to engraft certain graces of conduct upon his old, unregenerate nature. He aimed at the creation of a '*new man*,' who, of necessity, should live a new life. 'Make the tree good and his fruit good.'[1] The sequence is unfailing. 'Every good tree bringeth forth good fruit.'[2] It is this disposition as a whole, this new self, the pearl of great price, for which all else is to be sacrificed, if only it can be obtained. The ego is the determining factor. The man himself, what he is in the centre of his being, at the springs of thought and action —that is what counts in our Lord's eyes as all important. His sense of it made Him burn with indignation as He encountered the petty trifling of Pharisaic casuistry. With the great issues standing plainly before Him, with the meaning of the great realities ever present to His thought, He put His finger upon the things which matter. Morality, as He taught it, takes into account God, the soul, eternity. It is in relation to these verities that His standard of ethics was formed. The supreme need of man is to get into right relation with them. Nothing else matters. To stand right with God is to have the only secure foundation on which the moral life can be placed.

But the great difference between Christian ethics and other systems lies, after all, in the fact that while they present

[1] Matt. xii. 33. *v.* Weinel, *Bibl. Theol. des N.T.* p. 83.
[2] Matt. vii. 17.

an external code to be observed, but go no farther,[1] Christianity, with a code still more imperious and binding, gives the power to carry it out. It is a force within, as well as a law without.[2] If it requires a new birth, a fresh outlook, a new heart, it supplies these requirements, and with them the power to obey its commands. God never makes a greater demand upon us than we can respond to. We are not, as Christians, in bondage. We have not to make bricks without straw. The Christian standard of holiness is indeed always above and beyond us ; always out of our reach. Were it attainable, it would cease to be an ideal. The very *raison d'être* of an ideal is its unapproachableness. It becomes unnecessary, lifeless, an encumbrance, directly we touch it. Christ was not mocking us when He said, 'Be ye perfect even as your Father Which is in heaven is perfect.' He was setting before men an unattainable goal, that they might ever seek after it, ever unsatisfied, yet ever hopeful, eternity itself too short for the quest.

Is grace, the power to do the will of God—which thus distinguishes Christianity from all other ethical systems—is grace a failure because it cannot secure perfect correspondence with the ethical ideal ? It may be said to fail, if the result is tested at certain points. The Christian life is a progressive movement. But it would be as foolish to accuse it of failure because it *is* not what it is *becoming*, as to blame a child for lacking the strength and power of manhood. Grace itself is indefectible. 'I can do

[1] Cf. Gal. iii. 21. If Jewish law was powerless, still more was every other system. There is the same contrast of powerlessness and power in Jo. i. 17. 'The law was given by Moses, but grace and truth came by Jesus Christ'; an instance of the influence of Pauline teaching on the Fourth Gospel. The Law could command—and that was all. Grace, *i.e.* help to obey, came by Christ. *v.* Holtzmann, *Einleitung in d. N.T.* p. 427.

[2] 'The Sermon on the Mount kills, to use St. Paul's language, as relentlessly as the Law.' Strong, *Christian Ethics*, p. 22. True, but He who delivered it as the final code of human conduct 'knew what He would do' to make it work. It goes far beyond all existing codes in the depth and severity of its requirements. It makes demands on thought and desire as well as on conduct. It is more difficult of fulfilment than the law of the Old Covenant. But He who spoke it had within Himself the power to fulfil it, and that power He was to send forth in the promised gift of His Spirit. He might well lay down so searching a code for His people : for He knew that in His strength, and in the possession of His Spirit, they would show in their lives that it was a law which could be kept—not, indeed, in every detail at every moment—but in its broad and general spirit. Cf. 1 Jo. v. 18.

all things through Christ that strengtheneth me,' cried St. Paul. But grace has to work on a stubborn and intractable material. Hindered, thwarted at every turn, it can only produce, here and now, *the beginnings* of better things. The same Apostle, who throbbed at one time with the touch of the might of Christ, exclaims at another time, 'Wretched man that I am, who shall deliver me from the body of this death?' And yet he does not despair, 'I thank God through Jesus Christ.' It is the great paradox of the Christian life—boundless power checked at every point by human conditions—the strange dualism that runs through everything, waiting for the unifying moment for which all creation waits, when God shall 'be all in all.'[1]

And then, with all the imperfection and failure that attend the struggle, there is the undoubted strength and confidence which proceed from union with Christ. 'He that abideth in Him, sinneth not.' St. John characterizes this condition as one which sin does not disturb. The general habit of the man who is rooted and grounded in Christ is that of sinlessness. He may and does sin, as a matter of fact, on occasion. But the isolated act is out of agreement with his settled habit and purpose. Abiding in Christ is a condition which is unfavourable to sin.

The advantage of Christian ethics over every other system is due to another cause. It takes into account the origin as well as the fact of sin. It looks facts in the face and is able to deal with them. Man is a fallen being. Not that the frailty and weakness of man are unknown to the moralists of Judaism and indeed of every higher ethical system. But Christianity traces the cause of sin to its historic source in a distant past,[2] while it

[1] 1 Cor. xv. 28.

[2] The almost entire absence of reference to the Fall in the Old Testament is one of its most remarkable features. The tradition has hardly left a trace in the religious thought of Israel. It seems as though the realization of the promise of the Prot-evangelium (Gen. iii. 15), in the Person of the Incarnate Saviour, was required to bring home to men the fact that their present condition is due in great part to a definite break with God, to a Fall. 'It is difficult to conceive how life could have been possible under the old conditions, if all the meaning and all the cost of sin had been understood before its power was destroyed by the Death and Resurrection of Christ.' Strong, *Christian Ethics*, p. 215. The rendering of Job xxxi. 33, 'Like Adam' (A.V. and R.V.), and Hos. vi. 7, 'Like Adam' (R.V. but not A.V.), is too uncertain to prove reference to the Fall. Allusions to dust as the serpent's food in Mic. vii. 17, Is. lxv. 25 may be derived from the tradition in Gen. iii.: but we have to wait for the Book of Wisdom before we get any clear reference to Satan as the active agent,

points for confirmation of its theory to the experience of every enlightened conscience.

It is to St. Paul that we owe the first clear view of the connection of sinful experience with the Fall of the typical representative of mankind. The story of Genesis iii. is presupposed in every word of the Gospel account of the temptation of Christ: but it is not directly referred to. The bruising of the serpent's head was already going on while our Lord was casting out devils. At the return of the Seventy Disciples, He sees in vision the discomfiture of the evil one. But St. Paul makes the Fall of Adam, with its consequences, the background of his conception of the restoration of humanity by 'the Second Man, the Lord from heaven.' It accordingly forms a leading feature of his theology. The story which had lain almost unnoticed in the tradition of his people had recently come to life again in their later literature. St. Paul seems to have been led by it to study the ancient record of the way in which sin entered into the world, bringing spiritual, if not physical, death [1] in its train. But along with the primal cause of guilt, the disobedience of the pair who stood at the head and source of humanity, and in whom moral responsibility and consciousness of the will of God—'the law' of Rom. vii.—first came to be recognized, St. Paul saw its transmission by heredity to every succeeding member of the race. Mankind are 'in Adam' as the child in the parent; and the race is solid.[2] There is the taint of sin in everyone. It is there, although it may never be awakened into activity. It is there, not from any personal fault, but as part of an inheritance. When we come of age to discern right from wrong, the flaw betrays

who brought death into the world through envy of the favoured position of man. Wisd. ii. 24. In the part assigned to Satan by the authors of 1 Chron. xxi. 1 and Job, and by Zechariah iii. 1, there is no allusion to the story of Genesis, although it may well have been in their minds at the time of writing. In 4 Ezra, a work of the first century A.D. (Jewish, but non-Christian), we find clear reference to Gen. iii. (4 Ezra iii. 21, 22). It has been argued that the lateness of the work does not destroy its use in showing what was the belief of the Jews, as to the results of the Fall, in pre-Christian times. *v.* Bernard in Hastings' *D.B.* i. p. 841.

[1] If St. Paul here (Rom. v. 12) means physical death, he is *apparently* in opposition to science: but, as Illingworth remarks, 'we have not the means of knowing what the action of a sinless personality upon an otherwise mortal body might be.' *Christian Character*, chap. i. p. 7.

[2] 'He regards himself as the subject of what is related in Gen. iii. of the parents of the race.' Holtzmann, *N.T. Theol.* ii. p. 47.

itself. Sooner or later, though we know the good, we choose the evil. Over and over again, the story of the Fall repeats itself in ever new and varying form ;[1] but with the one great difference that, whereas to Adam the impulse to disobey came entirely from without, sin now finds an ally ready to acquiesce, in the very citadel of the heart and will. With Adam, there was the power to sin, because his will was free. With us, as a consequence of his yielding, who summed up in himself the race of which he was father, there is not only the power but the tendency to sin.

But this tendency is not to be regarded as poisoning every faculty of our being. It is not a necessity of our nature that we should sin. Otherwise actual sin would bring no guilt in its train. The sin lies in the deliberate choice of what we know to be contrary to the will of God.[2] To the child the will of God is manifested in that of the parent. His sole criterion of right and wrong is exhibited in the authority of father and mother. When self-will asserts itself against what he knows to be their will, the corrupt tendency begins to operate.

And the taint remains even in 'the regenerate,' in spite of the baptismal washing. The corruption of our nature is never wholly lost in this life, however advanced in holiness a person may be. The 'old Adam' reappears at times : hence the inconsistencies and weaknesses of the saints. 'Elias was a man subject to like passions as we are.' Once only has the world looked upon a sinless character, a life without a flaw. Only one man has appeared without sin, shielded from the dread heritage by the manner of His birth.[3]

It is a distinctive feature of Christian ethics that it takes account of this hereditary tendency to evil ; and that it does so without, on the one hand, so exaggerating the influence of heredity as to deny the freedom of the individual to sin or to forbear from sinning, and without, on the other hand, so minimizing its effects as to allow that we can, if we will, by our own unaided efforts and without the grace of God, turn to Him in love and service.

[1] Cf. *Apoc. Baruch*, liv. 19, 'Non est Adam causa, nisi animae suae tantum : nos vero, unusquisque fuit animae suae Adam.' *v.* Charles, *Apocrypha and Pseudepigrapha of the O.T.* ii. p. 477 ; Sanday and Headlam, *Romans*, p. 137.

[2] Original sin, therefore, does not destroy our responsibility.

[3] *v.* Church, *The Gifts of Civilisation*, p. 56 f.

In the world there are always to be met these opposing views of the corruption of man's nature. The determinist denies the moral responsibility of creatures, who enter life bound by the chain of inherited weakness, and grow up the victims of circumstance. Pelagius reappears as the champion of freedom and a power for righteousness which, if it existed, would render superfluous the Incarnation and the Cross.

Christian ethics faces the facts of human nature, and because it faces them, is able to suggest a remedy. To ignore the entail of human weakness and liability to err is to be blind to the need of Divine grace: while a gloomy fatalism destroys all power 'to lay hold on the hope set before us.'[1] Christianity is a religion of humility and trust. It measures the forces against us with unsparing fidelity. It is no less careful to enumerate the stores of grace which are to be found in the armoury of God.

This double attitude, recognizing what is hostile as well as what is on our side, results in an ethical system which meets every fact of human life. No problem of conduct is too hard for its decision if it be fairly appealed to. There may arise at times obligations which appear to conflict. An honest determination to see and act up to the right will generally show the course that should be taken. Casuistry, as it has appeared at certain epochs and among certain sections, has won a bad name for itself as sophistical and elusive, arguing a desire to play fast and loose with the declared will of God, to compromise principle and to avoid compliance with clear and certain duty. There is a Christian casuistry, on the other hand, which only seeks in difficult questions to bring action under the law of God, to determine everything by the will of Christ. But, as a rule, especially where our own action is concerned, first thoughts are best. To deliberate is often to palter with the voice of conscience, to cast about for an opportunity to evade obligation. Hesitation is fatal.

A readiness to face the facts of human nature, its sinfulness and its capacity for amendment, is thus one of the chief characteristics of Christian ethics as compared with all previous systems; and it is to St. Paul, more than to anyone else, that belongs the merit of bringing it about.

But to understand ourselves and our position in the sight of

[1] Hebr. vi. 18.

God is a small part of what is required of us. When the Apostles came before the world with the proclamation of the Gospel, they presented for its acceptance a perfect life, lived under the conditions of ordinary human life, subject to its weakness and exposed to its temptations, yet a life 'holy, harmless, undefiled, separate from sinners'—the complete example of what human life was intended to be. They preached Christ, and every succeeding age, by the mouth of its worthiest exponents, has owned that all which is best in human life met in its fulness in His Person. When the Church went farther than this and, under the guidance of its first teachers and by the inspiration of the Holy Spirit, called Him God and Lord, nothing was thereby taken from the completeness of His humanity, or from the force and reality of His example. He was no less man because He was recognized as God. The Temptation was a real experience, and to be real it implied the possibility of His yielding to it. He *might* have sinned; though we cannot imagine the possibility being translated into fact.

Christian ethics thus offers us a perfect example, that we 'should follow His steps, Who did no sin.' But how is this to be? The presentation of an ideal does not mean its fulfilment. A power to realize in human life and conduct the pattern set before it, a force which should enable yearning and desire to pass into action, was needed. It is the belief of the Church that this power has been given; that, in the Pentecostal outpouring of the Holy Spirit, One, Who from the dawn of creation had moved and worked in the world towards the spread of truth and light, had now come, *as the Spirit of Christ*, and in consequence of His atoning work, in a manner not possible before, to unite men to His sacred humanity and thus to give the power to live over again the Christ-life.

After all, that is the distinctive feature of the ethical system of Christianity. It goes upon the belief that a new power has entered into life, the power not merely to appreciate and admire a perfect life of holiness, but in some measure, by union with that life, to live it over again. This conviction lies at the root of St. Paul's declaration, 'I live, yet not I, but Christ liveth in me.' The Christian, in so far as he is true to his name and profession, is a fresh embodiment and realization of the life of Christ.

From this incorporation into Christ, which is effected by His Spirit, flow all the gifts and graces that adorn the life of the Christian man. Of these the chief is love; and this is only to be expected, seeing that the motive and mainspring of the Incarnation itself was the love of God. If, therefore, the Christian life is regarded as a life lived in union with that of Christ and by the power of His Spirit, it is only natural that love, which formed the moving power in man's redemption, should be the quality of most value in all who belong to Christ—the one vital and necessary gift without which 'all our doings . . . are nothing worth.'

But there is another reason for its pre-eminence in the ethical character. Love is the master-key which unlocks every treasure and secures the possession of all other graces. He who loves his brother will not defraud or injure him. He who loves God will not shrink from His service. Nothing ensures the right attitude to God and man as love. It is 'the one thing needful,' because, having it, we have all. It is 'the very bond of peace and of all virtues.' It is 'the fulfilling of the law.'

There was love in the world before Christ came to be the full revelation and embodiment of it. The yearning after God is nowhere more intensely felt than in the Psalms. He is the one desire of the saints of the Old Covenant. Their longing amounted to a passion for Him: 'When I awake up after Thy likeness, I shall be satisfied with it.' 'My soul is athirst for God, for the living God.'

But with the coming and the work of Christ, the whole conception of love was lifted to a higher plane. Such an exhibition of love as He presented in His life and death made love the one indispensable gift for all who claimed to follow Him and belong to Him. It became the inspiring form and the fulfilment of the Christian life—the life in Christ. On the Cross it was seen that, in its highest forms, love commands self-sacrifice. Careless of consequences to self, it finds all its happiness in its object. 'Christ pleased not Himself.' If this principle, so demonstrated on the Cross, is fairly worked in the relation of man to God and man to man, every problem of human conduct will receive its solution. He who loves, as Christ loved, will find that he is living in correspondence with the will and law of God. Rebellious passions are tamed; wayward fancies brought back; forbearance and consideration rule his intercourse with others.

The love which, before the appearance of Christ, tended to be fanatical and limited in its expression, was broadened and humanized after its full glory was revealed upon the Cross. It is to the religion of the Incarnation that we owe the final revelation of the being of God. It was the message of the Old Testament that God loves. It is the New Testament which assures us that 'God is love'—that when we speak of love we are entering upon holy ground; when we speak of God, we call up a vision of love at its highest range, the embodiment of all that is most tender and true.

It follows that love has been rescued for ever from all the unworthy and carnal associations that have wronged it, and which still presume to claim its name and sanction. Love implies readiness for sacrifice. It was so in God's primal thought for man's redemption, and in Christ's response to that thought. Mere human, unsanctified love is often the unbridled expression of an undisciplined self-will. When thwarted, or opposed, it freely turns to hate. Self has been the real object all along. The assumed object was but the external form which self took.

So it comes about that, under the Gospel, men are living under a rule sterner far than that of the law. It must be so. Perfect love has been revealed. Supreme self-sacrifice in the Person of the Incarnate Son has been manifested. And such love is a fire. It consumes what refuses to be blessed by it. It sets an example which every Christian, as a Christian, is bound to make his own. Against its purity every secret sin—the look, the thought, the half-formed desire—is exposed in its sinfulness. The sternness of the Sermon on the Mount is due to the fact that the Preacher is the Incarnate Love. He can demand no less of those who follow Him. Not overt and acted sin merely, but sin in the making is what He forbids. The old law could deal with actual, practised sin. It needed the sin-bearer Himself, Who is Love, thus to search the heart and to legislate for the inmost springs of thought and action.

Love is thus 'the bond of perfectness.' Love to God in Christ, to man for Christ's sake, is the flower and crown of Christian ethics. We have seen how it appeared in the unity of the primitive community and in the care for every member, when 'the multitude of them that believed were of one heart and of one soul: neither said any of them that ought of the things which he possessed was his own.'[1] At other times and under different circumstances it takes another form. Love can be stern and ruthless and still be love. Where tenderness would weaken and spoil, it is treason. Hard measures often prove the truest affection. For love, when unselfish, as it must always be if true to its character, seeks the best interest of its object.

St. John makes love of the brethren the test of our love to God. 'He that loveth not his brother whom he hath seen, how can he love God Whom he hath not seen?'[2] A heart that is steeled against one's fellow-men is in no mood to open itself to God. Thus, in the view of St. John, it is vain to speak of religion if there is something wrong with the central element of morals.

Love, whether to God or man, is not original. It is a response to an existing love. 'We love Him because He first loved us.'[3] Nothing shows more clearly than this that, according to the Christian view, morality is dependent on religion;[4] that it is religion in practice; that the love of God towards us is the moving spring of all moral thought and action, which return to their source, as the rivers to the sea that gave them birth. There is no safeguard, apart from religion, that morality will rise to any higher level than that of a kindly interest in the welfare of others and a wise precaution in the management of a man's own life. In time of stress and trial, the sanction which lacks a religious basis is apt to fail. 'But the strong, tenacious fibre of Christian character has not yet failed. The serious love of the unseen Christ . . . has not yet died out. It still wields its power over the wills of men. By God's mercy, God be thanked,

[1] *v.* p. 428. Acts iv. 32.

[2] 1 Jo. iv. 20. Apart from Christ, this argument would be pointless. The readiness to love a fellow-man seems to have no bearing upon our relation to God. Man is fallible, often disappointing and vexatious. God is infinite in wisdom and goodness. How can the withholding of love for what is unlovable argue our incapacity to love One Who is perfect—our Maker and Sustainer? The difficulty is resolved in Christ. Our unlovable brother is seen in the Christian relation. He is one with us in Christ. The call to love him is a voice from the Cross. If we turn a deaf ear to it, 'how can we love God'?

[3] 1 Jo. iv. 19. v. *Odes of Solomon*, iii. 3.

[4] Cicero saw this: 'Atque haud scio, an pietate adversus deos sublata, fides etiam et societas humani generis et una excellentissima virtus, justitia, tollatur.' *De Natur. Deor.* i. 2. 4.

it has yet great things to do. It has asked and received the sacrifice of richly equipped and noble lives; it still asks and receives the sacrifice of lives that might have been spent amid all that modern life can most innocently give, to the hard and distasteful tasks for which modern life also so urgently calls; it may be, that last sacrifice that man can offer—"greater love hath no man than this, that a man lay down his life for his friends." This—this "charity that never shall fail"—this is the finish and crown of the religious character, as it was new-created in Christ, as it can be on earth. This, while we are here in the flesh, is to have the mind of Christ.'[1]

[1] R. W. Church, *The Discipline of the Christian Character*, pp. 138, 9.

CHAPTER XXIX

THE CLOSE OF THE APOSTOLIC AGE

Our view of the rise of the Christian religion is bounded by the lives of the first Apostolic witnesses of our Lord's life on earth. When the last surviving Apostle left the scene of his labours, the Church may fairly be said to have started in full sail upon her voyage through the centuries. The hour of dawn is over. The record of the origin of Christianity is closed. The history of Catholicism is in full course.

The passing away of the men to whom our Lord directly committed His cause forms an epoch which corresponds to some extent with the crisis of His own departure from the world. The work was entrusted to other hands than those which had first taken it up. From Christ to His witnesses. From His witnesses to the Church at large. Here are two unequal, yet analogous, moments of crisis in the life of Christianity.

The death of the first Apostolic witnesses involved the cessation of that *χαρίσμα* to which the inspiration of Scripture is generally referred. However wide and liberal our view of the inspiring influence of the Spirit of God upon the minds of men ; however generously we may be disposed to regard the distribution of His gifts of light and leading, we cannot fail to see the wide and deep gulf which parts the writings which have found a place in the Sacred Canon from those which lie outside it. We pass into another realm when, from reading St. Paul or St. John, we take up a work of the sub-Apostolic age, St. Clement, St. Ignatius or the Pastor. It is not a difference of time which causes this change. St. Clement, at any rate, wrote while St. John was yet alive. Nor are these sub-Apostolic writings destitute of lofty thought and spiritual teaching. But they are lifeless and uninspiring when we turn to them from the creative work of Apostolic men, and we note the unerring instinct of the Divinely guided Church which has excluded them from its roll of Scripture. In the one class of writings we detect the presence of the Holy Spirit, Who is speaking through His chosen instruments, and Who gives to their message a force and authority which are wholly irrespective of literary power or craftsman's skill. In the other class, we acknowledge the edifying and interesting work of good men, who have been taught of God, but whose words claim no such deference and respect as the Apostolic writers can command. We pass from the vitalizing, creative period of Christianity to the reproductive, methodizing era.[1] When St. John died, no more original material was forthcoming. Henceforth men could combine, systematize, arrange ; but the deposit of the Faith had been already given. All things necessary for the glory of God in the salvation of man had been imparted to the keeping of His Church. The Faith had once for all been delivered to the saints. It was now for them to use and live by. The Christian religion might be developed and applied in the ages to come. But in its essence it was complete. And with the period of its completion we may bring the story of its origin to a close.

Another reason for this decision lies in the fact that, with the exception of a few incipient forms of heretical growth, the Church was one consistent whole while the Apostles lived. Disunion, perversion of the truth, heresy and self-assertion came soon, but as yet there was no disruption. The heresies of the Apostolic age and the divisions which appeared locally, as at Corinth, were a warning of what self-will could do if it had free scope. There are intimations of this in the writings of St. Paul and St. John.[2] But, speaking generally, we may say that the seamless coat was not yet torn. The unity of the Body of Christ had not yet ceased to be a reality. We may close our study of Christian origins before that disastrous issue comes in sight.

But, while allowing their full weight to these considerations,

[1] I find a similar line of thought taken by Gwatkin, *Early Church History to A.D. 313*, i. p. 98, 'There is no more striking contrast in the whole range of literature than that between the creative energy of the apostolic writers and the imitative poverty of the subapostolic.'

[2] 1 Cor. i. 10 ; xi. 18, 19 ; Tit. iii. 10 ; 1 Jo. ii. 18, 19 ; iv. 1 ; 2 Jo. 7.

we are met with a difficulty. So far as we know, the life of St. John was prolonged far beyond the limit of time which is usually assigned to the Apostolic age. It ran on into the sub-Apostolic period and formed a connecting link between the two epochs. This fact alone shows how difficult it is to apportion a set time for Christian origins. In one sense, while St. John lived, the age of the first witnesses to Christ—'the Apostolic age'—was running its course. Yet, in all other respects, the sub-Apostolic age—the era of those who saw and conversed with Apostles, but not with Christ—has begun.[1] While, therefore, we bear in mind the 'tarrying' of St. John, we shall regard the period from A.D. 70–100 as the age of those who had not seen Christ, but had been in touch with those who saw Him: it is mainly sub-Apostolic.

At the dawn of the critical year A.D. 70, which was to see the final overthrow of Judaism as the authoritative exponent of the true religion, of the Temple as the central house of prayer for all nations, and of Jerusalem as 'the city of the great King,' the Church of Christ had already lost well-nigh every one of its Apostolic leaders. St. Peter and St. James, St. James the Lord's brother, St. Paul, had all yielded up their lives as martyrs. Other Apostles had either departed on missionary work to the East, or had died.[2] The government and direction of the Church had almost passed out of the hands of Apostles. The age of episcopacy—of presbyters who exercised larger functions than belonged at first to their office—was yet to come in. What was the condition of the Church in this critical period of its fortunes? We are obliged to answer this question with some hesitation. It is only here and there that we can find any direct contemporary information. We are therefore partly dependent on the light reflected upon the period by subsequent writers, such as Justin Martyr, St. Ignatius and one or two others. Their evidence can only be used where it is clearly representative of a state of things which has been for some time in existence; otherwise it might prove to have no bearing upon the conditions of our period.

[1] Men like St. Clement of Rome, Papias, Polycarp, Aristion. Cf. C. H. Turner in *Quarterly Review*, July 1914, p. 9, 'It is impossible to isolate the Apostolic from the sub-Apostolic Church and to understand them apart.'

[2] 'The sixth decade robbed Christendom of all its great leaders.' V. Dobschütz, *Probleme des apost. Zeitalters*, p. 110. But as he says, 'One of the Apostles at least had according to old tradition survived this limit. John must have seen the end of the century.' *Ib.*

The Epistle to the Hebrews, the Epistles of St. John and St. Clement of Rome and the *Didache* are perhaps the only direct contemporary sources of information.[1]

The central scene of the Church's life has undergone a remarkable change. The war with Rome, ending in the destruction of Jerusalem and the Temple, had made the city impossible as the home of the leading Jewish Christian community. The candlestick was removed and never set up there again in the same prominence. Henceforth Antioch, Rome, Ephesus, not to speak of other cities, become the chief centres of the Church's work and influence.

It is difficult to estimate too highly the importance of this change. It threw the whole weight of the developing forces of Christianity into the leading centres of thought and life. It freed the Gospel from the constraining effect of Judaistic narrowness and reaction. It set Christ before the world as the Saviour of mankind, rather than as the Jewish Messiah. It brought the Gospel into contact with Roman statesmanship and law, with Greek philosophy, with problems of industry and commerce. Wherever thought was most alive, and men most active and progressive, there appeared the preacher of the Gospel and there were set up the worship and the service of God manifest in Christ. Everywhere, in all the chief cities of the Empire from Spain to the Euphrates, the Cross was being preached as the only measure of the power and riches of the world. The words of Christ—not yet recorded by St. John but, one may think, often brought to his recollection by what was passing—are already in process of fulfilment, 'I, if I be lifted up from the earth, will draw all men unto Me.'

Before we investigate the details of Christian life and worship at this period, we should consider what were the characteristic

[1] Indirectly the Fourth Gospel throws light upon the period and in certain points reflects the condition of things under which it was composed. Cf. the writer's references to 'the Jews.'

Von Dobschütz criticizes Wernle's *Die Anfänge unserer Religion* and Dibelius for anachronisms in their use of evidence. As he says, 'It cannot be considered fair to the peculiar character of primitive Christianity to combine it with the Christianity of the succeeding period.' *Probleme des apost. Zeitalters*, p. 121.

notes of Christianity as a whole, towards the close of the first century.

By what we know of the theology of the later Epistles of St. Paul, we may be certain that among the leaders of Christian thought—if not fully among the rank and file—the Person of our Lord was the object of worship and adoration in the Church of the closing years of the first century. God was regarded as completely revealed in Him.[1] No doubt many people had to feel their way gradually to a recognition of the truth. It was not to be expected that all would change their convictions as suddenly as St. Paul at his conversion. Where the Jewish-Christian element was strong, it took time to get beyond the Messiahship of our Lord to His true rank in the Divine order. It was easier for men who came in from the Gentile world to grasp those distinctions in the Godhead, which later on were to become fixed by the formula of the Trinity.[2] The monotheism of the Jewish religion, with its sacred associations reaching back into the distant past and glorified by the brightest events in the history of the people, presented to some minds serious difficulty in the way of embracing the full Christian position.

The Greek had no such unifying and restraining influence to overcome. His past could furnish him with many an analogy which, if it did not help, would at any rate not hinder the acceptance of the full Christian faith. A few years after the close of the century, we have the letter of the younger Pliny, which incidentally and therefore the more forcibly assures us that, in his province of Bithynia, Christians met together to worship 'Christ as God.'[3] That which had been the belief of the leaders of the Church from the Day of Pentecost onward had passed into the creed of the common people.

As we see from the *Didache*, it had become the essential element of the baptismal rite.[4] This must have come about during the period which we are considering, if not earlier; for the *Didache*

[1] Cf. Gwatkin, *Early Church History to A.D. 313*, p. 279, 'The common life (of the Christians) rested not on the unity of God, nor even on His Fatherhood, but on faith in Christ as the Incarnate Son who died for men. This holds strictly for the first two centuries.'

[2] Theophilus of Antioch (*c.* A.D. 180) was the first Christian father, who used the formula, τῆς Τρίαδος. *Ad Autolyc.* ii. 15. We owe the Latin form to Tertullian about thirty years later.

[3] Plin. *Epistolae*, x. 96.

[4] *Didache*, vii.

was written about the close of the first century, and it describes what was a standing practice in the Church. We also find clear allusions to the belief in St. Clement of Rome [1] and in the Epistle of Barnabas.[2] But the writers are under the influence of the Old Testament as the authorized sanction and support of what they teach. The writings of Evangelists and Apostles had not yet taken their place as the formal exponents of Christianity. They were treated with the utmost respect,[3] but the time was not ripe for their admission to the rank assigned to the Old Testament.[4] Like the Apostles before them, the Apostolic Fathers employ the Old Testament as their Bible and read into it the Gospel story, before they bring out its meaning and apply it to the life and teaching of our Lord. So to speak, they christianize the Old Testament and then use it as a Christian handbook. In doing this they tread in the footsteps of our Lord Himself. He had shown by reference to Moses and all the Prophets that 'Christ ought to have suffered these things and to enter into His glory.' And on the Day of Pentecost, St. Peter declares that the doings of that marvellous day have already been foreseen by the prophets, whom his hearers regarded as men taught of God. Thus the Old Testament forms an introduction to the volume which, under the guidance of the

[1] *Ad Cor.* lviii. where the Three Persons are co-ordinated; *ζῇ γὰρ ὁ Θεὸς καὶ ζῇ ὁ Κύριος 'Ιησοῦς Χριστὸς καὶ τὸ πνεῦμα τὸ ἅγιον.* In the ancient homily which used to be called the Second Epistle of St. Clement, dated by Lightfoot c. A.D. 120–140, we have the remarkable saying, (1) *οὕτως δεῖ ἡμᾶς φρονεῖν περὶ 'Ιησοῦ Χριστοῦ ὡς περὶ Θεοῦ, ὡς περὶ κριτοῦ ζώντων καὶ νεκρῶν.* Such language presupposes a far earlier basis in thought. The allusion in Pliny's letter marks an intermediate step in tracing the idea back towards its origin.

[2] *Ep. of Barn.* xii. *"Ιδε πάλιν 'Ιησοῦς, οὐχὶ υἱὸς ἀνθρώπου ἀλλὰ υἱὸς τοῦ Θεοῦ, τύπῳ δὲ ἐν σαρκὶ φανερωθείς.* The date of the Epistle is *c.* A.D. 70–79 according to Lightfoot. Cf. c. vii. The writer does not express his belief in the Holy Spirit, although he quotes Is. lxi. 1, 2.

It is strange that Selwyn considers that the predominant use of the Old Testament in the Epistles of Clement and Barnabas illustrates the lingering of Judaistic errors within the Christian Church. *The Oracles in the N.T.* p. 426. The remarkable feature of the Epistle of Barnabas is the writer's strong opposition to Judaism and persistence in seeing Christ and the Gospel in every part of the Old Testament.

[3] Clem. Rom. xlvii. 1, 2.

[4] 'Great as the veneration for the Apostles was, there could not be the same feeling for new writings as for those which had long been hallowed.' Stanton in Hastings' *D.B.* iii. p. 530.

Holy Spirit, is beginning to take shape and to gather to itself the respect and authority accorded to the ancient Scriptures.

But we have also to take into account the reactionary element in the Church of this period. The fall of the Temple and the blow to the authority and prestige of the old religion, which accompanied it, had not put an end to the Judaizing spirit against which St. Paul had to strive so passionately. Until the appearance of the Fourth Gospel, the Church as a whole was in danger of relapse into a condition of faith and practice which would have ended in its becoming a mere Jewish sect. Our attention is called to this danger of apostasy by the Epistle to the Hebrews. Written when the Fall of Jerusalem was impending, the superiority of the Christian revelation to Judaism is emphasized. If we compare it with the Epistle of Barnabas, written a few years later, we see a difference of treatment, but the same solemn warning against clinging to the old religion, now that the perfect one has been made known.[1] How far the danger of reverting to the outworn faith lingered on in the Palestinian community, we have little means of judging, but just as the primitive Apostles and St. James the Lord's brother had, as Christians, continued to frequent the Temple, to observe its hours of prayer, to look with favour on circumcision, and generally to share in the religious practices of their fathers, so during the period from A.D. 70–100 there was a continual feeling of friendliness for the old system; and consequently a perpetual danger among the less instructed members of the Church, of a falling back from Christ to Moses, from the light of noonday to the twilight of the old Faith.

To this tendency within the Christian Church, the Fourth Gospel gave its death-blow. 'The Jews,' so often thus designated by the writer, appear as the persistent opponents of our Lord throughout His Ministry. The eschatology of the Gospel presents quite a different aspect from that of the Synoptics. The Messiah of the Jews is presented rather as the Saviour

[1] It is strange to find that both Epistles have been attributed to St. Barnabas. The contrast of their respective treatment of the Old Testament is so marked—Hebrews seeing in the Old Testament and the Law a discipline preparatory to the revelation of God in Christ; the Epistle of Barnabas seeing only a system misunderstood and perverted by the Jews. Their assignment to the same author is a literary curiosity.

of the world, the enlightening Reason, Who imparts whatever is best in the thought and life of mankind. There is no sign of that immediate return to Judgment which had been the constant expectation of the early Apostolic Church. Language of our Lord, in which He speaks of 'coming' to His disciples, is understood to refer to the gift of the Holy Spirit.

When He speaks of judgment, it is in one sense, that which was passed at the rejection of Himself and His message by the world. In another sense, it is reserved for the end—'the last day.' Even then, He will not need to judge. The words that He had spoken during His Ministry will suffice to condemn those who had rejected them.[1]

Thus the Fourth Gospel completed the release from the bondage of Judaism, which had been begun by St. Paul and continued by the author of the Epistle to the Hebrews. It brought Christianity out of the narrowing and reactionary groove in which the Palestinian community would have kept it. It presented the religion of Christ in a guise which made it possible for the new, progressive races of the world to accept it. If Judaic Christianity lingered still, it was left out of account. At home in the East, it failed to touch the West, and we may perhaps regard Mahommedanism as in some sort its legacy to after ages.

But the Judaistic elements of early Christianity achieved one great result before they passed out of the chief centres of the Church's life. They presented a barrier to the entrance of alien beliefs and practices. They helped to keep the central truths of Christianity pure in the great cities of the Empire, where rival creeds were contending for supremacy. The inheritance of faith in one God preserved for Christianity a safeguard against the false conceptions which, as we can easily understand, would be only too likely to attend the reception of the Divinity of Christ and the doctrine of the Spirit among men who had been accustomed to a multiplicity of deities. The stern monotheism of the Jewish Christians was thus a preservative against error at a critical time. In a certain sense, this influence lasted on through centuries and is not wholly extinct at the present day. It was well that the cradle of Christianity was Judaism; that it was nursed in the austere atmosphere of the Old Covenant,

[1] Jo. xii. 31, 47, 48. *v.* Bousset, *Kyrios Christos*, p. 188.

and not amid the hedonistic surroundings of Greek culture. To this fact we owe much of the lofty character of Christian ethics, the stern sense of duty which plays so large a part in the lives of good men, the puritanism in the best sense, which has marked the bearing and conduct of all the greatest Saints of every age of the Christian Church.

Indeed, it would be contrary to all historical analogy, if the religion of the Old Covenant, with its glorious past, its long line of prophets, lawgivers and priests, had become so merged in the religion of the new dispensation as to lose every trace of its former existence, and to part with every mark of its individuality. Temporary elements have gone: 'that which decayeth and waxeth old is ready to vanish away' said the writer of the Epistle to the Hebrews to men who lived in the very time of transition:[1] 'but the things which cannot be shaken remain'—the foundation truths and principles which lie at the heart of the new religion, and which it took over from the old. No one more strenuously opposed a return to Jewish externalism and to superseded beliefs and practices than St. Paul; but it was he who wrote of his people, 'to whom pertaineth the adoption and the glory and the covenants and the giving of the law and the service of God and the promises; whose are the fathers and of whom, as concerning the flesh, Christ came Who is over all, God blessed for ever.'[2]

When, therefore, the central place of our Lord in the Christianity of the close of the first century is considered, we have to remember that it was among Jews that this truth first obtained credence, and that it was by the persistence of the beliefs of the Old Covenant that it remained pure. The Catholic doctrine of the Holy Trinity has much for which to thank the old religion; for it was the monotheism of Judaism that kept the Christian Faith, as it came in contact with the exuberant mythology of the Graeco-Roman world, from losing its foundation doctrine—its one safeguard against polytheism and idolatry—the unity of the Godhead.[3]

[1] Hebr. viii. 13.

[2] Rom. ix. 4, 5.

[3] Wernle takes a similar view. 'Exclusiveness and intolerance were peculiar to Jewish monotheism. This was fortunate for the new religion, which was thus preserved from disappearing in the general confusion of religions.' *D. Anfänge unserer Religion*, p. 346.

The passing of the recognition of a third element of the Godhead into that belief in the Holy Ghost, which had become a fixed doctrine of the Church by the time the Fourth Gospel was written, is another characteristic of the closing years of the first century. In the Acts,[1] we meet with 'certain disciples' who had never heard His Name. They had to be taught about Him, before they could receive Christian Baptism and be made disciples in the full sense of the term. We have seen in what various ways the Spirit manifested His presence in the Church. Our Lord had promised that He should abide with His people for ever. But there was no promise that the visible signs of His presence were to continue. As in the case of the Resurrection, there was a blessing for those who, having not seen have believed. The life-giving presence of the Holy Spirit was soon to be apprehended by a faith unaided by outward demonstration and apart from striking visible effects. For the special gifts that at first accompanied Him soon began to cease. They were no necessary part of the Divine gift. So late as Irenaeus, we read of men 'speaking in all kinds of tongues,' [2] and of men who had the gift of prophecy. Irenaeus says that 'we hear of them.' The gifts are no longer generally diffused in the Church as they appear to have been at first. It was only here and there that men so gifted were to be found.[3]

There is no doubt that these spiritual gifts were a snare to some. St. Paul, in writing to the Corinthians, speaks warningly of their use. He has 'a more excellent way' to show them. When he enumerates 'the fruits of the Spirit,' he names not *χαρίσματα*, which arrest the attention and, if abused, minister to pride, but solid graces of character, such as found their chief exponent in the life of Christ.[4]

[1] xix. 1. [2] *Adv. Haeres.* v. 6, § 1. c. A.D. 185.

[3] But in *Adv. Haeres.* ii. 32, § 4, Irenaeus speaks of prophetic gifts, of healings of sickness and even of raising of the dead as taking place—indeed of χαρίσματα being daily exercised. It is to be noticed that Justin Martyr, writing thirty years earlier, speaks of prophetic gifts (προφητικὰ χαρίσματα) existing among Christians (there had been no Jewish prophet after John the Baptist, *Dial. c. Tryph.* xlix.), but he makes no mention of the various other χαρίσματα, of which the later writer speaks. *Dial. c. Tryph.* lxxxii. The statement of Irenaeus seems to be more rhetorical than precise and exact.

[4] Gal. v. 22. Gunkel, speaking of the danger to the Church in the presence of men whose spiritual gifts were not always to be controlled, remarks that what saved the Church was the influence of the historic Jesus preserving for

It may be questioned whether belief in the Holy Ghost as the Third Person of the Godhead, although a fixed possession of the Church by the close of the first century, was intelligently grasped by the people at large. Indeed, in every age of the Church there has been too much disposition to regard the Holy Spirit as a mere influence proceeding from God, as a form of His working, rather than as one of the Persons of the Godhead. Yet the authoritative voice of the Church, as expressed by its leaders, and as it spoke in the baptismal formula, proclaimed the complete and distinct Personality of the Holy Spirit, coordinating Him with the Father and the Son.

It is accordingly a leading characteristic of the period that men believed themselves to be under the direct rule of the Holy Ghost. The risen and ascended Lord had fulfilled His parting promise. The Church was 'endued with power from on high.' Descending from heaven, the Spirit moved everywhere. His presence was universal and all-pervading. Only hardness and obstinacy shut Him out. From the Day of Pentecost onwards, this was recognized; and the effect was marvellous. A favourite explanation of the glow and the animation which filled the veins of the early Church and quickened the life of thousands, is enthusiasm.[1] But it fails to account for the circumstances. The loss from sight and companionship of the leader of a great movement is not usually regarded as productive of a special wave of power, a sudden access of new life among those who are left behind. The temperament and attitude, the conduct and the words of the community sufficiently show the futility of such an explanation. There was no ostensible ground for enthusiasm in themselves, or in the circumstances in which they were placed at their Lord's departure. But the enthusiasm was there; the life was abundant and overflowing; the results were marvellous and known to thousands who were living when the Book of Acts was written. The only explanation which accords with the facts is that which is given, 'Jesus . . . hath shed forth this, which ye now see and hear.'[2]

When we turn from the belief of Christians of the closing

the Church its historical character. *D. Wirkungen des Heiligen Geistes*, p. 56. Cf. above, p. 412.

[1] Cf. p. 397. [2] Acts ii. 33.

years of the first century to its expression in their worship and their life, we find that certain rites have taken forms which, however modified to suit the requirements of other times, have never lost their essential elements. Baptism and the Eucharist are fully established. They are believed to emanate from the direct institution of Christ Himself; and their ministration has become a fixed and ordered means of imparting the grace and virtue of the redemption won for man by the Sacrifice of the Cross. As yet the rite is in each case very simple. It contains the fewest possible ceremonial acts. But those acts are vital to the being of the Sacrament. They cannot be dispensed with. They last on into the time when they become surrounded with ceremony and ritual; and they are still the essence of what is done, the root and kernel of the whole matter. Every man becomes a Christian through baptism into the Name of Father, Son and Holy Ghost—the Water and the Word; the cleansing stream regenerating the whole nature; the self-surrender to God implied in the invocation of the Three-fold Name.[1] However simple and brief the rite, every essential element is already there. There is no other way of entrance upon the privileges and responsibilities of the Christian life than the 'one baptism for the remission of sins.' All that is needed is in the possession and use of the Church of this early time. The allusions to it in contemporary writings and in writings which testify to a long settled custom are abundant, and suffice to show what was the common belief and practice of the Church of the closing Apostolic age.

No less clear are the indications of the universal prevalence of the Eucharist during this period. Here again the ceremonial rite is of the simplest, but it contains the whole permanent element of the Sacrament. No addition of ritual, no

[1] On the question of Baptism in the name of Jesus Christ and Baptism in the name of the Holy Trinity, *v.* p. 468 f. The allusions in the *Didache* (c. vii.), point to a custom already well established. It is taken for granted that it is universally practised. Strong proof is thereby afforded to the genuineness of Matt. xxviii. 19 as a saying of the Risen Lord. 'Some look on the mention of the Trinity (as in Justin Martyr, *Apol.* i. 61 and in the *Didache*) as a development: but there is no need to understand baptism "into Christ" as implying an earlier formula of baptism into Christ only, and therefore no reason to doubt that the baptismal formula of Matt. xxviii. 19 is a genuine saying of the Lord, or that it was regularly used from the first.' Gwatkin, *Early History of the Church to* A.D. *313*, i. p. 248.

development of doctrinal meaning, has changed that element.[1] In 'the breaking of the bread,' for which the first disciples met together after their Lord's Resurrection, was contained the whole Sacrament which the Catholic Church receives and holds to-day. For the term covers more than it expresses.[2]

The writer to whom we owe an early account both of the institution and of the meaning of the Eucharist, took a large share in its ordering and development. St. Paul found it a regular meal to which those who were able brought their contributions. 1 Cor. xvi. 2, compared with such passages as Acts xx. 7, points to a weekly keeping of the Feast.[3] There was as yet no presiding minister, such as we meet with in Justin Martyr's account of it.[4] So near in time and memory was the Last Supper, that no one had taken upon himself to assume the position of the Great Consecrator.[5] It was essentially a common meal.

Like all such common meals it was open to abuse and perversion. It was possible to mistake its true end and purpose. In the Church at Corinth, the social element of the Feast had

[1] As Heitmüller says, 'The rites remain ; the views of their meaning change.' *Taufe und Abendmahl im Urchristentum*, p. 65.

[2] As baptism in the name of the Lord Jesus was the typical, distinctive term for what was in reality baptism in the name of the Father, Son and Holy Ghost, so 'the breaking of the bread,' as we gather from what passed at the Last Supper and from the reflected light of such an account as that of Justin Martyr (*Apol.* i. 66) upon earlier practice, was a brief summary of a larger connotation. It included the cup. The pouring out of the Saviour's blood was the consequence of the wounding (breaking) of His body, and the one involved the other. 'Since the recollection lingered chiefly round the act of the breaking of the bread (at the Last Supper), the meal seems to have received the name "The Breaking of the Bread."' Heitmüller, *Taufe und Abendmahl im Urchristentum*, p. 62. *v.* above, p. 422.

[3] Since the above was written, I find that Mr. C. H. Turner says: 'The weekly Eucharist was both primitive and universal. The custom of daily Eucharists was neither universal nor perhaps earlier than the third century.' *Cambridge Mediaeval History*, i. p. 158.

[4] It is, of course, quite unhistorical to say that 'From the earliest times a valid Eucharist meant the presence of a priest.' *v.* W. E. Barnes in *Quarterly Review*, July 1914 ; Robertson and Plummer, 1 *Ep. to Cor.* p. 313.

[5] Heitmüller ingeniously argues from the language of St. Paul, where he tells the Corinthians of the words spoken by our Lord at the Institution, that as yet there was no fixed formula employed in consecration. Had there been one in common use, St. Paul would not have reported the words thus for[illegible]lly. He would simply have reminded the Corinthians of them. *Taufe u.* [illegible]*mahl im Urchristentum*, p. 44.

so far gained the upper hand that the element of worship had sunk into the background. Revelry, pride and self-glorification were asserting themselves. Men came together as to a club feast. They forgot that it was 'the Lord's Supper,' and they needed to be reminded of the circumstances under which it was instituted. St. Paul was content to rebuke them in more or less general terms in his letter. The details he reserved for the visit which he was looking forward to pay them.[1] How he 'set the rest in order,' we do not know; but we may be sure that what he laid down as essential for the due administration of the Lord's Supper in the Church of Corinth quickly became a law to the Pauline communities generally, and did much to fix for the closing years of the first century the mode of its observance in the Church at large.

A regulation laid upon his converts by the Apostle was, if we may judge from later usage, the appointment of one to preside over the common meal. This seems to have arisen in the first instance from a desire for due order and solemnity in administration of the Eucharist. The authority of a man respected by every one would ensure that seemliness which had been so wanting in the Church of Corinth. We have no means of determining the precise character or rank of the president. At first an Apostle, if present, or an elder; towards the close of the century, as the Episcopal office begins to emerge from the ranks of the elders, a bishop would naturally preside. As the beginnings of liturgical service appeared, the presiding elder became the mouthpiece and representative of the gathering, in whatever prayers or praises were used to give expression to the common worship of the Church in the Sacred Feast. Ignatius regards the validity of the Eucharist as secured by the presence of [illegible] Bi[illegible][2] or his deputy.

As the first [illegible] closing, the Eucharist has attained the character [illegible]nt, rather than a feast of good fellowship. The n[illegible]n is heard. It has become an act of remembranc[illegible] death of Christ, as the 'one sacrifice for sins,'[3] [illegible] God; while its celebration on the Lord's Da[illegible] close connection with the Resurrection of Ch[illegible] hope which it gave that those, who [illegible]ined to Christ, would share in all

[illegible]ially [illegible] bend- [illegible]d *Smyrn.* viii. [3] Hebr. x. 12.

the benefits of His death and in His triumph over the grave. It was just at this time that the last surviving Apostle was recording in his Gospel our Lord's own assurance—'Whoso eateth My Flesh and drinketh My Blood hath eternal life and I will raise him up at the last day.'[1] We may be sure that the teaching of Christ, which was then being brought to the knowledge of the Church out of the inspired remembrance of the aged Apostle, powerfully affected the general conception of the Lord's Supper and raised it to a higher place in the reverence and observance of the Church.

Closely connected with the Sacraments is the question of the origin of liturgical forms of prayer and worship. Is there any trace of them to be found during the closing years of the first century? At the root of all Liturgies, defining and limiting their scope and object, lay the Lord's Prayer. The baptismal confession formed the kernel of the Creeds. The words of institution were drawn out into the Divine Office. There, roughly speaking, we have the original elements of the liturgical worship of the Church. During the period which we are considering, these early rudiments of prayer and confession received little accretion. Their bulk was hardly increased. The need for fuller and more detailed forms of worship was scarcely felt. Men had the substance of their religion already contained within these brief formulae. It was when erroneous teaching had begun to make itself felt, that formal creeds came into being; when the new thoughts of God, that had been created by Christianity, were more fully realized, that a more copious expression of devotion and worship was required. And this state of things lies beyond the limits of our inquiry.

But along with the distinctively Christian elements of liturgical worship, place must be allowed for what Jewish Christianity took over from Judaism. Hours of Prayer—stated times of private devotion—were familiar to all devout Jews;[2] while the ordinary Jewish grace, used still by Christians with the recollection of the Lord's Supper, made every family meal an Eucharist.[3]

[1] Jo. vi. 54. [2] *v.* above, p. 425.

[3] For the Jewish grace, *v. The Jewish Encycl.* art. 'Grace at Meals.' Cf. Lk. xxiv. 30; 1 Cor. x. 31. In Clem. Rom. lix. is a prayer largely modelled on Old Testament thought and language. Cf. the Jewish evening prayer, Taylor, *Pirqe Aboth*, p. 177.

It was only natural that, as the Bible of the Jewish Church was taken over by the Church of Christ, liturgical forms and private prayers should also be adopted.

The beginning of the Church's Liturgies can be traced here and there in the New Testament.[1] At the time of which we are writing, the Church, while possessing the Lord's Prayer and its inheritance of devotional forms which had been current in the Temple and in the Synagogues, had been gradually feeling the necessity of a more definite expression of its devotion and belief. It was during these years that the doxology was added to the Lord's Prayer. Here and there the rudiments of a fixed creed are noticeable.[2] A fuller conception of the Nature of the Godhead required a corresponding richness of liturgical expression. When the Personality of Christ became better understood and His place within the Divine Life more adequately realized, modification of long accustomed formulae was needed. As the Pauline teaching of life in Christ was being gradually appropriated through the ever widening circulation of his Epistles, worship directed to God was felt to be wanting, if the Saviour's Name had no place in it. There is no doubt that the decisive step, which this inclusion signified, was occasioned and sanctioned by recollection of the language of our Lord's own parting command and by the early incorporation of the idea into the baptismal rite.[3] But apart from this, the increasing recognition of the Divine Personality of Christ was the chief cause of the later liturgical enrichment and expansion.

In this broadening, or rather defining, of the object of worship, the Person of our Lord was no doubt the first to be considered: but we have no reason to think that the claim of the Holy Spirit to receive the adoration due to God alone would long be resisted. Not only the inclusion of His Name in Christ's last command, but the momentous occurrences of the Day of Pentecost pointed to His significance. If the Personality of Christ was more apparent at this stage of the evolution of Christian doctrine than the Personality of the Spirit, this is only what we should expect. The Incarnate Son had manifested His right to be considered as standing clear and distinct in the truth of His own being, within the circle of the Godhead. There had

[1] For the origin of Christian prayer, cf. p. 424 f.

[2] Rom. x. 9; 1 Tim. iii. 16.

[3] Matt. xxviii. 18 f.

been no such continued manifestation of the Divine nature and being of the Holy Spirit. Only at times, passing among men like the viewless breath of the summer breeze, or taking for an instant the form of a dove, or again, flashing in sudden gleam as of fire upon the head of an Apostle, One Who seemed but a form of Divine working—which, while always in harmony and union with the will of God, was yet distinct in His operation from the Father and the Son—did occasionally manifest His personal existence, and according to teaching which was becoming known in the Church, could only be rightly named as God the Holy Ghost.

Can we substantiate this view by reference to statements which show how thought was tending during these years? We should expect to find them, if they exist, under the form of creed, or of prayer. First in order and by way of summing up what has gone before, let us take what bears on the position of Christ and His place in Christian thought.

There is little doubt that the admission or confession that Jesus is the Messiah and the Son of God formed the immediate preliminary to the act of Baptism.[1] The naming of Christ by the baptizer or the baptized, or both, was an integral part of the rite, and it formed the germ from which sprang in time the fully developed creed of the Christian Church. A further step in the process is indicated by the two conditions which St. Paul lays down for assurance of salvation—confession that Jesus is Lord and belief in His Resurrection.[2] This is perhaps the earliest form of a creed, in the full sense, that has come down to us. It contains the two great Christian verities—that Jesus is Divine and that He rose from the dead.

In the Pastoral Epistles we have a more detailed summary of the faith of Christians.[3] The reality of the Incarnation, its manifestation here on earth, the witness borne to it by (*a*) the Holy Spirit, (*b*) the angels, (*c*) believers, the transference of the Incarnate Life to heaven; all these 'mysteries of piety' are celebrated.[4]

[1] Acts viii. 37 is a witness to the practice. Cf. Acts x. 48.

[2] Rom. x. 9.

[3] 1 Tim. iii. 16. 'A fragment of an early Church song, in which the community expressed its confession to Christ.' B. Weiss, *Bibl. Theologie des N.T.* p. 458.

[4] The mention of the actual manifestation (Epiphany) of the Incarnate Saviour perhaps shows the existence of an incipient form of docetism in the

By the time that St. Clement of Rome wrote his Epistle to the Corinthians in the closing years of the century, the place of our Lord in the faith and adoration of the Church had become fully established. 'Let us fear the Lord Jesus, whose blood was given for us.' 'To Him be the glory and the majesty for ever and ever.' He is the channel through which grace and peace come from Almighty God. He is 'our Salvation.'[1] In one remarkable passage the writer co-ordinates the life of the Father, of the Lord Jesus Christ and of the Holy Spirit in a manner which looks back, through the influence of such passages as 2 Cor. xiii. 13, to our Lord's parting words.[2]

Along with this witness to early doctrine, we may place the language of the *Didache,* which bears its independent testimony to the Divine honour paid to the Son and to the Holy Spirit during the period under consideration.[3]

The conclusion to be drawn from these passages is irresistible. As the first century was closing, the worship of Christ as God, the confession of Him as Saviour and Redeemer, the reality of His Incarnate life as the manifestation of God, were already in the full possession of the Church, and were finding expression in set forms of prayer, in symbolic rites, in professions of faith and in sacraments.

What is true of the early recognition of the place of our Lord in the Christian religion is, to a somewhat less extent, true of the reception of the Holy Spirit as an object of faith and worship. We have seen the reason of a more hesitating acceptance of His position in the Godhead; and incidents, such as those related in the Acts,[4] show that it was only by degrees that He came to be generally worshipped as a Person of the Trinity, and that His function in the Divine ordering of the universe, as well as His part in the salvation of man, were recognized by the Church at large.

The passages which co-ordinate the Holy Spirit with the Father and the Son form the starting point for the study of

period in which the hymn was composed. By the time that 1 John was written, the danger had become fully developed. The spirit of the Anti-Christ was identified with the denial that Christ had appeared in the flesh. 1 Jo. iv. 3.

[1] Clem. Rom. *ad Cor.* xxi.; xx.; xxxvi.

[2] *Ib.* lviii.; Matt. xxviii. 19.

[3] *Didache,* vii.

[4] xviii. 25; xix. 2.

the gradual acceptance of His Divine Being. It is a question whether baptism was at first regarded as imparting the Holy Spirit. St. Paul's teaching on the nature of the life in Christ was probably the groundwork of the conception that baptism carried with it the gift of the Spirit.[1] Certainly from the time of the Apostle onwards, the ordinary Christian was held, in virtue of his baptism into Christ, to be a temple of the Holy Ghost; and to seal and confirm this view came the record of our Lord's discourse with Nicodemus,[2] which for ever made it certain that the work of the Holy Spirit was closely bound up with baptism, and that it ordinarily produced regeneration into a new life in those who received it.

How far the work of Christ was distinguished from that of the Holy Spirit during this period, it is not easy to say. The Holy Spirit is frequently spoken of as the Spirit of Christ and in one place at least, He seems to be identified with our Lord,[3] so close is the connection between Them and so intimate Their relationship in effecting the redemption and sanctification of man. It was perhaps this closeness of connection which, for a time, prevented the clearness of discrimination that was required for the expression of worship directed to the Holy Spirit. At any rate, there is not the same decisive evidence for it as for the worship of Christ.[4] It is only to be expected that the custom of praying to God through the mediation of the Son would cause the worship of the Father and the Son to be more conspicuous a feature of the liturgical practice of this period than the worship of God the Holy Ghost. But this is far from saying that at the close of the Apostolic age, the true position and significance of the Holy Spirit had not been realized. The evidence is quite to the contrary. Not to speak of the great place which the Spirit occupies in the Fourth Gospel, we find St. Clement of Rome saying in reference to Isaiah li., 'the Holy Spirit spake concerning Him (Christ),' implying pre-existence.[5] And he

[1] *v.* Heitmüller, *Taufe u. Abendmahl*, p. 21.

[2] Jo. iii.

[3] 2 Cor. iii. 17, 'The Lord is that Spirit.'

[4] In the *Didache*, besides the allusion to baptism in the threefold Name, which shows how early the practice came about, there is an allusion to our Lord's saying as to the sin against the Holy Ghost (c. xi.); with one or two curious statements about 'speaking in the Spirit' and 'ordering a table in the Spirit' (c. xi.).

[5] *Ad Corinth.* xvi. 2. Cf. *ib.* xiii. 1.

speaks of 'an abundant outpouring of the Holy Spirit' as of One Who had been from of old.[1]

The use of the Temple—while it stood—and of Synagogues by the Jewish-Christian communities must not be lost sight of, in forming an estimate of the growth of liturgical worship in the Church at large. When St. Paul and St. Barnabas were at Antioch in Pisidia, about fifteen years after the conversion of the former, they 'went into the Synagogue on the Sabbath day and sat down.' They took part in the service and after the reading of the law and the prophets in the ordinary course, the rulers of the Synagogue sent one of the ministers to them, as men likely to have some special 'word of exhortation for the people.' St. Paul was always ready to avail himself of any opportunity of preaching the Gospel, especially when circumstances of place or occasion supplied a striking background and setting for his message. So now he was glad to be able to show how the Scriptures, which they had just been reading, had found their fulfilment in Jesus of Nazareth.

From this custom of the reading of the Old Testament and the following word of exhortation we may trace the origin of the lessons and the homily, which in time became part of the services of the Lord's Day in the Christian Church, and formed the narrative and descriptive setting for the worship, giving it its rationale and tending to keep it within the limits prescribed by accepted doctrine and teaching.

We have therefore to regard these years as witnessing the assembling of materials, historical, formal, spiritual and doctrinal, which during the following century came to build up the liturgies that arose in the great Churches of East and West, in Antioch and Alexandria, in Rome and Lyons.

The principle of fixed forms, to express and embody the universal elements of Christian worship, was not so rigid as to exclude varieties corresponding with differences of circumstance and temperament, among widely differing communities. But it gradually came to be recognized that the needs of order and of edification could both be met by the use of settled forms of worship; not to constrain and hamper the free play of feeling and devotion, but to ensure the sympathy and co-operation, as in a common act, of all the worshippers.

[1] *Ib.* ii.

As much of early Christian common worship was suggested by that of the Temple and the Synagogue, so was the form which its expression took. Already in 1 Cor. xiv., St. Paul speaks of singing as a mode of worship in the Church. Later he urges the use of 'Psalms and Hymns and spiritual Songs';[1] while we have the assurance of Pliny that 'early on a fixed day, Christians were accustomed to meet together and sing a hymn to Christ as God antiphonally' (*secum invicem*). This is what Christians themselves told him that they were in the habit of doing in Pontus and Bithynia.[2] The custom would be of still earlier origin in the Churches of the large cities. This adaptation of music to the worship of the Church was doubtless taken over from the worship of the Temple. Besides the Psalms, which formed the hymn book of the Jewish Church, there is reason for thinking that more distinctively doctrinal songs of adoration were early used in the Christian assemblies.[3]

Along with the worship of the community is to be placed the reading of the Scriptures. We have seen that the Church at once stepped as by right into the inheritance of the Old Testament, and that even the New Testament itself bears traces of the acceptance of certain of its writings as possessing an authority corresponding to that of the Old Testament.[4] As yet there is nothing in the way of a Canon of the New Testament. Only, a peculiar sanctity and weight was thought to be attached to writings of Apostles and of Apostolic men.[5] Any writing which was believed to report sayings of our Lord would at once be regarded as entitled to respect. We know from the preface to St. Luke's Gospel that many writings of a Gospel character were floating about in the Christian communities at about the middle of the first century; and as the Epistles of St. Paul became known to proceed from him and to bear all the authority of the most influential of the Apostles, they too would win a place for themselves in the estimation of the Church.

But as yet there is no hint of any attempt to gather sacred writings together into a 'New Testament,' which should correspond, in the Christian Church, to the Old Testament of the

[1] 1 Cor. xiv. 15; Col. iii. 16; Eph. v. 19.
[2] Plin. *Ep.* x. 96.
[3] *E.g.* 1 Tim. iii. 16.
[4] *v.* above, p. 455.
[5] *v.* Harnack, *Dogmengeschichte*, i. p. 110.

Jewish Church. That task belonged to the future. Only it is to be remarked that the judgment of separate communities, which was already discriminating between writings that bore the marks of having been given by the Holy Spirit and those which bore no such signs of inspiration, was singularly upheld by the consentient verdict of later times. The New Testament Canon is so far anticipated by the fact that prominent writers of the beginning of the second century possess and value the chief books of that Canon, such as the Gospels, certain Epistles of St. Paul, the Apocalypse and the First Epistles of St. Peter and St. John.[1]

The process of discrimination, by which books of supreme and lasting value were gradually separated from those of temporary or minor importance, lies within the next century. It was distinctly a work of the Church, whose collective judgment formed by the contributory estimates of separate communities, was felt to be guided by the Holy Spirit.

Another feature of the closing years of the century is the passing away of a ministry of general authority and the rise of an order of local and defined administration. Apostles, Prophets, Teachers belonged to the Church at large.[2] Their commission was world-wide, unfettered by limits of place or country. They had been sent to preach the Gospel, to make disciples of all nations. Their authority was recognized everywhere.

But, as the Church began to take the form of separate communities gathered in their own cities and towns, with their own needs of sacrament and worship, there arose the want of a more fixed and settled ministry. The Apostolic office probably came to an end in the person of St. John the Divine. The last of the eyewitnesses of Christ passed away. Prophets too and Teachers, as the glow of enthusiasm kindled

[1] For instance, Papias, who wrote about A.D. 100, possesses the Gospels. Ignatius, in the early years of the second century, is acquainted with the Book of Acts (*Ep. ad Magn.* v.), so is his contemporary Polycarp (*Ep. of Polyc.* i.), who also quotes 1 Pet. (*ib.* i.) and 1 Jo. (*ib.* vii.). Cf. Wernle, *D. Anfänge*, pp. 435, 6.

[2] 'The Apostles and Prophets meet us in the earliest age as the two supreme orders of the Christian ministry. Together with the Teachers they form the great triad of the First Epistle to the Corinthians. . . . After the beginning of the second century, the two orders disappear.' Turner, *Studies in Early Ch. Hist.* pp. 15, 16.

by the outpouring of the Spirit began to abate with the process of time, seem to have ceased to exercise peculiar gifts of teaching and foresight. The Faith had been delivered to the Saints. It was for the Church to cherish, to uphold it and to live its life.

Extraordinary gifts and special endowments, necessary as they had been in the first years of the new religion, were giving place to the ordinary offices which satisfied the requirements of a more settled Church life. With this change was witnessed the birth of ecclesiasticism, and all that it entailed.

What view should we take of this transition from the creative period of Christianity to that of its imitative activity?[1] Are we to regard it as but another instance of the decay and degeneration which, in this world, so often follow upon the inauguration of a new movement for good? Are we living in a time of less grace? Do we stand at a disadvantage, as we compare our spiritual outfit and our opportunities with those enjoyed by the men of the first century? Was the age of miracle, when God visibly manifested His power, a golden age to be looked back upon with yearning regret?

These questions seem at first sight to compel an affirmative answer. We appear to stand on a lower plane. At times it is as if God had 'forgotten to be gracious.' There is not the same sense of His nearness. Loss of His presence, if loss there be, must bring with it a corresponding loss of power and hope. But a moment's reflection will convince us that neither a simple affirmative nor negative can meet the situation. There were both loss and gain. Loss, certainly, in the departure of Apostolic men, who from their historic intercourse with our Lord and their plenary endowment of His Spirit, were in a position to strengthen, enlighten and guide the Church, as it emerged from the experiences of the first age and entered, somewhat solitary as it might seem, on its course through the centuries. Loss, too, in the inevitable reaction from the fervid and exalted state of men who were manifestly impelled and inspired by the Holy Spirit. Loss, again, in the exchange of quickening movements of early zeal for the more humdrum duties of ordered daily life. Human nature cannot maintain an abnormally high level of excellence for an indefinite period. There are bound to be moments of recoil. And this is especially the case when a large

[1] Cf. above, p. 572.

mixed body of people is in question. Time and again, old habits and trains of thought assert themselves, and there is a constant tendency to lower the standard of spiritual endeavour, in conformity with the insistent pressure of the surrounding world.[1]

The early Church did not escape these dangers. They were hardly perceptible in the period of which we speak. But their beginnings were there, and very soon they developed into movements of thought quite foreign to the mind of Christ and His first followers. Thus, the roots of the heresies, which were so soon to trouble Christendom, are already to be traced in controversial passages of the later Epistles of St. Paul and in the Epistles of St. John. In the personal ambition of Diotrephes, we can already detect the love of power and the worldly aims which have so often marred the healthy exercise of the episcopal office.[2] Thus, within the period of the composition of the New Testament and in the lifetime of an Apostle, one of the worst evils of ecclesiasticism has made its appearance. The ministry has become an opportunity of self-aggrandisement. The spirit of Him Who said 'I am among you as he that serveth' is already being forgotten. In all this there is loss.

Did the lapse of time and the necessary change in points of view bring no gain? Is the march of history only a continuous record of decline? Is the golden age wholly in the past? Are no gleams of dawn to be seen in the Eastern sky? To say so would be to lose sight of the general providence of God, of the power of the exalted Christ and the promised guidance of His Spirit. It would mean that God had failed, and His purpose been made of none effect.

But against the incipient signs of decay and loss there is to be set the rapid spread of the Gospel in the provinces of the Empire and in Rome itself. There was thus afforded a positive proof of the presence of the Holy Spirit and of the attractive power of the Cross. As St. Paul had long ago written,[3] 'whether in pretence or in truth Christ is preached.' And wherever he was preached He won His victories, and multitudes pressed into His Kingdom. Then, along with the accession

[1] *v.* Wernle, *D. Anfänge uns. Religion*, p. 481.

[2] 3 Jo. 9. On the bearing of this passage upon the rise of the monarchical episcopate, *v.* Salmon, *Introduction to the N.T.* p. 284.

[3] Phil. i. 18.

of new converts from every known race and nation, came the accumulation of varied religious experiences, confirming the reality of the great historic past and proving that it was not mere enthusiasm, but the power of God, which was moving among men. This became more apparent, as Christianity was brought more and more into rivalry and comparison with the other religions which were competing for the allegiance of the Roman world. But it was already evident as the first century was closing.

Perhaps it may be said that, if Christianity lost in the intensity of its life, it gained in diffusion and in adaptability to new conditions; if it lost in fervour, it gained in soberness and strength. The irregular and emotional outbursts of spiritual ecstasy, which played so great a part at Corinth, were gradually ceasing to take the first place in men's estimation of the meaning of Christianity.

The disturbing influence on life, which the immediate expectation of the end of the age and the return of the Messiah had had on the first and second generations of disciples, was succeeded by patient performance of daily duty, and by a return to calm and even continuance in well-doing. It was gradually realized, through the teaching of St. Paul, and still more through acquaintance with the Fourth Gospel, that our Lord's teaching on the subject of His return had been interpreted too strictly and literally as a question of time, and that time wholly in the future. Whereas, to the believer, every great dispensation is a separate coming, and every event in life a sentence of acquittal or of condemnation, according as we use or abuse it. Thus, feverish and excited expectation gave place to the calm assurance of a certain hope to be fulfilled in God's own time.

To this extent then there was gain, as those who had direct contact with the historic origin of the Faith were succeeded by men who were in a position to claim the last Beatitude of the Saviour, because they had 'not seen and yet have believed.' [1] For all we know, there is a greater blessedness than they enjoyed, who walked with Christ on earth, in the faith and devotion of those who can say of Him, 'Whom having not seen we love.' [2]

[1] Jo. xx. 29. [2] 1 Pet. i. 8.

CONCLUSION

In the preceding pages we have traced in outline the rise and early fortunes of the religion of Christ. With the conviction that its own historic documents form the most trustworthy guide to what took place, we made a brief examination of the Sources that lie before us in the writings of the New Testament, endeavouring to estimate their value as evidence of what actually occurred. While profoundly convinced that in the Christian religion a new and revolutionary force broke upon the world, it was felt that, as a movement, it could only be understood when studied in close connection with the thought and life of the ages which preceded it. For, if new and unique in character, it was no isolated phenomenon, separate from all that had gone before and out of touch with the general movements of contemporary thought and life. It is the peculiar glory of the religion of Jesus Christ that it meets and can satisfy every lawful aspiration of humanity; while it embodies and confirms every most characteristic truth that has been arrived at by the human mind. In a certain sense I can say Christianus 'sum: humani nihil à me alienum puto.'[1] Everything that belongs to the true worth and dignity of man finds its complete exponent in the Person of Christ. In Him met the converging lines of all that was best in the life and thought of the ancient world. From Him—the pure source and fountain of all goodness—flow the streams that make glad the City of God, that fertilize the fields which whiten to the harvest of His coming Kingdom. If He has fulfilled the longings of the Old world, His life and example have set the norm for the thought and action of the New. Standing historically in the centre of the ages, He rules and judges the present and the past. His Cross and

[1] Ter. *Heaut.* i. 1. 24.

Open Grave have for ever set the standard by which all values must henceforth be estimated. The seat of judgment is His by right, 'because he is the Son of Man.' [1]

Such we believe to be the conclusion forced upon us by a fair and unbiassed study of the New Testament documents—a conclusion supported by the experience of the Christian ages: and it carries with it the conviction that He, Who could stand thus in world-history, must be as unique in His Person as in His Life and its results.

Coming from heaven to earth, from the Throne to the Manger and the Cross, He found a family, a home, a country prepared for Him. With that preparation He entered upon the inheritance of a long historic past and, mingling with His contemporaries, He shared to an extent their interests and their thoughts.

But it is also true that His entrance into the world constituted an epoch and meant a new departure. The Incarnation was the coming of the Divine and the Eternal into the conditions of earth and time. The man Christ Jesus was not the product of the ages which preceded His coming, although the completeness of His humanity bore witness to His share in their effects. If He lived on earth as the child of Mary, His Personality was that of God the Son. To bear this in mind, is, we believe, to remain open to the impression which truth and fact combine to convey.

This double character of its Founder is reflected in His religion. It is in the world, as He was in the world; but, like Him, it is not of the world. It is not the mere outcome of earlier ages of religious evolution. Its essential principle is from above. There was nothing in the religion or philosophy of the past capable of producing it. In its inner being it came down from heaven. It was 'born from above.' [2] And what is true of the religion itself is true of every faithful adherent. 'If any man be in Christ, he is a new creation.' [3]

But like Christ, the Christian Faith came to live and operate in the world for the world's sake. Its history is therefore largely intermixed with mundane things. If it were not so, there could be no history to record. A religion wholly spiritual, quietistic, mystical, would be without incident. There would be nothing to furnish material for narrative. It is of the principle of the

[1] Jo. v. 27. [2] Jo. iii. 7. [3] 2 Cor. v. 17.

Incarnation that the Divine life both in Christ and in His Church is manifested in form and symbol. It acts and reacts upon what may be seen and touched. This interaction forms a large part of the material of history. It is the course of the Kingdom of God through the world that forms the annals of the Christian Church; and the earliest stages of its career have come before us in the preceding pages.

As a living organism, endowed with the presence of its risen Head and instinct with His Spirit, the Church of Christ moves and grows along with the movement and development of life and thought. It is always open to receive new light. It has no repugnance to ascertained fact. It has no conflict with knowledge. It does not hesitate to revise its methods where they are shown to be outworn, to correct its dogmatic statements, if they are proved to be irreconcilable with truth and fact.[1]

But, as planted in the world by Christ and established by His Apostolic witnesses, the Church is ever looking back to its first age for the unchangeable matter of its belief and practice. There may be religious life where there is no hold on the Incarnation and the Resurrection; but unless we turn our backs upon all that its greatest exponents have ever taught, *it is not the religion of Jesus Christ.*

To interpret ancient modes of speech in terms of modern thought, to adapt a definition which had ceased to define, in such a way that it may still achieve its purpose, is the task of the living, Spirit-bearing Church from age to age. But this task can only be carried out in loyalty and honour, when the interpretation and the definition are true to the fixed and unalterable substance of 'the Faith which was once for all delivered unto the Saints.'

It was to show how that sacred deposit was formed and illustrated in the life of the first century of Christendom, that these pages have been written. Only by constant recourse to 'the mind of Christ,' as revealed in His own Life and Teaching and as reflected in the witness of His Disciples, can we form any true representation of the Rise of our Religion.

[1] 'In an age of movement and discovery such as our own, it is the duty of the Church to bring the unchangeable faith of the Gospel into relation with the revelations of science and research.' Swete, *The Ancient Creeds in Modern Life*, p. 26.

INDEX

GLASGOW: PRINTED AT THE UNIVERSITY PRESS BY ROBERT MACLEHOSE AND CO. LTD.